T0076203

Mac OS X
Leopard

Scott Meyers and Mike Lee

Apress®

Mac OS X Leopard: Beyond the Manual
Copyright © 2008 by Scott Meyers and Mike Lee

ISBN-13 (pbk): 978-1-59059-837-5

ISBN-10 (pbk): 1-59059-837-7

ISBN-13 (electronic): 978-1-4302-0255-4

ISBN-10 (electronic): 1-4302-0255-6

Printed and bound in the United States of America 9 8 7 6 5 4 3 2 1

Lead Editor: Jeffrey Pepper
Editorial Board: Steve Anglin, Ewan Buckingham, Tony Campbell, Gary Cornell, Jonathan Gennick, Jason Gilmore, Kevin Goff, Jonathan Hassell, Matthew Moodie, Joseph Ottinger, Jeffrey Pepper, Ben Renow-Clarke, Dominic Shakeshaft, Matt Wade, Tom Welsh
Senior Project Manager: Tracy Brown Collins
Copy Editors: Damon Larson and Kim Wimpsett
Associate Production Director: Kari Brooks-Copony
Production Editor: Laura Esterman
Compositor: Dina Quan
Proofreaders: Erin Poe and Greg Teague
Indexer: John Collin
Artist: April Milne
Cover Designer: Kurt Krames
Manufacturing Director: Tom Debolski

Distributed to the book trade worldwide by Springer-Verlag New York, Inc., 233 Spring Street, 6th Floor, New York, NY 10013. Phone 1-800-SPRINGER, fax 201-348-4505, e-mail orders-ny@springer-sbm.com, or visit http://www.springeronline.com.

For information on translations, please contact Apress directly at 2855 Telegraph Avenue, Suite 600, Berkeley, CA 94705. Phone 510-549-5930, fax 510-549-5939, e-mail info@apress.com, or visit http://www.apress.com.

The source code for this book is available to readers at http://www.apress.com.

Contents at a Glance

Contents

PART 1
Getting to Know Leopard

CHAPTER 1

Working in Leopard: The Aqua Interface

PART 2
Customizing and Administering Leopard

CHAPTER 5

Connecting Peripherals to Your Mac 99

CHAPTER 6

Common Leopard Maintenance 121

CHAPTER 7

Backup, Synchronization, and Recovery of Data

CHAPTER 8

Leopard Security

PART 3
Communications and the Internet

CHAPTER 9

Connecting to the Internet

PART 4
Working with Applications

PART 5
Getting to Know Darwin

CHAPTER 19

Extending the Power of Darwin 329

PART 6

Networking Leopard

CHAPTER 20

Leopard Networking 351

PART 7
Leopard Development and Scripting

CHAPTER 23

Mac OS X Automation with Automator and AppleScript 401

CHAPTER 24

Mac OS X Development: The Application Frameworks 421

CHAPTER 25

Mac OS X Development: The Tools 447

PART 8

Cross-Platform Solutions

CHAPTER 27

Appendixes

About the Authors

SCOTT MEYERS has worked in and around the computer industry, beginning as an Apple sales specialist and consultant, for more than 12 years. He has since moved on to various other jobs including web design and development, and editing books on web development, open source, and Apple technology. He is a Select ADC (Apple Developers Connection) member and a huge fan of Mac OS X, which brings together his love of Apple's traditionally best-of-class GUI and applications with the unrivaled power of UNIX and open-source technologies and applications.

Scott lives outside of Indianapolis, Indiana, with his wife, two kids, and a cat and a dog. When not working or writing, he enjoys photography and playing guitar through amplifiers he built himself.

For comments, questions, or feedback about this book, Scott can be contacted at scott@beyondmac.com. Answers, updates, and errata can be viewed at www.beyondmac.com/.

MIKE LEE, the World's Toughest Programmer, has been bending computers to his will since the mid-'90s. As majordomo of Delicious Monster Software, he spends most of his time working on Delicious Library or answering support e-mail. His next project is a nonprofit software company dedicated to raising money and awareness for Madagascar and the world's few remaining lemurs.

Mike and his wife are originally from Honolulu, but currently live in Seattle where they are raising two cats. Mike's hobbies include weightlifting, single malts, and fire.

Mike can be contacted at mike@atomicwang.org.

Acknowledgments

First of all, I must thank my family: Sara Beth, Ethan, and Isabel—writing this book was a large time commitment that took me away from them much more than any of us expected going into this.

A big thanks goes to the people at Apress: Tracy, Jeff, Kim, Damon, and Laura, who kept me on track and helped turn my often incoherent rambling into a real book.

Also, thanks to Mike Lee for finding the glitches and nuances in Leopard that I missed and overall making this a much better book.

Finally, thanks to all the folks at Apple past, present, and future who got me started with an Apple II back in the day, and continue today to make computers more powerful, more usable, and just plain better. Today Apple seems to be one of the few companies that can create a product that induces a sense of childlike wonder combined with a sprinkling of techno-lust . . . something either neglected or just unobtainable by most others.

Scott Meyers

I'd like to thank my wife, Mary, for keeping me sane, my friend Lucas for keeping me sincere, and my mentor, Wil, for giving me a chance to write Macintosh software for living. Thanks to everyone at Apress for letting me be involved in this project, with extra special thanks to Scott for putting up with my abuse. Thanks to everyone at Apple, especially the evangelists.

Thanks to Greg and Ann-Marie for giving me the strength to take on a Buick and win.

Finally, thanks to Rich, Cabel, Steven, Robert, Dirk, Brent, Gus, Daniel, Joe, and the rest of the development community. Thanks for accepting me as one of your own and constantly inspiring me to strive for greatness.

Mike Lee

Introduction

After two and a half years of Tiger, Mac OS X Leopard is finally here, with hundreds of new and improved features. *Mac OS X Leopard: Beyond the Manual* gets you up and running with Leopard quickly, and then proceeds to explore features, both old and new, that can help users get the most out of their Macs.

To begin with, Part 1, "Getting to Know Leopard," takes a detailed look at Leopard's environment, including common Aqua elements and the Finder, and then moves on to explore Leopard's file system.

Next, in Part 2, "Customizing and Administering Leopard," we begin with a detailed look at all the system preferences included in Leopard. Then we move on to adding peripherals to your system, performing common system maintenance, and backing up and synchronizing system information and files. Finally, we take a look at keeping your Mac safe and secure.

Part 3, "Communications and the Internet," begins by illustrating the many ways to get Leopard connected to the Internet. After that, we take a look at the applications included in Leopard, which provide a gateway to the Internet, including a detailed look at Safari, Mail, and iChat.

Part 4, "Working with Media and iLife," goes on to provide a look at how OS X applications work in general in Leopard, and then provides a look at a number of applications included with Leopard. After that, we provide a solid introduction to both Apple's popular iLife '08 applications and iWork '08.

Part 5, "Getting to Know Darwin," jumps in and teaches you how to use Darwin, the underlying UNIX system buried beneath the slick Aqua interface. We provide a detailed introduction to taking advantage of Darwin. This includes real-world examples and explanations of using the most common Darwin commands and showing you how to customize your Darwin environment to suit your needs and desires. Then we show you how to add new applications and tools to Darwin and take advantage of the powerful scripting utilities to accomplish all sorts of tasks.

Part 6, "Networking Leopard," looks at many of the more powerful networking services and options available in Leopard, ranging from simple file sharing to accessing a wide range of remote servers and even running a full-fledged Apache web server.

Part 7, "Leopard Development and Scripting," takes a look at the development tools, frameworks, and features included with Leopard. This begins with an introduction to AppleScript and Automator to streamline computer tasks, and moves all the way through a tour of Apple's Xcode development tools for application development.

We finish off the book with Part 8, "Cross-Platform Solutions." Here we provide useful information for not only working with other non-Mac environments, but also for how to run Windows and Windows applications on your Mac instead of or side by side with Leopard.

Whether you're new to Mac OS X or just new to Leopard, upon completing this book you should be armed with the knowledge of all the powerful features, both obvious and not so obvious, that Leopard has to offer to make your computing experience both more enjoyable and more productive.

## PART 1

Getting to Know Leopard

## CHAPTER 1

Working in Leopard: The Aqua Interface

Whether you are new to OS X or just new to Leopard, the first step to getting the most out of your computer is to learn a bit about the Aqua interface in Leopard. Apple has designed what many people think is the most attractive, user-friendly interface of any popular computer operating system today; however, if you come to OS X after years of using Windows or some other operating system, you will likely encounter a number of features that are different and perhaps even confusing. Also, even if you are just making the upgrade from Tiger or an earlier Mac OS X version, you will immediately notice a few differences in Leopard. This chapter will go over the interface basics of Leopard and show you how to get the most out of it, specifically:

- The menu bar
- The Finder and the desktop
- The Dock

The Menu Bar

The menu bar may seem like an odd choice as the first topic to cover in this book; however, it is one of the primary user interface (UI) elements for both controlling and getting information in OS X. It is also the UI element that is most unique to OS X (and actually the Mac OS since its inception). The menu bar (shown in Figure 1-1) is divided into three primary areas: the Apple menu, the application menus, and the menu bar extras.

Figure 1-1. The OS X menu bar in Leopard

The Apple Menu

The Apple menu on the far-left side of the menu bar (shown expanded in Figure 1-2) is a special menu containing a number of system-level commands and resources that are particularly handy to have easily accessible. This includes the About This Mac command; shortcuts to software update; the System Preferences command; shortcuts to Dock preferences; and the Recent Items command (including shortcuts for applications, documents, and servers); the Force Quit command that will allow to immediately quit an application; the various Sleep, Restart, and Shutdown commands; and the Log Out *User* command. Most of these are fairly obvious as to what they do; however, some additional information about some of these items may be helpful.

The About This Mac command opens a window (shown in Figure 1-3) that gives you some fairly self-explanatory information about your computer. Clicking the light gray text under the large "Mac OS X" that reads "Version 10.5" will cycle through additional information, including the exact operating system build number and the computer's serial number (this is a much easier way to get your serial number than searching around for it on your actual computer). The More Info button in the About This Mac window will launch the System Profiler application that contains all sorts of information about your computer and the software installed on it.

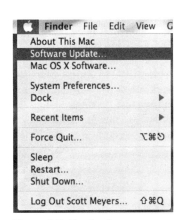

Figure 1-2. The Apple menu   **Figure 1-3.** About This Mac window

The Recent Items command opens a submenu that by default shows you the last ten applications, documents, or servers you accessed. You can adjust these defaults in the Appearance panel in System Preferences (we'll talk about System Preferences in depth in Chapter 5). You'll also see an option here to clear all items if for whatever reason you don't want that information to display.

The Force Quit command opens a new window that shows all the currently running Aqua applications. From this window you can select any of those applications to quit immediately. By immediately, we mean right away—no saving files or anything. The application will just quit. About the only time you may find yourself needing this is if an application freezes up (or in Apple lingo "stops responding") or if you need to relaunch the Finder (force quitting the Finder is the easiest way to restart it).

> **NOTE** You may notice that some menu items have an ellipsis (...) after them, and some don't. According to Apple's Human Interface Guidelines (http://developer.apple.com/documentation/UserExperience/Conceptual/OSXHIGuidelines/index.html), items with the ellipsis will require some additional user interaction to complete a task. In general, this means it will either prompt you or open a window with additional options. Other items common in menus are the sideways triangle on the far right, which indicates the menu item will open a submenu, and of course keyboard shortcuts are viewable for a number of menu items.

Application Menus

Moving just to the right of the Apple menu begins the application menus. This is where people new to Macs tend to get thrown off; you see, in OS X there is only one application menu bar, and this is it. The application menus, however, are dynamic in the sense that the information in one menu bar will reflect the application running in the foreground. So if you are using Microsoft Word, for example, the menu bar will reflect that (Figure 1-4). If you switch to the Finder or another application, the menu bar will change with you.

Figure 1-4. The menu bar's application menu presents Microsoft Word's menus when you're using Microsoft Word. Compare this to the Finder's menus in Figure 1-1.

Many menus are shared from one application to another; additionally, the general arrangement of the menus should be consistent from one application to another. The first menu to the right of the Apple menu will always reflect the name of the current foreground application (sometimes referred to as the application that has *focus*). Almost all proper Aqua applications have at least the following menus: *Application Menu*, File, Edit, Window, and Help. Interface Builder, part of the Xcode tools, by default sets up the following application menus: New Application, File, Edit, Format, View, Window, and Help. Everything between the Edit and Window menus tends to vary from application to application.

NOTE Strangely, though Interface Builder defaults to an order of menus that puts Format before View, many applications (Microsoft Word, and even Apple's own Mail application) tend to switch that order.

The five most common menus tend to serve the following purposes:

Application Menu: This menu identifies the application and usually contains the option to access the application's preferences and other options. This also contains the Services menu item, one of the most overlooked features of OS X.

TIP The Services menu is a powerful way to leverage the power of external services inside any application. By default Apple provides a number of services (Summarize is one of the most interesting). However, many applications also make some of their features available through the Services menu. We encourage you to play around with this, because it's a powerful feature that too few people take advantage of.

File: This is the menu where you generally create new documents or open, save, and print existing application documents.

Edit: The Edit menu contains the standard Copy, Paste, Undo, Find, and Replace commands. By default, it also contains the Spelling and Grammar menu items; however, many applications dispense with these.

Window: The Window menu manages multiple open windows from an application.

Help: The Help menu (Figure 1-5) contains a list of help documentation for the application and OS X in general. The help search feature, new in Leopard, provides an immediate dynamic contextual help system to help you find just the right help or item you need to find.

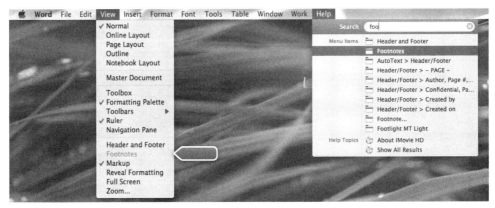

Figure 1-5. Leopard's improved help system can even help find hidden menu items.

NOTE One unique feature of OS X applications that relates to the menu bar is that since the menu bar is separate from the application window, the application can (and usually does) run even if no windows are open. This is one of those big WTF (Wow That's Fascinating) moments that people have when coming to the Mac from Microsoft Windows. With Windows, when you close a window (usually by clicking the X button on the far-right side of the title bar), the application closes along with the window. This is not so for document-based applications in OS X. In OS X if you close the document (usually by clicking the X button on the far-left side of the title bar), then the document closes, but the application itself is probably still running. To actually close an application in Leopard, you generally must explicitly quit it from the application menu (or by using the Cmd+Q keyboard shortcut or contextual menu from the Dock).

NOTE Contrary to the previous note, sometimes applications do quit when you close the window. This is one of those further head-scratching moments in OS X. The reason is that in OS X there are different application types. There are *document-based applications*, which usually follow the previous rules, and then there are other *applications* that don't (always). The general rule is that if you can have multiple windows, then you can have none (that is, document-based applications), even while the application is running. However, if your application provides only a single window, then when that window is closed, the application quits. Examples of default Apple applications that quit when the windows are closed are System Preferences, Dictionary, and Font Book.

Menu Bar Extras

On the far right of the menu bar is where you will find a number of menu bar extras. These are special menus that are available at all times that can provide information as well as quick access to certain functions. The magnifying glass icon on the far right is the Spotlight icon where you can access the Spotlight search feature of Leopard (covered in depth in Chapter 4); this icon is ever present and immovable. You can move the other menu extras around by Command-clicking them and then dragging them. If you drag them out of the menu bar, they will be removed from it. Most of the menu item extras that are available by default in Leopard are tied to System Preferences, so if you accidentally remove one, you can usually add it again in the appropriate System Preferences panel.

Besides the menu bar extras available from System Preferences, some additional extra menus are available. A couple of examples are the Script menu that can be added from within the AppleScript Utility and an iChat menu available from the iChat preferences.

NOTE The Script menu makes a large number of useful prewritten AppleScripts available from the menu bar (and of course you can add your own AppleScripts to the menu). This is a wonderful menu to include if you use even a few AppleScripts on a frequent basis.

Finally, a number of third-party applications provide menu bar extras. Most add information and access to specific features of specific applications; however, some are specific menu bar extra applications that can be configured to make various customizable things always available from the menu bar.

The Finder (and the Desktop)

The Finder is an application that makes all other applications and files findable. It's designed to allow you to find whatever you are looking for on your Mac and then get out of your way so you can work (or play, create, or whatever you do on your computer). Most of the work done with the Finder is done in the Finder window, shown in Figure 1-6.

Figure 1-6. The Finder window showing a typical home directory

As you can see, the Finder window is divided into three areas: the toolbar on top, the sidebar along the left of the window, and main viewing area that takes up most of the window.

The Finder's Toolbar

The toolbar (Figure 1-7) provides some buttons and a search field for working in the Finder. The arrows on the far left move you forward and backward through your Finder history in the same way as in most web browsers. The four buttons grouped together alter how the Finder displays items. The button with the eye icon will open the selected Finder item in Quick Look. The button with the gear icon will open a menu with some Finder options in it, and all the way on the right side is a search box that will help you find any item on any connected hard drive (using Spotlight). We'll talk about the different Finder views and Quick Look later in this chapter.

Figure 1-7. The Finder's default toolbar

> **NOTE** Like most toolbars in Aqua applications, the Finder's toolbar can be customized by
> right-clicking (or Control-clicking) the toolbar and selecting Customize Toolbar from the pop-
> up menu.

The Finder's Sidebar

The sidebar in the Finder window (Figure 1-8) is divided into four
areas:

Devices: This is where any attached file systems will show up.
This includes connected disk volumes, your iDisk, and any
attached network volumes.

Shared: This is where any shared network files or devices will
appear.

Places: By default this contains a list of your personal
directories. You can add or remove any files or folders here
that you want.

Search For: New for Leopard, this area contains saved Spotlight
searches. Saved searches in the Finder are similar to smart
folders; however, rather than the folder showing up in the file
system, the saved searches show up only in this part of the
Finder sidebar.

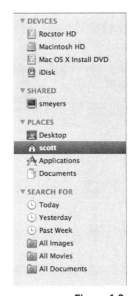

Figure 1-8.
The Finder's sidebar

The Finder's Views

The most important part of the Finder window is the viewing area; it is here that you actually
access what you want to find. Depending on your needs, the Finder has four ways to view the
items available to your computer: as icons, as a list, in columns, and, new for Leopard, in Cover
Flow view.

Using the Finder's Icon View

Icon view is the more traditional Mac OS view of folders, files, and applications. This view
shows the contents of one folder at a time, allowing you to transverse into other folders by
double-clicking them (or selecting them and using the Open command or Cmd+O keyboard
shortcut). To move up the directory path in Icon view, you can use the Go ➤ Enclosing Folder
command (or the much easier to use Cmd+up arrow keyboard shortcut). The Icon view defaults
are generally fine for most things; however, like many other views, this view can be tweaked to
look or behave differently using the view options presented when you select Show View Options
from the View menu or contextual menu (or when you press the Cmd+J keyboard shortcut). Figure 1-9 shows the Finder's Icon view along with the view's Options window open beside it.

Figure 1-9. The Finder's Icon view with the view's Options window open beside it

The options available to tweak the Icon view include the following:

Always open in Icon View: This causes the folder to always open in Icon view, overriding any system-wide defaults.

Icon size: This makes the icons in the view bigger or smaller.

Grid spacing: This adjusts the amount of space between the icons.

Text size: This adjusts the font size of the label text.

Label position: This moves the label text either below or to the right of the icons.

Show Item Info: This toggles extra information about items (that is, how many items are in folders, how much space is available on a storage system, how big an image file is in pixels, and so on).

Show icon preview: This toggles whether to show a thumbnail of certain files or to use the generic icon for the recommended application.

Arrange by: This selects how items are arranged in the view; Name is the default and will arrange item alphabetically, but at times other options may be preferable. (Date Modified, Date Created, Size, Kind, and Label are other options.)

Background: This allows you to change the view's background to a different color or even an image file.

Use as Defaults: This final option becomes available if you make any changes. Clicking this button will effectively make the changes carry over to all noncustomized folders; otherwise, the changes you make will be reflected only in the current folder.

Using the Finder's List View

The next view in the Finder is List view (Figure 1-10). This view has a number of advantages over the standard Icon view in that it presents more information about each Finder item, and it allows you to expand folders to see their contents without leaving the current folder. You do this by clicking the sideways-triangle symbol to the left of a folder item.

Figure 1-10. The Finder's List view with the view's Options window beside it

The view options for List view differ somewhat from the options in Icon view; the different options available in List view are as follows:

Always open in List View: This causes this folder to always open in List view.

Icon size: Rather than scaling the icons as in Icon view, in List view you can choose only Large or Small.

Show Columns: This allows you to choose which columns should be shown.

Use relative dates: When selected, the date columns can use terms such as "Today" and "Yesterday" rather than the actual date all the time.

Calculate all sizes: This causes the computer to calculate the sizes of all items, even other folders (by adding up all its contents). In many cases this can be a time-consuming process.

> **TIP** To sort the Finder items in List view, you can click any column header, and the column will determine the sort order. For example, to sort items by the date they were last modified, just click the column header Date Modified.

Using the Finder's Column View

The third view is Column view. This view was introduced in the first version of OS X and is based on the File Viewer from NeXTSTEP and later OPENSTEP (from which OS X descends). Column view (Figure 1-11) is nice in that it reveals the whole file system path that leads to the Finder item you are viewing. Additionally, when you select a nonfolder item in Column view, the last column will reveal a preview of the selected item along with some general information about it.

The view options for Column view are fairly limited, and the only new option is Show Preview Column, which, when checked, shows the last preview column.

Figure 1-11. The Finder's Column view with the view's Options window beside it

Using the Finder's Cover Flow

The final Finder view is the new Cover Flow view. Cover Flow view (Figure 1-12) is essentially a split window with a standard column view on the bottom; the top, however, provides a scrollable display that allows you to "flip through" previews of all the items shown in the column view below. Sometimes, when dealing with a large number of files, this is a helpful tool for visually identifying the file you want to find.

The Cover Flow view options mimic the options presented in List view since that is the view provided beneath the Cover Flow view area.

Figure 1-12. This is Cover Flow view in the Finder; most of the view options are the same here as in List view.

Common Finder Tasks

Although the Finder is a great tool for browsing around your computer, to be a useful file management tool in a modern operating system, the Finder needs to perform a number of additional tasks. Luckily, the Finder in Leopard performs all the basic tasks necessary plus a few handy extras.

> **NOTE** Many of the relevant commands in the Finder's application menu are available from a contextual menu that pops up when you right-click (Control-click) a Finder item or Finder window. The contextual menus will present different options depending on what options are available for any given item you right-click. This includes most of the relevant menu commands, as well as some special commands that may not be available from the Finder's menu, because some applications install a special "contextual menu item" that allows special features of that application to become available in contextual menus. Using contextual pop-ups should be very familiar to users of Microsoft Windows.

Viewing and Opening Documents and Applications

Double-clicking any item icon (or using the Cmd+O keyboard shortcut) in the Finder will open it. If the item is a folder, the Finder will open that folder in the current Finder window. If the item is an application, then that application will launch. If the item is a document, then the Finder will open that document with its preferred application.

> **TIP** If you want to open a folder in a new Finder window, you can hold Command while double-clicking the folder.

The preferred application with a document is usually the application that created the document. If the creating application is unknown or not present on your computer, then the Finder will make a guess based on the type of document it is. Occasionally you may want to open the document in an application other than the one the Finder thinks is best, and you can do this in numerous ways:

- Open the document from within the desired application.
- Drag the document on the desired application icon in the Finder or on the Dock.
- Right-click the document to open the pop-up contextual menu, and choose an alternate application from the Open With menu.

If you'd like to permanently change the default application for a specific file or all files of a specific type, select the file (or a file of the desired type), and select Get Info from the Finder menu, the Action toolbar item, or the pop-up contextual menu by right-clicking the document. This will open the Info window (Figure 1-13), and from

Figure 1-13. The Info window, opened by selecting Get Info from a menu

there you can select the desired application from the Open With drop-down menu. If you'd like to make all files of the same type open in this alternate application, click the Change All button.

Sometimes you might just want to preview a document, without opening any application. Leopard adds a new feature called Quick Look that allows you to do just that. To activate Quick Look, just select the desired document in the Finder, and hit the spacebar (or click the Quick Look button in the Finder's toolbar or press Cmd+Y). This will immediately open any supported document type in a hovering window for your viewing pleasure. You can even select a full-screen view (Figure 1-14) that will cause the document to fill the screen for distraction-free viewing.

Figure 1-14. Quick Look's full-screen viewing

NOTE The previewed document is not actually opened in the creating application but rather in a separate preview generator; therefore, occasionally you'll see some differences between the Quick Look preview and how the document will appear when opened in its actual application.

Moving, Copying, and Creating Aliases of Finder Items

Besides opening and viewing files, the Finder is also used for managing your documents and applications. Management is done in the Finder by simply dragging and dropping items around where you want them.

CAUTION One issue that may occur when you move an application from its original, installed location is that occasionally it's expected to be there. This is especially true with (but not limited to) Apple's own applications that occasionally won't update correctly if they are not located in the same folder in which they were installed. This doesn't mean you can't organize your applications into subfolders in the application folder; however, if you notice issues with an application that you've moved around, then you may want to move it back. Also, it's best to leave Apple applications where they are.

If rather than just moving a file you want to make a copy of the file, you can do this by holding the Option key while you drag the item. (You should notice a green button with a plus sign appear while you are dragging to indicate you are making a copy.) Holding Cmd+Opt while you drag will create an alias of the Finder item you are dragging.

> **NOTE** If you are moving a file from one volume to another, the Finder will, by default, automatically create a copy rather than simply moving the file. You can override this behavior by holding the Command key while moving the item.

If you want to create a copy of an item in the same folder as the original, you can use the File ➤ Duplicate command from the Finder's menus or use the Cmd+D keyboard shortcut (or select Duplicate from the item's contextual menu). You may also create aliases by selecting File ➤ Make Alias or pressing the Cmd+L keyboard shortcut. One final way to create a copy of a Finder item is to use a standard copy-paste operation; select Edit ➤ Copy (or press Cmd+C) to copy an item, and select Edit ➤ Paste (or press Cmd+V) to paste it wherever you want.

> **NOTE** Aliases are the OS X equivalent of shortcuts in Microsoft Windows. Rather than creating a copy of an item, OS X creates a link that points to the original Finder item. This is used when you want to keep one original Finder item yet you want to access it from different places in the file system.

Renaming Finder Items

To rename a Finder item, you need to first select the item and then click the name of the Finder item. If you do this too quickly, though, the system may recognize this as a double-click and open the item. Once the item is selected for editing (the name will become highlighted in a rectangular edit field), you can edit the text as desired. Alternately, you can just select a Finder item and then hit the Return key; this will toggle the name for editing without the need to time your second click.

> **CAUTION** When the name is selected for editing, the entire name minus the file extension is selected, so any typing will immediately overwrite the original name. If you want to just tweak the name, you can use the arrow keys or your mouse to position the cursor where you want to insert or delete text without overwriting the whole name.

You can also rename Finder items in the Info window (which we talk about later in this chapter).

> **CAUTION** Certain Finder items, such as applications and default system folders, should not be renamed. Renaming the default folders can cause all sorts of unexpected and undesirable results, and renaming applications can cause them to stop working correctly. As a general rule, you can rename any of your documents and any folders you create, but you may want to think twice about renaming other items. If you do happen to make a mistake, you can use the Undo command (Command+Z) to reset the name to it previous state.

Creating New Folders and New Smart Folders

Sooner or later it's likely you'll want to create new folders to help organize your documents or other Finder items. The easiest way to create a new folder is to select File ➤ New Folder from the Finder's menu or use the Shift+Cmd+N keyboard shortcut (or the contextual menu item). This creates a new folder with a rather generic name, so you'll probably want to rename it right away, and then it's ready to go.

To create a smart folder, select File ➤ New Smart Folder from the Finder's menu, or use the Opt+Cmd+N keyboard shortcut. This will open a New Smart Folder window (Figure 1-15) that allows you to set the search parameters for your smart folder using steps similar to defining mail rules. The process of creating a smart folder is a subset of the Spotlight feature, so we'll cover this in more detail in Chapter 3 where we cover Spotlight.

Figure 1-15. The New Smart Folder window

Getting (and Altering) Information About Finder Items

If you want to get more information about a particular Finder item, then the Info window (shown in Figure 1-13 earlier in the chapter) is the place to go. The Info window allows you not only to view information about a Finder item, but it will also allow you to add or alter information and attributes about the item. To open the Info window, select an item in the Finder, and then select File ➤ Get Info from the Finder menu (use the Cmd+I keystroke or the contextual menu item). At the top of the Info window, the name, size, icon, and last modified date for the item appear. Table 1-1 describes the basic structure of the Info window.

Table 1-1. Sections of the Get Info Window

Section	Description
Spotlight Comments	This is a text field that allows you to add any comments about the item. These comments are searchable in Spotlight.
Kind	This tells the item's type: Folder, Application (for applications, it will let you know whether the application is universal or PowerPC), or Document.
Size	This gives the size of the item (including the number of items in folders).
Location	This gives the directory path of the item's location (including the original location for aliases).

Continued

Table 1-1. Continued

Section	Description
Created	This is the date when the item was created.
Modified	This is the date when the item was last modified.
Label	This shows the item's label, which is editable, allowing you to set or alter the item's label.
Share Folder	This check box allows you to share a folder and its contents with other users of your computer and network (appears only if Kind is Folder).
Stationary Pad	This check box for documents causes a selected document to always open as a copy of itself. This essentially sets up the document as a template.
Open using Rosetta	This check box allows you to run universal applications in PowerPC emulation mode if you are using an Intel-based computer.
Locked	This check box locks a file so it cannot be modified in any way as long as it remains locked.
Time Machine	If you have Time Machine set up, this shows the last time Time Machine backed up the file; this includes a Back Up This Item check box that causes the item to be backed up even if the item is otherwise excluded from Time Machine.
Name & Extension	This is an editable text field that shows the item's full name (including the extension), which is immediately editable. OS X uses the file's extension as one way to choose what application can open a file, so changing the extension may change how a document is opened (possible making it unreadable). A check box allows you to choose to show or hide the file extension in the Finder.
Open With	Discussed earlier in the chapter, this allows you to change the ownership of a document from one application to another application.
Preview	This shows a preview of the item (this will play back supported audio and video files).
Languages	For applications, this shows what localizations (that is, languages) the application can run in.
Sharing & Permissions	This allows you to view and alter the abilities of any users and groups to access the item. The ability to view and alter this information depends on the permissions you have. In general, you must be the file's owner or an administrator to edit this information.

> **TIP** If you want to replace the icon of any Finder item, you can do this by selecting the icon at the top of the Info window and then pasting the new icon over it. Should you ever change your mind, you can delete the custom icon, which will cause the item to return to its default icon.

Compressing (Zipping) Finder Items

Often, especially when you want to send files via e-mail to someone else, you may want to compress or archive a file. OS X allows you to create .zip files from within the Finder. You can do this easily by selecting the item (or items) you want to compress and selecting File ➤ Compress from the Finder's menu or using the Compress contextual menu item. If you want to create an archive of multiple items to be zipped into a single .zip file, just create a folder containing all the desired files and then compress the folder.

> **NOTE** These days, many files and media formats are already compressed, so compressing, say, a single .jpg or .mp3 file won't cut down on the file size much, if any (in fact, some will actually be a tad larger). Still, if you are sending lots of files, even if they are compressed, it's a good idea to compress them together anyway since, even though the total file size might not decrease much, it may leave more free space on your computer because of the nuances of how files are stored on your disk.

By double-clicking a .zip file, the Finder will automatically expand the compressed item.

> **NOTE** By default the Finder uses the included Archive Utility to create and open compressed items. By default Leopard can handle many types of compressed items via Archive Utility; however, there are some compression and encoding types that require third-party software to open. This includes the SIT format, which was once the most popular compression format for Macintosh systems prior to OS X Tiger. .sit files will require StuffIt expander available at http://www.stuffit.com/mac/index.html or some other third-party compression application (including many decent free applications).

Backing Up and Burning Items to a Disc

We can't overemphasize the importance of backing up the data on your computer. The one truth of all storage devices is that someday they will fail, and when they do, they will likely take all the data stored on them along with them. Backing up data can be a bothersome task; however, Leopard introduces Time Machine, which makes the whole process easier (almost pain free), provided you have an extra hard drive to which to back up your data. Still, sometimes you may want to burn some or all of your data to a CD or DVD for a more permanent "offline" backup.

> **NOTE** Chapter 7 is devoted to backing up and syncing data. There we will cover Time Machine in depth as well as other backup strategies.

You can create backup data discs in the Finder in a few ways. First, you could simply select the data you want to back up in the Finder and select File ➤ Burn Items to Disc from the Finder menu. This will prompt you to insert a disc and upon doing so will open a burn disc window (Figure 1-16) to allow you to name the disc and set the burn speed. Then, simply clicking the Burn button will start the process.

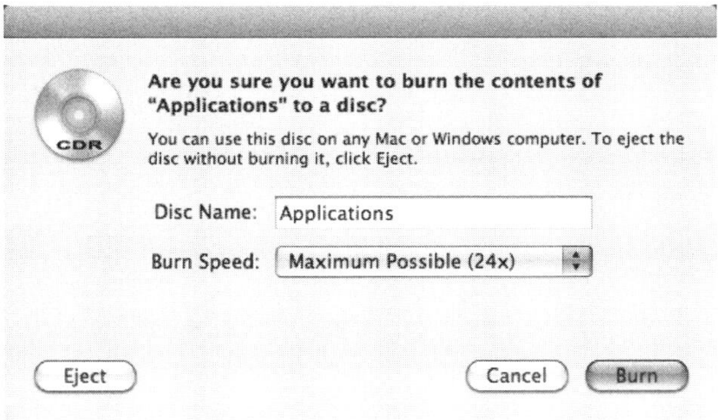

Are you sure you want to burn the contents of "Applications" to a disc?

You can use this disc on any Mac or Windows computer. To eject the disc without burning it, click Eject.

Disc Name: Applications

Burn Speed: Maximum Possible (24x)

Eject   Cancel   Burn

Figure 1-16. The burn disc window

> **NOTE** If you select more data than will fit on the disc you insert, you will get a warning telling you that the data is "too large to fit on the disc." OS X will ask you then to remove some data and try again. You may need to use a larger disc (if you are using a CD-R try using a DVD-R instead), or you may need to select less data at a time and make multiple burns.

Two other similar ways to burn data to a disc are to create a burn folder and to just insert a blank, writable disc into the computer and select Open Finder in the Action drop-down menu (Figure 1-17). You can create a burn folder by selecting File ➤ New Burn Folder from the Finder menu or from the contextual menu. Then you can drag any files you want to burn into this folder (which will automatically create an alias to the original). If you inserted a writable disc and selected the Open Finder action, the disc will mount, and you can then drag any items you want to burn on it onto the disc icon on the desktop. Either way, when you are done, you can click the special burn button from either of these locations to start the burning process (see Figure 1-18).

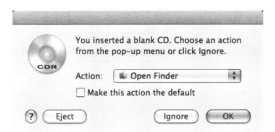

Figure 1-17. Pop-up window asking what action should occur when you open a blank, writable disc

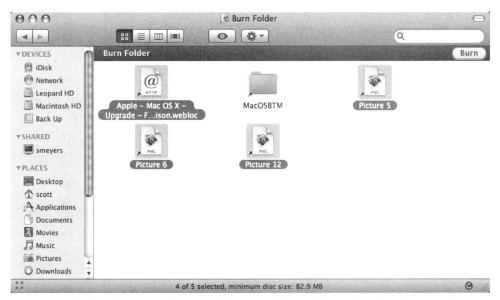

Figure 1-18. The burn button is in the upper-left corner of the Finder window. The information bar at the bottom keeps track of how much space you will need on the disc to burn the items.

Labeling Finder Items

For many years Mac OS has had the ability to label Finder items, and that tradition continues. Labels allow you to colorize Finder items as a way to sort them in the Finder; additionally, labels can have names associated with them (setting the names is covered later in this chapter). To label a Finder item, you can select it in the Finder and then select the appropriate label from the File ➤ Label item in the Finder menu.

In Icon and Column views, the label color will highlight the item's name with the selected color; in List view, it will highlight the item's entire row. Items in the Finder can then be sorted by label, and labels are an additional search parameter for smart folders and Spotlight.

> **NOTE** When sorting items by label in the Finder, the sort order is determined alphabetically by the label name, not by the color. This may be something to keep in mind when naming labels.

Choosing the Go to Folder Command

If you ever need to go directly to a specific folder in the Finder, you can use the Go ➤ Go to Folder item in the Finder menu, which will open a dialog box prompting you for a directory path. Although sometimes it may be easier to navigate there through the Finder, this option can come in handy if you know where you want to go.

> **NOTE** As you will learn later in the book, many folders are usually hidden in the Finder. If you know about these folders, you can use the Go to Folder to take you to these hidden directories.

Choosing the Connect to Server Command

The Go ➤ Connect to Server selection in the Finder menu is similar to the Go to Folder command, but instead of opening a folder on your computer, it can open network resources using a variety of protocols including FTP, HTTP, NSF, SMB, CIFS, AFP, or others (including a user's iDisk). To connect, just enter the network resource's URL into the dialog box, and it will connect. If the resource requires login credentials (name, password, and so on), you will be prompted for that information.

The Desktop

The desktop (shown in Figure 1-19) is the main backdrop for Leopard. Although it has some unique options, it works the same as any Finder window in Icon view. The items on it are in fact located in the Desktop folder in your home directory. Some of what makes the desktop unique is that the items placed on it are always there for easy access, and it can automatically display connected items such as hard drives, removable media, and even network resources on it. The view options available for the desktop are the same as those available to a Finder window in Icon view with the exception of selecting a desktop background. Setting the desktop background is handled through System Preferences, which will be covered in Chapter 4.

Customizing the Finder

Besides altering the view options for each of the Finder's views, you can apply a number of additional preferences that affect the Finder as the whole. The Finder preferences (like most application preferences) are in the main application menu. In the case of the Finder, that's Finder ➤ Preferences (the default keyboard shortcut to open the preferences of any application is the Cmd+, shortcut). The Finder's preferences are divided into four sections, as covered next.

Figure 1-19. Leopard's default desktop with the Dock at the bottom and the menu bar at the top

Setting General Options

Table 1-2 describes the Finder's General preferences (shown in Figure 1-20), which cover a few general Finder behaviors.

Table 1-2. Finder General Preferences

Preference	Description
Show these items on the Desktop	This offers three check boxes to determine what sort of devices will automatically show up on the Desktop.
New Finder windows open	This is a drop-down list that determines where a newly opened Finder window will start by default (this is where you begin when you open a new Finder window from the Finder's File menu or when you click the Finder icon in the Dock).
Always open folders in a new window	This check box, if checked, will cause all folders clicked in the Finder to open a new window rather than to open the contents of the folder in the existing window.
Spring-loaded folder and windows	This is a nice feature in OS X that helps in moving Finder items. When activated, if you drag and hold a Finder item over a folder for a period of time, that folder will spring open to reveal its contents. This way, you can move an item into a deep folder structure without first having to open the destination folder beforehand. The Delay bar indicates how long it takes for the folder to spring open.

Figure 1-20. Finder general preferences

Customizing Labels

The Labels tab in the Finder preferences (Figure 1-21) allows you to customize the names of the various colored labels. To change a label's name, just edit it in the text field next to appropriate color.

Customizing the Sidebar

The Sidebar preference tab (Figure 1-22) allows you to select what items automatically show up in the Finder's sidebar. Since you can drag in or drag out various folders anyway, most of these options include more dynamic, nonfolder items.

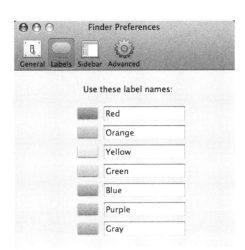

Figure 1-21. The Labels settings in the Finder preferences

Figure 1-22. Finder preferences, Sidebar options

Setting Advanced Options

The final Finder preferences tab are advanced options (Figure 1-23) of which there are four fairly self-explanatory check boxes:

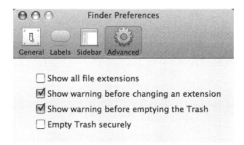

- Show all file extensions
- Show warning before changing extension
- Show warning before emptying the Trash
- Empty Trash securely

Figure 1-23. The Advanced Finder preferences

> **NOTE** The "Empty Trash securely" option actually writes over the disk space where the Trash items are located, making it nearly impossible to recover the items once they are deleted. This differs from a normal Trash empty procedure, which just lets the computer know that the space where the file exists is available for writing over, so until something overwrites that same area on your disk, that data could be recovered with the right software. The "Empty Trash securely" option takes more time to complete, especially if you are deleting a large amount of data.

The Dock

The final interface element we'll look at in this chapter is the Dock (shown in Figure 1-24). The Dock application allows you to keep your favorite applications a click away, manages the applications you have running, provides a place to access your favorite folders and documents, and also holds your Trash can for deleting Finder items you are done with.

Figure 1-24. The Dock shown with Leopard's default items

The items on the Dock are completely customizable; the only two elements that are bound to the Dock are the Finder item and the Trash item (Figure 1-25). The Dock is divided between application icons and other items by a faint dashed line resembling a crosswalk (called the *abbey road graphic*). We cover the types of items on the Dock in the next sections.

Figure 1-25. Minimal Dock with all optional items removed

Favorite Application Icons

Beginning on the far left of the Dock are the application icons. The first one on the far left is always the Finder icon, but the ones that follow are entirely customizable. To add one of your favorite applications to the Dock, just select the application in the Finder, and then drag the icon onto the Dock where you'd like it to be. You can also click and drag any icon already on the Dock to another location on the Dock or off the Dock entirely. To launch any of the applications on the Dock, just click them. Right-clicking (Control-clicking, or clicking and holding for those still using one-button mice) any Dock icon will open a contextual menu that varies on the application, whether it's running or not.

Applications that are open have a little bright blip under the icon (like a light shining up on the icon).

> **NOTE** You can't remove the icon of a running application from the Dock; if you try, it will spring back to the Dock. This, however, will cause the item to leave the Dock when the application quits.

Open Applications

Anytime you open an Aqua application, the icon for that application will be added to the Dock just to the right of your other docked applications (provided that it isn't in the Dock already). By clicking any open application icon on the Dock, you will make that the active application. Additionally, if that application has no open windows, then usually a new window will open when you make that application active. Upon closing any application not normally found in the Dock, the icon on the Dock will disappear.

Folders and Stacks

In previous versions of OS X, you could add folders to the Dock so that its contents were easily available. In Leopard, you can still add folders to the Dock; however, the behavior has changed, since the folders on the Dock are now turned into stacks.

Stacks are a new feature of Leopard that allow you to group a collection of Finder items and place them all together on the Dock for easy access. To create a stack, just select two or more files from the Finder, and drag them into the area between your application icons and the Trash (being careful not to actually drag them into the Trash). Those files will appear as a stack of single icons on the Dock. Clicking the stack in the Dock will expand the stack, making all the items accessible to you. Depending on the number of items in the stack, the stack will either expand to a single column of items (Figure 1-26) or expand to a row of items (Figure 1-27). Right-clicking a stack will allow you to rename it. To add an item to a stack, just drag the Finder icon onto the stack to which you want to add it. To remove an item from a stack, just expand the stack, select the item, and drag it out of the stack.

A folder dragged onto the Dock looks and behaves very much like a stack, with a few important exceptions. First, while stacks sort items manually (generally newest items appear first, but they can be moved around in the stack), folders sort items based on the Name, Date Added, Date Modified, Date Created, Kind, or Label items (selectable from contextual menu). Second, if you select a folder in a stack, that folder will open in a new Finder window; if you click a subfolder in a folder, the content of the subfolder will appear in the Dock rather than a separate Finder window (allowing you to navigate to subfolders from the Dock). If you want to view the folder in a Finder window, there is a special item in the Dock folder items called Show in Finder (shown earlier in Figure 1-26). Finally, although you can manipulate the item of a stack from the stack, folders are protected and can be modified only from within the Finder.

By default, OS X starts you out with the Download folder placed on your Dock.

Figure 1-26. A folder with a few items

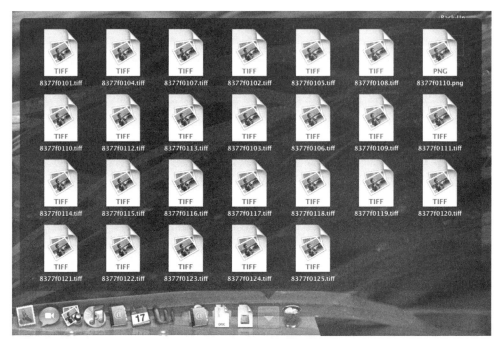

Figure 1-27. A stack with many items

Minimized Windows

Occasionally you may have what seems to be too many application windows on your screen at one time. By clicking the Minimize button in the upper-left corner of any window, the window will shrink down into the Dock and out of the way. (By default, that's the yellow button that will reveal a – when you mouse over it; these three buttons are commonly called the *window widgets*.) Clicking the minimized window in the Dock will expand the window to its previous size and position on the screen.

The Trash

The final item on the Dock is the Trash. Rather than immediately deleting Finder items, in OS X you generally move an item to the Trash when you are done with it. Then when you are ready, you empty the Trash to permanently delete items. This two-step process adds a fail-safe to keep you from permanently deleting a file accidentally. You can drag any item into the Trash (or use Cmd+Delete), where it will remain until you empty the Trash. To empty the Trash, you can right-click (or Control-click) the Trash and select Empty Trash from the menu, or in the Finder you can select Finder ➤ Empty Trash from the application menu.

One advantage of emptying the Trash from the Finder's menu is that it also gives you the option to securely empty the Trash, which makes the items you delete nearly impossible to ever recover, even with the most sophisticated utilities.

One other, strange ability of the Trash is that if you drag any removable media, external hard drives, or network resources on to it, rather than delete those items, it will actually eject, unmount, or disconnect the resource. This is actually the traditional way to do this, though it's especially odd for people new to Macs.

Dock Preferences

The Dock preferences affect the Dock's behavior. The Dock's settings are located in System Preferences (Dock panel) but are directly accessible from the Apple menu by selecting Dock ➤ Dock Preferences. Table 1-3 describes the preferences available for the Dock (Figure 1-28).

Table 1-3. Dock System Preferences

Preference	Effect
Size	This affects how big the Dock icons and the Dock will be.
Magnification	If selected, this affects how big Dock items will magnify when the cursor moves over them. This is useful if you have many small items in the Dock.
Position on Screen	This allows you to position the Dock on either side or the bottom of the screen.
Minimize using	This allows you to choose between two different effects, the Genie Effect and the Scale Effect, when you minimize items onto the Dock. This really has no effect on anything practical and is purely an aesthetic thing.
Animate opening applications	When selected, the application icons will bounce up and down in the Dock while the application is starting up. (Some people count the bounces as a metric as to how fast an application launches.)
Automatically hide and show the Dock	When selected, this will cause the Dock to disappear and remain hidden until you move the mouse down to the area of the screen where the Dock would normally appear at which time it will slide back into view to perform any regular Dock functions. This is nice in certain applications where you want to use the entire screen for the application and the Dock would normally get in the way.

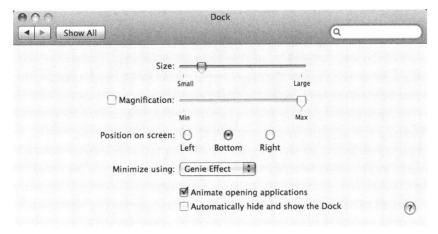

Figure 1-28. The Dock System Preferences

NOTE Many of these Dock preferences are selectable by choosing the Dock item in the Apple menu, by right-clicking the space just to the right of the application icons on the Dock, or by clicking and dragging on the Dock itself.

Summary

This chapter explained all of the basics you need in order to work inside the Aqua interface. Even if at first it seems strange (and there are certainly parts of it that are), as you get used to it, you will find that it in fact serves its purpose extraordinarily well (more so in most cases than any alternatives). Coupled with some of the other features that will be revealed as the book progresses, you'll find the Aqua interface to be a great foundation for a fun and productive computing environment.

Next, we'll cover the file system and explain where everything is.

## CHAPTER 2

The File System

This chapter will take you on a tour of the Leopard file system to discover what items exist in what folders and why. We'll cover the following in depth:

- The overall file structure of Leopard
- The top-level folders, including the System folder, Library folder, and Application folder
- Your personal home folder and its contents
- Other common folders
- Hidden folders

The Overall File Structure of Leopard

The file system for Leopard is pretty easy to understand. The file system starts at the root of your primary hard drive (the one from which you boot Leopard). From there, a series of folders descend downward, each with its own purpose. A basic view of the default file system is shown in Figure 2-1.

The file system is devised so that certain items belong in certain folders. For example, most of your applications should go in the Applications folder and most of your personal documents would go in the Documents folder within your home directory (which will be titled with your short username).

The term *path* is often used to describe where something is located in the file system. A path usually begins with a /, signifying that it begins at the top level of the file system, and then lists the folder path with a / between each folder. The exception to this is a path that begins with ~. This indicates that rather than beginning at the top of the file system, the path begins from your home folder. For example, the path to my Documents folder could be written either as /Users/scott/Documents/ or ~/Documents/.

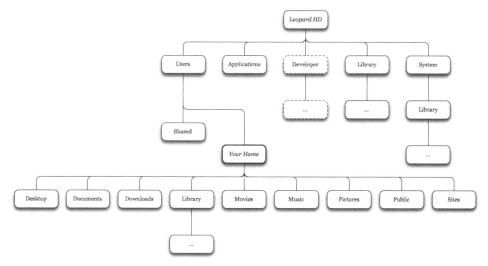

Figure 2-1. A simple view of Leopard's default file system

The Library Folders

One thing you may notice about the file system is that there are multiple Library folders. This is by design, and while there are many similarities between the contents of the Library folders, they are scoped differently.

> **NOTE** There are actually four Library domains, although generally you'll only see three Library folders. Some applications can contain their own Library folders that contain plug-ins or other information that is used only when that application is running.

The Library folders each contain the necessary support items for the applications on your system, as well as the system itself. These include things like preference settings, cache items, scripts, and screen savers. In practice, you almost never need to fuss with the contents of any Library folder; however, there are times when it may benefit you to do so (especially the Library folder in your home directory). That said, for each Library folder there are certain rules. We'll look at each of the three primary Library folders in general first, and then we'll explore common subitems contained in Library folders in general.

The Library and System Library Folders

The primary Library folder (/Library) and the Library folder contained in the System folder (/System/Library) have global scope. That is, their contents support every aspect of the system. Specifically, the System Library folder contains the items necessary for the system to operate, and the primary Library folder contains the items necessary for most applications, third-party hardware, and other items that affect every user on the system.

As a general rule, the System Library is sacred. Only Apple should install items in it, and only Apple should alter any of those items. As such, there is almost no reason for you (or me) to touch anything in there unless you are 100 percent sure you know exactly what you are doing and that doing it here is the only way to solve your problem. Changing anything here can cause very bad things to happen (or even worse . . . nothing at all).

On the other hand, there are times when it may benefit you to make a few changes to items in the main `Library` folder. This could be anything from installing a screen saver that you want to make available to all users of your computer to uninstalling some items left over from an old application or hardware device. That said, you should still be 100 percent sure of what you are doing before you do it. While errors here might not render your system unusable, they could certainly make it less usable.

> **CAUTION** Although sometimes you may want to clean out old unnecessary files that tend to build up in you `Library` folder, make sure that the items you remove are no longer used. Sometimes an item installed by one item is used by another item as well (this is especially true with certain common frameworks and components). Often it's better to err on the side of keeping an unnecessary item rather then accidentally deleting a necessary one.

Personal Library Folder

The `Library` folder inside you home directory (`~/Library`) is your own personal `Library` folder. This is where the system and individual application items that affect you are kept. This includes your personal system and application preferences, your mail settings (and actual mail), your Safari bookmarks, your iCal data, and much more. This `Library` folder is the preferred one for adding personal items such as screen savers, desktop backgrounds, and add-on scripts. This `Library` folder is also in the most need of an occasional cleaning; however, all the cautions just mentioned still apply.

Common Library Items

Each of the `Library` folders tend to share a number of subfolders that contain the same types of items; some of the `Library` folders also contain unique subfolders that have special significance. Table 2-1 points out a few common `Library` subfolders and explains their purposes.

Table 2-1. Common Library Subfolders and Their Purposes

Folder Name	Purpose
Application Support	This folder is the primary folder for applications to store their support files, usually in a subfolder named after the application. Additionally, some companies will store information that may be shared among different applications here (like Apple and Adobe). Also, some applications will store their data files here (as such, it's important to keep this folder backed up along with any other important data). In general, if you delete an application, then the support files contained here are safe to delete. Additionally, some application folders will contain subfolders where users may add plug-ins, scripts, or other features.
Audio	The Audio folder contains subfolders for audio plug-ins (Audio Units, VST, Digidesign, etc.) and other support items for audio applications (this includes all of your GarageBand loops and plug-ins).
Automator	The Automator folder in /System/Library contains many default Automator actions that are used within Automator to build more complex workflows. Additional Automator actions may be installed in either /Library/Automator or ~/Library/Automator (however, these folders will need to be created, as they don't exist by default).

Continued

Table 2-1. Continued

Folder Name	Purpose
Caches	The Caches folder exists in each of the Library folders. This is where the system or an application may store data that it refers to often—rather then reforming the data from scratch, it can use the data from the cache, saving time and system resources. While some people routinely clean out their Caches folders since the data there will be restored, some of the data stored there could take some time and resources to regenerate (and it will be regenerated), so there isn't much use in doing this, except for deleting caches for applications that no longer exist on your system.
Calendars	This folder, located in ~/Library/, is where calendar information is stored. This is mostly used by iCal, but the info is available to other apps that may utilize iCal information.
CFMSupport	This folder contains shared libraries that are required for the system and certain apps. The CFMSupport folders in general should be left alone unless you get specific instructions to add or remove an item.
ColorPickers	The ColorPickers folders are where color picker plug-ins go. Color pickers are the various color selection windows available to you when an Aqua application allows you to select a color. Leopard includes a few different color picker plug-ins: Color Wheel, Color Sliders, Color Palettes, Image Palettes, and Crayons. Other third-party color pickers are available for increased functionality or personal taste.
ColorSync	The ColorSync Library folders contain ColorSync profiles and support files. ColorSync is a Macintosh technology that allows color devices (monitors, printers, scanners, digital cameras, etc.) to be profiled so that color remains consistent from one device to another.
Components	Components are application plug-ins that provide useful features to the system and other applications.
Compositions	Items in the Compositions folder are movies or Quartz Composer files that provide animated backgrounds in applications like Photo Booth and iChat. In general, if you wish to add additional files for this purpose, you would create and add them to ~/Library/Compositions to make them available for you to use.
Contextual Menu Items	The items in the Contextual Menu Items folder are contextual menu plug-ins. These provide additional menu items for the contextual pop-up menus you get when you right-click (or Ctrl-click) Finder items.
CoreServices	The CoreServices folder, which resides in /System/Library, contains a number of interesting utility applications that are used by the system. Things like the Dock, the Finder, and even Spotlight are in here (yes, they are all just individual applications). Obviously, it would be strongly encouraged not to remove any of these items.
Cookies	The Cookies folder in ~/Library/ is where Safari (and perhaps other web browsers and WebKit-enabled applications) store cookies that are presented from web sites. The proper way to manage the contents of this folder is through Safari (the Show Cookies button in Safari's Security Preferences).
Documentation	This is where many applications store their documentation files, including the interactive help documents.

Folder Name	Purpose
Extensions	Extensions are items that add functions to the system. Extensions generally enable specific hardware features. Warnings about not messing with /System/Library/ items apply doubly here!
Favorites	This is a carryover from older versions of OS X. I've yet to find a single use for it in Leopard.
Filesystems	Leopard has an architecture that allows file system plug-ins. The items in the Filesystems folder provide Leopard with the ability to read and write to various file system formats.
Filters	Contains Quartz filters. These filters provide various means of manipulating an image's appearance.
FontCollections	Font Book allows you to group fonts into various "collections." This data is stored in the FontCollections folder.
Fonts	These folders are where all your fonts are stored. /System/Library/Fonts/ stores all the primary system fonts that Leopard needs. /Library/Fonts/ contains most of the other fonts that you wish to make available to all users and all applications. Any fonts stored in ~/Library/Fonts are available to you, but not other users.
Frameworks	Frameworks are the essential building blocks of most applications in Leopard. Most applications rely on a number of native OS X frameworks in /System/Library/Frameworks. Additionally, many third-party applications and utilities will require additional frameworks that will be installed in /Library/Frameworks.
Graphics	Like the Audio folder, the Graphics folder contains Image Units and Quartz plug-ins that provide additional graphics capabilities to many Quartz-enabled graphics apps.
Image Capture	This folder contains plug-ins and support devices that allow for the acquisition of images from external sources (scanners, digital cameras, etc.).
iMovie	This folder contains iMovie plug-ins and sound effects.
Internet Plug-Ins	The Internet Plug-Ins folder contains the plug-ins for Safari and other applications. These allow the browser to display specific types of content inline, such as Flash, Java, and QuickTime.
iTunes	This folder may contain iTunes plug-ins (such as visualizer plug-ins), audio plug-ins, and other files, including iPod and iPhone updates.
Java	The various Java folders contain the various core Java runtime libraries and extensions.
Keychains	The Keychains folder in ~/Library contains your keychains. These are the system's built-in technology for storing passwords and authentication information. These files are highly encrypted. The way to open and manages a keychain file is through the Keychain Access utility.
LaunchAgents	This directory contains launchd files that cause applications or services to activate when a user logs into the computer.
LaunchDaemons	The contents here are similar to those in the LaunchAgents folder; however, items in LaunchDaemons will activate when the system starts whether or not a user logs in.

Continued

Table 2-1. Continued

Folder Name	Purpose
Logs	Many of the applications and services in OS X generate log files that keep track of important events that occur during the execution of a particular service. These files are stored in the various Logs folders. All of these logs are accessible (to those who have proper permissions to read them) via the Console utility.
Mail	~/Library/Mail stores most of you mail account info and your actual Mail folders for Leopard's Mail application.
Modem Scripts	The Modem Scripts directory contains a number of files that initialize various brands of modems.
PDF Services	This folder contains the various PDF workflows available from the PDF submenu of the Print panel.
Perl	The Perl folders contain the required and additional libraries for the Perl scripting language.
Phones	This folder stores information about any (non-iPhone) mobile phones that you either sync with your computer (via iSync) or use as a modem.
PreferencePanes	This folder contains the individual preference panes that appear in the System Preferences window.
Preferences	The Preferences directories contain all the saved preference data for every application and system component. The preferences in /Library/Preferences/ contain system-wide settings and metadata, while the files in ~/Library/Preferences/ contain all of your personal settings and metadata for your environment to operate correctly. Deleting a preference file usually causes an application to revert to its default state, which will remove all you personal settings (certain applications that require registration codes for activation will often need to be reactivated as well). Almost every application you launch will create a preference file, so you tend to acquire a large number of them. Feel free to clean out preference files from applications you no longer use.
Printers	This folder stores information about your selected printers as well as other important printing system files.
PrivateFrameworks	This is another Framework directory that contains custom frameworks used for internal purposes.
Python	This directory contains additional Python libraries. (Unlike Perl, Python is compiled as a framework in Leopard, so the core libraries are stored in the /System/Library/Framework/ directory.)
QuickLook	This directory contains Quick Look plug-ins that allow developers to add new capabilities to Quick Look.
QuickTime	The QuickTime folder contains QuickTime components that enhance the capabilities of QuickTime (including third-party drivers).
Receipts	The /Library/Receipts folder contains records of installed applications. OS X uses the contents of this folder as sort of an odd package management system. This is used by the system in many ways, so it's best to leave it alone—the exception would be for removing any receipts of applications you have removed.

Folder Name	Purpose
Recent Severs	This folder keeps track of recent servers you've connected to through the Finder.
Safari	The ~/Library/Safari/ folder keeps track of Safari information, including you bookmarks, history, and values for forms.
Saved Searches	This folder contains the saved searches you perform from within Spotlight.
Screen Savers	This folder contains your screen savers. If you plan on adding any screen savers to you system, it's advisable to create a ~/Library/Screen Savers folder to install them in, rather than installing them in the /Library/Screen Savers folder.
Scripts	This folder contains AppleScripts that are accessible from various sources. If you plan on utilizing your own scripts, you should create a ~/Library/Scripts/ folder to contain them. Occasionally, individual applications will install application-specific scripts in a subfolder of Scripts.
ScriptingAdditions	This folder contains items that enhance the capabilities of AppleScript.
ScriptingDefinitions	This folder contains dictionary documents that are available from within the Script Editor. These documents provide information about AppleScript syntax and usage.
ServerSetup	This folder contains items that aid in the startup of specific server services. In the Leopard client (as opposed to the server version of Leopard), this folder predominately contains startup information for Postfix, an SMTP mail server included in Leopard.
Services	This folder contains service applets that are available to most Aqua applications from the Application ▶ Services submenu. Many of the services the system provides are kept here, while other applications may store services with the application bundles.
Speech	This folder contains items that are used by the OS X speech system, including the various speech voices.
Spotlight	This folder contains some Spotlight plug-ins that add to the search abilities of Spotlight.
StartupItems	This is an old mechanism for starting up applications and services in OS X. This has been replaced by the launchd system, so most of the items that once went here have been moved to the LaunchAgents or LaunchDaemons folders.
Tcl	Like Perl and Python, Tcl is a scripting language that is used by the system as well as some other common third-party add-ons. This folder is where the Tcl (and Tk) libraries are stored.
User Pictures	This folder contains user images that are used as the default login icons that are selectable when you add an account.
WebServer	/Library/WebServer is a folder used by the Apache web server installed on Leopard. This folder contains the default Apache root document folder, Documents, as well as the CGI-Executables folder. This is one Library folder that we will talk more about (in Chapter 20).
Widgets	The Widgets folders are where all your Dashboard widgets are stored.

While there are other folders in your various Library folders (and often third-party applications will install their own), Table 2-1 covers most of the default ones. Before moving on, we'd like to give just one more mention that, in general, if you're unsure of what an item in one of your Library folders is, just leave it alone.

The Applications Folder

The Applications folder, as you may have guessed, is the recommended folder for installing applications. Keeping all your applications in this folder makes things fairly easy to find. If, however, you find that you have many applications and this folder starts to get cluttered, it's common to create your own subfolders to organize types of applications. For example, you might create /Applications/Games/ for any games you install or /Applications/Graphics/ for any graphics apps you install. This sort of organization makes it easy to find what you are looking for.

> **TIP** One common practice is to drag your Applications folder onto the Dock—that way you can easily access all of your applications from the Dock without having to dig through the Finder.

> **CAUTION** Some applications don't like to be moved from where they are installed. For the most part, any moved application will function just fine; the problem is that sometimes, when it comes time to update your application, the update utility expects the original application to be in a specific location. This is especially true of Apple's default applications that are frequently updated with the Software Update utility. If you do move an application into a subfolder and something strange happens when you try to update it, you can usually move the application back to its original location and redo the update with no harm—it's just a bit inconvenient. As a general rule, if an installer installs an application, it's best to leave it where it's installed (although installers often provide an option to install in subfolders). If you install an application manually by just dragging it into the Applications folder (as is often done), then it's probably safe to put it anywhere you want.

The Users Folder and Your Home

The other default folder at the top level of a fresh Leopard install (aside from Applications, System, and Library) is the Users folder. This is where each user's personal folder resides. This personal folder is usually referred to as the Users home directory (or just home). Inside of the Users folder will be a home folder for each of the system's users (named after the "short" name chosen when the account was created) and a Shared folder. The Shared folder is a place where certain applications will install some information common to all users, but it's used infrequently. Your home directory, however, is where you generally keep all of your documents, and where all of your personal settings are stored.

Your home folder, by default, starts out with nine subfolders: Desktop, Documents, Downloads, Library, Movies, Music, Pictures, Public, and Sites. Each of these folders has a specific purpose, as explained in Table 2-2.

Table 2-2. Default Home Folders and Their Descriptions

Folder	Description
Desktop	The contents of this folder are the items that appear on your desktop.
Documents	This is the primary folder for you to store all your document files. When you go to save or open a document from within an application, this is usually where it will start you out.
Downloads	This is a new addition to the default folders in Leopard (although in the past, most people created one of their own). Most Leopard-compliant network/Internet applications will default to downloading items into this folder.
Library	As described previously, most of your personal system and application settings are stored in this folder.
Movies	This is the default folder where imported videos and iMovie files will be stored. It's worth pointing out that movies and videos that you buy from the iTunes Store are actually stored in the Music folder!
Music	This is where your GarageBand and iTunes files are stored by default.
Pictures	This is the default folder for most of your images. This is where iPhoto and other photo applications will store their files by default.
Public	This is a special folder where you can store files that you wish to share with others on your computer or your network. Inside of this folder is a Drop Box folder where others can leave you files as well. To share files with users on your network, File Sharing must be enabled in the Sharing Preference pane.
Sites	This is the default folder for your personal web pages if Web Sharing is turned on in the Sharing Preference pane. Web Sharing is covered in Chapter 20.

These default folders cover most of your personal folder needs (although subfolders are common in each of these). Occasionally, you may want to add another folder for a specific need, and that's fine—this is after all your home.

Other Common Folders

We've covered most of the default folders you'll interact with in Leopard, but there are some other common folders you may encounter.

One of the most common other folders is the /Developer folder, which is present if you install the Xcode tools during or after your Leopard installation. Contained in this folder are all the Developer applications, documentation, and other items necessary to develop your own Mac OS X applications.

A couple other common folders that may present themselves are the /opt and /sw folders. These are special folders that are used by certain popular projects such as MacPorts and Fink. Both of these projects are covered in Chapter 19, where you will learn more about these folders.

Hidden Folders

The folders mentioned previously barely scratch the surface of the whole file system on Leopard. The thing is, most of the other folders and contents are hidden from the Finder. These hidden files are mostly part of the UNIX system on which Leopard runs (largely referred to as the Darwin subsystem of OS X). Later, in Chapters 18 and 19, we'll devote a large part of our discussion to Darwin and the UNIX underbelly of Leopard.

If you are curious as to these hidden files, the following AppleScript can toggle the visibility of hidden Finder items:

```
tell application "Finder" to quit
try
    do shell script "defaults read com.apple.finder AppleShowAllFiles"
        set OnOff to result
on error
        set OnOff to "0"
end try

if OnOff = "0" then
        set OnOffCommand to "defaults write com.apple.finder AppleShowAllFiles 1"
else
        set OnOffCommand to "defaults write com.apple.finder AppleShowAllFiles 0"
end if
do shell script OnOffCommand
delay 1
tell application "Finder" to launch
```

To run this script, open the Script Editor (found in /Applications/AppleScript/), type the preceding script into the editor, and then click the Run button. Then have a look in the Finder and relish all the other folders and items that appear. Run the script once more to hide these items again. Feel free to create a Scripts folder in your ~/Library/ folder and save this little file there as "Toggle Hidden" or some such name, so that it will be available to you later.

> **NOTE** Most hidden files are there for a purpose, and are likewise hidden for a purpose. Usually this purpose is to protect the files from accidental disturbance by casual users. It's generally best to leave hidden files alone, at least until you learn what they do and how to work with them properly (some of which will be covered in this book).

Summary

Now that you've had a glimpse of how everything is organized on your computer and learned how to move around it, we're going to take a brief side track in the next chapter to point out a few of the unique features in Mac OS X, including some new features introduced in Leopard, such as Spotlight, Dashboard, Spaces, and Expose.

## CHAPTER 3

Using Spotlight, Exposé, Spaces, and Dashboard

Leopard has a few additional interface features that are definitely worth mentioning that haven't been covered yet in other chapters:

- Spotlight
- Exposé
- Spaces
- Dashboard

Searching with Spotlight

Spotlight, which was introduced in Tiger (Mac OS X 10.4), is a system-wide search tool that locates any items on your computer that match your search criteria. In Leopard, Spotlight improves upon and adds a number of features, including the ability to save searches as smart folders that are easily accessed from within Spotlight and the ability to search computers on your network (provided they allow such access). In Leopard, Spotlight becomes a seamless, integral part of how you work with your system.

> **NOTE** When you first install Leopard, Spotlight is not immediately available. Before Spotlight is ready, it must index your entire system. This can take several hours to complete. While Spotlight is indexing, your hard drive will spin a lot, your system will get hot, and the computer's fan (if it has one) will probably start running full speed. Oh, yeah, there will also be a pulsing black dot inside Spotlight's magnifying glass icon in the upper-right corner of the menu bar that indicates Spotlight is indexing.

Performing a Basic Search in Spotlight

To perform a Spotlight search, you can either click the magnifying glass in the upper-right corner of your screen or press Cmd+spacebar. This will open a simple drop-down text field for you to type your search (Figure 3-1). As you start to type, the drop-down field will expand to reveal

Figure 3-1. Spotlight's search field

possible matches for your search (Figure 3-2). As you refine your search, the matches will dynamically change to the most appropriate choices.

Once you have finished typing your search phrase, the top results matched will be revealed for you, organized by type. Depending on how specific your search is, there could be only a few possible matches; however, often there are more matches than fit in the simple drop-down menu. Selecting the Show All item will open a special Finder search window containing all the results from your search (Figure 3-3). This window will also allow you to further refine your search.

> **TIP** There are a number of keyboard shortcuts to help you move around the list of search results without having to reach for your mouse or trackpad. The up and down arrow keys will (as you may assume) move up and down one item at a time. Using the Cmd key with the up and down arrows will move up and down through the file types. Pressing Cmd+left arrow will insert a cursor at the beginning of your search term, and pressing Cmd+right arrow will insert the cursor at the end of your search term to edit or revise it. Finally, if Spaces is not active, pressing Ctrl+up arrow will move to the top of the list highlighting Show All, and pressing Ctrl+down arrow will move to the bottom of the list highlighting Spotlight Preferences. (If Spaces is active, it will by default use these shortcuts to switch spaces, and this function will override Spotlight. You may be able to duplicate this effect, though, with Fn+arrow keys.)

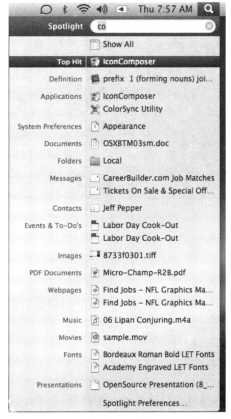

Figure 3-2. Spotlight reveals top matches for your search as you type.

Refining and Saving Your Searches

Whether you start with a simple Spotlight search and, as discussed earlier, choose the Show All option or you start a search directly in the Finder's search field, you will be presented with a special Finder search window (shown in Figure 3-3) that will allow you to refine and save your searches. The Finder's search window and regular Finder window are different in two ways. First, since you are dealing with search results, the items shown are not necessarily located in a single folder but rather can be collected from all over your hard drive and attached file systems. Second, there is a search bar and perhaps some refinement bars present at the top of the Finder view area that allow you to refine your searches.

There is always one primary search bar at the very top that will allow you to set the scope of your search; this can be your entire computer, a specific folder, or a shared resource. The specific options depend on a few criteria; for example, This Mac is always an option, which will cause the search to include your entire computer. The following option is a folder: if you are performing your search via the Spotlight icon, this folder will be your home directory; if you are performing the search from the Finder, then this folder is the folder from which you are performing the search. Other search options may include specific shared or network resources on which you have permission to perform searches.

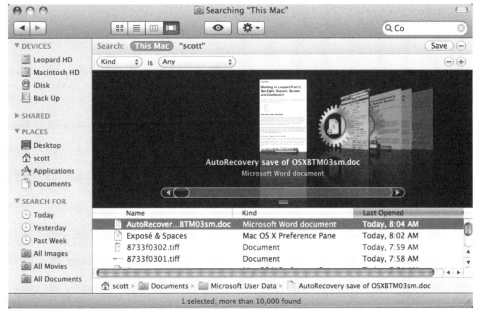

Figure 3-3. Show All will open a special Finder window revealing every item that matches your search.

To the far right of the topmost search bar is a Save button that will allow you to save your search for future use, and then there is a + or - button that will allow you to add or remove additional search criteria. Each time you add criteria, a new bar will appear that will allow you to refine your search from a series of drop-down lists (Figure 3-4).

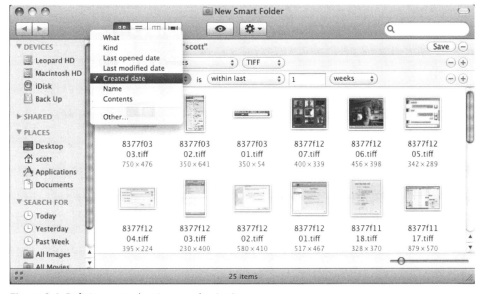

Figure 3-4. Refining a search using search criteria

Table 3-1 describes the general search criteria.

Table 3-1. Search Criteria to Refine Searches

Criteria	Description
What	Provides check boxes to determine whether the search should be limited to file names only and to system files. By default, the search will exclude system files; however, with all other files it will attempt to find the search string in any metadata, text within the item, and Finder comments as well as the actual file name.
Kind	This can help narrow down your search to a specific kind of file and includes the following options: Applications, Documents, Folders, Images, Movies, Music, PDF, Presentations, Text, and Other. Certain options will allow you to further refine the kind; for example, Images will allow you to narrow search results to specific image formats.
Last opened date	This will allow you to narrow search results to a date, or range of dates, when the item was last opened.
Last modified date	This will allow you to narrow search results to a date, or range of dates, when the item was last modified.
Created date	This will allow you to narrow search results to a date, or range of dates, when the item was created.
Name	This will allow you to match additional search strings against the name of the file.
Contents	This will allow you to match additional search strings against the contents of the file.
Other	This option will open a window with a number of additional search criteria that can be added to your search (Figure 3-5); many of these items are common metadata items or other common possible search criteria. Your actual list may change because of third-party applications that add their own data here.

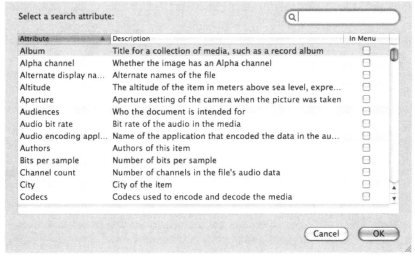

Figure 3-5. The Other search option opens a window that contains a large list of other common metadata and search criteria.

Once you have you search criteria set, you can select the specific item you are looking for in the Finder's Search view.

If you want to save your search, click the Save button in the top-left side of the view area. This will open a Save dialog box (Figure 3-6) that will let you save your search and if desired add it to your Finder sidebar.

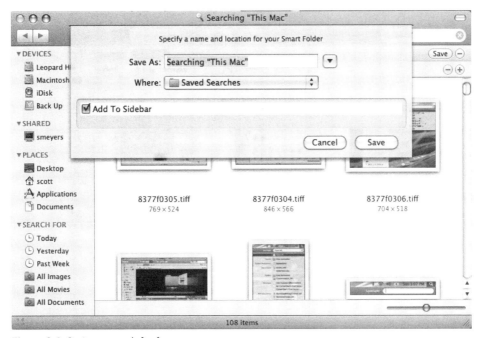

Figure 3-6. Saving a search for future access

Setting Up Smart Folders

The default locations for saving a search is in your ~/Library/Saved Searches folder. If you look there, you will see that saved searches are nothing more than smart folders. In fact, the process of setting up a smart folder is the same as refining and saving a search.

Using Spotlight Technology in Other Applications

Spotlight is a key technology in OS X, and developers are able to include its features into their own applications as they see fit. For example, digital asset management (DAM) applications can use it to help organize and find specific digital media files in a large collection. The Mail app includes Spotlight technology to help locate mail messages, notes, and to-do items stored in Mail. Spotlight is even cleverly included in the default help system and can be used to find and highlight application commands in the application menus (Figure 3-7).

Figure 3-7. Spotlight technology in the Help menu can help you find application menu items.

Using Exposé and Spaces

Besides Spotlight, some other nice features are built in to Leopard that can be summoned as necessary. The first two we'll talk about are Exposé and Spaces.

Exposé and Spaces help you find and manage open applications and application windows. Both Exposé and Spaces do this by manipulating your work area, but each of them does this in different ways.

Exposé

Exposé works within your current work area or desktop by moving, shrinking, and highlighting your current windows in ways that are incredibly useful, especially if you are working with many open windows at once.

Exposé provides three distinct views: "All windows" view, "Application windows" view, and Desktop view. Each view provides certain benefits.

You can trigger the "All windows" view (Figure 3-8) by default by hitting the F9 key. This view will shrink and arrange all the windows open on your current desktop so that they are all visible; from this view you can mouse over and select the particular window you'd like to bring to the foreground.

> **NOTE** On Apple computers, the F-keys (aka function keys) are often used for controlling things such as the brightness of the screen, the volume, and other features. This is especially true with MacBooks and MacBook Pros that by default have the F-keys set to control these features. In such a case you must use Fn+[F-key] to activate the desired F-key. If you would rather have the F-keys work as the F-keys by default, you can set this behavior in the Keyboard & Mouse preference pane.

Figure 3-8. Exposé's All windows View

The "Application windows" view (Figure 3-9) is similar to the "All windows" view, but it affects only the open windows of the foreground application. Triggered by the F10 key by default, it causes the windows of all background applications to be faded into the background while arranging and highlighting the windows of the current application. This is effective if you are working with many documents in a single application or if you have multiple Finder windows open.

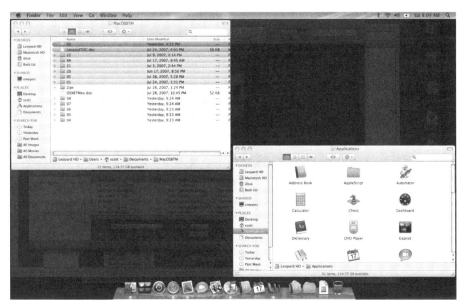

Figure 3-9. Exposé's "Application windows" view highlighting only the open Finder windows

The final Exposé view, triggered by the F11 key by default, is Desktop view (Figure 3-10). This "slides" all the currently open windows off the screen, making the entire desktop visible so you can access any Finder items located on it that may be blocked by the current windows. This is especially nice for people who tend to collect a large number of items on their desktops.

Figure 3-10. Exposé's Desktop view moves all the open windows to the side to reveal the entire desktop. The edges of the open windows remain slightly in view along the darkened edge.

NOTE The F-key defaults to control Exposé, Spaces, and Dashboard can all be changed in the Exposé & Spaces preference pane. Additionally, if you have a mouse with many buttons, you can easily map these features to mouse buttons.

Spaces

Spaces is a new feature in Leopard (though there have been third-party applications available for a while that provide a similar experience) that allows you to set up multiple working environments, or desktops, and switch between them. This is commonly referred to as creating and managing *virtual desktops*.

By default, Spaces isn't enabled, but its icon is on the Dock. Clicking the icon on the Dock the first time will prompt you to set up Spaces in the Exposé & Spaces preference pane (Figure 3-11). Clicking Set Up Spaces will open System Preferences to configure Spaces (Figure 3-12).

Figure 3-11. If you attempt to use Spaces before it's set up, you will be presented with a dialog box asking you to do so.

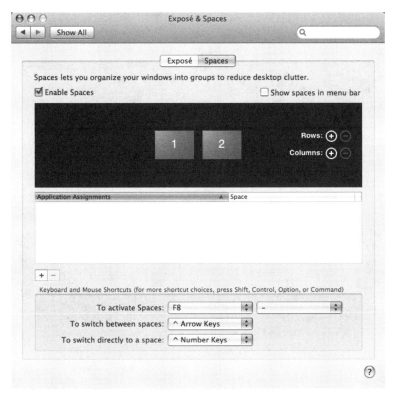

Figure 3-12. Spaces is set up in the Exposé & Spaces pane of System Preferences.

By default Spaces is set up with a row of two spaces. To add a row or column, click the appropriate + in the preference pane. The preference pane will show you a small illustration of your current layout with a label on each space to designate its appropriate number. If you select the "Show spaces in menu bar" option, it will use the designated number to display the active space and allow you to switch to other spaces via a drop-down menu.

Below the area displaying your spaces layout, you can set up applications so that they always open in a designated space. For example, you could have all your Internet applications open in one space and all of your office apps open in another. Switching to an application in the Dock, or opening an application, will automatically take you to the appropriate space.

To move from one space to another, you can "activate" Spaces either using the F8 key (by default) or clicking the icon in the Dock. This will present a view of all your spaces shrunk down to fit on your screen, very much like the "All windows" view in Exposé (Figure 3-13).

While Spaces is activated, you can select any window in the view and move it from one space to another, or you can select any space to make that space active on your primary screen.

You can also move windows from one space to another by selecting a window and dragging it to an edge of your screen where another space may be.

To quickly move from one space to another, you can use a series of other keyboard shortcuts. By default, pressing Ctrl and an arrow key at the same time will move you to the space in that direction. Specifically, pressing Ctrl with the right or left arrows will cycle through the spaces numerically, and pressing Ctrl with the up and down arrows will move up or down only if there is a valid space above or below to move into. If you know the space's number, you can move directly to that space pressing Ctrl and the spaces number (for example, pressing Ctrl+4 will move to space 4). When you use these keyboard shortcuts, a small overlay graphic will appear on the screen to illustrate where you are in the Spaces layout (Figure 3-14).

Figure 3-13. Activating Spaces will present you with a live view of all your active spaces.

Figure 3-14. A small overlay graphic will appear when you switch to a new space using the keyboard shortcuts; it highlights the space you have just entered.

NOTE The maximum number of spaces is 16, a 4×4 grid. This should most likely be more than enough spaces since in general it's probably best to utilize the fewest number of spaces necessary. Additionally, the keyboard shortcut won't work with spaces 10–16.

Dashboard

The final nifty Leopard feature we'll talk about in this chapter is Dashboard. Dashboard is an interface feature that, when activated, will bring forward a number of user-selectable widgets. A *widget* is a small, simple application that can do various things. Leopard ships with a number of widgets that can display the current time, give you the latest movie schedule for you area, control iTunes, and do much more.

By default, you activate Dashboard with the F12 key. When you do this, the active widgets will slide into view over your current desktop view (Figure 3-15).

Figure 3-15. Dashboard active with default widgets

To add a widget to your Dashboard, you can click the + sign in the lower-left corner of the screen when the Dashboard is active. That will open the widget bar across the bottom of the screen that contains all the Dashboard widgets currently installed (Figure 3-16). To add any of the installed widgets, select them and drag them off the bar onto the desktop. To remove a widget, click the X on the top-left of any widget when the widget bar is open. To move a widget, just click it and move it around to wherever you want, and it will reappear in your selected location each time you activate Dashboard.

> **NOTE** Holding the Opt key while mousing over a widget will also reveal its Close (X) button.

In addition to the widgets included with Leopard, many, many other widgets are available to download and install. A good place to look is www.apple.com/downloads/dashboard/. If you download a widget in Safari, it will usually recognize the file as a widget and ask you whether you'd like to install it. To manually install a widget, just stick it in your ~/Library/Widgets folder (you may need to create this folder if it doesn't exist). Once it's installed, it will be available from the widget bar. You can uninstall widgets by moving them out of the Widget folder. You can also deactivate widgets using the Manage Widgets widget that presents a list of all the installed widgets with check boxes that can be unchecked to deactivate any widgets.

Figure 3-16. Dashboard with the widget bar open at the bottom and the Manage Widgets widget open in the middle of the screen

NOTE Double-clicking a Dashboard widget in the Finder will also install the widget. If you are an administrator, it will prompt you whether you'd like it installed for yourself or for everyone. If you are a regular user, it will install it in your Library/Widgets folder.

Using the individual widgets varies from widget to widget; however, many widgets have settings hidden in them. To check a widget's settings, mouse over the widget to see whether a small *i* appears (usually in one of the corners). Clicking this *i* will cause the widget to flip over, revealing the widget information and settings.

In Leopard you can also add web clippings to your Dashboard from Safari. We'll talk about web clippings more when we cover Safari in Chapter 10, but as far as Dashboard is concerned, they generally behave like any other widget.

NOTE One new, behind-the-scenes feature of Dashboard in Leopard is that all widgets are run in the same process. Previously, every time you started a widget it would run in its own process, so if you ran a large number of widgets, you would notice a slowdown on your computer.

Summary

This chapter wrapped up our quick introduction to the basics of Leopard. The next part jumps into the basic administration of Leopard as well as how to customize Leopard to suit your needs. We'll begin by going through System Preferences in the next chapter.

PART **2**

Customizing and Administering Leopard

## CHAPTER 4

System Preferences

Many of the configuration and administration options for Leopard are located in System Preferences (Figure 4-1). In Leopard, System Preferences is an application that presents a collection of individual items called *preference panes*. Each preference pane presents configurable options for one specific facet of the OS.

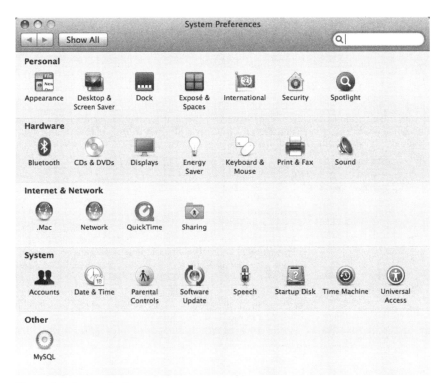

Figure 4-1. System Preferences

This chapter will give an overview of each of these preferences and explain what they all do. We will discuss them according to how they are categorized in System Preferences:

- Personal preferences
- Hardware preferences
- Internet & Network preferences
- System preferences

Some preferences will only be touched upon lightly, as they will be covered in depth later in this book.

NOTE There is also an Other category of preferences, which is where third-party system preferences are shown.

Personal Preferences

The first row of preferences in System Preferences contains the Personal preferences (Figure 4-2). These preferences together largely affect your personal environment and can be set differently for each user on your system.

Figure 4-2. The Personal preferences in System Preferences

Appearance

The Appearance preference pane (Figure 4-3) contains a number of options that control how certain aspects of your environment will not only look, but also behave.

Table 4-1 lists each of the appearance options and describes them.

Table 4-1. Appearance Options

Option	Description
Appearance	This option allows you to change certain visual elements from blue to graphite. In Leopard, many of the elements that had been affected by this preference have been replaced with a common black/gray appearance; however there are still many things that will be affected by this. The remaining elements that are affected by this are the window widgets in the top left of the title bars (switching from blue to graphite will cause the red, yellow, and green buttons to each change to become the same graphite color) and some other UI elements (e.g., the edges of drop-down option menus) will change from blue to graphite.
Highlight Color	This option allows you to change the highlight color of selected text in most applications.
Place scroll arrows	This option selects whether the scroll arrow in window scroll bars will be together (in the lower right of each scrollable window), or whether the arrows will appear at each end of the scroll bar.

Option	Description
Click in the scroll bar to	This option affects the scroll behavior when you click in an empty part of the scroll bar. Depending on your setting here, when you click an empty area of the scroll bar, the view will either scroll to the next page up or down (depending on where you click), or scroll directly to the relative location in the view where you clicked in the scroll bar.
Use smooth scrolling	Clicking this box will increase the smoothness in which items scroll by. It does this by using faster refreshes, so smooth scrolling comes at the cost of some system resources. On most newer machines, the effect of this is negligible.
Minimize when double-clicking a window title bar	This option does what it says. When selected, this will cause any window to minimize into the Dock when you double-click the title bar (personally, I preferred the window shades of earlier Mac OS systems).
Number of Recent Items	These three drop-down menus select how many items of each type will appear in the Recent Items submenu in the Apple menu.
Font smoothing style	This option controls font smoothing. Font smoothing rounds off fonts so the edges don't appear jagged, usually improving their appearance on the screen. Occasionally this can alter a font's intended look somewhat, and at very small font sizes it can cause them to become blurry—in which case, there is an option to turn off font smoothing for smaller fonts. In general, the defaults are fine, but you may wish to tweak these to your preference.

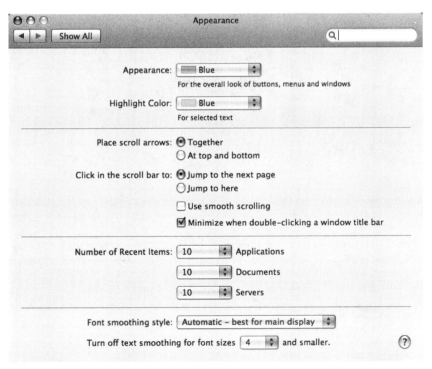

Figure 4-3. The Appearance preference pane in System Preferences

> **NOTE** Font smoothing in Mac OS X is noticeably different than font smoothing in Windows, and there are definitely proponents of each. In Mac OS X, the priority is preserving the look and spacing of the font so that the printed and onscreen text look identical. In Windows, the priority is placed on making the font most readable on the screen, even though that may mean that the onscreen font will be altered in unintended ways. As a result, the fonts in Mac OS X appear more accurate, but can seem a little soft or fuzzy, while the fonts in Windows look crisper, but the spacing and layout is often not necessarily as intended, and might not match the final output.

Desktop & Screen Saver

The Desktop & Screen Saver preference pane is where you go to change your desktop picture or alter you screen saver and screen saver settings. This pane is divided into two tabs: one that sets the desktop image (Figure 4-4) and one that contains all of your screen saver options (Figure 4-5).

Figure 4-4. The Desktop tab of the Desktop & Screen Saver preference pane sets your desktop background image.

The Desktop tab presents you with a selection of images to use as your desktop background. By default, Apple provides a wide selection of attractive backgrounds, classified into general categories. Clicking one of the folder items in the left column will present you a preview of all the images in the right viewing area. Selecting an image in the viewing area will automatically set the image as your desktop background, and put the preview image in the top image space with the image's name besides it.

The default background images are set with preselected aspects; however, if you choose one of your own images, a drop-down menu will appear that will allow you to alter the aspect of the image you choose. These aspects are described in Table 4-2.

Table 4-2. Desktop Image Aspect Selections

Aspect	Description
Fit to Screen	Fit to Screen will scale the image so that the entire image fits your screen. This option will not change the aspect of your image, so if your image is wider, empty space will appear above and below your image (the color of the empty space may be selected in the color swatch next to the aspect menu).
Fill Screen	This option will scale your image so that it fills the entire screen. This option won't adjust the aspect ratio of your image, either; however, rather than fill the difference with empty space, it will scale the image up to fill the empty space (possibly clipping off the edges of your image).
Stretch to Fill Screen	Stretch to Fill screen will scale the image to fill the screen, too. This option, however, will adjust the aspect ratio so that the entire image fills the screen. This may stretch your images contents oddly.
Center	This option will not scale your image; rather, it will just center your image on the screen. If your image dimensions are smaller than your screen dimensions, then empty space will appear around the image. If your image dimensions are larger than your screen dimensions, then the image will extend beyond the screen, effectively cutting off the edges. (You can select the background color that will be shown along the edges if visible.)
Tile	Like Center, this option will not scale your image at all; rather, it will align the top-left corner of your image with the top-left corner of the screen. If the dimensions of the image are smaller than the dimensions of the screen, then the image will repeat itself to the right and below itself over and over until it fills the entire screen.

This preference pane will automatically reveal any top-level images in your Pictures folder; additionally, it will show items from your iPhoto and Aperture libraries so you can select images from them. You can also add your own image folders by clicking the + button and selecting the folder you wish to add. Also, if you'd like, you can set your preferences so that your background image will change at regular intervals.

> **NOTE** The translucent menu bar in Leopard allows you to view parts of your desktop background that were previously hidden behind the menu bar. While this is nice, it also means that high-contrast areas of images behind the menu bar can make the menu bar items difficult to read. This should be kept under consideration when selecting your desktop backgrounds.

The Screen Saver tab presents a list of available screen saver *modules* on the left side of the window with a Preview area to the right. In addition to the individual modules, you can also select groups or libraries of images to be used as a screen saver.

To set up your screen saver, first choose the module you'd like to use. Some modules will have settable options; if the selected module has options, the Options button will be active. Once you have chosen the module and set its options, you can test it by clicking the Test button. This will activate the screen saver with your chosen module. To return, just wiggle the mouse or press a key.

Below the Preview area is the "Start screen saver" slider, which determines how long your system must be idle before the screen saver starts.

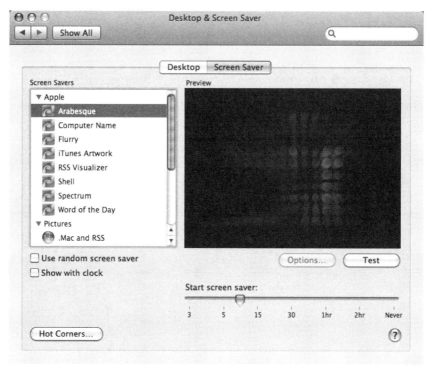

Figure 4-5. The Screen Saver tab of the Desktop & Screen Saver preference pane

NOTE Certain computers, particularly laptops, will power down the screen after a certain amount of idle time. If this time is shorter than the screen saver start time, then the screen saver will never start. If this is the case, you will receive a warning to this effect in the Screen Saver preference pane, along with a link to the Energy Saver preference pane, where you can control the sleep setting.

Following are some other screen saver options:

Use random screen saver: This option will randomly choose a screen saver module when the screen saver starts.

Show with clock: This will provide an overlay that presents the current time over the screen saver.

Hot Corners: This button will bring up the Hot Corner dialog, which allows you to assign certain functions to occur when the mouse cursor is moved into one of the corners of your screen. Two of the available options are Start Screen Saver and Disable Screen Saver (which will prevent the screen saver from starting if the mouse cursor is in the selected corner).

While the screen saver modules included in Leopard are nice, there are tons of third-party screen savers also available for download (try www.apple.com/downloads/macosx/icons_screensavers/). To install a new screen saver, just download the screen saver file and then double-click it. This will bring up a dialog box asking if you'd like to install the screen saver for just yourself or for all the users of your computer. If you select the option for just you, the screen saver file will be installed in ~/Library/Screen Savers/; if you choose to install it for everyone, it will be installed in /Library/Screen Savers/.

Dock

The Dock preference pane (Figure 4-6) presents options for configuring your Dock behavior. These options were covered in Chapter 1 of this book.

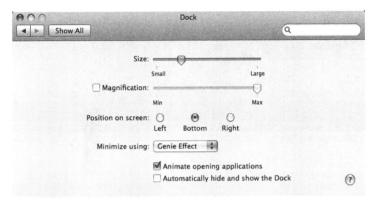

Figure 4-6. The Dock preference pane

Exposé & Spaces

The Exposé & Spaces preference pane (Figures 4-7 and 4-8) provides options for configuring Exposé and Spaces, as described in the previous chapter (Chapter 3).

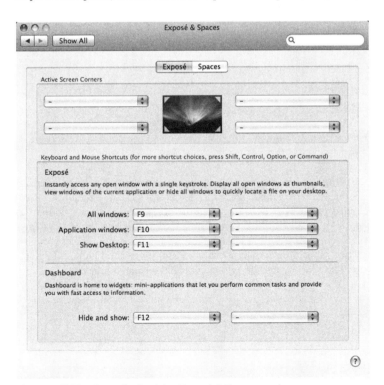

Figure 4-7. The Exposé tab of the Exposé & Spaces preference pane

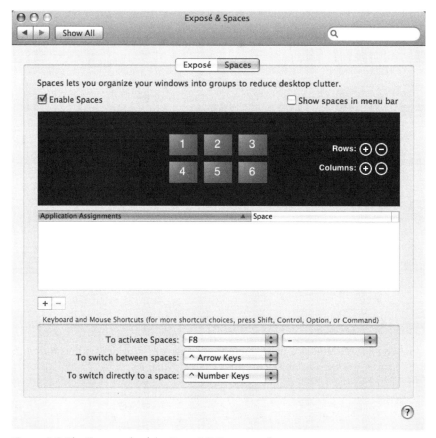

Figure 4-8. The Spaces tab of the Exposé & Spaces preference pane

International

The International preference pane controls the language and regional display settings of your computer. This preference pane has three tabs that control various settings: Language, Formats, and Input Menu.

The Language tab (Figure 4-9) allows you to set your preferred display language. The column on the left lists the activated languages, and you can drag them in the order of your language preference. For example, if I switched the order of English and Japanese, so that Japanese would appear first, then Japanese would become the default language for my system and all applications. If, however, an application wasn't localized in Japanese (i.e., didn't contain Japanese translations), then the application would attempt to find my second choice (English in this case). For the system or any application, the first available language will be used.

> **NOTE** *Localization* is a term referring to adding language information for a specific region in the world. Saying that an application is localized for the Ukraine means that Ukrainian language data was added to the application and is available to those who wish to use it. This isn't terribly difficult to do—in fact, if you encounter an application that lacks a localization that you favor, you may want to contact the developer about this. You could even easily help implement the proper localization if you so desire.

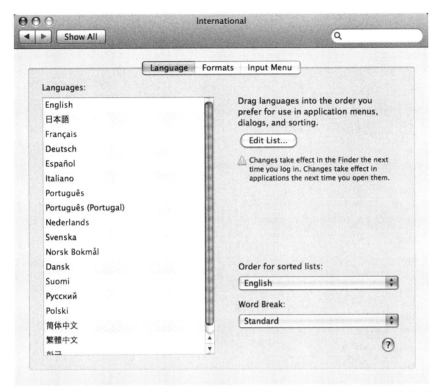

Figure 4-9. The Language tab of the International preference pane sets your default display language.

You may notice that while the default list of languages covers many languages, there are many more not covered. To add or remove languages from the list, click the Edit List button. This will bring up a dialog box with many more languages to choose from. Checking the box next to any of these languages will include that language in the default list.

Other options in this tab include the following:

Order for sorted lists: This determines the language used for sorting items in the Finder when you choose to sort items by name.

Word Break: This changes the behavior when you double-click a word in an editable text field. The Standard setting will highlight the entire word when you double-click it. If you use Japanese as your primary language, then the Japanese setting should be used. The final setting, English (United States, Computer), is intended specifically for programmers. It is a bit smarter about selecting words within syntax when using whitespace isn't the best way to determine where a word begins or ends.

The Formats tab (Figure 4-10) sets up default date, time, number, currency, and measurement unit settings for your computer. Selecting your region from the Region drop-down list generally sets these items accurately. For example, switching from United States to United Kingdom will alter the order of the date, switch to a 24-hour clock, change the currency from US Dollars to British Pound Sterling, and change the measurement units to metric. If, however, the default settings for your region aren't exactly what you want, most of these settings can be altered or customized (e.g., if you work for NASA, on, say, a Mars Climate Orbiter project, you might want to switch to the metric system). If you don't see the region that you want in the Region menu, try checking the "Show all regions" selection.

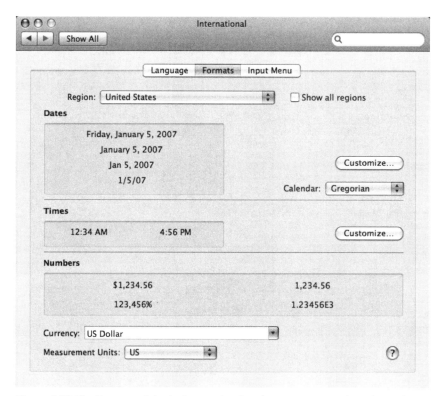

Figure 4-10. The Formats tab in the International preference pane sets how dates, times, numbers, currency, and measurements appear.

> **NOTE** It seems that whatever region you choose, the Calendar setting will stay set to Gregorian, so if you wish to use a different calendar system, you will need to set that manually.

While the Language and Formats tabs largely govern output and display, the Input Menu tab (Figure 4-11) is where you set up your input language and devices. The Input Menu tab is mostly a large list of items with check boxes. Each item represents an input palette, an input method, or an input device (specifically a keyboard). Checking the check box will activate an item. If more than one item is selected, the "Show input menu in menu bar" option will automatically be selected, allowing you to switch between different ways of inputting data easily from any application.

The input palettes (Figure 4-12) are special windows that appear on the screen and allow you to input characters by clicking them. The Keyboard Viewer palette is particularly interesting, since it shows how your keyboard is mapped and responds dynamically as you type on the keyboard. For example, if you press the Option key, the Keyboard Viewer will change to reflect the symbols available with the Option+*key* combinations. Paying attention to changes while playing around with this can teach you new tricks. For example, if you look at the changes while you hold the Fn key, you may notice a number of interesting functions (e.g., Fn+Del deletes the characters in front of the cursor rather than behind).

The input methods affect the behavior of inputting text, primarily for languages with very large character sets. For such languages, you will commonly enter two or more keystrokes to input a single character. These varying input methods facilitate this.

Figure 4-11. The Input Menu tab in the International preference pane sets the language input options for your systems.

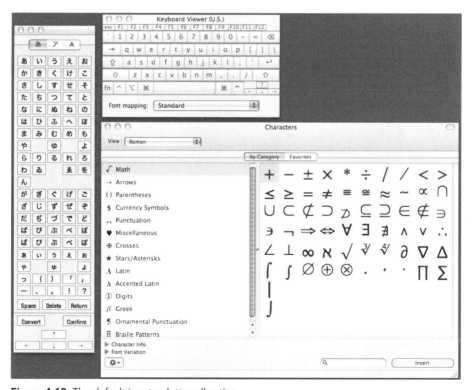

Figure 4-12. The default input palettes all active

Finally, the Keyboard items affect the keyboard layout. In general, this is to accommodate different language keyboards; however, you can use these options to remap any keyboard (even though in doing so the letters on the keys will no longer match the inputted character). While some of the remappings are extreme, some are subtler—for example, switching to a Spanish key map will only alter a few symbol keys (making common Spanish symbols easier to access). In addition to changing the input character maps of your keyboard, changing to certain languages will alter the direction of input—for example, switching to Arabic or Hebrew will cause the input to flow from right to left rather than left to right.

In general, if you need to enter text, characters, or symbols and you are not quite sure how, selecting either the Keyboard Viewer or Characters palette is a good place start to help you find what you are looking for.

> **TIP** If you use the Keyboard Viewer palette frequently, but don't want to fuss around with the International preferences whenever you want to access it, there is another, easier way to access it. The Keyboard Viewer itself is actually an application hidden away, but can be utilized just like any other application. To find the application, select Go ➤ Go to Folder... from the Finder's Application menu (or use the Shift+Cmd+G keyboard shortcut from the Finder) and enter **/System/Library/Components/KeyboardViewer.component/Contents/SharedSupport/** in the text field of the dialog box. Within this folder is the desired application, named KeyboardViewerServer. Double-clicking this will bring up the Keyboard Viewer palette. Now you may copy this application (don't move it, as the system needs it to be here) to wherever you want and treat it as any other application.

Security

The Security preference pane seems oddly placed in that most of its options affect the entire system rather than just your personal preferences. The Security preference pane provides three tabs: General, for general system security options; FileVault, for encrypting your personal home folder and all of its contents; and Firewall, which can help secure your system from network intrusion by limiting access to computer network services.

Chapter 8 is dedicated to system security, so these preferences and more will be covered there.

Spotlight

The Spotlight preference pane (Figure 4-13) helps you customize what types of items Spotlight will index, and in what preference you want the results of a search to be returned to you.

The Spotlight preference pane has two tabs: Search Results and Privacy. The Privacy tab (not shown) allows you to select folders that you want to prevent from being indexed. This can prevent information that you'd like to keep private from showing up in any searches of your system, or it can save system resources by indexing only the items that you are interested in indexing.

The Search Results tab provides a few more customization possibilities. First of all, it allows you to block certain types of files from appearing in a Spotlight search result. So, if you'd like to exclude mail messages from being returned in a Spotlight search, you can uncheck the Mail Messages item (this only affects system-wide Spotlight searches; messages will continue to be searchable from within Mail). Additionally, you can arrange the items in the Search Results list in the order that you'd like those items to be returned to you, so if you'd like all the matched images to appear before the matched contacts, just move the Images item above the Contacts item.

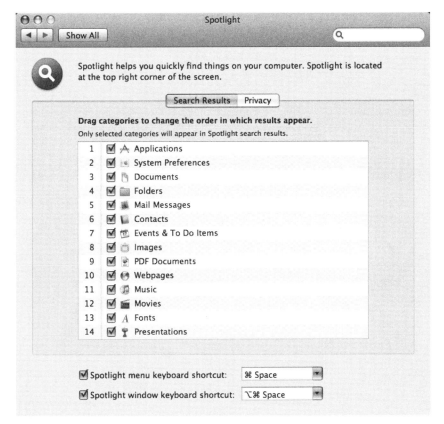

Figure 4-13. The Spotlight preference pane with the Search Results tab showing

The options below the window allow you to alter the keyboard shortcuts for activating Spotlight. In general, I'd recommend not doing this—since most applications are aware of the default shortcuts, it's unlikely that they would interfere with the defaults. If you change these, however, there may be times when the keyboard shortcuts you set do something unexpected.

Hardware

The row of preference panes below the Personal preferences contains the Hardware preferences (Figure 4-14). Here you will find settings for most of the hardware devices included with your computer.

Figure 4-14. The Hardware preference panes

> **NOTE** Most third-party hardware, and even some software, includes its own preference pane. These non-Apple preference panes will be included together at the bottom of System Preferences, in the Other Category.

Bluetooth

The Bluetooth preference pane is used to configure Bluetooth on your computer and manage any Bluetooth devices that have been paired to your computer. Connecting and managing Bluetooth devices is covered in the next chapter (Chapter 5).

CDs & DVDs

The CDs & DVDs preference pane (Figure 4-15) allows you to select what will happen when you insert certain media formats in your computer. The media formats that you can assign actions to include blank CDs, blank DVDs, music CDs, picture CDs, and video DVDs.

Figure 4-15. The CDs & DVDs preference pane

Displays

The Displays preference pane allows you to make adjustments to your computer displays. By default, there are two tabs in this preference pane: Display and Color.

The Display tab (Figure 4-16) allows you to set the display resolution and color depth for your display. Additionally, certain displays (predominately CRT monitors) will allow you to adjust the refresh rate, and others (predominately Apple monitors) will allow you to adjust the display's brightness from the control panel. Finally, if your computer has ambient light sensors (some Apple laptops), you can set an option that will automatically adjust your screen's brightness according to the brightness of your environment.

> **NOTE** These days, all the displays that Apple sells are flat-panel LCDs or newer LEDs. These are generally easier to set up than the older CRT monitors, since you don't need to hassle with refresh rates. Also, LCDs and LEDs are created to work best at specific resolutions (usually the highest resolution available), which makes choosing the best resolution easy as well.

The Color tab (Figure 4-17) allows you to manage the display's color profiles. A *color profile* is a data file that contains color information about a device or color standard. ColorSync uses these data files to match colors up so that an item appears consistent from one device to another. All this allows an image from your digital camera to appear on your screen the way the camera intended, and then allows the image you print out on your printer to match what you see on the screen. The trick, however, is to assure that your screen has the proper profile.

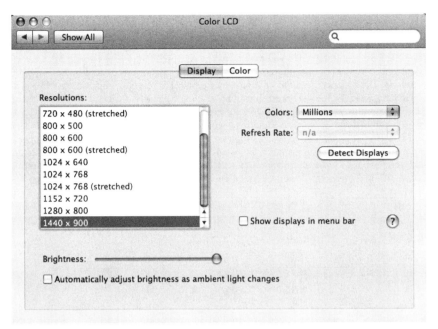

Figure 4-16. The Display tab of the Displays preference pane

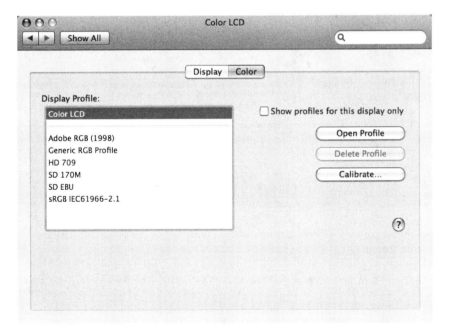

Figure 4-17. The Displays preference pane's Color tab helps you manage your display's color profiles.

Leopard provides some generic color profiles for Apple displays as well as some others; however, it's likely that you will want to calibrate your monitor, creating a custom profile for your display.

> **NOTE** Why calibrate your display? There are two reasons (and even if one doesn't apply to you, the other will). First, the generic color profiles that ship with Leopard are just that—generic. They are a decent average, but in reality each display is slightly different, so it's highly unlikely that the generic profile will match reality. Also, the generic profiles don't take into account your ambient lighting situation, which can have a big impact on how colors appear on your screen. The second reason to calibrate your monitor is to adjust the gamma of your display. *Gamma*, which is normally represented by a numeric value, is a bit like contrast, although a bit more complex (it's actually more like a curve, in design terms). Macs are traditionally set up with a gamma of 1.8, which is ideal for prepress designers whose final output will be on paper. However, the Internet (as well as the rest of the computing universe) tends to operate at a gamma of 2.2 (which seems a bit darker and has more contrast than 1.8). So, if you are a causal user, web developer, or photographer; or if you use your Mac for anything but prepress purposes, it's likely that you'll want to create and use a profile that utilizes a 2.2 gamma.

To create a basic profile, click the Calibrate button in the Color tab. This will open up the Display Calibrator Assistant (Figure 4-18), which will walk you through the process of calibrating your display.

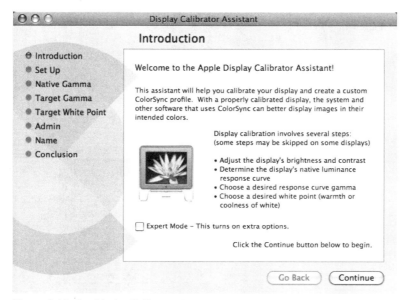

Figure 4-18. The Display Calibrator Assistant

Once the Display Calibrator Assistant is open, you can start a basic calibration by clicking the Continue button.

> **NOTE** You may notice that an expert mode offering extra options is available. If you are calibrating an older CRT, then the expert mode might work for you reasonably, but many of the expert tests are extraordinarily difficult to get right if you are using a flat-panel display (since color shifts as your angle of view changes). If accurate color matching is really important to you, I'd recommend picking up a hardware device that will calibrate your monitor for you. Something like the Pantone Huey will do an excellent job for less than $100.

Clicking the Continue button will take you to the screen where you select your target gamma (Figure 4-19). There are only two options in basic mode: 1.8 Standard Gamma and 2.2 Television Gamma. As stated previously, I'd recommend the 2.2 gamma option here.

NOTE As you may have noticed, clicking Continue skips two steps: Set Up and Native Gamma. Certain displays (predominately CRTs) will require extra steps to create a baseline for the calibration. If you find yourself confronted with these steps, just follow the onscreen instructions to work through them.

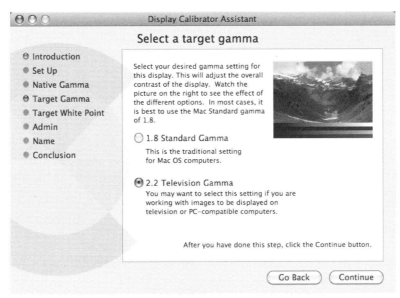

Figure 4-19. Selecting the target gamma in the Display Calibrator Assistant

Continuing on from the gamma selection will take you to the screen where you can set the display's white point (Figure 4-20). *White point* is the strangest and most difficult-to-grasp concept in color matching. Your eyes generally compensate for ambient light so that things that may not be white appear white. This makes setting the white point of your monitor a bit of a trick to do manually. In general, depending on the ambient light surrounding your computer, you will find a comfortable white point around 6000 to 7500 K (Kelvin, which is how white point is measured). For most modern displays, this should be right about where the native white point is, so unless you really know you don't want to use your native white point, I'd recommend using it.

NOTE Besides measuring white point in Kelvin (commonly referred to as the *correlated color temperature*), there are other common names given to certain white points, such as D50 or D65. D65 is also known as the Television white point, and is the default sRGB color space white point.

NOTE If you use a hardware device to calibrate your monitor, it will have a weird effect on the white point of your display—it will look wrong, even though it's likely spot on. This is your eyes playing tricks on you again (this is temporary, and lasts only until your eyes adjust to the new white point setting).

After you set the white point, click the Continue button. If you are a systems administrator, you will be prompted to choose if you'd like this profile to be available to users other than yourself; if not, you'll jump straight to the Name step, where you'll be asked to name your new profile (Figure 4-21). You can call your new profile anything you want, but I'd recommend something sensible.

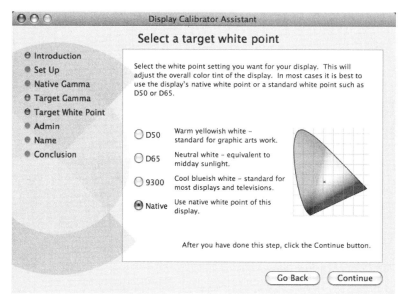

Figure 4-20. Selecting a target white point for your display

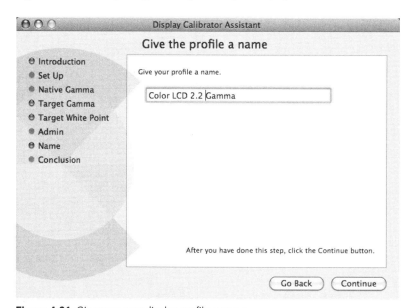

Figure 4-21. Give your new display profile a name.

Once you are done, click Continue. You will be presented with one last screen, essentially telling you that you're done. Click the Done button. When the assistant goes away, you will see your new profile as an option in the Display Profile area, along with any other profiles.

If you happen to have two or more displays hooked up to your computer, a third Display tab called Arrangement will appear (Figure 4-22). This provides a view area that lets you arrange your monitors next to each other, and a check box that allows you to mirror your displays. If the Mirror Displays option is checked, then both displays will have the same information on them. If the Mirror Displays option is unchecked, then the displays will act together as one large work area.

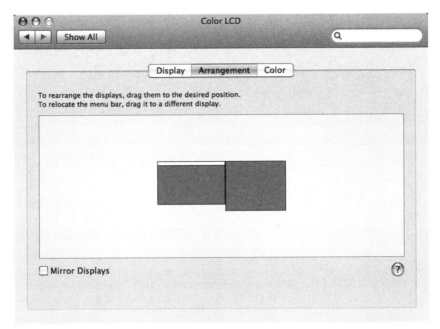

Figure 4-22. When you have multiple displays attached to your computer, the Arrangement tab will allow you to arrange the monitors into one large workspace.

When you have multiple monitors attached, the preference pane will open separate preference windows in each display, allowing you to independently set each display's preferences.

Energy Saver

The Energy Saver preference pane (Figure 4-23) allows you to adjust some power saving features for your computer. It does this by causing certain functions of your computer to sleep after a short idle period and by throttling overall performance of your system to conserve energy consumption.

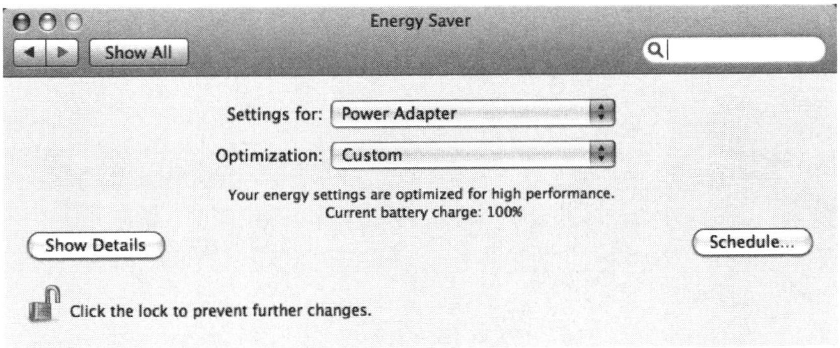

Figure 4-23. The Energy Saver preference pane

By default, the Energy Saver shows only a few options. The "Settings for" option is for portable computers and allows you to set up different energy saving profiles for running on battery power vs. running while plugged in. The Optimization option provides three preset energy profiles plus a custom setting. Table 4-3 describes the Energy Saver optimization settings.

Table 4-3. Energy Saver Optimization Settings

Setting	Description
Better Energy Savings	This is the most aggressive default energy savings setting. It will put your display to sleep after only 5 minutes, and your entire computer will sleep after 10 minutes.
Normal	This mode will put both your display and computer to sleep after 10 minutes of idle time. This provides the best balance between energy savings and performance.
Better Performance	This mode won't put your monitor to sleep until 20 minutes of idle time, and it will never put your entire computer to sleep.
Custom	This mode allows you to customize your power mode by setting the sleep times for your display and computer yourself. This mode can be set if you click the Show Details button, which will reveal two tabs presenting many options for customizing your Energy Saving options.

When you click the Show Details button, the preference pane will expand to reveal two tabs: the Sleep tab and the Options tab.

The Sleep tab (Figure 4-24) provides a number of sliders to control how long your system may idle before the display and computer sleep functions kick in. It also provides a rather vague check box about sleeping the hard drive, which will cause your drive to sleep when it is inactive (this depends on many things outside of idle time).

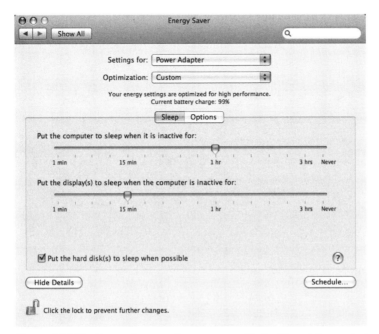

Figure 4-24. The Energy Saver preference pane with the Sleep tab revealed

The Options tab (Figure 4-25) provides a number of additional choices related to the Energy Saver. The Wake Options settings allow you to determine if the computer should wake up for specific network activity. The Other Options settings provide options for various other power-related aspects. The actual options listed here may vary depending on your system.

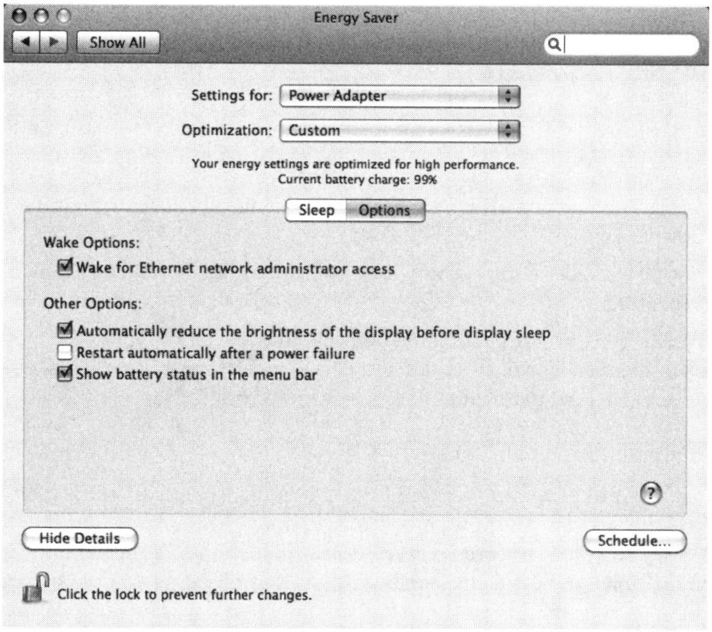

Figure 4-25. The Energy Saver's Options tab revealed

The Schedule button brings up a dialog box that allows you to designate times when you want your computer to go to sleep and wake up automatically. For example, if you use your computer in an office environment, you might want it to sleep in the evening after you leave and wake up in the morning just before you arrive.

One final option is the lock in the lower-left corner of the preference pane. This is the first time we've mentioned this in this book, although it's a common feature in many preference panes and applications. If you are an administrator on your computer, clicking this lock will lock the preference pane so that changes cannot be made to it until it is unlocked. Clicking the locked icon will present a standard authentication dialog box asking for your administrative password to unlock the preference pane. In general, if other people use your computer and you don't want them monkeying around with important settings, lock them.

Keyboard & Mouse

The Keyboard & Mouse preference pane controls the options for your mouse, keyboard, and trackpad. It is divided into five tabs each, providing options for your keyboard, trackpad, mouse, Bluetooth setup, and keyboard shortcuts.

> **NOTE** Certain tabs will only appear when certain hardware is available for your computer. For example, the Trackpad tab will only show up if you have a trackpad attached to your system. Even the Mouse tab won't show up until you attach a mouse.

> **NOTE** While the keyboard and mouse preferences cover most standard hardware, they are mostly designed for Apple keyboards, mice, and trackpads. If you are using a third-party mouse or keyboard, they may provide options not available with these preferences; additionally, some of the options here are specifically for Apple hardware features. For this reason, most third-party hardware comes with its own preference pane. Additionally, there are a couple of third-party drivers for mice and keyboards that offer different customization options that may suit you. (For example, I tend to be fond of my Logitech MX Revolution mouse, but find the included drivers . . . well . . . *insufficient*. For this reason, I use SteerMouse (`http://plentycom.jp/en/steermouse/index.html`) as my mouse driver.)

The Keyboard tab (Figure 4-26) provides options for your keyboard. The basic options are the following:

Key Repeat Rate: This slider controls how fast a letter will automatically repeat if you press and hold down a key.

Delay Until Repeat: This slider controls how long you must initially hold down a key until the letter starts repeating.

Modifier Keys: This button brings up a dialog box that allows you to remap the modifier keys (e.g., to switch the behavior of the Cmd and Ctrl keys for a more MS Windows–like experience). You can also turn these keys off (such as the dreaded Caps Lock key).

Other hardware-specific options include the following:

Use all F1, F2, etc., keys as standard function keys: On many Apple keyboards, the function keys have the alternate purpose of controlling things like volume, screen brightness, and other hardware features. These alternate functions are the default functions; to use the function keys as function keys, you must hold down the Option key. Checking this box reverses this behavior (i.e., the function key is the default, and Option+Fn will activate the alternate action).

Illuminate keyboard in low-light conditions: This is for special Apple keyboards (like those found on MacBook Pros) that allow the keyboard to light up. Selecting this box will cause the keys to light up in low-light conditions. A slider that will turn off the keyboard lights after a designated period of idle time follows this.

The trackpad on Apple Portables is an amazing thing. Despite its simple appearance, it packs a lot of power (yes, it only has one button, but it still works like a two-button mouse with a 3D scroll wheel). The Trackpad tab (Figure 4-27) allows you to configure all this goodness. The options and their descriptions are described in Table 4-4.

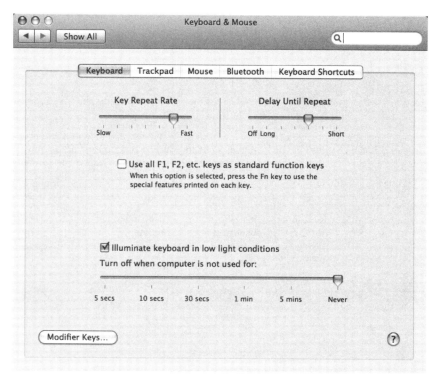

Figure 4-26. The Keyboard tab in the Keyboard & Mouse preference pane controls your keyboard.

Table 4-4. Trackpad Preferences

Option	Description
Tracking Speed	This slider sets how fast things happen on the screen in relation to how fast you move your finger(s) across the trackpad.
Double-Click Speed	This slider sets how much time is allowed between two clicks for it to count as a double-click, as opposed to two single clicks.
Trackpad Gestures:	These are options that cause special things to happen when you interact with the trackpad in certain ways.
Use two fingers to scroll	This option allows you to scroll vertically with two fingers on the trackpad.
Allow horizontal scrolling	This adds the ability to scroll horizontally with two fingers.
Zoom while holding	This allows you to set a key that, when used in combination with a two-finger drag, will zoom in on the screen. The Options button provides additional options for this function. It's important to note that this isn't the same as zooming into an image—this will magnify the entire screen.
Clicking	If this is enabled, a double-tap on the trackpad will act as a single mouse click.

Continued

Table 4-4. Continued

Option	Description
Dragging	This option allows you to double-tap, hold, and then drag an item from the mouse pad.
Drag Lock	This will lock an item that you've dragged until you tap on the item again.
For secondary clicks, place two fingers on the trackpad then click the button	This option allows you to use a secondary click (e.g., right-click or Ctrl+click) by clicking the trackpad button while two fingers are on the trackpad. This is an awesome feature!
Ignore accidental trackpad input	This helps prevent the cursor from moving around when you accidentally hit the trackpad (primarily when you are typing).
Ignore trackpad when mouse is present	This will ignore any trackpad input if you also have a mouse connected to your computer.

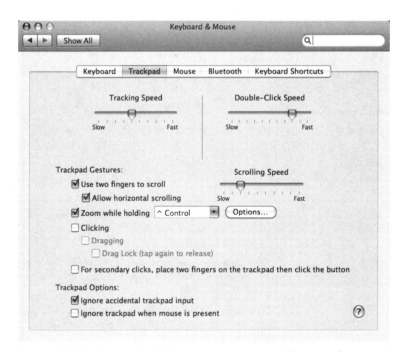

Figure 4-27. The Trackpad tab allows you to set up special features of your trackpad.

The Mouse tab (Figure 4-28) has a subset of the options available for the trackpad, with a few extras. For example, if you have a two- (or more) button mouse, you can alter which button will be used as the primary mouse button (nice for lefties). Also, if your mouse has a scroll wheel, there is a slider that controls the scroll speed—this covers both vertical and horizontal scrolling if available.

The Bluetooth tab (Figure 4-29) monitors any Bluetooth mice or keyboards that are connected to your computer. For each connected mouse or keyboard, this tab will give you the device's name and display its battery level. Additionally, this tab provides an option to allow Bluetooth devices to wake your computer. If you are relying on Bluetooth input devices, it's recommended that you select this option.

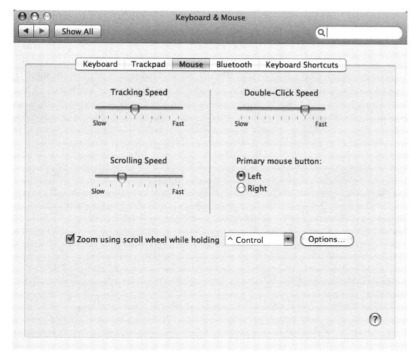

Figure 4-28. The Mouse tab on the Keyboard & Mouse preference pane

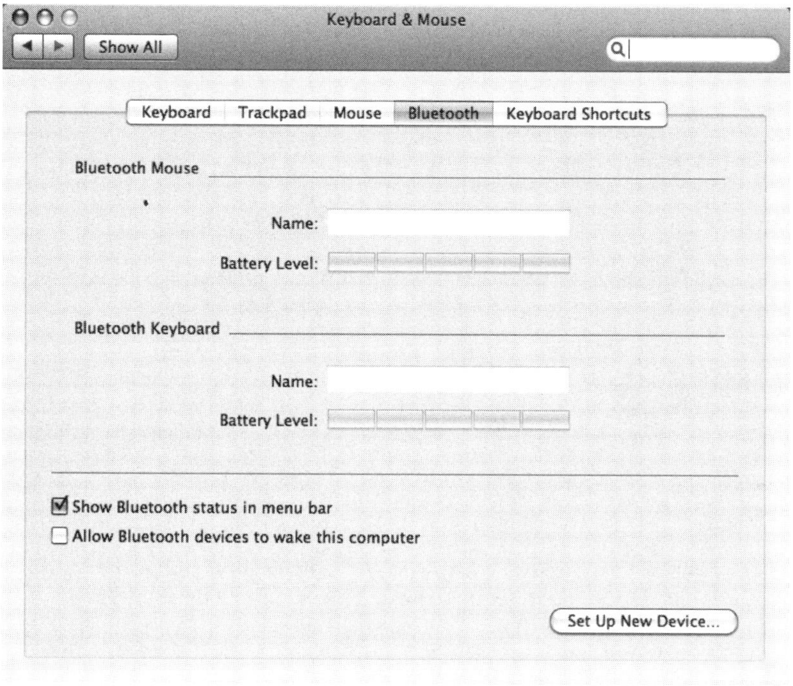

Figure 4-29. The Bluetooth tab of the Keyboard & Mouse preference pane

Many years ago one, of the biggest fears I heard from people about Macintosh computers was that they felt they needed to use the mouse for everything, while with Windows there tended to be a keyboard shortcut for just about everything. (Ironically, the other big fear was people wrongly assuming that Macs only work with one-button mice). The reality is that in Macs, there are keyboard shortcuts for all common tasks, along with some things you may not have thought of. The Keyboard Shortcuts tab (Figure 4-30) lists all of the system-wide keyboard shortcuts in one place. You can also change the default shortcuts here as well (although I'd recommend against this). Additionally, by clicking the + button at the bottom of the list, you can add a keyboard shortcut to any menu item in any application.

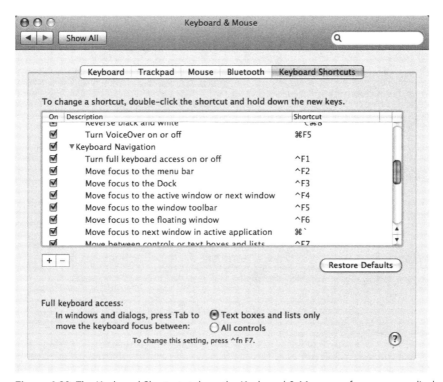

Figure 4-30. The Keyboard Shortcuts tab on the Keyboard & Mouse preference pane displays (and allows you to remap) a wide number of system-wide keyboard shortcuts.

> **NOTE** The ability to add a keyboard shortcut for any menu item in any application is a powerful feature. It can, however, cause all sorts of messiness if used haphazardly. Feel free to take advantage of this—however, be careful not to override existing, common keyboard shortcuts.

Print & Fax

The Print & Fax preference pane allows you to add and manage local and network printers, and if you have a modem, it allows you to set up fax capabilities. Setting up printers will be covered in detail in the next chapter (Chapter 5).

Processor

When you install the Xcode tools, the Processor preference pane will be placed in the /Developer/
Extras/PreferencePanes/ folder. Should you install this into one of the PreferencePanes folders in
one of your libraries, it will be available to you. The Processor preference pane (Figure 4-31) provides information about your computer's processors, and allows you to tweak some options (like
disabling processor cores, toggling napping (PPC chips), and other things that are of little to no
use for most people). In general, it's best to leave this alone unless you know what you are doing.
While altering anything here won't destroy anything, your computer processing power could suffer.

Figure 4-31. The Processor preference pane is part of Xcode's performance and optimization tools.

Sound

The Sound preference pane controls your sound input and output devices, and provides options
for system sounds and effects. The Sound preference pane has three tabs: Sound Effects, Output,
and Input.

The Sound Effects tab (Figure 4-32) allows you to set your alert sound (the sound your computer plays when it tries to get your attention—usually when something bad happens).

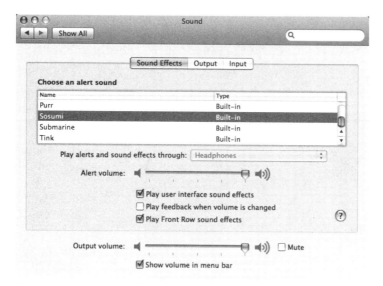

Figure 4-32. The Sound Effects tab lets you choose your system alert sound and provides a few options
for audio feedback.

The Output tab (Figure 4-33) allows you to select your primary output device (if more than one are available) and set the setting for the selected devices. At the bottom of the Sound preference pane is the Output volume slider, along with an option to show (and control) the volume in your menu bar.

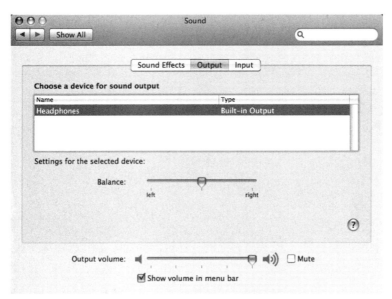

Figure 4-33. The Output tab in the Sound preference pane

The Input tab (Figure 4-34) in the Sound preference pane lists each of your available input devices and allows you to make level adjustments for the selected input device. Ambient noise reduction may help eliminate excess background noise; however, in some cases, it could also adversely affect the input sound quality.

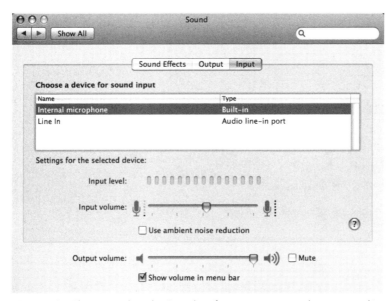

Figure 4-34. The Input tab in the Sound preference pane controls your sound input devices.

Internet & Network

The next section of System Preferences deals with Internet and network preferences (Figure 4-35). This contains your .Mac, Network, QuickTime, and Sharing preference panes. Each of these topics along with relevant preferences will be covered later in this book.

Internet & Network

.Mac   Network   QuickTime   Sharing

Figure 4-35. Internet & Network system preferences

> **NOTE** .Mac is covered in Chapter 15, network preferences are covered in Chapter 9 (and in more depth in Chapter 20), QuickTime is covered in Chapter 14, and sharing preferences are covered in Chapter 21.

System

The System section of System Preferences (Figure 4-36) contains the remaining preference panes that are installed with Leopard. The preference panes in the System section are Accounts, Date & Time, Parental Controls, Software Update, Speech, Startup Disk, Time Machine, and Universal Access.

Figure 4-36. The System preference panes in System Preferences

Accounts

The Accounts preference pane manages the all the system's users, including some of their settings and their login options. When an existing user is selected, there will be two tabs, Password and Login Items, each containing information about that specific user.

The Password tab (Figure 4-37), as the name suggests, allows a user to change their password by clicking the Change Password button. It also allows you to do the following:

- Change your user icon by clicking the icon image and selecting a new image from the drop-down list (or use the Edit Image selection to create a custom image).
- Change your user name by typing in a new name. (This, however, will not change your short name.)
- Add your .Mac account information if you have a .Mac account.
- View and edit your address book card in the Address Book application.
- Grant (or remove) administrator rights on the computer, provided that you are an administrator. (You cannot remove administrator rights from yourself.)
- Enable (or disable) parental controls for the user (provided that you have administrator rights).

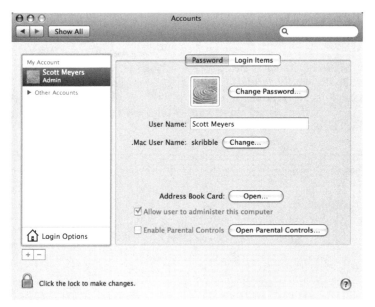

Figure 4-37. When a user is selected, the Password tab allows that user to change their password and other user information.

The Login Items tab (Figure 4-38) lets you manage applications, scripts, and other executable items that you want to start automatically when you log in to your computer. In general, what you will find listed here are background tasks that certain applications use to provide some sort of feature. You can, however, add your own items. For example, if you want the Mail application to start up immediately when you log in to your computer, you can add it to this list by clicking the + button and selecting Mail from the resulting dialog box.

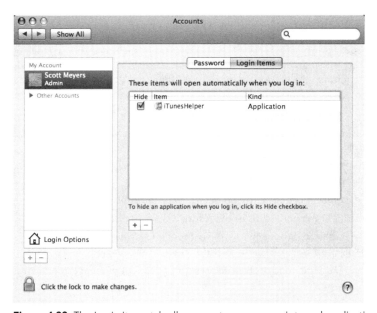

Figure 4-38. The Login Items tab allows you to manage scripts and applications that will automatically run when you log in.

Selecting Login Options (Figure 4-39) allows you to set options that govern login behavior. They are listed and defined in Table 4-5.

Table 4-5. Login Options

Option	Description
Automatic login	This option allows you to select a user who will automatically be logged in when the computer starts up. This is handy if you are the only user on a particular system. Disabling this option will require users to log in whenever the computer starts up. If "Automatic login" is set, that user can still log out, allowing others to log in.
Display login window as	This sets what a user sees at the login screen. The "List of users" option provides a list of all the users of the system. Clicking one of the user names or icons will prompt for a password. The "Name and password" option prompts for the user's name and password without revealing any of the user names. The "List of users" option is faster and more user-friendly, but the "Name and password" option provides slightly better security.
Show the Restart, Sleep, and Shut Down buttons	This will show the Restart, Sleep, and Shut Down buttons on the login screen, allowing these options to be used when no user is logged in.
Show Input menu in login window	This option provides a list to set different language options prior to logging in.
Show password hints	This will show the user's password hint after three failed login attempts. Obviously, there are security implications with this option.
Use VoiceOver at login window	This option will enable VoiceOver at the login window. VoiceOver causes any text under the mouse to be spoken through the computer. This is useful for the visually impaired.
Enable fast user switching	This option will add a user-switching menu to the right side of the menu bar, allowing you to switch from one user to another without logging out first. Setting the "View as" option to Menu will allow you to choose what information appears in this menu.

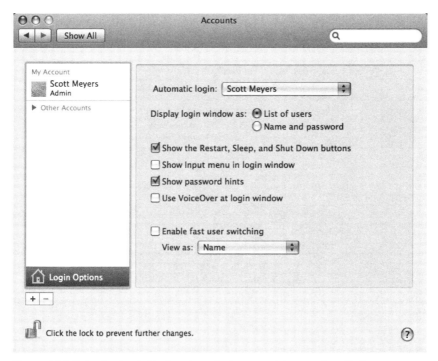

Figure 4-39. Selecting Login Options from the bottom of the user list will allow you to customize the login process.

Adding New Users to Your System

To add a new user to your system from the Accounts preference pane, first make sure that the preferences are unlocked, and then click the + button at the bottom of the user list. This will bring up a window (Figure 4-40) to enter the basic information for your new user.

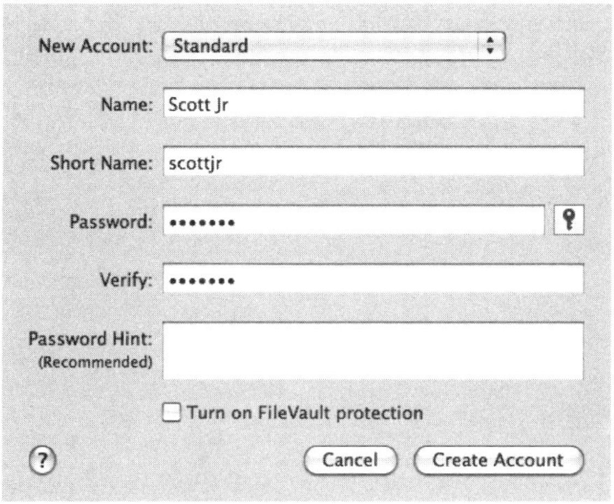

Figure 4-40. Information needed to add a new user

This window requires some basic information. To the right of New Account is a drop-down menu prompting for what type of account you are creating. Options include the following:

Administrator: This grants the user the ability to do just about anything they want on the system.

Standard: This allows the user to work fairly normally on the system, but won't let them do any tasks requiring administrator access.

Managed with Parental Controls: This allows the administrator to restrict the user in various ways using parental controls (covered shortly).

Sharing Only: This only allows access for remote file sharing; these users cannot actually log in through the login window.

Group: This is a special option that rather than creating a new user will create a group that existing users can be part of. You can allow access to files, folders, applications, and other system services based on the groups a user belongs to.

After you select the account type, just enter the name of the account, the short name, the password (twice), and a password hint if you'd like. If you are having trouble coming up with a password, you can access a random password generator (Figure 4-41) by clicking the key icon.

> **NOTE** The short name, once selected, cannot be changed. For all practical purposes, the short name is your actual user name for the system, and the name is just a familiar alias to it.

If you set up multiple users, a Guest account will automatically be added to your user list. The Guest account is a limited account with its own options (Figure 4-42).

Figure 4-41. Password Assistant will help you create a reasonably strong password for new accounts.

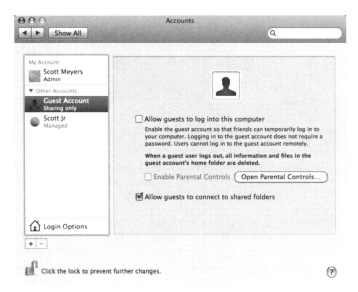

Figure 4-42. Guest account options

The Guest account can be configured in various ways. Selecting "Allow guests to log into this computer" will allow guests to log in and use your computer as a sandbox of sorts. They will have access to most applications—however, all settings and files they create will be wiped out when they log off. "Allow guests to connect to shared folders" will allow guests to access any shared folders on your system over the network. It's important to note that guests never need a password, so by allowing a guest access, you are essentially allowing anyone access to your system.

Date & Time

The Date & Time preference pane contains the system's date and time settings. These setting are broken up across three tabs: Date & Time, Time Zone, and Clock.

The Date & Time tab (Figure 4-43) simply allows you to either manually set the date and time of your system, or have it set automatically using one of Apple's timeservers. There are actually very few situations where you wouldn't want to set the time automatically (e.g., you have no Internet connection and thus the timeservers aren't available, or you want to fool your system into thinking the time is different than it actually is). If you choose to have the time set automatically, just select the closest Apple timeserver while connected to the Internet.

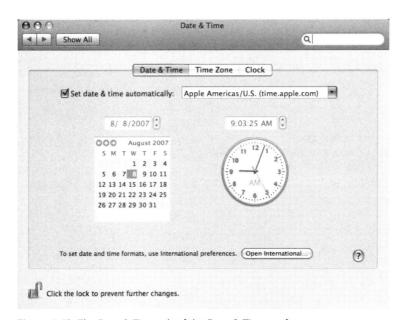

Figure 4-43. The Date & Time tab of the Date & Time preference pane

> **NOTE** There are other timeservers available besides the Apple timeservers that are listed. In fact, many organizations have their own timeserver on their network. You can utilize any available timeserver by entering its network address in the timeserver text field.

The Time Zone tab (Figure 4-44) allows you to select what time zone you are in. You can do this by entering or selecting a city from the Closest City drop-down menu/text field, or by clicking your location on the minimap. It's important to accurately set your time zone, even if you are manually entering your date and time information—otherwise, you may get incorrect time information.

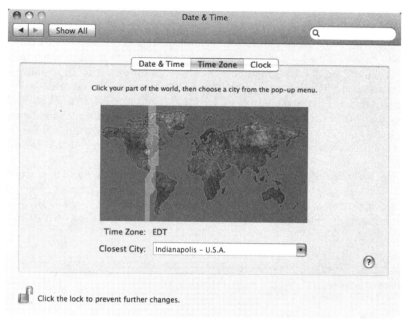

Figure 4-44. The Time Zone tab in the Date & Time preference pane

The Clock tab (Figure 4-45) provides a number of options that affect how the clock appears in your menu bar. There is a further option that will cause your computer to speak out the current time at designated intervals. These options are fairly explicit and shouldn't need much elaboration.

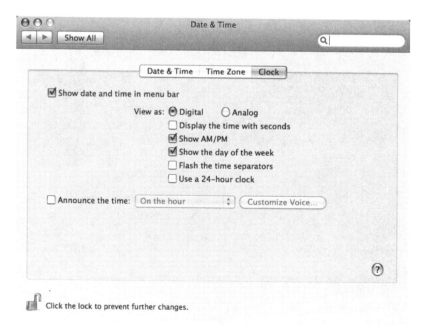

Figure 4-45. The Clock tab in the Date & Time preference pane allows you to set options for the clock in the menu bar.

Parental Controls

The parental controls allow an administrator to put in place a number of restrictions upon a user. These are generally thought of as a way for parents to limit the computing activities of their children, but could be used in any situation in which you want to restrict or monitor a user's activity on the computer. The Parental Controls preference pane lets you tailor the controls for any user account that has parental controls enabled. To set the controls, first select the desired user from the user list (if the list is empty, then you have no accounts with parental controls enabled), and then you can work through the five tabs presented to configure them. The five tabs in the preference pane are System, Content, Mail & iChat, Time Limits, and Logs (shown later in Figure 4-51).

The System tab (Figure 4-46) provides options that control how a user can interact with the system itself. The Use Simple Finder option will alter the Finder's appearance (Figure 4-47), removing many options and directories, and providing access only to a user's allowed applications and their documents. For old-school Macintosh users, this is similar to what At Ease used to provide.

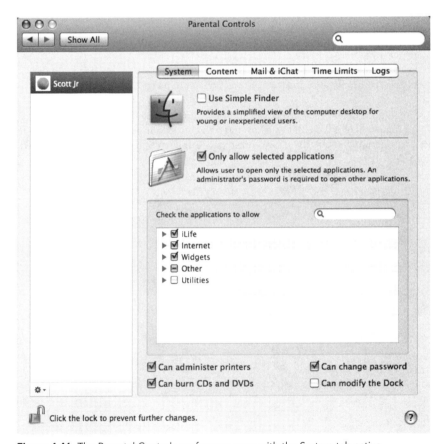

Figure 4-46. The Parental Controls preference pane with the System tab active

The "Only allow selected applications" option will only allow access to the applications (or groups of applications) selected in the following list. If you are using the Simple Finder, then only the selected applications will show up; otherwise, the user will be prompted for an administrator's password before launching an unselected application.

Figure 4-47. The Simple Finder

The remaining options, "Can administer printers," "Can burn CDs and DVDs," "Can change password," and "Can modify the Dock," are additional system actions you may choose whether to allow access to.

The Content tab (Figure 4-48) allows you to attempt to limit the content that the user has access to. The first selection limits access to words in the OS X dictionary. The Website Restrictions options offer three choices for attempting to manage web content:

Allow unrestricted access to websites: Will not block any web sites.

Try to limit access to adult websites automatically: Tries to filter out adult web sites using a variety of methods. While somewhat effective, this is not foolproof, and may both block sites that you don't find objectionable and let some objectionable content through. The Customize button allows you to fine-tune this behavior a bit by manually entering acceptable and unacceptable web sites.

Allow access to only these websites: Allows you to specifically enter the addresses of acceptable web sites. Only those entered will be accessible. Obviously, this will likely block lots of valuable information, while at the same time this is really the only way to block objectionable content with some certainty.

NOTE Content filtering has proponents and detractors from both political and technical points of views. As a parent of two, I have mixed feelings about this sort of technology— currently I don't use any content filtering, but I reserve the right to change my mind if I notice my kids doing something that really concerns me. That said, these filtering technologies are not foolproof, and should not be relied upon to protect your children or anyone else from unsavory elements of the Internet. The best advice I know of is to be honest with your kids about things they may encounter on the Internet, and explain what your values are and why. Most kids will get it.

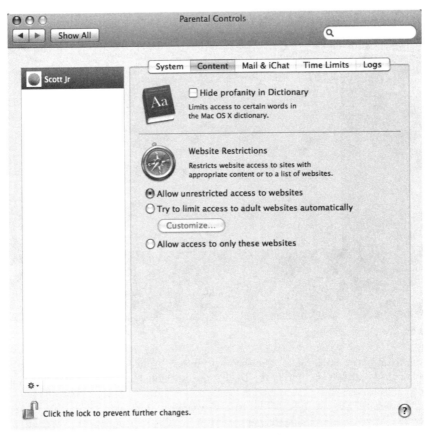

Figure 4-48. The Content tab in the Parental Controls preference pane

The Mail & iChat tab (Figure 4-49) allows you to specify addresses of select people who you allow the user to interact with through Mail and iChat. There is an option at the bottom that can be set to send a message to you every time the user attempts to contact someone who is not preapproved. This is a decent way to attempt to keep track of people that a user is interacting with online—however, this has no effect on web-based chats, or any other e-mail or messaging applications. As such, this is really only effective in combination with other controls.

> **NOTE** While online content won't jump out of your computer and cause you any physical harm, people are a different thing altogether. It's important to discuss, especially with children, that people on the Internet are not always what they seem, and are not all harmless. Personal information should not be shared with strangers, whether in chats, in e-mails, or on web sites. In my experience, knowledge and understanding are better at protecting our children and ourselves than depending on computer systems and blocking technologies.

The Time Limit tab (Figure 4-50) allows you to limit the time a user spends in front of the computer. It allows you to set daily limits for weekdays and weekends, as well as set specific times when the computer is off limits.

Figure 4-49. The Mail & iChat tab of the Parental Controls preference pane

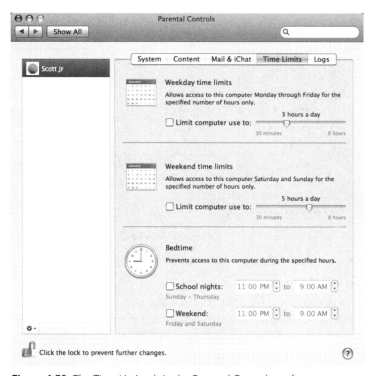

Figure 4-50. The Time Limit tab in the Parental Controls preference pane

> **NOTE** You may have discovered from my previous notes that I'm generally skeptical of most parental controls (especially the content filtering stuff). This is because I've never seen one that worked well and couldn't be worked around by a clever kid wanting to break the rules (of course, maybe you actually want to train your kid to become a skilled hacker). That said, I think there is something to setting time limits. Seriously, there are days when I wish my computer would kick me out after a certain amount of time using it.

The Logs tab (Figure 4-51) provides an account of certain activities that a user is engaging in on the computer. If you are concerned that a user is up to no good, then this will often let you check. It's a little Big Brother–esque, yet sometimes it's the only way to know for sure. The Logs tab reveals what web sites a user is visiting (including ones that are blocked) and what applications are being used, and keeps track of iChat chats.

Figure 4-51. The Logs tab on the Parental Controls preference pane keeps track of a user's activities.

Software Update

The Software Update preference pane (Figure 4-52) manages the Software Update features of Leopard. This allows you to set the frequency that updates are checked for automatically, and also provides a Check Now button to manually check for new updates.

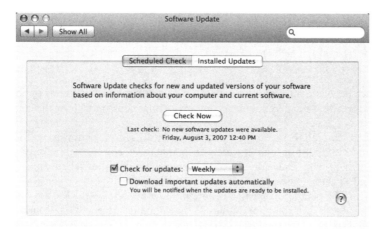

Figure 4-52. The Software Update preference pane

When you run Software Update (by clicking the Check Now button or using the Software Update item in the Apple menu), the Software Update window will open (Figure 4-53) and check for the availability of updated software. If updates are available, they will be listed in the window with a description of what the updates contain. To perform the updates, make sure the desired items are checked, and click the Install button in the lower-right corner of the window. This will download and install the updates. Certain system updates will require authentication to install, or will require you to restart your computer to complete—in either of these cases, you will be prompted accordingly.

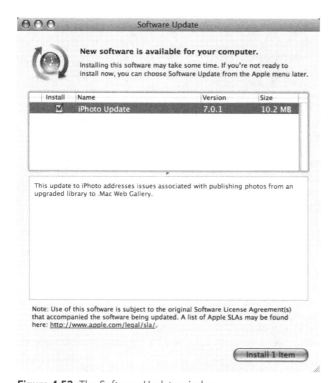

Figure 4-53. The Software Update window

The Installed Updates tab of the Software Update preference pane lists all of your past software updates.

Speech

The Speech preference pane contains two tabs: Speech Recognition, which contains options for responding to speech; and Text to Speech, which contains settings controlling how the computer speaks back to you.

The Speech Recognition tab (Figure 4-54) contains settings that control how to set the computer up to receive and respond to speakable items. To enable this feature, you first must set the Speakable Items option to On. Once the Speakable Items option is switched on, a small, roundish floating window with a microphone in it will appear. This will provide visual feedback for your speakable items. By default, to speak a command, first hold down the Esc key and then speak your command clearly into the microphone. If the computer accepts your command, it will carry out the command requested and provide you with acknowledgment as set up under the Upon Recognition setting. The Commands sub-tab provides a list of active command categories. Any time speech recognition is active, you click the small inverted triangle at the bottom of the small, round, hovering speech window, and select Open Speech Commands Window to view a list of available speech commands as well as a log of previous spoken actions.

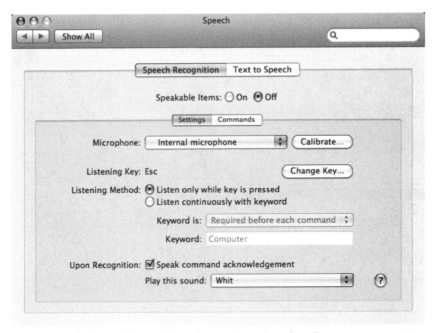

Figure 4-54. The Speech Recognition tab contains settings that allow your computer to respond to spoken commands.

> **NOTE** Apple speech recognition technology has been around for years, and has progressively gotten better; however, my results have always been mixed. While I find this fun to play around with sometimes (the Chess game included in Leopard responds to spoken commands), I don't find it particularly useful. Maybe I just have a terrible voice. As they say, "Your mileage may vary."

The Text to Speech tab (Figure 4-55) controls how your computer speaks to you. Here you can change your computer's voice and the speed at which it talks. You can then set up options that will cause your computer to speak certain items:

Announce when alerts are displayed: Causes your computer to read any alerts that pop up

Announce when an application requires your attention: Causes your computer to tell you when an application is awaiting your input or has some message for you

Speak selected text when the key is pressed: Allows you to set a key that will cause any selected text to be read back to you

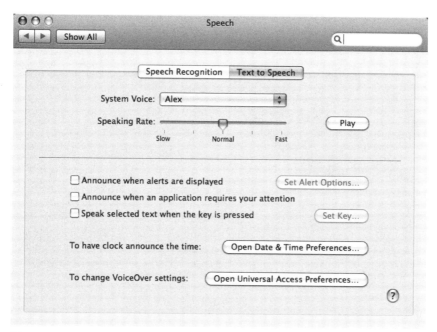

Figure 4-55. The Text to Speech tab in the Speech preference pane

Some applications have their own capability for reading back text as well. The important thing here is that the voice you pick on the Text to Speech tab will be the default voice used in all of the applications.

> **NOTE** Outside of some of the universal access uses of Text to Speech, this too tends to be more fun than useful. That said, speech has come a long way over the years—just compare the Fred Voice (one of the original voices) to the Alex Voice (a new voice in Leopard), and not even accounting for improvements in the underlying technology (of which there are many), you can hear the improvements. (Zarvox, by the way, is still my favorite voice.)

Startup Disk

If you have multiple bootable volumes connected to your computer, the Startup Disk preference pane (Figure 4-56) will allow you to select which disk to default to when starting your computer.

Figure 4-56. The Startup Disk preference pane controls which bootable volume the computer will use by default when starting up.

The startup disk selected here can always be overridden by special startup key commands (holding the Option key while starting your computer will allow you to choose to boot from any connected bootable hard drive).

One interesting option here is Target Disk Mode. This allows you to set up your computer so that the next time it's started you can connect to another Mac via a FireWire cable and use it as a hard drive. This is a handy option for copying files from one computer to another very quickly (this is covered in Chapter 21). (You can also boot your computer in Target Disk mode by holding the T key while starting your computer.)

Time Machine

Next is the Time Machine preference pane. This allows you to set up and configure Time Machine. (This is covered in Chapter 7.)

Universal Access

The Universal Access preference pane provides settings to assist people who have difficulty hearing, seeing, or otherwise working with their computer. This preference pane is divided into four tabs: Seeing, Hearing, Keyboard, and Mouse & Trackpad.

The Seeing tab (Figure 4-57) provides a number of options to assist people who have trouble seeing things on their computer screen.

VoiceOver, when activated, will speak out selected regions of the computer interface. First, it will identify the selected window, and then it will allow you to tab through interface features, speaking the name of each as you tab through. VoiceOver itself has many options and can be fully customized via VoiceOver Utility (Figure 4-58), accessible in the /Applications/Utilities folder, or by clicking the Open VoiceOver Utility button in the preference pane.

> **NOTE** VoiceOver is a very sophisticated piece of software, providing options for everything from minor audio assistance to full Braille output for the blind (and many options in between). VoiceOver Utility provides many options to customize this to whatever your needs are, and I'd encourage anyone needing this level of assistance to fully explore it.

Figure 4-57. The Seeing tab of the Universal Access preference pane

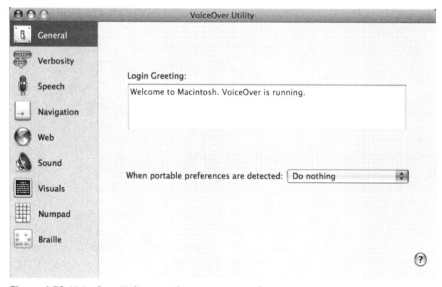

Figure 4-58. VoiceOver Utility provides many options for customizing VoiceOver's capabilities.

Zoom allows you to zoom in and out of the screen. This is an extension of the zoom functions for the mouse and trackpad discussed earlier, but it provides a few additional options and methods of zooming.

The Display section provides options that allow you to alter the display. This includes switching the display output to grayscale or color, adjusting the display's contrast, and even inverting the color scheme of the display (try Cmd+Option+Ctrl+8).

The Hearing tab (Figure 4-59) provides a few options to aid people with hearing issues. The primary option here allows you to flash the screen when an alert occurs. This option can come in handy if you work in a very loud (or very quiet) environment.

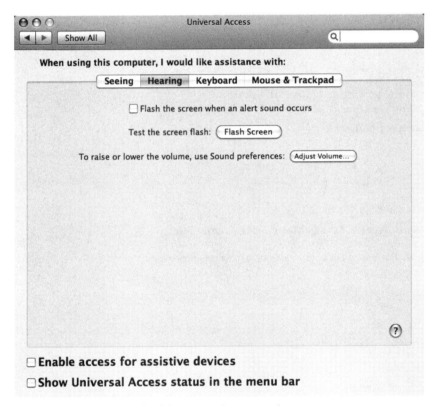

Figure 4-59. The Hearing tab of the Universal Access preference pane

The Keyboard tab (Figure 4-60) builds upon the keyboard options on the Keyboard & Mouse preference pane. Sticky Keys provides options for people who may have trouble holding multiple keys at once, so that they can more easily use keyboard combinations and shortcuts. The Slow Keys option helps the system ignore accidental key input.

The Mouse & Trackpad tab (Figure 4-61) provides options for people who have trouble using the mouse or trackpad. Mouse Keys allows you to use the keyboard's keypad to move the cursor around on the screen instead of the mouse. There is also an option to increase the size of the mouse cursor so that it's easier to track on the screen.

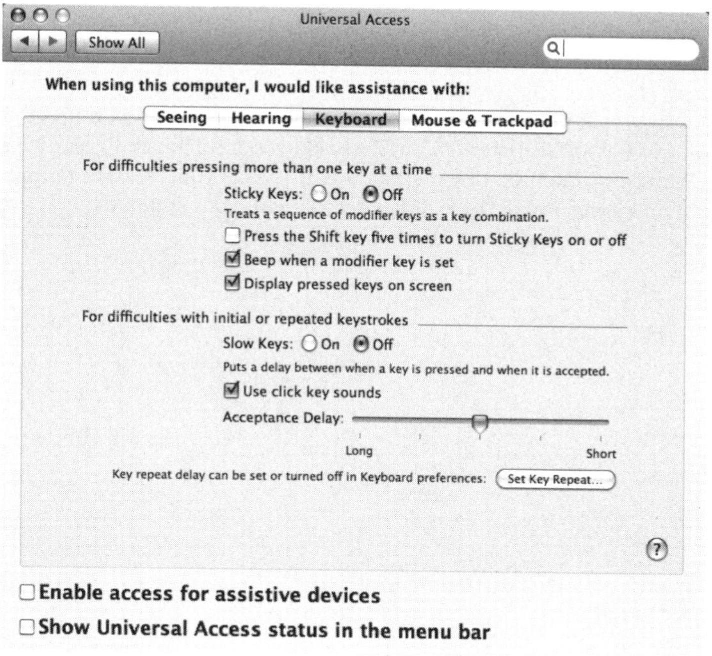

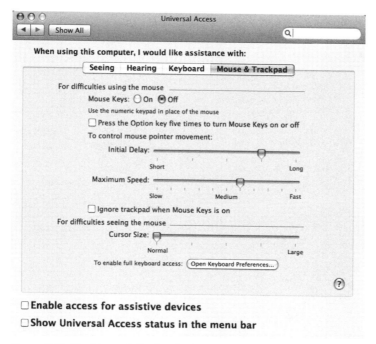

Figure 4-60. The Keyboard tab provides some additional keyboard options.

Figure 4-61. The Mouse & Trackpad tab on the Universal Access preference pane adds additional mouse and trackpad options.

Summary

We have covered a lot of ground in this chapter, and while we have saved a few things that need more elaboration than was possible here for later in the book, you have hopefully learned a number of ways to help set up your computer to work in a way that suits you. Next, as promised, we will look at connecting and using a range of external devices with your computer.

## CHAPTER 5

Connecting Peripherals to Your Mac

Today more and more features are built into computers than ever before. Most new Macs (except the MacPro and Mac mini) include features such as stereo speakers, decent microphones, and even video cameras all built in and ready to use. Still, oftentimes you need something else or want to improve on what you already have in your computer. Luckily for you, there is a range of hardware devices that can work wonderfully with your Mac (commonly referred to as *peripherals*). Since you have a Mac, you just need to plug in most of these items, and they work (that is, they're plug and play, as it was intended). However, with the complexity and features available for some of these external devices, occasionally you need to do a little more to get the most out of them. Additionally, these days, many peripherals connect over a network or wirelessly, so rather than plugging something in, you often need to tell your computer to look for it. This chapter addresses all of this, including the following:

- Printers
- Bluetooth devices
- External storage
- Other external peripherals

Printing in Leopard

The world we live in is getting increasingly digital, and yet the paperless world isn't quite ready for primetime. Thus, sometimes you may need to resort to actually printing things. To do this, you need to connect and configure a printer. You can connect your computer to your printer in a number of ways, ranging from physically through a USB cable to over a network. If it's over a network, whether wireless or wired, many protocols are available, and each handles printing a little differently. Luckily, Leopard makes all of this easy (or at least as easy as possible).

How "Print" Happens

In very general terms when you hit the Print button in an application, a few things happen:

1. You are often presented with a Print dialog asking you to choose which connected printer you want to print to and what printing options (if any) you'd like to utilize. When you have you made your selection, you click the Print button to print your document.

2. Once you hit Print, the printing system in Leopard (CUPS) takes your document and converts it to a language that your printer will understand. It does this using a translation file known as a *print filter*.

3. Once the file is translated, this translated file is put in a special block of memory called a *print spool* where the file is then streamed to your printer over whatever connection protocol is being used.

4. The printer, as it receives this stream, usually starts printing the file as it receives it. Because your computer can usually feed information to your printer faster than it can print, a lot of communication is necessary between your printer and your computer to regulate the flow of information. If your printer runs out of memory (and many less expensive printers have very little to begin with) and your computer keeps sending the data, then data will get lost, and you'll end up with a garbled mess . . . not to worry, this rarely happens these days.

In a nutshell, that's it. It sounds like a lot of complicated stuff going on, and actually there is, but luckily for you, all you need to worry about is step 1 and occasionally adding more paper and ink/toner to your printer. Of course, before you can print, you need to set up your printer.

Setting Up a USB Printer

The most common printers, and the easiest to set up, are basic USB printers. In general, to set up a USB printer, plug in the printer power cord, and then plug in a USB cable from your printer into one of the USB ports on your computer. Unless your printer is a super-new model or a really strange off-brand, it's likely that's all you need to do. Your printer is ready to use. If in doubt, take a look in the Print & Fax pane of System Preferences (Figure 5-1); if you see the printer you just plugged in listed and correctly identified, you are good to go.

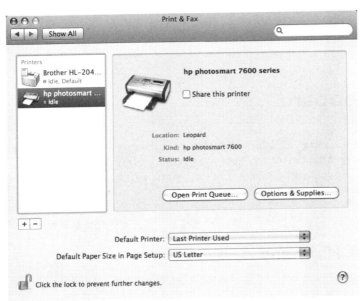

Figure 5-1. The Print & Fax pane of System Preferences showing the HP Photosmart printer we just plugged into a fresh Leopard install; there's no need to add any drivers or software or anything.

At this point, you may be skeptical that everything worked; in other words, that was too easy, right? You didn't even need to insert the CD that came with the printer. If you double-click the printer icon in the Print & Fax preference pane, the printer's Print Queue window (Figure 5-2) will open. This window provides information about your printer, including information about any documents currently printing or waiting to be printed (documents waiting in the print spool to be printed are called *print jobs*). If you want to test your printer, you can select the Printer ➤ Print Test Page command from the menu bar. If the test page prints, then all is well, and your printer is ready to use.

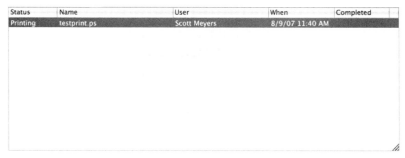

Figure 5-2. The printer's Print Queue window provides information about a specific printer connected to your computer.

So, what happens if things don't work or if your printer isn't recognized correctly when you plug it in? In this situation, you may need to install a driver for your printer.

Printer Drivers

When you install Leopard, by default it installs a large number of printer drivers. There are generally up-to-date drivers for most current and old printers from most printer manufacturers (including Brother, Canon, Epson, Fuji, HP, Lexmark, and others). The reason why your printer's driver may not be installed by default could be that your printer is too new, too old, or some other brand. Regardless, you may need to install a proper driver. Now, most printers come with a CD that includes the driver (and a bunch of other software) for your computer. We recommend that you *not* use this. Rather, go to your printer manufacturer's web site, and download the latest driver for your printer. Make sure it's for Mac OS X, and make sure it's for your version of Mac OS X. Then install this according to the manufacturer's instructions, and try again.

> **NOTE** Often printer drivers from manufacturers include more than what is really necessary for you to print. They often include special utility software and sometimes even strange graphics and printing software. By downloading the driver from the manufacturer's web site, you at least eliminate some of the extra software, and manufacturers may offer driver-only updates along with utilities and driver/utility bundles. In addition, occasionally during the install routine you can select a custom install and install only the driver. To print effectively, you almost always need only the driver. As for the utilities and other software, sometimes it's quite useful, and sometimes it's not. Occasionally the printer's utilities are just plain evil—lurking around in the background, popping up unnecessary windows, and eating away system resources. Whether you install these is up to you (provided you have a choice), but we tend to avoid these things unless necessary or unless we have found through experience that they are indeed useful.

Connecting to a Network Printer or Shared Printer

Printers in most companies as well as more and more homes are accessed through a network. These printers could be actual network printers, complete with network interfaces (either wired or wireless). Or they could be common USB printers attached to other computers on a network or a network print server (such as the ones built into Apple's AirPort and AirPort Express). Connecting to these printers ranges from almost as easy as connecting a USB printer to fairly easy if you know exactly what you are doing. We'll walk you through the general process using a real-life example of connecting to a networked Brother multifunction device (a fax/scanner/printer/copier).

The first step of adding a printer is to open the Print & Fax pane from System Preferences, and click the + button at the bottom of the printer list. This opens a Printer Browser window (Figure 5-3).

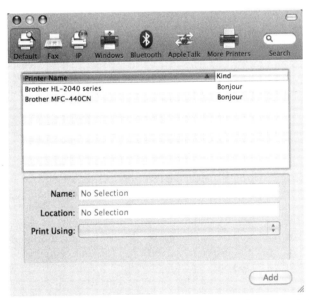

Figure 5-3. The Printer Browser window allows you browse and pick various types of printers to connect to.

As we look in the browser, we see Brother MFC-440CN listed, which happens to be the printer we want. When we select it in the list, our computer will try to find the name, location, and driver automatically. In this case, it succeeded (Figure 5-4).

Figure 5-4. After selecting the printer we want to add, Leopard automatically attempts to determine the name, location, and appropriate print driver.

NOTE You may notice that the Location field is blank; this is because the printer is connected using Bonjour (Apple's implementation of Zeroconf). Bonjour is a special networking technology that allows systems on a network to identify themselves and the services they offer in a flexible way without a central name server. Since this allows the location to be dynamic, it is not listed.

If the print driver is not found automatically, then you will need to select an appropriate driver manually for the printer. To do this, click the Print Using drop-down menu, and there you should first try "Select a driver to use," which will provide a list of all the currently available print drivers. If your driver isn't listed but you have it on your system, you can select Other, which will open a standard Open dialog box for you to locate and open the appropriate driver.

When your printer is selected and set up with the proper driver, click the Add button, and your printer will be ready to use (Figure 5-5).

NOTE If you are mostly but not quite sure you have everything set up correctly, don't panic. Try it. If something is wrong, you can adjust it later, or at worst you can remove it and start over again.

Ninety-nine percent of the time adding a printer is quite easy. But what about the other times—the times when your printer just doesn't get automatically recognized?

NOTE There tends to be a few ways to think about network printers. Some printers broadcast their presence (such as Bonjour printers), and they usually just show up in the default options of the Printer Browser window. Other printers, like those that use Windows and AppleTalk, are browsable; that is, you can navigate around the network to find available printers in the various Windows workgroups or AppleTalk zones. Finally, there are other types of network printers, and basically, you have to know where they are located on the network, and usually some more information about them, to connect to them.

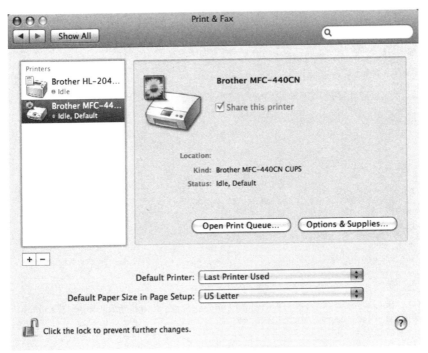

Figure 5-5. Our newly added printer shown in the Print & Fax preference pane

When you are attempting to connect to a network printer at work or in a large computing environment, or you are attempting to use a printer that is being shared by another computer, it might not just show up in the default printer listing in the Printer Browser window. When confronted with this situation, you need to find out what type of printer sharing is being used. The most common choice around homes and offices would be some sort of Windows printer sharing. Other less common network printer sharing protocols include the following:

AppleTalk: This is an older Apple networking technology that a large number of older network printers support. Connecting to an AppleTalk printer is similar to connecting to a Windows printer. AppleTalk printers can be set up under the AppleTalk options in the Printer Browser window.

Bluetooth: There just aren't that many Bluetooth printers available right now, but if you happen to have one, the Bluetooth printer should be easily discoverable if it's in range, at which point you will need to pair the device and select a driver. Only the discovery and pairing should differ from the process of connecting a USB printer or a Bonjour printer.

Internet Printer Protocol (IPP): Actually, this is fairly common since Common Unix Printing System (CUPS) is built around IPP, and CUPS (which, although an open source system, has recently become an Apple product after acquiring the CUPS trademarks and hiring the original developer, Michael Sweet) is the printing system used in Leopard and is the default printing system for many modern Unix and Linux systems. Microsoft also has IPP built into its printing services. Connecting to IPP printers within your local network is usually easy (in fact, that's what you are doing when you connect using Bonjour); however, occasionally the printer you are attempting to connect to isn't visible on the network, so in order to connect, you will need the printer's location (usually an IP address or even domain), and you may need to know the path to the printer (commonly called the *printer queue*). IPP printers can be set up under the IP options in the Printer Browser window.

Line Printer Daemon (LPD): This is an older Unix printing system that has largely been replaced by CUPS. To connect with an LPD printer, you will need its network address, and you will need to know the name of the print queue. An LPD printer can be set up under the IP options in the Printer Browser window.

Others: There is a handful of other, less common, mostly older, proprietary methods of connecting to a network printer. Leopard supports a number of these, including HP Jetdirect, Canon IJ Network, Epson FireWire, Epson TCP/IP, and HP IP Printing.

If you are connecting to a Windows network printer (shared or otherwise), click the Windows button, and then browse through the network until you locate the printer you want (Figure 5-6). It's unlikely that a driver will be selected for you automatically, so you will need to select "Select a driver to use" from the Print Using menu. When you select the appropriate driver, click the Add button.

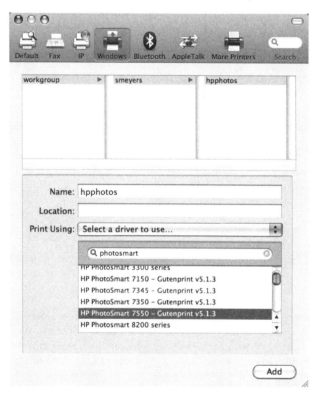

Figure 5-6. Browsing the Windows network for a shared or network printer

NOTE The HP printer we connected to over a Windows network is the same Photosmart 7660 that was immediately recognized when we plugged it in to our USB port. Interestingly, though, when we go browsing for the 7600 series driver, it doesn't exist in the list. So, what gives? Well, some printer manufacturers don't release proper CUPS drivers for their USB printers. Some reckon this is so people who want to print over the network will have to spend extra money for the network printer that has network drivers. We aren't saying this is so; however, with this particular series printer, HP updated the Windows drivers in such a way that it made it suddenly very difficult to use this printer over the network from Windows. As more and more devices come along that allow USB printers to be used over networks, we're not sure how this will play out, but it's something you should be aware of. Still, even though HP doesn't provide proper 7600 CUPS drivers, the 7550 driver works fine. Also, it's worth noting that since CUPS has been used in other Unix and Linux systems for a while, there are numerous "unofficial" CUPS drivers developed by pioneering individuals for many existing printers (the 7550 driver included in Leopard happens to be one of them).

NOTE PostScript printers should all print just fine by selecting the generic PostScript driver, though special features of the printers may not be available through generic (or unofficial) drivers.

Printer Options and the Print Queue

Once a printer is set up and working properly, there isn't much you need to do, but there are some options available to you in the Print & Fax preference pane. When you select a printer in the preference pane, the view area displays some brief information about your printer and also has one check box and a couple of buttons. The "Share this printer" check box will allow you to share this printer with other users on your network (provided that printer sharing is enabled in the Sharing preference pane). Below that are the Open Print Queue button, which will open the print queue just like double-clicking the printer icon, and the Options button.

Clicking the Options button will open a *sheet* (a special type of attached window) providing three tabs (Figure 5-7). The General tab provides basic information about the printer and the driver. The Driver tab lists your current driver in a drop-down list and allows you to select a new driver if you want. The Supply Levels tab can show you how much ink or toner is left in your printer; however, this relies on a number of variables and may not work accurately (or at all). The Supplies button at the bottom of this tab will take you to a web site to buy more printer supplies.

The Open Print Queue button will open the printer's print queue (shown in Figure 5-2). As mentioned, this will provide information about what print jobs are being printed or waiting to be printed. This will also let you pause the printer, delete print jobs, and even rearrange the order of awaiting print jobs. The Info button on the toolbar will open the printer Options sheet you saw in Figure 5-7. The Utility button will sometimes open a printer utility that allows you to utilize special printer features. The printer manufacturer usually provides the utility, and each one can vary greatly from another (if they work at all). The Supply Levels button again opens the Options sheet but with the Supply Levels tab selected (Figure 5-8).

In general, setting up a printer to work with your Mac is a fairly easy process. Even when it's not automatic, the features in Leopard tend to make it at least easier than may have been the case in the past (or is with other computer systems).

Printing from an Application

To use your printer, you usually just need to select File ➤ Print... from the menu bar (or press Cmd+P) in any application. This will open a standard print dialog box that walks you through the printing process. The default Print dialog (Figure 5-9) is simple, with only a few options.

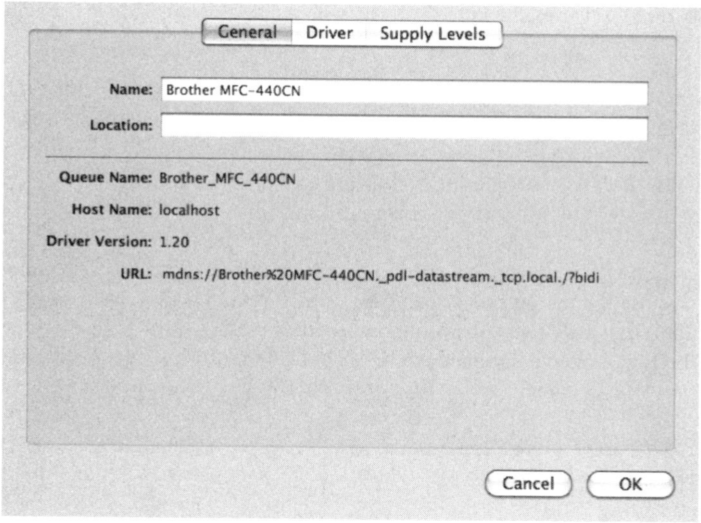

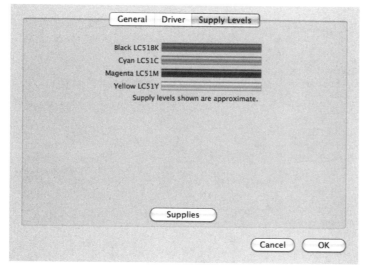

Figure 5-7. The printer Options sheet

Figure 5-8. The Supply Levels tab in the printer's Options sheet. With some printers, depending on the driver and the connection, this information may not be available.

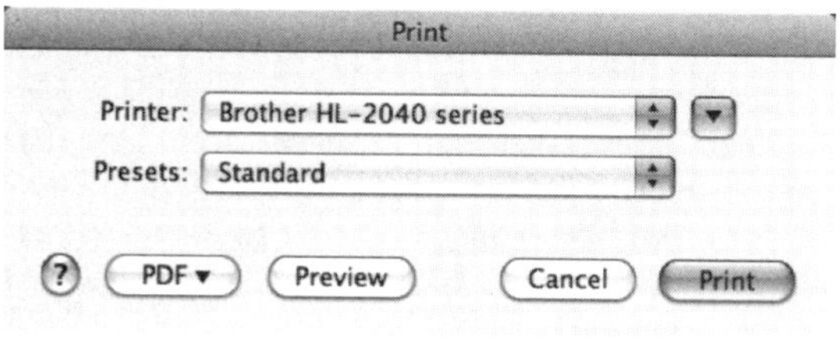

Figure 5-9. The default simple Print dialog box

> **NOTE** Many applications will open the Print dialog as a sheet, rather than a floating window, as shown in Figure 5-9.

If you have multiple printers connected to your computer, you can select the one you want to print to from the Printer drop-down menu (your default printer will be initially selected for you). The Presets button allows you select any preselected print options you may want to use. For most printers, Standard is the only initial option unless you save your own print options; however, many photo printers include a few other options (different size prints, borderless options, and so on).

Along the bottom of the Print dialog box are four buttons. Print will send your document to the printer. Cancel will close the dialog box without printing. Preview will open your document in the Preview application that will give you an onscreen representation of what the printed document will look like. PDF will open a submenu that will provide you with various options from creating a PDF file from your document.

> **NOTE** All of Mac OS X's graphics are PDF based; as such, you will find that it can create a PDF out of any document from the Print dialog without any additional software.

For more options for your printing, you can extend the Print dialog by clicking the inverted-triangle button (the Disclosure button) to the right of the selected printer. This will provide many more printing options (Figure 5-10).

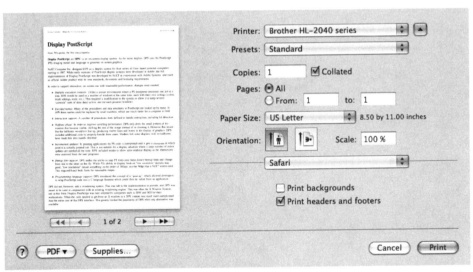

Figure 5-10. The extended Print dialog box provides many more printing options, depending on the print driver and the application.

The extended Print dialog provides a number of additional print options. The standard extended elements include a preview of the document, the ability to print multiple copies of the document, the ability to print only a range of pages rather than the entire document, the ability to adjust paper size and orientation, and the ability to scale the document up or down. However, numerous other options are available from the drop-down menu. This menu includes application options, options associated with your printer's features, color-matching options, advanced paper-handling options, scheduling options, fax options, and more.

Connecting Bluetooth Devices

Bluetooth is a technology that allows you to connect peripherals to one another. Unlike other common methods of doing this (USB and FireWire), Bluetooth does this wirelessly, and because of this, some additional work is necessary. The best place to begin connecting and setting up a Bluetooth device is from the Bluetooth preference pane in System Preferences (Figure 5-11).

Figure 5-11. The Bluetooth preference pane, with no devices set up

When no devices are set up, the preference pane will provide a Set Up New Device button right in the middle. There are various other areas in Leopard where you can set up Bluetooth devices as well. When you begin to set up a new Bluetooth device, Leopard will launch the Bluetooth Setup Assistant to help you through the process (Figure 5-12).

Figure 5-12. The Welcome screen of the Bluetooth Setup Assistant

The first screen of the Bluetooth Setup Assistant is a simple welcome screen. Clicking Continue will bring you to the next screen where you can select the type of device you want to add (Figure 5-13).

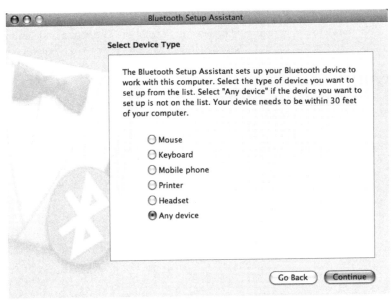

Figure 5-13. You can prompt the Bluetooth Setup Assistant to look only for certain devices.

By selecting a specific device on the Select Device Type screen, Leopard will attempt to recognize only that type of device on the search screen (Figure 5-14). Additionally, the remaining steps of the Bluetooth Setup Assistant will be tailored for setting up that type of device.

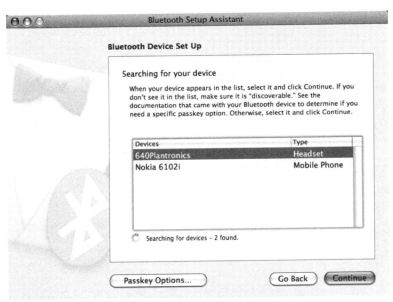

Figure 5-14. The Bluetooth Setup Assistant found two Bluetooth devices in range.

The Bluetooth Setup Assistant will attempt to discover any Bluetooth devices that are within range corresponding to the type you selected on the previous screen. If more than one device is discovered, you must choose the one you want to set up. When you have selected your device, click Continue to move to the next screen, which will attempt to gather all the information it can about your device (Figure 5-15).

> **NOTE** When the Bluetooth Setup Assistant first discovers a device, the initial name of the device may be a strange-looking string of digits. If you wait, this string will most likely become something a bit more familiar as the computer discovers more information about the device.

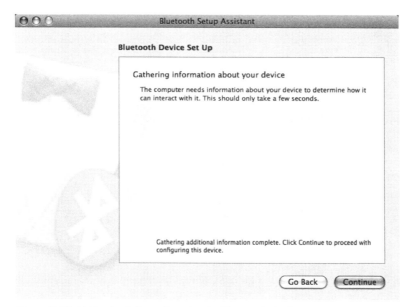

Figure 5-15. Gathering information about a Bluetooth device

Once the Bluetooth Setup Assistant is finished gathering information about your device, click the Continue button. This will often present a screen where you enter a passkey (Figure 5-16). The theory behind passkeys is that since various types of information can be passed from one Bluetooth device to another, then the connections between Bluetooth devices should occur only through paired devices. During the pairing process, each device must use the same passkey to assure a valid pairing. The complexity of the passkeys used to pair two devices tends to be consistent with the amount of risk involved with the pairing. (The headset used in this example has a simple static passkey hardwired into it. That is fine since the damage one can do by maliciously connecting to the headset is fairly limited.)

> **NOTE** The standard passkey for simple items such as headsets always seems to be 0000. So if you need to re-pair your headset, you may want to try this before you start panicking that you lost the instructions with the key on them.

Once the passkey is entered, click Continue. If the passkey is accepted, then you will move to the next screen, where you can specify which services you'd like to allow that are offered by the device (Figure 5-17). If the passkey is not accepted, then you will likely need to restart the process, making sure you have the right passkey and that the device you are connecting to is accepting connections.

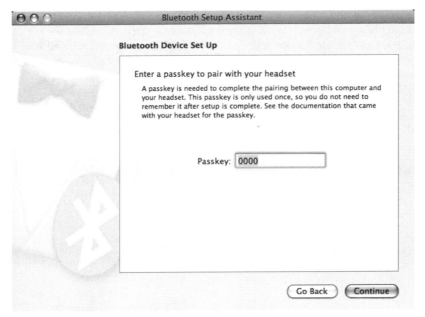

Figure 5-16. Entering a common passkey pairs our computer with the selected device.

Figure 5-17. Select what services you want to use from the device.

The number of services available varies greatly with the type of device you are connecting to. Bluetooth-enabled mobile phones can offer a number of services, while headsets and mice tend to offer one. Either way, select your services, and click Continue. *Voilà*! You have successfully added a Bluetooth device (Figure 5-18).

Figure 5-18. Finished successfully!

Once you are done, when you take a look in your Bluetooth preference pane, you can see that it has changed to display your Bluetooth devices (Figure 5-19).

Figure 5-19. The Bluetooth preference pane changes now that devices have been set up.

Now when you add different types of devices, this process will vary somewhat, especially the passkey part of this. For example, when you add a mobile phone, Leopard will provide a passkey that you must then enter into the phone to complete the pairing (Figure 5-20). Bluetooth printers, on the other hand, often have no passkey at all, allowing them to be browsable and used by all within range.

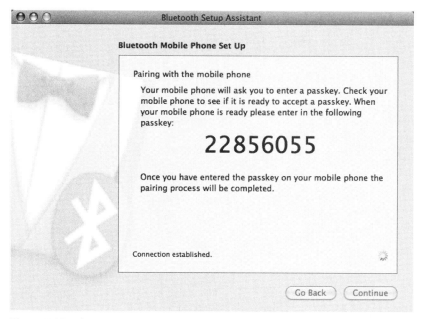

Figure 5-20. When connecting to a phone, Leopard will provide you with a longer, random passkey that you will need to enter into your phone to pair the devices.

Once you have paired certain Bluetooth devices to your computer, different applications can use them in various ways. For example, a Bluetooth-enabled phone (depending on the phone and the mobile services you subscribe to) can be used within iSync to sync your contacts and calendars on your computer with those on your phone, and it can also sometimes be used as a modem or a network device. Bluetooth headsets will be available through the Sound preferences, and other devices will be available in other areas.

Connecting External Storage

Ever since the advent of the floppy disk, and even the magnetic tapes before that, external storage has been a popular way of backing up and moving files, adding extra system storage, or even running entire operating systems. These days with the cost of large external hard drives dropping and the rampant use of thumb drives and even media devices such as iPods being used for storage, this trend continues.

Like most things, connecting to external storage in Leopard is easy. In fact, you just plug in the external storage, and it shows up on your desktop alongside your primary hard drive and any other storage media you have connected to your computer. To remove it, you first tell your computer to "eject" the media and then unplug it. Still, there are a few things worth knowing about: what the differences are between the different types of storage media and what all the available interfaces are and their advantages.

CAUTION To eject media in Leopard, you can either select Eject from the item's contextual menu, click the Eject button next to the item in the Devices section of a Finder window, or drag it into the Trash (to name a few ways you can do it). It's important to do this before you unplug the device, especially with external hard drives. If you don't and you just abruptly unplug the external storage device, you may have unplugged the device while it was still writing data, thus causing data loss and corruption and possibly even physically damaging the storage media.

Storage Media

The storage media is that actual mechanism that stores your data, of which there are three popular types: magnetic, optical, and flash.

Magnetic media includes hard drives, as well as tape drives and floppy drives. Today that primarily means hard drives, though high-end tape drives are still in use for large-scale backup and archive purposes by many organizations and institutions. Magnetic media is generally fast, is stable, can store very large amounts of data, and, these days, is relatively inexpensive. On the downside, it can be fragile and susceptible to damage from outside radiation and magnetism; it also isn't the most energy-efficient media, since moving parts are used in almost all cases.

Optical media includes CDs, DVDs, and an array of both newer, emerging and older, deprecated media types. Advantages of optical media include the cost of storage and the durability and flexibility of the media. Because of this, optical media is perhaps the best, cost-effective media for archival for most users. On the downside, optical media is traditionally slower in both reading and writing data, and most optical media is write-once media, meaning once the data is written, it can't be manipulated. There are today a number of rewritable optical formats; however, they tend to lose reliability after a number of rewrites. Optical media tends to require more power than other media types. Finally, although the technology exists (and is constantly under development) to increase the storage capabilities of optical media, the capacity is significantly less today than what is available with magnetic media.

Flash media is becoming more and more popular. Flash media is popular in many electronic devices for digital storage, including digital cameras, media players, iPods, mobile phones, PDAs, and more. It's also more and more popular as external computer storage for moving files from place to place with thumb drives. It's fast, durable (no moving parts to break), energy efficient (no moving parts, just shuffling electrons), and small. Despite all the advantages, it's expensive and limited in capacity; in addition, since it's newer, its long-term reliability is still in question. Still, technologically it has made the most gains of any storage media over the past few years. Capacity has increased, and costs have dropped dramatically.

Storage Interfaces

Besides the different types of storage media, several interfaces are available. When choosing an external storage device, it's important to pick one with an interface that will fit your needs. Table 4-1 lists the common interfaces.

The goal in choosing an interface is to pick the fastest one that provides what you want. If your new iMac supports FireWire 400, FireWire 800, and USB 2.0 but you also have an older iMac that supports only FireWire 400 and USB 1.1, then a FireWire 400 port would be the best common denominator (though you could get the FireWire 800 drive and buy a FireWire 800 ➤ 400 adapter to be prepared for your next computer).

NOTE Many external hard drives available today will include multiple interfaces. This is nice for maximum performance and connectivity, especially if you have computers of various ages.

Table 4-1. External Storage Interfaces

Interface	Description
USB	The USB interface is one of the most common interfaces, not only for storage but for many external peripherals. USB comes in three flavors (or versions really): USB 1.0, 1.1, and 2.0 (alternatively referred to as low speed, full speed, and high speed). These provide data speeds of 1.5 Mbit/s, 12 Mbit/s, and 480 Mbit/s. (Note the "bit" part! There are 8 bits per byte, so USB 2.0 really provides speeds *up to* 60 MB/s, for example.) Most USB ports, as well as most USB storage devices today, provide USB 2.0, but you really should check to be sure. USB 1.1 is sufficient for smaller thumb drives, but for hard drives the performance would be excruciating. Also note that older PowerPC (PPC) Macs will not allow you to boot from a USB device. Finally, USB 2.0 ports and devices are backward compatible with older USB ports and devices.
FireWire 400 (IEEE 1934a)	FireWire 400, also known as IEEE 1934a and as i.Link by Sony, is a technology originally invented by Apple to provide an alternative to SCSI for high-speed data transmission. It was quickly adopted as a standard A/V interface for sending digital A/V data from one device to another (camcorder to computer). It also, because of its cost and simplicity, quickly replaced SCSI as the external storage interface of choice for all but a few situations. FireWire 400 provides up to 400 Mbit/s transmission speeds, which in the real world makes it similar to USB 2.0. However, FireWire can support more devices on a single node than USB. At least one FireWire 400 port has been included with all Macs for quite awhile now, making this a good choice for external storage devices.
FireWire 800 (IEEE 1934b)	FireWire 800 doubles the performance of FireWire 400. The only issue with FireWire 800 is that while technically FireWire 800 is backward compatible with FireWire 400, they use different connectors, which makes the physical connection incompatible. So, although today only the new MacBooks and Mac minis lack FireWire 800, the original MacBook Pros and iMacs prior to the new aluminum ones didn't either. If you have FireWire 800, it's a great choice.
FibreChannel	FibreChannel connections are available as an option only on Mac Pros and Xserves, but they provide a blazing 4 GB/s transmission (for comparison, that would be 32,000 Mbit/s). This is used for Apple's Xserve RAID system and other high-end storage systems. It's awesome if you can afford it.
eSATA	External Serial ATA (eSATA) is a technology that extends the SATA bus for external use. SATA is what all new Macs use on the inside to connect hard drives. For external connections, though, although eSATA promises high-speed throughput of data, it currently has a number of real-world disadvantages over USB 2 and especially FireWire. eSATA is not included with any current Mac, though expansion cards are available for a number of Apple Macs.

No matter what interface or media is being used, it's important to remember that as long as the interface on your device matches up with an interface on your computer, you are good to go.

> **NOTE** When you get a new hard drive, you may want to partition or format it before you use it. We'll cover this in Chapter 6.

Connecting Other Peripherals

Besides printers, extra storage, and general Bluetooth devices, there are lots of other things available to plug into your computer for various reasons. Although it's impossible to cover each possible device here, we'll end this chapter with some general advice as well as a few specific instances where something unique will happen that relates to Leopard.

Whenever you connect a device to your computer, your computer must be able identify and communicate with the device. Most of the time your Leopard system will at least be able to identify the device; however, it may have no idea how to communicate with the device or how to make it work. A driver generally handles this communication process, and although Leopard ships with a large number of drivers and knows how to communicate with a large range of products, there are a large number of items that will need you to install a driver for them to work correctly. Usually, any device you purchase will include not only any necessary drivers but also supporting software and instructions on how to get your device working with your computer.

Occasionally there will be a product that will work well without an additional driver but certain features won't work (common among certain multifeatured mice and keyboards). In such a situation it's up to you whether to install the manufacturer's driver; in general, if you bought something for the features, then you probably want them to all work.

The following types of devices will require a driver to function properly:

- Scanners
- Input tablets
- Audio/MIDI interfaces and controllers
- Screen calibration devices
- Multifunction mice and keyboards
- Certain video interfaces
- Some printers

On the other hand, a large number of devices should work immediately after plugging them in (though some configuration or special software may be needed to do much with them):

- Digital cameras
- Video camcorders with a FireWire link
- Most Apple hardware
- Speakers and microphones (including USB headsets)
- Some USB/MIDI keyboards and adapters
- Storage devices
- Many standard mice and keyboards (including multibutton mice with a scroll wheel)
- Many printers

Occasionally some special action occurs when you connect a particular type of device.

Digital Cameras

Every type of digital camera we've ever connected to OS X has immediately been recognized. Additionally, when you connect a digital camera, you will be prompted for a specific action. By default, on a clean install of Leopard, when you attach a camera, the Image Capture application (Figure 5-21) will launch and walk you through options for copying images from your camera to your computer.

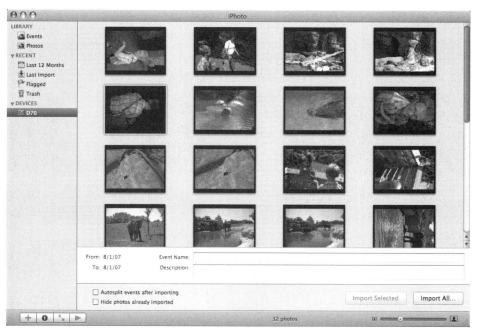

Figure 5-21. The Image Capture application is the default application for importing images from a digital camera.

If you've installed iPhoto (Figure 5-22) or Aperture, you will be prompted when you first plug in your camera as to what application you'd like to open by default in the future. If you select iPhoto or Aperture, then you can set those applications to download the images directly into their libraries.

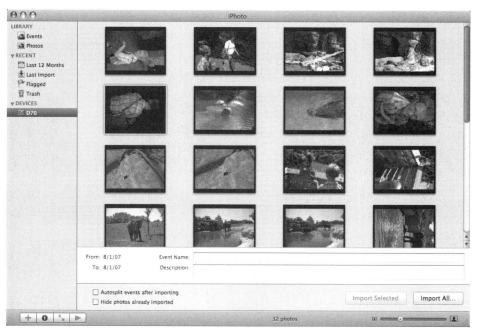

Figure 5-22. If installed, iPhoto can also be used to import images from your digital camera.

What you do with your images once they are imported is entirely up to you, though we will talk a bit about iPhoto '08 later in this book.

Input Tablets

Input tablets are another interesting input device, although they're generally used by graphic designers and artists with graphic applications. When you plug an input tablet in your Leopard computer, you will find that a new preference pane appears in your System Preferences: Ink.

The Ink preference pane (Figure 5-23) provides options for the Inkwell feature introduced in Tiger (Mac OS X 10.4). Inkwell is a handwriting recognition technology that allows you to write text with your input tablet, which the computer will then (attempt to) convert it into editable type:

this is an example 0 I text I entered with inkwell Csif

As you can see, it's still not perfect, but it's fun to play around with (and your handwriting may be better than ours).

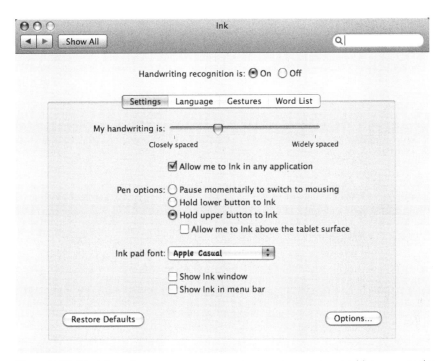

Figure 5-23. The Ink preference pane appears when you have an input tablet connected to your computer.

> **NOTE** Inkwell will not work until the proper driver is installed for your input tablet.

Summary

Now you shouldn't have too much trouble getting any external peripheral to work with your Mac (provided it was designed to work with your Mac . . . getting non-Mac-compatible devices to work goes beyond the scope of this book). Next we will move on to some general administration tasks for Leopard.

> **NOTE** A number of devices that don't make claims to work with a Mac will in fact work just fine, so if you have something laying around, give it a shot.

## CHAPTER 6

Common Leopard Maintenance

Leopard tends to do a pretty good job of taking care of itself; however, there are a few things that occasionally need attention, or that Leopard leaves up to you to take care of. The issues that we will cover in this chapter include the following:

- Disk setup and maintenance
- Application management
- Font management

Disk Setup and Maintenance

> **NOTE** The most important thing about hard disks is that they will all fail in time. Sometimes it is a slow death where they start making a loud clicking that gets progressively worse until they just stop working; other times there is no warning. If you want to keep your data, back it up. Buy an external hard drive (or two) and use Time Machine or some other utility. Really. As the saying goes, "Pay now or pay more later."

Hard drives—both the primary hard drive that came in your computer and any extras, either internal or external—are an essential part of your computer. If things go wrong with a hard drive, your system may stop functioning, or more importantly, you may lose data. Luckily, apart from the very real worry that your hard drive may (and someday will) eventually physically stop working, Leopard tends to take care of things on your drive, limiting the amount of routine maintenance needed to keep your file system and hard drive (and thus your data) healthy. Still, occasionally there are routines that you may want to run to verify that everything is OK. Additionally, someday you may wish to format, partition, or utilize a specific file system on one of the hard drives connected to your system. To manage your hard drives and take care of all of these functions, Leopard includes the Disk Utility application (located in /Applications/ Utilities/).

> **NOTE** There are two primary things that can go wrong on a disk: there's physical damage, which is when the disk mechanism fails and possibly crashes, and there's file system damage, which is when the data on your disk gets mixed up or damaged. Tools like Disk Utility can often detect and repair file system damage before it causes data loss. Physical damage to the disk is more permanent, and often irreparable (although in some cases the data can be recovered by special hardware and/or software).

> **NOTE** The term *disk crash* refers to the event when the arms that pass over the disk surface to read the data fall and literally crash into the disk's surface, causing irreparable damage. This used to happen with older disk mechanisms that would rely on the air force of the spinning disk to keep the arms up, so if the disks quit spinning suddenly before the arms could move back off the disk's surface (e.g., in a power failure), the arms would fall. Disk crashes like this don't happen with today's hard drives, but mechanical issues still arise, and disks do get old and eventually wear out (usually after years of service, though).

Disk Utility divides its abilities into five areas: First Aid, Erase, RAID, Restore, and Partition. First Aid provides a couple of general maintenance tools that can help identify and repair both file system damage and issues in which the system's file permissions become altered. The Erase tab provides the necessary tools to partition and format a disk using various supported file systems. The RAID tab allows you configure multiple disks to behave as one in various ways. The Restore tab lets you restore a disk image onto a disk. We'll cover each of these in the following sections. The fifth area is Partition; it appears if you select the entire disk, rather than just a volume in the list of devices on the left. The Partition tab allows you to split a single disk into multiple volumes.

> **NOTE** A *disk* is a physical device, whereas a *volume* is a file system written to a disk. The physical space on a disk can be divided up into different volumes (or even left as empty space). These divisions are referred to as *disk partitions*.

First Aid

The First Aid tab (Figure 6-1) allows you to run a few tasks to help identify and fix certain problems with your disk's file system. If you seem to be having issues with your disk or notice anything unusual about how it's running or storing data, this is the first place to go to try to solve the problem.

In the lower-right-hand corner are two buttons: Verify Disk and Repair Disk. Clicking Repair Disk will scan the disk to identify and repair many common file system errors. Although most of the errors it may find are in themselves minor, they can often cause bigger issues down the road. One gotcha here is that you can't repair the boot volume—you can, however, click the Verify Disk button to see if there are any problems with it, and if so, you can utilize the Repair Disk function from the Disk Utility application included with your Leopard DVD (just boot from your install DVD and run Disk Utility from there—don't, however, start a new install unless things are really hopeless). On occasion, the Repair utility will come across an issue it cannot repair. At this point, you have two primary options (well, three if you are the type of person who can just ignore a problem until it's too late). Before you decide what you want to do, you should first make backup copies of everything you value on your hard drive. Even if you already have a copy, make another one (I have personally had a primary disk and a backup disk fail simultaneously, and it was not a happy moment. Luckily I had another backup and only lost about a month of work; now I use a mirrored RAID for my backup). Once that's done, you can do either of the following:

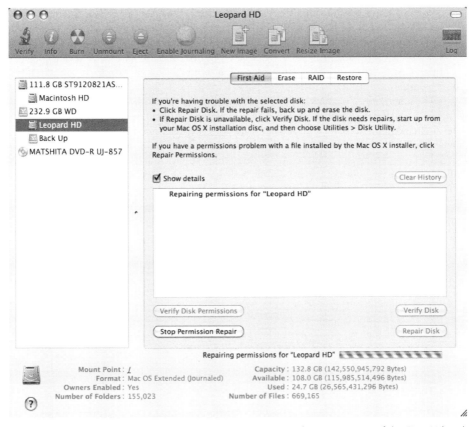

Figure 6-1. Leopard's Disk Utility repairing permissions on a volume using one of the First Aid tools

- Erase, reformat, and reinstall everything on your disk. This option takes a long time and will likely cause a few frustrating moments—and nothing will ever be quite the same. However, it should fix any file system problem, plus it can clean out some other gunk that can creep into your computer as you use it over a long period of time.

- Purchase and try some other disk utility software. There are two very good, easily obtainable disk utilities out there for Macs: TechTool Pro by Micromat (www.micromat.com/) and DiskWarrior by Alsoft (www.alsoft.com/DiskWarrior/). Both of these come on a bootable CD or DVD (you can even get a special bootable thumb drive with TechTool Pro), so you can boot them up and use them right away. The downside it that either of these will set you back about $100.

> **NOTE** Before you break out that checkbook, check whether you got AppleCare with your new computer (you did, didn't you?). If so, check the box it came with—inside is a CD with a special version of TechTool. It doesn't have all the features of the Pro version, but it might solve your problem, and at the very least, you can use this version to save some money when upgrading to the full Pro version ($59 vs. $98 on their web site).

So what happens if nothing works? Sadly, in that case it may be time to replace your hard drive. If your computer is covered under warranty or AppleCare, you should be taken care of. Otherwise, you'll either have to order a new hard drive and install it yourself (easy with a Mac Pro; not so easy, but doable, with a Portable or an iMac) or take it in and have someone else do it (an area Apple store is a good choice, or ask around . . . just make sure if you pay someone to do it that they are Apple certified).

The other pair of buttons on the First Aid tab, Verify Disk Permissions and Repair Disk Permissions, do what they say. In OS X and Leopard, each item in your system has a set of permissions that determine who can do what with the item, and in return what that item can do (a deeper look at permissions is covered in Chapter 18). Occasionally, for a variety of reasons, permissions get changed, and sometimes this causes applications to behave poorly or not work at all. In such a case, setting the permissions back to their defaults usually fixes the problem. To do this, just run Repair Disk Permissions and see if that fixes the problem.

NOTE It's not a bad idea to verify and repair disk permissions every once in a while. It's fairly quick and painless and can save you some unforeseen headaches.

Erasing and Formatting a Volume

The Erase tab (Figure 6-2) allows you to erase all or part of a disk.

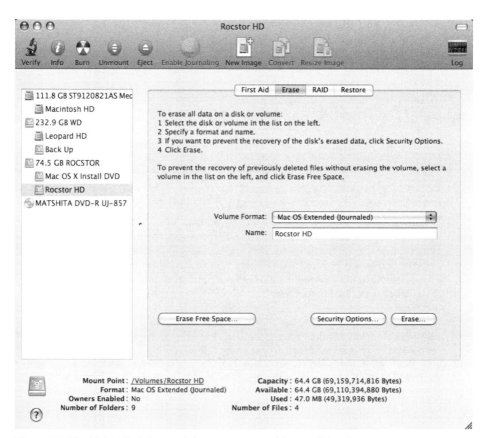

Figure 6-2. The Disk Utility's Erase tab lets you erase and format disk volumes.

You will use this in the following scenarios:

- If you just want to zap all the data on your disk and start over
- If you want to change how a disk is formatted
- If you actually want to wipe the data on your hard drive clean

In the case of the first two scenarios, you basically do the same thing: choose a format from the Volume Format list, choose a name for your new volume, and click the Erase button. This effectively reformats your drive. A simple format, however, does not actually erase your disk, it just erases the existing directory information. With the directory information cleared, your computer has no record of anything stored on it, so it just assumes it's empty and starts writing over old content, keeping track of the new directory information.

If you want to actually erase the content on your hard drive so it cannot be recovered, you have two options. If you just want to assure that any files you have deleted in the trash are actually gone, then you can use the Erase Free Space button. If you want to assure that the entire volume is erased when you format it, click the Security Options button prior to formatting it. Each of these buttons will allow you to choose between three different modes: zero out, 7-pass, or 35-pass of data. Each additional pass will assure that the data will be unrecoverable; however, it will also add a significant amount of time to the process (7 or 35 times the amount of time, to be specific).

Partitioning a Disk

Partitioning a disk is a similar process to formatting a volume; however, it allows you to create and format multiple volumes on the same disk at the same time. The Partition tab (Figure 6-3) appears when you select a disk from the list at the left.

To partition a disk, first select the number of partitions you'd like to create on the disk from the Volume Scheme drop-down list. This will split the disk into the chosen number of partitions, each with approximately an equal size. To resize partitions, simply drag the separator between two partitions in the visual disk partition view below the Volume Scheme menu, thus shrinking one while increasing the size of the other. Alternately, you can select a partition and enter a size in the Size text field to the right (this will also change the size of surrounding partitions). When you have your partition sizes correct, you may enter a volume name in the Name field and choose a file system from the Volume Format list. If you are sure you are ready, click the Apply button, and your selected partitions will be created and formatted as you selected.

> **NOTE** The file system you choose to install on a partition determines some of the types and capabilities of the systems that can be run on them. This is especially true when it comes to booting the computer. For example, through fancy software like VMware Fusion or Parallels, you can run Windows on an HFS partition, but you can only boot your computer into Windows (via Boot Camp) from an MS-DOS formatted partition.

The various file systems available in the format fields are the following:

Mac OS Extended (Journaled): This is Leopard's default file system (HFSJ or HFS+ Journaled).

> **NOTE** *Journaled partitions* keep track of what the disk is doing at all times. In the event that a disk transaction fails, a journaled partition may be able to piece together what was going on when the failure occurred so you don't lose any data.

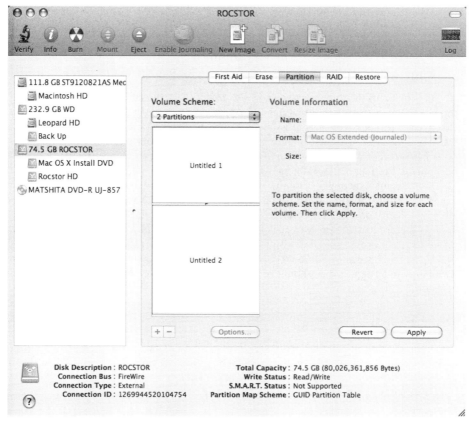

Figure 6-3. The Partition tab allows you to create and format multiple volumes on a single disk.

Mac OS Extended: This is Apple's previous default file system (HFS+).

Mac OS Extended (Case-Sensitive, Journaled): This is the same as HFSJ, but it adds case sensitivity to the file system (so, for example, *Apple* and *apple* would be recognized differently in the file system).

> **NOTE** While case sensitivity sounds like a good thing, it's not. It can make certain applications and computer functions behave poorly, and should only be used in situations where it's essential. The normal HFS+ file system, while it ignores case, preserves it, and that is generally sufficient, even in cases where case is important.

Mac OS Extended (Case-Sensitive): This is the same as HFS+ with added case sensitivity.

MS-DOS: This will use the FAT32 format, which is useful if you intend to physically share the volume with Windows systems.

Free Space: This will leave the partition empty and unusable until you reformat it later.

There are some additional file systems that are possible to utilize; however, at this stage they are considered experimental. These include what many believe to be Apple's next default file system, ZFS, which is currently only available if you download and install support for it separately from Apple's developer web site.

RAID

The RAID tab (Figure 6-4) allows you to configure multiple hard drives into a single volume (or RAID set name).

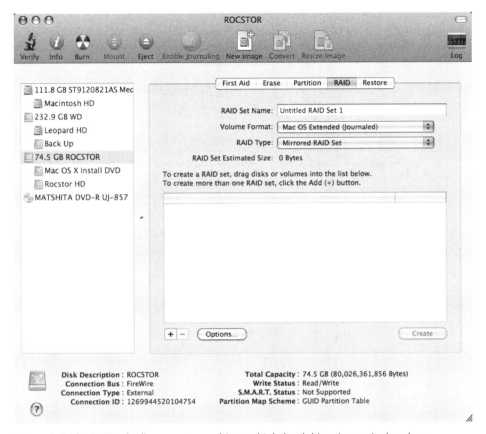

Figure 6-4. The RAID tab allows you to combine multiple hard drives into a single volume.

Disk Utility allows you to create three different types of RAID configurations:

Mirrored RAID Set (a.k.a. RAID 1): This will configure two hard drives of the exact same size in a mirrored array. This means that any data you store on the resulting volume will be physically stored separately on each drive, thus assuring that the data will be safe in the event that one of the drives fails.

Stripped RAID Set (a.k.a. RAID 0): This option will take two hard drives of the exact same size and combine them into one larger volume (equal to the size of both of them together). It will do this in such a way that alternating data is fed to each physical drive, thus greatly increasing overall disk read and write speeds. This is very popular with people who work with large amounts of data and large media files. On the downside, if either drive fails it will be difficult to recover any data from either drive.

Concatenated Disk Set: This will take any number of hard drives and combine them into a single volume spanning all the drives.

Besides these options, there are many other type of RAID configurations that are possible using third-party software or hardware. Many external drive enclosures that support multiple drives include hardware that makes different types of RAID configurations much more efficient.

Restoring Disk Images

A popular way of transmitting large files or applications from one computer to another, especially over a network, is to create a disk image. A disk image is essentially an archive of a disk volume that can be mounted like a disk. Occasionally, copies of CDs and DVDs can be stored and transmitted this way as well. The Restore tab (Figure 6-5) allows you recreate the image file on a disk volume simply by selecting a disk image, selecting an available volume that the image will fit in, and then clicking the Restore button. You should be aware that this will often overwrite the destination volume entirely.

> **TIP** If you work with sensitive data, one thing you can do is create a secure disk image containing this data and mount the disk when you need to work with the data. Then you can unmount the image when you are done with it, returning the data into a state of blissful encryption.

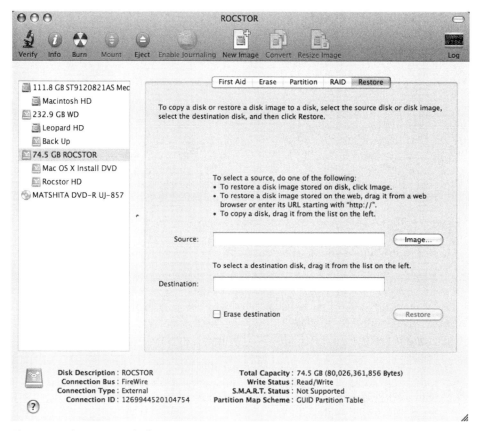

Figure 6-5. The Restore tab allows you to restore a disk image to a disk volume.

Burning an Image File to a CD or DVD

Certain disk images are actually images of CDs or DVDs, and as such, they (or any other appropriately sized image file) can, rather than be restored to a disk volume, be burned to a CD or DVD. To accomplish this, select Images ➤ Burn from the Disk Utility menu (or use the Cmd+B keyboard shortcut). This will first prompt you to select the appropriate image file from the standard open dialog, and then it will prompt you to insert the appropriate writable disk into your disk burner. It will then burn the image to disk.

Managing Applications

A computer without applications is like a car without tires—you can turn it on, but you can't go anywhere. As far as managing applications, there are three primary tasks that may require some thought: installing, updating, and removing them. While none of these are complicated, there tend to be different ways of doing each of these, and there are some extra things to look for when doing them.

Installing

Generally there are two ways that applications are installed on your computer: either by dragging and dropping the applications into your system, or by using an installer application.

You can install most simple apps just by moving them into your system (for a disk or mounted disk image), or by simply downloading and uncompressing them. There really couldn't be anything easier—just move that application where you'd like it (usually somewhere in the Applications folder), and use it.

Other applications come with an installer, which when double-clicked will walk you through the installation process, often providing you with some options as to where you'd like the application (and its parts) installed, and what parts of the application you'd like to install. In general, there is nothing tricky about this, and often it makes what could be a complex task really easy. The one gotcha here is that often an installer will install more than just the application—other items will often be installed along with it in places other than your Applications folder. This isn't inherently bad, but it is something to consider (especially when the time comes to uninstall the application).

> **NOTE** Occasionally, updaters and installers will prompt you for an administrator's password to install an application. This is usually when the application has to install some support items in the /Library folder or somewhere else where privileges are necessary to install items. (If you aren't an administrator, that's pretty much the entire system outside of your home folder, including the Applications folder). If you trust the source of the application, then you should have no worries; however, if you are not sure about the source of what you are installing, it might be a good idea to cancel the installation until you know more.

One thing to think about when installing an application is exactly where you want it. As mentioned, it's likely that you will want to install most of your applications in the Applications folder, but if you have lots of applications, it's not uncommon to create a number of subfolders in your Applications folder for certain types of applications. For example, you may want to put all of your graphics applications in one folder and all of your Internet applications in another. This organization is entirely up to you; Leopard should have no problem running an application wherever you install it. Since Leopard doesn't care too much where the application is, occasionally you may want to install an application elsewhere. It's not uncommon to keep a few personal applications somewhere in your home folder, and this is perfectly fine.

Updating

Like everything else in the computer industry, things are always changing, including the applications you use every day. For this reason, you will likely have to update them from time to time. There are different methods of updating applications that closely mirror the installation options.

Figure 6-6. A dialog box warning you that you are about to replace an older item with a new one

Sometimes, you just download an updated application and drag it into the same folder as the older version. This will usually cause the Finder to pop up a dialog that says that you are about to replace an older item with a newer one and asks you if this is OK (Figure 6-6). In this case, just click Replace if you'd like to continue.

Other times you may need to use an updater application to update an application (you'll usually use these if you used an installer in the first place). An updater will search your system for the older version of the application and then update it.

> **NOTE** For whatever reason (usually lazy programmers), certain updaters will not seek out the proper location of older versions of applications, and will instead install the update files where they assume the program to be (usually in the top level of the Applications folder). This may even create a new application item that only contains half the application (the new half), resulting in two items claiming to be the application: one broken and one outdated. The only fix for this is to delete the new item, move the original item where the installer thinks it should be, and then rerun the installer. Or at worst, delete everything, reinstall the original application, and then update it.

One other method of updating applications (and the system) is Apple's Software Update function. This will automatically check for updates and install them for most Apple-branded software (including system updates). Setting up and running Software Update is covered in Chapter 4.

> **NOTE** Where do you look for software updates? Some applications have options that will allow the application to check for updates when you launch them, and others don't. Either way, a good way to keep up on updates is to routinely check software update sites like MacUpdate (http://macupdate.com/) or VersionTracker (www.versiontracker.com/). If you subscribe to either of their RSS feeds, you can easily keep track of new applications and application updates as they are released.

Uninstalling Applications

Uninstalling applications, and I mean completely uninstalling applications, is a bit more complicated than installing them. Certain applications include an uninstaller application (and certain installer applications likewise include an uninstall option). If this is the case, then using this should be your first step. Otherwise, the first step is simply moving the application to the trash and emptying it. Either of these steps generally removes the application effectively; however, applications tend to leave behind some additional traces that you may want to get rid of.

> **NOTE** AppZapper (http://appzapper.com/) is an application that can help remove old applications completely. When you wish to uninstall an application, simply drag the application file into AppZapper, which will then look through your system for all those other pesky parts and related files.

Cache Files, Preferences, and Support Files

The first place to look for leftover files is in your `~/Library` folder, particularly in the `Caches` folder, the `Preferences` folder, and the `Application Support` folder.

The `Application Support` folder is a common place for applications to store all sorts of items that help them function. This should be stop one. Just take a look and see if the application you are removing has a support folder here (it will usually have the same name as the application itself.) If so, you may delete it.

> **NOTE** Before you delete support files, make sure you have any information that the application was storing for you backed up.

> **NOTE** Some applications will create their own support folder in your `~/Library` folder rather than in the `Application Support` subfolder.

After you clean out any application support files, check the `~/Library/Caches` folder. Here, many applications (especially network-enabled apps) store temporary cache files. These can take up lots of space, so you don't want to leave any unused cache files lying around.

> **NOTE** It's not a bad idea to delete the caches of all applications every now and then. Just make sure that the application isn't running when you delete the folder. The application should just create a new cache the next time it needs one. Cleaning out these folders can add a fairly significant amount of disk space.

The next place to look is your `~/Library/Preferences` folder. This folder keeps track of all your personal preferences for all your applications and many other system features; and every application, even if just launched once and closed, is likely to have created a file here. Finding the appropriate preference file is a bit tricky. Traditionally, there was no specific naming convention for preference files, so they were usually named after the application. Additionally, certain software developers would (and still do) create a folder here to store the preferences for all their applications (because some applications share preferences among similar applications). Today, however, there is a specific naming convention for most preference files that uses a reverse top-level domain for the developer, followed by the name of the application, followed by some sub-information if needed. So, for example, all the preference files for Apple products would follow the format `com.apple.appname.subpref`. Usually, these will end with a `.plist` extension indicating the type of file is a property list. Once you locate the appropriate preference for your deleted application, you may likewise delete it.

> **NOTE** Preference files are interesting to take a peek at. If you installed the Xcode tools, a special application, `/Developer/Applications/Utilities/Property List Editor`, was installed that makes browsing and editing these `.plist` files easy. Most `.plist` files are written in XML, which can be viewed in any text editor as well. While you should exercise some caution with preference files, you may discover preferences for certain applications that aren't otherwise accessible (hidden preferences).

> **NOTE** While it's not recommended that you regularly delete a preference file, if you do mistakenly delete one, it essentially resets the application back to the first time you used it. With some apps, this may cause no noticeable difference; with others, you may need to go through the setup or registration process again. While this may be inconvenient, it's rarely a big problem.

> **NOTE** Occasionally, an application may create some of these files in the `/Library` folder as well. Feel free to delete these as well.

Frameworks, Components, Receipts, and Contextual Menu Items

Besides the extra items mentioned previously that are installed and created by applications, a number of applications may install some additional support files. These include special development frameworks, special components, and contextual menu items. Most of these items can be safely deleted; however, you should use care when doing so.

Contextual menu items (which are often installed in the Contextual Menu Items subfolder in one of the Library folders) are items that enable some application-specific behavior to be accessible from a contextual menu. If you delete the application that the item is attached to, then it will cease to function; so obviously, if you find these "dead" items, you should delete them.

Components (found in the Components subdirectory of a Library folder) are generally not needed when you remove the application they are associated with either. The only problem is that these items are often named in such a way that it's hard to determine what component is attached to what application, and deleting the wrong one can cause an existing application to fail. In general, if in doubt, leave it alone. If, however, you are sure that you no longer need a component, you may remove it.

Frameworks are trickier. One application may install a third-party framework, and a subsequent application you install may also use that framework, so even if you delete the initial application that installed the framework, by removing the framework you could damage another application. As such, we generally recommend against uninstalling any frameworks unless you are absolutely sure that it's safe. Other than taking up some disk space, an unused framework won't interfere with your system in any way.

Finally, most installer packages leave behind a *receipt* (which is a copy of the package file) in the /Library/Receipts folder. When you delete an application, it's safe to delete any package files here associated with it. Removing receipts for existing applications could, however, affect the ability to upgrade the application in the future—and many update packages use receipt data to determine the necessity or eligibility for an upgrade.

Other Hidden Application Files

The last type of file that may be installed along with the application are hidden or obscure files. These files are installed for one of two reasons. First, some applications install files that are accessible from the command line—while these files are not normally viewable from the Finder, they are not specifically hidden from you (often applications will check with you before installing command-line tools). The other reason applications install hidden or obscure files is specifically so you don't find them; this is usually for licensing reasons and to prevent you from pirating the software or reusing timed-out demo versions of software.

The "hidden" command-line tools (which really aren't hidden; they just aren't immediately visible) can easily be removed from the command line (this is covered later in the book, beginning in Chapter 18). The other files—the ones that are actually intentionally hidden—are problematic. While they generally don't affect your system in any way (other than restricting the use of a particular application), the idea of them lying around bothers people.

While there are no specific instructions for finding and removing all of these intentionally hidden files, there are some suggestions:

- Look around your file system in the command line (see Chapter 18). Lots of files that are hidden from the Finder are easily revealed in the command line. If you find files in a Library folder or subfolder in the command line that you don't see in the Finder, they are probably being hidden.

- If you are really stumped, have an extra hard disk that you can use, and some time on your hands. Create two partitions on the disk and install a clean system on each. Then install the suspected application on one partition and compare the resulting file systems. If you do this correctly, then any additional files on the application partition belong to the application. (There are a number of ways of creating directory lists, including all files, and then comparing the lists using a variety of command-line and text-based tools.)

- Finally (and this should probably be the first step you try), search the Internet for information about the application and hidden files. Like most things, it's unlikely you are the first person to encounter this situation, and perhaps the answers you are looking for are already out there.

NOTE Even though you might not want these hidden files around once you remove the associated application, if you are currently using the application, it's likely that you need these files for it to work correctly, so use caution here and don't delete hidden files just because they are hidden—it's likely you won't like the results.

Managing Fonts

Fonts may not seem like something that needs to be managed too much, and in OS X, fonts don't tend to cause many of the issues that they have been attributed to in the past. Still, if you tend to accumulate lots of fonts, you may want to manage them for a number of reasons:

- To be able to easily find the exact type of font you are looking for quickly and easily from a large list of installed fonts

- To "turn off" unused fonts, since many applications (especially graphics apps and word processors) load all active fonts into memory when they launch (slowing up launch time and consuming memory)

OS X, beginning with Panther, included an application named Font Book that will help you manage your fonts. Font Book (Figure 6-7) provides the ability to find, preview, organize, and switch on or off all the fonts installed on your system.

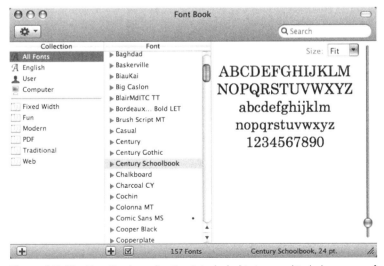

Figure 6-7. The Font Book application is included in Leopard to help manage fonts on your system.

The Font Book application is organized with two columns and a preview window. The first column, Collection, allows you to select and create sets, or collections, of fonts. The set you select in this column determines the specific font families that are displayed in the Font column. Selecting a font family or specific font from within a family will display that font in the view window.

To create your own collection, click the + button at the bottom of the Collection column, and give your collection a name. Then you can drag fonts displayed in the Font column into your new collection. When you select your set, only the fonts you added to it will appear in the Font column.

To add a new font, click the + button at the bottom of the Font column, and select the font file(s) to add.

To deactivate a font or collection of fonts, right-click the font or collection, and select the Disable option from the contextual menu. Alternately, you can select fonts in the Font column and toggle them with the small check box button at the bottom of the column.

When you deactivate a font collection, it will deactivate any fonts in that collection that are not present in any other activated collection. This prevents fonts from an active collection to be inadvertently disabled.

Fonts may be reactivated in the same manner.

One nice thing about creating groups of fonts, beyond that ability to activate and deactivate entire groups easily, it that the groups appear in the standard Cocoa font selection dialog box (Figure 6-8), making it easy to find specific fonts that exist within a particular collection.

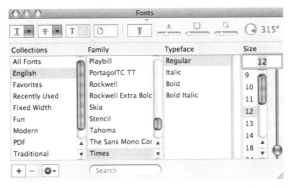

Figure 6-8. Font collections appear in the standard font selection dialog box, making finding a particular font easy.

Summary

This chapter has covered a few basic management tasks that you'll likely encounter at some point. The next chapter is going focus on a more specific maintenance task: keeping your data backed up and current.

## CHAPTER 7

Backup, Synchronization, and Recovery of Data

Most people who have been around computers for a long time have horror stories of disk crashes and data loss. And even if your story isn't horrific, you probably have an "Oh, $#!*!" moment or two when things go wrong and you lose an hour's or a day's (or more) worth of work. The thing is, the minute your hard drive was created, it started a countdown toward its mean time before failure (MTBF—a rating that measures the average amount of time before a hard drive fails); in addition, we as people tend to occasionally make mistakes, so we must make sure we have effective ways of backing up and syncing our data.

> **NOTE** You can read an interesting article about drive failure from eWeek at www.eweek.com/article2/0,1895,2099467,00.asp.

This chapter is dedicated to backing up and syncing data, not because it's a terribly long and complicated thing to explain (in fact, with the release of Leopard, it's really relatively easy) but because it's such an important topic that it deserves to be treated on its own. In this chapter, we will cover the following:

- The difference between backup and synchronization and what's appropriate in what circumstances
- Keeping your computer's data backed up using Time Machine
- Syncing your data with iSync and .Mac
- Other methods of backup, syncing, and data recovery

The Difference Between Backups and Synchronization

Before we go too far, it's important to distinguish between a backup and a sync. In overly simple terms, suppose you have two disks: disk A and disk B. If you back up disk A to disk B, you will make an exact copy of disk A onto disk B, thus preserving all the data on disk A. If you synchronize disk A with disk B, the information on each disk will be copied to the other, so each disk will have the same information, which is the sum of disk A + disk B. One special type of backup is a backup with an archive. In this case, when you back up disk A to disk B, the old information on disk B will be moved into an archive, not deleted, which is particularly useful since you can go back in time and recover files that have been previously deleted from disk A. If you are more of a visual thinker, these differences are illustrated in Figure 7-1.

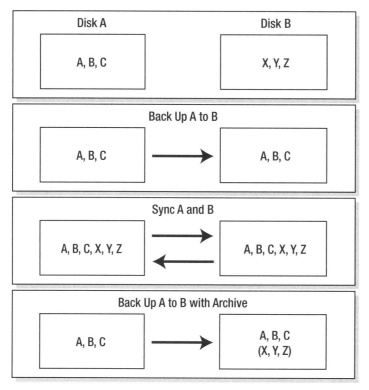

Figure 7-1. Differences between backups and synchronization

Generally, when you want to keep an extra copy of your important data in case something happens to your primary data store, then what you want is a backup. When you have two data stores that you need to keep current with each other, then what you want is synchronization. Either way, you are creating a redundancy that is important should one data source fail. One important note, though: creating a backup with archiving is the only way to effectively protect against file corruption. If you synchronize or simply back up a corrupted file, then you are just creating a new copy of a corrupted file, often overwriting an old, noncorrupted file.

Backing Up Your Data with Time Machine

Leopard introduces what seems to be a fantastic little backup utility called Time Machine. Time Machine provides data backups of all your information complete with a historical archive of data. The best thing about this, though, is that Time Machine does all of its work automatically in the background, making it painless. The disadvantage, though, is that in order to use Time Machine, you will need an extra hard drive connected to your computer for Time Machine to back up data to.

NOTE When deciding whether to invest in an external hard drive for Time Machine to use, ask yourself how much the data you keep on your computer is worth. You can easily find a nice-sized external hard drive these days for less than $100, and in our opinion, our data is worth at least that.

NOTE If you are desperate, you can set up Time Machine to back up to a different partition on your primary hard drive. Although this will provide some protection of your data as well as a nice historical archive of data, this will do nothing if your hard drive fails.

To set up Time Machine, you open the Time Machine pane in System Preferences (Figure 7-2). Click the Configure button to pick an attached volume for Time Machine to use, and then, if you'd like, add any volumes or folders you *don't* want Time Machine to back up. Finally, you have the options of skipping backing up system files and having your backup occur automatically. Skipping system files isn't such a bad idea, since if something really bad happens, you'll need to reinstall the system anyway and you have that on your DVD. The automatic backups are a personal preference. If you remember to back up manually (by clicking the Back Up Now button), then that's fine. If, however, you just don't want to think about it, leave the automatic backup checked.

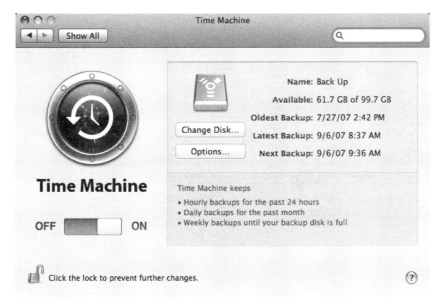

Figure 7-2. The Time Machine preference pane provides configuration options for Time Machine.

NOTE Once Time Machine is active, you can select individual items within the Finder and choose whether to include or exclude them from Time Machine backups in either the Get Info window or the contextual menu.

Once Time Machine is initially set up, it may take a bit of time to make the initial backup, but after that, the backups will be relatively short (unless you are doing backups manually and infrequently or you use a portable and attach your backup drive only every now and then). However, once things are moving, Time Machine is ready when you need it.

When you launch Time Machine, your desktop will fade away, and you will be brought into the Time Machine interface. If you launch Time Machine from the Finder, then a Finder window will be the main focus (Figure 7-3). You can navigate through the single Finder window normally, and you will find all the currently backed up Finder items. If you go to the far-right side of the window, though, you will notice a time line. If you click back through the timeline, the Finder window will change from showing you the latest backup files to showing you the files backed up as far back as you go in the timeline. If you want to restore any file from any time or place in the Finder, simply select it, and click Restore at the bottom. This will bring the item out of Time Machine and put it back in its original location in the Finder. If an item of the same name exists in that place, then you will be prompted to keep one or the other files or both files.

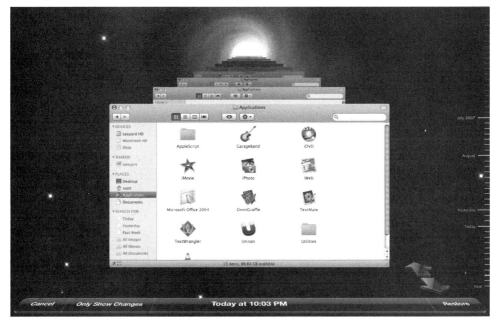

Figure 7-3. Time Machine browsing Finder items as they were backed up through time

> **NOTE** The timeline will go back pretty much as far as you let it. When you click the Configure button in the Time Machine preference pane, there is an option to delete files after a certain amount of time. If your backup volume is low on space, you may want to utilize this.

If you want to leave Time Machine without restoring any items, just click the Cancel button in the lower-left corner of the Time Machine interface.

One interesting aspect of the Time Machine is it will attempt to open Time Machine in the frontmost open window on your screen. If you double-click the Time Machine icon in your Applications folder, the Time Machine will open with a Finder window open to the Applications folder. On the other hand, if you are working in a Time Machine–enabled application and you open Time Machine from the Dock (either from an icon on the Dock or from a stack), an interesting thing will happen: instead of getting a Finder window, you will get an application window that you can browse backward through and restore changes in that application. For example, if you launch Time Machine while running the Mail application, then Time Machine will open with a Mail window (Figure 7-4), allowing you to go back in time and view old mail messages that have been deleted.

Figure 7-4. Opening Time Machine while Mail is running in the foreground opens Time Machine in Mail, allowing you to recover deleted Mail messages.

If you ever need to recover more than just a file or a few e-mail messages, Time Machine allows you to select and recover entire folders, or, yes, even your entire volume. Additionally, if you even have to reinstall your system from scratch, there is an option during the install that will recover information from a Time Machine backup disk (you can learn more about installing Leopard in Appendix B).

> **NOTE** Many people may point out that Time Machine actually goes beyond just backup and actually provides version control as well. *Version control* tracks changes of items over time so that you can recover older versions if something critically wrong happens in a new version. For developers, version control (or source code management [SCM]) is essential for creating stable software, and support for a number of version control systems including CVS, Subversion, and Perforce are built into Xcode. For more general project version control, Versions (www. versionsapp.com/) provides an easy-to-use interface for taking advantage of the Subversion version control system.

Synchronization

Besides backup, Leopard provides a number of ways for you to sync your data with the other computers or devices you use.

First there is iSync (Figure 7-5). iSync allows you to sync your calendars and your contacts with mobile devices. So if you are out and about and meet an old friend and enter their contact information in your phone, next time you sync your phone using iSync, that contact information will be added to your Address Book. At the same time, if you add a number of events in iCal, when you sync your phone with iSync, those events get entered into your phone's calendar.

Figure 7-5. iSync allows you to sync contacts and calendar information with mobile phones and PDAs.

To use iSync, first you must connect an acceptable device to your computer (you can find an up-to-date list of devices that are supported by iSync at www.apple.com/macosx/features/isync/devices.html). Once the device is added and recognized, it will show up as an item in iSync's toolbar. Selecting a device will allow you to set up the sync options. You can choose what items you want to synchronize and how to handle the initial sync. To start the synchronization process, hit the Sync Devices button in the top-right corner. If your device is found and ready to receive (you may need to do something on the receiving device as well), then the sync should occur. You will be notified of any errors as well as how many items have successfully been synchronized.

iSync is also used to synchronize your data with .Mac, but today .Mac allows all sorts of interesting synchronization options that far outshine iSync. .Mac (which is covered in more detail in Chapter 15) allows you to selectively sync a wide number of items from your computer through .Mac to any other computer. For example, if you use a Mac at home and a Mac at work, then through .Mac you can keep the following items synced with each computer:

- Bookmarks
- Calendars
- Contacts
- Dashboard widgets
- Dock items
- Keychains

- Mail accounts
- Mail rules, signatures, and smart mailboxes
- Notes
- Preferences
- Entourage notes

Together these options effectively re-create the environment from one computer to another and then keep the environments in sync with each other, creating a seamless transition from working with one to working with the other.

The items you want to keep synced must be selected for each computer you want to keep synced. This can be set up and configured on the Sync tab of the .Mac pane of System Preferences (Figure 7-6).

Figure 7-6. You can use .Mac to keep the environments of two or more computers in sync with each other.

NOTE One unique yet extraordinarily common sync is syncing an iPod or iPhone. Both of these sync from within iTunes. This particular case will be covered with iTunes in Chapter 14.

Other Methods of Backup, Sync, and Recovery

Besides these methods that are part of Leopard, you can use a range of other utilities, applications, and methods to protect your data. Some applications, such as Apple's Aperture, provide a means of backing up and archiving their data. Some people are in the habit of regularly burning archives of important files to CDs or DVDs, and there are many other applications out there to help with backup and recovery of your data. If Time Machine doesn't quite fit your needs (or for whatever reason you just don't like it), these are some other applications worth a look:

- Decimus Software (www.decimus.net/) makes three different backup applications depending on your needs: Synk Backup, Synk Standard, and Synk Pro. These apps range in cost from $25 to $45. Although the Standard version handles most common backup and synchronization tasks, the Pro version adds some very nice features and at $45 is the best bang for your buck.

- Qdea (www.qdea.com) has been making backup software for Macs for years. Their current Synchronize! X Plus and Synchronize! X Pro are also great products for a variety of backup and synchronization needs. These cost $29.95 and $99.95, respectively.

- EMC Insignia (www.emcinsignia.com), a division of storage powerhouse EMC, recently acquired Retrospect, a highly regarded backup solution for Macs. EMC Retrospect for Macintosh comes in four versions. The Express version, which is distributed only with hard drives from some manufacturers and resellers, provides basic backup capabilities. The Desktop version (about $120) provides everything you could want in a desktop backup solution. The Workgroup version (about $500) is designed to keep up to 20 networked computers all backed up. The Server version (about $800) provides backups for up to 100 desktop clients (this version supports clients running Macs, Windows, and Red Hat Linux).

What's most important—whether you use Time Machine, use Retrospect, or manually copy all your data onto thumb drives—is that you do *something* to back up your data. Just pick a system that works for you and go with it.

Summary

Now that you know how to protect your data from hard drive failures and accidental data loss, we'll move on to protecting your data and your computer from other threats.

## CHAPTER 8

Leopard Security

Besides protecting your data from hardware failure and accidents, in today's world, where computers tend to be always connected, it's also important to protect your data from other users—both on your computer and outside of it. This chapter deals with security, including the following topics:

- Passwords and keychains
- Data encryption and FileVault
- Other security features

Passwords and Keychains

Passwords are used time and time again on your computer: logging in to your account, checking your e-mail, visiting certain web sites, logging in to connected servers, and more. There are so many passwords that it becomes a chore to keep track of them all. To help manage all of your passwords, security certificates, and encryption keys, OS X includes a keychain feature to keep track of all of this information.

The Keychain Feature

Whenever you enter a password into an application that takes advantage of the OS X keychain, you will be prompted whether to save the username-password combination in your keychain. If you select yes, then the next time you log in, rather than getting a prompt to enter your username and password, the application will automatically use what's already saved in your keychain. Now your keychain will only use the passwords stored in it under certain circumstances:

- The keychain will only use data saved in the logged-in user's keychain, so your keychain is protected from all other users (excepting shared keychains).
- By default, passwords associated with a particular application allow only that application to access the password item in your keychain. Often when you update your application and attempt to use it, you will be prompted to update the key to work with the updated application (you will need to authorize the update).

- The key in the keychain is valid and unexpired. While this usually isn't a big problem for passwords, security certificates and encryption keys, which are also stored in the keychain, will often expire.

The keychain data itself is stored in a file in your ~/Library/Keychains folder. All sensitive data is well encrypted within the file. Should you ever need to view your keychain (or other keychains you have access to), Leopard includes the Keychain Access utility (in the /Applications/ Utilities folder). The Keychain Access utility (Figure 8-1) provides a way for you to view, edit, and configure individual entries stored in your keychain.

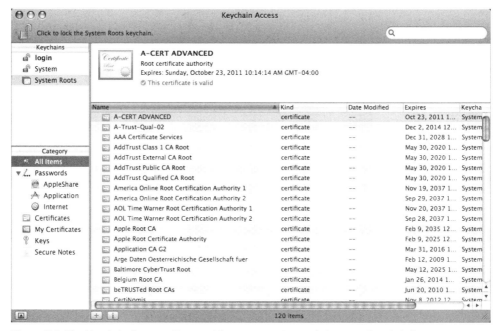

Figure 8-1. The Keychain Access utility provides a way to view and alter your keychain items.

The Keychain Access utility provides a column on the left where you can select the keychain you'd like to view (any available keychains will be listed there; your default keychain is the login keychain). Below the list of keychains is a list of categories of items that are stored in the keychain. The categories and their descriptions are covered in Table 8-1. On the right side is the view area, where, at the bottom, the individual items stored in the keychain are listed. Above that is a view that provides some basic information about the selected item.

Table 8-1. Categories of Items Stored in Your Keychain

Category	Description
Passwords	These are your passwords, which are broken into three subcategories: AppleShare: These are your passwords associated with file servers and other people's computers that you have accounts on. Application: These passwords are associated with specific applications. They can be used for just about anything, including Internet sites, but rather than being associated with the site they are associated with the application. Internet: These are your Internet passwords, which include certain web site login information, as well as mail accounts and other Internet server credentials.

Category	Description
Certificates	Certificates provide a method of verifying a site's credentials, certifying that a service on the Internet (or network) is who it says it is. This is based on a method of trust: there are a number of certificate authorities who issue certificates—assuming you trust the authority, then you can trust all of the certificates issued by that authority. A number of certificates from reputable issuing authorities are included in Leopard (these are viewable from the System Roots keychain). Occasionally you may be prompted by a web site to approve a new certificate, which is of course at your discretion (Figure 8-2). If the certificate checks out, it will be categorized here.
My Certificates	The My Certificates category also stores certificates, but rather than certificates that verify others to you, these certificates verify you to others. Using certificates to verify you are who you say you are is becoming more common, especially in situations where data integrity is essential. These sorts of certificates can be used in lieu of a password, or more often used in conjunction with a password (if someone walks up to your computer, the certificate is available but they may not know your password; on the other hand, if someone has your password, then they need physical access to your computer [or certificate] to do anything with it).
Keys	Keys are used for encryption. In general, there are many forms of encryption that use keys, but the essential idea is that communication on one end of the network uses one key to encrypt data that only a specific (often different) key on the other end of the network can decrypt. This is important because most bits of information passing through the Internet or a network can usually be viewed by many other computers and systems in between.
Secure Notes	Secure notes are different than most of the other items stored in your keychain, in that they are generally not used outside of the keychain. Rather, they just provide a way for you to store confidential notes in your keychain. The information here could contain credit card information or any other personal information you decide to limit access to.

Figure 8-2. When your system encounters a new certificate that it cannot verify, it will prompt you about whether you want to accept the connection. Selecting the "Always trust..." check box will add the certificate to your keychain.

> **NOTE** Cryptography and encryption are very big, complicated topics. A great book that does a good job of explaining them, including keys and certificates, is *Cryptography Decrypted*, by H. X. Mel and Doris Baker (Addison-Wesley Professional, 2000).

Double-clicking any of the items in your keychain will open up a window providing detailed information about that item. For items like passwords and secure notes, some details will be hidden, specifically the password and the actual content of the note.

The password items have a number of options spread out over two tabs: the Attributes tab and the Access Control tab.

The Attributes tab (Figure 8-3) provides the following information:

Name: This is just the name of the keychain item.

Kind: This is the category the item belongs to.

Account: This is the name associated with the account. Usually this field contains the username, but occasionally, especially for application passwords, it is used to represent something used similarly by the application.

Location: This identifies where the password is valid; this is commonly a URI pointing to the online resource for which the item is valid, but occasionally it is something else (a protocol, for example, or just something that has meaning to an application).

Comments: This field contains any comments associated with the item.

Password: This is where the password is shown. However, by default it is empty to protect the password. To view the password, you will need to select the View Password option and then authenticate yourself.

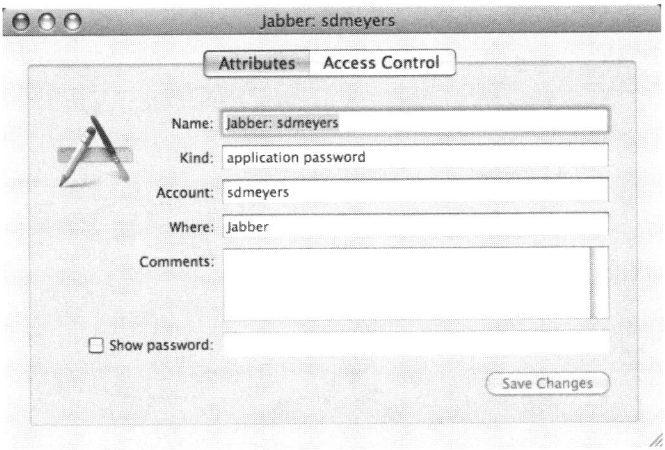

Figure 8-3. The Attributes tab of a password keychain item

> **NOTE** All of the fields in the Attributes tab are editable. If you are storing items here for your own reference, you may certainly edit these—however, if the item is being used by an application, altering this information may interfere with the normal operation of the application.

The Access Control tab (Figure 8-4) allows you to delegate what applications can access the keychain item, and whether or not you'll be prompted to approve any new application that wishes to use the information.

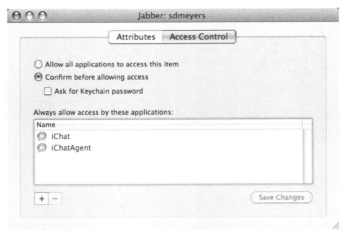

Figure 8-4. The Access Control tab controls how the information in the item can be accessed.

Creating Your Own Keychains and Keychain Items

While the keychain feature is designed to mostly run in the background to seamlessly manage passwords, keys, and certificates, it will also allow you to store your own information inside of it. You could store your own passwords and notes, and even keep track of serial numbers for registered applications.

> **NOTE** Besides using the keychain, there are other ways to securely store password and application data provided by third parties. Some interesting applications include Pastor (www.mehlau.net/pastor/) and info.xhead (www.xheadsoftware.com/info_xhead.asp), which are both nice stand-alone applications for securely storing password and registration data.

To add a keychain item, you click the little + button at the bottom of the keychain window, and a sheet will open so you can enter your information. By default, the sheet will be geared toward passwords. If you a want to create a note, select the Note group in the left column, and then click the + button. This will open up a sheet for entering your note. Alternately, you can select File ➤ New Password Item or File ➤ New Secure Note Item directly from the menu bar.

The password sheet (Figure 8-5) is fairly straightforward; you enter a name for your item, the account name, and your password. There are some interesting points here, though. For one, the keychain item name determines what the type of item will be. If you enter a URL, the item will be created as an Internet password; otherwise the item will be created as an application password. Finally, the bar at the bottom will extend to the right and change from red to green as you enter your password to indicate its strength.

The strength of a password is determined by common means that a malicious user may use to attempt to crack it. This determination consists of many variables, including the length of the password, uniqueness, and the type of characters used. Common names and words found in dictionaries are very weak, as a modern computer can run through a dictionary list of common words and passwords in a few minutes. Beyond that, short passwords take a relatively short amount of time to crack using *brute force* methods (which basically means using every possible combination of every letter, number, and symbol for each space). The difficulty of brute-force cracking increases dramatically with each additional character. It's good practice to attempt to mix uppercase and lowercase letters, numbers, and if possible, symbols, into your passwords. Additionally, passwords should be at least eight characters long.

Figure 8-5. The password sheet allows you to enter a password into a new keychain item.

> **NOTE** Ten years ago, an eight-character password was considered strong. Today, that would be a minimum acceptable in most situations. As computing power increases, passwords become increasingly less effective, since as password lengths increase, it becomes increasingly hard to remember them, and therefore less practical. For this reason, a number of password alternatives have been developed, and are gaining in popularity. These alternatives may be used to complement a password system or eliminate passwords altogether. These alternatives include smart cards and other hardware authentication devices, and biometric security measures (such as fingerprint readers).

When you choose to enter a secure note item to your keychain, the sheet that appears (Figure 8-6) asks for a name for your item and then includes a large text field for your note.

If you intend to store lots of personal information in a keychain, you may want to create a keychain separate from your login keychain to store information; this is easily done by selecting File ➤ New Keychain... from the Keychain Access menu.

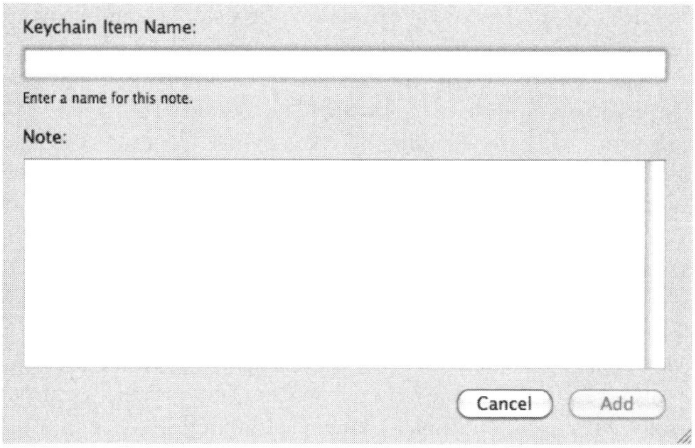

Figure 8-6. The keychain sheet for entering a secure note item

Other Keychain Options

There are a few other features associated with keychains that are available from the Keychain Access utility. These are described in the following sections.

Keychain Passwords

By default, your keychain password (the password you will need to unlock data such as passwords and notes in your keychain) is the same as your login password. This password can be changed for each keychain using the Edit ➤ Change Password for Keychain "*keychain*"... command.

Keychain Settings

The Edit ➤ Change Settings for Keychain "*keychain*"... menu item allows you to access some additional options for a particular keychain. These include the ability to lock your keychain after a certain amount of time, or when your computer goes to sleep (you will need to enter your keychain password each time you or an application attempt to access a locked keychain). This also provides an option to synchronize your keychain with .Mac, allowing you to share a keychain across multiple computers utilizing .Mac's sync features.

Keychain First Aid

If your keychain gets mucked up to the point that it no longer functions correctly, the Keychain First Aid selection under the Keychain Access application menu can help solve a number of problems. Depending on what First Aid options are set in the Keychain Access utility's preferences, running Keychain First Aid will rebuild your keychain file and reset most settings back to the defaults, including setting the keychain passwords back to the login password, and setting the login keychain back to the default keychain.

Data Encryption: FileVault

While the keychain feature protects your passwords while keeping them easily accessible, FileVault protects your data from others. FileVault, accessible from the FileVault tab in the Security System Preferences pane (Figure 8-7), encrypts the contents of your home folder, protecting them from anyone who attempts to access anything stored there.

The first step in enabling FileVault is to choose a master password by selecting the Set Master Password button. This will open up a sheet (Figure 8-8) for you to enter a master password that can be used to decrypt any of your computer's FileVaults. The reason for this is that if a user forgets their login password, then this master password can be used by an administrator to reset the user's password, allowing them to regain access to their home data.

Figure 8-7. The FileVault tab of the Security preference pane lets you turn FileVault on and off.

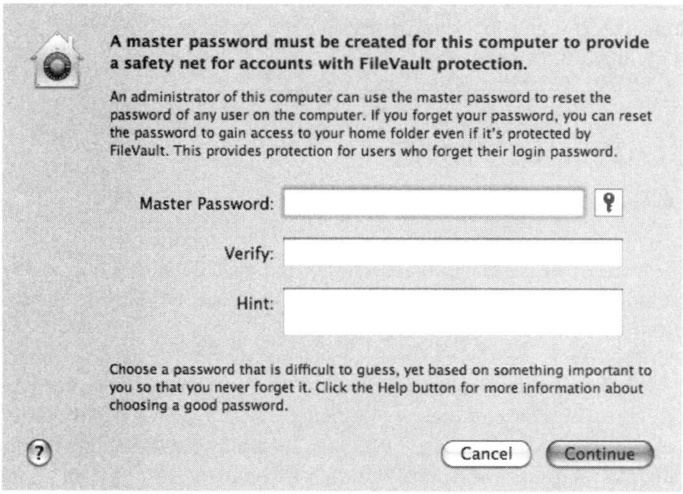

Figure 8-8. A master password is a safeguard that allows an administrator to reset a user's password. Without this, the entire contents of the user's home directory could be lost.

Once you've set the master password, click the Turn on FileVault button, and you'll be asked for various forms of authentication, including administrator and user passwords. Then you'll be presented with a sheet containing some final warnings about the limitations of FileVault-protected accounts and a couple more options (see Figure 8-9).

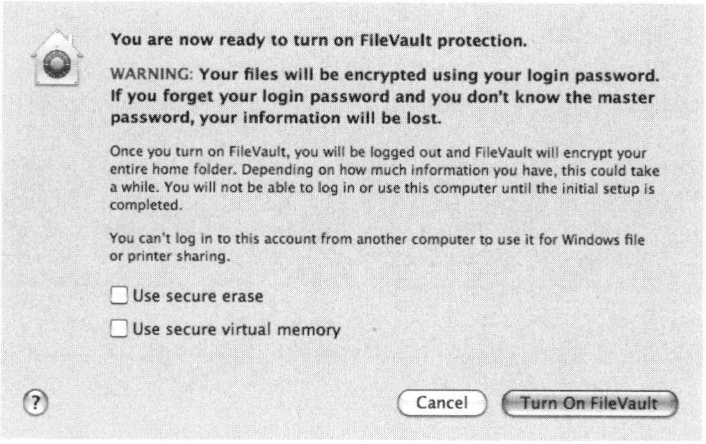

Figure 8-9. Last warnings and two more options before turning on FileVault

The "Use secure erase" option will cause the Secure Empty Trash option to be used by default when the trash is emptied. The "Use secure virtual memory" option will additionally overwrite any memory traces that may be on your hard drive to further protect all of your data. If you are ready to go, click the Turn On FileVault button.

When you initially turn on FileVault, you will be immediately logged out, as the system encrypts all of your data. Depending on the amount of data you have in your home directory, this process could take some time.

Once FileVault is set up, using your protected account will be pretty much the same, as your home directory data will be decrypted when you log in.

As mentioned, there are some disadvantages to using FileVault:

- File sharing of all types will be disabled for the FileVault-enabled account.
- Remote access will be disabled.
- There will be some minor performance issues, especially the time required to log in (as data is decrypted) and log out (as new data is encrypted and traces are cleaned up). Additionally, other minor delays for various tasks will occur.

NOTE FileVault provides some very serious data protection, and despite conflicting with some other features of OS X, if you must work in an entirely secure environment and data security is extremely important, this will help provide that. On the other hand, for most users, this will be overkill. If you simply wish to keep a handful of files encrypted, there are a number of utilities available that will accommodate you.

FileVault Considerations: The Good and the Bad

Besides what's already been mentioned, there are some serious considerations you should think about when deciding to use FileVault:

- While in general, passwords are required to access a user's data on a running system, there are ways to work around this, such as booting the computer in Target Disk mode. When using FileVault, your data is still encrypted, so even though someone may have access to it, they can't easily do anything with it.
- FileVault stores your entire home directory in a single encrypted file. If this file becomes corrupted due to a hard drive failure or something else, all your data will be lost.

- Since FileVault encrypts your entire home directory, it tends to encrypt lots of things that just don't need to be encrypted (e.g., the iTunes library). This presents a large performance penalty.

- If you use FileVault, you should also keep in mind that any backups should be encrypted as well. It doesn't do any good protecting your information on your computer if your backups aren't equally protected.

- If you occasionally need this sort of protection, it may be a good idea to create a separate account specifically for this purpose.

- If you need to protect only a limited amount of data, it may be a better idea to just utilize an encrypted disk image that contains the protected data, as this provides quite a bit more flexibility.

If you should change your mind, you can turn off FileVault by repeating the same steps used in turning it on.

Other Security Features

In very general terms, computer security is divided into physical security and network security. Physical security represents the security of your computer when someone is sitting right in front of it, while with network security, you are protecting your computer from a potential threat that could be halfway around the world. The trouble with these simple distinctions is that today they tend to blur a bit, especially with multiuser systems like OS X, where there is blurring between physical and network security with remote desktop technologies that allow many users to essentially have physical access to the system, even over a network.

The obvious place to begin looking for all of these is the Security preference pane in System Preferences. Here we have three tabs: General (Figure 8-10), FileVault, and Firewall.

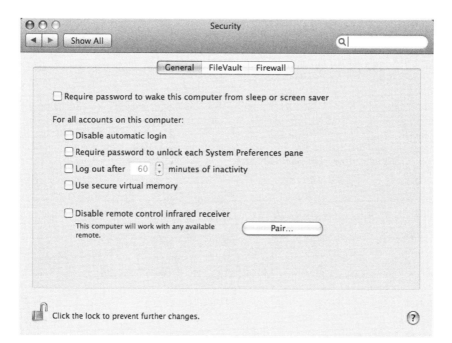

Figure 8-10. The general security options in the Security preference pane

The general security options cover a wide range of options normally associated with physical security. The options covered on the General tab of the Security preference pane are covered in Table 8-2.

Table 8-2. General Security Options

Option	Description
Require password to wake this computer from sleep or screen saver	This option will prompt for a password when the computer is awoken from a period of inactivity. This protects your system if you step away for a bit, leaving your computer on but unattended.
Disable automatic login	This option requires a user to log in when the system is turned on.
Require password to unlock each System Preferences pane	This will require an administrative password whenever someone attempts to adjust any system preferences.
Logout after X minutes of inactivity	This will log out any user who is inactive for a certain period of time.
Use secure virtual memory	This will overwrite any disk space used for virtual memory when the memory is no longer used.
Disable remote control infrared receiver	If your system includes a remote control (e.g., portables and iMacs), which is commonly used to control Front Row and other features, this option will disable this functionality. Additionally, the Pair button will allow you to set up your system to only work with a specified (paired) remote control.

The Firewall tab is associated with network security, and combined with sharing options can control what sort of network activity your computer will allow. This is covered in Chapter 20.

> **NOTE** Leopard ships with the firewall disabled—however, all network services are turned off. This effectively eliminates most potential network security issues from the outside since the system isn't accepting any incoming communications. However, certain applications may open their own network ports and run services on them. Usually, if they're from a trusted source, you'll be OK; but if they're from an untrusted source, look out! Additionally, outgoing networking will work fine by default, so you should have no trouble using your web browser, e-mail, or other network-enabled applications unless you are on a network with its own dedicated firewall. Again, caution should be used when using untrusted applications, since by default they would be free to transmit anything.

Finally, Leopard includes a range of additional features built into the system and various applications that will allow you to provide any level of data security you wish. For example, another way to protect your data is to put it on an encrypted disk image. You can do this by creating a blank disk image in Disk Utility and selecting one of the encryption options for it. This will prompt you for a password that will be necessary every time you attempt to mount the image.

> **NOTE** One other password option is setting a firmware password, which provides low-level system protection. In order to use this feature, you must copy over to your computer the Firmware Password Utility hidden in the `Applications/Utilities` folder on the Leopard installation DVD (insert and select the DVD in the Finder, and then use File ➤ Go To... and enter **Applications/Utilities** to view this). This will allow you to set a password that will be required for using most special boot sequences, including booting your computer in Target Disk mode and selecting an alternative boot device at startup.

Summary

OS X Leopard is built upon a naturally secure foundation, and coupled with a range of features, makes maintaining a secure system easy, and without lots of the headaches and pain associated with security. While this chapter covered mostly user-centric and basic system security, later we will cover network security in more detail. Additionally, we will continue to provide added security tips where applicable throughout the book.

The next part of the book will begin covering more of the day-to-day usability of OS X, beginning with utilizing the Internet with Leopard.

PART **3**

Communications and the Internet

## CHAPTER 9

Connecting to the Internet

One of the first things you may want to do once you get Leopard set up is to get it connected to the Internet. Depending on your connection, this could range from ridiculously easy to just fairly easy . . . at least as far as configuring Leopard goes. Essentially, there are three common ways to connect to the Internet today, and we'll cover each of them in this chapter:

- Connecting via dial-up
- Connecting via a broadband Internet connection
- Connecting to a high-speed Internet connection

We'll also cover how to set up networking profiles for different locations.

Connecting to the Internet Using Dial-Up Networking

Dial-up networking, once the king of Internet connections, seems to be fading away as broadband networks reach out across the world. Still, for some people in some situations, it's the best or only option available.

> **NOTE** It should be obvious that to use dial-up networking, you'll need a modem. Many slightly older Macs have internal modems, but the currently shipping Macs don't. Apple, however, offers an external USB modem as an option with all Macs that you just need to plug into a USB port. One other option for dial-up networking is that some mobile phone services offer network services that can be accessed via a Bluetooth connection. If you have a phone (and mobile service) that supports this, you may utilize this connection just about anywhere you get mobile service.

Setting Up Your Dial-Up Connection

Setting up your dial-up connection is usually done in three simple steps:

1. Make sure your hardware is connected and set up. An internal modem should be ready to go as soon as you connect an active phone line to it. An external Apple modem should be ready as soon as you plug it in. If you are using a Bluetooth phone for dial-up, you will need to make sure you have set up your phone as a Bluetooth device.

   NOTE When we talk about modems for dial-up, we are talking about a traditional Plain Old Telephone Service (POTS) modem. Cable modems do not require this setup, because most cable modems are simply routers. We will cover cable modems later in this chapter.

   NOTE Not all phone lines are POTS lines. Many companies these days have installed VoIP telephone systems, which although they look like pretty normal telephones and telephone plugs (RJ-11), they send a digital signal rather than an analog one. Additionally, some telephone companies have begun to install fiber-optic telephone lines, replacing the copper POTS lines. In either of these cases, a traditional modem will not work and could possibly be damaged if connected.

2. Collect the information you will need to connect to your dial-up account. Usually you will need three items:

   - The phone number for your access provider.
   - Your account username.
   - Your account password.
   - For a Bluetooth connection utilizing a mobile network, you will need the access point name (APN).

3. You must open the Network panel in System Preferences, select the appropriate device (Figure 9-1), and fill in the appropriate information.

Figure 9-1. To set up a dial-up connection, you just need to attach a modem and fill in the appropriate information in the Network preference pane.

Usually those three steps should get you connected (just click the Connect button and try it). Occasionally, though, your ISP will require some additional advanced options to be set up. Clicking the Advanced button will provide a sheet containing five tabs for setting advanced options. Of these five tabs, unless you have specific networking needs, you most likely need to adjust the settings on the Modem tab if you are having trouble connecting.

> **NOTE** For dial-up connections using your mobile phone's data connection, the phone number can vary from something like 99# to the APN used by your mobile access provider.

The Modem tab provides different information depending on your dial-up device. For a POTS modem (Figure 9-2), some common items you may need to adjust are the Model list that selects the proper modem script to initialize you modem. Ideally this should be set to Apple Modem (v.92) for an external Apple modem or to Internal 56K Modem (v.92) if you have an internal modem. However, your ISP's modem must be v.92 compliant for this connection (most today are). If you are having trouble connecting, you may need to fall back to an older modem protocol, so try the v.90 option, the v.34 option, and so on. The other option here that may affect the connection is the "Enable error correction and compression in modem" option. This option, when selected, provides added performance, but this must also be supported on your ISP's modem for it to work.

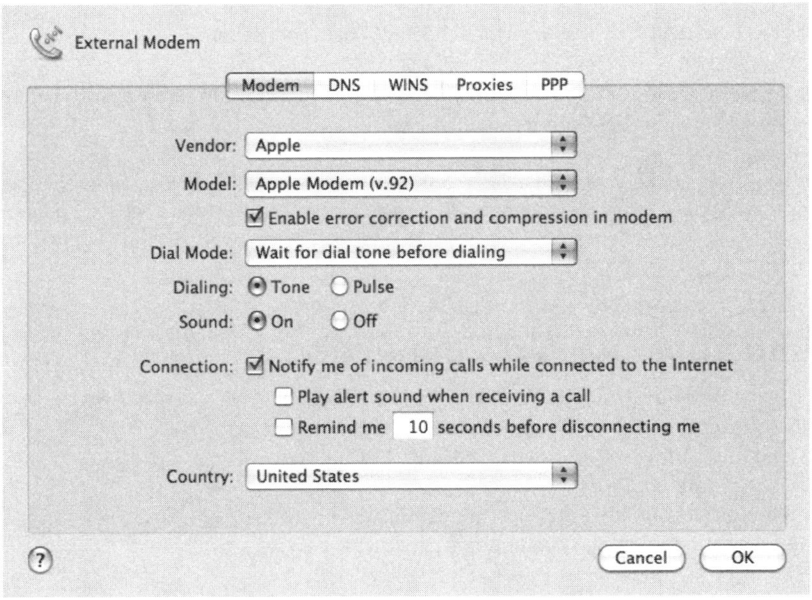

Figure 9-2. The advanced Modem options for a POTS modem

If you are setting up a Bluetooth dial-up modem, then the Modem options will be different (Figure 9-3). The model you select must correspond with your Bluetooth device; thankfully, Leopard adds support for most popular Bluetooth-enabled modems. Additionally, there is a place to enter your APN here.

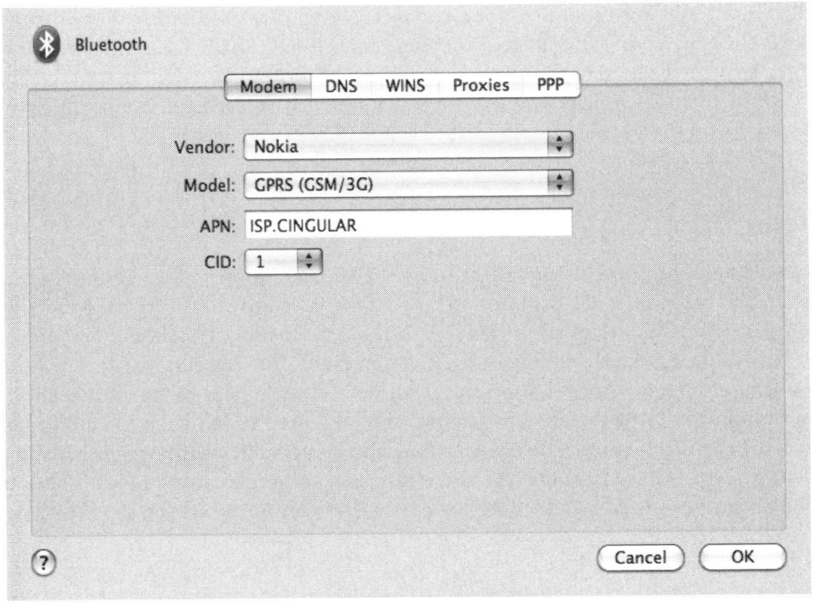

Bluetooth

| Modem | DNS | WINS | Proxies | PPP |

Vendor: Nokia

Model: GPRS (GSM/3G)

APN: ISP.CINGULAR

CID: 1

Cancel   OK

Figure 9-3. The advanced Modem options for a Bluetooth data connection

If you have everything set up for your Bluetooth data connection and are still having trouble connecting, change the CID and try again.

> **NOTE** The exact configuration for a Bluetooth data connection varies slightly for each model of phone and varies even more from one service provider to another (there are even different services for each service provider). This makes setting up this sort of connection a bit difficult to get right.

Initiating Your Dial-Up Connection

Once you have your dial-up connection set up, you'll still need to make the connection when you want to access the Internet. Apple has a couple of ways to do this besides hitting the Connect button in the Network panel in System Preferences each time you want to initiate a dial-up connection. One way is to simply select the "Select modem status in the menu bar" option in the Network preference panel. This will provide a menu item (Figure 9-4) that will allow you to initiate your modem connections quickly and easily from the menu bar.

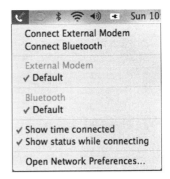

Figure 9-4. You can add a menu item that will allow you to initiate your modem connections from the menu bar.

> **NOTE** One application notably missing from Leopard is the Internet Connect application. This application, originally designed for dial-up networking, had over the years grown a bit redundant. Today, all the features of Internet Connect are now sensibly located in the System Preferences Network preference pane.

Setting Up Multiple Dial-Up Configurations for a Modem

If you use dial-up frequently, you may want to set up different configurations. Say, for example, you use one number to connect from home, another to connect when you are visiting your mother-in-law, and another when you travel elsewhere. To add a new configuration, simply select Add Configuration from the configuration menu in the Network panel in System Preferences, select a name for this configuration, and then fill in the details for this connection. When you are done, click Apply, and that configuration will be saved. Then you can select that, or any other saved configuration, from the Configuration menu in either the Network preference pane or the Internet Connect application; additionally, all of your configurations will appear in the modem status menu item.

> **NOTE** Many ISPs provide software to manage dial-up connections. Although these are usually easy to set up and use, they are often unnecessary and may not be 100 percent compatible with all versions of OS X. As with many things, there seems to be a trade-off. We recommend trying to set up dial-up networking as outlined earlier in the chapter.

> **NOTE** One potential exception to the previous note applies when dealing with mobile service data providers. As mentioned, these are not straightforward to set up, so if your service provider provides software or if you choose some third-party connection software, such as nova media's launch2net (www.novamedia.de), you may save yourself some time and aggravation.

Broadband (High-Speed) Network Connections

Broadband networking has come a long way over the years. Today broadband access is available almost everywhere, and the cost, on the lower end, rivals the cost of dial-up access. Many types of broadband connections are available; Table 9-1 covers some of the currently prominent technologies.

Table 9-1. Common Broadband Networking Technologies

Technology	Description
DSL	Digital subscriber line (DSL) is, along with cable, one of the most popular broadband technologies used today. DSL sends a digital signal over traditional phone lines, making it easily available to many existing phone customers. There are a number of variants of DSL; the most common today is asymmetric DSL (ADSL). The big drawback to ADSL is that its speeds start to diminish over distance, making this technology less effective for rural areas. ADSL also provides fast download speeds while limiting its upload speed; this makes it suitable for most home users but less useful for businesses. SDSL, on the other hand, provides the same upload and download speeds. ADSL is commonly referred to as residential DSL, while business DSL is usually SDSL.
VDSL	VDSL is a newer "very high-speed" DSL technology that is starting to be rolled out all over the world. This DSL technology is currently able to provide up to 100 Mbps upload and download speeds over traditional POTS copper wiring. As with DSL, this speed diminishes over distance; still, VDSL promises higher speeds and longer distances than earlier versions of DSL. (AT&T is rolling out VDSL as U-Verse to selected communities across the United States.)
Cable	Cable broadband is another big broadband technology used today. This provides access over existing cable TV lines. Unlike DSL, cable broadband does not lose its effectiveness over distances and traditionally has been able to provide faster data speeds than DSL; on the other hand, cable is also generally more expensive, and most cable companies provide cable broadband only to cable TV subscribers, raising the costs associated with cable even higher.
ISDN	ISDN is one of the original broadband technologies available to consumers. It provides faster-than-dial-up speeds; however, there are lots of higher costs associated with it. ISDN has for the most part been replaced with other less expensive, faster technologies today.
T1	T1 lines (also called DS1 and E1) are the traditional broadband, high-speed connections that are common in many commercial offices. Originally, T1 connections were special telephone lines designed to carry voice communications for large organizations; however, early in the expansion of the Internet, digital T1 lines were used to provide high-speed Internet connections. T1 lines are still in use in many businesses for both voice and data. The downside to T1 lines is that even today they are regulated and require special lines to be run to connect the provider with the user. This makes their costs high. There are also T2 and T3 lines, which are similar yet faster than the traditional T1 lines.
SONET	Synchronous optical networking (SONET) technologies are slowly replacing T1 as the commercial data connection of choice. Using fiber-optic lines to carry the digital information allows OC-x technologies to provide extremely high-speed data throughput over long distances (though at a very high cost).
Wi-Fi	Wi-Fi is a blanket term that covers wireless 802.11 technologies including Apple's AirPort technologies. Although the range of Wi-Fi is relatively low, in high density and commercial areas it is quite popular. (Being short range, Wi-Fi is usually used in conjunction with a hardwired broadband technology such as DSL, cable, T1, or OC-x.)
WiMAX	WiMAX is a new emerging wireless broadband technology that attempts to provide faster speeds and more important greater range than traditional Wi-Fi technologies.

Technology	Description
Satellite	Satellite broadband provides high-speed access utilizing satellites to provide the communication over great distances. Satellite broadband is generally slightly more expensive and slightly slower than other methods of broadband; it is a viable alternative especially in rural areas where other technologies are unavailable or prohibitively expensive. The big disadvantage of satellite broadband is a latency problem where a delay of 500 to 900 milliseconds is added to any other network latency transmitting the signal into space and then back again. Although this is not a big deal for casual Internet usage including web browsing and e-mail, it's a burden for real-time Internet activities such as VoIP (and it's a real killer for online gaming).

Besides the technologies listed in Table 9-1, a range of other technologies is available, and new ideas and technologies are constantly being developed. What's interesting about almost all of these, though, is the following:

- They all carry IP packets from point A to point B.
- In a broadband environment, most of these technologies (except in most cases wireless technologies) usually just bridge a gap between the Internet and a router on your end.

Because of this, the actual broadband technology has little to do with how you set up your computer to take advantage of it. When the broadband connection enters your home, office, or company, it is usually run into an Ethernet or Wi-Fi router, which in turn you connect to with your computer using standard TCP/IP networking.

TCP/IP Networking

TCP/IP networking consists of a collection of networking protocols collectively known as the Internet Protocol (IP) suite. In very general terms, Transmission Control Protocol (TCP) is responsible for application data carried over the Internet, and Internet Protocol (IP) is responsible for communication data. So although TCP carries the message, IP makes sure the message gets where it needs to go. When you configure your networking, you are essentially setting up your computer as a uniquely identifiable destination on the Internet for IP to successfully deliver TCP data to your computer.

The current IP protocol being used today is version 4. IPv4, in theory, addresses each computer on the Internet with a unique address made up of four series of numbers, called *octets*, that range from 0–255. A typical IP address may look like 153.29.250.112.

For those of you keeping count, this means IPv4 can address, in theory, only a bit more than 4 billion devices. When this was conceived in the early 1980s, a device was a computer, and 4 billion seemed like a lot. Today not only are there a lot more computers, but there are other devices such as phones, watches, automobiles, and more, that use TCP/IP. In addition, a significant chunk of those 4 billion address are reserved for special uses, and you may notice a problem . . . we are running out of IPv4 addresses.

According to IANA (the organization responsible for assigning IP addresses), the current projected date when all IPv4 addresses run will be around 2011 or 2012. This won't matter much if you go by the Mayan calendar, which says the world will end then anyway, but for the rest of us, it's a problem. Although there are a number of ways to extend IPv4 (IP Masquerading, NAT, and other technologies that are common today), a new version of IP, IPv6, has been defined and is currently being deployed. (The U.S. government is pushing for deployment for all civilian and defense vendors by the summer of 2008.) For comparison, IPv6 supports approximately 3.4×10^{38} addresses.

Configuring Your Mac for a Broadband Connection

For your Mac to function on the Internet, it must have the following information:

A qualified IP address: IP addresses are discussed in the "TCP/IP Networking" sidebar; this is a unique address that identifies your computer on the Internet so that all information being sent to your computer actually makes it there. You cannot (usually) just make up an IP address; it must be assigned, or else it will likely not work.

A subnet mask: A subnet mask is used to separate the network address from the host address. This can be further used within a network to create subnets; breaking up a host address into subnets allows more effective routing of IP traffic. An example of an IPv4 subnet mask is 255.255.255.0, and any IP address that shares the first three octets in the IP address is part of the same subnet. If all that sounds foreign to you, don't worry; just use the subnet mask your ISP or network administrator gave you.

A gateway address (or router): The router address (also known as a *gateway address*) is the IP address of the next upstream router.

A DNS server address: The DNS server is the primary server for your subnet that is responsible for providing DNS services. A DNS server is responsible for translating a domain name (that is, apple.com) into an IP address (in other words, 17.254.3.183). You can list multiple DNS servers if you would like, and if the first one is unable to resolve a domain name, then the next one listed will be consulted.

Search domains (optional): Search domains are an optional list of domains to search if a domain address cannot be resolved by any of the DNS servers. This can provide a shortcut on some networks as well, since it will allow you to address a computer by the host name alone.

NOTE IPv4 has set aside a number of IP address blocks as private addresses (10.x.x.x, 172.16.x.x, and 192.168.x.x). These private IP addresses are for the creation of private networks that utilize IP. Many routers (and firewalls) take advantage of these private IP addresses to perform network address translation (NAT, a.k.a. network masquerading). This allows the router to be assigned a valid Internet IP address yet assign all the computers behind it private IP addresses. The router can then act as a gateway between the private network and the Internet, providing each computer connected to the router with full Internet access without a dedicated IP address. Although initial implementations of NAT often carried with them some side effects, most current implementations of NAT provide Internet clients with complete functionality. Server processes running behind NAT, however, need special considerations and are limited. This can be used advantageously from a security point of view, and in fact, many firewalls use NAT combined with port forwarding to hide the actual server from the Internet.

NOTE Port forwarding allows the router or firewall facing the Internet to masquerade as a server while server requests are actually being passed along to other systems on the private network. This can be set up so specific services, which use specific ports, can be passed to specific systems. So, all e-mail traffic using ports 25 (SMTP), 110 (POP3), and 143 (IMAP4) could point to one server behind the router, while all web traffic using port 80 (HTTP) would be directed to another.

There are two primary ways to connect your computer to a broadband connection: Ethernet and Wi-Fi.

Making an Ethernet Connection

Prior to Wi-Fi, the most common way to make a high-speed connection was through Ethernet, and this remains popular today. For a while now, all shipping Apple computers came with built-in Ethernet capability.

An Ethernet connect is a physical connection where a cable will run from a router or modem into your computer. Depending on your broadband service and your local area network (LAN) setup, configuring your connection through Ethernet could be handled automatically through DHCP or BootP, or the configuration may need to be done manually. Additionally, some service providers (especially ADSL) use a connection called Point-to-Point Protocol over Ethernet (PPPoE) that, while creating a high-speed connection over Ethernet, is configured a bit more like a dial-up connection.

If you know you need to use PPPoE or configure your network connection manually, then you can get the proper configuration information from your service provider or administrator. Otherwise, just plug in the Ethernet cable and turn on your computer; a surprisingly large amount of the time, Dynamic Host Configuration Protocol (DHCP) is used and will configure your network information automatically. To check, take a look in the Network panel in System Preferences and see whether you are connected (Figure 9-5).

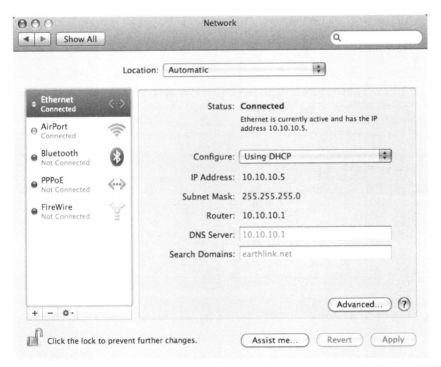

Figure 9-5. This Ethernet connection is configured and connected automatically using DHCP.

If the little bubble next to the connection in the left column of the Network preference pane is green, then your connection is successful. If it is yellow, then the computer detects that a cable is plugged in, but there is problem with either the physical connection or the configuration. If the bubble is red, then that service is not currently connected.

If DHCP doesn't work, then you will need to choose another way to configure your network. The configuration drop-down provides a list that includes the following:

DHCP: Dynamic Host Configuration Protocol (DHCP) is more and more common these days in almost every environment. Not only does it make setting up a system incredibly easy from the user end, but it also allows reuse of IP addresses and increased manageability from the administrative perspective.

DHCP with manual address: Usually DHCP will automatically assign a computer that connects to it the next available IP address it has at its disposal. It will lease this address to that particular system for a period of time (and usually continue to renew that lease as long as the system remains connected); however, after a period of time, it may issue the system a different IP address. For most situations, this is fine; however, occasionally a system needs a static IP address that won't change. This option allows you to pick a static IP address.

NOTE IP addresses need to be unique; even on a private network, every IP address needs to be different than every other IP address on that network. Because of this, when you manually assign an IP address, you should be careful that it doesn't belong to the block of IP addresses being dynamically assigned and that it isn't being used by another system on the network.

BootP: Bootstrap Protocol (BootP) is an older technology that was created to allow diskless workstations or thin clients to receive an IP address automatically from a server. DHCP is based upon BootP but is much more advanced (and complex).

Manually: This option requires that you manually fill in all the required networking information. In this case, you will likely be given specific information to use (Figure 9-6).

Off: This turns off the interface.

Create PPPoE Service: This will create a new PPPoE interface for configuring the PPPoE service (Figure 9-7). If this is required, your service provider will give you the necessary information for this (username, password, and perhaps a service name).

Figure 9-6. If you must configure your network manually, you will need to fill in all the required information.

Figure 9-7. A PPPoE connection works very much like a dial-up connection; however, it creates a much faster connection when active.

Making an AirPort Internet Connection

Today every computer Apple sells comes equipped with what Apple calls AirPort technology. What Apple calls AirPort, most everybody else refers to as Wi-Fi, or more properly 802.11.

> **NOTE** 802.11 or IEEE 802.11 is the proper name of the WLAN technology we are talking about here. Apple calls its implementation of this standard AirPort, and an industry group has formed outside the IEEE called the Wi-Fi Alliance that was created to help certify new incarnations of 802.11 before the IEEE officially approves them. Either way, in the big picture, whatever it's called, it usually refers to the same technology.

802.11 is a point-to-point networking technology that is used to create LANs that work like a traditional wired network without the wires. These are commonly referred to as *wireless LANs* (WLANs).

802.11 networks handle the network configuration in the same manner as wired networks; in fact, almost all 802.11 networks use DHCP to make this configuration automatic. The tricky part comes during the process of joining or connecting to the WLAN to begin with. This is because there are a number of different types of 802.11 networks; also, there are a number of types of security schemes available to limit who can join an 802.11 network and to encrypt the network data once the connection is made.

Types of Wi-Fi Networks

Currently, four common variations of 802.11 networks are in use today:

802.11b: This was what the original AirPort technology was based on and also what most people associate with Wi-Fi. It provides reasonably fast transfer speeds over a reasonably large area. It operates in the 2.4 to 2.5 GHz radio frequency range.

802.11a: 802.11a came out about the same time as 802.11b, provided faster transfer speeds, and used radio frequencies in the 5 GHz range, which cut down on interference from cordless phones, Bluetooth devices, and microwave ovens. However, 802.11a products started shipping late by which time the industry was already implementing 802.11b. As such, 802.11a never really caught on to the extent of 802.11b. (An ironic twist on this is that although Apple has never supported 802.11a, the current AirPort chips included with Intel-based Macs do support 802.11a.) 802.11a is not compatible with 802.11b or 802.11g.

802.11g: This is currently the most popular 802.11 variant. It is 100 percent compatible with 802.11b, but when used with 802.11g devices at both ends, it provides much faster transfer speeds and a slight boost in distance. Apple's AirPort devices (both in computers and base stations) quickly switched from 802.11b to 802.11g (Apple called this AirPort Extreme). The downside with 802.11g is that it still operates in the crowded 2.4 to 2.5 GHz radio frequency range.

802.11n: 802.11n is the newest version of 802.11 with shipping products, even though the actual specification has yet to be ratified. 802.11n increases transfer speeds about 45 and 25 the range over 802.11g, when used in 802.11n mode with other 802.11n devices. It can work in either the 2.4 to 2.5 or 5.0 GHz radio frequency range. 802.11n devices also can operate in three modes: Legacy, which supports 802.11 b/g and 802.11 a; Mixed, which supports 802.11 b/g, 802.11 a, and 802.11n; and then a pure 802.11n mode, which is necessary to take advantage of the increased speed and distances offered by 802.11n. Apple's newest AirPort Extremes as well as all new Core 2 Duo and newer Macs support a draft of this technology.

Wi-Fi Security Schemes

Besides the different types of actual networks, there are also different security mechanisms used to protect 802.11 networks. These include the following:

WEP: Wired Equivalent Privacy (WEP) was written as part of the 802.11 standard to provide access control and data security to WLANs. Standard 64-bit WEP uses a 40-bit encryption key; however, today 128-bit WEP is prevalent and supports a 104-bit encryption key. Although WEP is quite popular and does provide at least some protection from casual eavesdropping, from a security standpoint it is considered broken. Not only are the keys vulnerable (a WEP key can be cracked in a few minutes using readily available software from the Internet), but there are other inherent flaws in WEP that makes it unsuitable for situations where security and data integrity are a priority.

WPA/WPA2: Wi-Fi Protected Access (WPA) was created in response to flaws discovered with WEP, and it was quickly implemented and is based upon the IEEE 802.11i standard (WPA2 fully implements 802.11i, while WPA implemented most of it). WPA uses an improved encryption key, making cracking the key significantly more difficult than a WEP key, and improves data integrity checks lacking in WEP. WPA2 further increases the strength of the encryption key. WPA and WPA2 offer two modes of use: a Personal mode and an Enterprise mode. Personal mode works similarly to WEP in that there is a single preshared encryption key (PSK) used. In Enterprise mode a user must first log into a RADIUS server that assigns a dynamic key to that user. Not only does this provide excellent user access control, but by providing a unique key for each user, it provides excellent data security as well.

802.1X: This is an IEEE standard that is part of the same group as 802.11 (though it is not directly related). It is a method of authentication often used in conjunction with WPA2 Enterprise mode when authenticating the user to the RADIUS server.

LEAP: Lightweight Extensible Authentication Protocol (LEAP) was developed by Cisco for Cisco wireless routers. This requires the user to first log in with a username and password to receive a WEP key. Beyond the login, this operates similarly to WEP; as such, it is not used much anymore.

None: It is of course possible to have no security on a WLAN. This is referred to as an *open network*. Most public Wi-Fi access points are open networks (though some require registration and perhaps fees to access the Internet). The most important thing to keep in mind about using an open network is that there is no wireless encryption, so everything you send over the network is potentially viewable by those around you. As such, it's important to use encrypted connections to services you are accessing whenever possible.

Joining a Wi-Fi Network

You can join a wireless network either from the Network preference panel (Figure 9-8) or from the AirPort menu item (Figure 9-9).

Figure 9-8. Connecting to an AirPort in the Network preference panel

The first thing you need to do is assure you have powered on the AirPort in your computer. Once the network is on, you can click the Network Name drop-down list, which will list all the advertising Wi-Fi networks in range of your computer. Select the network you want join from the list, and then click Apply. If the selected network requires authentication or a password (key), you will be prompted to enter that information. If your password or authentication information is correct, then you will be immediately connected. If for whatever reason you want to adjust the network settings, you can access them by clicking the Advanced button.

A much more convenient way to join a Wi-Fi network is by selecting the "Show AirPort status in menu bar" option and using the menu item.

The AirPort menu item provides some additional information about your current connection as well as other available WLANs in your area. First, the icon in the menu bar will signify the strength of your current network signal; four bars is great, and one bar (which looks more like a dot) is not so good. In the list provided from the AirPort menu item, you can see a list of all the available networks divided by secured and open networks. If you hold your cursor over one of the network names, a tool tip will pop up showing the type of security used as well as the relative signal strength. Selecting a network from the menu will prompt you for any security passwords or authentication and then connect you to that network.

> **NOTE** WEP passwords are generally hexadecimal strings 10 digits long for 40-bit and 26 digits long for 104-bit keys. Apple, however, tends to use common "password" strings for passwords (which are then converted to hexadecimal strings). The thing is, if you are connecting to a WEP-secured WLAN and are given the hexadecimal key, when you type it into the Password text box, Leopard will by default assume you are entering a text password and convert the string you enter from a normal text string to a hexadecimal string. To prevent this from happening, you must start the hexadecimal string with a $ character. So if you are given 3B-2D-98-AA-32 as a hexadecimal string, you should enter **$3B2D98AA32** in the Password box.

Figure 9-9. The AirPort menu item will allow you to view and select any of the Wi-Fi networks in your location.

Creating Separate Networking Profiles for Different Locations

If you rely on DHCP for everything or you never move your computer around, then you can set up your network and live just fine with it. However, if you are using a portable computer and you need to connect multiple networks that use different settings, then you may want to take advantage of the Location feature. At the top of the Network preference pane, there is a drop-down list that by default is set on Automatic. While Automatic is selected, any changes you make to any of your network interfaces are saved in the Automatic location.

If you need to have multiple network configurations—one at home that is basically the same as the Automatic setting and one for work too where you are assigned specific networking information—then you can add a location from the drop-down list and configure the networking for that location as needed. Once you have multiple locations set up, a Location item will appear in your Apple menu that will allow you to switch your networking preferences from one location to the next.

Summary

This chapter covered what you need to get your computer connected to the Internet with your Mac. We attempted to skirt around some of the more complex networking issues, saving most of those for Part 6 of this book, which is dedicated to networking. The point is to get you up and running so you can follow along with the next chapters that cover Safari, Mail, and other Internet-related applications.

## CHAPTER 10

Browsing the Web with Safari

Leopard includes the latest version of Apple's web browser, Safari 3. Safari is a fast, standards-compliant web browser loaded with lots of useful features for getting the most out of the Web. The chapter will take a look at Safari and its capabilities, including the following:

- Safari basics
- Adding and managing bookmarks
- Tabbed browsing
- Downloading content from the Web
- Viewing PDFs
- Auto-filling form data
- Security
- Advanced browsing features
- RSS and syndication feeds
- Plug-ins and inline content
- Web clippings

Safari Basics

Safari is Leopard's default web browser, but you can install and use any other available Mac web browser as well (Firefox, Camino, OmniWeb, Opera, and many more exist. You could even whip up your own in Xcode without writing a single line of code!). However, most people who start using Safari tend to stick with it. Like most Apple software, Safari packs in a lot of useful features while still providing a clean, easy-to-use interface.

The Basic Interface

In general, Safari (Figure 10-1) appears and works like most other popular web browsers. By default, its toolbar is sparse yet functional, with only a handful of items (Back, Forward, Reload, Web Clip, and Add Bookmark buttons; an address field; and a web search field). Below the toolbar it has a Bookmarks bar to provide access to your favorite bookmarks or bookmark collections, as well as a way to access all of your bookmarks. Below the Bookmarks bar is the Tab bar, which appears when you are using the Tabs feature (you can leave it on all the time by selecting the View ➤ Show Tab Bar option from the menu). Below the Tab bar (if visible) is the Find Banner, which will appear when you use the Edit ➤ Find ➤ Find... (or Cmd+F) command. This allows you to find text within a web page, which in the latest version of Safari provides a revolutionary interface for finding what you are looking for. Below that is the main web view, where the web pages are rendered. Finally, at the very bottom is the Status bar, which provides some information about loading pages and hyperlinks.

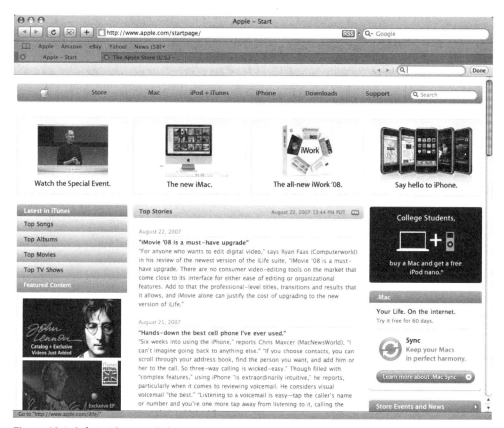

Figure 10-1. Safari with expanded view options

> **NOTE** By default, only the toolbar and Bookmarks bar are shown. The Tab bar will appear automatically when you are using more than one tab, and you must select View ➤ Show Status Bar (or Cmd+/) to activate the Status bar.

Right-clicking (or Ctrl+clicking) the toolbar and selecting Customize Toolbar... will open a sheet containing other buttons and items (Figure 10-2) that you can put on your toolbar. Some popular items include Home and Print buttons. From the Customize Toolbar sheet, you can add, remove, or reorganize any of these items on you toolbar. At the bottom of the Customize Toolbar sheet is a default toolbar, which you can use to return your toolbar to its default state.

Besides the options viewable in the window, like most applications, there are many menu items in the various menus provided. Table 10-1 provides a list of Safari menu items.

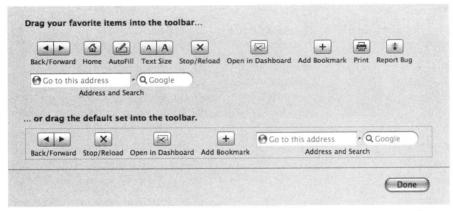

Figure 10-2. You can customize your Safari toolbar in a number of ways to suit your needs.

> **NOTE** Many menu items (as well as their keyboard shortcuts) are common among all Mac OS X applications. Occasionally, though, even common items have unique behavior in some applications and situations. For Safari, we will go over all the default options, but as we progress through the book, we will only cover options that are unique to the product or that haven't previously been covered.

Table 10-1. Safari Menu Items

Menu/Submenu Item	Keyboard Shortcut	Description
Safari		
About Safari		Provides general information about the running version of Safari.
Report Bugs to Apple...		Allows you to notify Apple engineers about any issues you encounter with Safari. It will ask you for the URL of the web page that affects Safari and then a description of the problem.
Preferences...	Cmd+,	Opens Safari's Preference window.
Block Pop-Up Windows	Shift+Cmd+K	Toggles Safari's ability to block those mostly unwanted pop-up windows that automatically spring up when you load some web pages. This doesn't prevent requested pop-up windows (ones that are initiated by you when you click a link) from displaying.
Private Browsing...		Toggles Private Browsing. When Private Browsing is activated, none of the pages you visit will be added to your browser history, and items will be removed from your browser cache and downloads (accepted cookies, however, will remain).

Continued

Table 10-1. Continued

Menu/Submenu Item	Keyboard Shortcut	Description
Safari (continued)		
Reset Safari...		Allows you to selectively reset (clear) a number items that Safari stores all at once. These include the history, cache, cookies, and AutoFill information.
Empty Cache...	Option+Cmd+E	Empties your browser cache.
Services		Provides a sublist of services that the system and other applications offer from within Safari.
Hide Safari	Cmd+H	Hides all Safari windows from the desktop. Safari will still run, and those windows will not close; they will just no longer be visible.
Hide Others	Option+Cmd+H	Hides all the open windows on your desktop except windows belonging to Safari.
Show All		Reveals all hidden windows.
Quit Safari	Cmd+Q	Quits Safari.
File		
New Window	Cmd+N	Opens a new browser window in Safari.
New Tab	Cmd+T	Opens a new tab in the current browser window.
Open File...	Cmd+O	Opens a file dialog box allowing you to open an file located on your computer in Safari.
Open Location...	Cmd+L	Highlights the Location text field in the toolbar, allowing you to type in a URL of a web resource you wish to open. (Pressing Return will then take you directly there, all without needing to move you hands from the keyboard.)
Close Window	(Shift+)Cmd+W	Closes the current browser window. If multiple tabs are open in the window, the default keyboard shortcut will change, as Cmd+W will only close the front tab. Also, if you are closing a window with multiple tabs, you will be prompted to verify your action.
Close Tab	(Cmd+W)	Closes the current tab. The Cmd+W keyboard shortcut will close the window if there are no tabs (or only one tab).
Save as...		Brings up a save dialog allowing you to save the current web page. You can save the page as a web archive, which will create a special file that includes all images and other data that can only be viewed properly in Safari on Mac OS X (currently Safari on Windows will not open this file), or as a source file (which will only save the text source of the page; however, you will be able to view the HTML file in any browser).

Menu/Submenu Item	Keyboard Shortcut	Description
File (continued)		
Mail Contents of This Page	Cmd+I	Opens the contents of the web page in a new Mail message so you can send it to others who can view HTML web messages.
Mail Link to This Page	Shift+Cmd+I	Opens a new Mail message with the link embedded to facilitate the e-mailing of the link to your recipients.
Open in Dashboard...		Allows you to select a region of the current web page to be added as a web clipping to your Dashboard (this is covered later in this chapter).
Import Bookmarks...		Allows you to import a bookmark file from another location on your computer (including bookmarks from some other browsers).
Export Bookmarks...		Exports your Safari bookmarks into a separate file for archiving or for importing into a different browser. The bookmark file you export will be a properly formatted HTML file, so you can use it in various interesting ways.
Print...	Cmd+P	Opens the Print dialog so you can print out the current web page. Since you can print to PDF, this provides another option for saving web content.
Edit		
Undo	Cmd+Z	Undoes the last change you made to a document. In Safari, this will usually apply only to editable content. If there is nothing to undo, this will be grayed out.
Redo	Shift+Cmd+Z	Similar to Undo, this command specifically undoes an undo.
Cut	Cmd+X	Cuts the selected document items, removing them from the document, but placing them in the clipboard for pasting elsewhere. In Safari, this works only on editable content.
Copy	Cmd+C	Copies any selected items into the clipboard. This will work on any selected items in Safari.
Paste	Cmd+V	Pastes the contents of the clipboard into any editable region.
Delete		Deletes any selected items in an editable region of your browser.
Select All	Cmd+A	Selects all items in the current area of focus (in Safari, this is usually the entire current web page).

Continued

Table 10-1. Continued

Menu/Submenu Item	Keyboard Shortcut	Description
Edit (continued)		
AutoFill Form	Shift+Cmd+A	Attempts to fill in a web form using data from the AutoFill feature in Safari. This feature is sometimes triggered automatically when you begin to fill out a form.
Find		Opens a submenu of the following items (i.e., the items from Google Search to Jump to Selection).
Google Search	Option+Cmd+F	Moves the focus to the Google search box in the toolbar so you can enter a term to search with Google.
Find...	Cmd+F	Opens up the Find Banner at the top of the web page so that you may search the web page for specific text.
Find Next	Cmd+G	Cycles forward through the web page revealing the next match to your Find search string in the web page.
Find Previous	Shift+Cmd+G	Cycles back through the page finding previous search matches.
Hide Find Banner	Shift+Cmd+F	Hides the Find Banner if opened.
Use Selection for Find	Cmd+E	Copies the selected text into the Find field (even if the Find Banner is hidden). You may then use the Find Next or Find Previous commands to cycle through matched or selected text.
Jump to Selection	Cmd+J	Automatically scrolls the web page up or down (if necessary) to recenter the page on the selected region.
Spelling and Grammar		Like Find, opens up a submenu of items relating to Apple's built-in Spelling and Grammar system.
Show Spelling and Grammar	Cmd+:	Opens the Spelling and Grammar window, which allows you to cycle through perceived errors in editable text. For each error it finds, it will offer advice on correcting it.
Check Document Now	Cmd+;	Checks the editable content of your document for spelling errors. It will underline any errors it finds with a small squiggly red line.
Check Spelling While Typing		Underlines perceived spelling errors in editable text with a small squiggly red line. Right-clicking (or Cmd+clicking) the word will bring up a contextual menu with potential correct spellings for the misspelled word.
Check Grammar with Spelling		Displays potential grammar issues when you check the document for spelling errors.
Special Characters...	Option+Cmd+T	Opens a character palette for selecting special characters that you may want to insert into a text field.

Menu/Submenu Item	Keyboard Shortcut	Description
View		
(Show|Hide) Bookmarks Bar	Shift+Cmd+B	Toggles the visibility of the Bookmarks bar.
(Show|Hide) Status Bar	Cmd+/	Toggles the visibility of the Status bar.
(Show|Hide) Tab Bar	Shift+Cmd+T	Toggles the visibility of the Tab bar. This only has an effect when no tabs are currently open (or if there is only one tab).
(Show|Hide) Toolbar	Cmd+| (Shift+Cmd+\\)	Toggles the visibility of the main toolbar.
Customize Toolbar...		Opens the Customize Toolbar sheet as described previously.
Stop	Cmd+.	Stops loading the currently loading page.
Reload Page	Cmd+R	Reloads the current page. This will cause the page to fully reload, overwriting any information in the cache.
Make Text Bigger	Cmd++ (Cmd+=)	Increases the size of the web page's text. This has no effect on images or other non–text inline content (like Flash).
Make Text Normal Size	Cmd+0	Returns text to the original (intended) size.
Make Text Smaller	Cmd+-	Makes the text in the web page smaller.
View Source	Option+Cmd+U	Opens the web page's source in a separate window.
Text Encoding		Opens a submenu providing different text encoding options for different language sets. This is useful if the default language isn't properly recognized automatically.
History		
Back	Cmd+[	Returns you to the last page you visited.
Forward	Cmd+]	Returns you forward after going backward.
Home	Shift+Cmd+H	Takes you directly to your home page as configured in your preferences.
Mark Page for SnapBack	Option+Cmd+K	Marks you current page as a SnapBack page.
Page SnapBack	Option+Cmd+P	Returns you to your SnapBack page.
Search Results SnapBack	Option+Cmd+S	Returns you to your last Google web search results page. This feature even works with searches performed directly from the Google web page.
Reopen Last Closed Window		Reopens the last window you closed. The window will open with any tabs that were closed with it as well.

Continued

Table 10-1. Continued

Menu/Submenu Item	Keyboard Shortcut	Description
History (continued)		
Reopen All Windows From Last Session		Reopens all previously opened windows from the last session (will return Safari to the state it was in the last time you closed it).[1]
Show All History		Opens a window allowing you to view all your previous browsing history. By default, this will include the browsing history as set up in Safari's general preferences.
Clear History		Clears you browser history.
Bookmarks		
(Show|Hide) All Bookmarks	Option+Cmd+B	Toggles open the bookmark window in the main viewing area. This is the same view as the Show All History view. This view allows you to view and organize all of your bookmarks.
Add Bookmark...	Cmd+D	Opens a small sheet that allows you to add a bookmark to the current web page to any of your bookmark folders.
Add Bookmark For These Tabs...		Allows you to add bookmarks for all the open tabs in a window at once.
Add Bookmark Folder	Shift+Cmd+N	Creates a new unnamed folder selected in the Bookmarks view.
Bookmarks Bar		Opens a submenu containing the bookmarks that you have on your Bookmarks bar (this may be turned off in Safari's preferences).[2]
Open in Tabs		Opens each bookmark stored in your Bookmark Menu collection in a separate tab at the same time. This could be a whole lot of bookmarks (Safari seems to have a limit of 200), so use this with care.
Window		
Minimize	Cmd+M	Minimizes the window into the dock. (This is the same as using the - window widget.)
Zoom		Zooms the window. (This is the same as using the + window widget.)
Select Next Tab	Cmd+}	Cycles to the next tab.
Select Previous Tab	Cmd+{	Cycles to the previous tab.
Move Tab to New Window		Opens the active tab in a separate window.
Merge All Windows		Consolidates all open browser windows into one window using tabs.
Downloads	Option+Cmd+L	Opens and brings to the foreground the Downloads window.

Menu/Submenu Item	Keyboard Shortcut	Description
Window (continued)		
Activity	Option+Cmd+A	Opens and brings to the foreground the Activity window.
Bring All To Front		Brings all of Safari's open windows to the foreground.[3]
Help		
Safari Help		Opens Safari help topics in the Help browser.
License		Opens a window containing the software license that Safari is released under.
Acknowledgments		Opens a window containing a list of acknowledgments for other projects that Safari is partially based upon.
Installed Plug-Ins		Opens a window listing all of the browser plug-ins currently active in Safari.

1 Following the Reopen All Windows From Last Session item, Safari will provide the last 20 history items (or bookmarks from the last 20 web pages stored in its history), followed by submenus containing your browser history over the last week.

2 After the Bookmarks Bar item, there will be list of bookmarks that are part of your Bookmark Menu collection.

3 Following the Bring All To Front item, each open window will be listed.

> **NOTE** Most of the Edit commands only work on editable regions of a web page (forms and text fields). If these items are not available, they will be grayed out.

> **NOTE** The clipboard (more appropriately called the pasteboard) is a special place in memory where cut and copied items are temporarily stored so that they can be reused (pasted) elsewhere. By default, this clipboard only holds one item at a time—each new cut or copy will overwrite the old item.

That covers the basics of the interface, including the menu items. Now we'll take a closer look at how to perform certain tasks in Safari.

Setting Your Home Page

Your Home page is the default web page that Safari will go to when it is initially launched. Out of the box, this is set for the Apple Start page (www.apple.com/startpage/), which provides Apple news and links to other Apple products and features. If, however, you'd like to open a different page (or no page) when you start Safari, then open the Safari preferences, click the General button (Figure 10-3), and set a few options:

New windows open with: This drop-down list allows you to select if new windows open with the home page, an empty page, the same page (i.e., the page that was last opened in Safari), or in Bookmarks view.

Home page: This text field allows you to enter the URL of any web page that you'd like to use as your home page.

Set to Current Page: Clicking this button will automatically enter the URL of you current web page into the "Home page" text field.

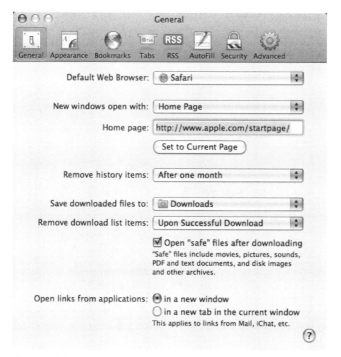

Figure 10-3. You can select your own home page on the General tab of Safari's preferences.

Searching the Web

If you'd like to perform a search on the Web, Safari by default provides a search field in the top right of the toolbar to enter a search string, which will open a page of search results from Google.

Bookmarks

Bookmarks provide a way for you to keep track of the web sites you visit that you'd like to return to (or keep track of for some other reason). Safari has a very nice bookmark system in place that allows you to keep an extensive collection of bookmarks well organized in folders and collections.

Adding Bookmarks

To add a bookmark of a page you are visiting, you can either select Add Bookmark from the Bookmarks menu, use the Cmd+D keyboard shortcut, or click the Add Bookmark button on the toolbar. This will open a bookmark panel allowing you to name and choose a location for storing your bookmark. You can also add a bookmark by selecting the URL from the Address field in the toolbar and drag it down to the Bookmarks bar, a specific bookmark folder or a bookmark collection in the Bookmarks view (Figure 10-4).

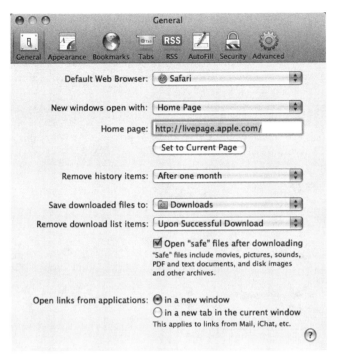

Figure 10-4. All of your bookmarks, bookmark folders, and bookmark collections are visible in Bookmarks view.

Managing Bookmarks

When you are in the Bookmarks view, you can organize you bookmarks in a way that makes the most sense to you. To enter the Bookmarks view, select the Show All Bookmarks item from the Bookmarks menu, use the Option+Cmd+B keyboard shortcut, or click the Show All Bookmarks button on the far left of you Bookmarks bar (the icon that looks like an open book).

> **NOTE** When viewing the items in the Bookmarks Bar collection, you may notice a column called Auto-Click, which contains a check box next to each folder item. When the Auto-Click feature is selected, rather than providing a drop-down list of bookmarks contained in that folder, all the bookmarks contained in the folder open in individual tabs when you select this item in the Bookmarks bar.

In the left column of the Bookmarks view, there are two areas: Collections and Bookmarks. *Collections* are special groupings of bookmarks or other related items. The Bookmarks Bar and Bookmarks Menu collections provide a place for you to store bookmarks so they are easily accessible from Safari, the contents in these two collections are fully customizable. Other collections provide access to links that are automatically collected. The Address Book collection contains all the URLs associated with contacts in your Address Book. The Bonjour collection contains a list of web sites on your network that takes advantage of Bonjour. The History collection provides links to you browsing history. All RSS Feeds it a collection of Links that lead to RSS feeds rather than traditional web pages.

Below the collections are you primary Bookmarks folders. Here you can add, remove, and move around folders, and store any bookmarks within them. This is a great way to store large amounts of bookmarks in an organized manner. It's important to note, though, that the bookmarks stored here are only accessible from this view. If you need quicker access to particular bookmarks, it's best to store those in the Bookmarks bar or Bookmarks Menu collections.

Bookmark Preferences

The Bookmarks tab in Safari's Preference window (Figure 10-5) provides a few options, primarily how to treat certain collections, but also a sync option.

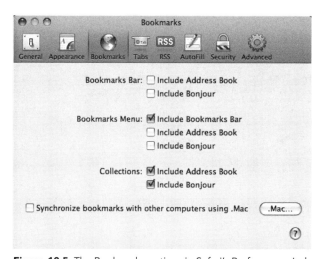

Figure 10-5. The Bookmarks options in Safari's Preference window

The Bookmarks bar and Bookmarks menu options allow you to select from a list of collections. Any selected collections will then appear as items in the selected element. The Collections options let you choose whether to include the Address Book or Bonjour collections at all.

The last option, if selected, will keep your bookmarks in sync with your .Mac account (and thus, in sync with other computers you use that also sync with .Mac). This is handy if you use many different computers and want to keep all your bookmarks handy from any of them. Also, enabling this provides you with an up-to-date backup of all of your bookmarks.

Tabbed Browsing

The Safari browser fully supports tabbed browsing, which allows you to open up and view multiple web pages at one time all in one window (Figure 10-6). For those of us with a history of browsing many sites at once, this is a massive improvement over shuffling around many separate browser windows.

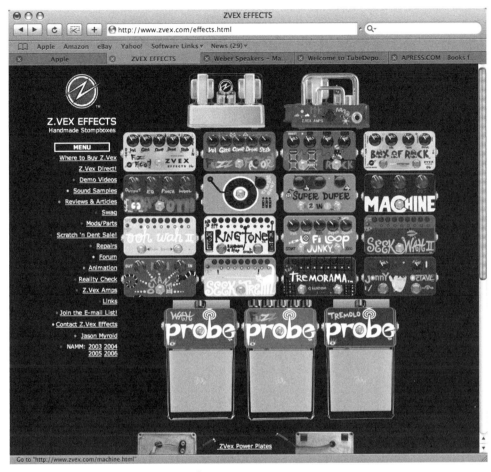

Figure 10-6. Safari running with many tabs open at once

The ability to use tabs is always present in Safari—however, setting a few options in the Tabs tab in Safari's preferences (Figure 10-7) can make using tabs more convenient.

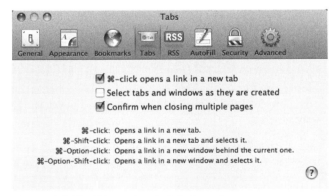

Figure 10-7. The Tabs options in Safari's preferences

One other option in Safari's preferences that has a direct impact on the use of tabs, but isn't in the Tabs section of the preferences, is the "Open links from applications" option on the General preference tab. This option allows you to configure Safari so that when you click a link in another application it will open that link in a tab in the current Safari window, instead of opening a new window each time (if no Safari window is currently open, then of course a new window will be created).

Creating New Tabs

To create an empty tab in a Safari window, select New Tab from the File menu (or use Cmd+T). Otherwise, depending on you preferences, new tabs can be created when you Cmd+click a hyperlink in a web page, or when you click a link in an external application.

> **NOTE** By default in OS X, mouse button 3, which is commonly the middle mouse button (or the scroll wheel when clicked) will open up new links in a new tab as well. Some mice (e.g., Logitech Revolution) have other default actions when you click the scroll wheel, though, so this behavior can vary both in hardware and third-party mouse drivers.

Moving Tabs

One new feature in Safari 3 is that ability to reorder tabs. To switch a tab's order, just grab (click and hold) the tab and drag it around the Tab bar where you want it in relation to other tabs.

Closing Tabs

To close a tab, you can either click the small *x* circle located on any tab, or use the Close Tab menu option in the File menu (or the Cmd+W keyboard shortcut) to close the active tab.

Other Tab Tricks

Tabs can also be dragged out of the window they are in, into their own stand-alone browser window or into another existing window. Conversely, a window can be dragged into another window to combine them into a singe window. Finally, if you have lots of open windows, you can use the Window ➤ Merge All Windows command to merge all your windows into a single window.

Downloading Content from the Web

Besides browsing the Web, Safari can also easily download content that it encounters on the Web. When you click a link in Safari that leads to a file that Safari doesn't traditionally display, Safari will automatically start to download the selected item, and the Downloads window will open up to display the download progress.

> **NOTE** Safari doesn't support all the popular protocols used today to download files, including BitTorrent, Gnutella, and others. If you wish to utilize this type of file download, you will need to get a third-party application like Lime Wire (www.limewire.com/), Acquisition (www.acquisitionx.com), or Transmission (http://transmission.m0k.org/).

> **NOTE** Chapter 21 covers all sorts of ways to transfer files from one location to another in more depth.

> **NOTE** Leopard will occasionally warn you, the first time you attempt to launch an application or open a file that you have downloaded from the Internet, that you should use some caution when opening unknown items on your computer.

On the General tab of Safari's preferences, there are a few options that affect how Safari downloads items:

Save downloaded files to: This option allows you to choose a folder to save all downloads in. By default, this is the `Downloads` folder in your home directory.

Remove download list items: This option allows you to choose whether downloaded items remain listed in the Downloads window until you manually remove them (using the Clear button), or whether this list should automatically be cleared when the download is complete or you quit Safari. Private Browsing overrides this option. Additionally, failed or canceled searches are never cleared automatically.

Open "safe" files after downloading: When this option is selected, items deemed safe will automatically launch when they have completed downloading. Not only does this include opening items like images and movies in Safari, but when this option is selected, archives will be uncompressed and disk images will automatically be mounted. This will not in any situation cause a newly downloaded application to automatically launch, though (that would be considered unsafe).

Viewing Image Files and PDFs in Safari

When Safari downloads certain types of files that it can display, it will (depending on the "safe" file option) open that item in Safari. When that item is a stand-alone image, if the image is larger than the Safari window it is opening in, then Safari's behavior is to scale the image so it fits in the window. If you click the scaled image, it will scale back to its original size, allowing you to scroll around to view it.

> **NOTE** One nice thing about this feature is that when you click a large image to zoom in on it, the image will zoom into the region you clicked in.

Besides images, Safari will display PDF files from the Internet for easy viewing (Figure 10-8). Additionally, Safari provides a nice toolbar overlay (Figure 10-9) that will appear when you move your mouse toward the bottom center of the PDF view. This toolbar allows you to zoom in and out of the PDF, open the PDF in the Preview application, and save the PDF file to disk.

> **NOTE** Besides the visible options, there are additional options available for both images and PDFs from the contextual menu.

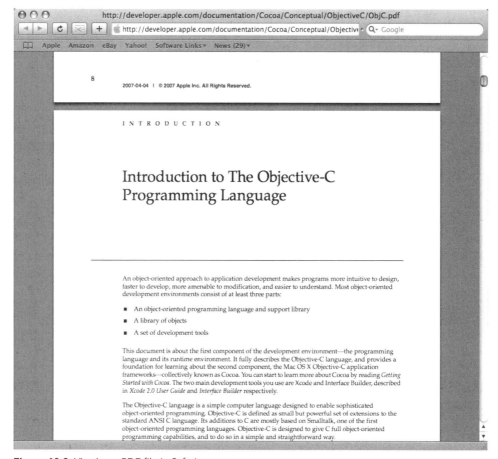

Figure 10-8. Viewing a PDF file in Safari

Figure 10-9. A small toolbar will appear at the bottom of the Safari view window when you are viewing a PDF to provide the ability to zoom, open in Preview, or save the PDF to disk.

Web Forms and AutoFill

Many functions of many web sites require that you fill out forms with data ranging from simple web site login information to shipping information and other contact info. While none of this is very hard, sometimes you wish this information would just fill itself in. Safari provides a feature called AutoFill that can help.

The AutoFill options are located under the AutoFill tab in Safari's preferences (Figure 10-10). Here you can select what type of information you would like Safari to save and fill in when you access many forms in a web site.

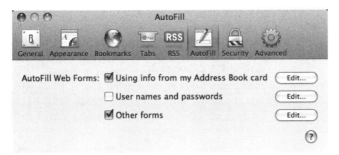

Figure 10-10. The AutoFill options in Safari's Preference window

Checking the "Using info from my Address Book card" option will enable you to use the contact information about you stored in your Address Book card to fill in that information when it is requested in an online form. This will detect fields like "Address," "email," and so on, and fill in the appropriate information. Clicking the Edit... button next to this option will open up the Address Book application to you Contact information.

The "User names and passwords" option, which is off by default, will store usernames and passwords for various web sites. It will tie specific username/password combinations to a particular web site and will only fill in the specific username/password combo for that specific site. This data is stored safely in your keychain so that it would be difficult for someone discover your password using devious means. However, if this is active, any user who has access to your account will be able to access any web sites protected by information stored here (unless you do not unlock your keychain). The Edit... button will allow you to view and edit web sites, and usernames associated with those web sites that are stored in AutoFill. Passwords are not shown (however, they can be viewed in your keychain with the Keychain Access utility).

If you check the "Other forms" option, data will be collected from forms on various web sites, and that information will be stored for reuse the next time you visit those sites. You can view what web sites AutoFill is storing data for by clicking the Edit... button.

AutoFill is clearly one of those things that, if enabled, adds a lot of convenience, but at the cost of some security.

Security

As more and more services and activities shift over to taking place on the Internet, and particularly on the Web, browser security becomes more and more important. Since its inception, Safari has proven to be one of the more secure browsers out there, and the version of Safari that ships with Leopard seems to uphold that level of security.

> **NOTE** Safari isn't without its security flaws. In the past, there was a potentially critical flaw that could cause some security headaches if a user had the "Open 'safe' files after downloading" option selected. Also, there were some potential issues discovered with the first public beta of Safari 3 for Windows. While there are no reports that any of these things actually resulted in a security breach, it underlies the importance of keeping your software up-to-date, as issues like these are usually quickly resolved after they are discovered. Additionally, besides Safari itself, certain plug-ins may possess their own security flaws.

Secure Browsing

To support a secure environment, Safari has built-in support for an array of protocols that assure the information you send and receive from a web site is encrypted. Safari supports the standard SSL versions 2 and 3, as well as TLS (Transport Layer Security, a newer, potential replacement for SSL). Whenever you have a secure connection between your browser and a web site, Safari will display a small lock icon in the top right of the window. Clicking the lock will provide information about the security being used, as well as the certificate information assuring that the web site is indeed what it claims to be.

> **CAUTION** It's not advisable to send any information you deem private or important over the Web unless you know who is on the receiving end and the connection is secured. This rule generally applies beyond the Web as well, and should be followed for all network communication. A secure connection doesn't guarantee the information you submit will be secure.

Blocking Web Content

Safari can also block certain types of web content, specifically any pop-up windows that are not only annoying, but may contain undesirable content. To enable pop-up blocking, you can select Block Pop-Up Windows from the Safari menu (or use Shift+Cmd+K). Safari tries to block only non-requested pop-ups, but if for some reason Safari blocks a desirable pop-up window, then you may need to toggle off this protection temporarily.

Besides blocking pop-ups, you can block other web content. On the Security tab of Safari's Preference window (Figure 10-11), you can disable JavaScript, Java, and plug-ins to further block potentially harmful content.

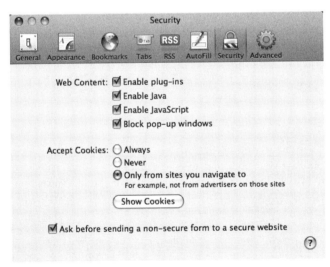

Figure 10-11. The Security options in Safari's preferences

> **NOTE** Disabling plug-ins, Java and JavaScript may make for a safer, and perhaps less distracting, web browsing experience, but by disabling these things you will also be losing a great number of features, and some web sites may become unusable. It comes down to your own personal security vs. hassle priorities.

Private Browsing

Another way to protect your information when browsing is to utilize the Private Browsing feature of Safari. When Private Browsing is enabled (by selecting Private Browsing... from the Safari menu), Safari will not save any of your browsing activity in the browser history or cache. This assures that people can't go into you computer and poke around at places you've been and items you've been browsing.

> **CAUTION** Private Browsing may overlook items in your Downloads window, specifically any canceled or incomplete downloads.

Cookies

HTTP is a stateless protocol, so when you connect to a web site, there are complications in carrying out complex transactions, since the protocol doesn't keep track of one particular user vs. any other user. There are, of course, many ways to work around this, but the most popular method today is to use a cookie to keep track of session data as well as other data (web site preferences and other information can be stored in cookies as well). As such, cookies are an important part of using the Web today, and while you can disable them, you will be losing out on a great deal of web functionality doing so.

> **NOTE** Since cookies became popular, there has been a large amount of paranoia about them, most of which is unfounded. Cookies can track your movement around a web site, and they can contain personal information, but a cookie is only valid for the originating web site, so any personal data stored in the cookie is data that you willingly submitted to that web site to begin with. That said, you may not want to leave cookies lying around on a computer in a user account that others have access to—but beyond that, they are perfectly safe and make the Web a much more interesting place to visit. Like plug-ins and so many other computing features, it comes down to a security vs. ease issue.

Safari has a number of options available to you regarding the accepting of cookies. In the Security tab of Safari's Preference window, you select when you wish to accept cookies: never, always, or only from sites you navigate to (which is the default and most sensible option). Additionally, the Show Cookies button will open up a window providing information about each cookie you have stored in your system. This view will also allow you to selectively remove individual cookies, or if you'd like remove them all.

Emptying the Browser Cache

The browser cache stores most of the content you encounter on the Web locally to help improve the browser's response time when revisiting a web site. While this is fantastic from a performance point of view, you might not want to leave all the items you were browsing lying around in your computer, as they may contain sensitive or private information (they can also take up a good amount of disk space, although that's not as big of a problem today as it was a few years ago). Either way, you may wish to occasionally empty you browser cache. To do this, just select the Empty Cache... item from the Safari menu or use the Option+Cmd+E keyboard shortcut. This will open up a dialog to confirm you want to empty the cache. Click the Empty button to empty it.

> **TIP** It is possible to disable the cache entirely. First you must enable the secret Safari Debug menu. The easiest way to do this is to open the Terminal application and enter `defaults write com.apple.Safari IncludeDebugMenu 1` on the command line when Safari is not running. Next time you launch Safari, there will be a new menu named Debug to the right of the Help menu. If you select Show Caches Window from the Debug menu and check the Disable WebCore Caches option, you will effectively turn off the cache.

> **CAUTION** The Debug menu has lots of fun options, many of which can be very useful if used in the proper context. However, used poorly, these options can cause all sort of problems with Safari and have an unfortunate effect on you web browsing experience. If you don't know and understand what you are doing here, it's best to leave it alone.

Advanced Safari Features

Safari has a few Advanced options located in its preferences (Figure 10-12) that are useful in certain situations.

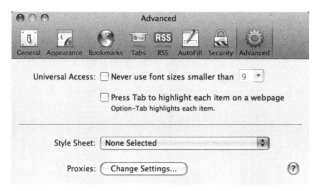

Figure 10-12. The Advanced Safari preferences

Universal Access

The Universal Access options on the Advanced preference tab allow you to adjust the minimum font size for readability, and to select between using Tab or the default Option+Tab to cycle through links *and* form items on a web page.

> **NOTE** The difference between the default Tab and Option+Tab is that, unless you set the "Press Tab to highlight each item on a web page" option, Tab will only cycle through form items (as well as the address field and search field on the toolbar), while Option+Tab will cycle through form items and hyperlinks.

Setting a Default Style Sheet

The Advanced Safari preferences also include the ability to use a specific style sheet that will affect every web page you visit. It's important to note that only text settings are imported from this style sheet to help improve readability, so the layout of each web site shouldn't be affected (unless large text settings cause items to wrap funny, which is really the fault of an inflexible web design(er), not Safari or the style sheet).

RSS Feeds in Safari

RSS (Really Simple Syndication) is a way for web sites to syndicate their content. This allows users to subscribe to a web site's RSS feed, which will contain any updates to the web site. This is great if you like to visit a large number of web sites frequently, because with RSS, instead of going to each site to see what's new, you can get a list of new items from all of the web sites and filter out what items interest you.

> **NOTE** When is RSS not RSS? When it's some other type of syndication standard. RSS has always had a few things that others found as weaknesses. This has resulted in two things: first, people adding content to RSS feeds that weren't covered by the RSS standard (Apple, for example, does this for iTunes podcast feeds); and second, people getting together and inventing new syndication standards, like ATOM. Most RSS clients, including Safari and Mail, support ATOM along with RSS—however, they still tend to refer to it all under the blanket of RSS.

Safari contains the ability to subscribe to RSS feeds as easily as adding a bookmark, and makes a suitable RSS reader with some nice features.

> **NOTE** In Leopard, Apple also added the ability to handle RSS in Mail, which provides a nice alternative to Safari's RSS feature. While some items referring to this will come up here, we will focus on how Safari handles RSS here, and how Mail handles RSS in the next chapter.

> **NOTE** Even though Apple provides a couple of good options for viewing RSS feeds, there are a number of other third-party applications specifically for handling RSS feeds (called news aggregators) that add some additional or unique features, or that may help you organize a large number of feeds in a more suitable way. One such reader is NetNewsWire (www. newsgator.com/Individuals/NetNewsWire/Default.aspx). NetNewsWire comes in a free lite version that is suitable for reading RSS feeds, and a full version that adds many extremely handy features. If you manage lots of RSS feeds, NetNewsWire is definitely worth checking out.

Adding Feeds

When you are browsing the Web in Safari, whenever you visit a site with an RSS feed, a blue RSS icon will appear on the far right side of the Address field in Safari's toolbar (Figure 10-13).

http://mydogateit.com/scott/blog/index.html   RSS

Figure 10-13. A web site that has an RSS feed associated with it will display a blue RSS box in Safari's address bar.

Clicking the RSS icon will either open the RSS feed in your browser, or open a list of all the feeds available if there are more than one. Select the feed you wish to subscribe to from the pop-up, and the news feed will open up in Safari (Figure 10-14).

> **NOTE** When you select an RSS feed from within Safari, the RSS feed will open up in the default RSS newsreader. If your default newsreader is not Safari (e.g., Mail or a third-party RSS reader), then something else will happen than what is described here.

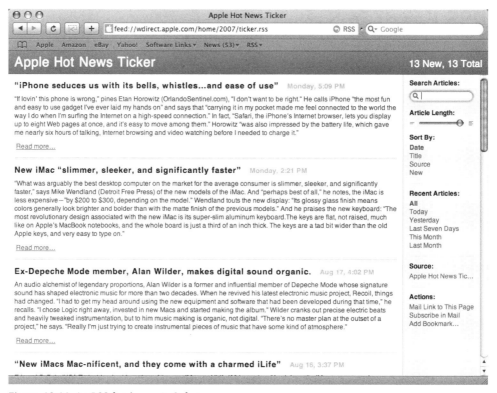

Figure 10-14. An RSS feed open in Safari

Once the feed is open, you can add the feed just as you would any bookmark (Cmd+D). Adding a feed will save the feed's location, but will not necessarily update the feed automatically (which is usually the desired result). Depending on your RSS options, you must add the bookmark to either your Bookmarks Bar collection, or your Bookmarks Menu collection for the feeds to automatically update. (You may want to create an RSS folder in one of these locations to store your favorite RSS feeds.)

> **NOTE** The Bookmarks view provides an All RSS Feeds collection that contains all the RSS feeds you have bookmarked. You can use this to view all your RSS feeds in one place.

> **NOTE** When you go to add the bookmark, you will notice an option to add the bookmark to Mail. This is provided if you wish to subscribe to the RSS feed in Mail as well.

Reading Feeds

Reading RSS feeds is pretty straightforward in Safari. If you select a specific feed, all of the current articles will appear in the Safari view area. If you select a collection of feeds by clicking View All RSS Articles in the Bookmark menu or from a folder list in the Bookmark bar, then all the articles from all the feeds will be displayed.

On the right side of the view area are some RSS options that apply to the feed(s) you are viewing. The Search Articles text field allows you to search for specific strings within all the visible articles. Below the Search Articles text field is the Article Length slider. This will limit how much of the feed summary to show. (RSS feeds themselves vary in how they summarize articles. Some feeds will give no summary at all, while others will send the entire article.) The Sort By options will adjust the order the articles appear in Safari. The Recent Articles option will adjust which articles appear in the view. For example, if you select Today, then only the articles that were updated today will be shown. The Source item shows where the feeds come from. If you select an individual feed, then the feed's URL will be shown; if you select a collection of RSS feeds, then the name of that collection will be shown. Finally, there are some actions available: Mail Link to This Page will open up a new mail message in Mail containing a link to the news feed or feeds being shown; Subscribe in Mail will subscribe to all the feeds in Mail (which is handy if you use Mail as you primary RSS reader).

Feed Options

The Safari preferences include an RSS tab containing some options for RSS feeds (Figure 10-15).

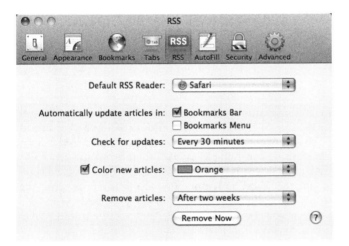

Figure 10-15. The RSS options in Safari's Preference window

The Default RSS Reader option provides a list of all the known RSS readers installed on your system. The application chosen here is the primary one that Safari will use to open RSS links in.

The "Automatically update articles in" options allow you to select whether you would like all the RSS feeds in your Bookmarks bar, Bookmarks menu, or both to be automatically updated. The "Check for updates" list determines how often these feeds will get updated.

The "Color new articles" option causes part of the article's information (Author and Date) to be colored in the chosen shade. This can help you identify new articles more easily.

Finally, while RSS feeds themselves often limit the number of articles that are contained in the actual feed, once downloaded Safari will keep track of all the articles until they are removed. The "Remove articles" list allows you to determine when Safari should automatically remove older articles.

Safari Plug-Ins

Safari in Leopard comes equipped with the most commonly used browser plug-ins, including Shockwave and Flash plug-ins, Java plug-ins, and a QuickTime plug-in that supports a wide variety of image, audio, and video media formats. Occasionally, however, you may come across some content on the Web that requires some other type of plug-in. Depending on the web site, you may be prompted to download and install the plug-in, or you may just be told that you are missing the required plug-in (and usually told which one you are missing). Two common plug-ins not installed by default are plug-ins for Real Media and for Windows Media. To get the Real Media plug-in, visit www.real.com/ and download the free RealPlayer for the Mac. This will include the browser plug-in. Things for Windows Media are a bit trickier, as currently there is no up-to-date version of Windows Media Player for OS X. However, a program called Flip4Mac, from http://flip4mac.com/, will install the necessary plug-ins to allow most Windows Media files to be played back both in Safari and QuickTime.

Beyond that, there are some other infrequently used plug-ins. Often when you encounter these, there will be information about what is necessary to view the content. Luckily, though, the days of plug-in madness have passed (i.e., the dot-com days when every wanna-be tech company had its own plug-in for its own proprietary format)—today, most of your plug-in needs should be fulfilled by the included plug-ins.

Web Clippings

Web Clippings, a new feature in Safari, allows you to select regions of a web page and add those regions to your Dashboard. The type of content can be anything that is contained in a web page, so this feature can really be interesting. For example, say you come across the listing of Yahoo's top 20 daily searches (http://buzz.yahoo.com/overall/). You can clip out the table displaying the results (Figure 10-16) by clicking the Web Clip button on your toolbar, or selecting the File ➤ Open in Dashboard... command, highlighting the desired content, and clicking the Add button. This will add the selected region to your Dashboard (Figure 10-17). Once placed, you can click the small *i* button on the clipping to add a border around it.

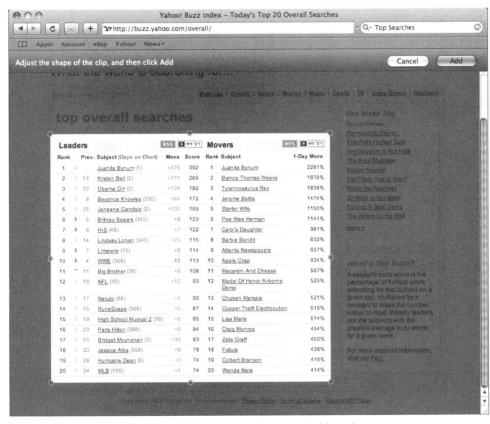

Figure 10-16. Selecting a region in a web page to add to your Dashboard

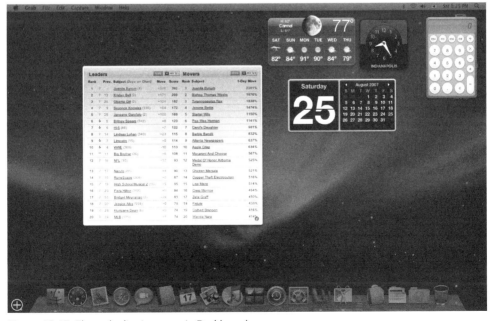

Figure 10-17. The web clipping open in Dashboard

Summary

Since Apple introduced Safari, it has been a quite capable web browser, but with Safari 3, Apple has introduced what is clearly one of the best, if not the best, web browser available on any platform today. Combined with its tight integration with Leopard, it's really a clear winner. Of course, there is much more to the Internet than the Web—in fact, for many people, e-mail is the most important feature of the Internet—so next we'll talk about Mail along with iCal and Address Book, which now all work together to provide a seamless way to manage your e-mail, news feeds, To Do lists, notes, and more.

## CHAPTER 11

Mail, Address Book, and iCal

The Mail application in Leopard has undergone some significant changes. Although it has always been capable of managing e-mail, the new version can also manage notes and RSS feeds. Additionally, Mail has improved integration with Address Book and iCal to help provide a unified time and contact management solution. In this chapter, we will cover all three applications:

- Mail
- Address Book
- iCal

Mail

Mail is Apple's e-mail application that has been part of OS X from its start. With each new release of OS X, Apple refines the Mail application a bit. With Leopard, Apple not only refined the interface a bit, but it also added a whole slew of new features.

Working in Mail's Interface

If you've used Mail in Tiger (OS X 10.4), then, despite a few noticeable interface tweaks and the inclusion of some new features (notes, To Do items, and RSS), you should be able to find your way around quite easily. If you are entirely new to Apple's Mail application or have used only a version prior to the version that shipped with Tiger, then you may need a quick overview of the interface of the Mail application in Leopard (Figure 11-1).

By default, Mail's main window is the Message Viewer window. It is presented in a traditional three-pane layout. The column on the left provides a hierarchical list of your mailboxes, folders, and other items. The top-right pane lists all the items contained in the mailbox or folder selected on the left, and below that is a view area to view any selected item in the top area. Basically, it's a traditional mail layout that is common among many mail clients and many other applications.

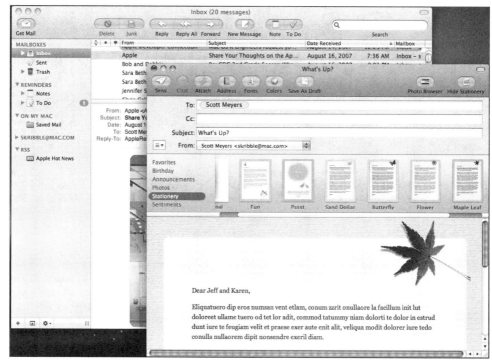

Figure 11-1. The Mail application in Leopard

Mail has a single toolbar that, like in Safari, can be customized with a wide array of optional buttons. Besides the toolbar, many commands and options are located in Mail's menus in the menu bar (Table 11-1).

Table 11-1. Mail's Menu Bar Items

Item	Keyboard Shortcut	Description
Mail		
About Mail		Provides version information about Mail.
Preferences...	Cmd+,	Opens Mail's Preference window.
Provide Mail Feedback		Sends information about your e-mail accounts to Apple that Apple can use to improve the product.
Services		Opens a submenu filled with commands and features of other applications that can be accessed from within Mail.
Hide Mail	Cmd+H	Hides all open Mail windows.
Hide Others	Opt+Cmd+H	Hides all windows on the desktop except windows used by Mail.
Show All		Reveals all hidden windows.
Quit Mail	Cmd+Q	Quits Mail.

Item	Keyboard Shortcut	Description
File		
New Message	Cmd+N	Opens a New Message window to create and send an e-mail.
New Note	Ctrl+Cmd+N	Opens a New Note window.
Add To Do	Opt+Cmd+Y	Switches to your To Do list and adds a new To Do item.
New Viewer Window	Opt+Cmd+N	Opens a new view window, which is the default Mail window.
Open Message	Cmd+O	Opens selected message(s) in a new window.
Close	Cmd+W	Closes the active window.
Save	Cmd+S	Saves new or edited notes or current e-mail messages as drafts.
Save As…	Shift+Cmd+S	Allows you to save a message or note as a separate file in a variety of formats.
Save as Stationary…		Saves an e-mail message you create as a template for other future e-mail messages.
Attach File…	Shift+Cmd+A	Opens a browser dialog box to select a file to attach to an e-mail message.
Save Attachments…		Saves incoming e-mail attachments to a location chosen by you (or you could just drag the attachments out of the message to your desired location).
Quick Look Attachments	Cmd+Y	Opens the attachment in Quick Look if the attachment is a supported type.
Add Account…		Opens a window to walk you through adding a new mail account.
Import Mailboxes…		Aids you in importing e-mail messages from other Mail mailboxes or even other e-mail clients.
Add RSS Feeds…		Opens a dialog box to add URLs of RSS feeds you want to subscribe to in Mail.
Print…	Cmd+P	Opens the Print dialog to print a Mail item.
Edit		
Undo	Cmd+Z	Undoes your last command.
Redo	Shift+Cmd+Z	Undoes your last undo.
Cut	Cmd+X	Cuts the selected item or text, placing it in the clipboard.
Copy	Cmd+C	Copies the selected area or item, placing it in the clipboard.

Continued

Table 11-1. Continued

Item	Keyboard Shortcut	Description
Edit (continued)		
Paste	Cmd+V	Pastes the item in the clipboard in the selected location.
Delete	Cmd+Del	Deletes the selected item; if the item is a message or note, the item will immediately be moved to the trash. For a To Do item, the item will be immediately deleted.
Select All	Cmd+A	Selects all items or text in a view area or window.
Complete	Opt+Esc	Opens a list of possible words for the word you are typing.
Paste as Quotation	Shift+Cmd+V	Pastes the text in the clipboard into a new mail message formatted as quoted text.
Past and Match Style	Opt+Shift+Cmd+V	Pastes any text in the clipboard in a message matching the currently selected message text style.
Append Selected Messages	Opt+Cmd+I	Appends any selected e-mail messages into a new message.
Link		Opens a submenu containing items dealing with hyperlinks in mail messages.
Link ➤ Add...		Opens a dialog box to enter a URL to create a hyperlink in a mail message, which will either link the selected text or insert the URL if no text is selected.
Link ➤ Remove		Removes a selected hyperlink from a mail message.
Attachments		Opens a submenu containing options for dealing with attachments in mail messages.
Attachments ➤ Include Original Attachments in Reply		Includes in replies any attachments that are included with an original message when this is selected.
Attachments ➤ Always Send Windows Friendly Attachments		Encodes any attachments to be included in a manner that is compatible with most Windows mail clients.
Attachments ➤ Always Insert Attachments at End of Message		Always inserts attachments at the end of the message rather than allowing attachments to be inserted inline.
Find		Opens a submenu of Find options.
Find ➤ Mailbox Search	Opt+Cmd+F	Highlights the search text field in the toolbar to begin a string-based search for items in your Mail folders.
Find ➤ Find...	Cmd+F	Opens a dialog box to begin a search for a string within a message or note.

Item	Keyboard Shortcut	Description
Edit (continued)		
Find ➤ Find Next	Cmd+G	Selects the next match when using the Find command.
Find ➤ Find Previous	Shift+Cmd+G	Selects the previous match when using the Find command.
Find ➤ Use Selection for Find	Cmd+E	Begins a search using the selected text as the search string.
Find ➤ Jump to Selection	Cmd+J	Centers the selected region of an item in the window.
Spelling and Grammar		Provides the standard spelling and grammar options; one unique variation in Mail is the Check Spelling option.
Check Spelling		Provides a submenu to select whether to check spelling while you type, before you send a message, or never.
Speech		Opens a submenu to have the default system voice start and stop reading your mail message aloud.
Special Characters…		Opens a character palette to choose characters or symbols to insert in your text.
View		
Columns		Opens a submenu containing a list of message properties that can be viewed as columns in the message list area of Mail's View window.
Sort By		Includes the list of potential column items. Selecting one will cause your messages to sort themselves based on the selected field (alternately, you can just click the column header to sort your messages by that field).
Organize by Thread		Keeps messages that are part of the same message thread (which is a series of messages related to the same subject) together in the e-mail list view.
Expand All Threads		Reveals all messages in all threads.
Collapse All Threads		Collapses threads so that only the most recent message is shown (you can expand or collapse each thread individually as well).
Cc Address Field		Toggles the Cc address field for a new message.
Bcc Address Field	Opt+Cmd+[B]	Toggles the Bcc address field for a new message.
Reply-To Address Filed	Opt+Cmd+[R]	Toggles the Reply-To address field in a new message.

Continued

Table 11-1. Continued

Item	Keyboard Shortcut	Description
View (continued)		
Select		Opens a submenu of options for easily selecting messages that are part of the same thread.
Select ➤ All Messages in this Thread	Shift+Cmd+K	Highlights all the messages in a specific e-mail thread.
Select ➤ Next Message in this Thread		Selects the next message in the same e-mail thread as the currently selected message.
Select ➤ Previous Message in this Thread		Selects the previous message in the same e-mail thread as the currently selected message.
Message		Provides a submenu containing view options for individual messages.
Message ➤ Long Headers	Shift+Cmd+H	Reveals additional header information about each e-mail message.
Message ➤ Raw Source	Opt+Cmd+U	Reveals the entire contents of an e-mail message in plain text including all header information and all formatting.
Message ➤ Plain Text Alternative	Opt+Cmd+P	Views a message if it's sent with a plain-text alternative message.
Message ➤ Previous Alternative	Opt+Cmd+[	Displays the previous alternative format for the selected e-mail message.
Message ➤ Next Alternative	Opt+Cmd+]	Displays the next alternative format for the selected e-mail message.
Message ➤ Best Alternative		Selects the best alternative text format for viewing the message in Mail (this is the default).
Display Selected Messages Only		Hides all messages in the message list except those that you have selected (which is useful if used in combination with Select ➤ All Messages in this thread).
(Hide|Show) Mailboxes	Shift+Cmd+M	Toggles the visibility of the left column in the message view area, which contains the list of mailboxes and folders.
(Show|Hide) Deleted Messages	Cmd+L	Toggles the visibility of deleted messages in your Inbox. This option depends on both the type of server and your account settings.
(Hide|Show) Toolbar		Toggles the visibility of Mail's toolbar.
Customize Toolbar…		Opens a sheet allowing you to customize your toolbar with various alternate commands and options.
Mailbox		
Take All Accounts Online		Takes all of your e-mail accounts online.
Take All Accounts Offline		Takes all of your e-mail accounts offline.

Item	Keyboard Shortcut	Description
Mailbox (continued)		
Get All New Mail	Shift+Cmd+N	Checks for and retrieves any new messages from all online accounts.
Synchronize All Accounts		Synchronizes all IMAP and Exchange accounts, updating both remote and local mailboxes with any changes.
Online Status		Displays a submenu allowing you to view and toggle the online status of each account individually.
Get New Mail		Displays a submenu allowing you to choose a specific account to check for new mail messages.
Synchronize		Displays a submenu allowing you to choose a specific account to synchronize.
Erase Deleted Messages		Displays a submenu that presents options for removing deleted (trashed) messages permanently, including each individual account separately as well as a few other options.
Erase Deleted Messages ➤ In All Accounts	Cmd+K	Erases all deleted items in all accounts, including expunging messages from IMAP and Exchange servers (though server settings may override this).
Erase Deleted Messages ➤ On My Mac		Deletes any trashed messages stored in Mail's trash; this won't immediately erase any messages stored on remote servers (such as IMAP and Exchange).
Erase Junk Mail	Opt+Cmd+[J]	Permanently removes any junk e-mail messages stored in the Junk mailbox. For this option to be available, you must activate the "When junk mail arrives: Move it to the Junk Mailbox" option in Mail's preferences.
New Mailbox...		Opens a dialog box allowing you to name and choose a location for a new mailbox.
New Smart Mailbox...		Opens a dialog box to allow you to configure a new smart mailbox.
Edit Smart Mailbox...		Opens a dialog box allowing you to alter the selected smart mailbox's rules.
Duplicate Smart Mailbox		Creates a new smart mailbox with the same rules as the selected smart mailbox.
New Smart Mailbox Folder		Opens a sheet to enter the name of a new smart mailbox folder for organizing smart mailboxes.
Rename Mailbox...		Highlights the name of the selected mailbox or folder to be renamed.

Continued

Table 11-1. Continued

Item	Keyboard Shortcut	Description
Mailbox (continued)		
Delete Mailbox...		Deletes the selected mailbox. Depending on the type of mailbox, this may delete all the messages the mailbox contains as well. You will be prompted to verify this action.
Archive Mailbox...		Saves an archive file of the selected mailbox, which will allow you to import the mailbox and data back into Mail at a later date.
Go To		Opens a submenu of common mailboxes and folders. Selecting an item here will take you to that mailbox.
Go To ➤ In	Cmd+1	Takes you to Mail's Inbox.
Go To ➤ Out	Cmd+2	Takes you to Mail's Outbox.
Go To ➤ Drafts	Cmd+3	Takes you to Mail's Drafts folder.
Go To ➤ Sent	Cmd+4	Takes you to Mail's Sent Items folder.
Go To ➤ Trash	Cmd+5	Takes you to Mail's trash.
Go To ➤ Junk	Cmd+6	Takes you to Mail's Junk folder.
Go To ➤ Notes	Cmd+7	Takes you to Mail's Notes folder.
Go To ➤ To Do	Cmd+8	Takes you to Mail's To Do items.
Go To ➤ RSS	Cmd+9	Takes you to Mail's RSS feeds.
Use This Mailbox For		Opens a submenu that allows you to designate the specific purposes of mailboxes, such as storing mail drafts, trash, junk, and so on.
Rebuild		Rebuilds your mailboxes. This can help fix potential (or real) corruption and can help save space by reorganizing your mailbox files. It's good to use this every once in awhile.
Message		
Send (Again)	Shift+Cmd+D	If you are writing a new message, this option will be Send and will send the current new message. Otherwise, this option will be Send Again, which will allow you to resend the selected message from your Sent mailbox.
Reply	Cmd+R	Opens the New Message window all set up to send a reply to the sender of the selected message.
Reply All	Shift+Cmd+R	Like Reply, but in addition to sending your reply to the initial sender, the reply will also be sent to everyone included in the original message.
Reply With iChat	Shift+Cmd+I	Allows you to start a chat with the sender of a message if the sender.

Item	Keyboard Shortcut	Description
Message (continued)		
Forward	Shift+Cmd+F	Opens a New Message window with the current selected message pasted in it so you can easily forward that message to another recipient.
Forward as Attachment		Allows you to forward a message, but rather than pasting the original message in the New Message window, it will attach the original message.
Redirect	Shift+Cmd+E	Redirects a selected message to another recipient. This is very different from Forward in that the redirected message will be removed from your Inbox and sent to the recipient without comment. The original sender will remain as the sender (though it will be known that you redirected it). This option is handy for redirecting phishing messages to security personal and such.
Bounce	Shift+Cmd+B	Bounces a message you receive back to the original sender as if your account doesn't exist. Although in theory this sounds like a good way to make spammers think your e-mail address is no longer valid, the most annoying spammers probably don't use their own return addresses, so it's likely using this will just end up spamming some other poor random soul with a bunch of bounced messages.
Mark		Opens a submenu to provide options for marking or labeling e-mail messages in your mailboxes.
Mark ➤ As (Unread|Read)	Shift+Cmd+U	Toggles selected messages as being unread/read.
Mark ➤ As (Flagged|Unflagged)	Shift+Cmd+L	Toggles a flag for the selected messages, which is a common way to mark e-mail messages for follow-up.
Mark ➤ As (Not) Junk Mail	Shift+Cmd+[J]	Toggles the current message as junk mail or as not junk mail.
Mark ➤ As Low Priority		Marks the selected message as low priority.
Mark ➤ As Normal Priority		Marks the selected messages as normal priority.
Mark ➤ As High Priority		Marks the selected messages as high priority.
Move To		Opens a submenu containing a list of all of your mailboxes, allowing you to move selected messages into a different mailbox.
Copy To		Marks a submenu containing a list of all your mailboxes, allowing you to copy selected messages into a different mailbox
(Move|Copy) To "*x*" Again	Opt+Cmd+T	Moves another message into the mailbox used in the last Move To command.

Continued

Table 11-1. Continued

Item	Keyboard Shortcut	Description
Message (continued)		
Apply Rules	Opt+Cmd+L	Applies your mail rules to selected messages.
Add Sender to Address Book	Shift+Cmd+Y	Adds the e-mail address (and name if available) of the sender of selected messages to your Address Book.
Remove Attachments		Removes the attachments of a selected message.
Text Encoding		Opens a submenu allowing you to encode the text using different languages and character sets.
Format		
Show Fonts	Cmd+T	Opens the system font dialog to choose a text font for the selected text.
Show Colors	Shift+Cmd+C	Opens the system color palette to choose a color for your selected text.
Lists		Opens a submenu to help you format different types of lists in a note or message.
Style		Opens a submenu with options for formatting text in a note or message.
Style ➤ Bold	Cmd+B	Makes selected text bold or makes all new text beginning at the cursor position bold.
Style ➤ Italic	Cmd+I	Makes selected text italic or makes all new text beginning at the cursor position italic.
Style ➤ Underline	Cmd+U	Underlines selected text or makes all new text beginning at the cursor position underlined.
Style ➤ Outline		Makes selected text outlined or makes all new text beginning at the cursor position outlined.
Style ➤ Bigger	Cmd+[+] (or Cmd+[=])	Makes selected text bigger.
Style ➤ Smaller	Cmd+[-]	Makes selected text smaller.
Style ➤ Copy Style	Opt+Cmd+[C]	Copies the style of selected text.
Style ➤ Paste Style	Opt+Cmd+[P]	Pastes the previously copied style onto selected text.
Style ➤ Styles...		Opens a style pane displaying various system level styles.
Alignment		Opens a submenu providing text alignment options.
Alignment ➤ Align Left	Cmd+{	Aligns text to the left side of the text area. (This is the default text alignment for most languages.)
Alignment ➤ Center	Cmd+I	Centers text in the text area.
Alignment ➤ Justify		Aligns text on both sides.

Item	Keyboard Shortcut	Description
Format (continued)		
Alignment ➤ Align Right	Cmd+}	Aligns text along the right side of the text field.
Alignment ➤ Float Left		Floats the image in your message to the left of the text (allowing the text to flow along the right side of the image).
Alignment ➤ Float Right		Floats the image to the right of the text.
Alignment ➤ Remove Float		Removes the float from an image. Text will not wrap along the side of the image. This is the default.
Alignment ➤ Writing Direction		Changes the direction of the text. The default is left to right, which is most common; however, this will accommodate languages that flow right to left (including most Semitic languages such as Arabic and Hebrew).
Indentation		Opens a submenu that allows you to control the indentation of text blocks.
Indentation ➤ Increase	Cmd+]	Increases the indentation of text.
Indentation ➤ Decrease	Cmd+[	Decreases the indentation (and is valid only on indented text).
Quote Level		Opens a submenu to allow you to format blocks of text as quoted text.
Indentation ➤ Increase	Cmd+'	Increases the quote level.
Indentation ➤ Decrease	Opt+Cmd+'	Decreases the quote level.
Make (Plain|Rich) Text	Shift+Cmd+T	Toggles the formatting of the text in a message from plain text (which is no formatting) to rich text (which is actually formatted using HTML and allows formatted text and images). Traditionally, e-mail was all plain text, and today some people and e-mail clients still prefer it that way.

NOTE When sending a message using rich text from Mail, the Mail application will also include a plain-text version of your message for people who prefer plain text or can't or won't except rich text.

Window

Item	Keyboard Shortcut	Description
Minimize	Cmd+M	Minimizes the current window into the Dock.
Zoom		Zooms the current window.
Message Viewer		Selects the Message Viewer window (Mail's default window).
Photo Browser		Opens Mail's Photo Browser window that will allow you to browse iPhoto libraries for images to include in your messages.

Continued

Table 11-1. Continued

Item	Keyboard Shortcut	Description
Window (continued)		
Address Panel	Opt+Cmd+A	Opens a window containing an abbreviated view of contacts from your Address Book, displaying only their names and e-mail addresses.
Previous Recipients		Opens a window to keep track of all your previous message recipients. Whenever you start to type an e-mail address in a To, Cc, or Bcc field, the Mail application will use this list to attempt to autocomplete the name.
Activity	Cmd+0	Opens the activity viewer window showing any background activity taking place in Mail. Although this is still available, there is now an option to toggle mail activity in the left column of the Message Viewer window.
Connection Doctor		Opens a window that will check all the network connections used by Mail. This will help determine whether a network failure is on your end or on one of your mail servers. This will also help verify that all of your accounts are properly set up and working.
Bring All to Front		Brings all of Mail's open window to the foreground of the desktop.

Following these Window menu items, there will be a list of your currently open windows to choose from, which will vary depending on how many or what kind of windows you have open in Mail.

> **NOTE** The Help menu contains fairly standard help items for using Mail, so it isn't covered in this table.

Adding Mail Accounts

The easiest and most effective way to add a new e-mail account is to use the File ➤ Add Account menu option that will walk you through adding a new e-mail account step by step. You can also access this account setup walk-through when you add an account from the Accounts tab in Mail's System Preferences. The information you'll need to know varies with the type of account and the mail service you use.

The first bit of information you will need to know for all e-mail accounts is your e-mail address and your password (Figure 11-2).

Depending on your account, your name, e-mail address, and password may be all you need. New in Leopard, Mail will autoconfigure a number of accounts from popular ISPs and e-mail service providers, including .Mac, Gmail, Yahoo, Earthlink, and more. If you get the option to automatically set up an account, select the option, and let Mail do the rest.

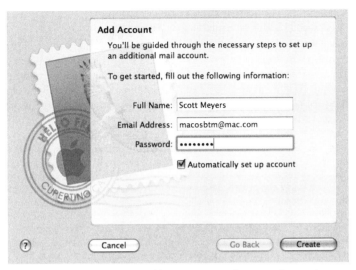

Figure 11-2. The first step in adding a new e-mail account is entering your name, e-mail address, and password.

If your account isn't automatically set up, then you'll need some more information to set up both your incoming and outgoing mail servers. To configure your incoming server (the one you receive your e-mail from), you'll need to know the following information (Figure 11-3):

- The type of server or protocol you are using: POP, IMAP, or Exchange.
- The address of your incoming mail server.
- If you are configuring an Exchange server, you'll also be asked for the address of the Outlook Web Access Server.
- You are also asked for a description, which is the name by which this account will be referred to in Mail.

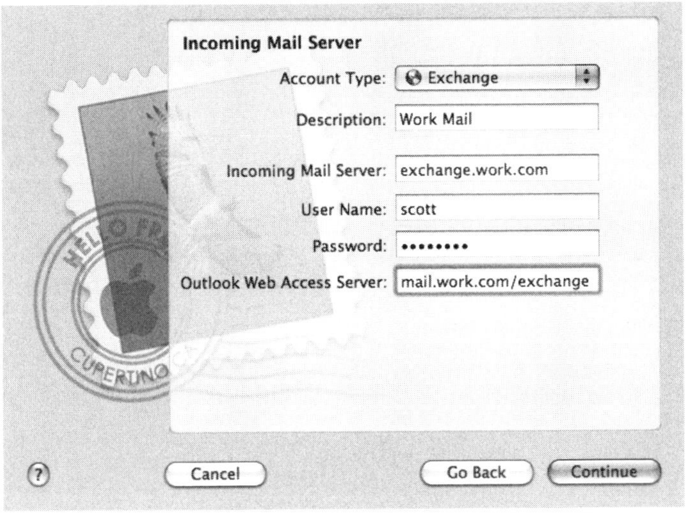

Figure 11-3. Initial configuration of incoming mail server

Once you've entered all your information and hit the Continue button, Mail will try to connect to the server and determine the best means of connecting to it. If this fails, then you will get a pop-up message warning you that Mail was unable to connect to the mail server. This usually means something was entered incorrectly or perhaps the mail server is down or not accepting connections. If you are sure everything is correct, you can click Continue again to move on.

At this point, depending on what happened when Mail contacted your incoming server, you may or may not be prompted to select your security settings. If you are, you should enter them here. We strongly encourage you to select SSL encryption.

> **NOTE** SSL encryption encrypts the data being passed between your computer and the server at the other end. Some services for whatever reason don't accept SSL encryption (or any other encryption) for e-mail. If this is the case, we strongly urge you to find another e-mail provider and *not* use the account lacking encryption. Checking your e-mail over an unencrypted connection and sending your username and e-mail address across the Internet in easy-to-read plain text for all, with a little know-how, to see is very, very bad. If you don't want to fork over money for a .Mac account or some other e-mail provider service that offers good, secure e-mail, you can always get a free, permanent, secure Gmail account at www.gmail.com (which may redirect you to Google—it's OK, Gmail is synonymous with Google Mail), so you have no excuses.

The next step is selecting your outgoing mail server for this account (Figure 11-4). Here you can either choose an existing outgoing mail server (one from an existing account) to use when sending mail from this account or enter the details of a new one. Usually you will want to enter the outgoing account information associated with the account you are setting up.

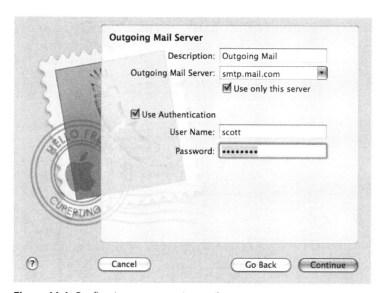

Figure 11-4. Configuring your outgoing mail server

NOTE Almost all outgoing servers will be Simple Mail Transfer Protocol (SMTP) servers. SMTP is what makes e-mail work by moving your message from SMTP server to SMTP server until your message reaches its destination. Unfortunately, as the name implies, it is very simple and very old. It was written for a day long ago when the Internet, and e-mail, was used mainly by educational, government, and research institutions. Spam wasn't a problem. Today, most SMTP servers have evolved to provide some checks in an attempt to limit spam, but the fundamental design of SMTP is to accept and route all e-mail as quickly and effortlessly as possible. As such, spam gets through. This presents some issues for nonspammers (well spammers too, but we don't care about issues they have). Certain public Internet connections routinely block SMTP traffic, so if you find yourself attempting to send an e-mail from a public place or even from work or a hotel room, you may find it doesn't work. In some cases, there is a special SMTP server you can gain access to (Mail will present you with the opportunity to change or add an SMTP server when it fails to connect to the default SMTP server tied with a particular account); other times, it's just not going to work. About the only real solution I've found in some of these situations is to send my message through a web mail interface.

Just like when you configure your incoming account, when you enter new outgoing account information, Mail will attempt to contact the server to acquire additional information about the server and to verify the connection when you click the Continue button. If Mail can't connect to the server, you will get a warning asking whether you'd like to continue. After you click Continue, you may or may not get the Security Options screen to set up a secure connection for outgoing mail. Unlike incoming mail, a secure connection is recommended only if your SMTP server requires authentication. You really want to keep your authentication encrypted. As for your message, it's going to eventually be passed around from SMTP server to SMTP server with no encryption anyway.

NOTE If you want to encrypt a mail message, a number of utilities can allow this, each with its own pros and cons. One of the most popular is Pretty Good Privacy (PGP) encryption. This is a public key encryption system that is widely distributed. In this system, each user has a private key and a public key. Any information encrypted using the public key can be decrypted using only the private key. Commercial versions (www.pgp.com) and open source variations based on OpenPGP are available.

Upon completion of entering your outgoing mail information, you will be presented with a summary of your new account information (Figure 11-5). If everything is correct, hit the Create button to create your new account.

Figure 11-5. Preview your e-mail account information, and hit Create to create your new account.

Receiving and Managing E-mail

Receiving, reading, and managing e-mail messages are the main tasks that most people are occupied with when using their mail clients. Mail provides some nice features for this whether you deal with a few messages from a single account every day or you deal with hundreds from multiple accounts.

Checking and Reading New E-mail

Mail is set up, by default, to automatically check for new e-mail in each of your active, online accounts every five minutes. This interval is adjustable on the General tab of Mail's System Preferences (Figure 11-6) from the "Check for new mail" drop-down list. Of course, you are always free to manually check your e-mail by clicking the Get Mail button in Mail's toolbar or by using one of the Get Mail options in the Mailbox menu.

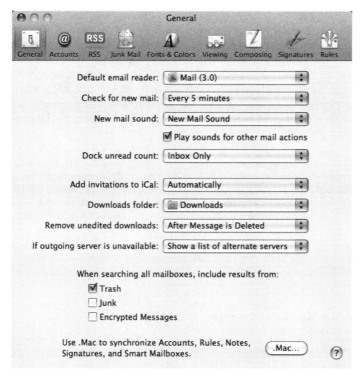

Figure 11-6. The General tab of Mail's preferences

By default, when Mail discovers new messages for one of your accounts, the new messages are downloaded into the Inbox associated with the account, and the "new mail" sound will play, notifying you of new mail. Additionally, the number of unread messages in your Inbox will appear on the Mail icon in the Dock (known as *badging*), as well as next to your Inbox. Unread messages in the message list area of the Message Viewer window will be flagged with a small blue dot that will go away when you select the message to read.

> **NOTE** In the Mailboxes area along the left side of Mail's Message View window, Mail provides a single Inbox that will expand into separate Inbox folders for each account. This allows you to view your messages from different accounts either together by selecting the Inbox item or separately by account by selecting one of the subitems under Inbox.

When you select a message, its contents will appear below the message list area in the message view area of the Message Viewer window. You can scroll through it there, or if you double-click the message item in the message list area, the message will open in a separate window.

Dealing with Junk E-mail

Mail has a built-in system to help you identify and deal with junk mail, or *spam*. This system is actually quite genius and can be trained to be as accurate as any spam/junk filter out there. The key point is that it must be trained. By default, Mail's junk filter is pretty average as far as filters go, but as you mark missed messages as Junk and mislabeled good mail as Not Junk, Mail will learn over a fairly rapid period of time what you consider to be junk and what you don't.

Most of the configurable options regarding how junk mail works are contained on the Junk Mail tab of Mail's preferences (Figure 11-7).

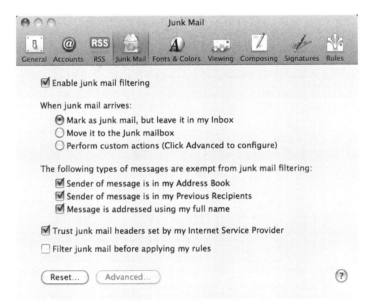

Figure 11-7. The Junk Mail tab provides options regarding how Mail deals with mail it considers to be spam.

The first option on the Junk Mail preferences tab is to enable junk mail filtering. Below that are options for what Mail should do with e-mail it considers junk. The "Mark as junk mail, but leave it in my Inbox" option is the best choice when you are first training Mail as to what you consider junk and what you don't. When you think Mail is identifying junk mail at a good rate, you can alter this setting. The "Move it to the Junk mailbox" option will create a new mailbox called Junk where, when this option is activated, Mail will store junk mail rather than your Inbox. The final option, "Perform custom actions," will allow you to set up a custom mail rule for dealing with junk mail when you click the Advanced button. We cover setting up mail rules in the "Creating Mail Rules" section.

> **NOTE** The Erase Junk Mail menu item in both the Mailbox menu and the contextual menu available from the mailbox area of the Message View window will cause any messages stored in your Junk mailbox to be immediately deleted—not stored in the trash, but gone. This is both a handy way to rid yourself of trash and an easy way to accidentally rid yourself of an important message that was flagged as Junk by mistake.

Next you can choose certain criteria for messages that should never be marked as Junk. You can exempt mail from people in your Address Book, people in your Previous Recipients list, or e-mail that is addressed using your full name. Exempting people listed in your Address Book and Previous Recipients list is usually safe; however, we find that for whatever reason lots of junk mailers tend to know our full names, so this option is bit more questionable.

The "Trust junk mail headers set by my Internet Service Provider" option allows Mail to look at certain e-mail headers that are commonly used by ISPs and mail servers to rate the probability that a message is junk. The results of using this option are mixed depending on your mail server.

> **NOTE** We leave this option checked since it covers all our accounts; however, one of our primary e-mail accounts has its own junk mail quarantine, and we find that when we release a message from this quarantine, Mail will flag it as Junk when it hits the Inbox since the headers identifying it as Junk on the mail server are still intact.

The "Filter junk mail before applying rules" option will identify mail as junk before looking at any other rules. This option could prevent rules from running on messages that Mail considers junk. If this option in unchecked, then, unless you specify a custom junk mail action, the junk filter will work after your mail rules are run, thus allowing them to affect all messages.

The Reset button will reset all of your junk mail options and reset all the junk mail training you have done.

Creating Mailboxes and Folders to Store E-mails

Besides your Inbox and other special-purpose mailboxes and folders that Mail creates for you, it's likely you'll want to create your own to organize any saved messages, as well as notes you store in Mail.

> **NOTE** In Mail, folders are synonymous with mailboxes. Mailboxes you create will actually appear as folders, and although you can store both mail and notes in them, they are still generally called *mailboxes* in Mail.

To create a new mailbox, simply select Mailbox ➤ New Mailbox from the menu bar or select New Mailbox from the menu that appears when you click the + button in the lower left of the Message View window. This will open a dialog box with a text field to enter the name of your new mailbox and a drop-down list for you to choose where you want the mailbox to be created. In general, new mailboxes are stored On My Mac (that being your Mac), which means they are kept locally. If you have access to an IMAP mail account (which includes .Mac as well as any Exchange servers you have added), then you can also create folders on the remote mail server this way (since IMAP stores your mail remotely). This will make those mailboxes and the items stored within them accessible from any computer you have set up to access that account.

Once you create mailboxes, if you want to change its location, you can by selecting and dragging the mailbox where you'd like it. To further add to the flexibility, mailboxes can be nested (that is, mailboxes can reside in other mailboxes).

In addition to your standard mailboxes, you can also create smart mailboxes in Mail that will dynamically contain messages based on the rules you define for your smart mailbox. Setting up a smart mailbox in Mail is similar to setting up a smart folder in the Finder. It's good to know that like smart folders, messages added to smart mailboxes aren't moved there; the message will still remain in its regular mailbox as well.

Creating Mail Rules

Mail rules can help you deal with large amounts of e-mail by automatically performing tasks on individual messages that meet certain specified criteria. To view your rules, go to the Rules tab in Mail's preferences (Figure 11-8).

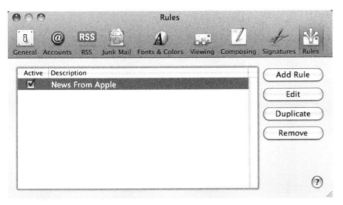

Figure 11-8. The Rules tab shows you your existing rules and allows you to edit them or create new ones.

The Rules preference tab allows you to view your existing rules, activate or deactivate each of them, and reorder them. There are also four buttons that allow you to create new rules (Add Rule), edit an existing rule (Edit), create a copy of a rule as a starting point for a new rule (Duplicate), or delete a rule (Remove).

The activated rules will be applied in the order they are listed on either each new message as it arrives or on selected messages when the Message ➤ Apply Rules (Opt+Cmd+L) is applied. The order of the rules is significant since the last-run rule will have precedence over previously applied rules. Additionally, each rule has the option of preventing further rules from being executed. To reorder your rules, simply drag them in the order in which you want them executed.

> **NOTE** Rules are generally applied to mail in a certain folder, so if one of your rules happens to move a message into a different folder, the following rules will not be processed for that message.

To create a new rule, click the Add Rule button, and a sheet will open for you to begin creating the rule (Figure 11-9).

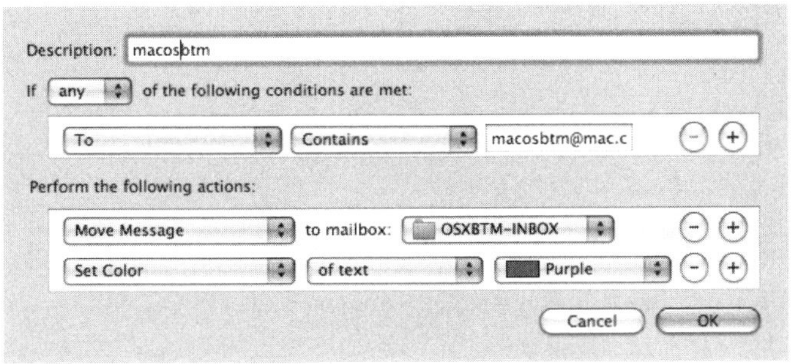

Description: | macosbtm |

If [any ▼] of the following conditions are met:

[To ▼] [Contains ▼] [macosbtm@mac.c] ⊖ ⊕

Perform the following actions:

[Move Message ▼] to mailbox: [OSXBTM–INBOX ▼] ⊖ ⊕
[Set Color ▼] [of text ▼] [■ Purple ▼] ⊖ ⊕

[Cancel] [OK]

Figure 11-9. The rule sheet allows you to fill in your rule's criteria for new rules or allows you to edit existing rules.

A rule has three parts: the description (or name), the conditions when the rule's actions are applied, and the actions that will occur when the conditions are met.

The description can be any name you want to use to identify the rule.

You can set the conditions so that the actions will trigger when any of the conditions are met or all of the conditions are met. To add a condition, click the + button next to any existing condition, and a new blank condition will appear below. To remove a condition, click the - button next to the condition you want to remove.

You can add and remove actions the same way as adding and removing conditions (the + and - buttons). Some special actions available are Run AppleScript, which will allow you to run any AppleScript, making the possibilities of what you can do here rather immense, and "Stop evaluating rules," which will immediately halt running all further rules for the current message.

Adding iCal Events from Mail

Often people will e-mail you important dates that you want to add to one of your iCal calendars. Mail makes this easy.

You can receive an event in two ways. First, if the event is sent to you as an iCal event attachment, just double-click the attachment, and iCal will open the event and ask you which of your calendars you'd like to add the event to.

More interesting, though, is that Mail can now recognize dates in the text of a message. If you hold your mouse over a date listed in a message, the date will become outlined and act as a small drop-down menu allowing you to add the date to iCal (Figure 11-10).

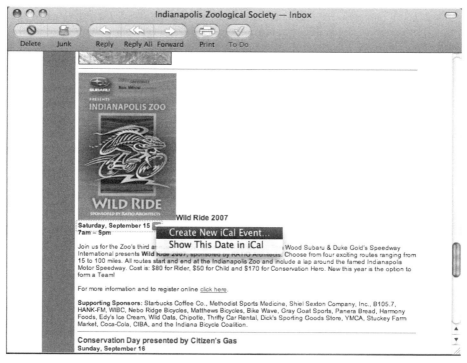

Figure 11-10. You can click any date in a message's text to add a new iCal event.

When you select Create New iCal Event, a small pop-up sheet will appear for you to fill in the details of the event (Mail will try to fill in some information based on the information it can get from the message), as shown in Figure 11-11.

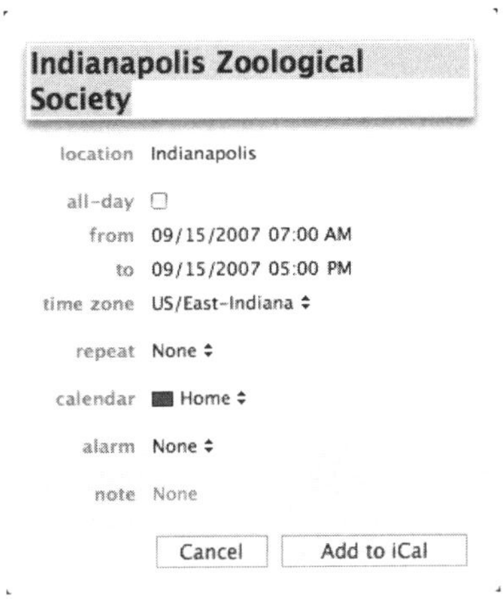

Indianapolis Zoological Society

location	Indianapolis
all-day	☐
from	09/15/2007 07:00 AM
to	09/15/2007 05:00 PM
time zone	US/East-Indiana ⬍
repeat	None ⬍
calendar	■ Home ⬍
alarm	None ⬍
note	None

Cancel   Add to iCal

Figure 11-11. Mail will open a sheet allowing you to fill in the details of your new event.

When the details are correct, click Add to iCal, and your new event will be added.

Sending E-mail

Sending e-mail is a pretty straightforward task: you create a new message; type your recipients, subject, and message; and hit Send. Mail in Leopard adds some new (for Mail) possibilities to your messages, though, such as the ability to use stationery to apply a theme to your message.

Creating a New Message

To start a new message, select File ➤ New Message (Cmd+N) from the menu bar, or click the New Message button on Mail's toolbar. This will open a blank New Message window (Figure 11-12).

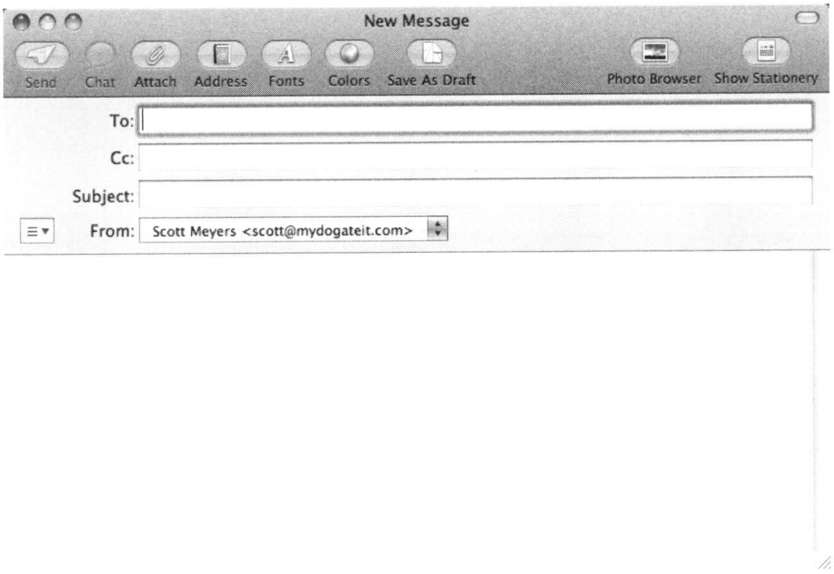

Figure 11-12. Mail's New Message window

To start, you must first fill in the To and Cc (and/or Bcc) fields with the names of your recipients and fill in the Subject field with the subject of the message.

> **NOTE** The To field is traditionally for the primary recipients of a message. The Cc (which stands for *carbon copy*) field is for including anyone else you want to "keep in the loop." The Bcc field (which stands for *blind carbon copy*) is where you can add recipients that will be unknown to all other recipients including other Bcc recipients.

> **NOTE** By default, certain fields including Bcc, Reply-To, and Priority are hidden. The small drop-down menu to the left of the From field will allow you to reveal these fields as well as any other header information you'd like to add (via the Customize option).

As you fill in recipient information, Mail will attempt to autocomplete the names or address you are typing using information from your Previous Recipients list and Address Book. If you enter a name in the one of these fields that Address Book has multiple e-mail addresses for, you can click the name to select which e-mail address(es) you'd like to use. Additionally, if you click the Address button in the New Messages toolbar, you will get a list of all the names and e-mail addresses contained in your Address Book.

The From field allows you to select from which of your accounts you'd like the message to be sent. The initial account listed will be the one belonging to your default e-mail address listed in the My Card Address Book information. By default, the address used will be the one belonging to the last-viewed mailbox, which has the effect of ensuring that any message you reply to will come from the account to which it was sent. You can alter this behavior in the Composing section of Mail's System Preferences.

After you have filled in the required fields, you can start typing your message in the large text area. By default, the message text will be formatted using rich text (which in Mail is HTML). This allows you to style your text using different font styles, colors, and sizes (accessible from the Fonts and Colors buttons on the toolbar or from the various options in the Format menu bar's submenus). Additionally, you may include inline images in your message.

To add an image to your message, you can drag and drop the image file from the Finder into your message, or you can use the Photo Browser built into Mail to browse your iPhoto library for an image to insert.

To add an attachment to your message, you can drag and drop the file in your message, or you can select the files you want to be attached from the dialog that appears when you click the Attach button on the toolbar (or you can select File ➤ Attach File... or press Shift+Cmd+A).

> **NOTE** There is a preference to use Windows-friendly attachments. This option is selected by default, and it is likely that you will want to keep it selected unless you are 100 percent sure the person you are sending an attachment to is using a Mac.

When you are done with your message and are ready to send it, just click the Send button in the toolbar, or select Message ➤ Send (Shift+Cmd+D) from the menu bar, and your message will be sent using the outgoing server set up for the chosen account.

If for some reason your outgoing mail server is unreachable, Mail will prompt you to either try again later or try sending the message using one of the other outgoing mail servers you have set up for other accounts. If you want to try again later (maybe you have limited Internet access or SMTP is being blocked), the message will be saved, and Mail will attempt to send the message later.

If you are working on a message and you aren't ready to send it, when you close the message, Mail will ask you whether you'd like to save the message as a draft. If you select Yes, the message will be saved in your Drafts mailbox (if one doesn't exist, it will be created). You can select the message from your Drafts mailbox later to finish and send it or delete it.

Using Mail Stationery

The Mail application in Leopard adds the ability to apply themes to your e-mail messages using what Apple calls *stationery*. When you are creating a new message in Mail, if you click the Show Stationery button on the toolbar, a special area will slide open between the header fields and the message text to reveal a selection of stationery.

As you select a specific stationery, the stationery will be previewed in the message area. Usually stationery consists of a background, image area, and text area. The text area is where you type your message. In general, the photo areas are meant to be replaced with your own images. To replace the placeholder image with your own image, just drag a new image from the Finder or the Photo Browser into the image area, and the placeholder image will immediately be replaced with your chosen image. Besides the images, some of the backgrounds (such as Birthday Daises) have different options that are available by clicking the background.

> **NOTE** Stationery items are really just bundles of specially formatted HTML documents and images. Therefore, it's possible to create your own. However, the exact process of packaging them is a bit complex. Mail does allow you to save new messages as stationery so that you can use them as the basis for future messages.

Replying To and Forwarding a Message

Besides creating a new message from scratch, you can also send mail by replying to or forwarding existing messages. The primary difference between a reply and a forward is that a *reply* will be, by default, directed to the initial sender (and other original recipients if you choose Reply All), where when you *forward* a message, it is usually addressed to someone not part of the initial e-mail thread.

When you reply or forward a message, the original message is usually included (or quoted) in the reply. The original message(s) are usually indented and formatted in a special way (formatted as quoted text), leaving room at the top of the message for you to add your own text to the e-mail thread.

> **NOTE** When you *redirect* a message, you are not adding to or continuing the thread so much as you are just passing the message on to someone else as you received it.

Creating Notes and To Dos

New in Leopard, Mail has the ability to store notes and To Dos. Notes are a fantastic way to keep track of just about anything and can be stored right alongside your mail in any mailbox. To Dos, on the other hand, are a bit more restrained and exist only in the To Do "mailboxes" in your Reminders area. The neat thing about the To Do list in Mail is that it is the same To Do list used in iCal, so you can create a To Do item in Mail and view it in iCal, and vice versa.

To create a new note, just click the Note button on the Messages View toolbar, or select File ➤ New Note (Ctrl+Cmd+N) from Mail's menu bar. This will open a New Note window (Figure 11-13), which is ready for you to start entering your information.

One super-nice feature is that notes can contain any images or attachments; additionally, you can add To Do items to individual notes (which will then appear in Mail's To Do list and in iCal's To Do list). Once you have completed your note, hit the Done button or save it by selecting File ➤ Save (or pressing Cmd+S). The name of the note that will appear is the first line of your note.

Each saved note is an individual item that can be moved into any other mailbox. You can even drag copies of your note from Mail into the Finder.

To create a new To Do item, click the To Do button on the toolbar, or select File ➤ New To Do (Opt+Cmd+Y). This will create a new item in your To Do list and ask you for the title, due date, priority, calendar, and whether you want to set an alarm for it (pretty much the same information you are asked in iCal).

> **NOTE** Interestingly, by default the keyboard command to create a new To Do item in Mail (Opt+Cmd+Y) is different from the keyboard shortcut in iCal (Cmd+K). This is rarity in the Mac world, and it wouldn't be surprising if in the future one of these changes so they are the same.

Reading RSS Feeds in Mail

Another new feature in the latest version of Mail is the ability to subscribe to an RSS feed in Mail. If you set your default RSS reader to Mail (either in Mail or in Safari's RSS preferences), then whenever you select an RSS link, you will be prompted to add the news feed in Mail. Otherwise, you can use options in Safari to subscribe to a feed in Mail or add the URL of an RSS feed in the dialog box that appears when you select File ➤ Add RSS Feeds… in Mail's menu bar.

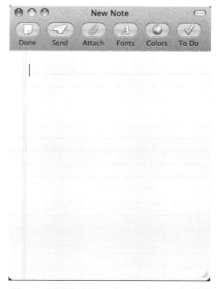

Figure 11-13. A New Note window in Mail waiting for information

When you initially subscribe to an RSS feed in Mail, it will appear in the RSS area in the Mailbox column; however, when you select a feed, an arrow will appear to the right of it that will bump the feed up to your Inbox. This will not only add new RSS items to your Inbox but will also notify you when new RSS items are downloaded.

In general, feed items appear and behave as messages, while feeds behave as individual mailboxes. You can even sort your feeds into separate mailboxes to help keep them organized (and read many feeds at once).

If you want to unsubscribe to a feed, you can select Mailbox ➤ Delete Feed… from the menu bar (or Delete Feed from the feed's contextual menu), which will delete the feed and remove any items.

Address Book

Address Book (Figure 11-14) is Mac OS X's primary tool for managing contact information. It allows you to add contact information about individuals and organizations, create groups, and even access networked directory services.

The Address Book in Leopard provides a three-column view by default (but also has a view that contains just the address card). The Group column is where you can create groups to contain multiple contacts, the second column contains the names of individual contacts, and the last area contains the address card for the selected individual.

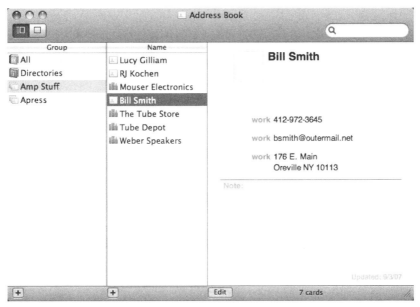

Figure 11-14. Leopard's Address Book

Adding and Editing Contacts

You can get new contacts into your Address Book in a few ways. One way is to simply import them from another device or file. The other way is to manually enter them.

You can import contacts to Address Book by syncing your Address Book through .Mac, Exchange, or Yahoo or by using iSync to sync Address Book to a mobile device. Syncing through .Mac, Exchange, or Yahoo can be configured from within the General tab of Address Book's preferences.

You can also import contacts from various files including vCards (which are a standard way of sharing contact information among many contact management clients), LDIF files (which are a standard format for exchanging LDAP data), or even comma-separated value (CSV) or tab-delimited text files. Finally, you can also import contact data from Address Book archive files. Any of these can be imported using the File ➤ Import submenu on the menu bar; additionally, you can drag vCard files into Address Book to import them or simply double-click them in the Finder, provided that Address Book is the default application for dealing with vCards. (Additionally, if you drag a contact from Address Book, it will be exported as a vCard.)

If you need to add a new contact from scratch, either click the + button at the bottom of the Name column, select the File ➤ New Card menu, or press Cmd+N. This will create a new empty contact card ready to edit in the card view area (Figure 11-15).

> **NOTE** The card view area has two modes: an edit mode and a view mode. By default, Address Book opens with cards in view mode that will hide empty fields and restrict the editing of the contact fields (clicking a field name in view mode will generally open a menu with options pertaining to the type of field it represents). Address Book will switch to edit mode when you create a new contact. In edit mode, clicking a field will select it for editing; additionally, all default template fields will be visible even if they are empty, and you will be able to add new fields. To toggle between the modes, click the Edit button beneath the card view area.

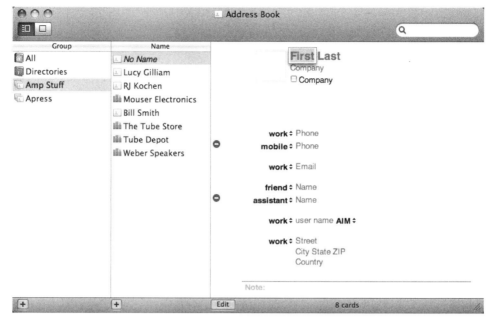

Figure 11-15. Address Book with a new contact card waiting to be filled in

When the new card is created, it will reveal all the fields set up in the template. To fill in a field, simply click the grayed-out text describing the field, and type the proper information. Most fields include a drop-down list (or lists) that describes the nature of the field, generally whether the information is associated with home or work and other descriptive information that can help differentiate between similar information. Additionally, in edit mode many fields will be preceded with a red - and or green + field, which will allow you to add or remove fields of similar data. For example, if you fill in all the e-mail address fields available, you can click the + button to the left of the last e-mail field to add a blank e-mail field below the last one.

If you are looking for a specific field that is currently not listed in the card, you can add a number of fields from the Card ➤ Add Field menu. This includes fields such as birthdays and other dates (which can be added to iCal) and other common contact fields.

If you find you are consistently adding information fields that are available but aren't listed in the default contact card template, then you can change the card template on the Template tab of Address Book's preferences.

If you'd like to associate an image with a contact, you can drag an image into the image field of a contact (the gray shadow of a head next to the name).

If the contact is primarily a business or organization, selecting the Company option will list the company name in the Name column rather than the person's name associated with the card (if there is one).

Learning About My Card

One special card in the Address Book is the card that represents you and your information. This information is used for all sorts of things in the system and various applications, so it's good to keep it up-to-date. If you'd like to set a different card, for whatever reason, as My Card, you can use the Card ➤ Make This My Card option in the menu bar.

Creating Groups

You might want to create contact groups for several reasons: to create mailing lists, to make it easier to find particular contacts, or to just keep things organized. To create a group, just click the + button beneath the Group column, and a new group will be created. To add contacts to the group, you can drag existing contacts from the Name column to the group item in the Group column, or you can create new contacts from within the group.

Once the group is created, you can right-click the group name to export the vCards of the group, send an e-mail to each member of the group, or edit the group distribution list, which will determine which e-mail addresses are used when you send a group e-mail.

Sharing Contacts

Address Book allows you to share your contacts with specific people through .Mac. To enable this feature, you must turn on sharing on the Sharing tab of Address Book's preferences, and then you must select which other .Mac member you are allowing to view (and optionally edit) your contacts.

Viewing Shared Contact Lists

If you have permission to view a shared Address Book through .Mac, select File ➤ Subscribe to Address Book from the menu bar, and then enter the .Mac member information of the person whose Address Book you'd like to share. If you have permission to view these contacts, then they will show up as a group in your Address Book.

Besides .Mac address sharing, Address Book can also display contact information being shared through LDAP or any network directory service to which your computer has access. If you have access to an LDAP server, you can fill in the appropriate information on the LDAP tab of Address Book's preferences. To configure other directory services, you will need to use the Directory Utility in the Applications/Utilities folder. Any of these resources will appear under the Directories item listed in the Group column.

> **NOTE** Names for directory services will appear only in response to a search string, occasionally a very specific search string. Ideally, if you find you need to contact certain people listed in a directory service often, drag their information from the directory service section into a group or the All item to add that person to your local Address Book. If you really must browse a directory that you have access to, you can use the Directory Utility application in the Applications/Utility folder.

Printing Labels and Envelopes

One nice hard-to-find feature of Address Book is the ability to print labels or envelopes for a specific contact or a group of contacts. To find this feature, select the contact or group you want to print labels or envelopes for, and then select File ➤ Print (Cmd+P) from the menu bar. Make sure to expand the Print dialog (Figure 11-16), and select Address Book from the Print Options menu. This will reveal a number of options to not only print labels and envelopes but also to print nicely formatted contact lists or small address book pages.

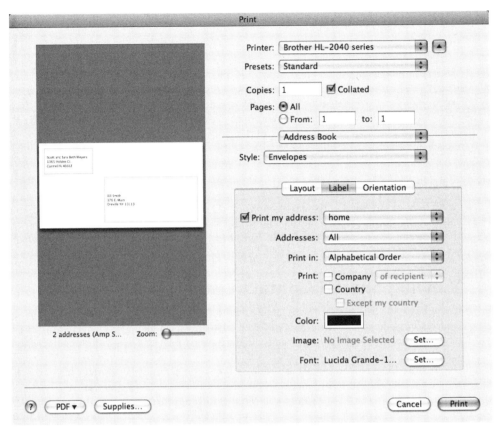

Figure 11-16. Address Book has print options that automatically print envelopes, labels, and contact lists.

iCal

Of all the updated applications in Leopard, iCal (Figure 11-17) has gone through some of the most significant interface changes. Though many are subtle, others significantly affect how you access and work with events in iCal.

The iCal interface has become extremely streamlined in Leopard while adding some nice new features. The iCal window by default has a simple toolbar that allows you to scroll forward and backward through time, change your calendar view, center the view on the current day, and search text in your calendar. The calendar view by default has a column on the left that contains your Calendar list at the top and a Mini Months calendar at the bottom, and to the right of the column is the main calendar view. At the bottom of the view area is a group of buttons below the Calendars list column that will add new calendars, toggle the Mini Months view, and toggle the Notifications view. In the lower-right corner is a button to toggle the To Do list, which, when visible, will appear as a column to the right of the main calendar view.

In the latest version of iCal, the information sidebar is gone; now event information will pop up when you double-click the event item in the calendar view. This pop-up window will reveal event details and let you edit the event information.

Figure 11-17. iCal in Leopard (Week view)

The view buttons in the toolbar (and the associated menu bar items) control the calendar view and whether it will display a single day, a week, or a whole month. The Day view (select View ➤ by Day or press Cmd+1) provides the most information, at a glance, about any events that are occurring that day, and if you have a very crowded calendar, it's about the only view that will help you make sense of it. In the Month view (select View ➤ by Month or press Cmd+3), there is limited space to provide much information about a single event, but it does give you a nice view of future and past dates (and makes scrolling to a future or past date much quicker, though the Mini Months calendar could serve this purpose as well). The Week view (select View ➤ by Week or press Cmd+2) provides a nice compromise between the two. In the end, you will likely find the view, or combination of views, that generally works best for how you work.

Adding Calendars to iCal

A nice feature of iCal is the ability to add and display multiple calendars at the same time within iCal. This feature is not only useful as a way to organize your events, but it also allows you to selectively share and view certain types of events.

By default, iCal starts you out with two sensible calendars: Home and Work. However, if you'd like to add another, simply click the + button below the Calendars List area, select File ➤ New Calendar (Opt+Cmd+N) from the menu bar, or select New Calendar from the contextual menu that appears when you right-click in the Calendar list. This will create a new calendar and highlight the name for editing. If you select Get Info from a calendar item's contextual menu, then you can add a description for that calendar and select a display color that all events associated with that calendar will appear in.

If you'd like, you can also organize calendars into calendar groups. To create a calendar group, select File ➤ New Calendar Group (Shift+Cmd+N) from the menu bar or New Group from the Calendar list area's contextual menu. Then you can drag individual calendars into that group.

Adding and Editing Events

You can add an event in a number of ways. Selecting File ➤ New Event (Cmd+N) will add a new event item to the selected date in the calendar, and in month view you can double-click a date or select New Event from the contextual menu. In any of those cases, you will likely need to double-click the event and edit it. In the Day or Week view, you can actually click and drag across a time frame to create a new event for that time.

> **NOTE** Initially, all events will be created in the calendar selected in the Calendar List area, like most other event properties, but this can be edited later.

Figure 11-18. Editing an iCal event

Once your event is created, it's likely you'll want to edit it. To edit an event, double-click it to open the Event Information pop-up, and click the Edit button to put the window into edit mode (Figure 11-18). The Edit window will allow you to change the date and times associated with an event, change the calendar the event is associated with, set an alarm to go off reminding you of the event, and make the event repeatable.

This mode will also allow you to tag the event as an All-Day event, which will list the event differently in the calendar view and allow the event to span multiple days.

Finally, you can add attachments, notes, and URLs to the event to help you keep associated files and information tied to the event.

When the event information is complete, just click Done.

If an event gets rescheduled or needs to be moved for any reason, rather than having to go into edit mode, you can change the date and time of the event by dragging the event from one time slot in the calendar to another.

Using To Dos

Besides events, iCal (now in tandem with Mail) also keeps track of To Do items. To view your To Do items in iCal, either click the button in the lower-right corner of the iCal window or select View ➤ Show To Do List (Opt+Cmd+T). This will open your To Do list along the right side of your calendar view. To Do items in iCal are essentially the same as they are in Mail (though the keyboard shortcut to create a new To Do item in iCal is different—Cmd+K).

Inviting Others to Events and Appointments

In an event's edit mode, there is also a section for adding attendees. By clicking here you can add any number of people you want to add as attendees for your event. Any attendees who are listed in your Address Book are automatically sent an invitation to the event.

> **NOTE** Attendees who you are inviting need to be in your Address Book for them to get an invite, so if an attendee isn't listed there, it's best to add the information to your Address Book before you send out the invite.

Adding Time Zone Support

iCal has a nice time zone support feature that is not activated by default, but if you often travel or deal with people in other time zones, then this is fantastic feature to use. Activating time zone support is as easy as selecting the "Turn on time zone support" option on the Advanced tab in iCal's preferences. Once the support is turned on, you will notice that a small time zone drop-down list will appear in the upper-right of iCal's main window above the search field. You can alter this field to reflect the time zone that iCal is in. Additionally, events will gain a time zone setting. With time zone support enabled, iCal will automatically alter event times based on the time zone of the event and the time zone of iCal.

Subscribing to Other Calendars

Sometimes you may want to subscribe to a calendar other than your own. For example, you may want to subscribe to a calendar that provides the schedule of your favorite baseball team's games, or you may want to subscribe to a calendar that contains all the common U.K. holidays.

Often, organizations will post calendar links on their web sites where you can just click a link and iCal will automatically open and add the calendar. Other times you may need to use the Calendar ➤ Subscribe (Opt+Cmd+S) menu bar option that will open the dialog box and allow you to enter the URL in the calendar file.

To get started, select the Calendar ➤ Find Shared Calendars option from the menu bar. This will open your web browser to an Apple web site were Apple makes available a number of common shared calendars (including MLB baseball schedules and U.K. holidays).

Sharing Your Calendars

Besides subscribing to other calendars, sometimes you may want to share one of your calendars. To enable other people to subscribe to your calendar, you must have access to .Mac or a Web-DAV server to publish your calendar. If you have access, then you select a calendar and select Calendar ➤ Publish from the menu bar. This will open a sheet asking for information about where and what you want to share. Once the calendar is shared, you can pass the URL to anyone who you want to view it.

Learning About iCal and CalDAV

There are lots of issues with sharing calendars, as outlined previously, but the biggest one is that it's a little too static; in other words, calendar information doesn't freely flow back and forth. Many calendaring systems avoid these issues, but most of them are fairly proprietary systems, so there are interoperability problems. To solve this, Apple and a number of other organizations have joined together to create the CalDAV standard, which provides a standard way to handle calendaring systems in a client/server environment.

In this system, calendars are stored on a central calendar server that makes everyone's schedules available to everyone else (with the security frameworks in place at the organization). The big advantage to this is that it facilitates scheduling and even planning in a much more effective manner.

It just so happens that iCal in Leopard supports CalDAV (and Leopard Server provides a nice CalDAV-based calendar server called iCal Server). If you have access to a CalDAV server, you need to set up the account information on the Accounts tab in iCal's preferences. This will add a calendar to iCal representing the calendar on the server.

Once this is all set up, then you can select Window ➤ Availability Panel to view the availability of other users of the calendar server. Using this makes scheduling meetings with a number of others a snap; in fact, iCal can use this to automatically find the next time that everyone is available for a meeting.

Summary

Mail, Address Book, and iCal have worked well at their respective tasks since their inception, but in Leopard they reach new levels of functionality and, more important, seamless integration. Next we'll cover Apple's instant message client, iChat, which is, in some circles, replacing e-mail as the Internet communication method of choice.

iChat

Instant messaging has been gaining popularity over the last few years as the Internet communication method of choice for many situations. iChat is Apple's default instant messaging client in Leopard and has lots to offer. First, it's compatible with AIM (AOL Instant Messenger) as well as Google Chat, two of the biggest instant messaging networks out there. Second, it adds lots of cool features that go beyond simple text chat, including voice and video chat. Finally, it's easy to use and well integrated with other Leopard applications. In this chapter we'll cover the following:

- Getting an iChat account
- Logging in with your account
- Adding and managing buddies
- Text chat and instant messaging
- Voice and video chat
- Using iChat with other programs
- Customizing iChat
- iChat Theater
- File Transfers

Getting and Setting Up an iChat Account

Since iChat supports various instant messaging (IM) services, there are many ways to get an account that will work with iChat. However, to be effective, the people you wish to chat with must be using the same service as you. While Google Chat is growing, AIM is still the number one IM service available, and it is also the service that .Mac utilizes, so chances are if you are using iChat, you'll want an AIM or .Mac account.

> **NOTE** If you already are, or ever have been, a .Mac member, or have had an AOL/AIM username, then you already have an IM account that will work fine with iChat.

To get an AIM account from AOL, you'll need to go to http://aim.com, select the Get a Screen Name option, and go through the registration on that site. Being a faithful Mac user, you may opt to get a .Mac account instead.

> **NOTE** There are two reasons to go the .Mac route instead of the AIM route. First, Leopard can take advantage of .Mac in many ways, and if you wish to take advantage of all these, you'll need a .Mac account anyway. Second, AOL has been around for a very long time, and all user-names must be unique, so you stand a much better chance of getting a username that doesn't resemble scdmeye27653 or some other unrecognizable mess if you go through .Mac, where there are likely more sensible screen names available.

To get a .Mac username, you just need to sign up for the .Mac trial (at http://mac.com). Even if you choose not to extend the .Mac trial offer, the name you choose when you register will still be valid indefinitely for iChat.

Once you have an account, go to the Accounts tab of iChat's preferences, as shown in Figure 12-1. Click the little + button beneath the Accounts column. This will open up a sheet for you to enter your account information, as shown in Figure 12-2.

On the Account Setup sheet, you first must pick your account type. This will either be .Mac Account, AIM Account, Jabber Account, or Google Talk Account. Below that, you will be asked for your username (Member Name, Account Name) and password. Additionally, if you are using a Jabber server, you will be prompted to enter the server information. The Get an iChat Account option will take you to the .Mac registration page in your web browser.

When you have entered the required information, click Done, and your new account will appear in the Accounts column of the Accounts tab in iChat's preferences.

> **NOTE** There is one other type of account that iChat can use that does not need to be configured—that's Bonjour. The Bonjour account will automatically use your Leopard account info to identify you and will find any other iChat users on your LAN who have their Bonjour account activated. Bonjour is a great way to IM people in your organization a few offices away, or one of your children upstairs in their room blaring music loudly with their door closed.

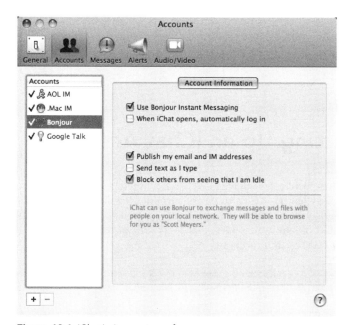

Figure 12-1. iChat's Accounts preferences

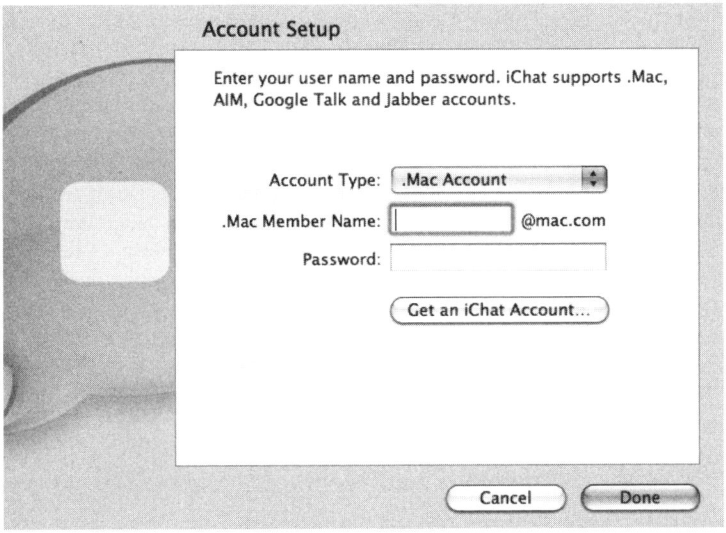

Account Setup

Enter your user name and password. iChat supports .Mac, AIM, Google Talk and Jabber accounts.

Account Type: [.Mac Account]

.Mac Member Name: [   ] @mac.com

Password: [   ]

(Get an iChat Account...)

(Cancel)   (Done)

Figure 12-2. The Account Setup sheet used to add new iChat accounts

Depending on the account type for each account listed in your Accounts column, there will be some additional configuration options. The key options you'll want to know about are the "Use this account" and "When iChat opens, automatically log in" options. "Use this account" enables the account and lists it the File ➤ Accounts submenu. The "When iChat opens, automatically log in" option is fairly obvious: when you launch iChat, iChat will automatically attempt to log in to the account.

Some accounts also have security options associated with them; these options generally enable you to restrict how other people view your status when you are online.

Logging In to Your iChat Account and Setting Your Status

Logging in to your iChat account(s) is a fairly easy process. Obviously, if you have selected the option to have your account automatically log in when iChat launches, then you really don't have anything to do. However, to manually log in and log out, all you have to do is toggle your account in the File ➤ Accounts submenu.

When you log in, an account window will open up that will allow you to access account IM features for that account and view your buddy list, as shown in Figure 12-3.

The top of the account window provides your account status. The top line will provide the name you have associated with the account, or your "handle" (which is another way of saying your screen name, or account name). You can toggle between the two by clicking the name/handle. To the left of your name is your online status: a green dot means

Figure 12-3. An iChat account window, with a buddy list

you are online and accepting IMs; a red dot means you are online, but you are not accepting incoming IMs; a faint gray circle means you are online, but are invisible (people can't see you are online); and no dot means you are offline.

Below the name is your online status message. Your status message and current online status will be visible to anyone (unless you limit the visibility of your status in the account's security preferences). To change your status or message, click the status message and select a new status from the pop-up menu. You can set a custom status message by selecting Custom Available... or Custom Away... from the menu, and then typing in anything you want. Selecting Edit Status Menu... will open a sheet where you can create, edit, or delete the status messages that appear in the pop-up, and change whether and how iChat remembers your custom status messages.

To the right of your name is your picture, also known as your buddy icon. Your initial picture is the same icon you have associated with your account and your contact info in Address Book. To change your picture, drop an image on the current picture, or click it to bring up a list of recent pictures. From the Recent Pictures sheet, you can also select Edit Picture... for more options, including taking a snapshot with iSight.

If you have audio or video chat enabled, a green audio or video icon will also be visible.

Adding and Managing Buddies

Each account maintains a buddy list to keep track of friends, family, and associates who have IM accounts. To add a buddy, click the + button at the bottom of your account window and select the Add Buddy... option or select Buddies ➤ Add Buddy... (Shift+Cmd+A) from the menu bar. This will open up a sheet for you to fill in information about your new buddy, as shown in Figure 12-4.

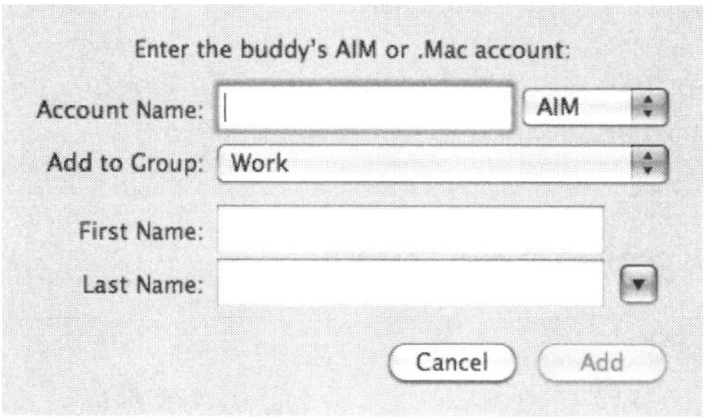

Figure 12-4. The Add Buddy sheet in iChat

Address Book is integrated with iChat. If your buddy is already listed in your address book, iChat will autocomplete the Add Buddy form as you type. Clicking the blue disclosure button to the right of the Last Name field will expand the sheet into a people picker. Selecting an Address Book card will associate it with that buddy. You can also drag contacts from Address Book into your buddy list to add them.

To help you keep track of your buddies, you can organize them into groups. To create a group, click the + button at the bottom of the account window and select the Add Group... option. A small sheet will open up and ask for the name of your new group. Enter the name and click Add to add the group. To change or delete groups, select the Edit Groups... option from the Account + menu.

When you add a buddy, you are asked what group you'd like them to be in. If you'd like to change the group, simply select and drag your buddy into a new group. If you'd like to rearrange the order in which your groups appear, grab their headers and drag them around.

In iChat's View menu, there are a number of options about how to display offline buddies. You can hide them, display them in their regular groups, or coalesce them into a special offline group.

The View menu also lets you choose whether to use groups at all; whether to display your audio or video status; whether to display buddies by full name, short name, or handle; and whether to sort buddies by name, availability, or not at all.

▌ **NOTE** For more options, see the "Customizing iChat" section, which follows.

Communicating with iChat

While iChat started as a fancier version of AOL's Instant Messenger client, it has evolved into a multi-protocol communication powerhouse. The traditional features are still there, but they are joined by advanced audio and video chat modes, and augmented by integration with other programs on the system. Right- or Cmd+clicking a name on your buddy list reveals a long list of options, each one representing a different method of communicating.

▌ **NOTE** In addition to the buddy list's contextual menu, you can also initiate communications with selected buddies from the Buddies menu on the menu bar, or by the menu items' associated keyboard shortcuts.

Text Chat

The first option is Invite to Chat... Selecting this opens a new chat window. Typing a message and pressing Return will cause a window to pop up on your selected buddies' screens inviting them to chat. If they accept, you will be able to type messages back and forth, forming a conversation, as shown in Figure 12-5.

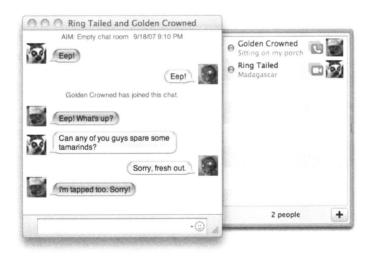

Figure 12-5. Multiple-participant chat room in iChat

The chat window displays your conversation as it happens, with the users' buddy icons and text balloons indicating who said what. To enter a message, just type your text in the text field at the bottom of the window. When someone is typing, a gray thought balloon will appear next to their buddy icon, so you know they're formulating a response and not just ignoring you.

That the chat option is first on the list suggests it's iChat's preferred method of communication. This is a not a coincidence, as the chat mode offers several conveniences over traditional IM.

Chats can involve more than two people. Selecting multiple buddies when initiating a chat will send invitations to everyone. Anyone who joins that chat will be able to participate in the conversation.

Chat mode uses a chat room metaphor, similar to Internet Relay Chat (IRC). That means people can be invited to join at any time and leave as they please. As long as one person remains in the chat room, the conversation will remain open.

Even if you're only talking to one person, chat is a still a good mode because you always have the option of inviting more people—more like a natural conversation. Imagine if you were in a coffee shop talking to a friend when another friend came in. How silly it would be to have to leave the coffee shop and come back for them to join you!

> **NOTE** You can chat without using your buddy list. To start a chat with someone who isn't on your buddy list, select File ➤ New Chat... (Cmd+N) from the menu bar and fill in the information in the pop-up dialog box. To join a chat room by name, select File ➤ Go to Chat Room... (Cmd+R) and type the name of the room. If a room by that name does not exist, it will be created.

Instant and Direct Messaging

Instant messaging is hardly a new invention. Indeed, it's limited person-to-person connection could be called a step backward, as it has more in common with the old UNIX `talk` command than with the sophisticated chat rooms of IRC. Still, what it lacks in features, IM makes up for in simplicity and ubiquity.

Figure 12-6. Direct messaging over Bonjour in iChat

In iChat, selecting Send Instant Message... or Send Direct Message... works almost identically to Invite to Chat...; in fact, the window will still say you are "chatting with" your buddy, as shown in Figure 12-6. Don't be fooled; IM has fewer options than a true chat. While you can hold multiple IM conversations, you can't have three or more people talking at a time, nor can you add participants as you can with a chat.

To add to the confusion, if you try to send an instant message to multiple buddies at once, you will actually start a chat session, even though your selected Send Instant Message..., not Invite to Chat...!

Direct messaging is identical to IM, with one subtle behind-the-scenes difference. Whereas IM uses a central server to route messages, direct messaging establishes a direct connection between two computers.

The main advantage of direct messaging is enhanced privacy, but IM has its own advantages. It's older and more common, so it's more likely to be understood by chat clients other than iChat. It's also less prone to interference from network settings and firewalls.

> **CAUTION** Direct messaging enhances privacy, but it cannot be considered secure, because it doesn't use encryption to protect the content of your messages. To read more about secure chatting, see the "Customizing iChat" section, which follows.

Ironically, the IM central server also provides an advantage over both direct messaging and chatting. Since instant messages are directed to a single person, the server can store them until that person logs on. Thus, you can send instant messages to people who are offline.

> **NOTE** Double-clicking names on your buddy list will always start a conversation, but the mode used depends on the situation. If multiple buddies are selected, double-clicking always launches a chat. If a single buddy is selected, double-clicking will start an IM session, unless you are communicating via Bonjour, in which case double-clicking will use direct messaging.

Audio and Video Chats

Like you, people in your buddy or chat participant lists with video chat enabled will display a camera icon. Clicking this icon will invite them to video chat and present you with a video preview window, giving you a last chance to get the spinach out of your teeth. If they accept, you will see a picture-in-a-picture video screen.

> **NOTE** If your buddies can only support audio chats, they will have a telephone icon. Clicking this icon will invite them to audio chat instead. If a buddy can't support either, they will not have an icon. If, however, they have an icon, but it's grayed out, that means they are already in a video chat.

As with text chat, video chat can support multi-way conferencing, as shown in Figure 12-7. Depending on the speed of your computer's processor, you can video chat with as many as three people simultaneously. Chat participants can be selected when you start the chat, or they can be invited late by pressing the + button.

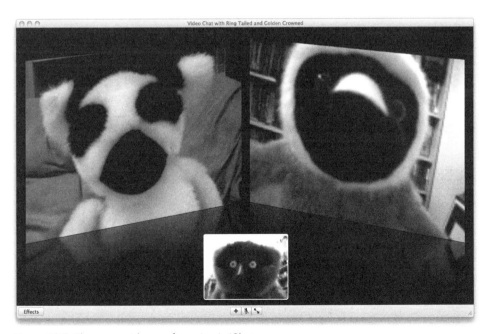

Figure 12-7. Three-way video conferencing in iChat

Adjacent to the + button is a mute button, which will disable the audio portion of the chat. To the right of the mute button is a button for going into full-screen mode. To the far left is the Effects button, which toggles a menu of real-time effects you can apply to your video, as shown in Figure 12-8.

The Video Effects window can also be summoned by selecting Video ➤ Show|Hide Video Effects (Shift+Cmd+R) from the menu bar. To select an effect, click it. To remove the effect, click the original effect in the middle of the page.

There are a few pages of effects, which you can navigate by using the arrow buttons on either side of the panel. There are also several blank spots on the last page where you can insert your own effects.

Figure 12-8. The Video Effects window in iChat

Background Effects

Video effects that have an outline of a person in them are background effects. If you select one, iChat will ask you to step out of the frame while it analyzes the background. It will then replace the background with full-motion video. When you step back into the frame, it will appear that you're standing in front of the new background, as shown in Figure 12-9.

Figure 12-9. The results of applying background effects in iChat

For best results, select an even, neutral background. A white wall works well. Make sure your clothes have sufficient contrast from the background (unless you *want* to look like a floating head). If you see spots where the background shows through, select Video ➤ Reset Background (Option+Cmd+R) from the menu bar and try again. It also helps if you don't move around too much.

All in all, the background effects are probably not going to convince your boss you're hard at work at the office while you sip margaritas on the beach, but it may certainly add a fun flare to your Friday meetings.

Variations on Video Chat

Clicking a buddy's video icon always launches video chat, even if all you want is audio chat. Fortunately, there are several other ways to launch audio and video chats, the most obvious of which is to select Invite to Video Chat or Invite to Audio Chat from the buddy list's contextual menu, or from the Buddies menu in the menu bar.

If a buddy does not have audio or video chatting enabled, these menu items will become Invite to One-Way Video Chat and Invite to One-Way Audio Chat. That means, for example, you can still originate a video chat with them, and they will be able to see you, but you won't be able to see them.

You can also click the telephone and camera buttons on the bottom of your buddy list to launch that type of chat with the selected buddies. Pressing the text button is equivalent to double-clicking; it will launch some kind of text-based communication, depending on context.

iChat also works with other AIM video chat clients, most notably AOL Instant Messenger for Windows, assuming the users have the appropriate hardware. At this time, however, AIM doesn't have a separate audio chat feature that works with iChat.

Mobile Text Messaging

Most mobile phones support text messaging via the Short Message Service protocol, also known as SMS, or simply "text messaging." iChat has two ways to participate in text messaging. First, you can send a text message to a buddy by selecting Send SMS... from the buddy list contextual menu, or Buddies ➤ Send SMS... from the menu bar.

In order for the Send SMS... command to be enabled, you must have a phone number set for your buddy in Address Book, and that number must be labeled as "mobile." If the number is labeled as anything else, including home, main, pager, or a custom label, it will not work in iChat.

Sending an SMS message will launch a chat window just like sending an instant message. If your buddy sends a response, it will show up in the chat window, as expected. If you have since closed the window, iChat will open a new one. However, this is not a true instant message, so if your buddy tries to respond after you've closed iChat or logged out, they will receive an error message.

Another way to communicate with iChat from your mobile phone is to enable mobile forwarding on your AIM account. This is done online, but you can get to the appropriate web page by clicking the Configure AIM Mobile Forwarding... button in iChat's account preferences. The process is simple; you enter your phone number and AOL sends a confirmation code to your phone. Enter the code on the activation page, and you're done.

With mobile forwarding enabled, you will never go offline. If anyone sends you an instant message, it will be converted to an SMS text message and sent to your phone. Your responses will be returned in the chat window, much like the Send SMS feature.

In iChat, buddies who are receiving their messages via mobile forwarding will have a gray "broadcasting" symbol next to their names, as shown in Figure 12-10. Their availability dot will be clear to light gray in color, and they will have the status message they had when they logged out.

Figure 12-10. A buddy using mobile forwarding in iChat

> **CAUTION** Most mobile plans limit the number of SMS text messages subscribers can send and receive, and some even charge a fee for each message. Keep this in mind before using mobile messaging features from iChat.

File Transfers

One nice feature of iChat is the ability to send a file to someone you are chatting with. If you'd like to send a file, select Buddies ➤ Send File... (Option+Cmd+F), which will open a file dialog to select the file you wish to send. Once the file is selected, the person you are sending the file to will get prompted to accept the file. When they accept, the download will begin. Likewise, if you are being sent a file, you will be prompted in your chat window to accept or decline the item. If you accept, the file will be downloaded to your system.

Figure 12-11. Pictures are usually rendered in place in iChat

You can also drag files from within the Finder to names in your buddy list, or into the input field of an open chat. Certain types of files, such as images and PDFs, will be rendered in place, as shown in Figure 12-11.

To save the image, drag it from the chat window to the Finder. If the image is large, it will be scaled down in the chat window; but when you drag it, you will save the original file as if you had just transferred it.

Since moving files around in iChat has become so common, Leopard adds a File Transfers window, much like the one found in Safari. This window contains a list of files, their transfer status, and a magnifying glass icon you can click to jump to the file in the Finder. The File Transfers window will launch automatically as needed, but you can also summon it from the menu bar by selecting Window ➤ File Transfers (Option+Cmd+L).

Screen Sharing

Screen sharing allows you to view and control another user's computer from a window on your own machine. It's a great way to show something to a friend, collaborate with a colleague, or provide technical support for a family member.

You can initiate screen sharing from within iChat by selecting Share My Screen... or Ask to Share Remote Screen... from the buddy list contextual menu or the Buddies menu bar item. You can also click the Screen Sharing button on your buddy list. That's the one on the right side that looks like one rectangle overlapping another.

Screen sharing is actually one of Leopard's Sharing networking features, so it's discussed in much more detail in Chapter 21.

> **NOTE** The Share My Screen... and Ask to Share Remote Screen... menu items will change to reflect the buddy you have selected, so don't be surprised if you actually have to click Share My Screen with Alice... or Ask to Share Bob's Screen....

Integrating with Mail

Mail and iChat represent two different ways of communicating that are nevertheless complementary. You might start writing an e-mail message and realize it would be better said over iChat. Or you might want to iChat someone, but they're not online.

For situations like these, iChat and Mail both make it easy to use the other. In iChat, selecting Send Email... from the buddy list context menu or the Buddy menu bar item will launch Mail with a new message to that buddy, assuming you have their e-mail address in Address Book.

If you are reading or composing mail to a buddy who is available in iChat, their name will display a green availability dot. Mail includes Reply With iChat among the options available from the message contextual menu, the menu bar, and an optional toolbar icon.

Advanced Status Messages

Despite their name and original purpose, iChat's status messages have become a handy way to announce things to your friends without having to specifically address them. Since status messages can't be too long, it's often handy to just set your status to a link, which your friends can follow if they want to know more.

In iChat, friends with URLs in their status messages will display a small gray circle with an arrow on it, as shown in Figure 12-12. Clicking the arrow will launch the URL in Safari. You can also launch the URL by selecting Open URL from the buddy list contextual menu.

Figure 12-12. A buddy with a URL status message in iChat

> **NOTE** If a buddy is selected, the Open URL menu item will change to reflect the name of the URL—so in the example in Figure 12-12, the menu item would actually read "Open http://savethelemur.org."

Another popular use for the status message is displaying the current song you're listening to in iTunes. You can set this to update automatically by selecting Current iTunes Song from the status message pop-up menu. If your buddy is taking advantage of this feature, their status message will have the same gray circle and arrow as with a URL, except clicking it will take you to that track in the iTunes Music Store.

> **NOTE** You might expect the Open URL menu item to take you to a buddy's home page, assuming it's listed in Address Book, but it does not. It also doesn't work with the Current iTunes Song feature.

Customizing iChat

There are a lot of options packed into iChat's Preference window. While you can certainly use iChat without going through the preferences, you'd be missing out on a lot of functionality. Here is a quick tour of what you can do from the various preference panels.

General

- Change the default IM application, allowing you to use iChat to facilitate not using iChat.
- Optionally show your iChat status in the menu bar by adding a miniature version of iChat to the menu bar as a menu bar extra, from which you can monitor and change your status, watch your buddy lists, and launch chats.
- Set options to auto-reply when you are away, which basically functions as an answering machine for iChat. You can let people know what you're doing, and they can continue chatting, effectively leaving you a message for when you get back.
- Set "Animate buddy pictures," which will restore one of the more polarizing features of AIM: the use of animated GIFs as buddy icons. This was absent for a long time in iChat, because a lot of people find them annoying.
- Automate your status changes, such as changing your status to "available" when you wake your computer from sleep, automatically logging out of iChat when you use Mac OS X's fast user-switching feature, and keeping IM accounts logged in even when iChat is closed.

Accounts

- Add and remove accounts, as well as activate and deactivate accounts without actually removing them from the list.
- Allow iChat to automatically log in to your accounts when you open iChat.
- Allow your account to be logged in to from multiple machines. If you log in to an account from a second machine (or session or client), AOL will prompt you to log out of the existing session remotely.
- Use a special "recent buddies" group to remember people who chat with you but are not in your buddy list.
- Configure mobile forwarding to receive instant messages on your phone, as discussed previously.
- Set privacy options, including the ability to block specific people, preventing them from seeing you online or sending you messages.
- Enable encrypted chats, so people cannot access private information by intercepting your chats. This option is only available with .Mac accounts.

Messages

- Change the color of your word balloons and the font used in your text chats. You can also override other people's word balloon and font choices.
- Set a keyboard shortcut to immediately bring iChat into focus, which is handy if you always keep iChat running in the background so people can get in touch with you. This is particularly useful combined with iChat's Dock icon, which will display a badge showing you the number of pending unread messages.
- Automatically save chat transcripts to a folder, which is handy if you need to remember things you talk about in your chats. This is discussed in more detail in the "Nifty iChat Features" section later in the chapter.

- Collect chats into a single window, also known as tabbed chatting. This is also discussed in more detail in the "Nifty iChat Features" section.
- Remember open chats when you close iChat, so you can pick up where you left off the next time you open iChat.
- Watch for your name in incoming messages, automatically highlighting your name in chats. This is quite useful if you hang out in a chat room where the conversation doesn't necessarily revolve around you.

Alerts

- Set custom alerts so you can keep watch on iChat when it's in the background without actually having to switch to it.
- Play sounds, use the speech synthesizer to make announcements, or bounce the Dock icon in response to specific events.
- Run AppleScripts, which means you can pretty much make your computer do anything in response to iChat events.

Audio/Video

- Preview your video window prior to starting a chat, or just use your computer as a really expensive mirror.
- Set the microphone you're using, or set up a Bluetooth headset for better sound quality and privacy during audio or video chats.
- Set a bandwidth limit to prevent performance problems on your network.

Nifty iChat Features

In addition to being a versatile chat client and communication center, iChat has several additional features to add utility and a bit of fun to your conversations.

iChat Theater

Leopard introduces iChat Theater, which lets you use iChat's video chat feature in conjunction with external applications. For example, you can give a Keynote presentation or present an iPhoto slideshow from within iChat, as shown in Figure 12-13.

The effect is not unlike starting a video chat and pointing the camera at the screen while running an application, except that the application feeds video directly to iChat, so neither you nor the person you are chatting with have to have a video camera in order to use iChat Theater. The application you share is your only video source.

My personal favorite use of iChat Theater is true to its name: watching a movie with my wife even though one of us is traveling. Depending on your network connection, your mileage may vary.

Figure 12-13. Sharing an iPhoto slideshow in iChat Theater

The one big caveat of iChat Theater is that applications you share have to implement the functionality. It's not something that comes for free. Fortunately, many of Apple's applications already work with iChat Theater, so you can get some use out of it while third-party developers catch up.

The easiest way to use iChat Theater is to select File ➤ Share a File With iChat Theater... from the menu bar. iChat does a pretty good job of parsing many files you'd like to share without having to invoke another application.

You can also enter iChat Theater from within other applications. For example, in Keynote, you can select View ➤ Play in iChat Theater from the menu bar. This will present the current presentation in iChat Theater.

Tabbed Chat

The nice thing about iChat vs. the telephone is that you don't have any awkward silences. If you don't have anything to say, you can just not type anything. Then, if something comes to mind, you can send it along and it will be appended to the conversation as if no time had passed (except, of course, for the telltale timestamp).

That means you can have several chats happening at once, potentially causing a lot of clutter, and making it difficult to know which window needs your attention. Leopard introduces tabbed chats, which collect all your chat windows into one, as shown in Figure 12-14.

The tabs are actually a list of chats, not unlike a buddy list. If someone has something to say, a miniature word bubble will appear, making it clear which tab needs your attention. To switch chats, just click the appropriate tab.

Figure 12-14. Tabbed chat helps you manage multiple conversations.

Saving Your Chats

Another advantage iChat has over the telephone is the ability to save your chats. If someone gives you a to-do list, or you have a late night trans-Atlantic brainstorming session with your colleagues in Amsterdam, you can save the chat by selecting File ➤ Save a Copy As (Cmd+S) from the menu bar.

Alternately, if you have a really bad memory and you just want to automatically save all chats, you can set this in the preferences.

To open a chat, just select File ➤ Open... (Cmd+O) from the menu bar and navigate to the saved file, or, if it happened recently, find it in the File ➤ Recent Items submenu.

Smileys

One of the biggest problems with text chat is that you can't convey emotions. The best accepted solution to this problem was invented in 1982 by a computer scientist at Carnegie Mellon University named Scott Fahlman. His simple proposal, known today as "smileys," or "emoticons," are small text drawings representing facial expressions. For example, a statement meant to be taken as tongue-in-cheek can be followed by a smiley face, rendered as =).

In iChat, text smileys are replaced with small pictures. Hence, typing =) will insert a yellow smiley face graphic. You can also insert smileys by clicking the smiley face icon in the input field of a chat window, or by selecting Edit ➤ Insert Smiley from the menu bar.

If you're a traditionalist, or you frequently use iChat to discuss programming code or other sources of nontraditional punctuation, you might find this feature annoying. Luckily, you can turn it off by selecting View ➤ Messages ➤ Hide Smileys from the menu bar.

Alternatives to iChat

While iChat is great, it's not the only game in town. There are several other competing IM applications, each with their own protocols, features, strengths, and weaknesses. Most of these have Mac clients you can download and use, including MSN Messenger and Yahoo Messenger.

Another popular solution is to use a multi-protocol communication tool that understands all the major chat protocols. Adium is by far the best of these. Adium is Mac-only and open source, and the guys who work on Adium are really cool, to boot.

Adium supports AIM, Google Talk, MSN Messenger, Yahoo Messenger, Jabber, Bonjour, and several other protocols I've never even heard of. It has a slick interface, it's easy to use, and best of all, it's free. You can get Adium at www.adiumx.com/.

Finally, for those who like what iChat has done for their long-distance bill, but miss the whole telephone experience, there's Skype. Unlike iChat, Skype can actually place voice calls to standard phones. Skype has a nice Mac client, which you can download from www.skype.com/.

Summary

iChat is a fun and useful tool for keeping in contact with people all over the world instantly. While there are still times when e-mail is preferable to IM, this is becoming a more important means of communicating on the Internet.

Now that we've covered most of the Internet tools that come with Leopard, you should be all set for about 90 percent of what most people use computers for these days. Of course, you probably didn't buy a Mac just to surf the Internet (although it's a good choice if you did). The next section of this book will deal with some of the other applications that come with Leopard, as well as touch upon iLife and iWork.

## PART 4

Working with Applications

## CHAPTER 13

Application Basics

Y ou've already worked with a number of applications in this book, and although each application is unique in many ways, they all tend to share some commonalities. In this chapter, we will cover some of these common features that aren't covered elsewhere in the book so that whatever application you are using, you will have a good grasp of how to do certain tasks (and have a good starting point for figuring everything else out). These tasks include the following:

- Installing an application with a standard installer
- Using the file dialog (opening and saving files)
- Choosing a document's default application
- Using the Services menu

> **NOTE** Most of these tasks are the same across applications because they all rely on the same common frameworks to perform these functions. That said, some applications will not work in all the ways described in this chapter because the developer decided for whatever reason to do things differently. In those cases, we can only hope that the developer came up with something so obviously easy that it doesn't need description or that the developer documented the differences sufficiently.

Installing an Application Package

In Chapter 6, we covered the basic ways of installing an application; some applications you can just drag onto your hard drive and they are ready to go, while others come in packages that will walk you through an installation. Applications are generally packaged either when they require more complex installations than simply moving an application bundle where you want it or when multiple options are provided when you install the application. If you just click through the installer, though, you may miss these options. Although every package you install will be slightly different, the general process is similar, so the best way to show how this works is to walk you through some of what you may encounter.

Starting the Installer

An installer package is usually distributed on a disk image or even a CD or DVD. Upon opening the disk (image), you will usually see one or more packages (Figure 13-1). Double-clicking the package will begin the installer.

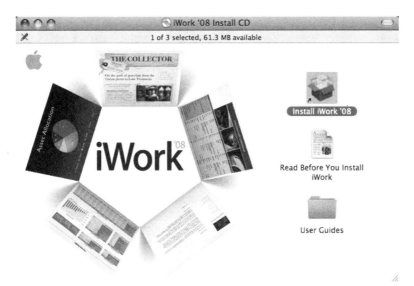

Figure 13-1. The iWork installer package (actually an alias to the .mpkg file)

> **NOTE** There are two similar-appearing types of package files; some have the .pkg extension, and others have the .mpkg extension. The .mpkg files are special metapackages that generally contain a number of smaller .pkg files. The installation of both types will be similar; however, the .mpkg file often will have more available options

When you double-click the installer package, Leopard's Installer application will start and begin the installation process. One of the first things the Installer may do is check your system to verify it is suitable for installing the application (Figure 13-2).

Figure 13-2. Some packages must check your system before they can begin the installation.

After the system check (if necessary), the Installer will generally present you with a few screens of information about the application. This generally includes up to three items: an Introduction screen, a Read Me screen, and a Software License screen.

The Introduction screen generally just welcomes you to the installation application and summarizes the software you are installing. The Read Me screen contains more in-depth information about the application(s) you are installing. Often readme files will contain some important last-minute information about the software, so they're worth the read. Following that, you may be presented with a software license, which when you click Continue will prompt you with a sheet asking whether you agree or disagree (you have to agree if you want to install the software).

After you click through the first informational screens, you will begin the proper installation part.

Customizing Your Installation

One of the first choices you will need to make is the volume you want to install the software on (Figure 13-3). If you have only a single partition on a singe hard drive, you don't have much of a choice to make; if you have volumes, then the available volumes will be indicated, and you can choose where you want to install the software.

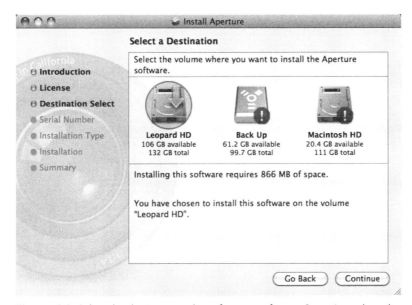

Figure 13-3. Select the destination volume for your software. Sometimes the only available volume will be your start-up disk.

After you select your volume, the next step is often the Installation Type screen (Figure 13-4). (There may be steps in between the Destination Select screen and the Installation Type screen. For example, Aperture presents a screen to enter your user information and serial number after you select your destination and click Continue. Other applications will prompt you for this information when you first launch the application.)

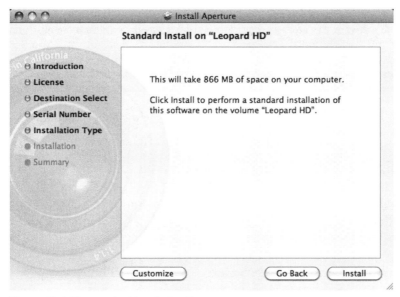

Figure 13-4. The standard Installation Type screen

The first screen you are presented with during the Installation Type selection is the Standard Install screen (this used to be called the Easy Install). By clicking Install here, you tell the Installer to install the application with all the basic components needed by most people. If, however, you'd like more control over what gets installed, you can click the Customize button, which will change the Standard Install screen into the Custom Install screen (Figure 13-5).

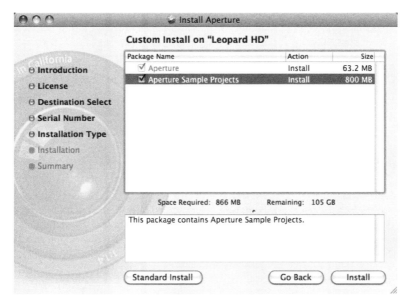

Figure 13-5. The Custom Install screen will provide various options for customizing your installation.

Depending on the package, the options available to you will vary greatly, but generally the Custom Install screen will let you add or remove optional components to/from your install and may also provide a column to customize the installation folder on the selected install volume (otherwise, the default install will be either directly in the Applications folder or in a subfolder in the Applications folder).

Whether you choose the standard install or custom install, once you click the Install button, the installation will begin.

When the installation is complete, you will often be presented with a screen letting you know that your installation was successful.

> **NOTE** An application package, like many applications, is actually a bundle of various pieces. To look inside a package, select Show Package Contents from the contextual menu. One particularly interesting file you will find inside is the BOM file (usually called `Archive.bom`). What's interesting about this is that it contains a listing of all the application parts and where they go. To view this information, use the `lsbom` command-line tool.

File Dialogs: Opening and Saving Files

One common feature found in most applications is the file dialog. This window (and variations of it) is used throughout the system, primarily for opening and saving files.

The simplest file dialog is often used to open a file (Figure 13-6). Essentially this provides a mini-Finder view to browse the system and select the item you want to open.

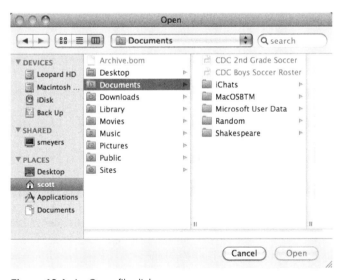

Figure 13-6. An Open file dialog

When you want to save a file, the file dialog is a bit different. The first difference is that the Save As dialog has a simple view (Figure 13-7) and an extended view (Figure 13-8).

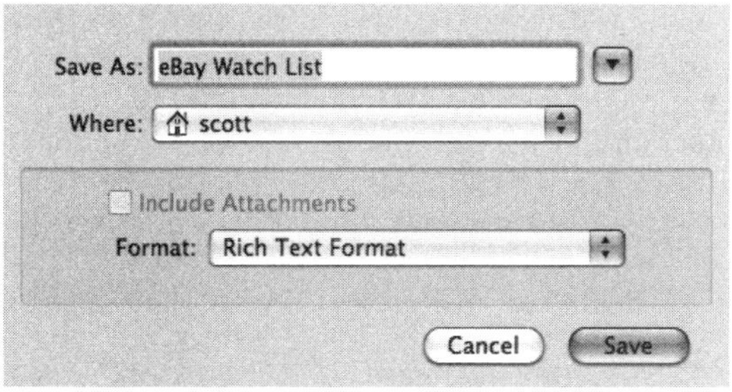

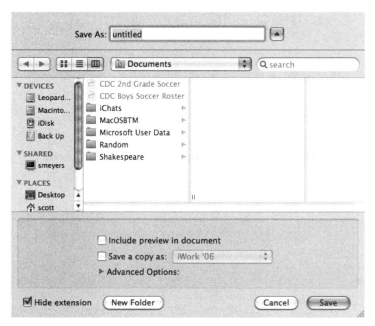

Figure 13-7. A simple Save As dialog

The simple Save As dialog simple asks what you'd like the name of the file to be and provides a drop-down menu of common and recent folders into which to save the file. Beneath that is an area with application-specific save settings. Clicking the disclosure triangle to the right of the Save As text field will expand the dialog into the expanded view.

Figure 13-8. An expanded Save As file dialog. The area between the file browser and the buttons allows developers to include their own save options; as such, what's contained will vary from app to app.

The expanded Save As dialog provides the Finder view just like the Open file dialog but adds the Save As text field as well as the application save settings.

> **NOTE** Save will save an existing file with changes, overwriting the old file. Save As, on the other hand, will prompt you for a new file name (and location) so you can save a duplicate or updated copy of the file while preserving the original. If the file doesn't exist, Save will work the same as Save As. In the past, occasionally Save would sometimes tack on new information to a file in an inefficient manner, creating larger-than-necessary files, and it was recommended that you use Save As to save a fresh file every once in a while to correct this bloat. However, this behavior is no longer common (though Word in Office 2004 does have an option to allow *fast saves*, which would reintroduce this issue).

Certain applications will present different options for opening and saving files, and there may be other uses for this common interface element.

> **NOTE** Other items similar to Open and Save, which are available in many applications, are Import and Export. The primary difference is that when you import or export a field, you are generally opening a file using a file format other than the application's native format (import) or saving an open file in a format other than the application's native format (export).

Other Common Application Features

Besides what we've covered previously in this chapter and elsewhere in the book, there are a few other useful things to know about when working with applications in Leopard.

Choosing a Document's Default Application

When you double-click a document, the document opens automatically in the default application for that document. This application is usually the same as the one that created the document, but not always. If you want to specify what application a document will open in, you can select from a list of compatible applications from the Open With submenu from the document's contextual menu. The default application will be listed first, followed by any other application the system identifies as being able to open that type of file.

> **NOTE** If you drag a file over an application's icon in the Finder, this will usually cause the application to launch and attempt to open the file or files you dragged on it. If the application can't open that particular file type, unexpected results could occur.

If you'd like to change the default application associated with a specific file, or even all files of the same type, you can select the new application in the Open With section of the file's Get Info window. Selecting the Change All button will make that application the default for all files of that type.

> **NOTE** There are a few things that OS X looks at when determining what application to use to open a particular file: the file's extension (which may be hidden) and any Finder metadata or attributes associated with the file. Some files that are received from another computer or created in a non-Aqua application (a Darwin application, for example) may have none of these. In this case, you will be prompted to find a suitable application to open that file.

> **NOTE** Occasionally you will not be able to open a file if the creating application doesn't exist on your computer. In that case, you may be able to import the document from within another application. However, if the application is not compatible, you may get strange results.

Using the Services Menu

The Application ➤ Services menu provides a way for the system, and other applications, to offer features that are accessible from within any other application. A number of these services even have system-wide keyboard shortcuts. For example, if you are reading some text in an application, you can select a word or phrase from that text and hit Shift+Cmd+F to automatically open a Google search on that phrase.

There are all types of useful features in the Services menu, and many new applications will add services of their own to this.

> **NOTE** Services are not available from all applications, even though the Services menu is present. This has to do with the developer of the application not taking the time to enable this feature. If you find yourself using one of these applications and missing this feature, you should let the developer know how you feel.

Using AppleScript and Automator

Most OS X Aqua applications expose at least some of their abilities to AppleScript and Automator to allow savvy users to extend the functionality of the application or to utilize the features of the application in an automated workflow. This ability can be put to some very powerful uses and is covered in much depth in Chapter 23.

Summary

Most of what we have covered in this chapter applies to most of the applications you will use on Leopard. That said, developers have a lot of freedom to change the behavior of any or all of the features covered in this chapter. Next, we'll cover some common applications that are part of Leopard.

## CHAPTER 14

Apple Apps Included with Leopard

I f Leopard came preinstalled on your new computer, then you'll find all sorts of software, including all of iLife and some third-party applications, already there. If you purchased the Leopard DVD and did a clean install of it on your computer, you won't find quite as much software, but you will find a number of applications that are important and useful. This chapter is going to go over some of these applications that are particularly useful, including the following:

- QuickTime Player
- iTunes
- Preview
- Photo Booth

QuickTime Player

QuickTime itself falls into two general areas: there's all the QuickTime technologies that exist behind the scenes in the system that make the music play and the videos go, and then there's QuickTime Player (Figure 14-1), which provides an application for viewing QuickTime media.

By default, QuickTime Player is simply a viewer for various media types, including, of course, QuickTime movies, but also a wide range of other video, audio, and image formats. Generally, when you double-click a media file that QuickTime Player is set to play back, it will open automatically and start playing the file.

> **NOTE** QuickTime Player is only one way to play back QuickTime media. QuickTime can also be embedded in web browsers and integrated into other applications (for example, iTunes is essentially a special-purpose media player based upon QuickTime).

There are a number of ways to extend QuickTime Player's capabilities. First, you can upgrade QuickTime to QuickTime Pro, which will unlock a number of features in QuickTime Player, including the ability to export media into other formats, and some basic media editing capabilities. Beyond that, QuickTime provides the means to add special plug-in files (called codecs) that will allow QuickTime to play back other media formats.

Figure 14-1. A video playing in QuickTime Player

NOTE If you generally just want to view content, then you will likely not need to upgrade to QuickTime Pro. However, if you plan on doing any video conversion or editing, you'll find that QuickTime is a good way to handle certain tasks, so you may want to consider it.

iTunes

iTunes (Figure 14-2) is one of Apple's most successful software products ever. Originally designed as a simple music library and playback application, it has since moved beyond just music, and now includes the iTunes Store and the ability to handle not only Internet streaming radio, but also video. Beyond that it is the primary interface used to sync up your iPod and iPhone with your music, video, and contact and calendar data.

While iTunes is feature rich, it's still easy to use. The iTunes toolbar provides the basic controls to start, stop, and control the media playback, while the main window area is designed to select and manage your media.

The main window provides a column along the left side to select your media libraries (sorted by type) and your playlists, along with a selection to take you to the iTunes Store. The main window area to the right is where you can view your media in a number of different ways.

TIP One particular way to find a song, album, or artist quickly is to use the browser accessible from the menu bar by selecting View ➤ (Show|Hide) Browser (Cmd+B). When used, the browser will appear at the top of the main window (Figure 14-3) in all views except the Cover Flow view.

Figure 14-2. iTunes using the Cover Flow view

Figure 14-3. Viewing your iTunes library by album with the browser visible

Importing Media into iTunes

In order to take advantage of iTunes, you must first import your media into it. The way this is done depends on what sort of media you are starting with. If you already have a collection of supported digital media files (including MP3, AAC (Advanced Audio Coding), and MOV), then you can just use the File ➤ Import... command from the menu bar.

> **NOTE** The Advanced tab in iTunes preferences contains a number of options that are relevant to importing media. For example, under the Advanced ➤ General tab, you may want to select "Copy files to iTunes Music folder when adding to library" and "Keep iTunes Music folders organized," which will keep all of your iTunes media organized in its own location without affecting any of the original files you import.

If you are importing your music from a CD collection, iTunes will automatically convert your audio CDs into MP3, AAC, or other formats, and import them into your library. The options available to you are located on the Advanced ➤ Importing tab in iTunes preferences.

> **NOTE** Which settings are best for importing your CDs is mostly a personal choice. If you are a true audiophile with lots of hard drive space, then of course Apple Lossless format is your best choice (it makes an exact copy of the audio with no loss in quality whatsoever, yet still occupies only half the space as a CD audio file). For everyone else, it becomes a space, quality, and compatibility issue. AAC and MP3 are both compatible with most digital media players; however, MP3 would still be the default if maximum compatibility is an issue. Many people feel that AAC provides better playback quality at the same compression over MP3 (and at higher compression I tend to agree). I find that 256 Kbps AAC provides excellent audio files while saving considerable disk space over uncompressed (or lossless) formats, while 128 Kbps AAC provides good enough sound quality for most situations and allows you to cram lots of music on your iPod. For MP3s, I find 192 Kbps files to be good enough, but I find 128 Kbps MP3s to have quite noticeable audio issues.

Once you have your import preferences set up, when you insert an audio CD into your computer, it will show up in your iTunes library, and (at least the first time) a pop-up window will appear asking you if you'd like to import the CD into your iTunes library. If you send away the pop-up window (either momentarily or permanently), you can still import your CD by clicking the Import CD button in the lower-right-hand corner of iTunes.

> **NOTE** When you insert your CD, if you are connected to the Internet, iTunes will seek out information about the CD you inserted and automatically fill in the CD and track details (unless you turned this feature off on the Advanced ➤ Importing tab of iTunes preferences). If for some reason the details are wrong, or you'd like to change them, then select the track (or tracks) you wish to alter and select Get Info from the contextual menu. The Get Info box will not only reveal more information about the tracks and album, but will allow you to freely edit the information.

The other way to get music into your iTunes library is to buy it from the iTunes Store (Figure 14-4) (formerly know as the iTunes Music Store, but then they started selling videos, too).

The iTunes Store, which now ranks as one of the leading music retailers in the world, provides a huge selection of music new and old, along with an ever-increasing selection of movies, TV shows, music videos, and audio books. Most of this is for sale, although there are occasionally freebies available for download.

Figure 14-4. The iTunes Store in iTunes

To buy music from the iTunes Store, you must first sign in with your Apple ID (if you have a .Mac account, that info is also your Apple ID unless you've previously registered using some other information).

iTunes Store files, DRM, and iTunes Plus

Traditionally, all the files you purchased from the iTunes Store were "protected" using a method of Digital Rights Management (DRM) called FairPlay. As far as DRM goes, FairPlay is fairly lenient, allowing any purchased files to be transferred and played on five different computers (the same five for all purchases, and each computer must be authorized). It also allows a playlist with that song to be burned to seven audio CDs, allowing unlimited syncs to iPods and iPhones, and the ability to stream the items to Apple Airport Express and Apple TV.

Still, traditionally, all the items you could buy were protected by DRM, which disturbs some people who feel insecure about the fact that Apple controls how their items are used. (Some are disturbed for valid if not paranoid reasons, some for nefarious reasons, and some for seemingly purely politically idealist reasons.)

Recently, Apple has reached agreements with some publishers to distribute some items not only free of DRM, but also of a higher quality than traditional iTunes music files. These files are called iTunes Plus files, and are common 256 Kbps AAC files. They tend to cost a bit more than the traditional DRM-protected files, but if DRM bothers you, it's the way to go (I think it's worthwhile for the added sound quality).

By the way, the iTunes Plus files do contain embedded information about who purchased the file, which should not bother anyone who wishes to use the files legitimately, but could be used to help identify people who are taking their purchases straight to Pirate Bay or some other file-sharing system.

NOTE While you can easily export your own iMovies and other QuickTime movies so that they will appear in iTunes (and sync with your iPod/iPhone), Apple doesn't provide a way to import DVDs into iTunes. This could be because Apple sells movies on the iTunes Store, but it's unlikely. More likely is that importing movies from DVDs is somewhat legally ambiguous. From a technical standpoint, it's perfectly legal to make a copy of a movie you own—however, to make a copy of a DVD, you must unencode the content, which may run afoul of the Digital Millennium Copyright Act (DMCA—a sloppy little law passed by government officials who either were getting big money from the MPAA, or more likely just weren't paying attention). Most right-minded people would agree that it's fine, but the movie industry and some others tend to disagree. Either way, if you wish to do this, it's usually a two-step process: ripping the DVD (or converting it for use from your hard drive), and then converting the video. I tend to find that using HandBrake (`http://handbrake.m0k.org/`) to convert a DVD to M4V format ready for my iPhone works just fine.

Sharing and Streaming iTunes Media

iTunes allows you to share your iTunes library with anyone else on your network. You can enable this from the Sharing tab in iTunes preferences. This will allow your library to show in the iTunes libraries of any other people on your network. Likewise, you can view and play songs from other users on your network who are sharing their libraries.

NOTE DRM-protected iTunes Store files can't be shared unless the receiving computer is one of the five computers authorized to play back your iTunes DRMed files. In fact, if you attempt to play one from an unauthorized computer, the music will stop.

Besides sharing your files, you can also stream your files. Music files can be streamed to AirPort and AirPort Expresses equipped with speakers, as well as Apple TV systems. Video can be streamed to Apple TV systems. To stream your files, select the output source from the drop-down menu in the lower-right-hand corner of iTunes.

To fully take advantage of Apple TV with iTunes, you must also set up Apple TV in the Apple TV iTunes preferences.

Syncing iPods and iPhones

When you connect an iPod or iPhone to your computer, the device will show up as a device in your iTunes library. Selecting the device will allow you to configure the settings, which will range from simple for an iPod shuffle (Figure 14-5), to more complex for an iPhone (Figure 14-6). After you set your settings, click the Apply button to resync your device with the new settings.

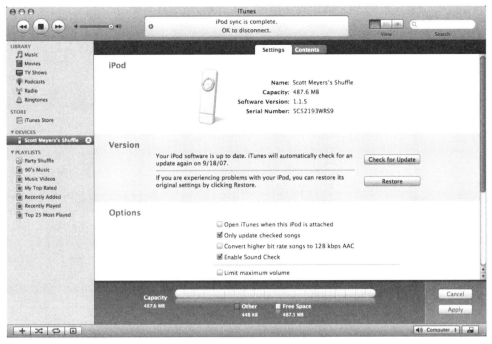

Figure 14-5. Device settings allow you to update and apply settings to iPods and iPhones. For an iPod Shuffle, there aren't too many options.

Figure 14-6. Due to its enhanced capabilities, iTunes displays quite a few more options when an iPhone is connected to it vs. an iPod Shuffle.

Preview

Preview (Figure 14-7) is to PDF and image files as QuickTime Player is to video. It provides an excellent alternative to Adobe's Acrobat Reader for viewing PDF files, complete with support for performing text searches, copying and pasting text from a PDF, viewing encrypted PDFs, creating bookmarks, page previews, and annotation capabilities. Beyond that, it's a multiformat image viewer allowing you to quickly open a wide range of image formats.

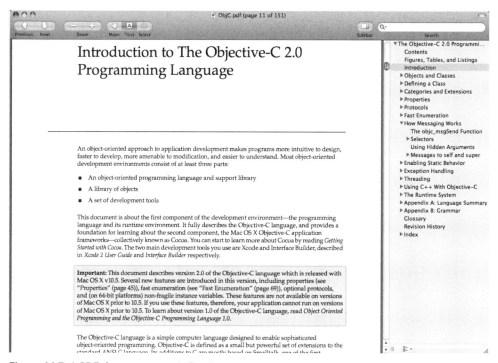

Figure 14-7. A PDF document open in Preview

Besides viewing images, Preview also has the ability to do some minor image editing, including image color adjustments, cropping, resizing, and saving in an array of image file formats.

Photo Booth

Photo Booth is a fairly silly yet highly entertaining application that takes advantage of the iSight camera that is attached to most new Macs (except Mac Pros and Mac minis). When you launch Photo Booth, it will automatically fire up the camera built into your computer and allow you to capture photos or videos.

Once Photo Booth is launched, you can switch between a single picture, four quick pictures (just like a real photo booth!), and a video mode using the button on the left below the preview area. You can also apply effects to the images or video by clicking the Effects button and scrolling through the effect previews. All the images and videos shot with Photo Booth will scroll across the bottom. Selecting an existing image will open it up in the preview area (Figure 14-8), allowing you to send the image to someone through Mail, add the image to iPhoto, or use the image as your iChat or Account icon.

Figure 14-8. A four-picture image previewed in Photo Booth

Other Default Leopard Applications

Leopard comes with a number of other applications for various purposes that aren't covered elsewhere in this book. These applications are described in Table 14-1.

Table 14-1. Other Applications Installed with Leopard

Application	Description
Calculator	This application provides not only a simple calculator mode, but also advanced scientific and programming modes. It also provides conversions to and from many systems of measurement.
Chess	This application provides a 3D chess set that puts you against the computer. It also supports voice recognition, which makes it interesting to play around with.
Dictionary	This is a handy application that provides dictionary, thesaurus, and Wikipedia references for a word or term either individually or together.
DVD Player	With a new, slick interface for Leopard, this application provides a great experience for watching DVDs on your Mac.
Front Row	Coupled with an Apple remote, this application provides a nice interface for controlling and viewing media on your computer from across the room.
Stickies	This application allows you to create sticky notes that will appear on your desktop.
TextEdit	This is a simple text editor with some basic word processing features.

Summary

Besides these basic applications, which range from indispensable to at least sort of interesting, Apple provides a number of other common applications, which we'll talk about in a bit. But first, we'll talk a bit about .Mac.

## CHAPTER 15

.Mac

.Mac (pronounced "dot Mac") is an online service provided by Apple that not only provides basic features such as e-mail, file sharing, and web site hosting but also provides a link between many OS X applications and computers. At the cost of $99 a year, you have to ask yourself, is this worth it?

That's a question you'll have to answer yourself, but first you need to understand more about what .Mac offers. After all, if all you want is an e-mail address (which .Mac offers quite nicely), Google, Yahoo, and others will give you one for free; however, if you are looking for a complete integrated service that provides added utility to your system and applications, then .Mac may be just what you need.

In this chapter, we'll outline how to set up .Mac and then outline just a few of the features of .Mac, including the following:

- E-mail
- Web hosting
- iDisk
- System syncing
- The Back to My Mac feature
- Application integration

Setting up .Mac

To set up a .Mac account, go to www.mac.com, and select either the Free Trial or Join Now option from the .Mac home page. This will take you to the sign-up page where you will be asked to enter some personal information and select your .Mac username and password. Although you can change your password at any time in the future, you are stuck with your username forever, so choose carefully. At this point, if you are joining .Mac, you will be prompted for billing information; otherwise, if you are just getting a trial account, you are all set.

One of the first things you'll want to do once you have set up a .Mac account is to enter your .Mac username in the Accounts panel of System Preferences. This will allow you to take advantage of all the features of .Mac from your computer.

> **NOTE** You can also view your account details, and even upgrade or renew your .Mac account, from the Account tab in the .Mac panel of System Preferences.

.Mac E-mail

In its humble beginnings, .Mac was thought of primarily as an e-mail service, and today it's still known for this. What's particularly nice about .Mac's e-mail is that it's convenient and easy to use from any computer with Internet access and a web browser.

Obviously, from your computer you can access .Mac mail in Mail (in fact when you enter your .Mac information into your account information, it gets added and set up automatically). If, however, you don't have access to your computer, you can view all your messages in a web browser in an interface similar to the Mail application (Figure 15-1).

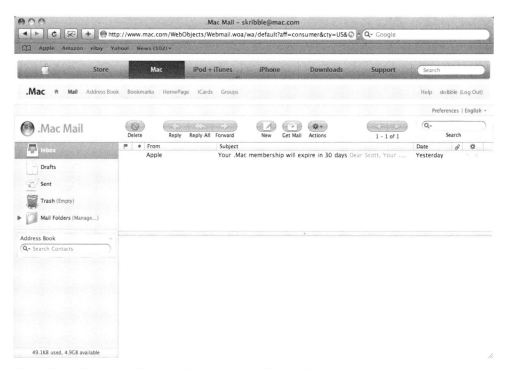

Figure 15-1. .Mac web mail looks and acts very much like the Mail app on your computer.

Besides making your .Mac mail available from a web interface, .Mac mail provides lots of options when you click the Preferences link at the top right of the web mail interface (Figure 15-2).

The General, Viewing, and Composing tabs in the .Mac web mail preferences generally allow you to set options that affect how the web mail interface looks and operates. The Aliases and Other tabs, however, provide some nice extra features.

> **NOTE** If you access your .Mac account from the Mail app and enable junk mail filtering in the .Mac web mail preferences, then you should also select the "Store junk mail messages on the server" option under the .Mac mail account options in the Mail app. This will ensure that your junk mail is in sync between your web mail and the Mail application.

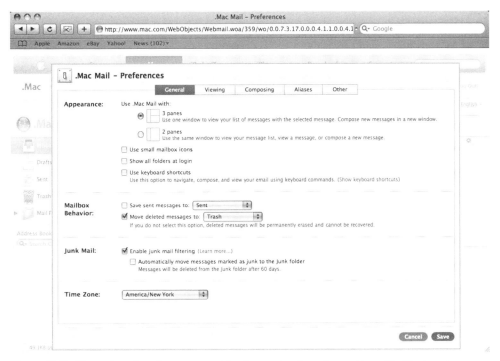

Figure 15-2. .Mac web mail preferences provide all sort of options for working with .Mac's web interface and some nice options for .Mac mail in general.

The Aliases tab allows you to set up aliases for your .Mac mail account. An *alias* is an alternate username that points to your real name. For example, if I wanted to create a new e-mail address such as macosbtm@mac.com that would send e-mail sent to macosbtm@mac.com to my existing .Mac mail account, I could go to the Aliases tab, and if that username was available, I could set it up as an alias. I can even make e-mail addressed to an alias show up in a different color for easy sorting and viewing.

The Other tab provides two more nice options: "Checking email from an external account" and Mail Forwarding. The first option allows you to set up .Mac mail to check and receive mail from a different POP account. This is useful if you have another POP e-mail account but want to check your e-mail from only one account (which is especially useful if you are away and want to check all your mail from a single web mail account). Mail Forwarding, on the other hand, will forward e-mail received by your .Mac account to another e-mail address. Also in the Forwarding section is an "Automatically reply to email when it is received" option, which is commonly used to reply to senders if you are away from your e-mail for a period of time.

Web Hosting

.Mac also provides you with an easy way to create and share your own web site on the Internet. Clicking .Mac's HomePage option will take you to a web page that will walk you through creating your own simple web site, which will be located at http://homesite.mac.com/yourusername/.

Besides using the .Mac web-based tools, you can create even more complex web pages that can be hosted in .Mac by using iWeb or other common web development tools (web sites created with other web editors can be uploaded directly to the Sites folder on your iDisk).

iDisk

Another feature provided by .Mac is your own iDisk, which is an online storage system that is tightly integrated into OS X (and Apple provides iDisk access tools specifically for Microsoft Windows as well). iDisk allows you to store, back up, and share files that are then accessible from any other computer connected to the Internet either by using a .Mac web interface, by using the Windows iDisk utility, or by using the OS X Finder.

> **NOTE** .Mac currently provides 10GB of storage that can consist of any content on your iDisk, your web pages, and your .Mac e-mail. This total storage limit has, since .Mac's start, been steadily increasing, and it is conceivable that the storage limit will continue to increase in the future. You can view your current and available storage space on the iDisk tab in the .Mac panel of System Preferences.

To share files using iDisk, you simply need to place them in the `Public` folder on your iDisk (all other folders are visible only to you on your iDisk). You can configure the access you give to others from the iDisk tab in the .Mac panel of System Preferences. The access can range from a free-for-all, allowing anyone to freely read and write to your iDisk (not the recommended option), to setting up a password to grant access to your iDisk to only those with the proper password.

Data Syncing

One nice feature that .Mac provides is the ability to keep user accounts on different Macs in sync with each other. Additionally, syncing certain data such as bookmarks, your Address Book, and your calendars will make that information available to you from .Mac's web interface.

You can select the information you want to sync with .Mac from the Sync tab in the .Mac panel of System Preferences (Figure 15-3).

By setting up multiple accounts on different computers to sync with the same .Mac account, everything will stay in sync from computer to computer.

Back to My Mac

With a .Mac account and Leopard, you can now take advantage of the Back to My Mac feature. This allows you to access the files on one of your Macs running Leopard (or higher) from any other Mac running Leopard on the Internet. To enable this feature, you first must turn it on in the Back to My Mac tab in the .Mac panel of System Preferences. After that, your computer's files will show up as a shared network resource on other Back to My Mac–enabled computers that share your .Mac account information.

Figure 15-3. You can choose which information you want to sync with .Mac.

Application Integration

One other great feature of .Mac is that it allows applications to utilize its services for an array of possibilities over the network. As you will learn, most of the iLife applications can take advantage of .Mac to provide a variety of features including photo sharing from iPhoto with the .Mac Web Gallery feature, creating .Mac web sites with iWeb, and more. Additionally, many third-party applications also can take advantage of .Mac.

> **NOTE** We will touch on iLife .Mac features in the next chapter. Chapter 23 includes more information on .Mac and network sharing and application integration.

Summary

Besides what we covered in this chapter, Apple and third-party developers continue to expand the types of services and application integration that make .Mac a useful part of the Mac experience. Next we'll cover iLife, which includes a number of applications that can leverage the features made possible with a .Mac account.

iLife '08

Apple's iLife '08 is an update to Apple's bundle of digital lifestyle applications. It is included with all new Macs from the Mac mini up to the Mac Pro, and can be purchased for the bargain price of $79. Included are applications for photo management and workflow (iPhoto), digital video editing (iMovie), audio and music production (GarageBand), web site creation (iWeb), and an application to take your media and create DVDs (iDVD).

This chapter will go over the individual applications contained in iLife '08 and discuss some of the new features in the latest version. We will cover the following:

- iPhoto '08
- iMovie '08
- GarageBand '08
- iWeb '08
- iDVD '08

iPhoto '08

iPhoto (Figure 16-1) has always been one of the premier consumer photo management tools available on any computer platform, and the latest version improves on almost every aspect of it.

iPhoto '08 is a complete photo workflow tool, allowing you to import and organize your photos, edit them, and then export and share them in a number of ways.

Photo Management

When you connect a digital camera to your computer and launch iPhoto (you can set iPhoto to launch automatically when you connect a digital camera in iPhoto's general preferences), your camera will show up as a device in iPhoto and give you a number of import options. By default, iPhoto will import all the images into a single event—however, you can select an option that will split up your photos into multiple events based on time if you choose.

Figure 16-1. iPhoto '08's mail window allows you to browse, organize, and work with your photos quickly and easily.

Events are one of the primary ways that iPhoto '08 divides and organizes your photos. They serves a similar role to rolls in previous versions of iPhoto—however, events are much more flexible, as you can move images from one event to another and can reorder entire events in your library.

Albums and *smart albums* provide another way to organize your photos. The key difference between albums and events is that a single photo can only reside in one event, while it can be placed in many albums.

Another feature included in iPhoto '08 is that ability to tag individual photos with titles, ratings, and keywords. Titles allow you to provide easily recognizable names to images without renaming the actual image file. This is very useful for those who use specific naming schemes for files (such as time and date information) that may not be very descriptive of the image content. Ratings simply allow you to quickly rate your photos from 0 to 5 stars, allowing you to find your very best (4- or 5-star) photos quickly at a later time. Keywords allow you to add searchable words that help describe your images; they can range from very specific names to general categories.

> **TIP** Keywords aren't very useful if you aren't somewhat consistent with them. If you use different words for every photo, then they quickly become out of control. However, if your keywords aren't specific enough, then they don't serve much purpose either. One suggestion is to jot down some general keyword categories (I start out with *People*, *Places*, and *Things* as my top-level keywords), and then add some subcategories (e.g., under *People*, you might have *Family*, *Friends*, *Celebrities*, etc.) and more specific information under that (specific names of people). The most important rule is to be consistent.

> **NOTE** As a general rule, keywords should be no more than 64 characters long. This length is based on the maximum length for IPTC (International Press Telecommunications Council) data. This is a standard format of transmitting image data along with digital images (either embedded or as "sidecar" XMP files).

> **NOTE** iPhoto keeps track of all your keywords. To view them, open the Keyword window (Cmd+K). You can use this window to add keywords to selected photos by clicking the keyword. You can even set up common keywords with their own keyboard shortcut to apply them quickly to any photo. This not only makes adding popular keywords easy, but is also a good way to keep keywords consistent.

Once all the data (titles, ratings, and keywords) are set up for your images, you can really take advantage of the search and smart album tools in iPhoto to find just the right image or images you are looking for.

Photo Editing

iPhoto '08 includes a range of easy-to-use image editing tools. To switch into Edit mode, click the Edit icon in the lower-left-hand corner of iPhoto. In Edit mode, there will be a number of editing tools listed along the bottom toolbar:

Rotate: Rotates the image 90 degrees counterclockwise. You may need to use this more than one time to rotate an image that needs it.

Crop: Allows you to select and crop an image.

Straighten: Allows you to slightly rotate a photo where the subject is slightly off skew.

Enhance: Provides some automatic image adjustments to attempt to improve the image.

Red-Eye: Provides a tool that can help eliminate red-eye in photos.

Retouch: Provides tools that can help mask blemishes or strange anomalies in photos (including dust specks).

Effects: Opens a window that provides a number of effects that may be applied to the photo.

Adjust: Opens up a window with a number of very high-quality image enhancement tools that give you precise control over levels, contrast, exposure, color, sharpening, and other sophisticated image editing features.

Any edits you make will be applied the image—however, iPhoto will preserve the original image so you can revert back to it at any time in the future if necessary.

Besides switching into Edit mode, all of the editing tools are available from the lower pop-up toolbar in iPhoto's full-screen mode (Figure 16-2).

Printing and Sharing Your Photos

Taking and organizing your photos is nice, but ultimately you'll likely want to share them with others, and iPhoto provides a number of ways to do this, both digitally and physically.

If you just want to share some photos with a minimum of fuss, you can select the desired images in your library and e-mail them to the desired recipients, print them from your own printer, or order professional prints using Kodak Print Service.

> **NOTE** The first time you order prints, you will need to set up an account for yourself. This is fairly easy, as iPhoto will walk you through the process.

For those who wish to share photos with a bit more flair, iPhoto has a number of ways to satisfy this desire. This ranges from creating simple slideshows of photos that can be played back in iPhoto or exported and played as QuickTime movies, to sending a selection of photos to iDVD to create a Photo DVD to share with friends and family.

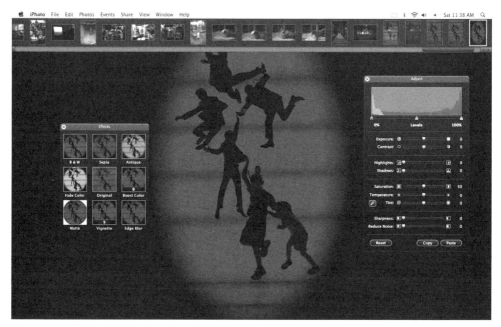

Figure 16-2. The image editing tools in iPhoto '08 are easily accessible in full-screen mode, which provides an uncluttered way to view and edit your images.

The new Web Gallery feature allows you to create a gallery that works with .Mac to create albums of photos online that can be shared with anyone who has a web browser and an Internet connection. Additionally, as you add more photos to a Web Gallery album in iPhoto, the .Mac Web Gallery will automatically be updated. Each Web Gallery album can be configured to provide a range of settings, from password protection to allowing people to upload their own photos to your gallery. An additional nice feature of Web Gallery is that it can format your gallery to appear on a range of devices including the iPhone. People can even subscribe to an album and view your images in iPhoto on their computer.

For a different way to share your photos on the Web, you can select an event, an album, or a collection of images, and send them into iWeb to create your own photo gallery there.

If you want a nondigital, interesting hard copy of your images, iPhoto allows you to create and order amazing photo books, cards, and even calendars from your photos.

iMovie '08

iMovie '08 is an entirely new application that differs significantly from previous versions of iMovie. iMovie '08 provides a new interface (Figure 16-3), designed to allow users to quickly and easily edit and assemble their home videos into wonderful home movies.

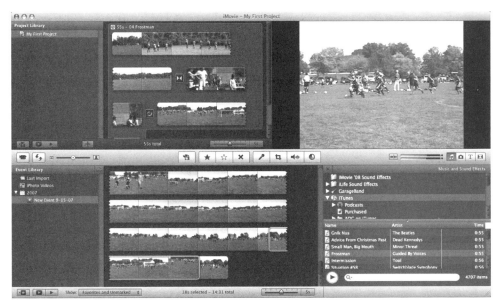

Figure 16-3. iMovie '08 and its new interface

> **NOTE** iMovie '08 has been criticized by some for lacking features that were found in previous versions of iMovie. And indeed there are a few things that are no longer available. However, the trade-off of losing a few features vs. the new, improved interface and ease of creating top-notch movies seems well worth it. As a fairly busy person with many ways to spend my time, I'd rather not spend extra time learning and navigating a more complex interface to create movies for one or two subtle features when I don't have to. In the past, iMovie just frustrated me, since it had the complexity of more advanced video editing applications without some of the features. Often if I wanted certain advanced editing features, I'd still have to reach for Final Cut Express or other more powerful multitrack video editing tools. With iMovie '08, Apple now provides a fast, easy alternative that's a pleasure to work with. Really to me, it's one of the coolest new breakthroughs in digital video since the now-defunct Digital Creations released EditDV. As a compromise of sorts, Apple still makes iMovie HD (a.k.a. iMovie '06), available for free to anyone who own iLife '08. See www.apple.com/support/downloads/imovieHD6.html for details.

To begin using iMovie, you simply import your video. If you are using a traditional Mini DV camcorder, iMovie provides the traditional interface for importing video directly from your camera (Figure 16-4). If you are using a new hard drive–based (or other media–based) camcorder, you can just import the video files directly from the camcorder's media and start working.

> **NOTE** iMovie '08 now fully supports MPEG2 and AVCHD out of the box, along with other traditionally supported video formats (DV, HDV, and MPEG4).

Once the video is imported, you can select your original or imported movie files from iMovie's Event Library, scrub through them, select the sections of video you want to include in your final movie, and drag them up to the project area in the order you want them. If desired, you can select and place transitions between clips, and add background sounds or sound effects to save to your new video—nice and easy with surprisingly wonderful results.

Figure 16-4. Importing video from a Mini DV camcorder

When you have finished creating your new movie, iMovie allows you to export it into a wide range of formats, plus you can use iDVD to create DVDs directly from your finished movie projects.

If you dig around, there are a number of additional tweaks you can make, but really this is designed for quick-and-easy movies. If you crave more control, your iMovie projects can be imported into Final Cut Express or Pro for additional touches.

iWeb '08

iWeb '08 is an application that allows you to easily create theme-based web pages and web sites with a WYSIWYG, layout-based interface (Figure 16-5).

To begin creating a web site with iWeb, you first select a theme from one of the many available themes in iWeb. Each theme also contains a number of page templates, including a Welcome page (usually the first page you want to start with), and special templates for blogs, movies, photos, podcasts, and more.

> **NOTE** iWeb is both easy to use for quickly creating nice template-based web sites, and extraordinarily inflexible if you wish to truly customize a web experience. That is to say it's a great tool for people who wish to build a web site without the need for learning HTML, CSS, and other web creation technologies, but if you are used to tools like Dreamweaver, Coda, or BBEdit, then iWeb probably won't be of much interest to you.

Figure 16-5. Building a Welcome page from a template in iWeb '08

Once you select a theme and a template to begin with, you simply start editing the template with your content, replacing the placeholder content as you go. To replace images, you can select any image from the Media Browser or the Finder and drag it over an image placeholder. To replace text, just select it and start typing. Most of the image and text boxes on the page can be selected and relocated by clicking an item and moving it where you want it to go. If you'd like to insert additional content, iWeb allows you to insert Web widgets, which includes Google Ad Words, Google Maps, and the ability to insert any HTML code into your page.

As you add pages to your web site, iWeb keeps track of the new content and automatically updates the links on all the related pages on your web site.

When you have done what you want, iWeb will automatically publish your web site, either directly to your .Mac account or to a folder on your computer that you can host from your computer or upload to another web site.

> **NOTE** Recently, Apple started offering domain web hosting through .Mac. This will allow you to use iWeb to publish web sites available at www.*yourdomain*.com through .Mac. The one downside to this is that, as of yet, this only covers web hosting—for e-mail services for that domain, you will have to look elsewhere.

GarageBand

GarageBand (Figure 16-6) is Apple's entry-level DAW (digital audio workstation). GarageBand lets you record, mix, and edit multiple audio and MIDI tracks together and then save them as audio files in a variety of formats. While GarageBand lacks some features of Apple's other DAWs (Logic Express and Logic Studio), it provides a number of professional-quality software instruments and effects coupled with reasonable track editing abilities (including volume, panning, and new track automation abilities) that can easily create professional-sounding recordings.

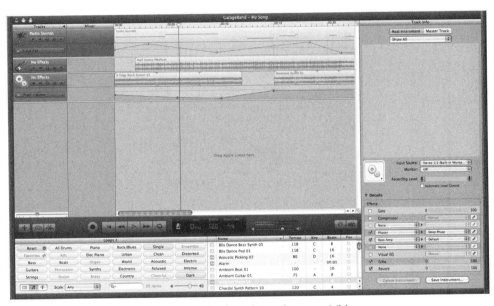

Figure 16-6. GarageBand '08 with the Track Info and Loop browser visible

Each track can contain either a software instrument track or a real instrument track. The software tracks contain MIDI information that is translated into sound based on the software instrument associated with it. Real instrument tracks contain actual sound files that can come from prerecorded music or loops, or can be recorded on the fly in GarageBand through an audio interface (including the built-in audio inputs if necessary).

GarageBand '08 allows you to record up to eight instruments (or eight tracks) at one time (provided you have an audio interface that supports this).

> **NOTE** If you are serious about recording, you should probably look into purchasing an audio interface for your computer. A decent two-channel USB2 or FireWire audio interface costs around $200 or so, and will provide you with much better sound quality than using your Mac's built-in audio port. Obviously, there are more expensive audio interfaces as well that include more features. Some companies that make good audio interfaces include TASCAM, Mackie (or TAPCO), M-Audio, Digidesign, and MOTU (Mark of the Unicorn).

New in GarageBand '08 is a feature called Magic GarageBand (Figure 16-7). Magic Garage-Band allows you to create a virtual backing band that you can play along with. With Magic GarageBand, you choose from a preselected number of musical styles and then assign the instruments and styles played by each virtual member. Then you can add your own music in the mix and record the whole thing.

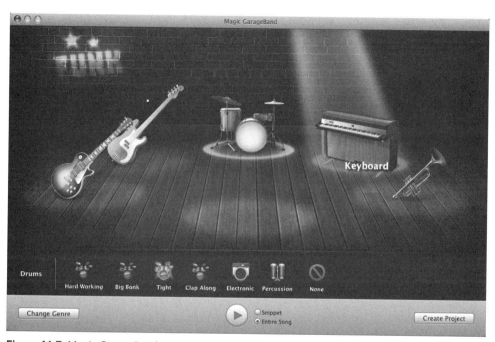

Figure 16-7. Magic GarageBand

Once you have finished with a song in GarageBand, GarageBand will allow you to export it to a number of different audio formats. Normally you would export it to iTunes, where you can use iTunes to play it back and then burn a selection of your songs to CD.

iDVD '08

There's more to creating a DVD than just having a great movie. You need menus and transitions and chapters and special features. iDVD '08 gives you the power to create amazing, professional-looking DVDs with very little effort. iDVD '08 (Figure 16-8) doesn't add any significant new features from a user perspective other than a few new themes. However, on the back end, iDVD has enhanced performance and the video quality of the final DVD, both welcome improvements.

Figure 16-8. With Magic iDVD, choose your media files and your theme, and let iDVD do the rest.

Despite the fact that lots of sharing of movies and photos and such is being done now more than ever on the Internet, iDVD is still great way to create DVDs for sharing or archiving your content (plus, sometimes it's preferable to crash down on the sofa in front of your big-screen TV than to huddle around a computer).

Summary

There's only so much room in an OS X book to cover things like iLife, but we wanted to give you a quick look at what's there. Most of these applications are fairly easy to pick up and use after just a little guidance, although you'll find as you dig deeper into each of these iLife applications that they offer quite a bit of power behind their easy-to-use exterior. In the next chapter, we'll take a look at Apple's other software bundle, iWork '08.

iWork '08

Apple has been producing office suites for its computers on and off since it introduced one of the first office suites for the Apple II called AppleWorks. Later, AppleWorks reemerged for the Macintosh computer from Apple's Claris subsidy, initially called ClarisWorks. It was renamed AppleWorks when parts of Claris were reabsorbed back into Apple (the remaining parts of Claris were formed into FileMaker, which makes the wonderful FileMaker Pro database). AppleWorks continued even after the first version of iWork was introduced in 2005 (though it hadn't had a significant upgrade since 2004), but shortly after the release of iWork '08, Apple declared that AppleWorks would no longer be sold. So today, iWork '08 is not only Apple's premier Office suite, but it's Apple's only one.

iWork '08 contains three common office components:

- Keynote '08, Apple's presentation software
- Pages '08, Apple's word processing and page layout program
- Numbers '08, Apple's new spreadsheet application

In this chapter, we will quickly introduce each of these applications.

Keynote '08

Initially released as a stand-alone software product in 2003, Keynote is presentation software that was allegedly developed at Apple specifically for Steve Jobs to use during his keynote presentations and other Apple events. Over the years, Keynote has gone through a number of revisions leading up to Keynote '08 (version 4).

Keynote '08 (Figure 17-1) ships with 35 themes to get you going quickly. Each of them provides a number of predesigned layouts (called *masters*) to suit most of your needs.

Getting started on a new presentation with Keynote is quite easy. When you first start a new presentation, you will be prompted to select a theme from the Theme Chooser (Figure 17-2). Once you select your theme, you will be presented with a blank presentation with only a single slide. As you create your presentation, you will add slides. Each slide can have its own layout depending on the best way to present your information. The preconfigured layouts can be selected from the Masters drop-down menu on the toolbar. To create your own themes or layouts, you can start with the White theme or Blank master and build upon it with the layout tools provided by Keynote.

Figure 17-1. Creating presentation slides in Keynote '08

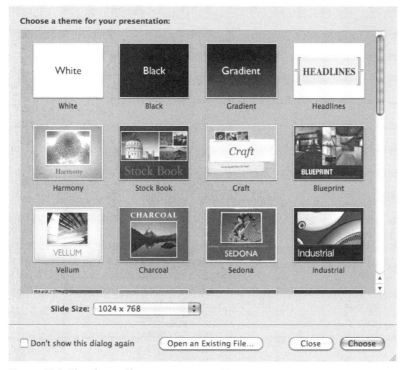

Figure 17-2. The Theme Chooser in Keynote '08

One great feature of Keynote is that when creating your presentations, you can utilize an extensive variety of images and other media types in your presentation. Additionally, Keynote has built-in tools for creating tables and charts. Together, these features allow you to create visually stunning presentations.

To go one step further, Keynote has a wide variety of animation and transition effects available. Keynote '08 even adds a smart build feature that helps you automatically build slick-looking animations for presenting images.

Besides helping you build your presentation, Keynote allows you to add comments and notes to each slide to help you with your presentations. Comments are like sticky notes that you can add to your slides as you go through them, maybe suggesting a change or something. Notes, on the other hand, are actual presentation notes. Your notes can either be printed or can be visible on one screen while using another screen for your presentation.

Once you have finished your presentation, you can select View ➤ Rehearse Slideshow to help practice your presentation. This will walk you through your presentation but with a timer visible so you can help pace your presentation within a given amount of time.

When you are ready for your presentation, hit the Play button (or select View ➤ Play Slideshow or press Opt+Cmd+P), and your screen will switch to a full-screen presentation. A click of the mouse will move you forward one screen or trigger the next animation event.

Besides using Keynote to present your presentation, you can print your presentation in various ways to hand out before or after your presentation. Also, you can export your Keynote presentations so they can be presented using a variety of methods including QuickTime, Power-Point, HTML, Flash, or even a special version for your iPod.

Pages '08

The first version of iWork (iWork '05) introduced Pages along with an updated version Keynote. Although it hasn't been around as long as Keynote, with its third release, Pages '08 is a stable, full-featured word processor as well as a very capable page layout tool.

As a word processor (Figure 17-3), Pages '08 provides most of the tools you will ever need in any situation, including footnotes, bookmarks, custom styles, grammar and spelling checking, the ability to generate a table of contents, and (new with Pages '08) the ability to track document changes during revisions.

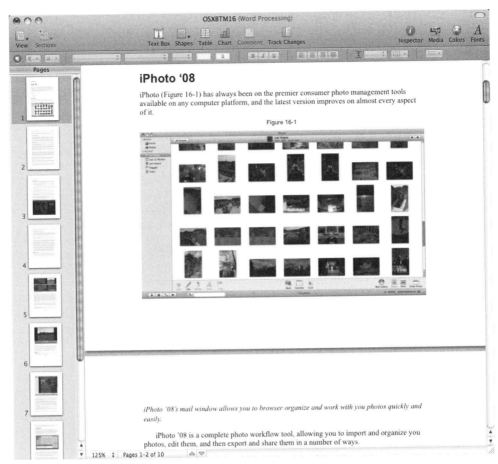

Figure 17-3. A document open in Pages '08 Word Processing mode

Besides great word processing capabilities, Pages '08 also has a Page Layout mode (Figure 17-4) for more creative documents such as newsletters and flyers. In Page Layout mode, text must explicitly be placed in text boxes that can be sized and formatted individually on your document. In Pages '08, text boxes can be linked so that overflow text from one text box can flow directly into another.

Just like many applications, Pages '08 provides a number of templates to start from, depending on the type of document you want to create. The different templates are divided into word processing documents and page layout documents and further divided into other groups (newsletters, letters, resumes, and so on).

NOTE The primary difference between Word Processing mode and Page Layout mode is that in Word Processing mode the entire editable page area (as defined by the margins) is essentially a large text field ready for typing that flows from one page to the next. In Page Layout mode, you must create text boxes before you can start adding text, and text boxes will flow only as you dictate. Text boxes and images can easily be added in Word Processing mode, while page-sized text fields can be added in Page Layout mode. In a way, they can both accomplish the same things, but one mode puts text ahead of design, while the other puts design ahead of text.

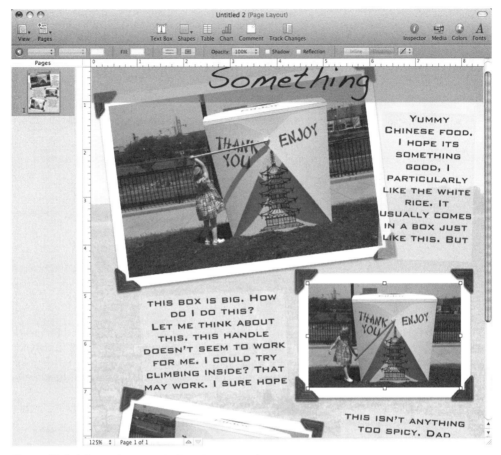

Figure 17-4. A Pages document in Page Layout mode

Pages '08 can import and export files to/from other popular word processors including Microsoft Word and other formats including PDF, RTF, and plain text. Occasionally, you'll lose some formatting when importing to or exporting from a different format; however, with Microsoft Word documents, the formatting for the most part remains; specifically, formatting, styles, and even revisions will be imported usually intact, but macros and special toolbars won't.

Numbers '08

Newly released with iWork '08, Numbers '08 is Apple's long-anticipated spreadsheet application. Although able to look and function like a traditional spreadsheet application, Numbers '08 provides its users with unprecedented control over organization and presentation not found in other spreadsheet applications.

A Numbers spreadsheet (Figure 17-5) is comprised of sheets, where each sheet can contain any combination of spreadsheet tables, charts, or other elements such as images, shapes, and text boxes.

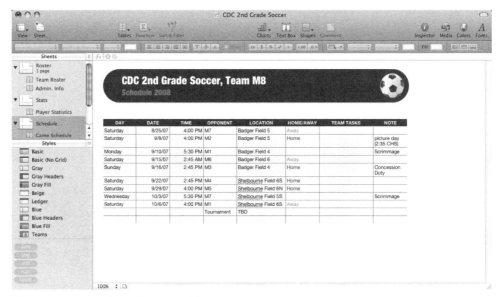

Figure 17-5. A typical Numbers spreadsheet

The main part of a Numbers spreadsheet is the spreadsheet tables. These tables function like most other spreadsheets where you label your rows and columns and then fill in the table with your data. Numbers provides various functions that can be performed on your data and then added to the tables. Data from within a table can be easily selected and transformed into a wide variety of charts and graphs.

Like the other iWork '08 applications, Numbers '08 provides a wide range of templates for personal, business, and educational projects.

Numbers '08 provides a wide range of options for sharing spreadsheet data. For example, Numbers '08 is able to import and export Microsoft Excel and comma-separated value (CSV) documents. It can also save documents in PDF and can export spreadsheets to iWeb for posting on a web site. Numbers '08 also provides a Print view that will let you preview how your spreadsheets will appear when printed, allowing you to rearrange data as needed to make sure everything fits the way you want it.

NOTE Although a first-generation product, Numbers '08 is fairly complete. There are, however, a few features that power spreadsheet users may find lacking. For example, Numbers '08 currently doesn't provide the sophisticated pivot tables commonly found in Excel spreadsheets.

Summary

Along with Numbers, iWork '08 now provides a credible alternative to Microsoft Office or other office suites for OS X users. It certainly is a more powerful replacement for the now officially end-of-lifed (EOLed) AppleWorks and should provide all the tools that most people will need for home, school, or work.

## PART 5

Getting to Know Darwin

## CHAPTER 18

Introducing Darwin and the Shell

Running behind the slick Mac OS X Aqua interface is a powerful component of Mac OS X called Darwin. This is Apple's name for the UNIX underpinnings of the OS. The most direct way to interact with Darwin and take full advantage of all those wonderfully powerful UNIX tools is through the use of the Terminal application (/Applications/Utilities/Terminal). When Terminal is launched, it will open up a terminal window running a shell program, as shown in Figure 18-1.

```
Terminal — bash — 80×24
Last login: Thu Sep  6 14:23:07 on ttys000
Leopard:~ scott$ █
```

Figure 18-1. The Terminal application running in Leopard

> **NOTE** In UNIX lingo, which applies to Darwin as well, using the command prompt is often referred to as running a shell, or running in a shell.

Darwin Basics

The first thing you need to know when working with Darwin is some of the common language used, in order to avoid confusion. Second, you need to know how files are organized; and finally, you need to know how to move around the file system.

> **NOTE** When we talk about files here, we are not just talking about the last text file you created; Darwin treats everything as a file. For example, a directory (a.k.a. folder) is a file that contains other files. Each file has a number of properties that will determine how the shell treats that specific file; if it's an application, the shell will launch it; if it's a directory, the shell will know that it can access other files contained in it. We'll cover file properties a bit later.

Darwin Semantics

To avoid confusion as the chapter proceeds, we should quickly go over some of the important terms used in Darwin and how they compare with terms used in the Finder. Table 18-1 defines a handful of terms used commonly in Darwin (and other UNIX systems), gives the Finder equivalent or alternate term, and adds any relevant notes. While there are many other terms you'll come across, these basics will be used repeatedly, so they are good to know.

Table 18-1. Darwin Terms Explained

Darwin Term	Finder or Alternate Term	Notes
File	File (and others)	Darwin treats all items, documents, directories, and applications as files; in the Finder, when we talk about a file, we are generally talking specifically about a document.
Directory	Folder	Folders are generally referred to as directories.
Root directory, or /	Top level of hard drive	Not to be confused with the root user, the root directory, which is represented by the / symbol, is the highest level of the Darwin file structure.
Root (user)	Administrator	In addition to the root directory, there is also a root user. The root user (also known as the superuser) has the ability to do just about anything in the Darwin environment, including irreparably destroying it. To maintain a secure system and avoid devastating problems, certain files require root privileges to read, write, and execute. While the administrator is the closest thing to root in Aqua, it's not quite the same, as root actually has more abilities.
Link (specifically a symbolic link)	Alias	A link in Darwin functions the same way as an alias does in the Finder (and appears as such when viewed in the Finder). While the function of a symbolic link and an alias are the same, it's worth knowing that they are implemented differently.

Darwin Term	Finder or Alternate Term	Notes
Alias	N/A	An alias in Darwin is a simple command set up in the shell that can trigger more complex commands or allow you to override the behavior of an existing command.
Directory path	N/A	The directory path is a representation of where you are in the file system, beginning from the root directory. For example, if your user name is scott, then the *path* to your home directory would be /Users/scott/ (your home directory can also be abbreviated to ~, as you will see later). The leading / represents the root directory.
Executable command	Application or script	Any command that's issued at the command line and causes something to happen can be referred to as an executable.
Command arguments, arguments	N/A	Arguments are additional, sometimes necessary information added to commands. Arguments don't affect how the command is run in the way options do; instead, they generally target the command to affect specific items.
Command options, options	Switches (DOS)	Command options are special arguments (usually preceded by a - and immediately following the command) that can change how a command is run. This is similar to setting command preferences for an Aqua application, but more flexible, as different preferences can be issued at runtime. For Windows and DOS users, these are like switches issued with a DOS or Windows command prompt command.
Process	N/A	A process is a running application or daemon (also known as a background process). In Leopard (and in fact most modern systems), there can be (and often are) hundreds of processes running at any one time.
Pipes	N/A	Pipes, represented by the | symbol, provide a way of stringing two or more commands together. *Piping* one command into another is a very powerful way to accomplish some otherwise very complex tasks. Pipes, along with redirection, are covered in more depth later in this chapter.

The File System

The Darwin file system shares the same folder structure found while navigating through the Finder in Quartz. However, while navigating through Darwin, you will notice a few differences. First, there are quite a few more visible items in the Darwin view. Second, you will find that your additional volumes (added hard drives, CD/DVD drives, Flash drives, etc.) are found a little differently.

The Darwin file system starts from root, which is symbolized by /. This is the highest level of the file system, and is essentially the same as viewing your primary hard drive in the Finder. A quick look in our root directory reveals the following items (the trailing / and @ symbols that follow have special meaning: / indicates that the item is a directory [or folder] and @ indicates that the item is a link [or alias]):

```
Applications/    System/      etc@              sbin/
Desktop DB       Users/       home/             tmp@
Desktop DF       Volumes/     mach_kernel       usr/
Developer/       bin/         mach_kernel.ctfsys var@
Library/         cores/       net/
Network/         dev/         private/
```

As you can see, all the basic Finder folders—Applications, Library, System, Users, and Developer (provided you've installed the Developer tools)—are there, along with a slew of other items. Some of these are merely system files that are of little interest to most people. Table 18-2 shows some common directory paths and describes what sorts of files are located in them.

Table 18-2. Common Darwin Directories and Their Contents

Directory Path	Contents
/bin	The /bin directory contains the core user executables that are necessary for the OS to function normally.
/etc (/private/etc)	The /etc directory contains the primary configuration files for much of OS X and its services.
/sbin	The /sbin directory contains the core administrative executables necessary for the OS to function normally.
/tmp (/private/tmp)	The /tmp directory is where the OS and many services and applications store data that is only used briefly and then discarded.
/usr	The /usr directory is a metadirectory that contains a number of subdirectories. Traditionally, these directories contain files that, while not necessary for the basic functioning of the system, are still often necessary for a system that functions the way one would expect it to. The truth is that these days, while the system would technically function without these files, most people would find it unusable. (Although it's not exactly the same, the /usr directory is to Darwin what the /Library folder is to Quartz.)
/usr/X11 (/usr/X11R6)	X11 is UNIX's traditional graphical interface. While it's seldom used in Mac OS X, some people may have uses for specific applications that rely on it. This is an optional install when you install Leopard, but if it is installed, this is where most of the parts of X11 live.
/usr/bin	Like /bin, /usr/bin contains user-level command-line executables. Many of the most common commands you will use are found in this directory.
/usr/libexec	This directory contains a number of special executables. This includes files that control tasks related to printing, networking, security, and the built-in web server.
/usr/local	This is yet another metadirectory. In the traditional UNIX way of doing things, this is where one would install any add-ons to the system that didn't come with it by default. Many third-party additions will still install themselves here. This directory doesn't exist by default in Leopard, but it's likely if you make much use of Darwin, it will be created sooner or later.
/usr/sbin	Like /sbin, this is a directory that contains administrative executables.

Introducing the Shell

The Terminal application (go ahead, fire it up) is essentially an empty window that can display and accept text input. In order for you to actually do anything, Terminal must run a shell program inside of itself. A *shell* is a specialized application that helps you interact with Darwin; it shares the same relationship to Darwin that the Finder shares with Quartz. By default, Leopard includes five of the most common UNIX shells: Bash, Korn, Bourne, Tcsh, and Zsh (the C shell is also listed as a shell—however, it is actually a link to Tcsh). Of the six, the shell Leopard uses by default is Bash.

> **NOTE** Originally, Mac OS X used Tcsh by default, but switched to Bash with the release of OS X 10.3 Panther. If you are new to working with UNIX shells, I'd recommend sticking with Bash, at least while you are learning. The lessons in this book, unless specifically noted, are all given using the Bash shell.

The first time you launch Terminal, you'll be greeted by some text similar to this:

```
Last login: Tue Sep  5 14:12:26 on ttyp1
Leopard:~ scott$ _
```

The first line tells you when you last logged in to Darwin (even if you've never logged in to Darwin before intentionally, you'll still get a message saying you did); followed by the default prompt for Bash. The default prompt (which, like most everything else in Darwin, can be changed) gives you some important information. First, it gives you the name of your computer, which is either assigned by your network or taken from the Computer Name field in the system's Sharing preference pane. Next, following the :, the prompt gives you your location in the file system (the ~ is a shortcut representing your home directory). Then the prompt gives you the username you are logged in as, followed by the $ prompt (which will change to a # if the user is logged in as the *root* user, otherwise known as the *superuser*). Finally, you get the cursor anxiously waiting your command.

As you will soon see, shells possess some hidden powers that can make your interactions with Darwin more pleasant and add a new level of power and flexibility to the command line. Before you look at the shell in more depth, though, you should first learn a bit about the Darwin file system as well as a few basic Darwin commands (walk before flying and all that).

Moving Around Darwin

One of the first things you need to learn about the shell is how to move around and view the file system. To do this, there are three basic commands to start with: ls, cd, and pwd.

ls

ls is the "list" command, and by default lists all the visible files in a directory. If you're familiar with DOS, it would be the replacement for dir. By default, the ls command looks something like this:

```
Leopard:~ scott$ ls
Desktop    Library   Music     Public
Documents  Movies    Pictures  Sites
```

The first thing you may notice is that by default all directories (folders), files, and executables (applications) look the same when using the ls command (of course, in this example they all are directories). That's because, as we previously mentioned, Darwin treats everything as a file. To differentiate between the different types of files, there are two primary options:

- ls -F will append special files with a symbol to determine their type. It will add a / to directories, a * to executables, a @ to symbolic links (aliases), and a few other symbols for other special file types.

- ls -G will colorize the output using different colors for different file types as well as other file options. For example, by default most directories will appear blue; however, world-writable directories will appear black with a yellow background. Likewise, most executables will appear red and most symbolic links will appear purple—however, if certain attributes are set, this will not always be the case.

> **NOTE** One thing immediately noticeable to users moving to Darwin from Linux is that certain command-line commands are slightly different. For example, to colorize your output in Linux, one would traditionally use ls --color, and in some cases the output colors are different. This difference exists because UNIX comes in many different flavors and occasionally there is slight deviation in commands from one to the other. For example, some UNIX tools are derived from the traditional BSD camp, and they differ in some subtle ways from tools from the GNU camp. Linux almost always chooses its tools from the GNU camp, while Darwin tends to favor the BSD camp. While in general the tools will work the same, there are a few cases where there are minor differences—colorizing ls is one of those differences.

Like most command-line commands, the options can be combined. For example, you can use -F and -G together:

```
Desktop/   Library/   Music/      Public/
Documents/ Movies/    Pictures/   Sites/
```

Other important ls options include the following:

- ls -l prints out a long list that will provide additional information about each file. We'll cover what everything here means later in the "File Permissions and Attributes" section of this chapter, but for now the results will appear to be something like this:

```
Leopard:~ scott$ ls -l
total 0
drwx------+  4 scott  staff   136 Sep  3 07:00 Desktop
drwx------+ 10 scott  staff   340 Sep  3 21:03 Documents
drwx------+  4 scott  staff   136 Sep  6 13:51 Downloads
drwx------+ 38 scott  staff  1292 Sep  2 22:44 Library
drwx------+  3 scott  staff   102 Aug 25 14:54 Movies
drwx------+  6 scott  staff   204 Aug 30 19:15 Music
drwx------+  4 scott  staff   136 Aug 25 14:54 Pictures
drwxr-xr-x+  4 scott  staff   136 Aug 25 14:54 Public
drwxr-xr-x+  5 scott  staff   170 Aug 25 14:54 Sites
```

- ls -a and ls -A print out a file listing that includes hidden dot files. There are two main types of files hidden on your computer—some that are by default hidden from the Finder, but will show up normally in Darwin; and others (the dot files) that are generally hidden in Darwin. These dot files (called that because they always begin with a .) are often preference or configuration files. They are usually hidden to reduce clutter and not for some nefarious purpose (although you may find that some Quartz applications utilize these hidden files to hide something they really don't want you to find). The main difference between ls -a and ls -A is that using ls -a will show two special files found in almost every directory—the . and the ..—which represent the current directory and the directory immediately above, respectively (these act the same as the . and .. files shown when issuing a dir command in the Microsoft Windows command prompt). A common ls -a on a home directory will produce quite a few more files than just a vanilla ls (three times as many or more is not uncommon):

```
Leopard:~ scott$ ls -a
.                       .bash_profile           Desktop
..                      .bashrc                 Documents
.CFUserTextEncoding     .gdb_history            Library
.DS_Store               .lpoptions              Movies
.MacOSX                 .parallels_settings     Music
.Trash                  .port_history           Pictures
.Xauthority             .sqlite_history         Public
.adobe                  .ssh                    Sites
.bash_history           .viminfo
```

While there are significantly more options available for the ls command, those are the most common, and should get you started on the right path. You may learn a few other options as you go along, and later you'll learn about the man command, which will allow you to learn more about the ls command (and most others) than you care to know.

Listing a Directory Other Than Your Current Directory

Besides ls's many options, ls will also accept a directory or file name as an argument. This allows you to view the contents of any directory without actually moving into that directory, or explore a single file's attributes (using the -l option). For example, if I'm in my home directory, but want to view the files in my Documents folder, I can do this by adding Documents as an argument. For example:

```
Leopard:~ scott$ ls -G
Desktop/   Library/   Music/      Public/
Documents/ Movies/    Pictures/   Sites/
Leopard:~ scott$ ls -G Documents
CDC Baseball/   Personal/       Stuff/      CDCrosters.pdf
Projects/       Work/           Rails/      Writing/
eBooks/         Microsoft User Data/
```

Furthermore, if I want to find out more about a specific file, I can enter a command like this:

```
Leopard:~ scott$ ls -l Documents/CDCrosters.pdf
-rw-r--r--   1 scott  scott  25739 Apr 24 09:39 Documents/CDCrosters.pdf
```

Now that you know how to list other directories, the next thing you may want to learn is how to move into them (virtually anyway).

cd

The cd command allows you to move from one directory to another (or as the command implies, it allows you to *change directories*). The cd command doesn't have any options, and only accepts a path name as its single argument.

> **NOTE** cd is kind of special in that, unlike ls, it is not an executable file—rather, it is a special type of command referred to as a *built-in command*. This command, along with a few others you will learn about, is a function of the shell, and not traditionally a separate executable file. Although most common built-ins like cd exist in all common shells, it is possible that a built-in command in one shell will behave slightly differently than one in another (cd isn't one of these—it behaves the same way in every shell I've used over the past 20 or so years).

To issue the cd command, simply type cd followed by your destination, like so:

```
Leopard:~ scott$ cd /
Leopard:/ scott$
```

If no argument is given, then cd will take you back to your home directory:

```
Leopard:/ scott$ cd
Leopard:~ scott$
```

Finally, if cd doesn't recognize the argument as a file or directory, it will tell you so:

```
Leopard:~ scott$ cd /blah
-bash: cd: /blah: No such file or directory
Leopard:~ scott$
```

This is an error statement, and most well-written functions and executables will provide some sort of error message if the information you provide doesn't make sense to them.

> **CAUTION** Just because well-written commands often give you an error message when you do something wrong, it's important to note that this only happens when the command has no idea how to parse the information you've given it. However, this will not prevent all erroneous commands from executing. If a command is recognized as valid, even if the information you enter isn't, the command will execute. While this is often harmless, it can have disastrous consequences (the rm command, as you will soon learn, deletes files immediately and permanently, and can cause all sorts of badness if used poorly).

pwd

The final command in this section is the pwd command. The pwd command returns your current working directory, as this information is by default available in your prompt (after the :). You may not need to use this command too often—however, it is useful in illustrating the file structure of the system and can come in quite handy when you need to pass your current path into a script. Also, it's possible that you may find yourself stuck in a foreign shell on a foreign machine, where you may actually need this. The basic pwd command looks like this:

```
Leopard:~ scott$ pwd
/Users/scott
```

In this case, pwd returns the absolute path of my home directory rather than the abbreviated ~ in the command prompt. This can come in handy on a foreign machine where you may not know where the home directory is located, or one where the path info isn't part of the prompt.

Being a rather simple command, pwd only offers two extra options:

- pwd -L will print the logical path to your working directory.
- pwd -D will print out the physical path to your working directory resolving any symbolic links. This is the default behavior of pwd.

Wildcards

Before moving on to more Darwin commands, we should have a quick lesson on wildcards and pattern matching. *Wildcards* are special symbols that when used with other commands can help limit or expand the results. Table 18-3 shows the three major wildcards and what they represent or match.

Table 18-3. Darwin Wildcards

Wildcard	Definition (Matches)
?	The ? used on the command line matches any single character.
*	The * matches any one or more characters in a file name.
[ ]	The [ ] matches any characters listed between the brackets; this can include a series of characters as well—for example, [1-p] would match *l*, *m*, *n*, *o*, and *p*.

To put this to use using what you learned previously, if we cd to /usr/bin and list out the contents using ls, we are struck with a rather large list of files (in this case mostly executable commands). Wildcards will allow us to selectively list out the directory contents in more manageable chunks. For example, if we just wanted to list the files that begin with *v*, we could use ls v*, like so:

```
Leopard:/usr/bin scott$ ls v*
vers_string* vi@        vim*        vimtutor*    vm_stat*
vgrind*      view@      vimdiff@    vis*         vmmap*
```

If for whatever reason we wanted to expand the search to include *b* and *v*, we could use ls [bv]*:

```
Leopard:/usr/bin scott$ ls [bv]*
b2m*          bg*            bzcat*         bzless*       vimtutor*
banner*       biff*          bzcmp*         bzmore*       vis*
basename*     bison*         bzdiff*        vers_string*  vm_stat*
bashbug*      bridget*       bzegrep*       vgrind*       vmmap*
batch*        bsdmake*       bzfgrep*       vi@
bbdiff*       bspatch*       bzgrep*        view@
bbedit*       bspatch_apple@ bzip2*         vim*
bc*           bunzip2*       bzip2recover*  vimdiff@
```

> **NOTE** Like most things in Darwin, the characters used within the square brackets are case sensitive, so [bv] would not match any *B*s or *V*s.

Finally, if we wanted to list all files with two-letter names that begin with any letter in the alphabet from *b* to *v*, we could use ls [b-v]? and get the following:

```
Leopard:/usr/bin scott$ ls [b-v]?
bc* cc@ ci* dc* ex@ fg* ld* m4* nc* nm* pl* ri* su* ul*
bg* cd* co* du* fc* id* lp* md* nl* od* pr* rs* tr* vi@
```

Working with Files and Directories

While most people are perfectly happy and comfortable working with files and directories in the Finder, there are some times when it's either necessary or advantageous to work with files in

Darwin. Of course, like all things before you are able to unleash the power of Darwin, you need to learn a few basic commands for working with files and directories. These basics are shown and described in Table 18-4.

Table 18-4. File and Directory Management Commands

Command	Usage	Description
cat	cat *filename*	The cat command lists the contents of a file. This command was originally written to perform concatenation functions, so if used improperly, this could have unexpected results.
head	head [-n #] *filename*	The head command allows you to display just the beginning of a long file using the -n option followed by the number of lines you wish to view.
tail	tail [-n #] *filename*	The tail command allows you to display just the end of a long file using the -n option followed by the number of lines you wish to view.
cp	cp *filename filecopy*	cp creates copies of files.
mv	mv *filename newfilename*	mv is interesting in that it is used both to move files from one location to another and to rename files.
rm	rm *filename*	rm permanently and immediately removes a file (or files).
mkdir	mkdir *newdirectory*	mkdir is used to create new directories.
rmdir	rmdir *directory*	rmdir is a special command used to delete directories. It's a safer option than rm in that it will not delete a nonempty directory (which at times makes it more frustrating as well).
touch	touch *filename*	touch will create a new empty file. (If the file, however, already exists, touch will merely alter the date it was last accessed.)

CAUTION Irresponsible uses of rm can result in very bad things happening—for example, if you happen to be utilizing root privileges (which, in general, you probably shouldn't), and happen to type rm -R /* at the command line, your system will immediately begin to delete itself and everything contained within it until it deletes enough of itself that it can't continue . . . ever. (By the way, the -R option stands for recursive, a handy option found in many commands.)

To illustrate how all of these work, I've created a test file named soliloquy4 in a directory named Shakespeare.

First we can use the cat command to view the file:

```
Leopard:~/Documents/Shakespeare scott$ cat soliloquy4
Tomorrow, and tomorrow, and tomorrow,
Creeps in this petty pace from day to day
To the last syllable of recorded time,
And all our yesterdays have lighted fools
The way to dusty death. Out, out, brief candle!
Life's but a walking shadow, a poor player
```

```
That struts and frets his hour upon the stage
And then is heard no more: it is a tale
Told by an idiot, full of sound and fury,
Signifying nothing.
```

Now if we weren't sure what this file was (or how long it was), we could use head to view just the first three lines:

```
Leopard:~/Documents/Shakespeare scott$ head -n 3 soliloquy4
Tomorrow, and tomorrow, and tomorrow,
Creeps in this petty pace from day to day
To the last syllable of recorded time,
```

Likewise, we could use tail to view the last three lines:

```
Leopard:~/Documents/Shakespeare scott$ tail -n 3 soliloquy4
And then is heard no more: it is a tale
Told by an idiot, full of sound and fury,
Signifying nothing.
```

NOTE Like many OSs these days, OS X keeps rather long log files about many of the things happening on the system. While there are many dedicated viewers for many of these files, these files are often very, very long. For such files, tail can be a godsend. For example, if you ran a busy web server for which you wanted to see the details of the last 50 hits, you could use tail -n 50 /var/log/httpd/access_log.

To make a copy of our file, we would use the cp command:

```
Leopard:~/Documents/Shakespeare scott$ ls
soliloquy4
Leopard:~/Documents/Shakespeare scott$ cp soliloquy4 macbethsolo
Leopard:~/Documents/Shakespeare scott$ ls
macbethsolo  soliloquy4
```

We could then create a new subdirectory:

```
Leopard:~/Documents/Shakespeare scott$ mkdir Macbeth
Leopard:~/Documents/Shakespeare scott$ ls
Macbeth/    macbethsolo  soliloquy4
```

and then move one of the files into our new directory:

```
Leopard:~/Documents/Shakespeare scott$ mv soliloquy4 Macbeth/soliloquy4
Leopard:~/Documents/Shakespeare scott$ ls
Macbeth/    macbethsolo
Leopard:~/Documents/Shakespeare scott$ ls Macbeth/
soliloquy4
```

We can also use the mv command to rename a file:

```
Leopard:~/Documents/Shakespeare scott$ mv macbethsolo tomorrow
Leopard:~/Documents/Shakespeare scott$ ls
Macbeth/  tomorrow
```

Next we could try to remove our Macbeth directory:

```
Leopard:~/Documents/Shakespeare scott$ rmdir Macbeth/
rmdir: Macbeth/: Directory not empty
```

Oops, first we need to remove any files in there:

```
Leopard:~/Documents/Shakespeare scott$ rm Macbeth/*
Leopard:~/Documents/Shakespeare scott$ rmdir Macbeth
Leopard:~/Documents/Shakespeare scott$ ls
tomorrow
```

Next, we can create an empty file with touch:

```
Leopard:~/Documents/Shakespeare scott$ touch nothing
Leopard:~/Documents/Shakespeare scott$ ls
nothing    tomorrow
Leopard:~/Documents/Shakespeare scott$ cat nothing
Leopard:~/Documents/Shakespeare scott$
```

More Essential Commands

There are literally hundreds of commands available at the command line, and it would take far more space than we have in this book to cover them all; however, as you progress through the rest of the book, you will learn a number of new commands when they are applicable to the topic at hand. In the meantime, there are a number of essential, or at least very useful, commands that you may want to know about that don't fit nicely in a future discussion in this book. They are covered here.

man

The man command is the command that will explain all others. If you want to learn more about the ls command, enter man ls, and your terminal will open into a special mode (called a *pager*) for reading man pages, which will look something like this:

```
LS(1)                        BSD General Commands Manual                        LS(1)


NAME
     ls -- list directory contents


SYNOPSIS
     ls [-ABCFGHLPRTWZabcdefghiklmnopqrstuwx1] [file ...]


DESCRIPTION
     For each operand that names a file of a type other than directory, ls
     displays its name as well as any requested, associated information.  For
     each operand that names a file of type directory, ls displays the names
     of files contained within that directory, as well as any requested, asso-
     ciated information.

     If no operands are given, the contents of the current directory are dis-
     played.  If more than one operand is given, nondirectory operands are
     displayed first; directory and nondirectory operands are sorted sepa-
     rately and in lexicographical order.

     The following options are available:

     -@        Display extended attribute keys and sizes.


 :
```

Now this is just the first page of the man page—you can scroll through the rest using either the arrow keys (to move up and down one line at a time), or the spacebar to move through one page at a time. When you are done, you can exit the man page by pressing Q on the keyboard.

> **TIP** Computers have come a long way since the man page system was created, and while reading a man page in the terminal is relatively easy for short and simple commands, for more complex commands that can scroll through 100 or more screens, this isn't ideal. One neat trick you can use is man -t *command* | open -f -a /Applications/Preview.app, which will open the entire man page of the command in Preview as a PDF file for immediate reading, printing, or saving. (The -t option converts the man page into a PostScript file, which you can then pipe into your Preview application, which converts the PostScript file into a PDF file as it opens it. Pipes are covered later.)

grep

The grep command searches through files or results for a specified string and then prints out the lines that contain a match. For example, using the preceding text file, we could print out all lines that contain "to" using the command grep to tomorrow. This is shown here:

```
Leopard:~/Documents/Shakespeare scott$ ls
nothing    tomorrow
Leopard:~/Documents/Shakespeare scott$ grep to tomorrow
Tomorrow, and tomorrow, and tomorrow,
Creeps in this petty pace from day to day
The way to dusty death. Out, out, brief candle!
```

ln

ln is the command-line utility for creating links. While there are different ways of linking files, what we are most concerned with are symbolic (a.k.a. soft) links (more commonly referred to as aliases, or shortcuts in Windows). To create a symbolic link, you use ln with the -s link, followed by the name of the source file and then optionally the name of the linked file.

> **NOTE** ln by default creates a hard link, which is most likely not what you want, so it's important to remember the -s option. For the technically curious, a hard link essentially creates a new file that shares its data with another (the source). If you edit one, the data will change in the other. If you delete one, the other will still remain with all the data intact. A symbolic link, on the other hand (like an alias or shortcut), creates a special "path" file that always refers to the original. If this original is deleted, the path is broken unless a new file of the same name replaces the original. A big difference in use is that a symbolic link can refer to a directory or a file on a different file system, while a hard link cannot.

Let's look at ln in action:

```
Leopard:~/Documents/Shakespeare scott$ ls
macbeth/ nothing
Leopard:~/Documents/Shakespeare scott$ ls macbeth/
soliloqy4
Leopard:~/Documents/Shakespeare scott$ ln -s macbeth/soliloquy4 tomorrow
Leopard:~/Documents/Shakespeare scott$ ls
macbeth/   nothing    tomorrow@
Leopard:~/Documents/Shakespeare scott$ cat tomorrow
Tomorrow, and tomorrow, and tomorrow,
Creeps in this petty pace from day to day
To the last syllable of recorded time,
```

```
And all our yesterdays have lighted fools
The way to dusty death. Out, out, brief candle!
Life's but a walking shadow, a poor player
That struts and frets his hour upon the stage
And then is heard no more: it is a tale
Told by an idiot, full of sound and fury,
Signifying nothing.
```

who

The who command tells you who else is logged in to the computer. Traditionally, this would just be you, since most personal computers would only allow one person to be logged in at a time (and this is how we still tend to use them). However, if you've turned on the Remote Login option in the Sharing control pane, it's possible for multiple users to actually be using one Mac OS system at a time. who also has a related command, whoami, which will also tell you your username if you ever forget. (By the way, your Darwin username is the "short" username you pick when you create your account.)

To see these in action on your system isn't always that exciting:

```
Leopard:~ scott$ who
scott     console  May 20 19:39
scott     ttyp1    May 20 20:17
Leopard:~ scott$ whoami
scott
```

> **NOTE** who may be considered dangerous by many systems administrators who feel it's a potential security breach to disclose too much information about the system or its users; for this reason, on many of today's servers, systems are in place to keep you from finding out who's really online at any time. Of course, the real cool (or if you're a systems administrator, real bad) command that is similar to who is finger. Traditionally, finger would allow you to find out all sorts of personal information about any user, not only those on your local machine, but you could actually "finger" anyone on any UNIX-type machine (and most other multiuser systems of the day). The finger command still exists on some computers and is even installed on your Mac (go ahead try it)—however, it's unlikely that you'll be able to find many machines on your network or on the Internet that will allow you to finger them or any of their users (for aforementioned security and even privacy fears). By default, Leopard will not allow any remote machine to finger you.

ps

ps allows you to view what processes are running at any given time on your system. By default, it shows limited information about all the services running from the terminal you are using (i.e., only the current Darwin process that you've started from your current terminal session). Until you really start digging into the power of Darwin, ps will likely just return your shell as your only process:

```
Leopard:~ scott$ ps
  PID  TTY TIME CMD
  310  p1 0:00.12 -bash
```

The important pieces of information here are the PID (process ID) and the COMMAND. However, with a few options, ps can give you lots of information about every command running on your system. The most common options are -a, -u, and -x (so common, in fact, that you can issue them without the -). This will most likely give you a long scrolling list of processes:

```
Leopard:~ scott$ ps aux
USER        PID %CPU %MEM     VSZ     RSS TT  STAT STARTED      TIME COMMAND
scott       304  5.7 -7.2  750344 150160 ??  S    8:15PM  13:46.39 /Applicati
scott       307  0.9 -0.9  374372  19368 ??  R    8:17PM   0:10.18 /Applicati
windowse     62  0.8 -2.4  907896  51124 ??  Ss   4:14PM   3:21.24 /System/Li
scott       305  0.1 -1.3  481400  26912 ??  S    8:16PM   0:06.38 /Applicati
root         31  0.0 -0.1   27840   2408 ??  Ss   4:14PM   0:00.03 /usr/bin/W
root         32  0.0 -0.4  303152   7440 ??  Ss   4:14PM   0:01.39 /Library/A
root         33  0.0 -0.1   27824   2052 ??  Ss   4:14PM   0:00.01 /System/Li
root         34  0.0 -0.1   27844   2328 ??  Ss   4:14PM   0:00.02 /usr/sbin/
root         35  0.0 -0.1   28564   2696 ??
...
```

This gives you much more information besides the PID and COMMAND (which is the full path, and as shown, is often truncated by the width of the terminal), including what USER is responsible for the process, how much of your computer's processor power the command is using (%CPU), and how much of the system's memory the command is using (%MEM). By default, the information is sorted so that the processes that are using the most processing power are listed first. If you want to filter this a bit to show only what tasks a specific user is running, you can use the -U option. For example, if you just wanted to see how many processes you are personally responsible for, you could use the following:

```
Leopard:~ scott$ ps aux -U scott
USER        PID %CPU %MEM     VSZ     RSS TT  STAT STARTED      TIME COMMAND
scott       304  6.0 -7.4  753864 154472 ??  S    8:15PM  15:51.65 /Applications
scott        71  0.0 -0.4  365144   7740 ??  Ss   4:15PM   0:04.67 /System/Libra
scott       244  0.0 -0.2  349524   3392 ??  S    7:39PM   0:00.14 /Library/Star
scott       245  0.0 -0.3   55632   5588 ??  Ss   7:39PM   0:00.42 /System/Libra
scott       248  0.0 -0.2   27840   3560 ??  S    7:39PM   0:00.03 /Library/Star
scott       250  0.0 -0.2   27936   3288 ??  S    7:39PM   0:00.06 aped
scott       257  0.0 -0.5  372004   9988 ??  S    7:40PM   0:00.95 /System/Libra
scott       259  0.0 -0.5  368044   9708 ??  S    7:40PM   0:02.27 /System/Libra
scott       260  0.0 -0.7  380848  14532 ??  S    7:40PM   0:01.14 /System/Libra
scott       265  0.0 -0.2  357976   4068 ??  S    7:40PM   0:16.47 /System/Libra
scott       266  0.0 -0.1  347028   2508 ??  S    7:40PM   0:00.06 /Applications
scott       267  0.0 -0.2  351700   3804 ??  S    7:40PM   0:00.18 /Applications
scott       268  0.0 -0.7  366848  14580 ??  S    7:40PM   0:01.44 /Users/scott/
scott       269  0.0 -0.1  348020   2864 ??  S    7:40PM   0:00.21 /Applications
scott       281  0.0 -4.0  476464  84268 ??  S    7:41PM   5:04.01 /Applications
scott       292  0.0 -2.2  410676  45744 ??  S    7:46PM   0:14.68 /Applications
scott       293  0.0 -0.5  372204  10168 ??  S    7:46PM   0:03.98 /Applications
scott       302  0.0 -0.1   38096   1184 ??  S    7:52PM   0:00.03 /System/Libra
scott       305  0.0 -1.3  481400  26916 ??  S    8:16PM   0:06.82 /Applications
scott       307  0.0 -0.9  374564  18976 ??  R    8:17PM   0:11.89 /Applications
scott       310  0.0 -0.0   27728    992 p1  S    8:17PM   0:00.13 -bash
scott       390  0.0 -0.9  383348  19312 ??  S    9:14PM   0:02.21 /Applications
scott        69  0.0 -0.4   82956   8256 ??  Ss   4:15PM   0:02.22 /System/Libra
scott       417  0.0 -0.2   75600   4112 ??  SNs  9:47PM   0:00.19 /System/Libra
```

NOTE A similar command to ps is top. The primary difference between the two is that ps takes a snapshot of processes when you run the command, while top stays active and continually updates itself. The Activity Monitor application in the Utilities folder provides a nice GUI to the top command (and presents some additional information as well, including disk usage, memory usage, and CPU usage).

kill

kill is used to stop a specific process. This can be necessary if you have a task that is running amok and you can't figure out how else to stop it (perhaps you are attempting to write your own application or script and it gets caught in a nasty loop).

To see this in action, we can intentionally create some very nasty background tasks using the yes command, which we will then kill.

> **NOTE** The yes command by default prints out y indefinitely as fast as possible. If you want to find out just how hot your computer will get before a fan kicks in, you can open up a few terminal windows (or tabs that were added to the Terminal application in Leopard) and run yes in each one. I'm not sure I'd recommend this if you are using a MacBook Pro while it is sitting on your lap, though . . . you might not like the burning sensation it causes. To stop yes from running the "correct" way, just press Ctrl+C, and it should stop.

To do this, we will first start running yes in the background twice, and then we will find out what the PID of each yes process is and kill it:

```
Leopard:~ scott$ yes > /dev/null &
[1] 480
Leopard:~ scott$ yes > /dev/null &
[2] 481
Leopard:~ scott$ ps u
USER    PID %CPU %MEM    VSZ   RSS  TT  STAT STARTED       TIME COMMAND
scott   481 96.8 -0.0   27376  476  p1  R    10:38PM    0:03.25 yes
scott   480 93.4 -0.0   27376  476  p1  R    10:38PM    0:05.20 yes
scott   473  0.1 -0.0   27728  784  p1  S    10:35PM    0:00.02 -bash
Leopard:~ scott$ kill 481
Leopard:~ scott$ kill 480
[1]-  Terminated              yes >/dev/null
[2]+  Terminated              yes >/dev/null
Leopard:~ scott$ ps u
USER    PID %CPU %MEM    VSZ   RSS  TT  STAT STARTED       TIME COMMAND
scott   473  0.0 -0.0   27728  788  p1  S    10:35PM    0:00.02 -bash
```

There are a few things I should explain. The yes command I entered, yes > /dev/null &, takes the output of yes and redirects it to /dev/null, which is a special device in most UNIX systems that is a black hole of sorts. Everything sent to /dev/null just goes away. The > is the redirect command, and the & tells the terminal to run this in the background. We will cover background tasks and redirections later.

Finally, you may notice the ps command shows that one yes process is using 96.8 percent of my processor and the other is using 93.4 percent, and these numbers don't seem to add up. The reason for this is that the %CPU shows the percentage for a single processor. Most Apple computers these days include at least two processing cores (including mine), so in this case one yes command is using 96.8 percent of one while the other is using 93.4 percent of the other (your mileage may vary).

Occasionally, a simple kill still won't stop a process; in that event, you'll need to use kill -9 to stop the process. The -9 signal runs kill in KILL mode. Common kill signals include the following:

1: HUP (hang up)

2: INT (interrupt)

3: QUIT (quit)

6: ABRT (abort)

9: KILL (unstoppable killing of process)

less (more)

less is a pager, which allows you to scroll through large amounts of text that may normally scroll right by you in the terminal. You learned how pagers worked with the man command, which automatically runs in a pager (which by default in Leopard is actually less)—however, sometimes it's useful to use a pager with other commands as well. For example, when we use the ps aux command, we are presented with lots of information scrolling right by; however, if we pipe the ps aux command into less, then we can scroll around our output just as we scrolled around our man pages. An example of this is the following:

```
Leopard:~ scott$ ps aux | less
```

USER	PID	%CPU	%MEM	VSZ	RSS	TT	STAT	STARTED	TIME	COMMAND
scott	304	5.9	-8.1	795272	170688	??	S	8:15PM	24:06.93	/Applicati
root	39	0.7	-0.3	30440	6192	??	Ss	4:14PM	0:05.56	/usr/sbin/
windowse	62	0.1	-2.2	902716	45600	??	Ss	4:14PM	5:30.36	/System/Li
scott	307	0.1	-0.6	372104	12548	??	S	8:17PM	1:10.59	/Applicati
root	31	0.0	-0.1	27840	2408	??	Ss	4:14PM	0:00.03	/usr/bin/W
root	32	0.0	-0.4	303152	7440	??	Ss	4:14PM	0:01.47	/Library/A
root	33	0.0	-0.1	27824	2052	??	Ss	4:14PM	0:00.01	/System/Li
root	34	0.0	-0.1	27844	2328	??	Ss	4:14PM	0:00.02	/usr/sbin/
root	35	0.0	-0.1	28564	2696	??	Ss	4:14PM	0:00.82	/usr/sbin/
root	36	0.0	-0.1	27580	1088	??	Ss	4:14PM	0:00.47	/usr/sbin/
root	37	0.0	-0.0	27288	1016	??	Ss	4:14PM	0:00.08	/usr/sbin/
root	40	0.0	-0.3	31852	5772	??	Ss	4:14PM	0:00.23	/usr/sbin/
root	41	0.0	-0.1	27776	2780	??	Ss	4:14PM	0:00.12	/usr/sbin/
root	42	0.0	-0.1	28324	1716	??	Ss	4:14PM	0:00.02	/usr/sbin/
root	44	0.0	-0.3	29268	5316	??	Ss	4:14PM	0:00.27	/usr/sbin/
root	46	0.0	-0.0	27864	880	??	Ss	4:14PM	0:00.15	/usr/sbin/
root	50	0.0	-0.0	27252	708	??	Ss	4:14PM	0:20.84	/usr/sbin/
root	54	0.0	-0.3	30744	6768	??	Ss	4:14PM	0:00.32	/usr/sbin/
root	55	0.0	-0.1	27676	2184	??	Ss	4:14PM	0:00.37	/usr/sbin/
root	63	0.0	-0.3	37828	5512	??	S	4:14PM	0:00.18	/usr/sbin/
root	64	0.0	-0.5	37028	9752	??	Ss	4:14PM	0:00.53	/System/Li
scott	69	0.0	-0.4	82936	8332	??	Ss	4:15PM	0:02.26	/System/Li
:										

Using the arrow keys, we can now scroll through our output, and when we are done, we can quit the pager and return to our prompt by pressing Q.

> **NOTE** Another older yet extremely popular pager was called more. Although more was very popular, it was lacking in many ways—for instance, it would only allow you to scroll down (e.g., you couldn't go back once you scrolled past something). Because of this, less has largely replaced more; however, for backward compatibility, the more command has been linked with less, so the more command still works (although it will actually run less).

find and whereis

find and whereis are two commands that work very differently, yet are both used to the same ends: finding something in the Darwin file system.

find by default takes a path variable and presents a list of matches. Additionally, if a match is a directory, find will traverse that directory as well (find / will return every visible file on your hard drive!). Using regular expressions and wildcards can effectively narrow (or broaden) your search as needed. A simple find example may be something like this:

```
Leopard:~ scott$ find ~/Documents/Shakes*
/Users/scott/Documents/Shakespeare
/Users/scott/Documents/Shakespeare/macbeth
/Users/scott/Documents/Shakespeare/macbeth/soliloquy4
/Users/scott/Documents/Shakespeare/nothing
/Users/scott/Documents/Shakespeare/tomorrow
```

Listing directories is nothing new, but find becomes very useful with its ability to search for matches of specific file properties, the most popular being the name of the file. To use find this way, we give find the directory we wish to traverse, and then enter the -name option, followed by our search string. For example, if we were looking for our soliloquy in our Documents folder, we could use the following:

```
Leopard:~ scott$ find ~/Documents -name "sol*"
/Users/scott/Documents/Shakespeare/macbeth/soliloquy4
```

Other properties that you can use as search parameters for find include the file's owner and its group.

> **NOTE** When using find, it's best to have a good general idea of the location of the file you are looking for. While it's perfectly acceptable to do something like find / -name "sol*", find is not a fast command, so in addition to getting a number of false hits and warnings (mostly Permission Denied warnings from subdirectories that find isn't allowed to look in), it would take a relatively long time to perform such a search.

Unlike find, whereis is tailored specifically for finding executable files. It does this by specifically searching the common places where programs live (primarily the various bin and sbin directories for a specific program name you enter). For example, if you wanted to see where the whereis command is located, you could do this:

```
Leopard:~ scott$ whereis whereis
/usr/bin/whereis
```

While this may seem trivial on a certain level, there are a couple of good reasons to use this. First, if you occasionally compile or install your own Darwin software (which we'll talk about in the next chapter), at some point you may end up with two copies of the same program, and whereis will help you find them so you can deal with it. Second, scripts written in languages like Perl, Python, or Ruby often want to know where the language executable is, and whereis is a quick way to determine that.

> **NOTE** Two other commands worth mentioning here are locate and mdfind. locate searches its database for matches to your query, which makes it quite a bit faster than find—however, it's possible that what you are looking for isn't in the database. mdfind is a command unique to Mac OS X that actually searches on Spotlight's metadata. This makes it very fast and powerful—however, there is one minor setback in that Spotlight doesn't always index items until they are opened in the Finder. So, for example, our soliloquy4 text file may not show up in an mdfind search (or Spotlight search), at least until it is accessed by a non-Darwin application. As such, mdfind wouldn't be a first choice for looking for something in the Darwin file system on the whole (however, it's an excellent choice if what you are looking for is visible in the Finder).

lipo

lipo is a command that has special meaning to Mac OS X universal binaries. When Apple switched hardware platforms from the PowerPC architecture to the Intel architecture, they introduced the *universal binary*, which allows the application to run natively on both platforms. Whether you are running an older PowerPC Mac or a newer Intel Mac, you probably don't need both types of code in your application. lipo allows you to take a universal application and "thin" it so that the resulting application will only run on one architecture. The advantage of this is that you can free up significant amounts of space on your hard drive by thinning your application. For example, if we delve into Sherlock.app (which in Darwin will appear as a directory, since most OS X applications are actually application bundles, or special directories containing all the pieces of the application) to the actual executable (/Applications/Sherlock.app/Contents/MacOS/Sherlock), we can see that its default size is 570 KB. If we run lipo using the -thin i386 option (since I'm using an Intel machine—if you are on a PowerPC computer, you would replace the i386 with ppc), we can shrink this file down to around 280 KB. That's a 50 percent savings of disk space by stripping away parts I don't need and will never use on this computer! lipo will thin a file by taking the initial universal binary executable, followed by the thin option, followed by the output option and the name of the output file. lipo always makes a copy of the original, and it's not a bad idea to back up the original file until you are sure that the thinned file works without error. An example of running lipo on Sherlock could look something like this:

```
Leopard:~ scott$ cd /Applications/Sherlock.app/Contents/MacOS/
Leopard:/Applications/Sherlock.app/Contents/MacOS scott$ ls
Sherlock*
Leopard:/Applications/Sherlock.app/Contents/MacOS scott$ du -hsk Sh*
572K    Sherlock
Leopard:/Applications/Sherlock.app/Contents/MacOS scott$ lipo Sherlock -thin i386 ➥
-output Sherlock.i386
Leopard:/Applications/Sherlock.app/Contents/MacOS scott$ du -hsk Sh*
572K    Sherlock
284K    Sherlock.i386
Leopard:/Applications/Sherlock.app/Contents/MacOS scott$ mv Sherlock ~/Documents/
Leopard:/Applications/Sherlock.app/Contents/MacOS scott$ mv Sherlock.i386 Sherlock
```

NOTE The du command is a simple "disk usage" command. When used with the -hsk option, it will simply show you how big a file or directory is from the command line.

Now I can run Sherlock to make sure everything works, and once I verify that it in fact does, I can run rm on the original Sherlock executable and gain back close to 300 KB of my precious disk space.

NOTE What happens if something goes wrong? Well, that's why we back up the original, which we can then just put back in place with no ill effect at all. By design, this should work without issue—however, as companies transition from PowerPC-only applications to universal applications, it's prudent to expect that somewhere, somehow, it's possible that something important could get lost in this process. It's never happened to me, but it's better to be safe than sorry.

NOTE lipo is actually used to create and get information about universal binaries, not to break them apart. The use of lipo to thin out universal binaries is more of a useful side effect than an intention.

Pipes, Redirection, and Background Tasks

A few more things we should cover before we move on are the ability to pipe one command into another, the ability to redirect output (or input) to and from a command, and the ability to run tasks in the background. We've actually done each of these things in some of the preceding examples, yet as they are quite powerful tools, I'll give a bit more depth here.

Pipes

Piping one command into another is a great way to make even the simplest Darwin tools do powerful things. We saw this previously when we piped the ps command into the less command. The pipe symbol is the | (which is the tall line that lives above the \ on a normal US Mac keyboard). In practice, this takes the first command and sends the output into the second. Commands like less rely almost entirely on the ability to pipe one command into it, and other commands become much more useful with this ability. For example, the ability to take commands that produce large amounts of output and pipe that content into a filter (like the grep command) can save lots of time and headaches.

Redirects

A *redirect* allows you to alter what happens to the output of a command, or alternately direct the content of a file into a command. The symbols for redirection are ‹ and ›. A very simple use of a redirect is to create a text file using echo, like this:

```
Leopard:~ scott$ echo "Hello my name is Scott" > name.txt
Leopard:~ scott$ cat name.txt
Hello my name is Scott
```

The echo command normally would just print out whatever you feed into it back to your terminal, but here we redirected the output to name.txt (which may or may not have existed).

> **CAUTION** If you are redirecting data into an existing file, the entire contents of that file will be replaced with the new data. So be very careful with this command.

If you wanted to redirect additional data into an existing file (rather than replace the content, which the > always does), >> can be used to append the new data to the old:

```
Leopard:~ scott$ echo " Hello Scott" >> name.txt
Leopard:~ scott$ cat name.txt
Hello my name is Scott
 Hello Scott
Leopard:~ scott$ echo "Ooops" > name.txt
Leopard:~ scott$ cat name.txt
Ooops
```

Background Tasks

Any Darwin command can be issued to run in the background with the & symbol tacked onto the end of the command. This is particularly useful when you want to start a command that may take a long time to finish, or when running a task that you want to keep running indefinitely. For example, if we wanted to use the find command to find something with the name motd somewhere on our system, knowing that this may take some time, we may want to run it in the background. Here's an annotated example of this:

```
Leopard:~ scott$ find / -name "motd" > found 2> found_err &
[1] 358
```

Here we start our find command in the background. We are redirecting our output to a file named found. Also, the 2> found_err will redirect any error messages to a file named found_err (otherwise, even though the command is running in the background, error messages would still spam our terminal).

```
Leopard:~ scott$ jobs
[1]+  Running                 find / -name "motd" >found 2>found_err &
```

The jobs command gives us a list of all of our background tasks and tells us their state (in this case our only task is running).

```
Leopard:~ scott$ fg
find / -name "motd" >found 2>found_err
```

The fg command will bring forward the first running task (which for now is our only task). Since the command is running in the foreground, we can no longer use the terminal unless we pause the process. We can do this using the Ctrl+Z key combo.

```
^Z
[1]+  Stopped                    find / -name "motd" >found 2>found_err
```

When we use Ctrl+Z, we are giving the message that our task has stopped. We can now resume this task in the background using bg.

```
Leopard:~ scott$ bg
[1]+ find / -name "motd" >found 2>found_err &
```

While this task runs, let's start another background task.

```
Leopard:~ scott$ (sleep 30; echo "done")&
[2] 359
Leopard:~ scott$ jobs
[1]-  Running                    find / -name "motd" >found 2>found_err &
[2]+  Running                    ( sleep 30; echo "done" ) &
```

Now we have two jobs running in the background, our find command is still chugging along, and we have our new command (which will wait, or sleep, 30 seconds, and then run the echo "done" command. Notice that each job has been giving a number. Our find command is [1] and our sleep command is [2]. To pull our sleep command into the foreground, we must specify that we want job 2:

```
Leopard:~ scott$ fg 2
( sleep 30; echo "done" )
done
```

Eventually, the sleep command will complete and echo "done" to the terminal. At this point, we can continue to use our terminal, and eventually we will get a message that our find command has completed:

```
[1]+  Exit 1                     find / -name "motd" >found 2>found_err
Leopard:~ scott$ cat found
/private/etc/motd
```

Working As Root

In Darwin, the root user is synonymous with the administrator, superuser, or all-knowing, all-doing, grand poobah. Working as root is sort of like splitting the atom: great potential for good, great potential for total destruction . . . in the case of root, that which gets destroyed can vary from an important file to all of your data and the OS itself. Traditionally, root has no boundaries and no restrictions, and can override all the security safeguards on the system. As such, you should never use it. (Sometimes, though, if it's your personal computer, and you really want to do certain things, you may have to).

> **CAUTION** With root comes lots of responsibility. Nothing short of a very powerful magnet sitting on your hard drive can mess up your system quite like a misplaced root command. As such, I cannot stress enough that root should be used sparingly and only when absolutely necessary.

So, when should you run a command as root? When there is no other way to run it. For example, when we ran our find command on the whole hard drive, we received a number of Permission Denied warnings. If we in fact wanted to search those protected files and directories, we would have to do so as root (or as the owner of the specific protected files or directories). Additionally, while you may be allowed to see and use many of the files and directories in Darwin, you won't be allowed to alter them or add new files to the directories. If you need to alter a configuration file, or install a new Darwin application in a specific location, or do one of the many other related tasks, you will often have to do so as root.

When the time comes to run a command as root, one generally doesn't log out and log back in as root (which Apple goes to great lengths to make very difficult to do anyway). Instead, the recommended way is to utilize the sudo command.

sudo

The sudo command (which means *substitute user do*) allows selected users to run any other command as the root (or any other) user, as specified in the sudoers file (located at /ect/sudoers).

To run a command as root (which is sudo's default nature), merely precede the command with sudo—for example, if I wanted to manually run the weekly maintenance script, I would do so like this:

```
Leopard:~ scott$ sudo /etc/periodic/weekly*

WARNING: Improper use of the sudo command could lead to data loss
or the deletion of important system files. Please double-check your
typing when using sudo. Type "man sudo" for more information.

To proceed, enter your password, or type Ctrl-C to abort.

Password:

...
```

As you can see, the first time you use sudo you are given a stern warning about the dangers of using sudo followed by a prompt for your password. Upon entering your password, the command will execute. The preceding warning will only appear the first time you use sudo—however, each time you use sudo, you will be prompted for a password, with one caveat: by default, sudo will save your password for a period of time (5 minutes is the default), so you won't have to reenter it for any subsequent sudo commands within that time period.

> **NOTE** The weekly maintenance scripts are among three script collections the system runs to maintain your computer. The other two are daily and monthly. These scripts are meant to run at their indicated intervals. However, this is based on the premise that your computer is always on! If you frequently turn off your computer (especially common for laptops), then it's possible that these scripts and their subsequent commands may never run. Thus, it may be beneficial to run these commands manually as indicated previously to help clean up and maintain your system. (The weekly and monthly scripts may take a few minutes to complete.)

By default, sudo will allow root and any user in the admin group to utilize it. If a nonadmin user attempts to use sudo, instead of their chosen command being executed, they will be presented with the following warning:

```
user is not in the sudoers file.  This incident will be reported.
```

To run a command as a user other than root, sudo offers the -u option, which you would use as follows:

```
sudo -u username command
```

On the slight chance that you really must execute a series of commands as another user and you'd like to maintain the user state for an extended period of time, sudo offers a the -s option, which will in effect start the shell as the specified user. Since this command starts a shell as the specified user or root, no additional command is necessary. By default, this is the equivalent of using the older su command. If you must use this (and it's recommended that you don't), it's important to remember to quit as soon as you are done—otherwise, you will remain in root state and are more likely to do something regrettable (or forget you are logged in as root and walk away from your computer for a cup of coffee or something and allow someone else do something perhaps even more regrettable)!

> **NOTE** Before there was sudo, there was su (substitute user). Rather than taking a command, su just dropped you into a shell as root or the specified user. For whatever reason, many old-time UNIX users still swear by the su command, and while these are generally intelligent people who can perform amazing computer tasks in their sleep, their stubbornness in regard to su is misplaced. You shouldn't use su on the Mac (and yes, it is there). su was written in a time of relative innocence, when mail servers didn't require passwords and spam filters didn't exist, when virus protection wasn't a billion-dollar industry, and "god" was an appropriate (and sadly all too common) password for the root user. Anyway, those days are gone, and su just doesn't provide the features and, more importantly, the security that sudo provides (such as fine-grained per-user and per-group customizability, sophisticated checks on timestamps and files to assure that nobody has tampered with the file, and more).

sudoers

The sudo defaults are sensible and appropriate for most computer uses. However, for servers or other computers with many users, sudo can be coaxed into providing very specific, fine-grained privileges to individual users or groups. To do this requires editing the /etc/sudoers file. The catch is that to edit this file, you must have root privileges and you must use a special editor named visudo. visudo is really a special mode of the Vi editor—or more specifically, Vim, which stands for *vi improved*, and is installed on Leopard in place of Vi. The easiest way to accomplish all this is to merely use the following:

```
Leopard:~ scott$ sudo visudo
Password:
```

This will immediately open up the sudoers file to be edited (assuming you understand how Vi works, which if you don't right now, I will explain in the next section).

Sadly, a discussion on the many specific tweaks that can be made to this file would extend far beyond the confines of this book. However, typing man sudoers will bring you to the man page for this particular file and will explain in detail things like the extended Backus-Naur form, what exactly it means, and how to put it to use.

Editing Files

Editing files in Darwin is just one of those things that you'll eventually have to do to get the most out of it. For the most part, using a normal Mac OS X text editor like TextMate (€39), BBEdit ($125), TextWrangler (free), or Smultron (free, donations accepted) may be your best bet—however, at times it may be handy or necessary to edit a file on the command line. Leopard ships with four command line–based text editors in Darwin: Ed, Vim, Emacs, and Nano. Ed is the original text editor for UNIX, but it has been surpassed in both usability and features by many newer text editors. Despite this, it is still included in most UNIX distributions since it has found a small niche within certain shell scripts. Each of the remaining three has its advantages, and what it comes down to for most people is a matter of taste and habit (i.e., once you start using one it becomes a bit frustrating to use another, since they vary quite a bit).

> **NOTE** Since we mentioned some GUI text editors previously, it's worth noting that many of these come with a command-line executable as well, so that you may open any file in them from the command line. Specifically, BBEdit allows you to install the bbedit command-line executable, and TextMate allows you to install the tm command-line executable. Each of these will open the file in the GUI application, but it makes it handy to do so from the command line. Also . . . obviously these won't help you much if you are accessing the machine remotely through a terminal window.

Vim

Vim is, as the name suggests, an "improved" clone of Vi (Visual Editor), which in turn is based on Ex, which is based on the aforementioned Ed (which was based on an even older text editor called QED). Vim is interesting to people new to command-line editors in that, like its predecessors, it is a dual-mode text editor. To get things done, you must switch between an insert or edit mode and a command mode. While this way of working with a text editor takes some getting used to, it's fairly easy once you get the knack of it. Also, Vim, Vi, or one of its clones is installed by default on almost every version of UNIX or Linux, so once you learn it, you can count on something like it to be installed on any UNIX (or UNIX-like) system you encounter.

> **NOTE** Vim specifically has a special third mode—*visual mode*—which can be toggled by typing v in command mode. Once in visual mode, you can move the cursor around normally—however, the text you move over will be selected. This mode is very handy for selecting text for precise copying and pasting.

When you launch Vim, you can either open an existing file, create a new file, or just jump into the editor without creating a file. The syntax is fairly straightforward:

```
vim [filename]
```

where *filename* is either an existing file or one you wish to create.

> **NOTE** In Darwin, vi, view, vimdiff, and ex all point to vim—however, they each cause Vim to exhibit different default behavior. vi and vim will both launch in normal mode, view will open a file read-only, vimdiff allows you to open multiple files at the same time so that you can compare them, and ex will open Vim in ex mode (the :vi command will return you to normal mode).

Vim will begin in command mode when opening a new or existing file; so, if we open the soliloquy file we've been working with earlier in the chapter, we will be presented with the following:

```
Tomorrow, and tomorrow, and tomorrow,
Creeps in this petty pace from day to day
To the last syllable of recorded time,
And all our yesterdays have lighted fools
The way to dusty death. Out, out, brief candle!
Life's but a walking shadow, a poor player
That struts and frets his hour upon the stage
And then is heard no more: it is a tale
Told by an idiot, full of sound and fury,
Signifying nothing.
~
~
~
~
~
~
~
~
~
~
~
~
~
"soliloquy4" 10L, 409C
```

Some things to note here are the following:

- The cursor begins on the first letter of the first line.
- Lines on the screen beginning with ~ indicate that the line is empty.
- The line at the very bottom of the screen is the informational display. Initially it displays the name of the file, how many lines the file contains, and how many characters the file contains.

In command mode, the keys and key sequences have special meanings. For example, we can move our cursor around the text using the arrow keys, or the H, J, K, and L keys (old UNIX keyboards didn't all have arrow keys). If we are searching for a particular word (for example, *candle*), we could use the search function, which is / followed by our search term. /candle followed by the Return key will move the cursor to the first letter of the first instance of *candle* that it finds. If we want to continue to search for the next occurrence of our search term, we can use an empty /, and then press Return. In this particular case, since there is only one occurrence of *candle*, the informational line at the bottom will tell us search hit BOTTOM, continuing at TOP. If there were more occurrences of our search term, / would continue to search forward in our text for them. To search backward, replace the / with ?.

> **NOTE** Searching in Vim is case sensitive. Also, in its search, Vim has its own special characters—for example, the . character is a wildcard, so if you were to search for, say, the period at the end of a sentence, you would need to escape the . with a \ (backslash). Otherwise, it would match every character in the document.

To actually enter text, you need to enter insert mode. You can do this by typing i, which will start inserting at the point where your cursor is. Alternately, typing I will begin inserting text at the beginning of the line you are on, and o will start you at the beginning of a new line immediately below the line your cursor is on. In insert mode, you can type as you would normally. To exit insert mode and return to command mode, press the Esc key.

> **NOTE** If in doubt which mode you are in, you can always press the Esc key to return you to command mode (pressing Esc in command mode has no effect). Additionally, the informational line at the bottom will present you with a big, bold -- INSERT -- message when you are in insert mode.

When you are done editing your file, you can save it (while in command mode) using :w followed by Return if you wish to save it with the name that you initially opened the file with. Alternately, you can use :w *filename* to save the file with a specific name.

> **TIP** To save some typing when saving files, you can use the % symbol to represent the initial file name. For example, if you opened a file named supertext, you could save it as supertext.new using :w %.new.

When your file is saved and you are ready to quit, you can quit using :q. Alternately, you can save and quit in one shot using either :x, :wq, or (my favorite) ZZ.

> **NOTE** Occasionally you will find that Vim won't let you simply save a file or quit for certain reasons—most commonly when you wish to quit and your file is unsaved, or you are attempting to save a file that was opened read-only. In either of these cases, the informational line will tell you why Vim is acting ornery and give you the option of overriding its warnings by appending ! to the end of your command. For example, to force quit an unsaved file, you need to use :q! rather than just :q.

Once you get used to working with two modes in Vim, the next thing you'll want to do is explore the features of the command mode. To help, Table 18-5 lists common command mode keystrokes and what they accomplish (this is by no means a complete list).

Table 18-5. Vim Command Mode Keystrokes Quick Reference

Keystroke	Action
Moving Around	
k or up arrow	Move cursor up one line
j or down arrow	Move cursor down one line
h or left arrow	Move cursor one space to the left
l or right arrow	Move cursor one space to the right
e	Move to end of word
b	Move to beginning of word
$	Move to end of line
0	Move to beginning of line
(	Move back one sentence
)	Move forward one sentence
{	Move back one paragraph
}	Move forward one paragraph
:n	Move to line *n*
nG	Move to line *n*

Keystroke	Action
Moving Around (continued)	
G	Move to last line in document
1G	Move to first line in document
Ctrl+f	Scroll forward one screen
Ctrl+b	Scroll backward one screen
Inserting Text	
i	Insert text before cursor
a	Insert text after cursor
I	Insert text at beginning of line
A	Insert text at end of line
o	Create blank line below cursor and insert text
O	Create blank line above cursor and insert text
r	Overwrite one character and then return to command mode
R	Begin overwriting text at cursor
Deleting Text	
x	Delete character under cursor
X	Delete character before cursor
dd or :d	Delete entire line
Searching and Replacing Text	
/*pattern*	Search forward for *pattern*
/ or n	Search forward for previous *pattern*
?*pattern*	Search backward for *pattern*
? or N	Search backward for previous *pattern*
:s/*orig*/*repl*	Replace *orig* with *repl* on current line
:%s/*orig*/*repl*	Replace *orig* with *repl* throughout entire document
Copying and Pasting Text	
yw	Copy word
yy	Copy line
y	Copy selected text (from visual mode)
dw	Cut word
dd	Cut line
d	Cut selected text (from visual mode)
p	Paste text

Continued

Table 18-5. Continued

Keystroke	Action
Saving and Quitting	
:w [filename]	Save file as filename (if no file name is specified, the file will be saved with the current name)
:q	Quit Vim
:x, :wq or ZZ	Save file and quit
:w!	Force save read-only file (if you have proper permissions)
:q!	Force quit changed file without saving
Other Commands	
Esc	Return Vim to command mode
u	Undo
J	Join two lines into one
:.=	Display current line number

Emacs

Emacs (or "GNU Emacs," as the faithful like to refer to it) is another popular text editor (perhaps it may be best described as a powerful runtime system with text editing capabilities). Emacs can do wonderful things provided you take the time to learn a rather large number of mystical key combinations (and learning a little Lisp helps too). In fact, people who love and use Emacs (who really should have a name to describe them—like "Trekkies" or something—since they tend to share the same sort of devotion) won't settle for anything less.

Unlike Vi, Emacs is a single-mode text editor; so, in that way, it's probably similar to most GUI text editors you may have used. However, since it lacks a GUI, you can't use your mouse to access the fancy features. That's where the crazy keystrokes come into play. In general, these keystrokes take the form of either the Ctrl key or the Meta key plus some other key (in Emacs, the shorthand for this would be something like C-k for Ctrl+K, or M-k for Meta+K). Usually, you would hold these keys at the same time. The gotcha here is that the Mac keyboard doesn't have a Meta key. You can fix this by selecting the "Use option as meta key" option in Terminal's Settings preferences (on the Keyboard tab, as shown in Figure 18-2).

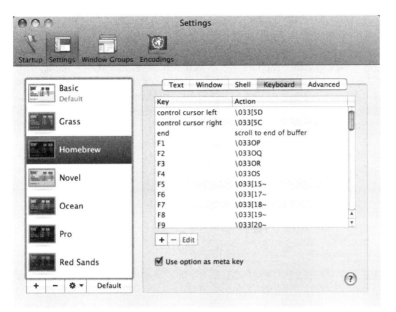

Figure 18-2. The "Use option as meta key" option selected in Terminal's Settings preferences

As with Vi (described previously), you can either open an existing file, create a new file, or just start with a scratch buffer when you launch Emacs using the emacs *[filename]* command. Opening our soliloquy file will produce the following output:

```
Tomorrow, and tomorrow, and tomorrow,
Creeps in this petty pace from day to day
To the last syllable of recorded time,
And all our yesterdays have lighted fools
The way to dusty death. Out, out, brief candle!
Life's but a walking shadow, a poor player
That struts and frets his hour upon the stage
And then is heard no more: it is a tale
Told by an idiot, full of sound and fury,
Signifying nothing.
```

```
-uu-:---F1  soliloquy4    All L1    (Fundamental)--------------------------
For information about the GNU Project and its goals, type C-h C-p.
```

Once the file is open, it's immediately ready to edit. To move around in the file, you can use either the arrow keys or some C-*n* keystrokes (C-f, C-b, C-p, and C-n). The Delete key works as you would expect, and you can enter text at the cursor just by typing.

To save the file, you can either use C-x C-s to save the file as its existing name, or C-x C-w *filename* to save the file as *filename*. C-x C-c will quit Emacs (it will prompt you to save any changed files first.) If you need to edit an additional file, you can use C-x C-f to open or create another file without quitting Emacs. Table 18-6 provides a handy list of a few common keystrokes and their effects.

Table 18-6. Common Emacs Keystrokes and Their Effects

Keystroke	Effect
Moving Around	
C-f or right arrow	Move one character to the right
C-b or left arrow	Move one character to the left
C-p or up arrow	Move one line up
C-n or down arrow	Move one line down
M-f	Move one word to the right
M-b	Move one word to the left
C-a	Move to the beginning of the current line
C-e	Move to the end of the current line
C-v	Page down
M-v	Page up
M->	Go to the end of the document
M-<	Go to the beginning of the document
C-u *n* C-n	Move ahead *n* lines
M-g g *n*	Go to line *n*
Searching and Replacing Text	
C-s *pattern* Ret (Return)	Search forward for *pattern*
C-r *pattern* Ret	Search backward for *pattern*
C-s Ret Ret	Search for next occurrence of previous pattern
M-% *orig* Ret *repl* Ret	Replace *orig* string with *repl* string (Emacs will prompt you for confirmation; press y to continue)
Copying and Pasting Text	
C-Spc (spacebar)	Set mark at cursor, which allows you to move cursor anywhere in the document, thus "selecting" text between mark and cursor (called a *region* in Emacs lingo)
C-w	Cut region
M-w	Copy region
C-y	Paste last cut or copied region

Keystroke	Effect
Saving and Quitting	
C-x C-w *filename*	Save file as *filename*
C-x C-s	Save file under current file name (will prompt to confirm overwrite of existing file)
C-x C-c	Quit Emacs (will prompt to confirm if current document has changed)
Other Commands	
C-x C-f *filename*	Open existing or new file in current buffer
C-h t	Start a built-in Emacs tutorial
C-x u	Undo

Nano

Nano is another handy command-line text editor in Leopard. What makes Nano special is that, compared to the others, Nano is relatively easy to figure out and use (the trade-off is that it lacks some of the more advanced (esoteric) features of Vim or Emacs, and while it's installed by default with Mac OS X (since Tiger), it's not as pervasive as Vim or Emacs.

> **NOTE** Nano is a clone of the Pico text editor, which is part of the fabulous command-line mail reader Pine. If you've used Pine in the past (or still do), you will find Nano immediately understandable. As an additional bonus, while many UNIX and Linux systems may not have Nano installed, it's just possible that they do have Pine installed, which will mean you may find Pico available where Nano isn't. Before Tiger, OS X included Pico, and today the pico command is still there, it's just aliased to nano.

One advantage of Nano is that the most common commands along with the keystrokes to invoke them are listed at the bottom of the screen (and the ones that aren't listed are easily looked up with the short yet concise built-in help). While the keystrokes may seem similar to Emacs in practice, the actual keys are different. Also, the common shorthand is different—while in Emacs, Ctrl+X is represented as C-x, in Nano, it's represented ^x (the ^ [carat] symbol means Ctrl).

Opening files in Nano is the same as opening them in Vi or Emacs. Just type nano *filename* at the cursor, and it will open up. Once again opening our soliloquy, we would see the following:

```
GNU nano 1.2.4   File: Documents/Shakespeare/macbeth/soliloquy4

Tomorrow, and tomorrow, and tomorrow,
Creeps in this petty pace from day to day
To the last syllable of recorded time,
And all our yesterdays have lighted fools
The way to dusty death. Out, out, brief candle!
Life's but a walking shadow, a poor player
That struts and frets his hour upon the stage
And then is heard no more: it is a tale
```

```
Told by an idiot, full of sound and fury,
Signifying nothing.
```

```
^G Get Help   ^O WriteOut   ^R Read File ^Y Prev Page ^K Cut Text   ^C Cur Pos
^X Exit       ^J Justify     ^W Where Is   ^V Next Page ^U UnCut Txt ^T To Spell
```

As you can see, at the top of the window Nano identifies the open file, and at the bottom it provides a list of common actions. The action list at the bottom will change based on circumstance—for example, when you go to save a file (using ^o), you will be prompted for the file name you wish to save our file as. The action list will also provide some other saving options (creating a backup, appending this file to another, etc.). With the short help file included with Nano, plus the adaptive action list shown, I'm going to forgo the table of commands since it would largely be redundant.

File Permissions and Attributes

File permissions are a central concept found in traditional UNIX systems. They allow one user to share files with everyone else on the system while still maintaining control of those files. The easiest way to view these permissions and attributes is with the ls -l command. For example, one line from an ls -l command may look like this:

```
-rw-r--r---   1 scott  scott    409 May 17 10:44 soliloquy4
```

The first string of 11 characters represents our permissions. Also of interest here are the file's owner (scott) and the file's group (also scott).

The first ten characters are broken down as follows:

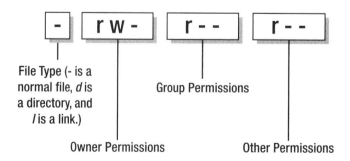

File Type (- is a
normal file, *d* is
a directory, and
l is a link.)

Owner Permissions

Group Permissions

Other Permissions

> **NOTE** The 11th character is special and indicates additional file attributes or security applied to the file. This will be covered in the "ACLs and Extended File Attributes" section.

Each of the permissions are either r, w, or x, signifying the ability to read, write, or execute (these are often referred to as bits). In the case of a directory, the execute bit signifies the ability to open the directory. The owner of any file can set these permissions as they see fit using the chmod command. Additionally, the owner can reset the group the files belong to to any other group the owner belongs to using the chgrp command.

The chmod command can be used one of two ways to set the permissions (also referred to as setting the mode), either literally or symbolically. The literal way is to specify the permissions as a string of numbers such as the following:

```
chmod nnnn filename
```

where *nnnn* is the combined value of permissions based on Table 18-7.

Table 18-7. chmod Literal Number Values

Value	Description
Basic Permissions	
400	Allows read by owner
200	Allows write by owner
100	Allows execute by owner
040	Allows read by group
020	Allows write by group
010	Allows execute by group
004	Allows read by everyone
002	Allows write by everyone
001	Allows execute by everyone
Advanced Mode Selectors (Optional, and Generally Not Recommended to Use Unless You Really Know What You Are Doing)	
4000	Sets UID on execution bit (execution of file will run with permissions of file's owner)
2000	Sets GID on execution bit (execution of file will run with permissions of file's group)
1000	Sets sticky bit

For example:

```
chmod 755 filename
```

would result in the *filename* having permissions -rwxr-xr-x.

The other, symbolic way, of setting permissions is to use chmod in the following way:

```
chmod [u][g][o]+/-[r][w][x] filename
```

where u stands for owner, g stands for group, and o stands for other (everyone); followed by + (for adding) or - (for denying) permissions (r, w, and x).

For example, if you had a file with the permissions -rwxr-xr-x, but you wanted to allow anyone in its group to also write to the file, you could just use the following:

```
chmod g+w filename
```

This would effectively just add write permissions to the group for *filename*.

Suppose you create a file and then wish to give special permissions to a group of people. By default, any file you create will have both the owner and group listed as you. You can change the group file to any other group that you belong to using the chgrp command with the following syntax:

```
chgrp group filename
```

To find out what groups you belong to you (and thus what's available to you), you can use the id command, like so:

```
Leopard:~ scott$ id
uid=501(scott) gid=501(scott) groups=501(scott), 81(appserveradm),
79(appserverusr), 80(admin)
```

So in this case, if I wanted to allow anyone in the admin group to be able to write to my soliloquy4 file, I could do the following:

```
Leopard:~/Documents/Shakespeare/macbeth scott$ chgrp admin soliloquy4
Leopard:~/Documents/Shakespeare/macbeth scott$ ls -l
total 8
-rw-r--r---  1 scott  admin  409 May 17 10:44 soliloquy4
Leopard:~/Documents/Shakespeare/macbeth scott$ chmod g+w soliloquy4
Leopard:~/Documents/Shakespeare/macbeth scott$ ls -l
total 8
-rw-rw-r---  1 scott  admin  409 May 17 10:44 soliloquy4
```

ACLs and Extended File Attributes

ACLs (access control lists) and extended attributes were introduced to OS X in Tiger (OS X 10.4), but while they used to simply be an option available to those who wished to use them, in Leopard they are used by default.

> **NOTE** ACLs will only be available on your system locally if you are using the HFS+ file system. For network shares, they can be used over AFP and SMB/CIFS.

ACLs allow fine-grained control of a file's access far beyond UNIX's traditional owner-group-everyone permissions. With ACLs you can control specific permissions for specific users or groups, and you can treat each user and group differently.

Specifically, each file on your system has one ACL, and each ACL may contain an ordered list of entries. Each entry sets specific permissions for a single user or group.

> **NOTE** If you have a user and a group with the same name, and you must differentiate these in an ACL, you may prefix the name with either user: or group: to specify which entity you are referring to.

Files with entries in their ACL will include a + in the 11th character in the permission listing when you use ls -l. If there are no ACL entries, but there are other file attributes for the given file, then the 11th character will contain an @. If there are no ACL entries or attributes, then the 11th character will contain a -.

To view the ACL associated with a file, use the -e option with the ls command—for example, if I look in my home directory:

```
Leopard:~ scott$ ls -le
total 0
drwx------+  5 scott  staff   170 Sep  7 10:35 Desktop/
 0: group:everyone deny delete
drwx------+ 11 scott  staff   374 Sep  7 07:53 Documents/
 0: group:everyone deny delete
drwx------+ 10 scott  staff   340 Sep  7 11:32 Downloads/
 0: group:everyone deny delete
drwx------+ 40 scott  staff  1360 Sep  7 10:39 Library/
 0: group:everyone deny delete
drwx------+  3 scott  staff   102 Aug 25 14:54 Movies/
 0: group:everyone deny delete
drwx------+  6 scott  staff   204 Aug 30 19:15 Music/
 0: group:everyone deny delete
drwx------+  4 scott  staff   136 Aug 25 14:54 Pictures/
 0: group:everyone deny delete
drwxr-xr-x+  4 scott  staff   136 Aug 25 14:54 Public/
 0: group:everyone deny delete
drwxr-xr-x+  6 scott  staff   204 Sep  6 18:17 Sites/
 0: group:everyone deny delete
```

When you look at the ACLs attached to the default folders in your home directory, you'll see that they are set to deny everyone from deleting them. Don't be afraid to try it; if you try a rmdir, you'll get a Permission Denied warning, and if you try to drag the folders into the trash, you'll get a warning telling you that that directory can't be modified or deleted.

To view a file's attributes, use the -@ option with ls.

> **NOTE** Most of the file attributes are strictly there for application and Finder support. You can add your own attributes for whatever reason you want, but for the most part in OS X they are there to support the Finder.

To add entries to or delete entries from an ACL, you use the chmod command with +a (to add an entry) or -a (to remove an entry). When you are adding an entry, the new entry will be added to the ACL. To remove an entry, you will need to specify the entry number using # *n* directives. Here are some examples of working with ACL entries:

```
Leopard:macbeth scott$ ls -l
total 8
-rw-r--r--  1 scott  staff  401 Sep  7 07:47 soliloquy4
Leopard:macbeth scott$ chmod +a "staff deny write,delete" soliloquy4
Leopard:macbeth scott$ ls -le
total 8
-rw-r--r--+ 1 scott  staff  401 Sep  7 07:47 soliloquy4
 0: group:staff deny write,delete
Leopard:macbeth scott$ chmod +a "scott allow read,write,delete" soliloquy4
Leopard:macbeth scott$ chmod +a "nobody deny read,write,delete" soliloquy4
Leopard:macbeth scott$ ls -le
total 8
-rw-r--r--+ 1 scott  staff  401 Sep  7 07:47 soliloquy4
 0: user:nobody deny read,write,delete
 1: group:staff deny write,delete
 2: user:scott allow read,write,delete
Leopard:macbeth scott$ chmod -a# 1 soliloquy4
Leopard:macbeth scott$ ls -le
total 8
-rw-r--r--+ 1 scott  staff  401 Sep  7 07:47 soliloquy4
```

```
    0: user:nobody deny read,write,delete
    1: user:scott allow read,write,delete
Leopard:macbeth scott$
```

The types of actions you can control in ACLs depend on the type of file. The following actions are settable for any file:

- delete
- readattr
- writeattr
- readextattr
- writeextattr
- readsecurity
- writesecurity
- chown

The following actions are settable for folders/directories:

- list
- search
- add_subdirectory
- delete_child

Finally, the following are available for nonfolder/directory items:

- read
- write
- append
- execute

More details about ACLs and controlling them are available in the chmod man page.

Customizing Terminal and the Shell

Once you start getting into using Darwin, you may want to make a few tweaks to both the Terminal application and your shell environment to streamline how you work. Before we leave this chapter, I feel I must cover these last few issues of customizing your Darwin experience.

Terminal Setup

The Terminal application that Apple ships with Mac OS X has gone through some pretty big changes for the Leopard release. These include the addition of features such as tabbed windows, which are very handy for those who work with multiple shells or must access many remote terminals at the same time. They also include the ability to save different window settings that control the appearance and behavior of your terminal.

One of the first things you may want to do when working with Terminal is adjust how it looks and make a few other tweaks (such as remapping the Meta key if you are a big Emacs user). The options to control your terminal settings are listed under the Settings tab of Terminal's preferences (Figure 18-3).

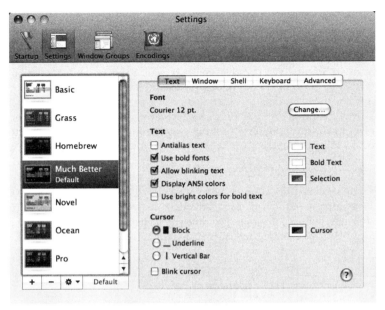

Figure 18-3. The Settings tab of Terminal's preferences

The Terminal settings preferences provide a number of different possible terminal settings listed in the column on the left. In the preferences, you can set options for each setting individually using the five tabs: Text, Window, Shell, Keyboard, and Advanced.

The Text settings control the font size face and colors. They also allow you to set the options for the terminal's cursor.

The Window tab allows you to set options for controlling the background color, title bar information, initial window size (set in character width and line height), and scrollback buffer.

The Shell tab allows you to set special shell startup commands as well as options about what happens when you exit the shell or try to close the window while a shell is still running.

The Keyboard tab allows you to set up key bindings, and lets you toggle the option to use the Option key as the Meta key.

The Advanced tab allows you to set a few other miscellaneous options pertaining to terminal emulation, bell actions, and text encoding options for foreign languages.

The other main Terminal preference tabs include the Startup tab, which allows you to select the default settings to use when Terminal launches, as well as what type of shell Terminal should use upon launching; the Window Groups tab, which allows you to save the behavior of multiple Terminal windows together as a group; and the Encodings tab, which allows you to select which text encoding should be made available to Terminal's settings.

Setting Up Your Shell Environment

Every shell has what is referred to as *environment*, which is basically made up of customized variables and commands that make the shell work the way you want it to. The Bash shell stores this info in a number of places. The variables that apply to everyone are stored in /etc/profile and /etc/bashrc. Additionally, you can make your own personal configurations to ~/.bashrc and ~/.bash_profile. As a general rule, things that affect your environment should go in the .bash_profile file and things that affect the shell specifically should go in the .bashrc file.

> **NOTE** Traditionally, things in the `profile` files would get read when you logged into a termi-
> nal, and things in the `bashrc` files would get read each time you launched a new shell. This isn't
> exactly how these things work anymore, but it's still nice to keep the content of each separate.

One common environmental variable that you may want to set is the $PATH variable. The
$PATH variable describes where your shell will look for executables when you attempt to launch
one from the command line. By default, your $PATH is set to include /bin, /sbin, /usr/bin,
/usr/sbin, and /usr/X11/bin (in the /etc/profile file). However, if you begin to install new executables, or even write your own, you may find that you need to add additional directories to
your $PATH. The syntax to add a directory to the $PATH is as follows:

```
$PATH=/new/directory:/another/new/direcotry:"${PATH}"
```

You can add as many directories as you need, separated by a colon. The "${PATH}" at the end
represents your existing path; without it, any of the default $PATH directories will be removed
from your $PATH. To have your path updated each time you launch a shell, it's best just to put this
info in your .bash_profile. For example, my current .bash_profile looks like this:

```
###   .bash_profile   ###

# a good place for environmental variables #

### $PATH ###

if [ -d /usr/local/bin ] ; then
        PATH=/usr/local/bin:"${PATH}"
fi
if [ -d /usr/local/mysql/bin ] ; then
        PATH=/usr/local/mysql/bin:"${PATH}"
fi
if [ -d ~/bin ] ; then
        PATH=~/bin:"${PATH}"
fi
if [ -d /opt/local/bin ] ; then
        PATH=/opt/local/bin:"${PATH}"
fi

### include .bashrc if one exists ###
if [ -f ~/.bashrc ]; then
        . ~/.bashrc
fi
```

Any line beginning with # is a comment. Here I use some of the built-in scripting functionality to check if common executable directories exist—if they do, then they are automatically
added to my $PATH.

The last part checks to see if I have a .bashrc file, and if I do, it includes that as well.

The bashrc files generally contain variables and commands that are specific to the shell. For
example, the default /etc/bashrc file sets the prompt variable. Other things that are generally
included in the bashrc files are common aliases and shell functions.

For example, my current OS X .bashrc file is simply the following:

```
###   .bashrc file   ###

#  This file is for shell-specific stuff                      #
#  $PATH and other env variables should go in the .bash_profile  #
```

```
### aliases ###

alias ls="ls -FG"
alias la="ls -FGA"
alias ll="ls -FGAl"

### functions ###

function pman() {
    man -t "${1}" | open -f -a /Applications/Preview.app/
}
```

Again, the lines that begin with # are comments.

Creating Commands with Aliases and Functions

The preceding sample .bashrc file shows a few aliases and a function. Essentially, these are both ways to create simple command-line commands that carry out more complex commands. In general, an *alias* is a way of creating a shortened version of a single command, while a *function* creates a command out of an actual shell script that may consist of many commands and simple logic.

Aliases are incredibly handy when you find you are using the same commands over and over and want to simplify them; you can even use them to essentially overwrite the default behavior of a command. Take the first alias listed previously:

```
alias ls="ls -FG"
```

This command creates the ls alias from the ls -FG command, effectively overwriting ls so that it will, by default, provide colored output and the benefits of the -F flag as well. The other two aliases in my .bashrc file also create aliases to other common ls options.

> **NOTE** You can create aliases at the command line using the alias command as well—however, if you don't save these to your .bashrc file, they will be gone once you exit that particular shell.

Functions, on the other hand, are more complex, as they are essentially simple shell scripts. Here's an example from the preceding .bashrc file:

```
function pman() {
    man -t "${1}" | open -f -a /Applications/Preview.app/
}
```

The first line defines pman as a function accessible from the command line, and everything between the curly braces defines what happens when we use the pman command. So, if I were to enter pman ls at the command line, the function would take the first argument, ls, and run man -t ls | open -f -a /Applications/Preview.app/, thus allowing me to simply open the man page of any command in the Preview application in one simple command.

Summary

Whew, there was lots of info in this chapter. While the aim wasn't to teach you everything about working with Darwin (which would be an entire book in itself just to scratch the surface), hopefully you now know enough to get around comfortably in Darwin, and more importantly, have a good base to build upon where you see fit. I will be using the info in this chapter to build upon in various upcoming parts of this book, beginning with the next chapter where we will take a quick look at adding to the abilities of Darwin by creating our own simple scripts and adding new programs from other sources.

## CHAPTER 19

Extending the Power of Darwin

After the previous chapter, we hope you are at least somewhat comfortable working in Darwin. In this chapter, we'll move on and show how to extend the power of Darwin by covering the following:

- An introduction to shell scripting
- An overview of Perl, Python, and Ruby, which are three powerful scripting languages included with Leopard
- How to find and install a range of additional applications using MacPorts and Fink
- How to custom compile a Darwin application from the source code

Getting Started with Shell Scripting

Shell scripting has been a staple in Unix since the first shell. A shell script allows you to add a series of shell commands to a file so that these commands can be easily run over and over. You can see an example of the value of this by examining the start-up process of Leopard. During the start-up, the shell script /etc/rc is started; this file begins a series of processes that effectively start up, configure, and maintain many of the necessary OS and networking functions that occur during start-up.

> **NOTE** It's not recommended that you edit this /etc/rc since it's possible that your system will not start up correctly if you make a mistake; however, you'll see that toward the bottom of this script there is a check for the existence of /etc/rc.local. If this file exists, it will include it and execute any scripting contained in it. If you want to include your own scripts that will execute every time you boot the OS, this file should be created if it doesn't exist (which by default it doesn't), and your additional start-up scripts should be added to it.

Writing a shell script can be as easy as just listing a series of any of the commands you may enter at the command line; however, shell scripts can also accept external variables and may contain simple if...then logic and loops. I'll briefly explain all of these things, but first let's take a look at a sample shell script (the line numbers are for reference and shouldn't be typed into your script):

```
 1:  #!/bin/sh
 2:
 3:  # togglevis
 4:  # A shell script to toggle the visibility of hidden files in the Finder
 5:
 6:  set `ps acx | grep Finder`
 7:
 8:  show=`defaults read com.apple.finder AppleShowAllFiles`
 9:
10:  if [ $show -eq 1 ]; then
11:      defaults write com.apple.finder AppleShowAllFiles 0
12:      kill $1
13:  else
14:      defaults write com.apple.finder AppleShowAllFiles 1
15:      kill $1
16:  fi
```

> **NOTE** For those of you who really hate line numbers in programs because they prevent you from copying the text out of an e-book and running it, later in this chapter there will be a Perl script that you should be able to tweak (when you are done with this chapter) to strip them out automatically.

This script will toggle the visibility of hidden items in the Mac OS X Finder, which is done by setting the hidden Finder preference AppleShowAllFiles to 1 (to show all files) or 0 (to hide hidden files) and then restarting the Finder to immediately enact the change.

> **NOTE** Truth be told, this script doesn't exactly restart the Finder. The script instead just kills the Finder. OS X, depending on the Finder, notices this and restarts the Finder for you.

The first line, #!/bin/sh, often referred to as the *interpreter line*, is important for all scripts because it points the shell to the executing script interpreter.

> **NOTE** On Leopard, /bin/sh and /bin/bash are both Bash shell executables. Most shell scripts in OS X (and generally in Unix) are written for the Bourne shell (sh) for compatibility across various Unix platforms (of which almost all have the Bourne shell installed). The Bash shell itself (a.k.a. Bourne Again SHell) is 100 percent backward compatible with the Bourne shell, with some extra features borrowed from the C shell and Korn shell. The general scripting syntax we are covering in this chapter is mostly Bourne shell compatible; however, there may be certain commands issued inside a script that are specific to OS X.

Lines 3 and 4, like all script lines beginning with # (except the sh-bang line), are comments. These are included to provide a clue about what's going on for anyone reading the script. Comments have no effect on how the script runs and in this respect are purely optional elements. It is a good habit to use comments, not only for others who may be looking at your script but also for yourself should you have to look at a script weeks, months, or even years after you wrote it. Here the first comment line gives the name of the script, and the second comment describes what the script does.

Line 6 shows us two things, the use of the set command and the use of backticks (`) in scripts. In a shell script, anything within backticks is executed, and the result is passed to the script (this is called *command substitution*). The set command sets the arguments used in the script just as if they were entered at the command line. So, line 6 takes the results from the ps acx | grep Finder command (which would be something like 261 ?? S 0:00.93 Finder) and makes them our arguments (of which there would be 5). The importance of line 6 for the rest of the script is that it specifically assigns the PID of the Finder to our first argument that can then be accessed as the variable $1.

Line 8 sets the variable show to the result of the defaults read com.apple.finder AppleShowAllFiles command. defaults provides a way to access and alter Mac OS X user default settings from the command line. In this case, we use it to read the AppleShowAllFiles value stored in the com.apple.finder preference to determine the existing setting (0 or 1) so we can then toggle the setting. If the AppleShowAllFiles value doesn't exist yet in your Finder preference file, you will get an error similar to this:

```
2007-06-26 12:24:00.175 defaults[1180]
The domain/default pair of (com.apple.finder, AppleShowAllFiles) does not exist
togglevis.sh: line 10: [: ==: unary operator expected
```

In this case you can ignore this, since the script will continue and actually create this value. However, if you continue to get errors after this (or if you get a vastly different error), then something else is wrong, and you should check your script closely.

Lines 10 through 16 provide a conditional if...then...else statement and provide the expected actions based on the condition. First, in line 10 we check to see whether the show variable (which is the set value of com.apple.finder AppleShowAllFiles) is 1; if it is, then we move on to line 11 where we change com.apple.finder AppleShowAllFiles to 0. Then in line 12 we kill the Finder using $1, which we set in line 6. If the condition in line 10 is false (the show variable is not 1), then we move on to the else part of the script, and in line 14 we set com.apple.finder AppleShowAllFiles to 1 and then kill the Finder. Line 16 ends the if...then...else statement with fi (that's if backward).

The script ends when it runs out of things to do.

There are a few ways to run this script: one is to pass the script to the shell executable as an argument, and the other is to make the actual script executable. Passing the script as an argument to the shell looks like this:

```
leopard:~/bin scott$ sh togglevis
```

If you want to have access to the script easily from anywhere, though, you must first make the script executable and make sure it's in a directory that is included in your $PATH (as discussed in the previous chapter). For example, we've placed this file in our own bin directory, which you can see is set in our path with the following statement:

```
leopard:~/bin scott$ echo $PATH
/opt/local/bin:/Users/scott/bin:/usr/local/bin:/bin:/sbin:/usr/bin:/usr/sbin
```

To make it executable, we use the chmod command:

```
leopard:~/bin scott$ chmod u+x togglevis
```

Now provided the script is in your path, you can use togglevis as you would any command from the command line.

Variables

Variables in shell scripts are generally reserved for use from within the script itself unless they are explicitly exported as environmental variables. Environmental variables (which include things like $PATH) are variables that are available to all shell scripts and programs, where shell variables are available only within your script.

Setting a variable is quite easy; just create a variable name, and set its value like this:

```
aVariable=Value
```

> **NOTE** The possible names a variable can have are virtually endless, but there are some rules. First, although the name can contain letters, numbers, or underscores, it's best that they begin with a letter (and they can't begin with a number, since that is reserved for command-line argument variables). Second, variables obviously can't share a name with a reserved word, which is one of the many words that have special meaning to the shell. Finally, by convention, environmental variables are often written with all capital letters, and shell variables are traditionally written in all lowercase letters, but of late many people use camel notation, which starts out lowercase but uses a capital letter where a new word begins. An example of camel notation is aVeryLongVariable.

It is important not to include spaces around the = when declaring your variables; if you do, you will get an error.

If you want to make your variable an environmental variable, then you must export it using the export command. Usually this is done immediately after the variable is declared, which can be done all on one line like this:

```
ENVVAR=Value; export ENVVAR
```

After the shell exports the variable, it will be immediately available for any program or shell script until the parent shell process exits. (In other words, every time you launch a new shell, you will need to redeclare and export the variable to use it again.) If you are planning on using an environmental variable over and over, it may be best to declare it in your .bash_profile file so it gets declared each time you launch your terminal or a shell.

Argument Variables

Some of the most commonly used variables are ones you don't need to declare at all. These are variables passed to the script as arguments from the command line when the script is called. For example, if you were to run an executable script called ascript, you could pass arguments to the script when you call it, like this:

```
leopard:~ scott$ ascript arg1 arg2 arg3
```

Here the arg1, arg2, and arg3 values are automatically assigned to variables $1, $2, and $3 so they can be used as needed in the script.

> **NOTE** In many computer languages, counting begins with 0, not 1. Command-line arguments in scripts are no exception. In scripts, $0 is always the script itself and will return the complete path name of the executed script.

These special variables don't have to be passed in from the command line, though. Occasionally it may be advantageous to create and control these arguments from within the script. This can be done by using the set command (as we did in our example shell script earlier). The set command will replace all command-line arguments with the arguments provided.

> **NOTE** set is a fairly complex command in Bash with lots of different capabilities. If you use set alone on the command line, it will list every environmental variable and function available to you in a nice, readable format. Used with options, set allows you to toggle many shell attributes. If you are interested, the gory details of all the possibilities for this command begin on page 51 of the Bash main page and continue until about three-quarters of the way through page 53. Also of note, set behaves differently in other shells; for example, in csh you would use set in place of export to create environmental variables.

Command Substitution

Another way to assign a variable is through command substitution. This allows you to work with the result of any shell command by enclosing the command with backticks (the ` character below the Esc key on most Mac keyboards). This allows you to take advantage of any shell command, making up for most of the shell's natural shortcomings. For example, the Bourne shell doesn't have built-in capabilities for simple arithmetic; however, using command substitution, you can take advantage of command-line executables that do this for you anyway, like this:

```
#!/bin/sh
x=2
y=3
z=`expr $x + $y`
echo $z
```

This little script uses the `expr` executable to do the math for you and then prints 5, which is what you'd expect.

> **NOTE** The Bash shell actually does have built-in arithmetic capability, so if you were so inclined, you could replace the z=`expr $x + $y` line with let z=$x+$y and get the same results.

Controlling the Flow

The ability to control the flow of a script makes it much more adaptable and useful. There are two primary ways to control the flow of a script: *conditionals*, which will execute commands if certain conditions are met, and *loops*, which can repeat commands over and over a predetermined number of times.

Conditional Statements

There are two common conditional statements available in shell scripts: `if` statements and `case` statements. An `if` statement checks to see whether a condition is true or false. If the condition is true, then a block of code is run; if it is false, an `else` block is run. The whole thing looks something like this:

```
if [ condition ]
then
     condition is met block
else
     condition not met block
fi
```

The `fi` at the end signals the end of the `if` statement.

One other thing that can be added to respond to multiple conditions is the `elif` condition. This allows you to create logic like this:

```
if [ condition1 ]
then
     condition1 block
elif [ condition2 ]
     condition2 block
elif [ condition3 ]
...
else
     no conditions met block
fi
```

One thing to keep in mind is that once the condition is met, the script will execute that block and then exit the if block entirely, so if condition1 is met, the script will not check for condition2 or run the code in that block.

There are a number of ways to create conditional statements; one of the most common is to use a mathematical test condition as listed in Table 19-1 (the Bash alternate expressions will work only with Bash and not a traditional Bourne shell).

Table 19-1. Mathematic Test Expressions for sh and Bash

Expression (sh)	Bash Alternate	Result
$x -eq $y	$x == $y	True if $x is equal to $y
$x -ne $y	$x != $y	True if $x is not equal to $y
$x -lt $y	$x < $y	True if $x is less than $y
$x -gt $y	$x > $y	True if $x is greater than $y
$x -le $y	$x <= $y	True if $x is less than or equal to $y
$x -ge $y	$x >= $y	True if $x is greater than or equal to $y

Another common conditional statement is to check on the existence of a file or directory. This is especially handy if you are creating workflow or other scripts that interact with the file system. An if statement that checks for the existence of a particular file would look like this:

```
if [ -e /path/to/file ]
then
    If file exists do this
else
    If file doesn't exist do this
fi
```

Here the -e option checks for the existence of the file. Table 19-2 lists some possible options.

Table 19-2. Common Options for Testing File Attributes in Shell Scripts

Option	Result
-e *file*	True if the file exists at all
-f *file*	True if file exists and it is a regular file
-d *file*	True if file exists and it is a directory
-r *file*	True if file exists and it is readable
-w *file*	True if file exists and it is writeable
-x *file*	True if file exists and it is executable

It is also possible to test multiple conditions using *logical and/or* statements. This allows you to check either whether multiple statements are all true or whether one of many statements is true. This is done using either && or || (that's the long bar over the \ key) between the conditions. [condition1] && [condition2] will return true if both conditions are true, while [condition1] || [condition2] will return true if either condition is true.

One final common conditional is to utilize the exit status of a command. Every command you run will provide an exit status; that's usually a 0 if everything went smoothly and some other number if something went wrong. if knows about this, so you can use statements like this:

```
if command
then
    if command exits normally do this
else
    if command resulted in an error do this
fi
```

Another way of dealing with multiple potential conditions is the use of the case statement. A case statement looks at a variable and responds differently depending on its value.

A case statement is generally much easier to use then an if statement; however, it's a viable alternate only if you are dealing with multiple similar outcomes that may be stored in a singe variable. A case statement looks like this:

```
case "$caseVar" in
    1) command(s) to run if the value of $caseVar is "1" ;;
    2) command(s) to run if the value of $caseVar is "2" ;;
    dog) command(s) to run if the value of $caseVar is "dog" ;;
    *) command(s) to run if none of the previous cases matched, "*" is a wildcard ;;
esac
```

Loops

Now that you've learned a bit about how to selectively run or not run a command based on a condition, we will cover how you can run a command over and over with loops. There are three main types of loops for shell scripting: while, until, and for loops.

The while and until loops are similar in idea, but they do the opposite in practice. Each of them takes a condition (similar to the if statement); however, where the while loop will run a block of code as long as the condition is true, the until loop will run as long as the condition is false.

> **CAUTION** Poorly written loops can have the adverse effect of running forever. If you are running a script from the command line, it's easy enough to stop such a runaway script with Ctrl+C, but if this is part of a background or start-up script, things can get more complicated. Therefore, it's a good idea to test your scripts from the command line before you place them in start-up files and such.

A simple while loop could look like this:

```
#!/bin/sh
x=1
while [ $x -le 10 ]
do
    echo $x
    x=`expr $x + 1`
done
```

This script will simply go through the while loop, printing the value of $x and then increasing the value of x by 1 as long as the value of $x is equal to or less than 10. If we switched while to until, the loop would skip entirely since our declared value of x (1) would immediately be less than or equal to 10.

> **NOTE** Like if statements, while and until loops can also evaluate multiple conditions using logical and (&&) and or (||) statements.

The other common loop is the for loop. Rather than relying on a true/false condition like the while and until loops, a for loop iterates over all the elements in a list. For example, a simple script to echo back the command-line arguments could look like this:

```
#!/bin/sh

echo "The command line arguments given to $0 are: "
for x in $@
do
    echo $x
done
```

> **NOTE** $@ is a special variable that contains each command-line argument together in a single variable.

You may find that there is situation where you need to get out of a loop before it completes, which is accomplished with either the break or continue command. The break command will immediately stop the current loop pass and exit the loop process entirely (that is, the script will continue immediately following the loop). The continue command will cause a halt in the current pass through the loop but will continue the loop process if the conditions are still met.

Input and Output

Many scripts you write will need to provide output, and often you may want a script to prompt for input as well. In the previous chapter, you learned most of the basics you need in order to output text either to the terminal or to a file using the echo command (with redirection if you want to write the output to a file), but there is also the printf command that provides more options in how your output is presented. To get information into a script, you can use the read command, which will provide a prompt at the command line for input.

The following script (enhanced from previously) shows how read and printf work (line numbers have been added for reference):

```
 1: #!/bin/sh
 2:
 3: printf "Please enter your input here: "
 4: read input
 5: set $input
 6: c=$#
 7: printf "You entered The following: "
 8: for x in $@
 9: do
10: c=`expr $c - 1`
11:     if [ $c -gt 0 ]
12:     then
13:         printf "\"$x\", "
14:     else
15:         printf "and \"$x\".\n"
16:     fi
17: done
```

When you run this script, you get something along the lines of this:

```
Please enter your input here: hello goodbye dogcow
You entered The following: "hello", "goodbye", and "dogcow".
```

The first thing you may notice is that unlike the echo command, printf does not automatically add a linefeed to each statement. By using printf in line 3, the prompt for the read statement appears on the some line rather than the line below.

The read statement is on line 4, and it's fairly easy: the read command followed by a variable to contain our input (cleverly called input).

In line 5 we set the input as our primary script arguments.

Line 6 starts a counter and starts it with $#, which is a special variable that tells the total number of arguments assigned by set in line 5.

Line 7 provides some text for our output.

Line 8 begins a for loop that will iterate through each of the arguments set in line 5. The $@ is another one of those special variables that contains all of our arguments in a single variable. In this case, $@ and $input will contain the same values.

Line 9 starts the for loop.

Line 10 decreases the value of our counter by 1.

Line 11 uses an if statement to see whether our counter is greater than 0. The counter is set up so that when it hits 0, the loop will be on our final input argument, so we continue the loop on line 13 until we reach the last of our inputs and then switch over to line 15.

Line 13 uses the printf statement to print one of our arguments surrounded by quotes. To get the quote to print, rather than get interpreted as the closing or opening of the text we are printing, we need to *escape* the ". We do this by preceding the quote symbol with a backslash (\) . printf knows a number of these formatting escape characters (which are actually borrowed from the C programming language) and will automatically expand them into their proper form when printing. Table 19-3 lists the common escape characters.

Table 19-3. Escape Character Expansion

Escape Character	Name	Output Result
\a	Alert (bell)	Activates the terminals bell. Depending on your Terminal preferences (set on the Advanced tab of the Terminal Inspector), this will either flash the terminal screen or make an audible noise (or both or neither). By default the terminal window will flash.
\b	Backspace	Moves the cursor back one space.
\f	Form feed	Clears the screen. Traditionally this would eject the current sheet of paper and start a new sheet.
\n	Newline	Moves the input to the beginning of the next line, like hitting Return.
\r	Carriage return	Moves the cursor back to the beginning of the current line; any further input would overwrite what's already there.
\t	Tab	Moves the cursor one tab space to the right.
\v	Vertical tab	Moves the cursor down one line; however, unlike \n, it will not return to the beginning of the line.
\\	Backslash	Prints the backslash character.
\'	Single quote	Prints a single quote character.
\"	Double quote	Prints a double quote character.

If our counter is set up properly (and there aren't any other glitches in our script), line 15 will run on the last of our input values, also printing it surrounded by quotes, but then instead of placing a comma (as if to continue the list), it will print out a . and then a newline character.

Line 16 then ends the `if` statement, and line 17 ends the loop and thus our little script.

One thing not shown here is that the `read` command can actually assign different variables to the input, where, for example, each input value would be assigned its own variable . . . well, that is if we assume that the number of variables and the number of words are the same. If we had the following `read` statement:

```
read a b c
```

and entered this:

```
one two three
```

then $a would be assigned the value `one`, $b would be assigned the value `two`, and $c would be assigned the value `three`. In the event we set `read` to accept three variables and we get four or more input terms, the last `read` variable will absorb all the remaining values.

> **TIP** If the integrity of your `read` variables is important and you want to protect against additional input, you could assign an additional `read` variable to suck up all the extra data. So if you really wanted only three input values, you could set up `read` with four variables and then just use the first three, thus essentially ignoring all the excess input.

One final useful related tidbit is the ability to merge an entire file into a script. This is done quite easily with the dot (that is, period) command. If you paid attention, you saw this in our sample `.bash_profile` file toward the end of the previous chapter where we used this:

```
if [ -f ~/.bashrc ]; then
        . ~/.bashrc
fi
```

Here we first check to see whether our desired file (`.bashrc`) exists and is a normal file. If so, we include it with the . `~/.bashrc`. And that's it. This is a handy way to create complex scripts where you can write entire parts as separate files and then include them all together to effectively run as one.

> **CAUTION** If you do combine scripts together, be careful with your variables. If two different script files use the same variable names and are then included together, unexpected (often bad) things can happen.

Advanced Scripting with Perl, Python, and Ruby

Shell scripting is very useful and fairly powerful for many things; however, there are a number of more powerful languages for writing scripts than the shell. Leopard comes with three of the biggest and most powerful scripting languages in use today: Perl, Python, and Ruby. Given the breadth of these languages (which are often referred to as *interpreted* programming languages or very high-level languages [VHLLs], rather than just scripting languages), it would be impossible to properly teach you how to use them in all their glory in this chapter. Although these languages are fairly easy to learn to use (some perhaps more so than others), the space (and time) needed to cover all of this goes beyond what is available in this book. Still, for those of you who are familiar with these or those of you looking to expand your programming repertoire, it would be remiss not to talk a bit about these languages and how they work within OS X.

Each of these languages shares a number of benefits vs. more traditional compiled languages such as C, C++, Obj-C, and Java, including ease of use, portability, and immediate feedback (since there is no compilation). Since they are scripting languages, all you need to write them is a text editor, and each of these languages is free and well supported across a wide range of platforms and devices. The other side of this coin is that interpreted languages such as Perl, Python, and Ruby (and shell scripts for that matter) have a few disadvantages vs. their compiled brethren: they lack the performance of a well-optimized compiled program; they are not as well suited for low-level programming tasks; and if you choose to distribute your script, you are also revealing all your source code, which makes scripting languages less inviting for commercial applications.

> **NOTE** Performance is a tricky matter. Although a well-optimized compiled program will always outperform an interpreted program (at least on the initial execution of the program), because of caching, the advanced subsequent execution of interpreted programs can easily match that of the compiled programs. Additionally, because of hardware advances, the real-time difference between the two is rapidly diminishing (though never quite reaching equality). Interestingly, certain programming technologies such as Java and some .NET technologies are both compiled and interpreted. This could lead one to assume that these would share the faults of both compiled and interpreted languages such as added development complexity and time and less than optimal performance. Although this may be true, they also gain a few benefits such as portability and source code obfuscation. (That's not to say that if a language *can* be portable, it actually is.)

Perl

Perl (which stands for Practical Extraction and Report Language) is currently the leading interpreted language used today (though Python and Ruby have been gaining on it over the past few years). Perl, as its name seems to imply, was initially designed to work with large chunks of text: to read in information and to parse it and/or manipulate it in meaningful ways. Thus, when the World Wide Web came into being with all of its marked-up text, Perl, combined with CGI, was uniquely suited to work with all of this data and manipulate it in fun, interesting, and useful ways. As a web language, Perl's popularity began to grow rapidly.

As a language, one of Perl's greatest assets, and also one of its greatest weaknesses, is its fantastic flexibility. It prides itself on providing multiple ways to solve any given task—Perl's motto is T.M.T.O.W.T.D.I. ("There's More Then One Way To Do It"). In the hands of a skilled programmer, this flexibility can unleash wonderful things, but it can also create a lot of unintelligible, unmaintainable code (thus giving Perl the unflattering reputation as a "write-only" language). The truth is that although Perl allows you to write some very ugly code, you can also write very clean, understandable code in Perl. Most important, though, when you have a problem, Perl usually can provide a way to solve it. For example, let's say we wanted to simplify numbering lines in source code (you know, because we're writing a book, and sometimes it's nice to refer to line numbers). Rather than going through each code listing and manually entering numbers, we could easy whip together the following script in Perl:

```
#!/usr/bin/perl -w

foreach my $file ( @ARGV ) {
    my $n = 0;
    open (OFILE, $file) || die "Sorry, $file can't be opened: $!";
    open (NFILE, ">num_$file");
```

```
        while ( <OFILE> ) {
            $n++;
            print NFILE sprintf("%3d: ",$n), $_;
        }
        close OFILE;
        close NFILE;
    }
```

This script allows us to enter any number of scripts as arguments at the command line, and it will go through each one of them numbering every line and formatting the output back into another file with the same name prefixed with num. If we ran this script on itself, we'd get this:

```
 1: #!/usr/bin/perl -w
 2:
 3: foreach my $file ( @ARGV ) {
 4:     my $n = 0;
 5:     open (OFILE, $file) || die "Sorry, $file can't be opened: $!";
 6:     open (NFILE, ">num_$file");
 7:     while ( <OFILE> ) {
 8:         $n++;
 9:         print NFILE sprintf("%3d: ",$n), $_;
10:     }
11:     close OFILE;
12:     close NFILE;
13: }
```

One other fantastic feature of Perl, which may be its ultimate strength, is that because of its maturity, it has built up a large collection of code libraries (called Perl *modules*) that can help you solve almost any task you can think of. Additionally, it has created a system around these libraries called the Comprehensive Perl Archive Network (CPAN) that provides an effective way of accessing these modules for your code. For the OS X user, included in CPAN are a number of modules for using Perl to manipulate Apple applications such as iTunes and iPhoto, as well as for accessing AppleEvents from Perl and more.

For the ultimate in OS X/Perl programming, there is also a project called Camel Bones (http://camelbones.sourceforge.net/index.html) that brings together a range of OS X/Perl–specific libraries, frameworks, and modules, allowing you to do things such as create Aqua interfaces for Perl scripts and use Perl in Cocoa applications instead of Obj-C.

Leopard ships with version 5.8.8 of Perl, which, as of this writing, is the latest stable version of Perl. Somewhere on the horizon is Perl 6, a complete rewrite of Perl that promises not only a new and improved interpreter but also many updates to the language. For more information about Perl, the best place to start is the official website: www.perl.org. If you'd like a book on Perl and you are completely new to programming, we recommend *Beginning Perl, Second Edition* by James Lee (Apress, ISBN 1590593912), which, despite being the same publisher as this book, we had nothing to do with. For a slower, gentler introduction, try *Teach Yourself Perl in 24, Third Edition* by Clinton Pierce (Sams Publishing, ISBN 0672327937), which, despite being from a different publisher, one of us had a hand in editing.

Python

Python, although not as well known as Perl, has been around for almost as long, but while Perl got to ride on the web wave because of its text-processing abilities, Python, being designed as a general-purpose scripting language, was often overlooked. Because of its more general-purpose beginnings, in many areas, especially surrounding math and science, Python was just the thing developers needed.

Python possesses a number of features that differentiate itself from Perl. First, Python was designed as an object-oriented scripting language (Perl gained reasonable object-oriented capabilities in version 5; however, on a whole Perl is still used very much as a functional programming language). Second, unlike Perl, the style of writing scripts is very strict. Proper indentation of code, whitespace, and line breaks have specific, essential meaning to Python. This often makes existing Python code much easier to understand than most Perl code, but dictating a strict style has also caused a few issues through Pythons evolution (and of course has caused a few "free thinking" individuals to shun the language).

Python has been around on the Mac for a while (beginning with MacPython even before OS X). Today, like Perl, it's a standard part of Darwin. Unlike Perl, Python is developed as a framework, rather than a traditional Darwin application. This makes Python available for Cocoa programming as well as Darwin development right out of the box.

Learning Python is fairly easy with lots of books and online tutorials available. One of the best places to start is the Python tutorial at http://docs.python.org/tut/. One nice part about learning Python is that it comes with its own interactive interpreter, which will start when you type python at the command line without arguments. Not only is this a great tool for learning the language, but it can be very handy for unleashing the power of Python for common tasks. We use the Python interpreter all the time as a calculator (we find it much faster and more flexible to use than the GUI calculator for most things). A session with the Python interpreter could look like this:

```
Leopard:~ scott$ Python
Python 2.5.1 (r251:54863, Jun  4 2007, 18:21:31)
[GCC 4.0.1 (Apple Inc. build 5450)] on darwin
Type "help", "copyright", "credits" or "license" for more information.
>>> x=2
>>> for y in range(11):
...     y*x
...
0
2
4
6
8
10
12
14
16
18
20
>>>
```

As you may devise from this, you can accomplish a lot of stuff with very little code. Once a programmer learns the nuances of Python, they generally find themselves creating code at a significantly faster pace than with most other languages.

Ruby

Ruby is the new kid in the family, but it's making quite a showing, largely because of the buzz surrounding Ruby on Rails (RoR), a very nice web application framework written in Ruby. Ruby shares many similarities with Python in general and on Leopard. Both are object oriented (in Ruby everything becomes an object), both are relatively easy to pick up, and both include an interactive interpreter for playing around with code (Ruby's interactive interpreter is not built into the language in the same way that Python's is; to get to the Ruby interactive interpreter, you use the irb command). For OS X developers the most important similarity is that they are both compiled as Cocoa frameworks, which makes them available for Cocoa development as well as Darwin development. Despite the similarities, Ruby is different from Python most noticeably semantically but also syntactically.

Because Ruby is a newer language, it seems to have learned to avoid a number of issues and perhaps shortcomings that Perl and Python have had, while at the same time incorporating new ideas that weren't mature when Perl and Python were conceived. On the other hand, because of its relative newness, Ruby has not been tested as much as Perl or Python and as such may not be as hardened as them. For example, there are those who think Ruby does not scale (in a performance sense) as well as Perl or Python.

> **NOTE** Much of the performance talk about Ruby may stem from the fact that nobody has actually used Ruby on a massively large scale. Ultimately, as a new language evolves, it will be tested, and in certain areas, it will fail or perform poorly; however, as it grows, those issues will be resolved. Ruby seems to be hovering around those last performance hurdles, but we won't know whether it's actually there until someone does something with it. Python may be considered the most scalable scripting language today, but it wasn't considered that until people realized just how much it could handle (a large amount of Goggle's back end allegedly runs on Python, which one would assume puts the question of Python's scalability to rest).

We'll be looking at Ruby, specifically Ruby on Rails, a framework for web development, later in this book. To learn more about Ruby in general, check out *Beginning Ruby* by Peter Cooper (Apress, ISBN: 1590597664). If you are looking for specifics on Developing Ruby Cocoa applications, documentation is included with the Xcode Tools installation (/Developer/ Documentation/RubyCocoa/).

Installing New Darwin Software

Although scripting is a good solution for simple problems, or new problems, often it's easier to just use a program that someone else has already written. Since Unix and related operating systems (such as Linux) have been around for a very long time and continue to be popular, for many of the tasks you may want to accomplish, an existing application or program may already be available. Best of all, many of these programs are available for free and are waiting for you to install them. Some are available simply by downloading an OS X installation package and installing them like any other OS X app (MySQL is a popular database that is available in many formats, including an official OS X installation package), but many more are available either as a precompiled binary (that is, a ready-to-run program) or more commonly (and often preferably) as a source package. This gives you some options; you could download the source package, configure it for your specific needs, and then compile the source code into an application optimized for your computer. You could try to locate a precompiled binary and install that (and hope that it works right). Or you could take advantage of either Fink or MacPorts (formally known as DarwinPorts), which are two systems of finding, installing, and maintaining third-party Darwin applications. This ultimately boils down to preference, but if you haven't already formed your own, we suggest you try things in this order:

1. An official binary release, if available, would be the first choice. This should make installation trivial and effective and should make for easy upgrades if needed. Additionally, any other applications that may rely on the application would probably assume the official release.

2. If an official version is not available, check either Fink or MacPorts (you'll most likely want to pick one and stick with it) to see whether the application you are after is available. Both Fink and MacPorts, once properly set up, will provide you with a way then to download and install the application. These systems will also assure that any other applications or libraries that the application depends on are installed as well and will provide an effective way to upgrade the apps or uninstall them if you no longer need them.

3. If you need a highly customized version of an app, or want to sidestep Fink or MacPorts for whatever reason, then you can download the source code and compile the application yourself. This will assure that the app is good to go; however, if you go this route, you will need to manually assure that all dependencies are covered, and all further maintenance of the package will need to be made manually.

4. Installing a random precompiled binary should be a last resort and should generally be avoided unless it comes from a trusted reliable source and it was compiled for your specific system; that is, an application compiled for Tiger (OS X 10.4) might not work right on Leopard (OS X 10.5). There are very few cases where this is recommended.

> **NOTE** A good source of finding official binaries, or at least reputable ones, is from Apple's website at `www.apple.com/downloads/macosx/unix_open_source/`. Here Apple provides lots of Unix and open source software and utilities to download.

MacPorts and Fink

As mentioned, the preferred way to get a large amount of Darwin goodness is through either Fink or MacPorts. To take advantage of one of these, though, you first must choose which one to use. In a side-by-side feature comparison, both of these come out pretty similarly. Fink, however, offers binary installation and source installations, where MacPorts uses source installs all the time. Fink also includes a GUI to install packages called Fink Commander. The main difference, though, is how these programs actually do what they do. The Fink project is based on the Debian packaging system from the Debian Linux Projects, while MacPorts is loosely based on FreeBSD's ports system.

Fink

Fink (`http://finkproject.org/`) was designed to bring the world of Unix to Mac OS X using tools provided by the Debian Project. Fink is designed to keep everything it does relegated to the `/sw` directory where it won't interfere with any of the default Mac OS X settings or applications.

The easiest way to get started with Fink is to download the binary installer package from its website and install it. During installation, Fink will prompt you for the administrator password so it can add some paths to your $PATH. Once the installation package is done with its installation, you should open your Terminal and issue the following commands to initialize Fink:

```
fink scanpackages; fink index
```

Once those two commands are finished running, before you start installing, you should make sure Fink is up-to-date. If you have installed the Xcode Tools package (that is, Apple's developers tools), the best way to do this is to issue the following command:

```
fink selfupdate
```

When prompted, select the rsync option (option 1). This will start a process of downloading, compiling, and installing the latest version of Fink. Once it's done, you're good to go.

Table 19-4 lists some handy commands to work with Fink.

Table 19-4. Fink Commands (Assumes Xcode Tools Are Installed)

Command	Action
fink list	Gives you a list of all the available packages. This is a long list, so you might want to do something like fink list > finkapps to create a text file called finkapps (or whatever you want to call it) containing the package list that can be pursued in a text editor, Preview, or even Quick View.
fink describe *someapp*	Prints a description of *someapp*.
fink install *someapp*	Downloads and installs *someapp*.
fink --use-binary-dist *someapp*	Downloads and installs the binary version of *someapp*, thus skipping the install phase.
fink remove *someapp*	Removes *someapp* from your system. The -r option will remove all dependencies as well.
fink purge *someapp*	Removes *someapp* from your system, along with all the configuration files.
fink cleanup	Removes obsolete and temporary files, freeing up disk space. By default this includes any old .deb files as well as any existing source files.
fink update-all	Updates all your installed Fink packages to their latest versions.
fink selfupdate	Updates the actual Fink package to its latest version. Upon its first use you will be prompted to select either rsync or CVS; rsync is the recommended option.

If you don't have the Xcode Tools installed for some reason and you still want to use Fink, you certainly can, but rather than using fink at the command line, you would be best served using either the apt-get command or dselect. dselect will allow you to scroll through a text listing of packages and manually select the ones you want to install. apt-get works more like the fink command and can be used as described in Table 19-5.

Table 19-5. apt-get Commands (for Binary Package Management in Fink)

Command	Action
apt-get update	Updates the listing of binary packages. This command must be run to initially get a list of packages for apt-get. After that it should be run periodically to keep the list updated.
apt-get install *someapp*	Installs *someapp*.
apt-get remove *someapp*	Removes *someapp*.

❚ NOTE Most packaging applications will require you to use sudo to install and remove packages.

MacPorts

MacPorts (www.macports.org) originated as the DarwinPorts project and was originated at Apple as the quasi-official way to manage additional Darwin applications. As such, it was rumored that sooner or later DarwinPorts would be integrated into Mac OS X. As of yet this has never happened; instead, recently, the project was renamed to MacPorts. MacPorts is part of Mac OS

Forge (http://macosforge.org), which is a larger project that hosts many of the open source projects specific to OS X. Other Mac OS Forge projects include Bonjour, the Darwin Streaming Server, WebKit, xnu (Darwin's Kernel), and Calendar Server. Apple sponsors all of these projects.

From a user perspective, MacPorts works similarly to Fink from the command line. Unlike Fink, MacPorts does not have an option to install precompiled binaries, so to use MacPorts, you must have the latest version of the Xcode Tools installed. Many MacPorts applications also assume you have installed the X11 packages and the X11SDK (both included on your Leopard as an option in the Leopard install).

MacPorts by default installs itself, and all the packages you install with it, in the /opt/local directory, so to effectively use MacPorts, you'll need to add /opt/local/bin and /opt/local/sbin to your $PATH. Additionally, if you are planning on using the X11 applications from MacPorts, you should add the line export DISPLAY=:0.0 to your .bash_profile as well.

Once all of that's out of the way, you can download the latest MacPorts binary installer from macports.org.

Like with Fink, once the installation is complete, the first thing you should do is to make sure everything is up-to-date. To do this, run the following command in the terminal:

```
sudo port selfupdate
```

> **NOTE** Why would you need to update something you just downloaded? Well, binary installer is packaged together only at certain intervals, while the updating of software is constant. By performing a self-update, you ensure that you are catching any new packages that have been added since the binary package was assembled.

This will update the entire ports system. Once you start using MacPorts, you should continue to periodically run this command to make sure you are working with a current version of MacPorts and that you have a list of all the current applications.

Once your environment is set up and you have the latest updated version of MacPorts installed, it's quite easy to use MacPorts with the commands listed in Table 19-6.

Table 19-6. MacPorts Commands

Command	Action
port list	Returns a list of all available ports.
port search *searchstring*	Returns a list of available ports whose name matches *searchstring*.
port info *appname*	Returns information about the port named *appname*.
port variants *appname*	Occasionally a port will have multiple options; if so, this command will list the additional port options available for the port *appname*.
sudo port install *appname*	Installs the base *appname* port.
sudo port install *appname* +*option1* +*option2*	Installs the port *appname* with *option1* and *option2*.
port installed	Returns a list of installed ports.
sudo port selfupdate	Updates the base port package as well as list of ports.
sudo port outdated	Lists outdated installed ports.
sudo port upgrade *appname*	Upgrades port *appname*.
sudo port upgrade outdated	Upgrades all outdated installed ports.

Continued

Table 19-6. Continued

Command	Action
sudo port uninstall *appname*	Removes the port *appname*.
sudo port clean *appname*	Removes the build files for *appname*, which is a good way to free up disk space after you install a port.

> **NOTE** So, you may ask, what's really better, Fink or MacPorts? The answer is that it probably doesn't matter much these days. We use MacPorts since it's familiar to us and for some historical reasons that have no significant relevance anymore. Today, as far as we can tell, they are both equally good at doing what they do, and either of them is better than none of them.

Compiling Software from the Source Code

With the maturity of Darwin in Leopard combined with the availability of most popular open source software through either MacPorts or Fink, it's rare you would ever need to compile software from source code (unless of course you are actively developing software, in which case you probably know all the information we're about to relate, plus a good bit more). Still, if you really want to try a bleeding-edge program that hasn't found its way to Fink or MacPorts or you think you must compile an application with just the right options, then you want to compile your own application from source code.

> **CAUTION** Compiling your own software from source code is not for the weak. Things will often just not work as they should, and it could take some time and research to figure out how to get something built correctly on your computer. Sometimes, things won't work at all (unless of course you want to dig into the code yourself and tweak it). If you are easily frustrated, then we suggest that the benefits of compiling your own program might not outweigh the mental anguish you could be setting yourself up for.

Compiling your application from source code generally requires three steps: configuring, building, and installing. Usually these steps are fairly automated and, with the exception of the configure stage, are usually pretty much the same.

> **NOTE** To be honest, there is often a fourth step: figuring out what went wrong when one of the three primary steps fails. We'll talk about this too.

Before you start any steps, though, you need to get the source code. This can usually be found on a project's web site or through a source repository such as SourceForge (www.sourceforge.net).

Step 1: Configure

For the user building an application for their own use, the configure stage is the most important part of the whole build process. This is where you can customize the application for your specific needs and your specific system. The first part of configuring your build is to see what configure options are available. You do this by going into the primary source folder and typing the following:

```
./configure --help
```

which will return a whole list of configure options. Most of these options either have sensible defaults or are automatically set during the configure stage. The things you want to look at are the optional features to see whether any of them would be useful to you.

> **NOTE** Certain programs require that your system provide specific libraries or other applications to compile correctly, and this is especially true for certain options you may want to build into your application; these are what are referred to as *dependencies*. MacPorts and Fink will usually solve dependency issues automatically when you install apps using them, but when you are compiling things yourself, you need to make sure these dependencies are satisfied.

If you think you don't need any options, you can usually configure your build by just typing this:

```
./configure
```

If you want to include options, then you would type something like this:

```
./configure --with-option1 --with-option2 --enable-feature-x [...]
```

Either way, when you press Return, the configure script will run and attempt to create a *makefile*, which will guide the actual build and install process (together referred to as the *make process*). For a complex program, the configure script can take a few minutes or even longer to do its work, during which time lots of text will scroll by, letting you know what's happening. Upon successful completion, the text will often issue a message saying that the configure completed successfully and perhaps giving some additional build advice. If something goes wrong, the text may or may not give you a clue as to what needs to be fixed.

> **NOTE** If something goes wrong, it's not always going to be easy to fix. Scrolling through the configure text may reveal a missing library, or it may indicate it cannot figure out what to do with your system. A missing library can usually be found and installed (sometimes it's there, but configure can't find it in which case you may need to specify the library path as a configure option). Sometimes there is a specific issue and if you poke around support forums, you can get an answer. Sadly, sometimes it's just not going to work on your system.

Step 2: Build

If the configure stage went without issue, the next step is to build the app. This should be as easy as typing the following:

```
make
```

Yep, that's it. Now go get a cup of coffee, stretch your legs, play a game on your Wii, or whatever, while your computer compiles your program. OK, although these days it could take your computer anywhere from a few seconds to a few hours to compile a program, for a moderately complex application it usually takes only between 5 minutes to 30 minutes depending on your computer.

If you have a newer Intel-based Mac, there is a trick to significantly speed up this process. Since even the lowliest Intel-based iMac has at least two processor cores, to use them both, just add -j 2 to the end of make. make -j 4 will work if you have four cores (a quad G5 or two dual-core Intel chips), and so on.

> **NOTE** Again, occasionally things will go wrong. Unfortunately, an error during the build process is usually even more difficult to track down than during the configure stage. If you notice the build failing in a specific area of the build that you identify with a configure option, you may try not enabling (or disabling) that particular option. If you really aren't using any strange options (or none at all) and this is a fairly popular program, then it's likely someone else is having the same issues, and if enough people are having these issues, then it's possible someone out there has a solution.

Step 3: Install

Usually, if you are dealing with a stable version of a popular application, things go smoothly and your configure and build stages happen without issue (or without major issues anyway), after which it comes time to install your program. This is also a very easy process; just type the following:

```
sudo make install
```

That should do it.

Most software compiled this way will install software in the /usr/local/ directory. By default this directory doesn't exist in Leopard, so you may want to create it. If, however, you want to install your software (or parts of it) somewhere else, this can usually be configured as a configure option.

To sum up, the quick and easy way to compile a program you downloaded as source code is often as easy as this:

```
./configure
make
sudo make install
```

Summary

We covered a whole lot of stuff in this chapter, from writing to shell scripts to compiling an application from source code. The point here wasn't to make you an expert at any of these things, but more so to familiarize yourself with some of the power that Darwin brings to the Mac world. The most important parts of this chapter were the ones on MacPorts and Fink, though, so pick one of these and install it. Then should you ever need to install and use something like, say, figlet, you'll be just a few commands away from being able to do this:

stich:~ scott$ **figlet Neat huh?**

PART 6

Networking Leopard

## CHAPTER 20

Leopard Networking

The Mac is known for making it easy and safe to get online. Under the hood, Mac OS X has all the networking power of UNIX. The Internet and UNIX go way back, growing up together. You might even say they were made for each other. Like any UNIX system, Mac OS X comes with a full set of networking tools built in:

Firewall software: Improved with Leopard to make it easier than ever to keep your computer safe on the Internet

Monitoring tools: To keep an eye on what your computer is doing, online and off

Network utilities: For inspecting your packets from the UI or the command line

AirPort utilities: For setting up and managing wireless networks and shared resources

> **NOTE** This chapter assumes you've already managed to connect your computer to the Internet. If you haven't gotten that far, see Chapter 9.

Setting Up the Firewall

The Mac has a well-deserved reputation for being safe on the Internet, but that doesn't mean you should be careless. The simplest thing you can do is set up the built-in firewall.

A *firewall* arbitrates incoming connection requests based on the requested port, the source, and the intended recipient. It's not unlike a lobby security guard in that it doesn't limit the ability of packets to leave; it only cares about things trying to come in from the outside.

To change your firewall settings, launch System Preferences by selecting System Preferences... from the Apple menu. Then click the Security preference pane and select the Firewall tab, as shown in Figure 20-1.

> **NOTE** In Tiger, firewall settings were part of the Sharing preference pane.

In order to be effective, security has to be simple. The firewall in Mac OS X has never been particularly complicated, but Leopard's firewall has been significantly simplified from Tiger.

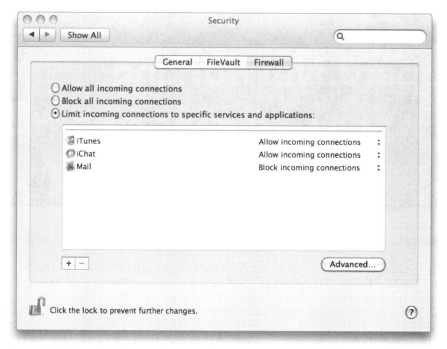

Figure 20-1. Firewall settings in System Preferences

On the BSD level, Mac OS X has switched from running ipfw to running socketfilterfw. Aside from eliminating the hassle of manually configuring ports, the socket filtering method is more accurate, because it filters packets based on where they are going, rather than which port they are coming into.

The new firewall has very few configuration options. First, there's the level of firewall activity. Your choices are to allow all connections, which is rarely a good idea, or to block all connections, which would be a good idea if all you do is surf the Web, but a bit draconian otherwise.

> **NOTE** There are a few times when it might be necessary to have the firewall allow all connections. If you're behind a dedicated firewall, it might be redundant. If you're having trouble connecting to another machine, you might need to temporarily disable the firewall. Finally, your network administrator, who has the last word on network configuration, might ask you to keep it open.

Figure 20-2. Automated firewall management dialog

The best option is usually to limit incoming connections to specific services and applications. You can add and remove applications and set whether incoming connections should be allowed or denied.

What makes the limit option so compelling is that you don't need to actually add any applications to the list. When you launch an application, it will let you know if it wants access through the firewall with a dialog, as shown in Figure 20-2.

Selecting Always Allow will add the application to the list with incoming connections allowed. Selecting Deny will also add the application to the list, but with incoming connections blocked. Should you change your mind, you can edit the settings from the Security panel.

Similarly, if you enable a network service from the Sharing panel in System Preferences, that service will automatically be added to the firewall's list of allowed applications.

There are also a couple of advanced firewall settings that can be accessed by clicking the Advanced... button on the security panel. This will pop up a sheet, as shown in Figure 20-3.

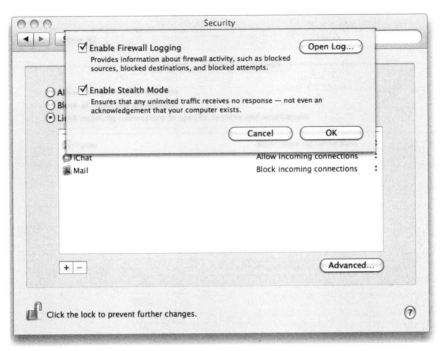

Figure 20-3. Advanced firewall settings sheet in System Preferences

The first preference, Enable Firewall Logging, keeps a log of all firewall activity. This is a good way to see who's been trying to connect to your computer, and is always an interesting read. You can get to the log by clicking the Open Log... button next to this preference, but you can also access the log directly using the Console utility in /Applications/Utilities.

The second preference is to enable stealth mode. Essentially this means your computer ignores pings, giving it the appearance of being off or disconnected from the network. Logic dictates this should make you some percentage safer.

Some people say that stealth mode won't make you any safer, and certainly it makes your computer uncooperative with the protocols of the Internet. Since none of those people are named Bruce Schneier, I generally ignore them.

That is to say, I run stealth mode. People don't need to ping my computer, regardless of the way the Internet is supposed to work. If you find yourself running network diagnostics or have your machine set up as a server, you'll probably want to disable stealth mode.

NOTE Machines on a local network that uses network address translation (NAT) aren't usually visible to the Internet, but depending on your network, you might want to run stealth mode anyway. The people on a home network are probably more trustworthy than the people on the open Wi-Fi at a coffee shop.

Monitoring Network Traffic

Raising the firewall is a good first step, but nothing beats basic situational awareness. If your computer was infected with malware and participating in zombienet denial-of-service attacks or sending out spam, would you know?

I like to know what my computer is doing, which is why I love *Activity Monitor*, located in /Applications/Utilities. Activity Monitor lets you know what's running and how much memory and CPU it's taking up. It also lets you monitor when things are writing to disk or sending and receiving traffic over the network, as shown in Figure 20-4.

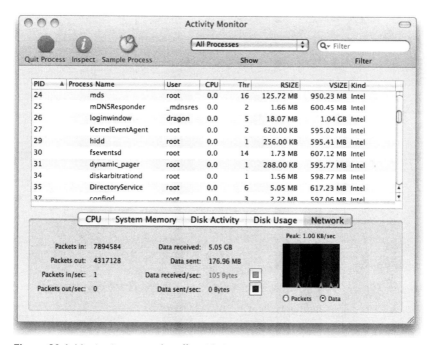

Figure 20-4. Monitoring network traffic with Activity Monitor

Activity Monitor has a convenient animated Dock icon, so even when the monitoring window is not open, I can keep an eye on packets traveling over the network. If I see a lot of activity and I'm not actively using the network, I want to know why.

> **TIP** A lot of root and system programs have arcane invocations that can make it hard to tell what a given program in Activity Monitor actually is. You can Google the program name, or you can look it up on such convenient lists as Amit Singh's Mac OS X Hacking Tools: www.kernelthread.com/mac/osx/tools.html.

If you want to take network monitoring to the next level, you need to check out Little Snitch, by Objective Development. Little Snitch complements your firewall by letting you know when applications try to send data from your machine.

Why might an application send out packets? If it's iChat or Mail or Safari, it probably has a legitimate reason. On the other hand, there are a lot of other reasons you might not be in total agreement with, such as phoning home with personal information the developer thinks it's OK to take without asking.

You can also use Little Snitch to selectively allow or block individual servers. For example, you might allow Safari to connect to a web page you are trying to view, but not allow it to connect to a site hot-linked from that page, such as an advertising or tracking network.

Like the firewall, Little Snitch has a list of rules you can build on the fly via notifications, as shown in Figure 20-5. Unlike the firewall, Little Snitch has a lot of configuration options, being designed for more advanced users. Even so, it's still a Mac application; you can install and run it without bothering with any of that stuff.

Figure 20-5. Little Snitch noticing an application sending out packets

Unlike the built-in firewall and Activity Monitor utility, Little Snitch costs $25. Like all good software, it comes with a free demo mode. Download it from the developer's site (www.obdev.at/) and give it a try. I think you'll agree it's well worth the price.

Network Utilities

Every UNIX distribution comes with a full compliment of networking tools, and Mac OS X is certainly no exception. Generally you have to go to the command line to use UNIX tools, but Apple has bundled the most common network utilities into a graphical application aptly named Network Utility, which lives in /Applications/Utilities.

Network Utility encompasses seven areas of functionality. Each lives in its own tab, with several subfeatures delimited with pop-up boxes, as shown in Figure 20-6.

Info

Chances are your computer has several network interfaces. Most Macs have an Ethernet port, an AirPort card, and a FireWire bus, all of which are capable of connecting to the Internet.

The Info panel lets you get statistics on all of your network interfaces, such as their hardware (MAC) and Internet (IP) addresses, their make and model, whether they're active, and at what speed they are connected. You can also see how many packets they've sent and received, and how many errors and collisions they've logged.

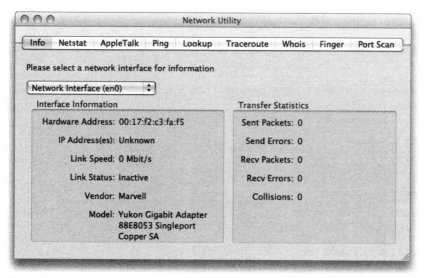

Figure 20-6. Exploring the Net with Network Utility

Netstat

Netstat, as its name implies, provides network statistics, in four varieties.

Routing Table: This is a map of known nodes from which your packets can begin their long trek across the Internet. This is not unlike checking Google maps to find out where your local post offices are.

Statistics: This is a comprehensive list of statistics by protocol. This is the long version of the simple numbers displayed by Activity Monitor and the Info tab. If you're curious to know how many inbound ipsec6 packets failed due to insufficient memory, here's where you can find out.

Multicast: This many-to-many communication protocol is used primarily by enterprise networks, though it's also used by mDNS, peer-to-peer technologies, and Internet Relay Chat (IRC). If you want to monitor your multicast memberships or packet statistics, Netstat is there for you.

Socket States: Every connection on the Internet uses a socket, which is the combination of your computer's IP address and a port. It's not a bad idea to see who's connecting to your machine and what they're up to.

AppleTalk

AppleTalk is an obsolete suite of networking protocols that Mac OS X supports for backward compatibility. Being built for the Internet, Mac OS X generally relies on TCP/IP for its networking needs. Still, should you find yourself participating in an AppleTalk network for some reason, Network Utility has a set of tools to help you keep tabs on your packets.

Ping

Ping is a diagnostic tool that uses the Internet Control Message Protocol (ICMP) to determine your ability to reach a given IP address, be it another computer or something like a router. The theory behind Ping is that any machine that receives a ping is supposed to echo it back. Unfortunately, Ping has been abused by malware in the past—hence stealth mode.

To use Ping in Network Utility, enter an IP address or domain name. Ping will then list the pings as they return, along with how long it took them to traverse the network. This is useful in any number of ways.

For example, if your web site goes down but your web host responds to pings, you can deduce that the host program crashed, but that the server is OK. If the server does not respond to pings, you can assume something is wrong on a hardware level.

Similarly, if your server responds by IP address, but doesn't respond by domain name, you can deduce that something is wrong with the domain name system (DNS). Further investigation would be needed to determine if the domain name has expired, or if there is something else going on. These can be determined elsewhere in Network Utility.

Lookup

The Lookup tab combines the `nslookup` and `dig` tools to query DNS, which converts human-readable web addresses to the numerical IP addresses used by computers. The information returned by Lookup varies by host, but at the very least you can use it to get the IP address of a given server name.

Traceroute

Traceroute maps the path of packets as they travel to a given server address. Aside from being kind of interesting, it's a useful diagnostic tool. When a server is unreachable, there's no way of knowing where the packets are being stopped. By using Traceroute, you can figure out who you need to call to get traffic flowing.

Like Ping, Traceroute has been abused by nefarious forces, so some servers will block Traceroute requests. Even so, you can usually get to the outer bounds of a given network, which will certainly tell you *something*, so Traceroute remains a good thing to have in your toolbox.

Whois

As opposed to the tools in Lookup, which convert domain names into IP addresses, Whois queries domain registries to determine who owns them. There are a couple of reasons why you might want to know this.

If your site is down and your server is reachable by IP address, but not by domain name, one possibility is that your domain name has expired or has been stolen. Checking the Whois information will let you know for sure. If Whois checks out OK, you can begin suspecting something is wrong with the name server itself.

Should you find your packets are being stopped at a certain node via Traceroute, Whois will tell you who you need to call about it. It's also a good way to see if a domain name is available, and if it's not, to see when it expires. There's no sense putting up good money for a domain-watching service if the registration is not going to expire for another five years.

As with many parts of the Internet, Whois registries have been abused. Putting your name, e-mail address, home address, and telephone number where anyone can get them is a potential privacy concern.

As such, some registrars now offer anonymous registration, whereby they will register the domain in their own name on your behalf, preventing people from getting any useful information about you. As with any such tactic, this certainly improves security by some degree, while breaking the Internet by another.

Finger

In the halcyon days of yore, when Spam was just a delicious luncheon meat and the Internet was just a military research project, a computer scientist named Les Earnest wrote a program that would take an e-mail address and "point out" who it belonged to by giving you the person's name, whether they were logged on, and where their home directory was.

When the Internet opened for general use, people soon found less earnest uses for Finger, and the protocol was eventually abandoned. The tool still exists, but mainly as way to generate the words *Connection refused*.

Port Scan

You should probably be noticing a theme with Internet tools. That is, they can be used for good or evil. Of all the tools in Network Utility, nothing fits this profile like Port Scan.

In a nutshell, Port Scan tries every port on a given machine and reports back which ones are open. This is handy information for potential attackers, which makes it handy information for potential victims.

It's also useful for figuring out, say, why a particular Internet service is not working, as having its port closed will render any Internet application silent.

Advanced Networking with Darwin

As discussed in Chapters 18 and 19, the underlying BSD system, accessible from the Terminal application, is the place to go for advanced hacking. Many networking utilities have more options than are available from within Network Utility.

There are also esoteric, specialized, and third-party tools that don't have graphical versions and, as such, can only be run in Terminal. Even simple utilities like Ping are at your disposal, as shown in Figure 20-7.

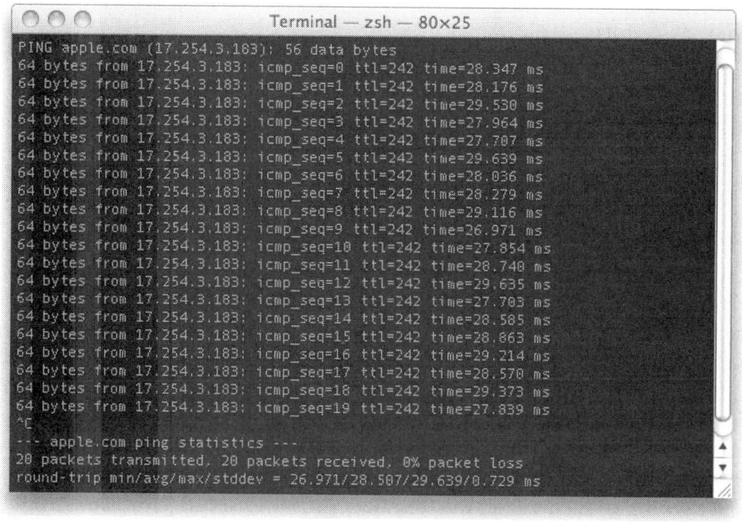

Figure 20-7. Running network tools from the command line in Terminal

So, while Network Utility is a good place to start, when you're really ready to become a network power user, open Terminal and start reading man pages.

> **NOTE** Some good Darwin network utilities to read up on would be `ifconfig`, which lets you configure your network interfaces, similar to the Network panel in System Preferences; and `tcpdump`, which lets you examine the contents of network packets, and replaces the popular `tcpflow` application.

Wireless Networking with AirPort

I would be remiss not to mention two very important networking tools that come in a pretty graphical package—AirPort Utility and AirPort Disk Utility—both of which live in `/Applications/Utilities`.

AirPort Utility replaces the old AirPort Setup Assistant and AirPort Admin Utility programs with a single, attractive, easy-to-use application. AirPort Utility also adds several new features, and makes it easier to manage multiple AirPort base stations.

At its most basic, AirPort Utility will show you which AirPort base stations are operating in your area, their names, IP and AirPort addresses, and which standards and firmware versions they support, as shown in Figure 20-8.

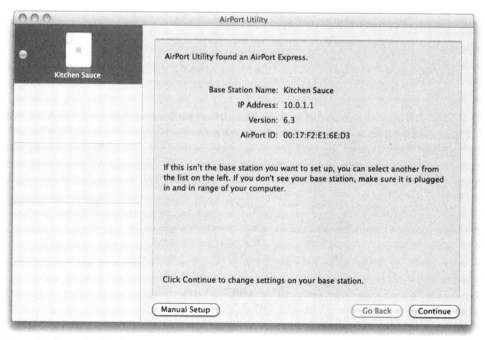

Figure 20-8. Apple's lovely graphical AirPort Utility

If one or more of the base stations in range belong to you, you can rename them and change their settings.

The availability and usefulness of settings in AirPort Utility will vary depending on which model of AirPort base station you have, its firmware version, and the peculiarities of your Internet provider. There are, however, a few notable groups of settings you should pay particular attention to:

Profiles: These are groups of settings you can easily switch between. This is handy if you travel with an AirPort base station so you can, say, share an Internet connection, as discussed in the next chapter.

Wireless Security: Unless you're intentionally running an open access point, you need to protect your network by setting up encryption and a password from the Wireless tab of the AirPort panel. There are several encryption standards in common use, but you should probably choose one based on Wi-Fi Protected Access, such as WPA2 Personal. AirPort's recommended setting is WPA/WPA2 Personal, which supports the older version of WPA for backward compatibility. If you have machines that do not support WPA2, you can use this setting, but in general, you want to limit the abilities of your AirPort base station to those needed by machines you own.

CAUTION If at all possible, avoid using a standard based on the Wired Equivalent Privacy (WEP) protocol. It's better than nothing, but at this point, even a moderately competent attacker can crack a WEP key with ease. If you have to use WEP to support older hardware, make it habit of frequently changing your password. You should also steer clear of WPA2 Enterprise, which requires a special RADIUS server far beyond the means and needs of the everyday user.

Radio Mode: This single setting resides right above the security options on the Wireless tab. As an AirPort base station will support up to four wireless standards, you should check this to ensure you're using the smallest, fastest set of standards that will meet your needs. For example, if all your machines have an 802.11n AirPort card, supporting the a, b, or g standards will needlessly slow the network down, beside making it all the more usable by uninvited guests.

DHCP: From this panel, you can limit the range of IP addresses DHCP uses, the length of a DHCP lease, and set a custom message displayed when people log in to your base station.

Logs and Statistics: AirPort Utility lets you monitor your network usage. For example, you can see a list of all the computers connected to the base station, including their MAC and IP addresses.

Port Forwarding: Typically your AirPort base station will have a single public IP address shared among the private addresses of your network. In order to reach a service on an individual machine from outside the local network, you have to map it to a port on your AirPort base station in a process known as port forwarding. We'll come back to this in a moment.

Remote Printing: By connecting a printer to your AirPort base station, you can allow any machine on the network to use the printer. This is an improvement over standard printer sharing because it doesn't require a host computer.

AirPort Disks: Similar to printer sharing, you can connect USB hard drives to your AirPort base station, which will allow them to be shared by people on your network.

Hard disk sharing is a really cool feature, particularly if you have a laptop. However, unlike a printer, hard drives contain personal data, which raises privacy issues. Apple lets you set up user accounts, password protection, and permissions on shared drives. That way multiple people can use the same drive without having access to each other's data.

Apple includes a second utility for dealing with remote hard drives. AirPort Disk Utility, shown in Figure 20-9, is not for setting up shared hard drives, but for managing how your computer deals with them.

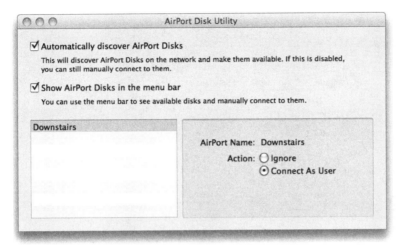

Figure 20-9. Managing shared hard drives with AirPort Disk Utility

AirPort Disk Utility has two simple options. You can elect to automatically discover AirPort Disks, instead of having to connect to them manually. You can also elect to show a menu bar item that gives you a list of available AirPort Disks in the area.

AirPort Disk Utility also has a list of all known AirPort Disks, which base station they are on, and whether you want to mount them when they are in range, or ignore them.

Port Forwarding

A typical home or small office network will have a single machine, usually a router, connected to the Internet by a public IP address. That machine, in turn, will share its Internet connection with other machines on the network. Rather than having public IP addresses, the machines on the local network use local addresses. Aside from saving the significant expense of having multiple IP addresses, this gives the network added security, since machines without reachable addresses are essentially invisible to anyone outside the network.

Normally this is a good thing, but not always (for example, if you decide to use your computer to serve web pages, which is the topic of Chapter 22). Invisibility is not a good trait for a public web server. In order to receive requests and send out pages, your web server must be reachable by the outside world. The best way to deal with this problem is to set the router to forward any incoming packets on a certain port to the web server, which can then fulfill the requests and send out the necessary data. This process is known as *port forwarding*.

Of course, the router can't forward packets if it doesn't know where to find the server, so the first step is to give your machine a static IP address. You can either use a hybrid method such as DHCP with a manual address, or you can just set the entire address manually.

To set up a static IP address, open the Networking panel of System Preferences. Select the network interface your machine will use to connect to the Internet. Since servers need to stay in one place in order to effectively serve, this will probably be a desktop machine connected by Ethernet.

That said, there's no technical reason why you can't serve your pages over another interface, such as AirPort. In fact, I'm going to use AirPort in this example, for reasons that will become clear. In either case, click the Advanced... button to reveal the Advanced Settings sheet, and then click the TCP/IP tab, as shown in Figure 20-10.

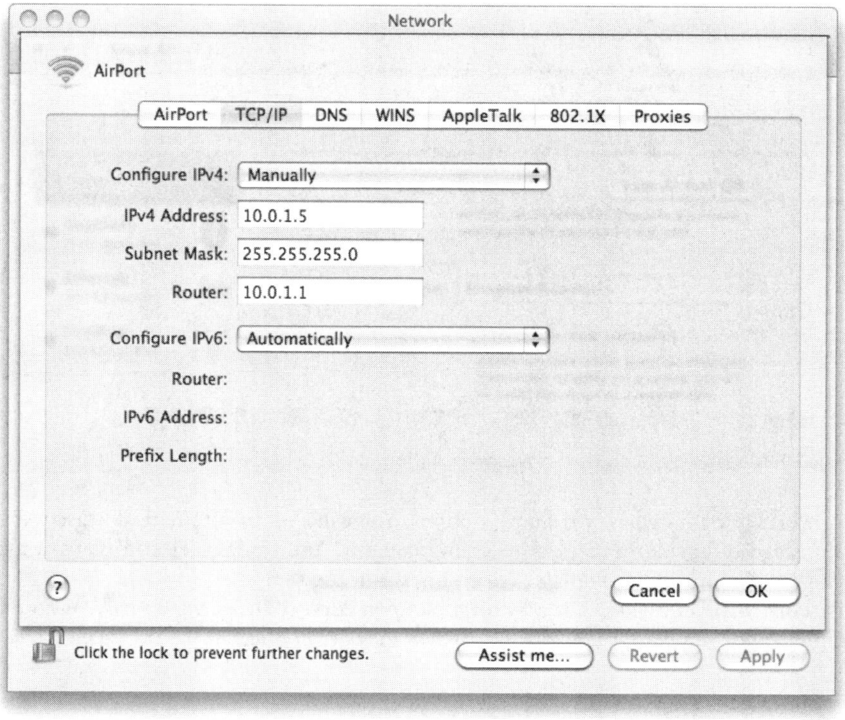

Figure 20-10. Setting up a static IP address in System Preferences

Make a note of your IPv4 address, subnet mask, and router address, as well as which ports you're trying to access. In the case of serving web pages, the default is 80, so if you changed it earlier, make a note of that. It's not a bad idea to confirm from within the local network that the socket you will be forwarding to works, which will make testing the forwarding that much easier.

Once you've got the IP address set and the ports open and tested, configure your router to forward messages on the appropriate ports to your machine's IP address and local port. How do you do that? I have no idea. Every router is different, so you'll have to read the manual or search the Internet for the exact information. That said, Apple's AirPort base stations are DHCP-enabled routers, so I'll set one up as an example. Open AirPort Utility and sign in to the base station that connects your web server to the Internet.

Click the Manual Configuration button, select the Advanced panel, and then select the Port Mapping tab. You can also reach this tab by clicking the Configure Port Mappings... button on the NAT tab of the Internet panel. Either way, the port mappings are just a list of ports. To add yours, click the + button, and then fill out the form, as shown in Figure 20-11. The Public Port Number(s) field lists the ports you want forwarded. In this example, I'm assuming my ISP blocks port 80, so I'm mapping port 8080. Of course, there's no reason we couldn't map them both, just in case.

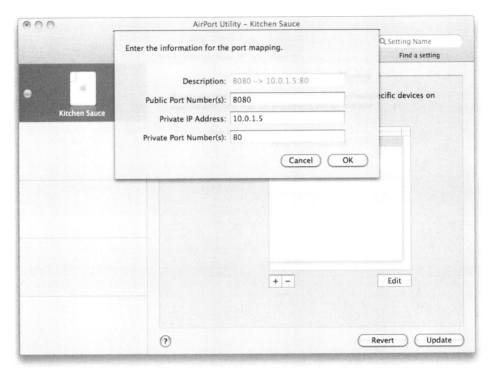

Figure 20-11. Setting up port forwarding in AirPort Utility

The Private IP Address field lists the IP address of the machine receiving the packets, which is to say, your web server. Enter the IP address you gave it in System Preferences. Finally, enter the port you want to receive the packets on in the Private Port Number(s) field. Click the OK button to dismiss the sheet, and then click the Update button to commit your changes. After the base station reboots, test your forwarding by accessing your web site using the outside IP address.

Summary

From the Finder to the command line, Leopard's built-in tools give you the power to monitor every aspect of the network. Third-party tools extend those abilities even further. Apple also includes specialized tools for dealing with AirPort networks and the specialized resource sharing they can provide.

Of course, connecting to a network is only of limited use unless you can actually connect to other machines. In the next chapter, we'll explore ways to connect your Mac to other machines, whether they're next door or on the other side of the world.

## CHAPTER 21

Working with Remote Servers and Networks

Chances are you connect to remove servers and networks every day without really thinking about it. When you open your favorite web browser to read the news, check the weather, or catch up on the blogosphere, you're sending out packets of information requesting data. Those packets adhere to a particular protocol, in this case the Hypertext Transfer Protocol, and they traverse networks around the globe seeking the particular port at the particular address of the particular server that has your requested content.

The server will consider your request and, if all goes well, package the information you've requested and send it flying through the vast network of networks until it ends up back at your machine. Most people probably never realize how much work they're doing just by slacking off on the Web!

Making the Connection

The Web is just one part of the Internet, which is in turn just one type of network. There are several other reasons to connect to another machine, each with its own capabilities, methods, and protocols. Fortunately, Mac OS X has networking built right in. In fact, it's quite possible that, as with surfing the Web, you won't even have to think about the fact you're using a remote machine.

Navigating in the Finder

The easiest way to browse your local network is in the Finder. Machines that have enabled an appropriate type of sharing, such as file sharing, will be listed in the Finder window under the Shared category, as if they were part of the system.

Selecting the machine in the Finder will display a visual representation of that system's options. If you can connect to the system remotely, a Connect As button will let you do so. The available folders, including any public folders, will be listed by user account, as shown in Figure 21-1.

If the machine has screen sharing enabled, the Share Screen button will let you activate it. Although built-in screen sharing is new to Leopard, it was previously available as part of the Apple Remote Desktop application, which has roots going all the way back to Mac OS 8.

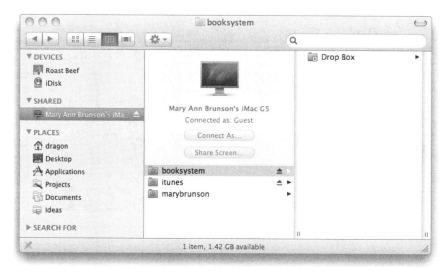

Figure 21-1. Browsing the local network in the Finder

The upshot is Leopard's screen-sharing feature can connect to machines that are not running Leopard. Both Tiger (10.4) and Panther (10.3) come with the necessary client software already installed.

When you make a screen-sharing connection, you will be prompted for a username and password. Upon authentication, the system will launch an application named Screen Sharing. Its main window will contain a live, interactive image of the remote computer's desktop. Depending on the remote computer's settings, you can take control of the cursor, launch and use applications, and manipulate files.

The Screen Sharing application has a few preferences worth checking out. By default, the remote screen is scaled to fit your screen, data is minimally encrypted to improve network performance, and drawing quality is adjusted on the fly depending on the quality of your connection. You can instead elect to view the screen at full size, to encrypt all data, or to draw the screen at full quality regardless of performance.

> **NOTE** This section deals only with connecting as a client to machines that already have a network service available. We'll discuss how to enable your machine as a server in the "Sharing" section later in this chapter.

Connecting Directly

The Finder's network browsing is limited to machines on your local network, but the Finder can address any machine, local or remote. As long as you can resolve an IP address or a domain name to it, you can connect to it directly using the Finder's Connect to Server window, as shown in Figure 21-2.

Launch the Connect to Server window from the Finder's menu bar by selecting Connect to Server from the Go menu, or press Cmd+K. To connect to a machine, type its address in URL form into the Server Address text field. If you intend to connect to the machine on a regular basis, click the + button to add it to the Favorite Servers list.

In the previous section, we connected to a machine using the Connect As button in the Finder. We could have also established that connection directly by typing the machine's URL, like so:

```
afp://10.0.1.5
```

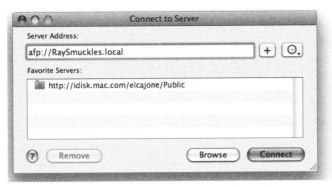

Figure 21-2. Connecting to a server by name in the Finder

Connecting to a machine in the Finder will use the default protocol. Connecting directly allows you to explicitly specify the protocol. Valid protocol declarations include the following:

afp: The Apple Filing Protocol is the standard protocol used for addressing remote volumes in the Finder. Although it is Apple's standard, AFP support is available for many operating systems, including Windows, NetWare, and several flavors of UNIX and Linux. If you do not specify a protocol, afp is assumed.

at: AppleTalk is an obsolete networking protocol that is included for backward compatibility. Previous versions of AFP used AppleTalk behind the scenes, but modern AFP uses the Virtual Network Computing standard on top of standard TCP/IP.

nfs: The Network File System protocol is a remote file access protocol developed by Sun Microsystems. It is similar to AFP and is available for several flavors of UNIX, as well as for operating systems such as NetWare, Windows, and, of course, Mac OS X.

smb: The Server Message Block protocol is the Windows equivalent to AFP. From within Windows, it's referred to simply as Microsoft Windows Network. The SMB protocol is sometimes called Samba, though technically Samba is a free reimplementation of SMB and not simply another name for the same thing.

cifs: The Common Internet File System, despite its name, is actually just a rebranding of SMB to reflect changes Microsoft made to the protocol since its invention at IBM. It was submitted, but not accepted, as an Internet standard. It can be considered to be the same as SMB.

http: The Hypertext Transfer Protocol is the standard protocol of the World Wide Web. Taking advantage of the ubiquity of the Web, HTTP is used for transporting more than web pages. For example, the WebDAV standard is used to mount remote file systems over HTTP. This is the same standard used when connecting to iDisk, which we'll discuss in the "Connecting to .Mac" section of this chapter.

https: The secure version of HTTP is not a true protocol. Instead, it simply refers to the use of standard HTTP over a connection that has been encrypted by either the Secure Sockets Layer (SSL) or Transport Layer Security (TLS) protocol.

ftp: The File Transfer Protocol is a very old standard for moving files from one computer to another. Because of its age and that it's compatible with every known operating system, it's in widespread use all over the Internet.

ftps: Analogous to HTTPS, FTPS refers to the use of regular FTP over an SSL or TLS connection.

Conspicuously absent as available protocol declarations in the Connect to Server window are sftp, the Secure Shell File Transfer Protocol; svn, the Subversion file transfer protocol (although Subversion can be transacted over other protocols, such as HTTP); and file, as used in standard file URLs. The absence of file URLs is notable not because they have much meaning in a dialog intended for connecting to servers but because they are used extensively throughout the system. Using them in the Connect to Server window simply returns an error.

Connecting in Darwin

Although using a computer's graphical interface via screen sharing is relatively new, the concept of using one computer to log in to and control another computer remotely is anything but. UNIX is, by its very nature, a remotely controllable operating system, and old-fashioned shell-to-shell networking is very much alive in Terminal, as shown in Figure 21-3.

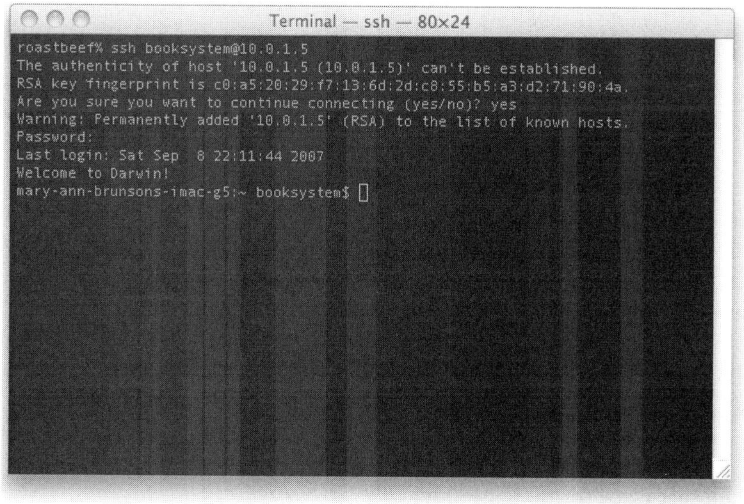

Figure 21-3. Remote computing by Secure Shell in Terminal

To connect to another machine, open Terminal from /Applications/Utilities. From the command line, invoke ssh with the username and address of the machine you want to connect to, separated by the "at" sign. For example, to connect to a machine at the local IP address 10.0.1.5 with the username booksystem, you would type this:

```
ssh booksystem@10.0.1.5
```

NOTE You don't have to use a local IP address or an IP address at all. Anything that can be resolved on the Internet is valid, including standard and local domain names.

If you are connecting to a machine for the first time, you will be asked whether it is safe to proceed. Confirm this by typing yes. Unlike most UNIX programs, you have to type the entire word. You will then be prompted for a password and then, assuming you can authenticate properly, presented with a welcome message and the command prompt.

From this prompt you can create, delete, and alter files and folders, as well as list, run, and kill processes. You can even launch new shells and Secure Shell into other servers. It's the same as if you were sitting at the remote machine typing into a Terminal window.

This can have unexpected consequences. For example, any DNS resolution will be in terms of the remote machine. If you have domains listed as default, local hosts, or discrepancies in the closest name server's routing table, the remote machine might behave differently than would your local host.

To log out of the remote server, type exit. This is the same as exiting any shell, so bear in mind that if you've launched a new shell from within the Secure Shell, typing exit will not log you out. Fortunately, when you log out of a Secure Shell session, Secure Shell will let you know the connection is closed. If you don't get that confirmation, assume you are still logged in.

Remote login via Secure Shell can be enabled from System Preferences, as discussed in the "Sharing" section later in this chapter.

> **NOTE** Secure Shell replaces the older Telnet application. Both programs accomplish the same thing, but ssh uses encryption to ensure an attacker cannot view your data in transit. Most machines do not allow insecure access, but Telnet remains in the UNIX toolbox for backward compatibility.

Darwin also includes an ftp program for using the File Transfer Protocol to move files between machines. As opposed to shell access, which allows for all manner of shenanigans, FTP access is much more limited, restricting user privileges to basic file operations.

To use FTP from the command line, simply type ftp. Unlike Secure Shell, FTP can be invoked without actually opening a connection. To connect to a remote machine, type open, and then, when prompted, enter the address of the machine, your username, and your password.

Unlike the Finder's Connect to Server menu, Darwin does not have an ftps command, but it does have an sftp command, which works just like the regular ftp command. However, although opening a connection and supplying your username at invocation time are optional in ftp, they are required in sftp.

```
sftp booksystem@10.0.1.5
```

Enter your password when prompted, and then proceed as normal.

Whatever the advantage to using sftp, moving files back and forth in the terminal is almost too complicated to make it worthwhile, but if you really want to know, type man ftp or man sftp in the terminal to read all about it. A much better idea would be to use a dedicated FTP client.

Third-Party Solutions

The Finder was designed to be a file browser, so it's a great way to take advantage of remote file protocols, such as AFP, SMB, and WebDAV. However, just as you wouldn't use the Finder to surf the Web, it's also ill-suited for dealing with the peculiar needs of FTP and related protocols. Instead, it's best to turn to third-party solutions.

Transmit

I've used a lot of FTP clients on a lot of different platforms, but one application stands head-and-shoulders above any other: Transmit (www.panic.com/transmit/). This award-winning application is available only on the Mac and was written by Panic, a Portland-based, Mac-only software company held in the highest esteem by developers and users alike.

As shown in Figure 21-4, Transmit has a simple, native drag-and-drop interface that belies its power. Under the hood Transmit has a robust file transfer engine that works with all manner of protocols, including FTP, FTPS, SFTP, WebDAV over HTTP and HTTPS, and Amazon S3. It also deals with such vagaries as proxies and passive mode.

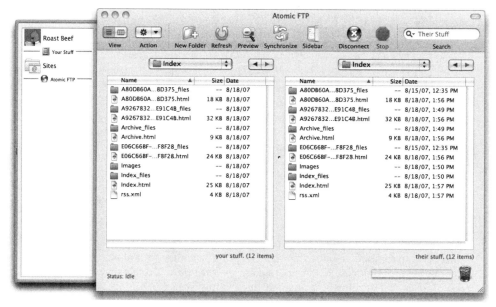

Figure 21-4. Connecting to an FTP server with Transmit

Other features in Transmit include directory synchronization, bookmarks, and remote viewing and editing. What really makes it worth the price is the level of integration it has with Mac OS X, including the Dock, iDisk, Bonjour, Dashboard, AppleScript, and Automator. It also works with .Mac's syncing feature so your bookmarks are always backed up and in sync.

Transmit is available for $29.95. You can download it from Panic's web site and try it free for 15 days, after which time certain features are limited.

> **NOTE** Several free and open source FTP clients are also available for the Mac, such as NcFTP (www.ncftp.com) and CyberDuck (http://cyberduck.ch/).

BBEdit

One of the most common uses of FTP and other file transfer protocols is for uploading content to a web server. Some applications have file transfer capabilities built in to streamline your workflow.

Bare Bones' BBEdit (http://barebones.com/products/bbedit/) is probably one of the oldest and most respected text editor on the Mac. It has the kind of understated interface over tremendous power beloved by veteran users of the great UNIX text editors Emacs and Vi. But it also has the convenience and easy approachability of a graphical application, as shown in Figure 21-5.

BBEdit's features are too numerous to enumerate, but suffice it to say it's not only a great text editor but also a great web page editor. Germane to the subject at hand, BBEdit can open and save files to a remote server via FTP or SFTP, eliminating the need for a separate file transfer protocol.

BBEdit is $125 but has a demo mode and significant discounts for students and users of previous versions. Bare Bones also makes a free "lite" version called TextWrangler. Although it lacks the most advanced features of BBEdit, TextWrangler has BBEdit's best features, including the FTP functionality.

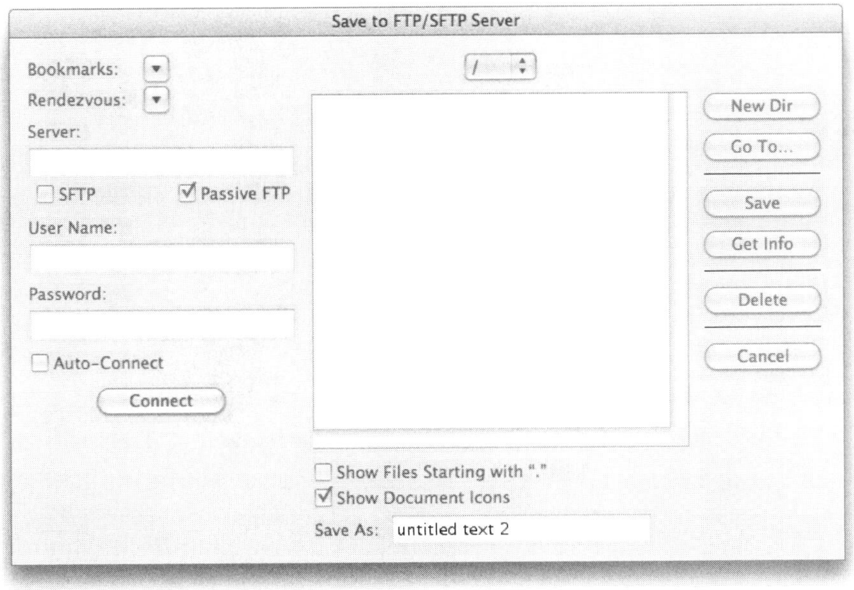

Figure 21-5. Saving a file directly to a server in BBEdit

Connecting to .Mac

As Transmit and BBEdit demonstrate, integration is the order of the day for many native Mac applications. As the Finder's built-in networking demonstrates, this is also true of the system in general. However, when it comes to simplicity through integration, nothing compares to Apple's .Mac.

NOTE If you're not familiar with .Mac, check out Chapter 15.

Connecting to .Mac is easier than connecting to other Internet hosts. You don't have to access it with Terminal or Transmit, because the interface is built into Mac OS X. You also don't have to deal with online control panels or configuration files because all that is handled from within System Preferences, as shown in Figure 21-6.

iDisk

If you create a web site in iWeb, which is part of iLife and included free on every new Mac, you can publish your home page to .Mac with one click. If you use another program to create your web pages, you can just mount your .Mac server space, known as iDisk, and copy, move, or delete files in the Finder.

If you have a bunch of pictures in iPhoto and you want to share them with your family, you can publish them straight to .Mac. You can also use .Mac to share movies you make in iMovie or music and podcasts you make in GarageBand. Using .Mac is all about putting things on the Web without ever having to actually deal with the Web.

Figure 21-6. Setting up .Mac in System Preferences

Much like your home account, your .Mac account contains a public folder. If you want to put something online for a friend or co-worker, you just copy it to your public folder. If you have a friend who puts something in their public folder for you, you can mount their public folder in the Finder as well.

To access your iDisk, click its icon in the Devices section of any Finder window. The Finder's menu bar also contains an iDisk submenu under the Go menu. You can use that to connect to your iDisk, another user's iDisk, or another user's public folder. You can also jump to your iDisk by pressing Shift+Cmd+I.

If your friends don't have a Mac, let alone .Mac, that's OK. With a few clicks, you can set up a file exchange site so people can download and upload files to your public disk from their web browser, as shown in Figure 21-7. If you'd rather not have your public disk be entirely public, you can password protect it.

Back to My Mac

In Leopard, Apple introduced a new feature called Back to My Mac. When you turn Back to My Mac on, the .Mac server keeps track of where on the Internet your computer is. Should you find yourself at work or school having left your big presentation sitting on your desktop, no worries. With Back to My Mac, you can log into your machine remotely and access the missing files.

To use Back to My Mac, select the .Mac pane in System Preferences, and then choose the Back to My Mac tab. Click the Start button to make your computer accessible from the Internet. Then, click the Open Sharing Preferences button to move to the Sharing pane. From here, enable screen sharing, file sharing, and other services you'd like to be able to access remotely.

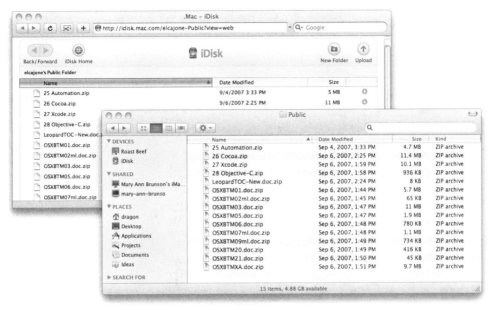

Figure 21-7. Navigating an iDisk in the Finder and Safari

> **NOTE** For more information on the various sharing services, see the "Sharing" section later in this chapter.

Third-Party Integration

A platform is only as strong as its third-party development. Even though Apple writes a lot of great software and bundles most of it for free with every new Mac, what really makes the platform amazing is how much great third-party software there is. Development on the platform is strong, competitive, and innovative.

It's the same story with .Mac. Apple doesn't hog it all to itself. Rather, Apple has opened it up for development and encouraged developers to incorporate .Mac into their applications. Many developers do, and why not? Customers love being able to use .Mac, and providing a great user experience is what makes great software.

Third-party software can (and does) take advantage of .Mac to back up and sync the data on all your machines. For example, Panic's Transmit uses .Mac to sync bookmarked FTP servers, and Bare Bones' Yojimbo uses .Mac to sync bookmarks, notes, and other stored data. Third-party developers also take advantage of .Mac's ability to get your stuff on the Web with little to no effort on your part.

I'll give you a personal example. My company makes a piece of software for organizing your personal media collection called Delicious Library. In Delicious Library 2, we added a feature called Web Publishing. This is probably the number-one requested feature, and it's definitely the biggest selling point of the new version. When we won the Apple Design Award for Best Leopard Application, this was the feature the judges showed off.

When you publish a collection, you can send it to iWeb to deal with it as you will. If you have a server, you can set up an FTP account and upload it that way. You can also publish your collection to a folder and use Transmit to deal with it. In any case, it's pretty easy, but it takes a few steps and some configuration—that is, unless you have .Mac, as shown in Figure 21-8, in which case, you don't have to configure anything because all your .Mac account information is already known to the system. You can just hit the Publish button, and your collection will be turned into a web page and uploaded to your .Mac account. When it's done, you can visit your collection online and send the link to your friends to check it out.

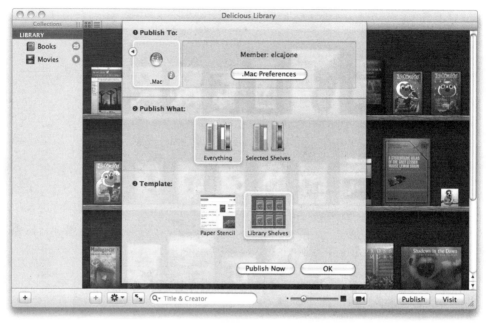

Figure 21-8. Publishing to .Mac in Delicious Library 2

If your friends are using Delicious Library as well, your collection will automatically be added to their computers so they can browse your media from within Delicious Library. You don't have to take any additional steps. All of that stuff is handled automatically by .Mac.

Informal Networking

It wasn't that long ago when there was no Internet to which regular people could connect. Back then, setting up a local area network in your house was far too expensive to be feasible, and wireless networking wasn't even something most people could fathom. Yet, whenever two people had a file they wanted to exchange that wouldn't fit on a 1.44 MB floppy disk or they wanted to play some head-to-head Doom, they were always faced with the same problem: how the heck do we connect these two computers?

Even when the Internet was well established and routers were cheap, creating a small, informal network between two or three computers was always a big challenge. Fortunately, the modern Macintosh makes these arrangements, known as *ad hoc networks*, extremely easy to set up and use.

Target Disk Mode

The first question you have to ask yourself is, why do I want to connect two computers? A lot of times, as then, it's to exchange files. Whether it's to copy some work from a laptop to a desktop or to move some videos from a desktop to a TV server, people are forever connecting two machines just to facilitate getting files from computer A to computer B.

In this case, a network is not actually necessary. Any two Macs with FireWire ports can take advantage of a special FireWire trick called *Target Disk mode*. To put a computer into Target Disk mode, hold the T key while booting, or select Target Disk mode from the Startup Disk pane of System Preferences. The machine will boot, but instead of a login screen, the computer's monitor will display the FireWire symbol.

When it's in Target Disk mode, a computer is treated as just another FireWire peripheral. That means if you plug it into another computer, that machine will mount the targeted machine's drives as if they were regular external drives, as shown in Figure 21-9. This includes the hard drive, as well as connected drives such as the DVD drive.

Figure 21-9. Mounting a machine in Target Disk mode in the Finder

To copy, move, or delete files, just do so in the Finder as you would with an external drive. You can also read or eject removable media in the usual way. Even with gigabit Ethernet, which is theoretically faster, a direct connection with a FireWire 800 cable is pretty much as fast as it gets when it comes to moving files.

> **NOTE** Somewhat counterintuitively, the proper way to bring a computer out of Target Disk mode is to hold down its power button until it shuts down. However, like any other external drive, you must remember to eject it from your machine first.

Target Disk mode can do some pretty interesting things. Since Mac OS X can boot from a FireWire drive, you can boot your computer as a different machine by putting that machine in Target Disk mode. That means you could put your laptop into Target Disk mode and boot your Mac Pro from its drive so you'd be using your laptop, except it would be your Mac Pro. Then you put the Mac Pro into target Disk Mode and use it from your laptop.

Why would you ever do that? Well, maybe your laptop got run over by a car and the screen is busted but the mechanics are still good. That sounds far-fetched, but it's actually a documented occurrence. Or maybe your friend brings over a Mac mini, and you want to boot it up but you don't have a monitor. As long as you have your laptop, Target Disk mode is all you need.

AirPort

If both machines have AirPort cards, it's easy to connect them. One machine can create an ad hoc AirPort network by simply selecting the Create Network option from the AirPort menu bar item, as shown in Figure 21-10. After giving it a name and an optional password, other people can join the network from the AirPort menu bar item as well.

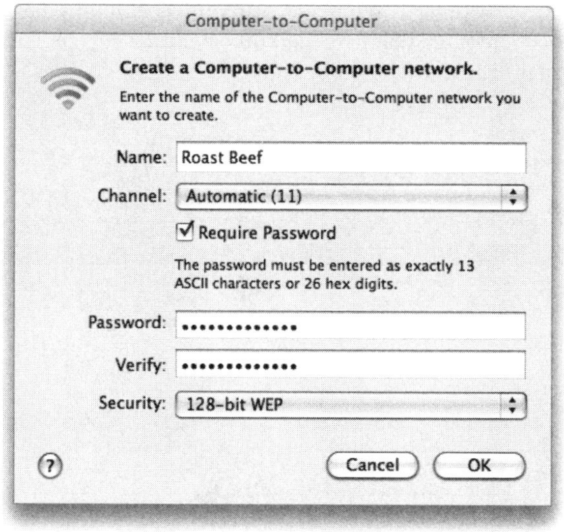

Figure 21-10. Creating an ad hoc network with AirPort

If you don't use the AirPort menu bar item, you can accomplish the same thing through the Network pane of System Preferences. Simply select the AirPort icon on the sidebar, and then, from the Network Name drop-down menu, select Create New Network. Other AirPort users can connect the same way.

I've never had a lot of luck setting up Wi-Fi on non-Macintosh computers, but since AirPort is just Apple's brand of Wi-Fi, it's at least theoretically possible to connect to Windows machines the same way.

> **NOTE** Unfortunately, AirPort's ad hoc networking doesn't support WPA, so you're stuck with easily cracked WEP encryption instead. Try not to talk about too many state secrets over an ad hoc network.

FireWire and Ethernet

If you don't have AirPort or want a faster way to connect, you can always plug the two machines together with FireWire. Aside from Target Disk mode, FireWire is actually a full network interface. After connecting the two machines, open the Networking pane of System Preferences.

You will have a self-assigned IP address. It doesn't really matter what it is, as long as the other person's self-assigned address is not the same. If it is the same, one of you should edit the last number so it's different.

Ethernet works the same way. Connect two machines, check the IP addresses, and change one if necessary. With Ethernet there is a trick, however. Some types of Ethernet cables are specially designed for connecting two machines directly. These so-called crossover cables are typically green in color.

If you're both using Macs, it doesn't matter whether you're using a crossover cable or not. If you connect two Macs with a standard cable, they will automatically cross over their Ethernet connections, so it makes no difference at all. If you're trying to connect to a machine that isn't a Mac, be aware that you might need the special cable.

Assuming you have the latest versions of each and the proper cables, there's no particular advantage between FireWire and Ethernet as network adapters. There is, however, an advantage to having two network adapters.

You can connect your computer to another computer using one and then connect your computer to a different computer using the other. By switching off between the two, you can chain together any number of computers into an arbitrarily long daisy chain.

Bonjour

Once your machines are connected, you can do any of things you would be able to do on a local area network, including connecting via the Finder and addressing each other directly by IP address or the .local name setup in the Sharing pane of System Preferences.

More important, Bonjour will work. If you need to exchange a file or communicate in some way, iChat's Bonjour window will enable you to do that, as shown in Figure 21-11. Many net-workable Mac applications provide support for Bonjour, so if you're connecting your machines to go head-to-head on some network-enabled game, check to see whether it supports Bonjour. If it does and you can manage to somehow connect one machine into the other, you're good to go.

Figure 21-11. Simple file transfer with Bonjour in iChat

Whether you're connected directly, via a LAN, or by the Internet itself, there's a lot more you can do than pass files back and forth in iChat, share a printer, or play a game of Quinn. To enable most of it, though, you'll have to learn to share.

Sharing

If this chapter has taught you anything, it should be that there are a lot of different ways to connect to a server. Even though the standard version of Mac OS X is called the *client* version, in UNIX the line between client and server is tenuous at best. With Mac OS X, if you can be a client, you can probably be a server. To see this for yourself, open the Sharing pane in System Preferences, and read the long list of services you can offer, as shown in Figure 21-12.

Selecting a service from the list on the left will open status and preference information on the right. To activate or deactivate a service, toggle the check box next to its name. System changes, such as opening the relevant port and making necessary adjustments to the firewall, are done for you.

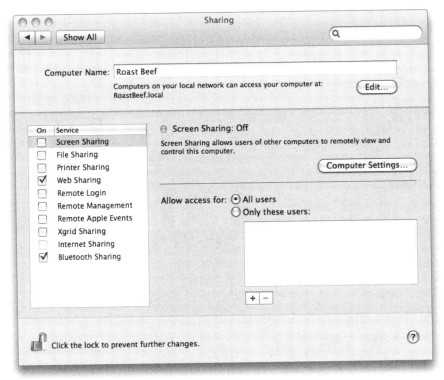

Figure 21-12. Many ways to share your Mac in System Preferences

Although each type of sharing has a description, it's not necessarily obvious exactly to which protocols or services they relate. Make sure you have the right service before you check the box and run out the door, or you might be in for an unpleasant surprise.

Screen Sharing

This allows people to connect to your machine using Leopard's built-in screen sharing, but not Apple Remote Desktop. It bears noting that screen sharing is more than just being able to see your machine. People who share your screen can actually use your computer as if they were sitting at it, as shown in Figure 21-13. It's the graphical equivalent of logging in with ssh.

Options include explicitly naming which users can connect using this protocol, whether people can request to control the screen, and whether to protect screen control with a password. Note that turning on screen sharing will cause your computer to become browsable from the Finder, so don't turn it on unless you need it.

When might you use screen sharing? Traditionally, its primary purpose is administrative. Apple Remote Desktop is, above all, a tool to help system administrators manage a network of machines. By bundling screen sharing with Leopard, Apple is expanding it to more informal uses. For example, if your mom calls you for tech support, you can just show her how to update her web page in iWeb instead of trying to describe it over the phone.

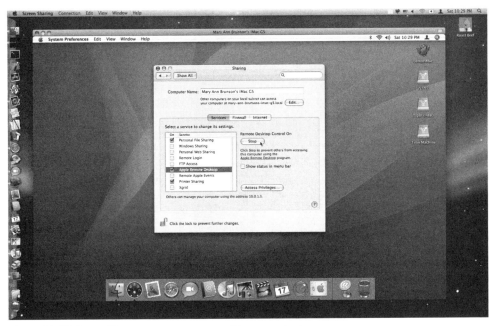

Figure 21-13. Controlling a remote computer with screen sharing

File Sharing

When you connect to another machine in the Finder, you are using file sharing. In previous versions of Mac OS X, different protocols were listed separately. In Leopard, AFP, FTP, and SMB are all covered by the same service. You can decide which protocols are allowed by clicking the Options button.

In addition to the protocol list, you can decide which folders you'd like to share and explicitly list which users should be allowed to connect to your machine. As with screen sharing, enabling file sharing will make your machine visible on the local network, so make sure you need it before activating it. Also, SMB requires storing passwords in a less-secure way than Mac OS X prefers, so make double-sure you need to let people connect to you with SMB before activating it.

Access to folders and files on your machine is determined by the permissions and access lists you've already set up. If you'd like to exchange files with other people on the network without having to worry about all that stuff, you can use the default Public folder, which is set up automatically on each new account.

By default, people who connect to your machine can read files from the Public folder, but they cannot edit or delete them, and they cannot put files in the Public folder itself. Within the Public folder, there's a folder called Drop Box, which works in the opposite way. People can put files in the Drop Box folder, but they cannot open the Drop Box folder to access the files it contains.

If you have a file you want people to access, simply put it in the Public folder. If someone else needs to give you a file, they can simply drop it in the Drop Box folder. It doesn't get much easier than that!

Printer Sharing

When printer sharing is enabled, printers connected to your machine are also connected to the network. Other machines on the network can see the printer in the printing system and negotiate the protocol on their own, though experience suggests it will usually end up being Bonjour. If you have a desktop machine hooked up to the printer, this a great way to print from your laptop.

Web Sharing

This simple, ambiguous name covers a lot of ground—so much ground, in fact, the entire next chapter is devoted to it. In a nutshell, though, web sharing means you will host web sites from your machine.

Remote Login

Unlike file sharing, which covers all manner of file transfer protocols, Remote Login specifically enables Secure Shell. Although Remote Login is conceptually similar to screen sharing (and sounds similar to Remote Desktop), as far as the Sharing pane is concerned, they are completely unrelated. The only option is an access control list.

Remote Management

Not to be mistaken for Remote Login or screen sharing, Remote Management controls whether people can connect to your machine using Apple Remote Desktop. Options are almost identical to screen sharing.

Traditionally, a given protocol used a given port, so enabling access to a particular service was an all-or-nothing affair. As discussed in the previous chapter, Leopard's new firewall is able to route or block requests at the application level. As such, even though Apple Remote Desktop and screen sharing use the same protocols, they can be enabled, disabled, and configured separately.

Remote Apple Events

The Apple Events system underlies interapplication communication, as used by AppleScript. To control a remote machine with AppleScript, therefore, a machine would have to respond to remote Apple Events. This would be useful if you were trying to use AppleScript to automate some administrative task over a network.

Xgrid Sharing

Apple's Xgrid application is used to distribute programming tasks over a network, creating an ad hoc supercomputer. If your company uses Xgrid, you'll need to enable Xgrid sharing. Otherwise, you can safely ignore it.

Internet Sharing

Contrary to what you might be led to believe by its ambiguous name, enabling Internet sharing does not allow you to connect to your computer from other computers on the Internet. Rather, it allows you to share the Internet from your computer with other computers.

The typical Mac has at least three network interfaces: Ethernet, FireWire, and AirPort. At any moment, only one of those interfaces is usually connected to the Internet, while other interfaces could be connected to another computer or even an entirely different network. By enabling Internet sharing, you're able to let the computers on one network interface connect to the Internet on another.

For example, a typical setup might have the Internet coming into your home via a cable or DSL modem, which, in turn, is connected to an AirPort base station. All the computers in your home would then be connected to the AirPort base station, sharing its Internet connection.

With Internet sharing, you could instead plug one computer directly into the modem via Ethernet and then use that machine's AirPort card to create an ad hoc network that other computers could use to share the Internet connection, eliminating the need for the AirPort base station altogether.

This kind of setup is particularly convenient when you are away from home. If your hotel room has an Internet connection via Ethernet, several people can share that connection without having to pack an AirPort base station or other network hardware.

Bluetooth Sharing

Although it's usually associated with headsets and other simple gadgets, Bluetooth is a general short-range wireless standard that can connect two machines with file systems, such as two computers, or a computer and a phone. To move files around over a Bluetooth connection, you'll need to enable Bluetooth sharing, though connecting a Bluetooth device will usually activate Bluetooth sharing for you.

Summary

When it comes to connecting to remote machines, you have a lot of options. Networking is built into the Finder, and .Mac takes this even further, integrating the entire web publishing experience into the Mac's legendary interface. Third-party applications expand this integration by offering direct connections to the Internet, either through .Mac or by directly incorporating Internet technology such as FTP and Secure Shell.

Networking is no longer a one-way street with clients and servers having immutable, predefined roles. Any Mac has the pedigree of a server built right into System Preferences, whether it's to simply share a file, to allow remote access to the machine, or to take on a more permanent role.

In the next chapter, we'll explore a particularly common sharing scenario: setting up a web server on your Mac. Whether creating an intranet, building a test platform for development, or hosting a web site from your home or office, you'll see that serving web pages on Mac OS X is easy to do but endlessly configurable.

## CHAPTER 22

Leopard As a Web Server

There are several reasons why you might want to host a web site on Mac OS X. Probably the most common is so you can develop web sites on your local machine before uploading finalized updates to your server.

Apache

Mac OS X comes with the world's leading open source web server, Apache 2, already installed. All user accounts on your machine can host a Sites folder, which contains that user's personal home page, as shown in Figure 22-1.

Figure 22-1. The default web site in Safari

Before you can actually load a user's personal home page, you must activate web sharing from the Sharing preference pane, in System Preferences, as shown in Figure 22-2. This is extremely simple: just check the Web Sharing box. There are no options.

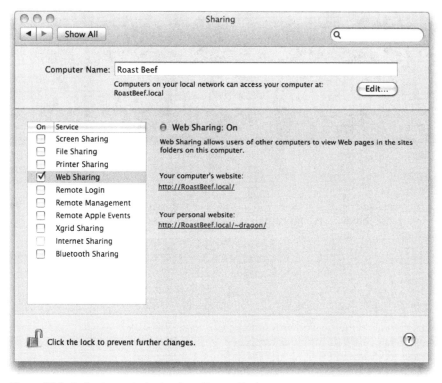

Figure 22-2. Activating web sharing from System Preferences

> **CAUTION** Turning on web sharing is an all-or-nothing proposition. If you turn web sharing on for one account, it will be on for all accounts. To change this behavior, see the "Configuring Apache" section, which follows.

Accessing Your Site

Your local web server is accessed like any other web server—that is to say, by IP address. You can use the standard loopback address, 127.0.0.1, but if another user on your network were to try to access your site at 127.0.0.1, they would get their own machine.

If you'd like to view your page from other computers on your local network, you can use the .local address, which you can assign from the Sharing pane. However, this depends on machines resolving DNS via multicast, so it might not work, depending on the configuration of your network.

If nothing else, you can access your machine by its local IP address. To determine your IP address, open the Networking pane of System Preferences, and then select the appropriate network interface from the list on the left. The status will list your IP address, as shown in Figure 22-3. You can get the same information from the Info tab of Network Utility.

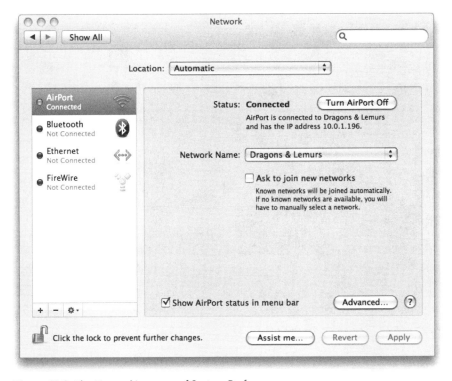

Figure 22-3. The Networking pane of System Preferences

> **TIP** Which network interface is the appropriate one? Chances are, you only have one active interface, which will have a green light next to it. If you have multiple active network interfaces, pick one that's connected to the network you are trying to access the machine from.

Depending on your network, you may or may not be able to access your machine from elsewhere on the Internet. How can you find out? Your first clue is your IP address. If it starts with 10, 169, or 192, it's most likely a local address assigned by a connection sharing protocol such as DHCP.

If it's something else, it might be reachable. Your best bet is to phone a friend and see if they can access your site by IP address.

Customizing Your Site

As nice as the default personal home page is in Leopard, you'll probably want to add your own content. Using your favorite web design tool, publish your content to your local Sites directory. The next time you visit your local address, your new site should be there, as shown in Figure 22-4.

If you get a 403 Forbidden message, chances are you do not have permissions on Sites or its contents. In general, folders serving web sites need to be readable and executable by everyone, while web documents and files should be readable by everyone.

Set the appropriate permissions on your Sites folder and its content using the Finder or the command line, and then try loading your page again. If it still doesn't work, your user site might not be configured correctly (see the "Configuring Apache" section, which follows).

Figure 22-4. A customized local home page in Safari

Document Root

In addition to the user sites located at ~username, your machine also has a site, as shown in Figure 22-5. This site's content is located in the Apache server's document root. Unlike the logical ~/Sites location, the default document root is /Library/WebServer/Documents.

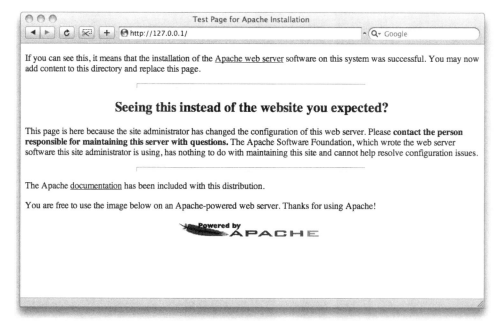

Figure 22-5. The site at Apache's document root

If you're developing web content, you probably want your local server setup to mirror your remote setup as closely as possible. Since ~username sites went out of fashion with Geocities, you probably want to use the document root.

If you're the only user on your computer, that's certainly an option. However, writing personal project files to a directory with administrative privileges is potentially problematic, and /Library/WebServer/Documents is not exactly a convenient location to have to remember.

There are a couple of options. The easiest method, which I recommend, is to simply create a symbolic link that points the expected document root to your local Sites directory.

> **NOTE** Symbolic links and shortcuts are similar in concept but very different in practice. Links are a UNIX file system construct, while shortcuts belong to the Finder. Using a shortcut to redirect your document root will not work.

To redirect your document root using symbolic links, navigate to the /Library/WebServer directory. Move aside the original Documents folder. You could delete it, but simply renaming it to something like OldDocuments will do the trick.

Launch the Terminal application from /Applications/Utilities, or, if you're a true power user, from the Dock. Invoke the following command:

```
sudo ln -s ~/Sites /Library/WebServer/Documents
```

This means, using superuser privileges (sudo), create a link (ln) that is symbolic (-s) from my local Sites directory (~/Sites) at the path /Library/WebServer/Documents.

Since you're using sudo, this will prompt you for your password. After entering it, invoking ls on /Library/WebServer will show a file called Documents. In the Finder, it will appear to be a shortcut. Loading the root site in your browser of choice should show your personal home site.

> **TIP** Your browser may have the old page cached, so you might need to reload or even empty your cache to see the change.

Configuring Apache

Since Apache is a UNIX application, it doesn't have a convenient GUI preference pane, nor does it use a standard Macintosh property list. Rather, it has its own configuration file in its own directory using its own peculiar scheme.

Fortunately, the configuration file, like everything else about Apache, is well documented and, honestly, not that complicated. The default home pages all contain links to the Apache manual, as does the dire warning that begins the configuration file itself. You can always just go straight to Apache's documentation home page: http://httpd.apache.org/docs/.

> **NOTE** The name of the Apache HTTP server has an interesting history. Originally, httpd was the NCSA HTTP Server, a project at the National Center for Supercomputing Applications. When its creator, Robert McCool, left NCSA, the project stalled. A group of developers continued working on patches for the NCSA code base, creating "a patchy" HTTP server in its stead.

Apache's configuration files live in the directory /private/etc/apache2. Unless you've turned on the ability to see invisible files in the Finder, you'll have to navigate there in Terminal. Listing the contents of the directory shows the file we've come here to see: httpd.conf.

> **NOTE** Although it's called Apache, the name of the UNIX executable is httpd, which reflects its role as a background process (daemon) that serves the Hypertext Transfer Protocol.

Open `httpd.conf` in your text editor of choice. I personally recommend using BBEdit, or its free equivalent, TextWrangler. With BBEdit, you can use the disk browser to easily navigate here, since it can see the hidden folders. It will also take care of overwriting the old file, which is read-only. That said, you can also use Nano, Emacs, or Vi, as detailed in Chapter 18.

The configuration file is very long, but don't be scared. Lines that start with the pound sign are comments, which is to say they are ignored. The file mainly consists of hints explaining what the various sections do. There's very little actual content here, and even less you have to worry about.

ServerRoot

Much as UNIX considers ~ to be a shortcut for your user directory, the `ServerRoot` command tells Apache where it should look for any files that are not explicitly named. Since these files are all for its internal use, there's really no need to change the default value.

Listen

Like any server process, Apache listens on a particular port or socket. Normally, it answers any incoming calls on port 80. If you need to change the port for some reason, or you want to bind to a specific IP address, you can edit this.

One particular use for Listen is to limit who can see your page. Remember how I said you could load your page by one of several means? What if you don't want people to be able to load your page elsewhere on the network? By binding Apache to 127.0.0.1:80, you will only be able to view the page locally. Dialing in to the actual IP address would simply return an error page.

Another use for the Listen directive is to use a port other than the default. For example, your ISP may block access to port 80 in an effort to prevent you from running a web server from your home. You could instead bind to port 8080.

You can bind to multiple ports and sockets by issuing multiple Listen directives. So, for example, to view the site locally on the standard port, but to let others only see it on a secret port, you could say this:

```
Listen 127.0.0.1:80
Listen 1984
```

You could then load your site by simply pointing to 127.0.0.1, but someone else on the network loading your site would get an error unless they knew to append the correct port to the end of your IP address. So, for example, if your IP address were 10.0.0.1, they would have to point their browser to `http://10.0.0.1:1984`.

Dynamic Shared Object (DSO) Support

This is a fancy name for the LoadModule directive. *Modules* extend the functionality of Apache. There are several modules loaded by default. We will come back to LoadModule when we are ready to add PHP to our web server.

User/Group

Since Apache operates on your system, it needs to be able to access files. You could run it as root, but that would be a security risk. Instead, Apache runs as the user `www` as part of the group `www`. Should you want to change this, you would do that here. Honestly, though, you probably don't need to.

VirtualHost

If you've got a web site running on a host somewhere, chances are you're not on a dedicated server. Lucky for everyone involved, you can run multiple sites on a single machine using a feature called *virtual hosting*.

Virtual hosting is off by default, but if you want to configure multiple sites to run on your machine, perhaps because you work on multiple sites and would like to access them all separately, you can do so.

Incidentally, the different user sites built into Mac OS X, while similar to virtual hosting, are actually a different feature.

ServerAdmin

One of the nice things Apache does is automatically generate index and error pages for you. Since these pages may require action by the server administrator, they will include an e-mail address. That address is given with the ServerAdmin directive.

ServerName

Similarly, the ServerName directive is how the server refers to itself. This would typically be the domain name and port, or possibly the IP address. Since this information can be determined automatically, it's commented out by default. Should you find yourself actually serving web pages to the public, you should define it explicitly.

DocumentRoot

This directive tells Apache where to start serving pages from. That is to say, it defines which directory on the host machine is represented by / in the web address. Directories attached to / will be similarly mapped to directories on the host machine.

By default, document root is set to `/Library/WebServer/Documents`, so loading `http://127.0.0.1/` loads the contents of `/Library/WebServer/Documents`. Loading `http://127.0.0.1/Site/Welcome.html` loads the file `/Library/WebServer/Documents/Site/Welcome.html`.

By replacing the file pointed to here with a symbolic link, we basically use the file system to fool Apache into loading a site different than it expects. We could accomplish the same thing by changing the DocumentRoot directive to the following:

```
DocumentRoot "/Users/username/Sites"
```

Each method has its advantages. Creating a symbolic link leaves the configuration file untouched, which makes it that much harder to mess up.

The nice thing about setting the document root in `httpd.conf` is that it's portable. As long as you use the same user name, your configuration file will work on any machine. It also doesn't rely on file system trickery, which makes it seem more pure. At the end of the day, it really doesn't matter which one you use.

Permissions

There's no actual "Permissions" directive, but that's the best term I can think of to describe the several entries that follow. These define the options for directories and files on the system. A notable entry is the Options FollowSymLinks directive, which is on by default, and which allows our symbolic link trick to work.

There are several more entries that block web visitors from being able to see certain types of files, such as hidden files that begin with a dot or the Mac OS X resource files.

One thing to keep in mind is that there are permissions entries for every known directory, including the document root. If you change a directory elsewhere in the configuration, you will have to be sure to change its permissions entry as well. This is one of the reasons why using symbolic links is easier than editing the configuration file.

DirectoryIndex

Easily missed amidst all the permissions directives, the DirectoryIndex directive defines the default index file name. That is to say, when a user simply points to a directory, which file do they get? The default is index.html, which is why you don't have to type index.html all the time when you're surfing the Web.

If you decide to start using PHP or some other technology that requires you to use a different file name or extension, you can edit this. By including multiple listings, you can give several possible defaults. Apache will server up the first one it finds. For example, to serve index.html by default, but to serve the old Microsoft FrontPage standard, welcome.html, as a backup, you would say the following:

```
DirectoryIndex index.html welcome.html
```

If nothing listed in DirectoryIndex exists, visitors will see a listing of everything in the directory. To prevent that, you can put a failsafe at the end of the DirectoryIndex directive, such as a reference to a file in your root directory telling people to stop poking around in your directories:

```
DirectoryIndex index.html welcome.html /lost.html
```

Logging

There are several directives related to logging. You can customize where logs are kept, how much logging Apache should do, and what format log messages are in. These are best kept to the default values, but if you spend a lot of time reading your logs and you develop an opinion on some aspect of logging, here is where you can flex your will.

Redirects

Much like the DocumentRoot directive, the Redirect, Alias, and ScriptAlias directives let you map the URLs people request to your file system.

Redirect will actually cause the browser to request a new location. This is useful if you've permanently moved a file to elsewhere on the system. Alias will cause a given path to look outside the normal document root hierarchy.

For example, you might want to give the outside world access to your Pictures directory (for some reason) by mapping requests to www.yoursite.com/pictures to /Users/username/Pictures. You could, of course, also accomplish this with symbolic links, assuming you allow FollowSymLinks on the directory.

ScriptAlias is like Alias, but it applies specifically to directories that contain executable scripts, rather than simple documents.

DefaultType

Most of the Internet uses MIME types to determine how it should deal with files. Since most web servers serve web pages, it's appropriate to leave this set to the default, text/plain.

> **NOTE** MIME stands for Multipurpose Internet Mail Extensions. Like most of the Internet, it has been expanded beyond its original purpose.

What makes this directive interesting is actually the list of AddType and AddHandler directives, which allow you to add support for certain types of files. The list is begun with a TypesConfig directive that points to an external list of types, stored by default in /private/etc/apache2/mime.types.

Most webmasters meet the types section when adding PHP support, as the traditional php file extension is not handled by default—although on Leopard, this is handled for you in the PHP configuration file.

ErrorDocument

If you ever go poking around the coolest sites on the Net, they always seem to have these sexy custom error pages, so pulling a 403: Access Denied doesn't jar you from the overall design of the site. The ErrorDocument directive lets you point to custom pages and scripts.

If you define a custom error document, be sure to actually implement it, lest your users not only be treated to a generic error page, but also be blighted with the ever embarrassing "Additionally, a 404 Not Found error was encountered while trying to use an ErrorDocument to handle the request."

Include

Apache configuration is typically split into multiple files. External files are referred to using the Include directive. For the purposes of scope, you can consider the entire text of an included file to be inserted where the Include directive is used.

This is important, because the general rule with Apache is that the last word is the one that's obeyed. So, if an included file disagrees with the main file, the one farther down the list is going to win. If you find some configuration detail is not working, despite being clearly documented, make sure you're not being overridden by another file.

Of particular importance is this line:

```
Include /private/etc/apache2/extra/httpd-userdir.conf
```

Editing this file reveals two things. First, it uses the UserDir directive to tell Apache that every user's personal root is their Sites directory. If, for example, you are from the old school and you'd prefer this directory to be called public_html, this is where you'd set that up.

Second, this file in turn includes all .conf files contained in the directory /private/etc/apache2/users. Listing that directory reveals a series of files of the form *username*.conf, where *username* is a username on the system.

Each of these files contains a permissions directive.

```
<Directory "/Users/username/Sites/">
    Options Indexes MultiViews
    AllowOverride None
    Order allow,deny
    Allow from all
</Directory>
```

Again, *username* refers to the actual user name dealt with by the file.

By default, all directories on your system are forbidden, except for those explicitly named. This directive makes the named user's Sites folder readable and sets up a few options. Were this file to be missing, you would not be able to access your site, regardless of system-level permissions.

When you turn on web sharing, these files are created by default. By editing the files, you can disallow certain users the ability to host sites. You could even remove the main include, disabling all user sites, while giving yourself the document root.

> **NOTE** While disabling the explicit permissions on a user directory will do the job in a round-about way, the proper way to enable or disable users is with the UserDir directive. See the Apache documents for more information.

Whenever you change Apache's configuration file, you will need to restart Apache. The easiest way to do this is with Terminal, using the special Apache control program, `apachectl`.

```
sudo apachectl -k graceful
```

This will restart Apache gracefully, which is to say, it will let it finish what it's doing, shut down, and then restart.

If you try to restart Apache, but it's not already running for some reason, it will just start. If you've messed up the configuration file it will usually let you know on restart. Otherwise, you should be ready to test your changes.

PHP

There have been a number of schemes to create dynamic web pages since the Web first came into being in 1993. Some of these rely on the client to execute. Most notable in this regard are Dynamic HTML (DHTML) and its modern equivalent, Ajax. While it's beginning to recover, client-side scripting has traditionally been hampered by compatibility issues in the aftermath of the browser wars.

Server-side scripting schemes include CGI and Server Side Includes (SSI). However, both of these have been largely rendered obsolete by PHP. Unlike CGI and SSI, PHP is a hypertext pre-processor. That is to say, it's a page that runs a script, but ultimately serves plain HTML.

Since it is open source, PHP is the preprocessor of choice on UNIX systems running Apache. Indeed, PHP has been implemented as an Apache module, and comes installed, but not activated, by default on Mac OS X.

To properly ensure PHP is installed, we need to have a PHP page. The best test page is a simple PHP Info page. It relies on PHP to be working, so it's a good test, and it gives us a lot of information about our PHP installation, so it's actually useful.

Create a PHP Info page in your favorite text editor, and save it to your document root as `index.php`. All you need to include is a single call to PHP's built-in `phpinfo` function:

```
<?php phpinfo() ?>
```

Then, load the page in your browser of choice by pointing to `http://127.0.0.1/index.php`. You have to point to the page explicitly, because otherwise you'll get the default index page, `index.html`.

> **NOTE** You can, of course, also save the PHP info page to your home `Sites` directory.

Loading the page in your browser, you're greeted with the entirety of its source, as written. That's because Apache doesn't know what a .php file is, so it's serving it as its default MIME type, `text/plain`.

To enable PHP, we simply need to uncomment a single line of text from the Apache configuration file.

```
#LoadModule php5_module        libexec/apache2/libphp5.so
```

Since it starts with #, it's a comment and is ignored. Delete the # and save. Back in the day, we'd also have to tell Apache how to handle the file type and look for `index.php` by default, but all that stuff is now handled automatically by the included php5.conf file. Just restart Apache and, as the saying goes, there is no step 3. The PHP Info screen should now display properly, as shown in Figure 22-6.

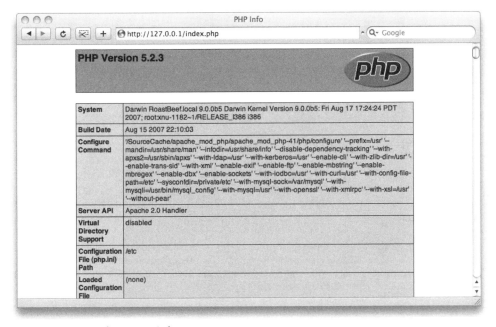

Figure 22-6. PHP Info page in Safari

Examining the PHP Info page will tell you a lot about how your server is set up. It's a good idea to run it on both your local machine and your remote host, so you can be aware of any differences between versions, features, or configuration options that might affect you.

To learn more about PHP, including an extensive manual with installation and integration guides, visit PHP's official web site at www.php.net/.

Database

Traditionally, a web server consists of four components. There's the operating system, the web server daemon, the scripting engine, and the database server. Mac OS X, Apache, and PHP cover three of those four out of the box. Whether the database requires any additional work depends on your needs.

SQLite

Mac OS X Leopard comes with SQLite installed and running. SQLite is a fast, simple, light-weight database that is quickly gaining popularity with web developers. It's compatible with the same Structured Query Language (SQL) used by nearly every other database in the world. More importantly, it's directly addressable from PHP.

Aside from the fact that SQLite is already set up for you, it has the major advantage of being the same database server used throughout the system. Applications written with Core Data can use SQLite as their backing store. That means you can share a database between your Core Data application and your PHP web site without ever having to touch SQL.

> **NOTE** For more information on Core Data and other application development topics, see Chapter 24.

If you're serving web pages from your machine, or if your remote host has SQLite (and the requisite PHP modules) running, you're good to go. Run `sqlite3` from the command line to access the included management program. You can also learn more by visiting `http://sqlite.org/`.

MySQL

If, however, you want to be like everyone else and run MySQL, you're going to have to install it yourself. Fortunately, MySQL maintains a Mac OS X installer package on its web site, `www.mysql.org/`. To install MySQL, simply download the disk image that matches your architecture and run it.

> **NOTE** At the time of this writing, there is no Leopard version of MySQL available on the download site. This may change by the time you get there, but in either case, the 10.4 version can be made to work with one minor tweak. See `http://www.beyondmac.com/2007/10/30/php-mysql-on-leopard-mysqlsock-location/`.

> **NOTE** Apple also provides a good tutorial on getting up to speed with MySQL, including installation and initial configuration. See `http://developer.apple.com/internet/opensource/osdb.html`.

Although it's available in more traditional tarball format, I downloaded the more Mac-like disk image installer package. This contains an installer for the database server itself, and a separate installer if you'd like MySQL to start automatically. If you're running a web server, that's probably a good idea.

Once it's installed, you can start the MySQL server from the command line. It's installed in `/usr/local`, which is not in the default path, so to run any MySQL tools you will have to actually go into the directory, or use the full path:

```
sudo -b /usr/local/mysql/bin/mysqld_safe
```

After entering your password, the server will start. The `-b` flag on `sudo` invokes the server as a background process. At your option, you can eliminate the background flag on your first run just to make sure everything is copacetic.

Alternately, if you installed the startup item, you can use it to start the MySQL database:

```
sudo /Library/StartupItems/MySQLCOM/MySQLCOM start
```

Finally, the installer includes a MySQL preference pane for System Preferences, as shown in Figure 22-7. Double-clicking will install it. The preference pane tells you whether MySQL is running, lets you start and stop MySQL, and includes a setting to automatically start MySQL at boot time.

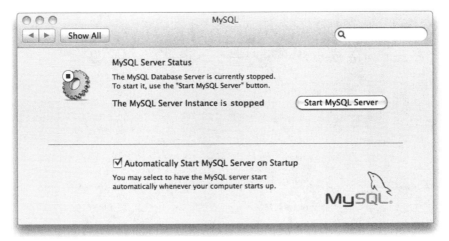

Figure 22-7. The MySQL pane in System Preferences

By default, MySQL sets up a root user with full access and no password. In other words, until you do something about it, your MySQL installation is completely unsecured. The first thing to do after starting the server is to lock down that root account. The easiest way to do this is with the MySQL command-line admin tool:

```
/usr/local/mysql/bin/mysqladmin -u root password "newpwd"
```

where *newpwd* is your new password.

> **NOTE** Aside from the root user, there are also two anonymous accounts with unsecured root access. However, these accounts can only access databases whose names start with test_, and only from the localhost, so they are not much of a risk. Still, if you are actually planning on serving pages professionally, you should lock or remove these accounts. See the online MySQL manual for more details.

Once it's installed, the default MySQL client program can be invoked from the command line, like so:

```
/usr/local/mysql/bin/mysql -u root -p
```

The -p flag will cause MySQL to prompt you for your password. Once you enter it, the command-line client program will launch. Type help to get a list of available commands, and type quit to exit.

MySQL also makes a set of graphical administrative tools that can be downloaded and installed separately, as shown in Figure 22-8. The graphical package contains a manager, a query tool, and a Dashboard widget for monitoring the health of your database. If you love command-line database management, more power to you. For the rest of us, the GUI is a really nice addition.

> **TIP** To connect to your local machine's MySQL server in the graphical administrator, use the host name localhost.

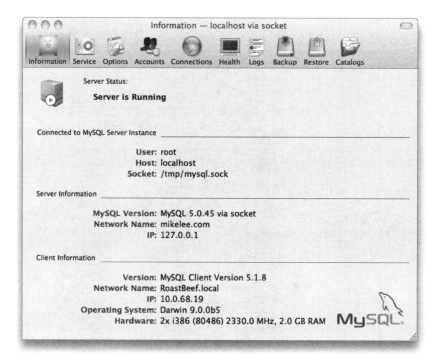

Figure 22-8. MySQL's graphical database administration tool

PHP and MySQL are expected to run together, so once you have MySQL running, PHP will notice immediately. Reloading your PHP Info page will confirm this. Beyond that, accessing MySQL in PHP, setting up user accounts in MySQL, and the sometimes maddening, sometimes magical world of database programming are beyond the scope of this book. Fortunately, there is no end of online resources, and there are several excellent books, including *Beginning PHP and MySQL 5*, by W. Jason Gilmore (Apress, 2006), *PHP and MySQL Web Development*, by Luke Welling and Laura Thomson (Sams, 2003), and *MySQL*, by Paul DuBois (Sams, 2005).

PostgreSQL

While SQLite concentrates on pure performance, and MySQL maintains a good mix of performance and added support for advanced features, PostgreSQL has always been conceived as an enterprise-level solution. It has the most advanced features (e.g., stored procedures), but is still free open source software.

As it is intended for experts, PostgreSQL lacks the hand-holding niceties of MySQL. Fortunately, Mark Liyanage maintains a Mac OS X installer package of PostgreSQL at www.entropy.ch/.

For more information on PostgreSQL, visit its official home page at www.postgresql.org/.

Apple also has a page about PostgreSQL at http://developer.apple.com/internet/opensource/postgres.html.

> **NOTE** Open source server technology is frequently referred to as LAMP, which means Linux, Apache, MySQL, and PHP. Of course, there are open source flavors of UNIX other than Linux, but I guess UAMP doesn't have the same ring to it.

Domain Name Tricks

Were you so inclined, you could set up a DNS server . . . but why? Chances are your registrar has a name server, so providing you have a static outside IP address, you can simply have them point to it and start welcoming visitors to your self-hosted web site.

However, not everyone has the need to spend the money on a static IP address. Especially when you consider that the cost of getting one is greater than the cost of professional web hosting. If you're setting up a web host just because it's fun, because you want to save money, or because you're doing local development, paying for a static IP address is overkill.

Custom Domains Without DNS

You can actually override DNS at a local level. Mac OS X maintains a list of known hosts in a file called /private/etc/hosts. Editing this file will let you map web addresses to IP addresses. Why would you do this?

First, looking at IP addresses all day is boring. That's why DNS was invented, after all. It's much more fun to give your local network machines fun names at imaginary top-level domains. Then you can surf over to http://mike.is.awesome.

Second, if you are developing web pages locally, you might run into a problem with absolute paths. That is to say, if you have a link pointing to www.mydomain.com/somefile.php, your browser will want to go to the remote version, rather than the local version you're developing.

The hosts file is the first place your machine looks when it tries to resolve a domain. Rerouting calls to mydomain.com or www.mydomain.com to your local machine is easy. Just open /private/etc/hosts in your favorite text editor, and then add the following line:

```
127.0.0.1 mydomain.com www.mydomain.com
```

Just remember to edit the hosts file back to normal before trying to surf the Web, or strange things might happen. For more information on the hosts file, invoke man hosts in Terminal.

> **CAUTION** It's OK to add things to the hosts file, but don't edit any of the existing entries. The system has that stuff there for a reason.

Dynamic DNS

What if you want to serve a personal web site from your home, but you don't want to pay for a static IP address? You could just update your registration every time your address changes, but given the time it takes for DNS changes to propagate, you could be looking at a lot of downtime. Even for a home project, that just looks sloppy.

A better option is to use a dynamic DNS service. There are many cheap-to-free services, such as No-IP (www.no-ip.com/) and FreeDNS (http://freedns.afraid.org/), that will let you point a domain name to your dynamic IP address. Unlike a standard name server, dynamic DNS services keep a very short refresh time on their name servers, so changes propagate quickly.

Other Considerations

Serving web pages is simply not that difficult a task. Even a Mac mini can do so with aplomb. As your needs grow, you will probably want to add an uninterruptible power supply and a RAID to protect your data. You'll also want a broadband connection with a high upstream speed and a static IP address.

Here are a couple more things worth checking out:

Mac OS X Server: If you're running a site as a hobby, or as a small business, the standard "client" version of Mac OS X is all you need, but Apple does produce a server version of Mac OS X, aimed at the enterprise. It has some additional administrative features that, while available in UNIX form, have been wrapped in that great Mac OS X user experience. If you're using Mac OS X as a server, you might look into it. Visit `www.apple.com/server/macosx/` for more details.

Ruby on Rails: While PHP is a popular way to create web applications, it's far from the only game in town. One platform that's rising fast is Ruby on Rails. Ruby is an object-oriented programming language, not unlike PHP 5. Rails is a development framework written in and for Ruby. Both are included with Leopard. See `http://developer.apple.com/tools/rubyonrails.html` for more information.

Summary

With its open source and UNIX roots, Mac OS X is built from the same stuff as the Internet itself. It's no wonder the Mac is such a great platform for web development. Whether you're serving web pages to the public right from your desktop, or just building a development environment on your laptop, Mac OS X comes with everything you need, and adding more is easier than ever.

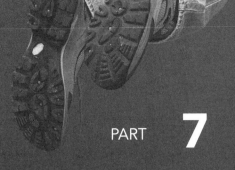

## PART 7

Leopard Development and Scripting

## CHAPTER 23

Mac OS X Automation with Automator and AppleScript

W hen you have some boring, repetitive task to do, you probably wish you could foist it off on an intern or on a really smart robot. If you have to collate reports or fold brochures, we can't help you, but if you're doing something on your computer over and over, we've got good news.

Figure 23-1. Otto, the mascot and application icon for Automator

Meet Otto, the friendly automation robot built into Mac OS X, shown in Figure 23-1. If you give him a step-by-step list of things to do, he'll do them for you with the speed and accuracy computers are designed for, leaving you to the creative and interesting tasks to which your brain is better suited.

From the Applications directory, double-clicking Otto launches Automator. This intuitive but powerful automation tool lets you drag and drop instructions, which can be saved as workflows and launched anytime you need to get things done.

Automator

Upon launching Automator from the Applications directory, you will be greeted with a template panel, as shown in Figure 23-2.

Automator's templates center around the types of data you will be working with; the categories are Files & Folders, Music & Audio, Photos & Images, and Text. There is also a Custom option, which just starts you with a blank workflow.

Once you select a starting template, Automator will let you select where the data is coming from. Typically, the choices will be an iLife application, elsewhere on your machine, or the Internet.

You'll then select when the data will be provided. Your choices boil down to providing the data as part of the workflow, obtaining the data automatically at runtime, or asking the user for the data. Don't sweat these choices too much, because you can change them later.

For the purpose of demonstration, select the Text template. Then, from the "Get content from" drop-down menus below, select User Input and "Ask for text when my workflow runs." Then, click the Choose button.

Figure 23-2. Creating a new Automator workflow

Workflows

A program written in Automator is called a *workflow*. A workflow is a step-by-step list of simple instructions, called *actions*. Workflows can also contain small bits of reusable data, called *variables*, but we'll return to that. Actions resemble windows in that they contain a title bar, a content view, and a tabbed details view.

The title bar, which has the action's name and icon, has a disclosure triangle on the left that will collapse and expand the action. Double-clicking the title bar has the same effect. On the right side of the title bar is an X icon. Clicking this icon will remove the action from the workflow.

> **CAUTION** Clicking the X icon removes the action without warning or confirmation. You can undo this by selecting Undo from the Edit menu or by pressing Cmd+Z.

The action's content view will typically contain preferences or other configuration options in the form of drop-down boxes, text fields, table views, and so forth. Your workflow contains a single action, Ask for Text, as shown in Figure 23-3. This action will prompt the user to enter some text. Set the question text to "What keyword shall I search for?" Leave Default Answer empty, but check the "Require an answer" box. Leave the buttons labeled as Cancel and OK.

To run this simple workflow, click the Run button in the toolbar. You'll be presented with the dialog you designed, as shown in Figure 23-4. Automator will pause execution of your work-flow and wait for you to deal with the dialog. Enter a search term, and click the OK button.

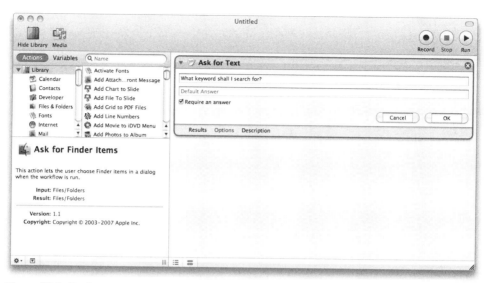

Figure 23-3. Configuring an Automator action

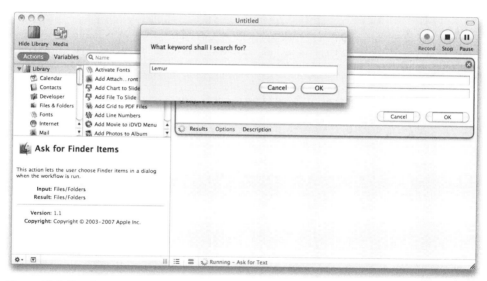

Figure 23-4. Running an Automator workflow

Once the dialog is dismissed, Automator moves to the next action. Since there are no more actions, the workflow stops. Below the content view is a tabbed details view. Clicking a tab will expand the details view, while clicking the tab again will collapse it. Clicking the Results tab will show you your search term, as shown in Figure 23-5.

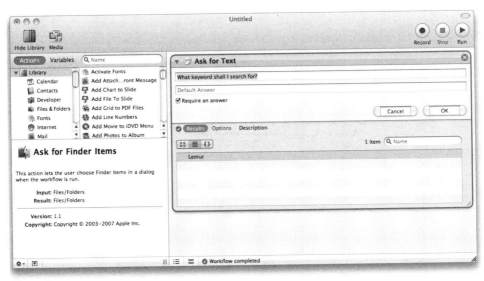

Figure 23-5. Examining the results of an Automator action

There are three tabs:

Results: When you run a workflow within Automator, you can examine the results of an action on this tab. This can include complex results such as images. There are several views within the Results tab, though which ones are available will vary depending on the type of data produced.

Options: Unlike the action's own options, which are presented in the content view, these options are Automator preferences. Usually the only option will be to show the action occurring when the workflow is run, which can be useful when testing the workflow but would probably be annoying when actually using it.

Description: This is the same information presented in the sidebar's detail pane when an action is selected. It gives the name and icon of the action, a description of what it does, and details such as the kind of input it requires, the kind of output it produces, its version, its copyright information, and so on.

So, you ask the user for a search term, but it's not very interesting as it is. You need more actions so you can do something with this data.

Actions

Actions are the basic unit of work in Automator. The typical action takes some piece of data, asks an application to perform some task with that data, and produces the results. The results can then be fed into the next action until the work is done.

Actions that are available to you are contained in the Library sidebar. You can hide or show the sidebar with the Hide/Show Library button in Automator's toolbar. You can also select Hide/Show Library from the View menu.

The Library sidebar has two tabs: Actions and Variables. Each tab has two columns. The leftmost column has folder-like groups. Selecting a group will show its contents in the right column.

You can filter the items showing in the right column by typing in the search field at the top of the column. Selecting an item in the right column will show a description in the details pane at the bottom of the sidebar. The details pane can be shown or hidden by clicking the disclosure button in the lower-left corner of the window.

You can create your own groups and smart groups from the group view's context menu or from the action (gear) menu in the lower-left corner of the Automator window.

In Tiger, actions were grouped by which application provided them. In Leopard, the actions are grouped by the category of data they work on:

Calendar: iCal calendars, events, and To Do items.

Contacts: Address Book contacts information.

Developer: Xcode, SQL, CVS, and other developer tools.

File & Folders: Finder items and tasks, including moving, copying, and deleting items; setting the desktop picture; and setting Spotlight comments.

Fonts: Font Book management tasks and metadata.

Internet: Web and RSS data, including extracting, filtering, and loading URLs.

Mail: Mail tasks, such as getting, filtering, displaying, and sending e-mail messages.

Movies: QuickTime, iMovie, iDVD, and DVD Player actions.

Music: iTunes and iPod actions, as well as the immensely useful Text to Audio File action.

PDFs: Preview actions for creating, controlling, or extracting data from PDF documents.

Photos: iPhoto, Preview, and QuickTime actions for getting, manipulating, and organizing photos. This also includes actions for controlling digital cameras and the iSight web camera.

Presentations: Keynote actions for controlling slide show presentations.

Text: TextEdit actions for creating, editing, and working with text documents.

Utilities: System services and Automator control actions, such as burning a disk and presenting different kinds of dialogs, as well as the immensely useful Run AppleScript, Run Shell Script, and Run Workflow actions.

Other: Theoretically, this group would contain actions that somehow don't fit into other groups. In practice, it's up to developers to define which groups their actions should be sorted into. If this information is not provided, the action ends up here.

NOTE Your categories may differ based on which applications you've installed. For example, the Developer category probably won't exist if you haven't installed any developer tools.

With the default actions, grouping by application or grouping by category is a largely irrelevant distinction. Apple's included applications tend to center around a specific type of data anyway.

However, when you install third-party applications, they will often add actions to Automator. You can also download actions from the Web that may or may not use applications to do their heavy lifting.

The more actions you have, the more the category grouping becomes useful. You can toggle between application or category grouping from the "Arrange Actions by" submenu of the View menu.

Using Actions

Let's use our keyword to do a Google image search. There are lots of actions for working with web data, but there's no action to turn our keyword into a URL. However, there is a Run Shell Script action, and you can easily create a URL string in a shell script.

To add an action to your workflow, drag it from the sidebar's right column. When it is over the workflow area, the action will expand into a full panel. To rearrange actions within the workflow, simply drag them around.

From the Utilities group, drag the Run Shell Script action to the workflow. The Ask for Text action automatically connects to the Run Shell Script action. When a workflow runs, it executes each action sequentially, from top to bottom. If an action generates output, it's assumed to be the next action's input. This relationship is represented by the connection between the two actions.

If two actions do not connect, no data will flow between them. If you want an action to ignore the data coming from the action above it, select Ignore Input from the receiving action's context menu.

Select "/bin/bash" from the Shell drop-down and "as arguments" from the "Pass input" drop-down. Enter the following simple shell script in the text area:

```
echo "http://images.google.com/images?q="$1
```

This simple script will return the beginning of a Google image query URL (as determined experimentally in Safari), plus the first argument, which will be the output of the Ask for Text action: the user's keyword input. Running the workflow will produce the completed URL, as shown in Figure 23-6.

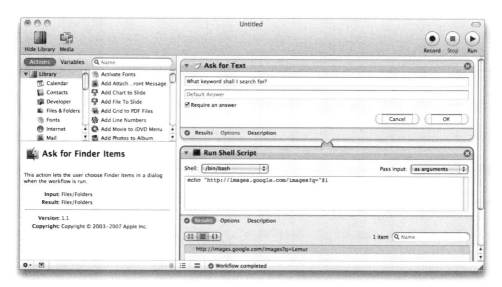

Figure 23-6. Running a shell script in Automator

> **NOTE** Shell scripting is covered in Chapter 19. Apple also provides a shell scripting primer, available online: `http://developer.apple.com/documentation/OpenSource/Conceptual/ShellScripting/`.

Once we have the URL to the search, we'll want to get the results. A Google image search will return a page of links. To extract the links from the page, drag the Get Link URLs from Webpages action from the Internet group. You might as well check the "Only return URLs in the same domain as the starting page" option.

The Google results page will have a lot of links besides the image results, so you'll want to apply a filter. Drag over a Filter URLs action from the Internet group. This uses a rule editor, similar to the one used in Mail. Again, by experiment, we determined we want links with URLs that begin with the following:

```
http://images.google.com/imgres?imgurl=
```

Running the workflow will show 20 URLs, as shown in Figure 23-7. Loading one of these URLs in Safari, you can see that these don't lead to the image directly. Rather, they lead to a multiframe Google results page that requires some clicking to get the image.

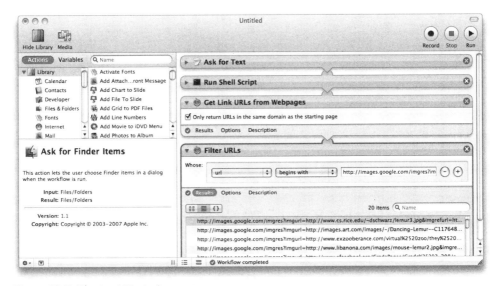

Figure 23-7. Filtering URLs in Automator

However, the URLs themselves contain the link to the image. Once again, you will have to turn to a simple shell script to extract the text you need. Add another Run Shell Script action, just as before, and enter this script:

```
for url in $@
do
    url=${url##*imgurl=}
    url=${url%%&*}
    echo $url
done
```

This script loops through the arguments and extracts the text between `imgurl=` and `&`, returning the image URL.

> **TIP** If you find it confusing having two actions called Run Shell Script, you can rename any action from its context menu.

To download the image, drag a Download URLs action from the Internet group, as shown in Figure 23-8. Note that when presented with a list of inputs, rather than a single input, Automator actions will automatically loop over the list item, eliminating most of the need for this most common programming control structure.

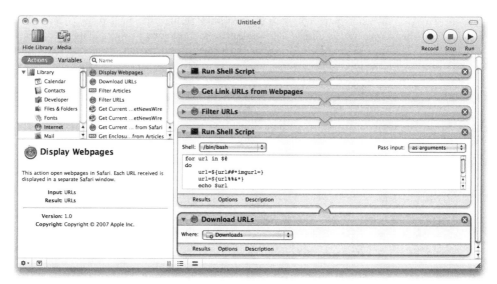

Figure 23-8. Downloading URLs in Automator

You could just download the images and open them in Preview, but that's boring. With a little more work, you can build a dynamic screen saver to present your downloaded images.

Setting Up the Keyword Screen Saver

You could try to do all this in Automator, but since it has to be done only once, you can just set up the screen saver manually and use the Automator workflow to generate the dynamic content. In the Finder, create a new folder in your `Pictures` folder called `Keyword Screensaver`, as shown in Figure 23-9.

Figure 23-9. Creating the Keyword Screensaver folder in the Finder

Rather than write a screen saver, you can just use the photo screen saver already built into Mac OS X. Select System Preferences... from the Apple menu, select the Desktop & Screen Saver preference pane, and then select the Screen Saver tab, as shown in Figure 23-10.

Figure 23-10. Setting up the Keyword screen saver in System Preferences

From the Screen Savers list on the left, select Choose Folder.... This will present you with a standard open sheet. Select the Keyword Screensaver folder, and click the Choose button. Finally, set up the photo screen saver as you want it. We recommend the new "falling pictures" display style, which is the second of the three styles.

With that set up, return to Automator. Drag the Get Specified Finder Items action from the Files & Folders group. You should do this before you actually download the images, so drag it to the top of the list. Click the Add... button, and find the Keyword Screensaver folder.

This new action connects to the Ask for Text action. This is not what you want. Rather, you want to store the value until you're ready to download the items. This is a perfect chance to use Automator's new variables.

Variables

Like actions, variables are grouped by category. Since they typically have nothing to do with applications, there is no by-application grouping option.

Date & Time: The current year, month, day, day of the week, and of course the date and time

Locations: Known folders, such as Applications, Documents, Downloads, and the current user's home directory

System: System information such as the computer's name, IP address, and operating system version

Text & Data: Generic variables for storing text and data

User: User information such as username, first name, last name, e-mail address, and .Mac account name

Utilities: Other useful values such as an AppleScript variable or a random number

User-definable variables in the sidebar will have a blue icon with a *V* on them. They will also appear blue in the workflow. Variables whose contents are determined entirely by the computer will have a purple icon with a gear on it in the sidebar and will appear purple in the workflow.

Just like with the sidebar, you can drag variables from the list into actions or the workflow. Variables are contained by the workflow but are used by actions, rather than accessed directly. As such, dragging a variable from the sidebar into an action will add it to that action, but dragging a variable into the workflow itself will create an action, Get Value of Variable.

> **NOTE** The Get Value of Variable action and the Set Value of Variable action are available from the Actions pane, in the Utilities category.

The bottom of the workflow pane contains a list of all its variables and their values, if applicable. Adding variables to the workflow automatically adds them to this list, but you can also create them in the list directly via the context menu. You can also edit variable names and values in the list.

From the Utilities group, drag in a Set Value of Variable action. From the Variable drop-down list, select "New variable..." and name it Image Folder, as shown in Figure 23-11. This will save the value of the Get Specified Finder Items action in the Image Folder variable, but you can also use the value immediately.

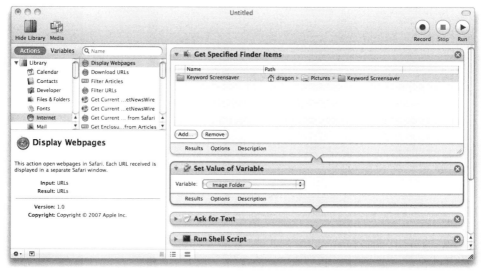

Figure 23-11. Setting the value of a variable in Automator

When you type a keyword and download images, they are going to be saved in the same folder as previous runs. Thus, your screen saver is going to remember all your previous keywords, diminishing the effect. Instead, you should clear the folder between runs so you always start fresh.

Drag a Get Folder Contents action from the Files & Folders group and then a Move Finder Items to Trash action. This will delete the folder's contents. Since Move Finder Items to Trash does not produce output, this also solves the problem of feeding bad information into the Ask for Text action, as shown in Figure 23-12.

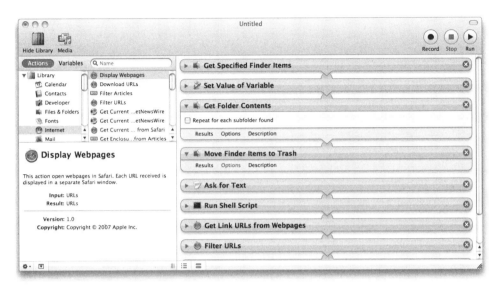

Figure 23-12. Emptying a folder in Automator

Now that you have a place to download your URLs, you can set the Where drop-down of your Download URLs action to Image Folder. Unfortunately, it's not in the drop-down. That's not a problem; simply drag the Image Folder variable from the variables list onto the drop-down, and it will be set for you, as shown in Figure 23-13.

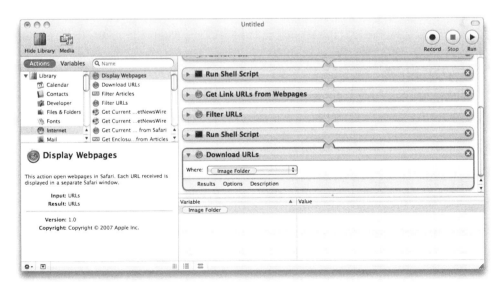

Figure 23-13. Using a variable in Automator

Finally, drag a Start Screen Saver action from the Utilities group, and click Run. Pretty cool, right? You can save your workflow and open it in Automator any time, or you can save it as application, as shown in Figure 23-14. Now you can keep it in the Dock and, whenever you want, launch a new screen saver depending on your mood.

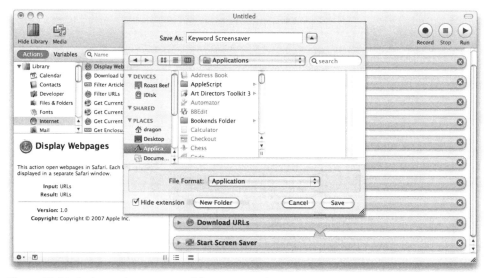

Figure 23-14. Saving an Automator workflow as an application

TIP You can drag the title of your newly minted application directly from the Automator window's title bar into the Dock.

When you're running an Automator workflow in Automator, it's pretty obvious what's happening. You can watch each action execute sequentially, examine the results, and watch the actions add messages to Automator's log.

When Automator is closed and you launch your application from the Dock, it's not immediately obvious that anything is happening. Since it takes a while to download all those images, it would be nice to have a status report. Fortunately, the Automator runtime does this for you automatically. When you run your new application, check out the status (and Cancel button) in the menu bar, as shown in Figure 23-15.

Figure 23-15. Automator workflow status in the menu bar

How Automator Works

Automator actions are actually tiny applications. They can be written as shell scripts, or they can be full-fledged programs written in Objective-C (and by extension, plain C). However, most Automator actions don't do very much, instead deferring to existing applications on the system.

Automator doesn't have any kind of magical ability to control other applications. It simply puts a convenient UI on an existing technology, the Mac OS X Open Scripting Architecture (OSA). You don't need to use Automator to take advantage of the OSA. You can also address it in its native language: AppleScript.

AppleScript

AppleScript is a simple programming language for controlling applications. Although Apple-Script and Automator are different around the edges, it's not a bad metaphor to think of AppleScript as writing Automator workflows in longhand.

To demonstrate that point, here is our Keyword Screensaver application written entirely in AppleScript:

```applescript
-- Remove any existing images
tell application "Finder"
    set _imageFolder to path to pictures folder
    set _imageFolder to folder "Keyword Screensaver" of folder _imageFolder
    delete every file in _imageFolder
end tell
-- Ask for Text
display dialog "What keyword shall I search for?" default answer ""
set _keyword to text returned of result
set _queryURL to "http://images.google.com/images?q=" & _keyword
-- Query Google
tell application "Safari"
    open location _queryURL
    set _timeoutInSeconds to 20
    delay 2
    repeat with _waitInSeconds from 1 to _timeoutInSeconds
        if (do JavaScript "document.readyState" in document 1) is "complete" then
            exit repeat
        else if _waitInSeconds is _timeoutInSeconds then
            number -128
        else
            delay 1
        end if
    end repeat
    set _searchResults to source of document 1
end tell
-- Extract image URLs from page source, then download them
set AppleScript's text item delimiters to "\",\""
set _rawResults to text items in _searchResults
set AppleScript's text item delimiters to ""
repeat with _text in _rawResults
    if _text starts with "http://" and _text does not end with "/images" then
        do shell script "cd ~/Pictures/Keyword\\ Screensaver;
        curl -sO " & quoted form of (_text as string)
    end if
end repeat
-- Activate screen saver
tell application "ScreenSaverEngine"
    activate
end tell
```

To use this script, open the Script Editor application in /Applications/AppleScript. The Script Editor is extremely simple. AppleScript goes in the main window, with runtime logging occurring below. The Run button in the toolbar parses, formats, corrects, compiles, and runs the script.

Even its biggest fans have to admit that AppleScript is a quirky language. Its English-like syntax makes it friendly to look at but tricky to write. Unlike C, which is rigid in its syntax,

AppleScript is quite loose, with several ways to say the same thing. The problem is, this leaves you guessing at the proper way to say something, with many grammatical constructions that seem like they should work but don't.

Hence, AppleScript tends to happen organically, with each phrase leading to a compile and test. If you're used to banging out pages of code between runs, you might want to reconsider that habit, or learning AppleScript is going to be a painful experience.

Analyzing the Code

Although AppleScript and Automator accomplish similar things, they don't exactly translate back and forth, so we have to do some things a little differently. It's probably best to just run through the code sample and point out some sights along the way.

Comments in AppleScript are preceded by --, like so:

```
-- Remove any existing images
```

Since it is mainly concerned with controlling applications, the central syntax element of an AppleScript program is the `tell` block:

```
tell application "Finder"
```

Each application's vocabulary is contained in a special *dictionary* file. When working with an application in AppleScript, the first thing you should do is open its dictionary by selecting Open Dictionary... from the File menu or by typing Shift+Cmd+O.

Variables can be named on the fly. Their values are set with the `set...to` construct:

```
set _imageFolder to path to pictures folder
```

There is no real way of telling what's a variable and what's a keyword, so we like to precede our variables with an underscore. That's just a personal preference, though.

The `path to` construct locates known folders. In this instance, we're trying to get a path to the user's `Pictures` folder, which in UNIX terms we would call `~/Pictures`.

Literal terms are enclosed in quotation marks, as are strings:

```
set _imageFolder to folder "Keyword Screensaver" of folder _imageFolder
```

Most objects on the system are considered containers for other objects. A folder that's inside another folder is `of` that folder. The `of` form can be extended to a ludicrous degree. You could refer to a character of a word of a paragraph of a document of an application, and so forth. You can also use the possessive form:

```
set _imageFolder to _imageFolder's folder "Keyword Screensaver"
```

AppleScript is a lot like LISP in that its only real data structure is the list. This underlies constructs like this:

```
delete every file in _imageFolder
```

You can also refer to things like the first file in the folder or file 3 in the folder. AppleScript also has explicit looping constructs, as you'll see later.

AppleScript is not whitespace sensitive, but it does use newlines to end its statements. Multi-line syntax structures, such as `tell` blocks, require `end` statements:

```
end tell
```

As a testament to the flexibility of the AppleScript language, the entire first `tell` block could also have been written as a single line:

```
tell application "Finder" to delete every file in (path to pictures folder)'s ➡
folder "Keyword Screensaver"
```

It's a bit awkward but still understandable. Note the use of parentheses to clear up syntactical ambiguities and the lack of end tell for the single-line version.

As expected, this displays the dialog:

```
display dialog "What keyword shall I search for?" default answer ""
```

The empty default answer clause gives you an empty text area for the user's input. Without it, the dialog would have just been informational. Note that the dialog is part of AppleScript itself, so it doesn't appear in any tell block.

This strange sentence is based on the fact that result is a secret keyword for the return value of the dialog called earlier:

```
set _keyword to text returned of result
```

Concatenation is accomplished with the & operator:

```
set _queryURL to "http://images.google.com/images?q=" & _keyword
```

We're not necessarily sure what type _keyword is, but it doesn't matter. Although AppleScript has variable types, a fact that occasionally rears its ugly head, most of the time type coercion happens automatically.

As before, this block could have been rendered as a single line:

```
set _queryURL to "http://images.google.com/images?q=" & text returned ➡
of (display dialog "What keyword shall I search for?" default answer "")
```

Automator has several convenient Internet methods that AppleScript lacks. Instead of fetching the results in the background and returning a list of links, you have to, somewhat tediously, open Safari and load the results page:

```
tell application "Safari"
    open location _queryURL
```

There's no way to know when the page is done loading, so you have to poll it. Since it might not actually load, you have to set a timeout:

```
set _timeoutInSeconds to 20
```

Since it will take at least a couple of seconds, you wait for 2 right off the bat:

```
delay 2
```

As mentioned, AppleScript has several looping constructs. This one iterates from one number to another:

```
repeat with _waitInSeconds from 1 to _timeoutInSeconds
```

AppleScript also has branching, via the if then...else if then...else construct. Although the then keyword is required, the Script Editor will fill it in for you if you forget it:

```
if (do JavaScript "document.readyState" in document 1) is "complete" then
```

Not unlike Automator, AppleScript can call other languages, though technically it's Safari, not AppleScript, that provides the do JavaScript functionality.

This is equivalent to the break statement in C. It is similar to, but not interchangeable with, end repeat, which ends the loop syntax.

```
exit repeat
```

All the operators have a long list of synonyms. Aside from is, you could say equals or use the mathematical equals sign:

```
else if _waitInSeconds is _timeoutInSeconds then
    error number -128
```

Error -128 means "User canceled." This will basically press the Cancel button for you after 20 seconds. Although AppleScript errors in practice are often obtuse, the language actually has decently robust error handling, including try blocks and targeted error handlers based on both the type of error and the object that caused it. Errors can include numeric codes, text descriptions, partial results, and more.

Since if statements and repeat statements are multiline, they require end statements.

```
    end if
end repeat
```

We are, admittedly, no AppleScript gurus. JavaScript has access to things like links, but there's no way we know of to pass an array of links from JavaScript back to AppleScript without writing some seriously funky JavaScript. Since that's not what we're going for, we're going to parse the links out manually in AppleScript. If it isn't obvious, there are several different ways to do this.

The Google image results page returns a massive string:

```
set _searchResults to source of document 1
```

Strings in AppleScript are basically lists. Aside from typical components such as paragraphs and words, strings have an amorphous text items component, which is defined as the components of a string as separated by the global text item delimiter.

> **NOTE** Although there is technically a list of delimiters, it's a list of one. Thus, we talk about the text item delimiter, but the actual keyword is pluralized. We set the delimiter to a single string, but behind the scenes, AppleScript will coerce our string into a single-item list.

If you examine the raw source of a Google image results page, it's not plain HTML but a bunch of JavaScript and other goings on. The URLs we want are quoted as part of a comma-separated list of parameters, so the easiest way to get at them is to split the string by the token ",".

However, strings in AppleScript are also quoted, so we have to escape the quotes within the string with backslashes, setting the delimiter to "\",\"":

```
set AppleScript's text item delimiters to "\",\""
```

This converts the string _searchResults into the explicit list _rawResults, which we'll loop through to filter out the URLs:

```
set _rawResults to text items in _searchResults
```

Although we declared _searchResults in a different try block, it's still in scope.

Since the text item delimiter is global, it is considered good form to set it back to the default, which is the empty string, "":

```
set AppleScript's text item delimiters to ""
```

This is a different loop construct, which enumerates the list, assigning each of its members to the named variable in turn:

```
repeat with _text in _rawResults
```

This is analogous to the `for...in` loop found in Objective-C and other languages. Since we're looking for a URL, we know it should start with `http://`:

```
if _text starts with "http://" and _text does not end with "/images" then
```

By observation, all the URLs in the source are either images or internal links that end with the directory `images`. Since it's easier to filter out a single word than it is to test for all the different permutations of all the file extensions of all the image formats, we did it this way. Your mileage may vary.

To test for the substrings, you can use the convenient string shortcuts `starts with`, `ends with`, and `contains`. Of course, we said `end with`, not `ends with`, but they mean the same thing. AppleScript has a lot of meaningless words you can add to make it seem more like grammatical English. For example, the word `the` and the pluralized verb form are both ignored by AppleScript.

There are a lot of ways to download a file, but the most reliable is the UNIX program `curl`. It's also a good chance to show off AppleScript's own `do shell script` command:

```
do shell script "cd ~/Pictures/Keyword\\ Screensaver;
curl -sO " & quoted form of (_text as string)
```

Note the double backslash, which will be translated into a single backslash when it's sent to UNIX, which will, in turn, escape the space in the file name `Keyword Screensaver`.

We used a semicolon to string multiple commands together. We explicitly cast the `_text` variable, which is a reference to a list item, to a string using the as keyword. We then converted that string to the `quoted form`, which basically means "make sure this is going to be something UNIX will not choke on" before concatenating it to the invocation for `curl`.

AppleScript will pause while `curl` downloads all the images so we don't have to bother polling it as we did with Safari. If we really wanted to be clever, we could use `curl` to download the results page as well and use `grep` to parse out the URLs. But, if we were going to do all that, we might as well write this tutorial in Perl.

Finally, we activate the screen saver and call it a night:

```
tell application "ScreenSaverEngine"
    activate
end tell
```

Automator vs. AppleScript

Given the choice between Automator and AppleScript for your automation needs, which one should you choose? These two tutorials should give you a pretty good idea of the strengths and weaknesses of each. In general, we'd say Automator is easier to use, but AppleScript is more powerful. Even with the features added in Leopard, such as variables and basic looping, Automator lacks the kind of control that AppleScript provides.

Still, for our dollar we'd pick Automator. You can pass things off to shell scripts, just like in AppleScript. You can also call AppleScript from Automator, giving you the best of both worlds. Mostly, though, if we wanted to program, we'd use Objective-C, which we'll get into in the next few chapters.

The biggest reason to use AppleScript is being comfortable with it. As with Automator, AppleScript can be compiled into applications. Apple's developer tools, Xcode and Interface Builder, have a feature called AppleScript Studio that lets AppleScript fans write graphical applications entirely in AppleScript.

What's amazing about AppleScript is not the language itself but what it does. Even in the high-performance world of professional software development, when you need to control another application, AppleScript is the first place to turn.

Application developers who write scriptable applications are a boon to the platform. Not only do they enable AppleScript gurus to work their magic, but they also contribute to Automator. With Leopard's new Scripting Bridge, it's even more important to be scriptable, because programmers in other languages can now address AppleScript's application hooks directly.

Automation saves people time and eliminates wasted effort, and the foundation of automation is interapplication cooperation. The more developers and users can leverage existing applications, the more our platform becomes extensible, flexible, and, that most important of attributes, usable.

More Information

If you think there's something to the phrase "Cult of Mac," you should see the zealots in the Mac automation community. I don't think we've ever written an AppleScript or a halfway decent Automator action without consulting at least one of the following sources:

Automator home page (http://automator.us/): Sal Soghoian is Apple's product manager for automation and is generally recognized as a, if not the, foremost expert on AppleScript and Automator. We can also personally attest that he is a character. All that aside, Sal's Automator page has everything you need to know, from the whys and wherefores of Automator to a massive collection of free Automator actions and links to other great Automator sites on the Web.

Automator Programming Guide (http://developer.apple.com/documentation/ AppleApplications/Conceptual/AutomatorConcepts/): This is Apple's official documentation on developing Automator actions. There's less here for the casual user, but the barrier to becoming a power user who can bust out custom actions is really not all that high. If you have any scripting or programming experience, you're practically there already.

AppleScript: The Comprehensive Guide to Scripting and Automation on Mac OS X, Second Edition by Hanaan Rosenthal (Apress, 2006): This is the ultimate tome on AppleScript and is, as of this writing, more up-to-date than even Apple's own documentation. Hanaan's critically acclaimed work will walk you step by step from automation neophyte to AppleScript master. It also makes a great footstool, on account of being huge.

AppleScript Essential Subroutines (http://www.apple.com/applescript/guidebook/sbrt/): This hidden page of useful AppleScript functions is the first place we turn when we get stuck trying to figure out how to do something. There's not a lot here, but what is here is solid gold.

AppleScript Language Guide (http://developer.apple.com/documentation/AppleScript/ Conceptual/AppleScriptLangGuide/): This is Apple's official documentation on AppleScript and quite possibly the oldest document on the entire Internet. Apple keeps saying it is going to update this as part of Leopard's AppleScript improvements, but it hasn't happened yet. We can understand the reluctance. With contributions by such notable minds as Mark Twain, Alexander Hamilton, and Sir Isaac Newton, this document is practically a national treasure.

AppleScript Users Official Mailing List (http://lists.apple.com/mailman/listinfo/applescript-users): Another official channel for all things AppleScript, the official mailing list is always a good place to get and give help.

Doug's AppleScripts for iTunes (http://dougscripts.com/): It sounds really specific, but iTunes is probably the most scriptable, and the most scripted, application in the world. As such, Doug's page may well be the largest repository of practical AppleScript on the Web. Having a simple relationship with iTunes, we don't think we've ever actually used one of these scripts for its intended purpose, but we've studied dozens of them. The people who write Doug's scripts are truly some of the cleverest, to say nothing of dedicated, AppleScript users around.

Summary

If you find yourself doing the same task over and over again, it's time to stop and think about automation. Using Automator or AppleScript might seem like a lot of trouble the first time, but once you learn how to use these powerful tools, your productivity will skyrocket, and you will truly earn the laurels of a power user.

If you've already mastered automation, need more than the OS can provide, or want to contribute to the platform by writing applications, plug-ins, or Automator actions, read on. In the next few chapters, we'll talk about the tools used by professional Macintosh application developers.

CHAPTER 24

Mac OS X Development: The Application Frameworks

What is it about the Mac that makes it so compelling? Almost anyone you ask will surely tell you the same thing: it's the user experience. But what does that mean? What lies at the heart of the Mac OS X user experience?

At the end of the day, it comes down to three things: ease of use, integration, and beauty. It should come as no surprise, therefore, that the major frameworks provided to developers center around these three concepts.

> **NOTE** Many of the things in this chapter have already been discussed from a user standpoint in previous chapters. This chapter, however, will view things from a developer's perspective.

Ease of Use

If you want to build an easy-to-use application, you need to start with an easy-to-use application framework. Smaller code is faster to write and easier to maintain, leading to fewer bugs, more features, and more time to spend optimizing performance and adding all those tiny details that Mac developers seem to always think of.

> **NOTE** A framework is the Mac OS X equivalent to a shared library, but it has a couple of advantages above and beyond simple code reuse:
> - It can contain non-code resources like images, documentation, and nibs.
> - It can have multiple versions side by side for backward compatibility.
> - It can be shared between running applications, saving memory.
> - It can contain references to other frameworks, creating umbrella frameworks.

If you want to build an easy-to-use application, therefore, the application framework of choice is Cocoa. Cocoa's motto, mission statement, and design philosophy is "Easy things easy, hard things possible." What makes Cocoa unique, however, is not just that it achieves this simple but powerful idea, but how.

Cocoa applications are better by design. Their graphical user interfaces are designed with a graphical user interface, Interface Builder, as shown in Figure 24-1. Their classes are built with

Objective-C, a revolutionary programming language that combines the design advantages of an object-oriented language with the flexibility of a low-level language, the dynamism of a scripting language, and a revolution in readability that almost makes comments obsolete.

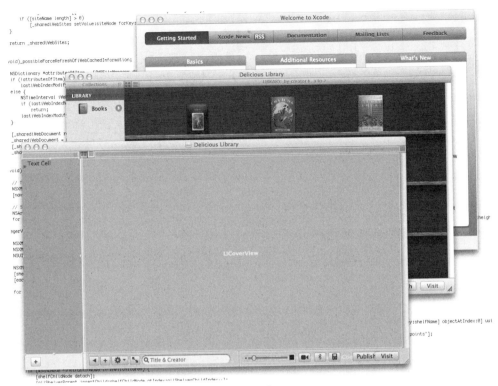

Figure 24-1. Great applications are built with great tools.

We'll talk about Interface Builder and Objective-C in the next couple of chapters. For now, let's focus on some of the frameworks that make creating professional applications in Cocoa so easy.

> **NOTE** Cocoa is only one of several application frameworks on Mac OS X, but you don't have to worry about whether something is technically Cocoa, a shared framework with a Cocoa interface, or part of another application framework altogether. You can use them all from your Cocoa application, thanks largely to the flexibility of Objective-C.

Application Kit

Just as its name implies, the Application Kit (or AppKit, as it is known to its friends) is a collection of prebuilt components common to many applications. Developers can cobble together a completely functional, if uninteresting, application by snapping together components, like those shown in Figure 24-2. Only Swedish furniture rivals the ease of assembly offered by AppKit.

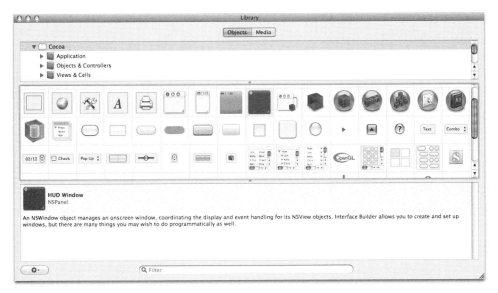

Figure 24-2. Cocoa components in Interface Builder

AppKit's components are not just tangible UI widgets like menus, windows, and buttons. Some of the other things AppKit provides are the following:

- Data visualization objects like tables, browsers, and matrices.
- Abstract objects like controllers, timers, and formatters.
- Document creation, management, and persistence.
- Text handling, including editing, spell checking, and typesetting.
- Graphics handling for images, multimedia, and animation.
- Functionality such as event handling, undo management, and threading.
- System interaction such as printing, pasteboard (clipboard) operations, and scripting.

Most of AppKit's features can be had with little or no code. Customization can be accomplished with simple configuration, either as needed by the developer, or at runtime in accordance with user preferences.

Despite all this simplicity, AppKit is also quite flexible. Because AppKit is object-oriented, anything it offers can be subclassed, letting developers customize as much, or as little, as they need.

Foundation

High-level application toolkits are all well and good, but even with all the basics and some of the not-so-basics done for you, you're still going to have to sit down and write some code. When that inevitability occurs, you need AppKit's fraternal twin, Foundation.

The Foundation classes are so legion as to be beyond the scope of this book. (Literally! Apple's Foundation documentation is over 2,200 pages long.) However, as you might expect, from 60,000 feet it looks a lot like a bulleted list:

- Basic data types such as strings, numbers, and raw data
- Specialized data types like dates, URLs, and time zones
- Basic collections like arrays, sets, and dictionaries

- Specialized collections like character sets, index sets, and pointer arrays
- Data loading—local and networked, synchronous and asynchronous
- Data manipulation, conversion, transformation, and formatting
- XML parsing, editing, and transformation
- System functions like run loops, threads, and timers
- Interprocess communications via pipes, ports, and notifications
- Language services like exceptions, garbage collection, and messaging

It's not called Foundation for nothing. AppKit and the rest of Cocoa are built on top of Foundation. This follows the general trend in Mac OS X development: Apple creates tools, and then uses those tools to make easy-to-use frameworks. Then, it gives developers the tools as well, so they can modify or add as they see fit.

Foundation, while extensive, might not seem so different from any other basic library. In practice, however, Foundation is designed with the same ease of use and snap-together design as AppKit. The classes try to maintain similar interfaces, so, for example, if you decide to refactor an array into a set, there's very little effort involved.

Since the interfaces are predictable, it's easy to keep Foundation in your head, despite its breadth. And since it's written in Objective-C, it's extremely easy to figure out how to use a method without having to constantly go back to the documentation.

As with AppKit, Objective-C also makes Foundation classes customizable via subclassing and categorization (one of the many tricks outlined in the section on Objective-C), so no matter what you need to do, you're rarely, if ever, stuck having to roll your own.

Core Data

A lot of people had a lot of reasons why Apple could never transition their architecture from PowerPC to Intel. Yet, when they did just that, most of those reasons ended up being non-issues. For example, the fact that the two architectures read bytes of binary code in opposite directions (the so-called endianness issue) ended up not affecting most developers at all.

The reason is abstraction. By using high-level frameworks like AppKit and Foundation, developers are protected from implementation details like byte order. The Core Data framework takes that idea a step further by abstracting applications from even their own data.

Traditionally, the system is ignorant of an application's objects and what they're doing. Whether you've got a word processing document, a photo album, or a dungeon-roaming adventurer in a mystical land beyond time and space, to the system they're all just ones and zeros. You can ask the system to write those ones and zeros to disk, and you can ask it to read them back, but when it comes to interpreting what they mean and how the user's actions affect them, you're on your own.

Core Data establishes a generalized object model. As long as your objects conform to that model, the system can tell enough about them to handle many aspects of their lives with little or no intervention on your part. For example, undo and redo, traditionally one of the harder problems to deal with, is free in Core Data.

One of the first things you learn in system design is how to plan your objects, their structures, and their relationships in an entity relationship diagram (ERD). Xcode, Apple's integrated development environment, even provides a graphical ERD tool, as shown in Figure 24-3. With Core Data, drawing an ERD doesn't just plan your objects, it also implements them. You can even drag entities out of the ERD into Interface Builder, and Core Data will generate your entire user interface!

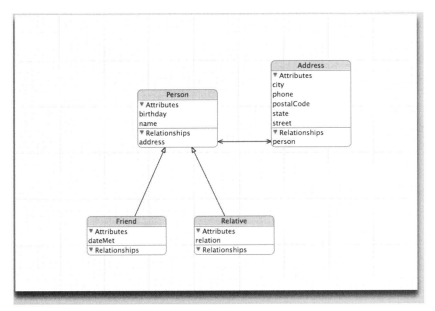

Figure 24-3. Core Data modeling in Xcode

Of course, Core Data is best known for persistence. When the user clicks the Save button, you've got to decide if that data is going to be written out in some binary format, converted to human-readable XML, or stored in a relational database. Each has its advantages and disadvantages, but choose wisely, for once you pick a persistence model, you're stuck with it.

Well, that's not entirely true. Nothing is going to stop you from throwing out your XML code and rewriting the whole thing to use relational database. Nothing, that is, except time, money, and a tremendous amount of wasted effort.

With Core Data, changing your persistence model is as simple as changing your mind. You haven't written any code to read and write data, nor to communicate with any database. Core Data handles all that dirty business for you, so if you want to develop with easily debugged XML, and then switch to a database for performance, you can.

And if you do decide to use a database, you don't have to worry about installing a database management system onto your users' machines, because all that stuff is already built into Mac OS X. Oh yeah, and you don't have to write, think in, or even be aware of the existence of SQL.

Image Kit

Sometimes an application's functionality becomes so beloved that it finds itself being copied, in whole or in part, in all kinds of other places. Consider photo management, once synonymous with iPhoto. Now you can take pictures in iChat, apply filters in Photo Booth, and view slideshows in Mail.

When this happens, Apple may factor out that functionality into a "kit" framework. Think of it as an application without an interface that you can embed into your own application. With Leopard's new Image Kit, you can embed all the photo management functionality of iPhoto in your own application, as shown in Figure 24-4.

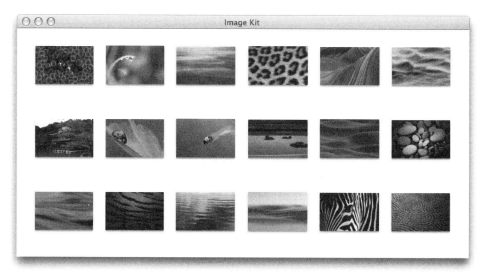

Figure 24-4. Image Kit's image browser in Interface Builder

Here are some of the classes provided by Image Kit:

- Browser for viewing a large number of images in a grid view, similar to iPhoto
- Slideshow for viewing and working with multiple images sequentially
- View optimized for images, with controls for zooming, rotating, and cropping
- Edit panel for changing image properties and applying some basic effects
- Filter application and UI elements for browsing and using filters
- Save panel addition that presents specialized options based on the format of the image data
- Picture taker, like the one found in iChat and Photo Booth

Aside from providing some great functionality, Image Kit is built on the latest Mac OS X graphics libraries. That means, aside from having the animated translucent look of a next-generation application, its interfaces are able to optimize performance for modern graphics cards, using things like hardware acceleration, when available.

Similarly, it uses the same nondestructive Core Image filters found throughout the system, so as Apple or other developers add new filters, your applications pick them up as well, with no extra effort on your part.

That also applies to image formats. Already, Image Kit can also handle icons, movies, PDF documents, and even Quartz Composer compositions.

NOTE For more information on iPhoto and Image Capture, check out Chapter 16.

Accelerate

Imagine yourself in the future, a happy and productive Cocoa programmer. You've already finished this book, including the section on Apple's optimization tools, so you knew better than to think about performance while you were blasting out your killer new application.

Now, ahead of schedule and under budget, you've carefully profiled away all the major performance bottlenecks, but one tight loop is giving your trouble. You reach for your book on assembly language . . .

Not so fast!

- What if Apple changes processors again?
- What if Intel introduces a new vector library?
- What if some of your users are still on PowerPC?
- What if someone invents a better algorithm?
- What if, somehow, people are still using this in the year 2000?

OK, that last one might not be a problem anymore, but it does illustrate the point: you don't know what's going to happen to your application, to computer science, or to hardware in the future. That's why hand-optimized code is a disaster waiting to happen.

I think you can see where I'm going with this. The Accelerate framework, as contradictory as it seems, is a high-level framework for low-level optimizations. That's like hiring an army of mole people who dream in assembly and think in algorithms, and will continue to do so long after your application has shipped.

That means you can answer all the "what ifs" with "who cares." You make one simple optimization and you're done. No matter where your application ends up in time or space, it will have the best performance available for that particular computer. Even as silicon science progresses, your application will get faster without your even being aware of it.

Here are some of the optimizations available in Accelerate:

- Image processing, including geometric and morphological transformations, histogram operations, and alpha compositing
- Digital signal processing on real and complex data types, including fast Fourier transforms, and vector-to-vector and vector-to-scalar operations
- A vectorized analog to the standard math library
- Linear algebra, including simultaneous sets of linear equations, eigenvalue and singular solution problems, and least-squares solutions for linear systems
- Routines that operate on matrices as if they were single variables

QuickTime Kit

At the heart of any modern operating system lies the ability to deal with *multimedia*. In case you're unfamiliar with the term, multimedia is a mid-'90s buzzword meaning "the mixture of audio, video, and text; be it local, remote, or streaming." Mac OS X has long been a frontrunner in multimedia. This is largely thanks to a very mature framework known as QuickTime, shown in Figure 24-5.

Figure 24-5. QuickTime as used by iTunes, QuickTime Player, and QTKit Movie View

Unfortunately, like much that is old, QuickTime had long been a holdout against the paradigm shift offered by Cocoa. This isn't a technical problem, as Cocoa programmers are able to access other frameworks, just as non-Cocoa programmers are able to access Cocoa.

However, having to leave the comfort of Cocoa for the dark recesses of old-fashioned procedural API is so much trouble, even for otherwise brilliant resources like QuickTime. Tiger finally corrected this with a brand new Cocoa interface to QuickTime, known by the euphonious nickname QTKit.

Here are some of the features of QTKit:

- Access to raw media data from local, remote, and streaming sources
- Object-oriented representations of media, tracks, and time ranges
- View subclass for displaying and controlling media
- Interface Builder object, which makes adding a full-featured media player to your applications a zero-code drag-and-drop operation

In addition, Leopard introduces QTCapture, which adds similar functionality to recording media. This includes the ability to control recording devices, such as the iSight camera now built into most Macs. For anyone interested in tapping the power of the iSight, I can attest firsthand: QTCapture will save you thousands of lines of code.

NOTE For more information on QuickTime, check out Chapter 14.

Integration

Much of what makes the Mac such a compelling experience can be summed up in one word: iLife. This suite of full-featured applications, included free with every new Mac (and the subject of Chapter 16) is not simply the sum of its parts. Rather, it's the integration between those parts.

Make some music in GarageBand. Use it as a soundtrack in iMovie. Burn your movie to disc with iDVD. Then, tell the world with iWeb. This kind of integration, which is a concept from the very core of UNIX, extends throughout the operating system.

Your own applications can and should take advantage of this. Not only does this provide an excellent "Mac-like" experience to your customers, it saves you the time and trouble of implementing features that are already served quite well by existing applications.

In order to help you leverage these applications, Apple provides a great number frameworks, including several new to Leopard. Here is a quick tour of some of the most useful.

Address Book

As strange as it might seem to those of us who spend all our time with machines, many of our users maintain a network of an entirely different sort: friends, family, coworkers, and businesses. To manage this pantheon of people, Apple provides an application called Address Book.

Rather than maintain separate lists for the people you get and receive mail from, call or text via your iPhone, and communicate with via iChat, everything is simply kept in Address Book. Your applications can participate via the framework known, appropriate enough, as Address Book.

In addition to being able to access the contact information stored in Address Book, the framework provides the ability to search, edit, and add contacts. For any social aspects of your application requiring human interaction, the work is already done for you. Leopard provides a prebuilt People Picker, as shown in Figure 24-6.

People Picker View

13 cards

Group	Name
All	Aaron Tuller
Accounts	Jon Szyperski
Business	Kaleiohu Lee
Family	Keith Dussell
Fight Club	Kevin Steele
Friends	Lucas Topher Newman
Monsters	**Mike Lee**
	Pat Castaldo
	Patrick Lee
	Robert T. Bakie
	Russell Popham
	Wayne Takabayashi
	William Jon Shipley

Figure 24-6. Address Book's People Picker view in Interface Builder

Finally, Address Book stores a special record known as a *Me card*, which contains a user's own contact information. By accessing the Me card, you can spare your user the trouble of providing their address, phone number, e-mail address, or home page, and simply present those fields for verification and, if necessary, correction.

> **NOTE** For more information on Address Book, check out Chapter 11.

Automator

Automator gives users the power to create automated workflows using *actions*, services provided by applications on the system. Automator can be thought of as AppleScript with an easy, drag-and-drop interface. Your applications can provide actions as well, with a little help from Xcode's Automator action template. Leopard takes that one further, and enables you to use Automator actions and workflows from within your application.

Moreover, the Automator framework even lets you embed Automator's drag-and-drop interface in your own application, using custom view and controller subclasses, as shown in Figure 24-7. From this interface, users can create standard Automator workflows. Or, if you prefer, you can create your own custom universe of components that just happen to borrow the convenient and familiar workflow concept.

Automator View

Drag actions or files here to build your workflow.

Figure 24-7. Automator view in Interface Builder

> **NOTE** For more information on Automator and automation, see Chapter 23.

DotMac Kit

To those of us who've been online since the first IP addresses crawled out of the sea, the services of Apple's .Mac subscription service are nothing new. E-mail, a home page, and a little space on a server somewhere are old hat. Still, .Mac manages to remain compelling, not with *what* it does, but *how*.

Normally, publishing things to the Web involves several steps and specialized file transfer programs. Using the WebDAV standard, the DotMac Kit embeds web services directly into applications. A user's .Mac account becomes less like a server and more like an online extension of their home folder.

Integrating with .Mac is a great way to add value for your users, and is probably the number-one feature that sets applications designed "for the Mac" apart from applications that are "Mac compatible." Fortunately, the DotMac Kit, also known as the .Mac SDK, makes adding this feature almost as easy as using .Mac itself.

The DotMac Kit breaks all operations into transactions. This means checking credentials, making sure a user's account is current, creating a directory, and moving files to and from the server are all encapsulated as transactions.

Transactions allow you to switch between synchronous and asynchronous modes as needed. There are a few places where switching modes is handy, but it's absolutely indispensable for debugging. There's also a compatibility interface for the truly lazy, which mimics the methods used by Cocoa's NSFileManager class. It doesn't have the same flexibility as transactions, but for simple actions or quick prototyping, it's quite convenient.

Calendar Store

As Address Book does for people, iCal does for events. Aside from the standard questions (What's going on? Where? When? Who's going to be there?), iCal events can include things like URLs, notes, and *alarms*: time-sensitive triggers that can do anything from popping up a reminder, running a script, and sending an e-mail. Using a colorful, easy-to-understand interface, iCal lets users manage all their calendar-related information in one place, as shown in Figure 24-8.

Again, just like with Address Book, your application can interact with iCal's data using the Calendar Store framework. New in Leopard, Calendar Store frees your application (not to mention your users) from the tedium of dealing with the same information in multiple places.

Calendar Store does more than just accessing, editing, and creating events. It also does the following:

- Manages Leopard's system-wide To Do list
- Notifies interested applications of any changes to the calendars
- Provides fast, flexible data-mining services using *predicates*: high-level, object-oriented queries used throughout Mac OS X

In fact, it's better to think of Calendar Store as what it really is: a central database. iCal just happens to be a conveniently prebundled client. Indeed, Calendar Store is based on CalDAV, an open networking standard that lets your users connect with server-side collaboration software, regardless of platform.

It also means your applications calendaring features need no longer bind users to iCal. Any application can use Calendar Store. In fact, Leopard provides several examples of this kind of integration. The next time you get a piece of e-mail asking if you're coming to the party on Wednesday, try clicking the text and watch iCal add that event, as if your host had sent you an iCal invitation.

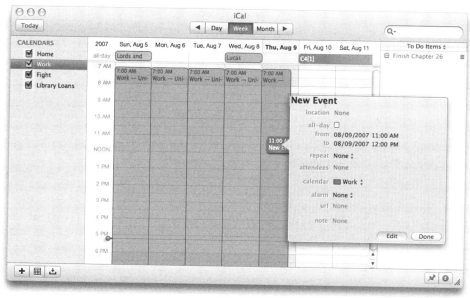

Figure 24-8. iCal in Leopard sports a new front end to complement its new back end.

Store, by the way, as in storage, refers to the high-performance database that enables the Calendar Store to work its magic. If you need a wiggly puppy page-a-day for your cubicle, you're still going to have to hit the mall.

> **NOTE** To learn more about iCal, see Chapter 11.

Instant Message

Mac users have long relied on iChat to keep them in constant communication with friends and business partners around the world. This innovative instant messaging client connects users by text, audio, or full-motion video. Your applications can take advantage of iChat using the Instant Message framework.

In basic usage, Instant Message allows you to incorporate iChat data, such as the contents of a user's buddy list and the online status of those buddies. This is how, for example, Mail lets you know that a person you are writing to is currently online, so you can simply chat with them instead.

Leopard introduces iChat Theater, which lets users turn their chats into multimedia presentations. Any application, including your own, can use the Instant Message framework to provide audio and video content to iChat Theater, as shown in Figure 24-9.

Figure 24-9. Sharing a photo with Leopard's new iChat Theater

Even if your application does not produce video in the traditional sense, the frame-by-frame access afforded by the Core Video framework, discussed later, makes it easy for you to provide static images to the video feed. iChat Theater and the Instant Message framework make it easy to turn your single-user experience into a collaborative multiuser masterpiece.

PDF Kit

Mac users have long been able to take advantage of Adobe's Portable Document Format. While other systems have required special tools for dealing with this universal format, Mac OS X has PDF support built in. Not only can users view PDFs with the bundled Preview application, they can create PDFs from any application via the Print panel.

The PDF Kit framework gives developers the ability to incorporate Preview's high-performance PDF rendering engine in their own applications. If you've ever used Preview, you know this goes far beyond simply displaying PDFs.

Interface Builder includes a PDF view, as shown in Figure 24-10. It has specialized behaviors, like crop, zoom, and rotate. PDF Kit also provides for document navigation, letting users jump to the next or previous page, the first or last page, or to an arbitrary page.

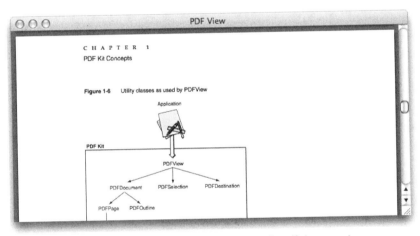

Figure 24-10. PDF Kit's view in Interface Builder is literally self-documenting.

Here are some other features PDF Kit handles:

- Annotations, which are additions to the page that are not part of the page itself, like sticky notes and editable text fields
- Encryption, including ownership, and permissions, such as limiting the ability to copy or print
- Outlining, which is an interactive table of contents showing the structure of a PDF document
- Pagination, which gives PDFs a familiar, book-like appearance
- Searching a PDF's content, as with Spotlight
- Selection, including the ability to highlight and copy text to the pasteboard

NOTE For more about Preview and Mac OS X's PDF capabilities, see Chapter 14.

Publication Subscription

Syndication is old technology that's recently taken the Web by storm. It works by letting people subscribe to *web feeds*—lightweight versions of their favorite web sites. These feeds can then be aggregated using specialized applications, like NewsGator's NetNewsWire, shown in Figure 24-11. Apple and others have expanded on syndication and found novel uses for its technology. In addition to Safari's subscription feature, iTunes's podcasts and iPhoto's album sharing are implemented using syndication.

Figure 24-11. NetNewsWire aggregates web content using syndication.

The bad news about syndication is that it encompasses several competing standards, such as RSS and ATOM. There are also different versions within each standard, such as RSS 0.9, RSS 1.0, and RSS 2.0. The good news is you don't need to care, thanks to Leopard's new Publication Subscription framework, known simply as PubSub.

PubSub handles the details of monitoring, downloading, and updating feeds, and then notifying interested applications when something changes. Because it's a central database for all syndication information, you can also ask PubSub for other people's feeds. For example, if you're interested in what feeds your user has bookmarked in Safari, PubSub can tell you.

Feeds are typically implemented in XML, and Cocoa's XML framework is quite good. Still, PubSub lets you treat the XML as an implementation detail, giving you a single, object-oriented interface to syndicated data regardless of the vagaries of format. Even if you don't subscribe to a feed, you can still use PubSub to parse it.

Spotlight

If you've been using a Mac (or reading this book), you know about Spotlight: Apple's integrated search utility that reunites users with their data across the vast cluttered landscape of their hard drives. To Mac developers, Spotlight presents a responsibility, as well as opportunity.

Spotlight has built-in support for most common data types, such as JPEG and PDF. If your application produces standard data, you don't need to do anything to take advantage of Spotlight. If, however, you're using a custom data type, you're going to need to provide a custom importer.

Spotlight importers are plug-ins that Spotlight uses to translate custom data types to the metadata it needs to work its magic. By providing an importer, you not only ensure users can find their stuff, but you also get to participate in Spotlight-based features like the Finder's smart folders, shown in Figure 24-12.

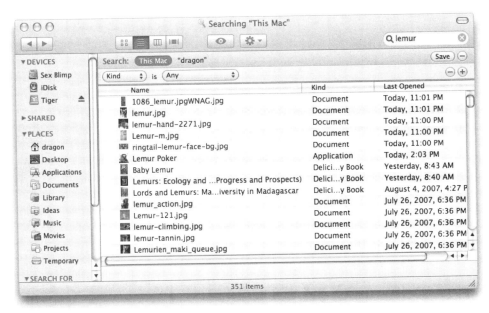

Figure 24-12. Spotlight's smart folders in the Finder

Fortunately, it behooves Apple to make providing an importer as painless as possible, so Xcode includes the *Spotlight Plug-in* template to get you started. There's also a Core Data template that includes a Spotlight importer.

From within your application, you can offer users a standard Spotlight interface. You can also query Spotlight's metadata database programmatically. Spotlight offers an Objective-C interface for building and executing object-oriented queries based on the NSPredicate class used throughout Cocoa. You can also set things like sort order, grouping, and whether you want to receive live updates if anything changes behind your back.

> **NOTE** For more information about Spotlight, see Chapter 3.

Quick Look

Quick Look provides rich previews of files, using a plug-in system similar to Spotlight. Known file types have plug-ins already installed, but custom types must provide a simple thumbnail and an extended preview. Users can then examine the file visually, even if the application used to create it no longer exists on the system.

Quick Look uses a two-level preview system. Documents can provide a thumbnail, which is a simple visual representation of the data. Often, this is just a static image stored in the document bundle. Once the thumbnail is loaded, Quick Look may present a preview. Unlike the static thumbnail, the preview can be nearly anything. Your preview might be your entire document as a PDF, or perhaps a QuickTime movie of your application in action. You can even generate dynamic content on the fly.

Quick Look is a good chance for your documents to shine, but if you do not provide a preview, users will get disappointing generic icons, like the white document icons to the right of center in Figure 24-13. Not only is Quick Look used in the Finder's column and Cover Flow views, it can also be activated by users directly.

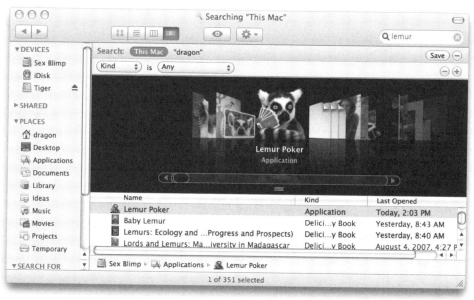

Figure 24-13. Spotlight's smart folders in the Finder, enhanced by Quick Look and Cover Flow

Scripting Bridge

The best way to integrate with other applications is through an official API, but when that nicety is not afforded to you, you can always use AppleScript. As discussed in the last chapter, AppleScript is the high-level language users can use to make applications do their bidding.

Unfortunately, AppleScript is not particularly fast. Using it in your application, while certainly possible, requires you to shift your brain mid-project into another language. When performance is a factor, developers have traditionally turned to Apple Events, the low-level system that lets AppleScript work its magic.

Somewhere on Earth I'm sure someone understands Apple Events, but by now you should know Cocoa programmers hate resorting to low-level programming. Apple, in its inimitable way, has simultaneously solved all these problems at once with Leopard's new Scripting Bridge.

Using Scripting Bridge is so easy it almost defies explanation:

1. Run the command-line tools sdef and sdp to generate Objective-C headers from another application's AppleScript dictionary.

2. Include the generated headers in your project.

3. There is no step 3.

Using the headers is like using any other header. You instantiate objects and manipulate their properties and methods using the standard Cocoa data types and structures. You can do this even if the program in question was not written in Cocoa and doesn't contain a single line of Objective-C.

Scripting Bridge is also a huge performance win. It's twice as fast as compiled AppleScript and about two orders of magnitude faster than uncompiled AppleScript.

> **NOTE** Scripting Bridge's underlying technology is also what enables Cocoa to be accessed from Ruby and Python.

Web Kit

Web Kit is the full-featured, open source, cross-platform, high-performance web page–rendering engine behind Safari. It's also used in Dashboard and Apple's help viewer. You can also find Web Kit in Xcode, and in Mail, as shown in Figure 24-14. In other words, Web Kit is everywhere. In fact, Web Kit is so ubiquitous that, as a developer, you'll probably manage to use Web Kit without even knowing it.

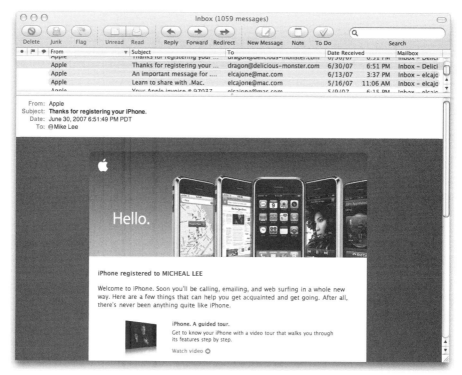

Figure 24-14. Mail uses Web Kit to display rich multimedia messages.

To understand why Web Kit is so ubiquitous, it helps to understand the technical problem of creating a formatted document. Text is easy; it's built into the very lowest levels of any operating system. Text alone, though, is far too boring for most uses.

A good document format will add typesetting information, such as font family, bold, and italics, different text sizes and colors, and effects like underlining. You also want structures like bulleted and numbered lists, outlines, and tables. Finally, you want to be able to embed things like images.

This is exactly what a web page is. Content and structure are defined by HTML (HyperText Markup Language), and display information is expressed by CSS (Cascading Style Sheets).

Documents encoded as web pages offer several advantages, and a lot of power, compared to other formats, such as Microsoft Word:

- They include built-in navigation via links (the *HT* in HTML).
- They are stored in plain text, so they be can created, viewed, and altered using standard tools in any programming language or environment.
- They use open standards that are not owned by, or subject to the whims of, a single company.
- HTML and CSS are free to use and implement without licensing or royalties.
- HTML and CSS are well understood by people all over the world.
- HTML can be made compatible with XML, which makes it extensible, and thus adaptable to myriad purposes.
- Using DOM and JavaScript, web pages can be made into dynamic, interactive, event-driven applications, as with Dashboard's widgets or Google Maps.
- Structure can be separated from style, so display characteristics can easily be changed without creator intervention.

This last point bears exploration. Your best writer can create the document while your best designer creates the style sheet. Every document in your company could exhibit the same style, which could be changed instantly and completely by editing a single style sheet. Your manual could have gorgeous visuals while remaining completely accessible to the blind.

Gaining all this power, thanks to Web Kit, is as simple as including a view in Interface Builder, as shown in Figure 24-15. Web Kit's extensive API offers low-level access to the various aspects of web pages and rendering behavior. Web Kit also provides a bridge between JavaScript and Objective-C, integrating web and desktop technology like never before.

Figure 24-15. Web Kit views in Safari and Interface Builder

> **NOTE** For more on Safari, see Chapter 10. For more on Dashboard, see Chapter 3.

Beauty

As a platform, the Mac has always been known as the place to be for graphics. Whether or not that's true, Mac OS X and its Aqua interface are certainly gorgeous. Applications on the Mac inherit the system's aesthetic brilliance for free, whether they are written in modern Cocoa, old-fashioned Carbon, or even a guest platform like Java.

That's because the application frameworks let developers build applications without worrying about any but the highest-level details of the graphics system. Little do they know that far below, OpenGL sits waiting for anyone who would dare traverse its sharp learning curve in the quest for pureness of power, flexibility, and performance.

Luckily, between these two extremes lies Quartz, the graphics compositing engine. Quartz can be accessed via a series of graphics frameworks that provide expressiveness with images, animation, video, and drawing, while still maintaining a good dose of abstraction from the nitty-gritty details of OpenGL routines and primitives.

When the free graphics from the application frameworks leave you feeling like you've gotten what you've paid for, it's time to peek beneath the shiny skin of your Apple and examine the power that lies at its core.

Core Animation

If a computer interface is more like the real world, it's more familiar, and therefore more usable. But computers are, in many ways, inherently alien to our everyday experiences. Contrast the instant on-off state change of a transistor to the slow opening and closing of a door.

The obvious solution is to smooth the transitions between state changes using animation. While simple in theory, the difficulty in implementing animation has long forced developers to compromise between the ideals of user interface and the realities of a deadline.

Leopard's new Core Animation framework frees developers from this drudgery and introduces a lightweight layer-based design metaphor. By enabling and encouraging experimentation, Core Animation may well make Leopard the biggest revolution in human interface design since 1984.

Layers encapsulate drawing properties like color, border, opacity, and a completely customizable shadow. They also contain geometric properties like size and position, and the full range of affine transformations. Layers can contain images, stacks of Core Image filters (which we'll get to in a moment), and an alpha mask. They can also be stacked and nested.

What really sets a layer apart is what happens when you change a property. Rather than just reflecting the new state, the layer animates the transition. Multiple properties can be changed at the same time. For example, a layer could simultaneously shrink, slide, rotate, and fade.

These animations are optimized to take advantage of hardware acceleration and other video card niceties, as well as being automatically threaded. Not only will the animation not block your main thread, but you can change a property while it is in the process of changing, and it will immediately be rerouted.

The animation itself is also encapsulated as an object, so aside from being adjustable in the usual ways, such as duration, animations can be subclassed to provide for things like keyframes or following a Bézier path.

As if all that weren't enough, you can take advantage of Core Animation without even writing code. Views can be layer-backed, and many layer properties are accessible from within Interface Builder, as shown in Figure 24-16.

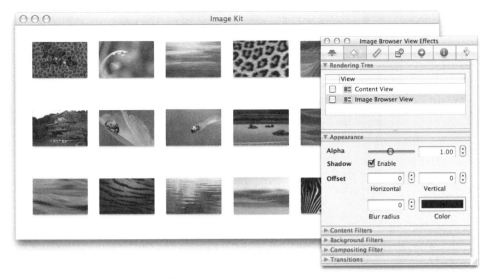

Figure 24-16. Core Animation's effects panel in Interface Builder

Core Image

If you've ever used Adobe Photoshop, you know how much fun image filters can be. Core Image takes the idea of image filters and runs with it, for results that are both amazing and amazingly useful.

Filters can range from the very simple, like a blur, to the very complex, like the new hologram effect, shown in Figure 24-17. Filters can also include operations not typically associated with filtering, such as cropping, resizing, or warping. Best of all, if there's no existing filter to meet your needs, you can write your own.

Core Image filters are nondestructive. Your images are not actually changed on disk. Rather, they are altered before being displayed on the graphics card, so you can undo or alter filters at any time, including runtime.

Core Image filters can be stacked, and the stacks are intelligently optimized to give you the same results with the least processing power possible. For example, if you have a Crop filter later in the stack, Core Image will apply it first, so you don't waste time processing pixels you're never going to see.

Core Image is available system-wide, which means you can apply its filters to anything, including video. Whether you're tidying up your pictures in iPhoto, applying a comic book effect in Photo Booth, pretending to be a hologram in iChat Theater, or fighting your way through glowing green gas in a video game, Core Image has you covered.

> **NOTE** Unfortunately the hologram effect did not make it into the final version of Leopard, but it lives on, thanks to the Internet. Google "Leopard Hologram" for instructions on how to restore it.

Core Graphics

Also known as Quartz 2D, Core Graphics provides basic drawing services throughout the system. This includes primitive drawing, with paths, shapes, colors, and the like; advanced drawing like shadows, gradients, and patterns; and transforms, bitmaps, transparency, masking, and compositing.

Because the underlying Quartz compositing engine is based on PDF, Core Graphics is also able to deal with PDF directly, including simple file operations like parsing and creation, as well as transforms, metadata access, and conversion from PostScript.

Figure 24-17. Photo Booth uses Core Image filters, including everyone's favorite: Hologram.

Core Graphics is blazing fast thanks to hardware acceleration, offloading as much processing as possible to the video card. It provides an abstraction layer, so you can deal with graphics directly, without worrying about how the actual processing will be done. Yesterday's machines will automatically ramp to CPU processing, and tomorrow's machines will take advantage of whatever heavy silicon they've got.

Even if you never use Core Graphics directly, you'll see its influence (and its prefix, CG) everywhere. For example, its width-agnostic floating-point scalar, CGFloat, replaces standard float and double types in many applications.

> **NOTE** In lieu of separate namespaces, frameworks use informal prefixes to give their members unique names. For example, consider three different classes for representing an image: CGImage, CIImage, and NSImage, from Core Graphics, Core Image, and Cocoa (formerly known as NeXTSTEP).

Core Video

When you think about it, video is more of a concept than a thing. When you say you have "a video," you really mean you have a VHS tape, or a DVD, or an MP4 file, or some of that new-fangled H.264 the kids are talking about. Video, while one simple term, actually encompasses a lot of complexity that the operating system protects us from.

On Mac OS X, this abstraction goes deep. With Core Video, developers can manipulate the individual frames of raw video, using a standard buffer to bridge differences between data types, and a pipeline of discrete processing steps for the ultimate in control.

Following are some things Core Video enables:

- Using Core Image filters
- Compositing video streams together
- Editing the content of frames
- Transforming the physical geometry of a video
- Mapping a video onto other surfaces or an OpenGL scene

Core Video also takes care of things most people take for granted, like making sure the picture remains synced with the sound, despite the vagaries of refresh rates, CPU operations, user interactions, and the myriad flavors of lag.

Image I/O

All this image processing is great, but that sort of assumes you have an image to work with in the first place. The formidable task of reading and parsing the myriad image formats out there used to be the job of Core Graphics. Eventually, the size of the task and the ubiquity of its need necessitated spinning off image interpretation into its own framework, called Image I/O.

Despite all the goings-on behind the scenes, the actual use of Image I/O is pretty easy to understand. You've got your *I*, which is to say, input, and you've got your *O*, which is to say, output.

For input, Image I/O introduces image sources, an abstraction from the raw data that contains multiple images, thumbnails, metadata, and important but easily overlooked things like color spaces. For output, Image I/O uses image destinations, which are like the same thing, in reverse.

If it sounds simple, that's because it is. Image I/O is simply the best, most efficient way to move image data into and out of your applications. There isn't much more to it than that.

Other Application Frameworks

Not everyone who develops *on* the Mac has the luxury of developing *for* the Mac, and not everyone writing Mac applications has the luxury of using Cocoa and Objective-C. Fortunately, on Mac OS X Leopard, applications written in any number of languages with any number of frameworks all live and work side by side, as shown in Figure 24-18.

Cocoa

Though primarily intended for development in Objective-C, Cocoa has been bridged to several other languages. Although C and C++ are not completely compatible, they share enough that C++ programmers can mix their native language with Objective-C via a hybrid known as Objective-C++.

Java developers have their own application framework, but there is a Cocoa Java bridge. It has been deprecated, but for those who learned Java as a teaching language, it's a great way to transition to Cocoa before learning Objective-C.

Figure 24-18. Cocoa, Carbon, UNIX, Java, Objective-C, Python, and C++ side by side

Python programmers can take advantage of PyObjC and the Python framework, enabling access to Cocoa alongside the many Python libraries. Xcode now includes Python templates to give Cocoa developers using Python the same head start as Cocoa developers using Objective-C. Indeed, developers have used Python with Cocoa to write entire commercial Cocoa applications that are indistinguishable for those written in Objective-C, as shown in Figure 24-19.

Figure 24-19. Madebysofa's Checkout was written in Python with Cocoa.

Ruby is the new hotness, and it ships with Leopard, alongside Rails, its development framework. Much like Python, Ruby is bridged to Cocoa and comes with a framework and many of the common libraries and tools Ruby programmers enjoy. Like Python, Ruby developers get their own Ruby Cocoa templates right in Xcode.

Carbon

When Apple bought NeXT in 1997, NeXT's operating system, NeXTSTEP, became the new Mac OS X. The old Mac OS, then on its ninth iteration, Mac OS 9, was deprecated, but not eliminated. To smooth the transition, the Mac OS 9 operating environment became a part of Mac OS X, called Classic. Mac users could use their old Mac OS 9 applications alongside native applications.

Eventually, everything deemed important became a native Mac OS X application, and Classic went away. For those newer to the platform, this is exactly what is happening with Rosetta, a Classic-like compatibility environment that allows users to run their old PowerPC applications. Eventually, everything will be a universal binary, and Rosetta too will go away.

The developer frameworks of Mac OS 9 likewise did not simply vanish. They were rolled into an application framework called Carbon, shown in Figure 24-20. For ten years, Carbon and Cocoa lived side by side. Cocoa continued to expand and mature, and new Carbon development slowed and eventually came to a stop.

Figure 24-20. iTunes was written with Carbon.

That being said, Carbon is not going away any time soon. However, new frameworks are being developed exclusively for Cocoa. For example, while the new 64-bit frameworks include Carbon, there is no Carbon UI. Rather, Carbon developers who wish to take advantage of new development, such as 64-bit, will have to do so with the Cocoa frameworks.

Fortunately, Carbon and Cocoa are compatible, so just as Cocoa developers can dip into Carbon, something that happens less and less as Cocoa has matured, Carbon developers can dip into Cocoa, something that will happen more and more as time goes on.

Java

Java is a cross-platform framework and eponymous object-oriented language. If you're a Java programmer, the Mac is a great place to work. The Java implementation on the Mac is the best one out there. It takes almost no effort to package a Java application to launch, look, and behave just like a native Mac application, as shown in Figure 24-21.

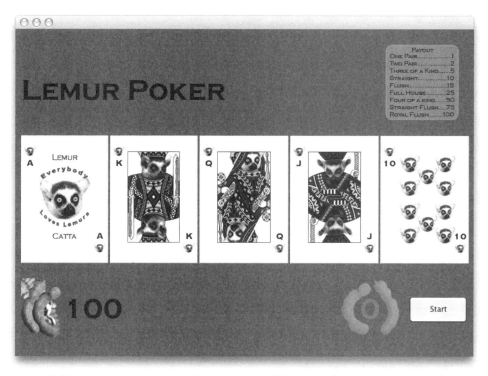

Figure 24-21. Java applications run just like native Mac OS X applications.

That said, with the Java-Cocoa bridge being deprecated, the Java language is not a good choice for writing native Mac applications. Furthermore, when you develop without regard for a particular operating system, you give up all the support that an operating system provides. It is a lot harder to program in Java than it is to program in almost any native application framework.

AppleScript

AppleScript is best known for automating tasks that use other applications on the system. It's also meant to be a very easy language to use, with an English-like syntax and very forgiving interpreter. With the improvements Leopard brings to AppleScript, we may well see a resurgence of this unique and useful language.

Xcode includes an environment, called AppleScript Studio, that adds graphical interface widgets to AppleScript. This enables power users who dabble in development with AppleScript to bridge the gap to creating full-fledged applications.

I **NOTE** For more information on AppleScript, see Chapter 23.

WebObjects

A kind of Cocoa for the Web, WebObjects is an enterprise-level product marketed by Apple for creating web-based storefronts and other services. It's included with the developer tools, but not installed by default.

BSD/X11

Lest we forget that Leopard is UNIX, applications and utilities can be written for and ported to Mac OS X, either as command-line BSD applications or as graphical X11 applications. If you're a scientific programmer, a Perl hacker, or have a huge white beard and pipe-scented suspenders, welcome to Darwin.

> **NOTE** For more on Darwin, see Chapters 18 and 19.

Ajax

Asynchronous JavaScript and XML (Ajax) is the best-known platform of Web 2.0. The basic idea is to extend the concept of a web page into a full-blown application by adding JavaScript: the dynamic, object-oriented language that is not at all related to Java.

However, like Java, Ajax is hardly specific to the Mac, but the Mac is a great platform for Ajax development. There are a lot of great tools for working with Ajax, and with other web technologies, that you can only use on the Mac, such as Apple's Dashcode, Panic's Coda, and BareBones's venerable BBEdit.

Ajax is used to create Dashboard widgets. Web Kit allows web technology to be embedded in any application, making Ajax a kind of lingua franca around the platform and beyond. Ajax is also the official development path for the iPhone.

Summary

Programming on the Mac is a lot like using a Mac, and how could it be any other way? When you see the thousands of top-notch applications by Apple and others that are available only on the Mac, it's inspiring. Whether you're a student, hobbyist, or professional, the Mac is a great place to live, and to code.

Whether you're programming for the Mac, or just a programmer who happens to develop on a Mac, Apple is working hard to keep you happy and productive. The application programming environment is only part of the story. In the chapters ahead, we'll sample some tools of the trade, and we'll meet Objective-C, Apple's secret weapon in the battle against deadlines.

## CHAPTER 25

Mac OS X Development: The Tools

Imagine if, when you bought your car, the trunk came fully loaded with every tool you needed to fix and maintain it. Not just a simple screwdriver and ratchet set, but the same specialized computer-driven data analysis and optimization tools used by professional mechanics. Believe it or not, this is the way computers used to be.

When the seed that would sprout into Apple was planted in Steve Jobs's parents' garage in 1976, it was part of a greater movement embodied by Silicon Valley's Homebrew Computer Club. Unlike the behemoths being developed by the slick suits down at IBM, the computers built by these hobbyist hackers were not meant to simply be operated. Rather, they were meant to be programmed, and by mere mortals.

Indeed, third-party software companies hadn't been invented yet, so even people who didn't know how to program still wrote their own programs, thanks to books and magazines with pages and pages of computer code that had to be typed verbatim. Even when software became something you simply bought and used, early personal computers were expected to come with the tools necessary to program them.

Yet somehow, as computer use became widespread, computer programming as an everyman skill faded until computers were considered nothing more than machines meant to run prepurchased software. Now, it's not uncommon to spend thousands of dollars on the tools necessary to develop software on a personal computer.

Apple, however, true to its homebrew legacy, includes its development tools, for free, with every copy of Mac OS X. The day you become a Mac user you've also gained the potential to be a Mac programmer, complete with a fully stocked toolbox.

Apple Developer Connection

If you're thinking of developing for the Mac, you should join the club, literally. The Apple Developer Connection (ADC) is Apple's official online resource for all things development. Before even installing Xcode, you should check it out online: http://developer.apple.com.

Aside from being the place to get up-to-the-minute information about the whys and wherefores of writing software on the Mac, ADC membership provides you with downloads and updates on all the tools you need: Xcode, documentation, example code, and software development kits for everything under the sun. It also gives you access to the Bug Reporter, but more on that later. Best of all, it's free.

> **NOTE** Professional software developers need more support and things like prerelease software. For them, Apple offers Select and Premier ADC memberships for a price. For our purposes, the free online membership is sufficient, but if you decide to make your living this way, it's well worth the cost of upgrading.

Installing Xcode Tools

To install the developer tools, known collectively as Xcode Tools, insert your Leopard installation DVD. It doesn't matter if it's the retail upgrade version or the restore version that came with your machine. Navigate to the Xcode Tools folder, and then double-click the XcodeTools.mpkg package. This will launch the installer. There's nothing unusual here, but don't overlook the easily missed Customize button.

Several optional installs are selected by default. Disclosing the Xcode IDE and Tools section reveals the Core Reference Library and Examples, which are good to have around, but Dashcode and Java Documentation are completely unnecessary unless you're planning on developing Dashboard widgets or Java applications, respectively.

> **NOTE** If you decide later you should have installed a tool, don't worry. You can run the installer again to add additional components.

The Xcode System Tools section is a bit more esoteric. The Distributed Builds Engine lets you create an ad hoc supercomputer to do your compiles. That's nice if you're a developer working on a huge project and your computer is connected to a network of machines that are also participating. For mere mortals, you should probably take a pass.

Analysis & Performance Tools and Command Line Support are always good to have around, but Mac OS X 10.3.9 Support and WebObjects should rightly remain unchecked, unless you specifically need them.

Speaking of Mac OS X 10.3.9 support, it bears note that if you're still writing pre-Leopard applications, you have another option. The latest versions of Xcode and its older brother, Interface Builder, are partially incompatible with, and therefore designed to run side by side with their previous versions. These are not included with Leopard, however, so if you need them, you'll have to dig out your Tiger disks.

Traditionally, developer tools went into the /Developer directory, right off of root, and adjacent to the /Applications directory. Furthermore, Xcode could only be installed on the boot disk, much to the chagrin of those reliant on external drives, multiple partitions, or networked storage. Leopard introduces the ability to choose your own installation destination, but unless you have some special need that's not being met by a root-level directory, you'll do well to stick to the default.

Once you've got everything configured, click Install, authenticate if prompted, and then go to lunch.

> **NOTE** No discs, no problem. You can always download the latest versions of the developer tools from the ADC web site.

Introduction to Xcode

Surfing into the newly minted Developer directory reveals a whole hierarchy of goodies, but with the possible exception of some reading material (About Xcode Tools.pdf), nothing in here is for you except the `Applications` subdirectory. Everything else is for Xcode's own use, so, unless you've got some special need, go straight into `Applications`.

The star of the show is the Xcode Integrated Development Environment, known to its friends simply as Xcode. Like any star, Xcode brings with it an entourage of supporting players, some of whom you may never meet, some of whom you will use every day.

If you develop software for the Mac, you live in Xcode. It is your editor, compiler, and debugger all in one. Xcode is built on open source tools, but, like Mac OS X itself, covers all that rich chocolate power with an easy-to-use candy shell. Xcode also serves as your project manager and research assistant, with integrated access to headers and documentation.

Don't be fooled! This brief description belies just how much Xcode does, and with Leopard, Xcode has been radically improved.

Xcode Preferences

The first time you launch Xcode, you'll be asked a few questions to set up the environment. Don't sweat these too much, as you can always change them in the Preferences window. Indeed, if you're like me, going to the preferences is the first thing you do. Do so now by selecting Preferences... from the application's menu, or by typing the standard keystroke, Cmd+,. This will bring up Xcode's extensive Preferences window, shown in Figure 25-1.

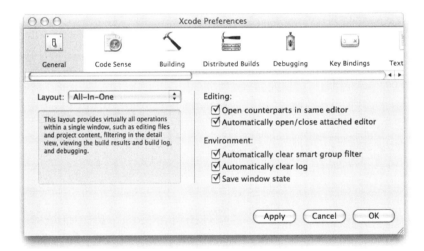

Figure 25-1. The Xcode Preferences window

Chances are you (or your boss) already has an idea of how things should be set up. Xcode has a lot of options for making things just so. These are divided into several groups, which scroll along the top of the window:

General:

- Adjust the positioning and grouping of windows.
- "Automatically clear log," when checked, clears the console between runs.

Code Sense:

- Code completion is requested with the Esc key, but you can also enable autocompletion and set the delay.
- Decide whether arguments are shown in suggestions or completions.
- Set the display and sorting of the editor's function pop-up list.

Building:

- Set where build products and temp files are located.
- Decide whether and how build, error, and warning logs are displayed.
- Set where and how Leopard's new error and warning bubbles are displayed.
- Decide whether to compile predictively, or in the presence of errors.
- Adjust autosave settings.

Distributed Builds:

- Decide whether and how to make your machine available for Xcode's distributed build system.
- Decide whether and to whom to send your own builds for distribution.
- As noted previously, distributed builds are only really worthwhile on very large projects with a lot of developers on a very fast network.

Debugging:

- Choose the colors used by the debugger.
- Set how and when to display the debugger.
- Adjust symbol and assembly display options.
- Decide whether to enable Leopard's new in-editor debugging.

Key Bindings:

- Set customizable shortcuts for menu items and other functions.
- There are prebuilt groups to make Xcode emulate other editors.

Text Editing:

- Toggle editor features like the gutter, line numbers, columns, page guides, and Leopard's new code folding and code focus features.
- Set selection behaviors around braces.
- Set default line ending and text encodings.

Fonts & Colors:

- Set fonts and colors used by the editor for every syntax element.
- There are also customizable sets here, but they don't emulate other programs so much as provide mood enhancement.

Indentation:

- Decide whether to use tabs or spaces, and the width and quantity of each.
- Decide whether and how to soft wrap text.
- Decide whether and how to apply automatic indentation.

File Types:

- Set the mapping of file types and which editor to use for each.
- Xcode can be used with any number of external editors.

Opening Quickly:

- Open Quickly is a command that allows you to open a file by selecting or typing its name, rather than by navigating the Open dialog.
- Opening Quickly is the customizable list of directories searched by the Open Quickly command.

Source Trees:

- Source Trees are global directories on your root file system where Xcode will look for project files and resources.
- Source Trees are managed via the Source Trees preference panel.

SCM:

- SCM stands for source code management, also known as version control.
- If you don't know what version control is, put this book down and Google it. It will change your life.
- Xcode supports CVS, Perforce, and Subversion.
- The Repositories tab is where you add your project servers.
- The Options tab contains preferences such as which editor to use for differencing and whether to autosave.

Documentation:

- Xcode's documentation system is fantastic, but none of its options are actually on this panel.
- This panel actually contains the various locations of documentation.
- I can only think of very contrived examples of why you would ever change this.

You might think that the Preferences panel is the only place to set up preferences for Xcode, but in fact Xcode has hidden preferences all over the place. Some of these are based on scope—for example, the different project and target settings. Others are based on tradition, such as right-clicking or Ctrl+clicking the toolbar to edit its configuration.

At the end of the day, while Xcode is much easier to use than traditional command-line tools, it's designed to be powerful, efficient, and endlessly configurable. If there's some way in which you want to exert your will over Xcode, don't assume it doesn't exist just because you can't find it. It's likely it does exist, but is hidden somewhere obscure.

Documentation

After setting up Xcode, you're greeted with the new Welcome to Xcode window, shown in Figure 25-2. Aside from assembling everything you need to start programming with Xcode, the welcome window uses RSS syndication to deliver up-to-the-minute news and documentation. This combines the accuracy and timeliness of web-based documentation with the convenience and accessibility of having the documentation right in Xcode.

Clicking A Quick Tour of Xcode is not only a good way to get acquainted with Xcode, but it's also a good way to meet your new best friend, the documentation window, shown in Figure 25-3. Like much of Xcode 3, this has been radically redesigned in Leopard.

There are several ways to get to the documentation window, aside from the Welcome to Xcode window. When in Xcode's editor, you can hold Option while double-clicking a term to automatically search for it in the documentation window.

You can also activate the documentation window by selecting Documentation from the Help menu. This means you can also launch it from the keyboard by typing Option+Cmd+?. That doesn't seem memorable, but it's really easy to type. Press the adjacent Option and Cmd buttons with your left hand and the adjacent ? and Shift buttons with your right.

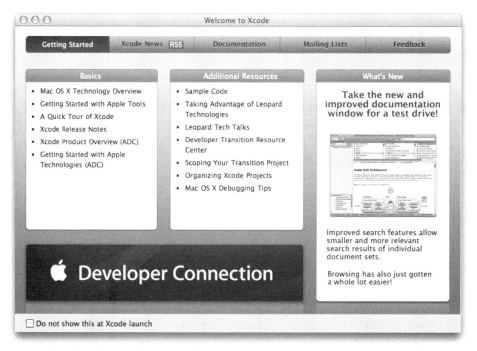

Figure 25-2. Xcode's new Welcome to Xcode window

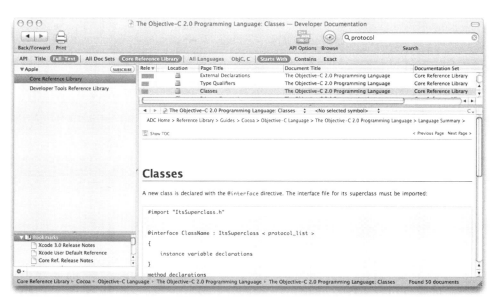

Figure 25-3. Xcode's documentation window

The operation of the documentation window should be pretty obvious. Type a search term into the box. Refine your search using the options below the toolbar. Results are displayed, sorted, and selected in the table view. The selected document is shown in the web view below, or in an external editor, as appropriate. The sidebar contains documentation sets and bookmarks.

Finally, Leopard introduces the Research Assistant, a floating documentation window intended to be kept open as you code (shown in Figure 25-4). You can activate the Research Assistant from the Help menu, or via an optional toolbar icon. When you click a term, the Research Assistant gives you context-specific help.

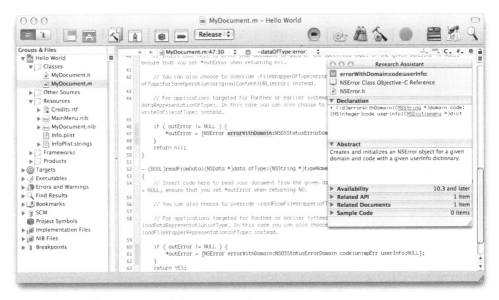

Figure 25-4. Xcode's new Research Assistant panel

Project Organization

Xcode organizes your projects into bundles called, appropriately, *projects*. To create a new project in Xcode, select New Project… from the File menu, or type Shift+Cmd+N. This will launch the Project Assistant, shown in Figure 25-5.

Figure 25-5. Project templates in Xcode's Project Assistant window

The Project Assistant presents you will a long list of project templates, organized into several categories:

Empty Project: This creates an Xcode project without applying any template.

Action: This includes templates for creating Automator actions with AppleScript, Cocoa, or Shell Script. There is also a template for defining new data types.

Application: This includes templates for creating AppleScript applications, Carbon applications in C or C++, and Cocoa applications in Objective-C, Ruby, or Python. In addition to basic application templates, there are templates for document-based applications and AppleScript droplets. There are also templates specifically for creating Cocoa applications backed by Core Data.

Audio Units: This includes templates for creating Core Audio plug-ins, known as Audio Units, in Carbon and Cocoa.

Bundle: While most projects end up as bundles, there are generic bundle templates for Carbon, Cocoa, and C++. This is useful for creating your own plug-ins, or for other bundle types not specifically addressed by other templates.

Command Line Utility: This includes templates for creating nongraphical programs to be run in Darwin. There are specific templates for writing programs with Core Foundation, the C framework that underlies Carbon and Cocoa; Foundation, the Objective-C framework from Cocoa; and Core Services, the C framework for many basic operating system services. There are also generic templates for writing utilities in C and C++.

Dynamic Library: Dynamic libraries are bundles of reusable code that can be loaded at runtime. Xcode's has dynamic library templates for Carbon, Cocoa, Ruby, BSD, and C++.

External Build System: This generic template allows developers to use Xcode to organize and edit their programs, but use their own build systems.

Framework: Cocoa frameworks are like dynamic libraries, except in addition to code they can contain other resources such as media files or Interface Builder's nib files. They also have built-in versioning.

Java: This includes templates for creating Java applets and tools, as well as standard, Java Native Interface and Java Web Start applications.

Kernel Extension: This includes templates for creating extensions to the lowest level of the operating system: the kernel. In addition to a generic template, there is a template for creating device drivers using IOKit.

Quartz Composer: We'll discuss Quartz Composer in its own section, but in a nutshell, Quartz Composer compositions are bundles of graphic and programming logic that can be used alone or in other applications. Xcode provides several templates for applications and plug-ins built around these compositions.

Standard Apple Plug-ins: Many Apple applications have plug-in architectures, allowing third-party developers to add functionality. To facilitate plug-in development, Xcode provides plug-in templates for Address Book, Xcode, Dashcode, Interface Builder, and Web Kit. There are also templates for creating bundled Core Image filters, called Image Units, as well as preference panels, screen savers, and sync schemas. If your application uses a custom data type, there are templates for creating plug-ins for Spotlight and Quick Look as well.

Static Library: Static libraries are bundles of reusable code that must be linked to at compile time. Xcode includes templates for creating static libraries with Carbon, Cocoa, and BSD.

You can't do much in Xcode without a project. From the Project Assistant window, create a new Cocoa document-based application named Hello World. You will be prompted to give the project a name and a location, as shown in Figure 25-6. I've created a ~/Projects folder in my home folder, adjacent my ~/Documents folder. I like to subdivide my Projects folder into general categories, but you can adapt this exercise to your own work style.

Xcode's project window is split vertically into two views. On the left is the Groups & Files sidebar, which organizes your project in a logical, hierarchical way. On the right is a details view that gives you more information on whatever is selected in the sidebar. While it's

Figure 25-6. Creating a project in Xcode's Project Assistant window

not immediately obvious at first, the right pane is actually further split horizontally. Centered at the bottom of the view is a small dot. Grabbing the dot with your cursor and dragging reveals the editor view, as shown in Figure 25-7. You can also reveal the editor by selecting a source code file in the sidebar, or by clicking the editor toolbar item.

Figure 25-7. Xcode's project window, with the editor pane revealed

Your new project already has a lot of content in its sidebar. These are Xcode's *smart groups*. Like iTunes, some of these are functional and built-in, while others simply serve to demonstrate the kinds of smart groups you can create yourself. Any of the preset smart groups can be toggled by right- or Cmd+clicking the sidebar to bring up its contextual menu, and then selecting Preferences.

Project Structure

The first thing in the sidebar is the Project Structure smart group. Note that this smart group is unique in that its displayed name will be the same as your project's. By default, it contains several subgroups, which look and behave like folders. These in turn contain all the source code and resources used by your project.

Groups are created, deleted, and renamed via the contextual menu. (Recall that the contextual menu is what pops up when you Ctrl+click or right-click an item.) The groups can be moved or nested by dragging them. Items within the groups can also be moved by dragging them.

It bears note that the groups within the Project Structure smart group have no actual relevance to your project, nor do they necessarily relate to the actual folders in your project's folder; they are only there for your organizational convenience.

Targets

Xcode's build system is organized into *targets*. A target contains the steps necessary to create a build product. Build steps include compiling source code, linking, and copying resources to the application bundle. By default, your project will only contain one target: the Hello World application.

Very complicated projects may contain additional targets, such as plug-ins, frameworks, command-line tools, or Automator actions. Simple projects don't have to worry about targets, as Xcode does a decent job of keeping a single target organized and updated.

Executables

Building a project isn't much good unless you can run and debug it. Since Xcode handles these tasks, it needs to know any arguments, environment variables, or debugging attachments you want added when you run. Any executable products of your project, such as the Hello World application, will be kept in the Executables smart group.

Upon selecting an executable in this group, typing Cmd+I will pull up an executable inspector where you can set things like arguments. As with targets, the default project will only contain a single executable.

Errors & Warnings

Sometimes a change can require so much code that by the time you can compile again, dozens of files have been touched. Even though Xcode 3 introduces error and warning pop-up bubbles, it's still nice to have a list of all the files that have something wrong with them. The Errors & Warnings smart group is just such a list. Any file with an error or warning on it will be added to this smart group until the next compile.

Find Results

The Edit menu item's Find subfolder reveals that Xcode has multiple levels of find. The familiar Cmd+F launches Single File Find, which does what it says. Typing Shift+Cmd+F (or clicking the magnifying glass toolbar item) launches Project Find. This is a bit of misnomer, as its focus can be broadened or narrowed from the project.

In any case, all Project Find search results are saved in the Find Results smart group. On large projects, where searches can take several minutes, this is a big time saver.

Bookmarks

Another problem plaguing large projects is navigating the hierarchy of folders to get to the files you're working on. To help you stay organized, Xcode lets you bookmark files. Bookmarked files show up in this smart group. To bookmark a file, right- or Cmd+click the file in the sidebar, details list, or editor to bring up its contextual menu, and select Add to Bookmarks.

SCM

If you're using version control in Xcode, any file that has been changed will be added to the SCM results details pane, as well as the SCM smart group. Items in the SCM smart group have version control commands in their contextual menu, which makes it easy to commit, revert, or diff a single file.

The SCM smart group's icon turns into a progress indicator during version control operations, so you can keep an eye on how your commit is going while getting ready to break things again.

Project Symbols

Unlike the other smart groups, Project Symbols doesn't have a disclosure triangle revealing a hierarchy of files. Rather, it's just there so you can select it and bring up its details panel. Doing so yields a list of every symbol, which is to say, every method, function, ivar, struct, global, typedef, protocol, property, and macro, as well as anything defined in a Core Data model or Interface Builder nib.

Why would you need a gigantic list of every symbol in the project? Who knows! But when the day comes, you'll probably be glad it's there.

Implementation Files/NIB Files

Aside from the built-in smart groups, you can create your own. Although they are functional and potentially useful, the Implementation Files and NIB Files smart groups are really samples of the kinds of things you could do. To create a smart group, select an option from the Project menu's New Smart Group submenu.

To edit an existing smart group, select Get Info from its contextual menu, or select it in the sidebar and type Cmd+I. Aside from defining a name, filter, and scope for the group, you can also set its icon. Regardless of whether that's useful, it's pretty cool.

Breakpoints

While running your program in the debugger, you may want to stop at a certain line of code to examine the values of variables, test some method calls, or just follow along line-by-line to see what's happening. To mark lines for the debugger to stop, or *break*, you set *breakpoints*. Breakpoints are also handy placeholders in their own right. To help you examine or jump to a certain breakpoint, they are all listed under the Breakpoints smart group.

> **TIP** Xcode also has a Favorites bar, which is similar to the Bookmarks bar in Safari. You can reveal the Favorites bar by selecting Show Favorites Bar from the Layout submenu of the View menu. Dragging files, groups, or smart groups to the Favorites bar will add them. Clicking an item in the Favorites bar will select it in the Groups & Files sidebar.

One thing I've noticed about Apple applications: they always include amazing templates. You can fire up anything in iLife or iWork and you already have a fully functional, if somewhat boring, web site, movie, song, DVD, presentation, or document. Xcode is the exact same way. Without typing anything, you've already started with a fully functional document-based application.

To see this for yourself, build and run your project by selecting Build and Run from the Build menu, typing Cmd+R, or clicking the hammer icon on the toolbar. In short order, you'll see a generic document, as seen in Figure 25-8.

If you're following along at home, you'll notice one difference between your application and the one in Figure 25-8. Namely, yours says "Your document contents here," and the one in the figure says "Hello World!" You can examine the source code all you want, but you're not going to find it.

Figure 25-8. Your first Mac application in action

That's because any graphical application doesn't really get going in Xcode until we take a detour to Interface Builder. Quit your application like any other—by selecting Quit from its menu or typing Cmd+Q. Then, from the project's smart group in the sidebar, find the Resources group and double-click MyDocument.nib to open it in Interface Builder.

Interface Builder

It's fitting that the first development tool for Mac OS X, back when it was still NeXTSTEP, was not a code editor, but an interface editor. Interface Builder made the process of creating a graphic user interface into a graphical experience.

Even though drag-and-drop user interface editors are now common, Interface Builder is unique in that it doesn't produce code. Rather, it creates freeze-dried interface objects in NeXTSTEP Interface Builder format, more generally known as *nibs*. These nibs are literally your application's interface. The same nibs you create in a project today will be deployed with your shipping application tomorrow.

Later, Interface Builder was joined by a younger sibling, Project Builder, now known as Xcode. Interface Builder remained separate, which is handy for interface designers, translators, and hackers who want to create or alter an application's interface without having to know or care about its source code.

While Xcode went through several iterations of improvement, Interface Builder was largely left as is, until now. Leopard's version of Interface Builder is completely rewritten from the ground up, breathing new life into this amazing tool. Interface Builder has four components, as shown in Figure 25-9.

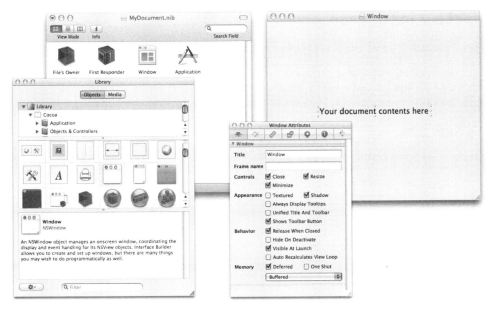

Figure 25-9. Editing a user interface in Interface Builder

The Interface

The nib is your interface, so it should come as no surprise that your interface elements are at the center of the nib's contents. When you open your nib in Interface Builder for the first time, you're greeted with the same document window you saw when building and running your nascent application. The window you see in the nib is the same window the user will be greeted with, but editable.

Double-click the words "Your document contents here" to edit the text field. Type the new text, "Hello World!" in its place. Since many interface elements have dynamic content that is difficult to render in edit mode, you can simulate your interface in normal mode by selecting Simulate Interface from the File menu, or by typing Cmd+R.

This launches your interface in Cocoa Simulator. You can interact with your interface to make sure it does what you expect when, for example, resizing a window. Resizing the window in Cocoa Simulator reveals an unexpected problem. The text area seems to be anchored to the bottom-left corner of the window, rather than doing what we would expect, which is to stay centered. We'll fix that in moment. For now, quit Cocoa Simulator by selecting Quit from the file menu or typing Cmd+Q.

Testing the interface by itself is OK for some tasks, but it doesn't show how the interface works with your application. For more complicated testing, you'll want to actually build and run your application. There are a few ways to do this. You can save your interface, and then quit Interface Builder, or switch back to Xcode to build and run, as we did before.

You can also build and run in Xcode from within Interface Builder itself. Save your interface by selecting Save from the File menu, or typing Cmd+S. Then select Build and Go in Xcode from the File menu, or type Shift+Cmd+R. This will send a message to Xcode (no doubt using Apple-Script) to build and run your application, just like you did earlier.

You should see your document window with your new text. You should also notice we still have that resizing bug. Quit your application in the usual way and return to Interface Builder. Select the text area with a single click. It's time to meet the Inspector.

The Inspector

Like any inspector panel, Interface Builder's Inspector allows you to see and change the attributes of your interface items. The Inspector is open by default, but you can always call it forth by selecting Inspector from the Tools menu, or by typing Shift+Cmd+I. To inspect an item, simply click it, and the Inspector's contents will change as appropriate. The Inspector's attributes are divided into several tabs.

Attributes

As interface objects are reusable, they have several configuration options. Although interface objects can be instantiated and configured in code, it's easier to set up as many attributes as possible in Interface Builder itself. This keeps the attributes with the objects they affect, and presents them in a visual way that often makes their effects easier to understand.

The Attributes tab is divided into subsections based on the object's inheritance. Our text field has several attributes, chief among them is its title, which is the text it displays. Editing the title will change the text just as you did by double-clicking and editing it in place. You can also set text attributes such as alignment, color, and whether to use *rich text*, which allows things like bold or italic formatting.

You can also set attributes on the text field itself, such as its border, whether it should draw a background, and if so, what color it should be.

Since your text field, as an instance of the class NSTextField, is a subclass of NSControl, the next subsection allows you to edit the attributes of a control. These include the text's direction, how it handles line breaks, and whether it is enabled or grayed out.

As NSControl is in turn a subclass of NSView, you can then edit view attributes like how it draws a focus ring to indicate it's the currently selected item, or whether it's visible at all.

Effects

As discussed in Chapter 24, many Core Animation effects are available from within Interface Builder. These are settable from the myriad subsections of the Effects tab. Since your text field is a view subclass, you can take advantage of Core Animation.

When a view uses Core Animation, we say it is *layer-backed*. Once a view is layer-backed, all of its subviews are also layer-backed. You can see the view hierarchy and decide at which level to activate layer-backing from the Rendering Tree subsection.

> **NOTE** Core Animation was originally called Layer Kit, because it uses a lightweight layer-based model. For whatever reason, Leopard's architects decided to emphasize the framework's easy animation over its nifty rendering model. Regardless of this change, we still refer to layers and call views that can use Core Animation "layer-backed."

Once your view is layer-backed, you can change its transparency and set a custom shadow from the Appearance tab. You can add Core Image filters from the Content Filters, Background Filters, and Compositing Filters subsections. Finally, you can affect the style of animation by setting custom transitions in the Transitions subsection.

Feel free to play with the various Core Animation and Core Image effects later if you like, but since none of this affects resizing (the task at hand), let's move on.

Size

The Size tab would be more properly called Geometry, as it affects more than just size. Nevertheless, this is where you need to go to set the resizing attributes of your text field. Much like the Attributes tab, you'll notice subsections based on inheritance. There are no special text field size attributes, so the first subsection comes from being a control subclass.

All controls come in three standard sizes: regular, small, and mini. Although you can manually change the size of a control and its contents, using one of the predefined sizes ensures that your controls will always match the rest of the system, regardless of design changes down the road. In general, Apple's Human Interface Guidelines suggest using regular controls whenever possible, reserving the use of the smaller controls for when space is at a premium.

> **NOTE** Did you think the Mac's usability was an accident? Far from it, every pixel has been sweated over by design experts and explained in excruciating detail in Apple's Human Interface Guidelines. These are required reading for any Mac developer, and also interesting for any user who'd like to get to know more about what makes using a Mac such a great experience. The guidelines, usually referred to as the HIG (rhymes with dig), are available in Xcode's documentation and online.

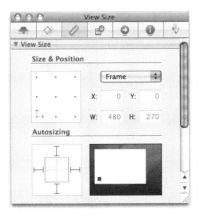

Figure 25-10. Changing Autosizing attributes in the Inspector

Moving down to the View Size subsection, you can set size and location based on any corner or edge, or the view's center. You can also align and center multiple views. What you really want is to change the autosizing behavior, as shown in Figure 25-10.

On the left side of the Autosizing section is a schematic representation of your view inside its superview. The inner rectangle represents your view. The vertical and horizontal arrows inside your view represent which direction you want your view to resize in. The struts connecting your view to the superview represent which sides of your view you want to be fixed in relation to the superview. The expected results of the settings are animated on the right.

By clicking the resize directions and struts in the schematic, you can change the effects shown in the animation. A little experimentation shows that removing all the struts will enable your text area to remain centered. Save and run the interface to verify that this is so.

Bindings

As you've seen, even simple controls like the text field have a lot of attributes. Some of these attributes are displayed to the user, such as the title. Other attributes affect the control itself, such as its size, or whether it's hidden. While you can set an initial state during the design of your interface, some attributes may need to change at runtime.

Traditionally, getting and setting a control's value was accomplished via an intermediary object, called a *controller*. A programmer would write *glue code* in the controller to perform the actual getting and setting of values.

Cocoa's *bindings* feature eliminates the need for this glue code by letting controls bind their values to other objects. For example, check boxes on a preference panel might be bound to the user defaults system. The value of a date field might be bound to the value of a date picker. Or, a user-editable value might be bound to a key in the document controller. Unlike traditional glue code, a bound value is always kept in sync automatically.

The Inspector's Bindings tab contains a list of bindable attributes. Within each binding, you can set the object, the key name, and several options. You can also set a value transformer to automatically convert between value types. For example, an object might have a URL attribute that you want to bind to another object's path attribute. Since URLs have their own class, NSURL, and paths are instances of the NSString class, you wouldn't be able to bind a URL to a path without the assistance of a value transformer.

Connections

While bindings allow you to make a connection between two objects' attributes, sometimes you have to make connections between objects themselves. For example, one object might wish to delegate some of its functionality to another object. When a user interacts with a control, such as a button, it must be able to notify its controller to perform an action. Other times, a controller might need a direct outlet to an object in the nib.

All of the connections an object can make are visible in the Inspector's Connections tab. In order to connect two objects, you simply Ctrl+click an object and drag. A line will appear between the dragging cursor and the object. If you drop the other end of the line onto another object, a pop-up window of that object's available connections will appear. Selecting a connection will establish the link between the two objects, which will be reflected in the Inspector.

Alternately, you can Ctrl+double-click an object to pull up its own connections panel, from which you can create connections, as shown in Figure 25-11. You can also begin connections from the Inspector itself. Finally, you can break connections in the Inspector by clicking the small *x* icon on the connection itself.

Figure 25-11. Establishing connections between objects in Interface Builder

Identity

In addition to attributes, objects also have a lot of metadata, which is configurable via the Inspector's Identity tab. You can change an object's class. If you change it to a class of your own creation, you can add actions and outlets, which you can then add to the class in Xcode with the synchronization options in the File menu.

You can give the item a description, for use by the Accessibility system. That way, for example, a person who has trouble seeing the screen can have the system describe your objects out loud. You can also set *tool tips*, which are the hints that pop up when a user hovers the cursor over an item for a few seconds. Finally, you can give the object a name, see its object ID, and write notes about it.

AppleScript

The AppleScript tab enables you to associate interface items with AppleScripts. Within a script, there will likely be several event handlers, which are AppleScript's equivalent to actions. You can specify which event handlers the control should call. Although AppleScript can be used by Cocoa applications, the primary purpose of Interface Builder's AppleScript interface is to let advanced users of AppleScript use Interface Builder to create graphical interfaces for their scripts.

The Library

When you tire of playing with the default text field, you're ready to check out the plethora of interface elements available in Interface Builder's Library panel. The Library panel's Objects tab is divided into three sections, as shown in Figure 25-12.

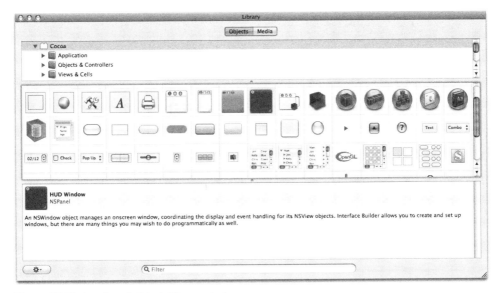

Figure 25-12. Interface Builder's Library window

The first section is a group list, which contains groups and sometimes subgroups of objects. The second section is an object list containing the objects available in the selected group. The third section simply contains a description of any object selected in the object list.

There are some cool tricks you can do with the Library panel. By dragging the divider between the group list and the object list all the way to the top of panel, the group list will become a pop-up. You can also group the object list by selecting Show Group Banners from the customization (Gear) pop-up menu on the bottom of the panel. You can also set up custom groups from the Gear menu.

The Gear menu will also let you change the display style of the object list. The default is to simply show representative icons. You can also chose to display the name of the object with those icons, or to display the icon, its name, and a brief description, making the description section unnecessary. You can collapse the description section by dragging the divider between it and the object list all the way to the bottom of the panel.

To use objects in the library, simply drag them from the Library panel to your interface window. There are a surprising number of objects at your disposal, as shown in Figure 25-13.

In general, objects in the library fall into several general categories:

Menus: This category includes menus and common menu items used in the application's menu bar. Custom menu items can also be used in other menu types, such as pop-up menus.

Toolbars: This category includes toolbars and common toolbar items, as well as a custom toolbar item.

Windows: This category includes standard, textured, and heads-up display windows, auxiliary panels, and a special compound item that will create a window with an auxiliary drawer.

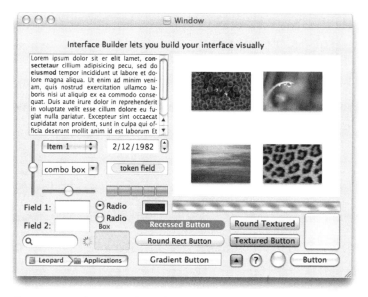

Figure 25-13. The range of interface items available in Interface Builder's Library panel

Controllers: Although nibs are typically associated with the view portion of the model-view-controller pattern, nibs can also contain controller objects. These controllers can be completely self-contained, or can be set to a custom class. A common use for controller objects in the nib is to stand in for collections in the main controller, since the traditional collection classes, such as NSArray, are not compatible with bindings. There is also a special *user defaults controller* to enable binding directly to the preference system.

Buttons: Interface Builder includes a wide variety of button styles. Technically, these are all the same NSButton object in different configurations. Using preconfigured buttons is a convenience, and it also provides consistency with other buttons in the application and system-wide.

Cells: When Application Kit was being developed, computers were much slower than they are today. As such, a lightweight alternative to views was necessary. Cells are lightweight objects contained and used by views and controls throughout Cocoa. Cells resemble common controls, including text fields, combo boxes, level indicators, and image views.

Formatters: Often the raw data behind a text field and what the user expects to see are two different things. The most common examples of this are dates, times, and currency. Formatters can be attached to text areas to alter the way their values are displayed.

Inputs & Values: The most general group in the library, all these objects have in common is that they display or alter some value. This includes several varieties of text field, as well as check boxes, combo boxes, sliders, progress indicators, and the color and image wells.

This group also contains the text view. In its default configuration, a text view resembles a multiline text field embedded in a scroll view. With a few clicks in the Inspector, a text view can be turned into a self-contained word processor, complete with formatting controls.

Data Views: These objects display and allow interaction with data that is too complicated to be dealt with by the objects in the Inputs & Values group. These include tables, outlines, and multicolumn browsers, as used by the Finder. This group also contains some views new in Leopard: the collection view, which displays a grid of other views, and the predicate editor, a visual list of rules like the one used in Mail.

Layout Views: This category includes views that provide layout but don't display data, such as split views, scroll views, tab views, and boxes. There is also a custom view object for adding your own NSView subclasses to the nib.

Special: In addition to the standard interface elements, there are many special views, controllers, and other objects provided by various APIs. Special groups included by default include Core Data, Web Kit, Address Book, Image Kit, PDF Kit, QuickTime Kit, and Quartz Composer. There is also a special Interface Builder template to integrate custom objects into the library.

The Nib

The main window represents the nib itself. While Interface Builder simply calls it Document, I'm going to refer to it as the Nib window. It offers three views: icon, list, and column, as shown in Figure 25-14. With the exception of Cover Flow, these are the same views used by the Finder.

Figure 25-14. Interface Builder's three nib views

Although you can navigate your view hierarchy by clicking around the interface itself, some items can be difficult to select. The Nib window's column view is especially convenient for selecting objects buried deep within subviews, especially as your interface becomes more complicated.

Views are typically contained in other views, but every hierarchy is going to contain an object that is not contained by anything else. The Nib window contains these top-level objects, which are typically windows or panels. The Nib window also contains special components for your convenience:

File's Owner: Although a separate entity in its own right, the nib is not simply floating in space. It's actually owned by your document class, MyDocument. In order to communicate with the document class, objects in the nib talk to the File's Owner object.

Application: Even though your nib has a direct line to its owner, sometimes its objects need to communicate with the application itself. The Application object facilitates that communication.

First Responder: Sometimes an object needs to communicate with whoever is responsible for performing a given action. For times like these, Mac OS X maintains a party line known as the *responder chain*. To put an event on the responder chain, objects in the nib can send them to First Responder.

Controllers: Controller objects are not views, so they can't be contained as subviews. As such, the Nib window contains any controllers in the nib. Indeed, while windows and panels can simply be dragged anywhere on the screen, controller objects must be dragged into the Nib window directly. The one exception is the user defaults controller, which will automatically be added to the Nib window should you bind an object to it.

Most application projects will require visiting Interface Builder at least once, if not several times. Anything that can be done within Interface Builder probably should be, since it will save a lot of code.

Still, as much as Interface Builder can do, chances are good you're still going to have to write some code. Let's close our interface and check out Xcode's editing and debugging features.

Programming in Xcode

In Chapter 24, we talked a lot about abstraction and how it protects developers from changes to the underlying system. Xcode is a big part of that abstraction. By getting as many programmers on Xcode as possible, Apple has been able to introduce things like universal binaries while minimizing extra work for developers. This, even more than the general persnickety nature of professional programmers, explains why Xcode is so configurable.

Since writing code is a form of word processing, many programmers become very comfortable with their editor of choice. As such, Xcode allows you to emulate the color schemes and key bindings of other editors, or to use other editors altogether. All that being said, Xcode includes a very usable editor. Xcode 3 introduces several niceties that make using Xcode's built-in editor all the more compelling.

The Editor

Xcode's editor can be invoked by selecting source code in the sidebar, and then adjusting the split pane. Double-clicking the source code will launch a new editor in its own window. Clicking the editor icon in the toolbar will open the currently selected source code within the main view itself, filling the entire right side, as shown in Figure 25-15.

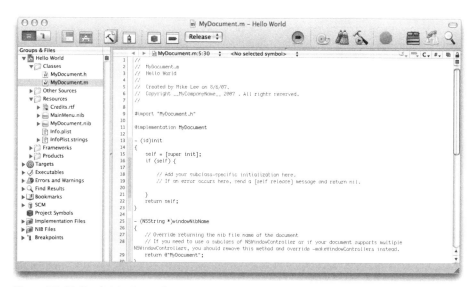

Figure 25-15. Xcode's built-in editor

Xcode's editor is designed to give you as much information as possible, without getting in the way of the task at hand. It accomplishes this by several different means, which we'll describe in the following sections.

Syntax Coloring

As you type, Xcode analyzes the syntax of your code and automatically colors the text based on what it represents. While the colors can be set to your personal preference, by default, keywords are pink, macros are brown, comments are green, numerical constants are blue, and string constants are red.

Since your code remains black, the colors help it stand out. It also helps you keep your strings and comments properly closed. If, for example, you forget to type a closing quotation mark, the bright pink color of your code will both indicate that something's wrong and give you an immediate idea of where the problem is.

Automatic Formatting

While whitespace remains optional in most languages, no programmer I've ever met would consider forgoing it. Xcode will automatically indent your code, and if you like, will even insert closing braces for you. Aside from keeping your code tidy and preventing premature wear on your Tab key, automatic formatting is another trick to help you notice mistakes early. Forgetting a brace or bracket will cause subsequent lines to format improperly.

Autocompletion

Terseness is the enemy of readability, but descriptive variable and function names take longer to type, cramping a coder's mind and hands. Autocompletion combines the best of both worlds. Typing just a few letters can produce descriptive, readable code. Autocompletion further saves time by inserting replaceable argument tokens in method names. Typing Cmd+/ will highlight the next token.

Again, this convenience also prevents errors. Assuming you pick the correct completion, the expanded text will always be correct, while typing out the entire name by hand is prone to human error. It's a good habit to always activate autocompletion, even when you've typed something out, just to make sure you didn't make a mistake.

The autocompletion suggestions list can be activated by pressing Esc. From Xcode's preference window, you can also choose to have autocompletion occur automatically if you pause while typing. Since that could quickly become annoying, the length of the pause is also customizable.

Code Scoping

Xcode 3 introduces a ribbon bar that runs alongside the main code editing window. The ribbon shows varying shades of gray depending on the scope of the code beside it. This gives a quick visual check that all your braces and brackets are properly balanced. If you need a little extra indication, hovering your cursor above the ribbon will extend its shading to the code itself, giving an exact indication of scope.

Code Folding

Xcode 3 also introduces code folding, which collapses a given scope in the editor. For example, a long if statement that doesn't apply to what you're trying to do can be collapsed into a single line. Similarly, functions and sections can be collapsed. The collapsing is syntax aware, and if you use the line numbering bar, the appropriate numbers will be skipped so you don't lose your place.

To fold your code, click the ribbon bar. When code is folded, a disclosure triangle will appear in the ribbon bar. Clicking this disclosure triangle will unfold that section of code.

Navigation

Though they're easy to miss, there are several navigation aids along the top of any editor view (shown in Figure 25-16). These make it easy to move between different areas of a file, or even between files.

Figure 25-16. Navigation controls on the top of Xcode's editor

On the left side there are back and forward buttons, a history menu, which lets you jump between recently edited files, and a function menu. The function menu lists any function, method, or class declarations, as well as defines, typedefs, and pragmas. Selecting an item from the function menu jumps to that item on the page.

You can add navigation aids to your page, which will then show up in the function menu. Perhaps the most common is the mark pragma:

```
#pragma mark This is some text.
```

This will cause any text after mark to show up in the navigation menu, like so:

```
This is some text.
```

As with anything else, you can jump to the mark by selecting it. If you group your methods by functionality, marks are a great way to add subheadings to set off the sections. You can also use the mark pragma to add separators to the menu.

```
#pragma mark -
```

You can add comments to the function menu by beginning them with certain special prefixes. These prefixes and some examples of their use are listed in Table 25-1.

Table 25-1. Xcode's Special Comment Prefixes

Prefix	Example	Result
//???:	//???: Is this really necessary?	???: Is this really necessary?
//!!!:	//!!!: This crashes every 3rd time	!!!: This crashes every 3rd time
//TODO:	//TODO: Implement the edge case	TODO: Implement the edge case
//FIXME:	//FIXME: The image no longer shows	FIXME: The image no longer shows

The editor's upper right has several small buttons. These reveal menus for jumping to bookmarks, breakpoints, includes, and other files that define the current class, including superclasses, subclasses, and categories. There is also a button to jump between the current class's header and implementation files.

> **TIP** You can jump between a class's header and implementation files by typing Option+Cmd+up arrow.

In the upper-right corner, there is a small lock icon. Clicking this icon will lock (or unlock) the current file, preventing accidental edits. Below the lock is a button that will horizontally split the editor into two independent views of the same file. Halves can be further split, and the split can be adjusted by dragging the divider. When an editor is split, a button will appear for rejoining the two halves.

Errors and Warnings

Traditional programming separates writing code from building programs. Although Xcode has always done both, it continued to require leaving the editor to see the results of a build, and then switching back and forth between modes to handle any errors or warnings from the build system. Xcode 3 finally merges these two modes with inline error and warning pop-up bubbles, as shown in Figure 25-17.

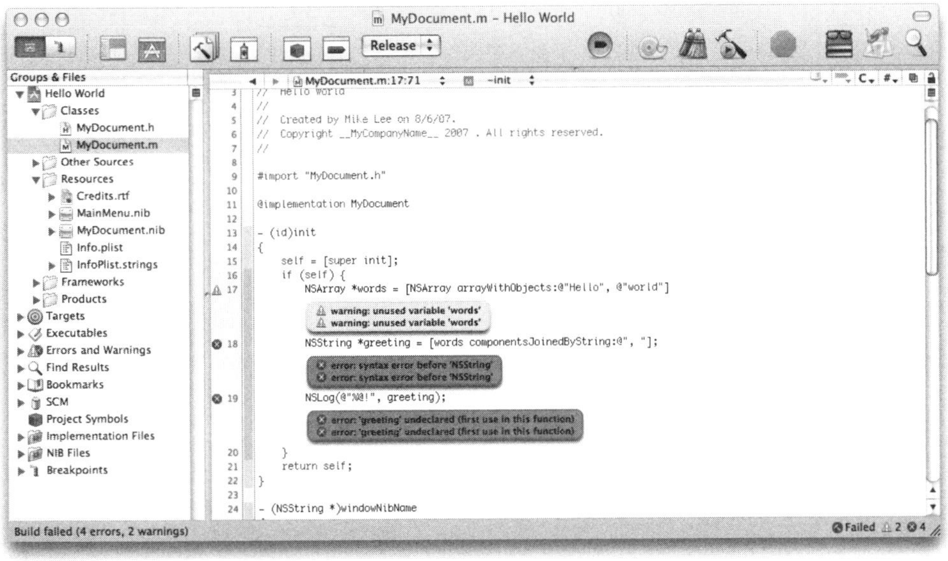

Figure 25-17. Xcode's new inline error and warning bubbles

You can hide or reveal the bubbles by clicking their icons in the gutter. Warning and error bubbles can also be toggled en masse via the View menu. You can also use the keyboard shortcut Cmd+= to move forward through the bubbles and Cmd++ (that's Cmd plus the + key) to move backward.

I cannot overstate what a tremendous improvement this is. The time saved by not having to switch contexts is enormous, especially for multifile edits.

> **NOTE** Using = to move forward and + to move backward seems counterintuitive. Shouldn't + move forward and - move backward? However, given the standard keyboard layout, + is actually Shift+=, so these shortcuts make good sense in practice, even if they seem weird in writing.

Debugging

No matter how good a programmer you are, you're going to have bugs. Whether it's a full-fledged crasher or just an unexpected result, getting to the bottom of things gets exponentially harder as a program grows in size and complexity. When reading the code and logging aren't enough, it's time to pull out the big guns. Xcode not only includes the GNU debugger, GDB, but integrates it into the interface in a way that's much easier than traditional command-line debugging.

Breakpoints

Debuggers, like vampires, cannot enter uninvited. To invite GDB into your program, mark your code with breakpoints. Setting a breakpoint is simple—just click the gutter that runs along the left side of the editor. This will add a blue pointer, representing the breakpoint. To toggle the breakpoint on and off, click it. To remove it, drag it from the gutter and it will vanish in a puff of smoke.

Normally, breakpoints are inactive and the program runs without paying any attention to them. To activate breakpoints, select Activate Breakpoints from the Run menu, or click the appropriate icon in the toolbar.

The normal reaction to a breakpoint is for the program to suspend execution before the line of code that contains the breakpoint. However, this is not the only option. Breakpoints can be set to only break on certain conditions, or to immediately continue after logging something to the console, running other GDB commands, making a sound, or even reading something aloud via text-to-speech. Unlike hard-coded logging, breakpoints can be set, removed, deactivated, moved, and edited on the fly.

Ctrl+clicking or right-clicking the gutter will bring up the breakpoint contextual menu, which has several additional options, including a list of predefined breakpoint behaviors. There is also a Breakpoints window where breakpoints can be set, removed, and edited. To launch the Breakpoints window, select Breakpoints from the Show submenu of the Run menu.

You can also set breakpoints outside your own code. A common trick among programmers is to create a breakpoint named objc_exception_throw. This will cause the program to automatically stop whenever it is about to throw an error. Since unexpected errors lead to crashes, this allows the programmer to examine the state of the program right before everything falls apart.

Xcode's Debugger Interface

When a program stops at a breakpoint, Xcode launches its graphical interface to GDB, as shown in Figure 25-18. From the GDB interface, the program's state and execution can be examined and controlled.

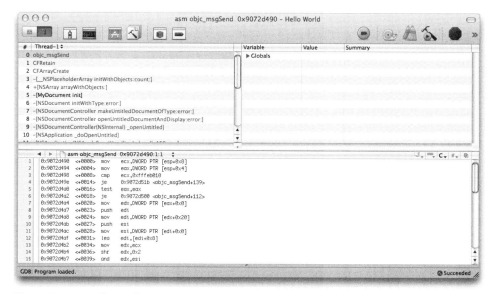

Figure 25-18. Xcode's traditional debugging environment

In the upper left, GDB shows the *stack*. Every time a method or function is called, it is pushed onto the stack. Each item on the stack is called a *stack frame*. The top stack frame is the current method. The next frame in the stack is the method that called it, and so on down the line. If the stack frame contains any variables, they appear to the right. This includes automatic variables, global variables, instance variables, and so on. Each variable's current value is listed beside its name.

Below the stack and variable views is an editor window with the current line of code highlighted. If the code is yours, you will just see a standard editor view. If the code is not yours, GDB will decompile it and show you the assembly.

You can continue executing the code, or you can step over it a line at a time, observing its effects. If the code is yours, you can edit it, but the edits will not take effect until the next build, and if you add or remove lines, the editor's display will no longer match the current line of execution, making its display inaccurate.

Beneath the editor is the GDB console. The console can be revealed by dragging the separator from the bottom of the screen, or by clicking its icon in the toolbar. The console will display any information being logged from the application or your breakpoints. Any errors or other feedback will also show up here.

More than just a message board, the GDB console is fully interactive. You can execute any GDB command. My personal favorite is print object, or po for short. The po command will take any expression and print the return value. In resolving an expression in Objective-C, GDB will send messages to objects. That means you can interact with your objects, change their values, or get information about them. While there are certain limitations to this, it's not unlike the interactive runtime environments enjoyed by users of noncompiled languages like LISP, JavaScript, Ruby, and Python.

Inline Debugging

Xcode's traditional debugging interface is very powerful, but it suffers from the same problem as the old build results system. That is, it interrupts the programming flow by taking you out of the editor and thrusting you into a different environment. Sometimes you don't need quite as much power as the full interface provides. For times like these, Xcode provides a new inline debugging interface, as shown in Figure 25-19.

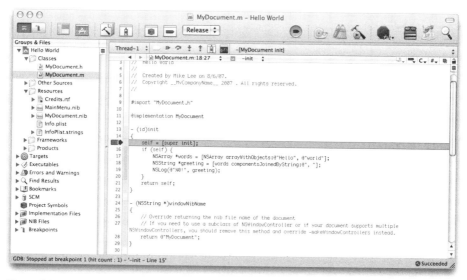

Figure 25-19. Xcode's new inline debugging environment

Since breakpoints are already built into the editor, those don't change. However, new minia-ture versions of the debugger's toolbar icons appear in the editor window when the application is running. These allow you to pause and continue execution, step from line to line, and so forth. The debugging bar also contains the current stack frame. Clicking it will bring up the full stack in a pop-up menu.

Hovering the cursor over a variable will pop up its current value in a tool tip window. By using a series of disclosure buttons, the variable's structure can be examined in depth. Highlight-ing an expression will reveal a small *i* icon. Clicking the icon will execute the expression and show you its return value.

Since the editor still competes with the running application for screen real estate, the inline debugging system includes a small floating heads-up display that will remain visible while you are testing the application. Should you run into a breakpoint that pauses execution, the heads-up display will expand to show the appropriate place in the source code, allowing you to take fur-ther action.

Other Features

That covers the basics of Xcode and Interface Builder, but what I haven't mentioned could fill a book. Xcode 3 in particular introduces a lot of cool new features we just don't have the time or space to cover. Here are a few topics you should look up in Xcode's documentation window:

Refactoring: Project aware find-and-replace and more

Snapshots: A cross between undo and version control

Text Macros: Prewritten code snippets

Templates: Allow you to customize Xcode's project templates

Targets: Allow you to leverage the power of Xcode's build system

Project Settings: Allow you to customize your project's every minute detail

Class Browser: An easy and interesting way to surf the libraries

Data Modeling: Allows you to interact with Core Data using entity relationship diagrams

Other Tools

While most application development takes place in Xcode and Interface Builder, the Developer folder contains many more tools. Some of these are complex applications that form entire devel-opment environments of their own, while others are simple utilities. Some have very serious and specific purposes, while others are just plain fun. Here are a few favorites.

Instruments

The newest member of the Xcode family, Instruments is quickly winning friends in the developer community. It uses an interface that is immediately recognizable to anyone who has used GarageBand. Debugging instruments are arranged into tracks, as shown in Figure 25-20. Several templates are provided, which can be augmented by an extensive library. The Instruments ses-sion can then be hooked into any process and recorded.

Most debugging tools are not useful to the general public, but Instruments is a notable exception. Not only is it simple enough for mere mortals to use, but specific sessions can be saved as templates and sent to users, who can execute them with minimal instructions.

Figure 25-20. Setting up a session in Instruments

Perhaps the most exciting instrument is the UI recorder, which uses the Accessibility framework to record a user's every action, as shown in Figure 25-21. The recording can then be sent back to the developer for analysis.

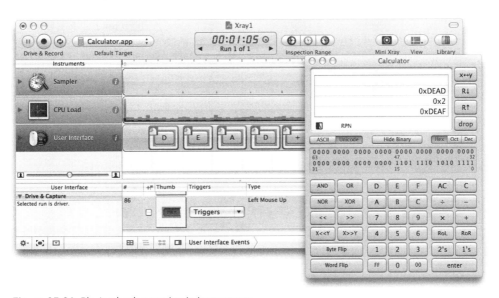

Figure 25-21. Playing back a session in Instruments

The potential of Instruments to change the way bugs are reported cannot be overstated. Imagine you have a problem with your car. Inevitably, when you take the car to the shop, the mechanic won't be able to reproduce it. Cars and software are equally difficult to fix without being able to reproduce the problem.

Now imagine being able to record yourself driving down the street. When you encounter the problem, you take the car to the shop and the mechanic can get into the car and press play. The car would then play back your drive exactly as it occurred. The mechanic could rewind and fast forward, or even pause and disassemble parts of the car frozen in time at the exact moment of the problem.

Once the problem is diagnosed and fixed, it could be played back to confirm that the problem no longer occurs. This is exactly what Instruments does for your applications. Whether you're the programmer who wrote the application, or a user who finds a bug in it, Instruments is very exciting.

Under the hood, Instruments runs on DTrace, an OpenSolaris project included in Leopard that provides probes in the very lowest levels of the machine. Thousands of these probes sit idle, causing no performance drain, waiting for the moment they are activated by masters of the arcane arts wishing to see the details of any process.

While using Instruments fortunately doesn't require grimoires, sacrifices, or learning the D scripting language, this open source engine means that the aforementioned arcane masters can create new instruments and share them with the community. As a further testament to the power of Instruments, several developer tools in Apple's toolbox have been replaced with Instruments templates.

Quartz Composer

Another tool that seems to have been designed by musicians, Quartz Composer is a visual environment for creating code-free graphical programs using a patch metaphor that should be most familiar to aficionados of the electric guitar. Instead of functions, Quartz Composer uses modules called *patches*. Patches take one or more inputs, change them in some way, and produce one or more outputs.

Patches are connected by dragging and dropping virtual cables, not unlike Interface Builder. By connecting the different inputs and outputs, users can create complex compositions, as shown in Figure 25-22. Quartz Composer compositions can be rolled into freestanding programs, used as screen savers, or incorporated into other, larger programs. It's also just a fun way to spend an afternoon.

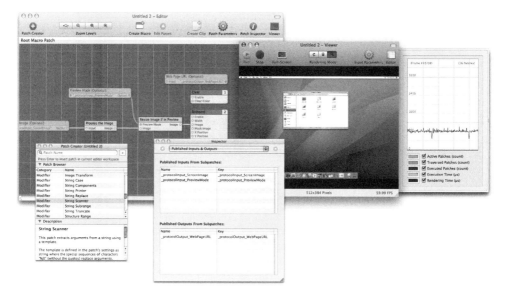

Figure 25-22. Visual programming in Quartz Composer

Dashcode

As the name implies, Dashcode is like Xcode for creating Dashboard widgets. It contains several templates for the most common types of widgets, including countdowns, maps, RSS feeds, gauges, and podcasts. It also includes a drag-and-drop library of common components, and a WYSIWYG editor for customizing your widget, as shown in Figure 25-23.

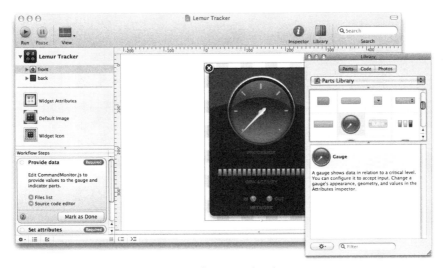

Figure 25-23. Designing a widget's interface in Dashcode

Under the hood, a widget is just a web page with HTML, CSS, and JavaScript code. Dashcode provides a code library of common functionality, as shown in Figure 25-24. Some 90 percent of the widgets out there today could be created in Dashcode without ever having to use the keyboard. That said, Dashcode also provides a solid JavaScript debugging environment, complete with member lists, breakpoints, and an interactive runtime.

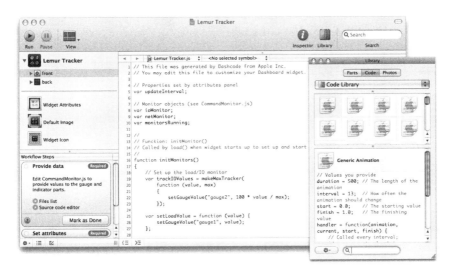

Figure 25-24. Editing a widget's source code in Dashcode

Core Image Fun House

When I explain Core Image filters to people, I just say, "You know, like in Photoshop." When Apple's Phil Schiller debuted Core Image during Steve Jobs's 2004 Worldwide Developer Conference keynote address, he needed something a little more tangible. To that end, some clever Apple engineer whipped up a fun demo called Core Image Fun House, as shown in Figure 25-25. The demo was so popular it was included with the developer tools.

Figure 25-25. Testing a filter stack in Core Image Fun House

Core Image Fun House is a simple application that allows you to load an image, and then apply a stack of Core Image filters. If you ever have to use Core Image, Fun House will save you a lot of time, which you can then waste by continuing to play with Fun House.

FileMerge

At its simplest, FileMerge is like a stereoscopic text editor. It opens two documents and shows you what's the same and what's different, as shown in Figure 25-26. You can select the left or right version of any differences, and save a merged copy.

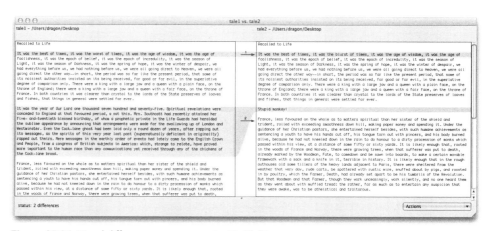

Figure 25-26. Visual difference management with FileMerge

If you're a single-person development house, you'll probably find it marginally useful if you can remember it's there. If, however, you ever find yourself in the kind of conflicted four-way pileup that can occur with multiuser version control, FileMerge might just save your life, your job, and your sanity.

IconComposer

Yeah, you could just set a TIFF file as your project's icon, assuming you're the kind of person who eats peanut butter sandwiches because jelly's too much hassle. Those of us in the know, however, want real Mac OS X icons in the ICNS format. Producing these professional-grade, resolution-independent, multiple-representation icons requires a special tool, as shown in Figure 25-27.

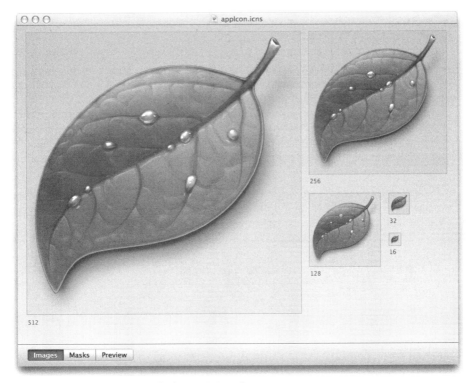

Figure 25-27. Panic's amazing Coda icon in IconComposer

For those who've never used IconComposer, it's a pretty simple process. Usually you create an icon in the largest size in Photoshop or what have you, and then drag it into IconComposer, which will generate smaller versions and alpha masks for you. For situations where your icon is illegible at smaller sizes, you can then create a simplified representation for those sizes, ensuring your icon looks great at any size.

For those who *have* used IconComposer before, the Leopard version is slightly different. Aside from a generally improved look and feel, the new IconComposer adds support for high-resolution, 512 pixel icons, as part of Leopard's move toward resolution independence.

Property List Editor

Property lists, known colloquially as *plists*, are files originally designed for storing properties, which is to say, preferences. When you set the preferences of a program in its preference panel, or via the command line's defaults command, you're editing that application's property list.

However, with the introduction of the XML plist format, these have become a handy way to store standard data structures, such as arrays and dictionaries, in an external, human-readable format. The Property List Editor is a convenient, schema-aware way to create and edit plists. It's also the only way to make heads or tails out of the older, but still useful, binary plist format.

Shark

Every developer wants their application to be fast, but the biggest mistake a programmer can make is writing their code for speed. Fast code is optimized code, and the lower a language is, the more opportunity for optimization there will be. Java offers few chances for optimization compared to C, and C is a snail compared to assembly language.

As fast as they might be, low-level languages are harder to read and take much longer to write. Even if you don't change languages, it's a shame to pick a library or function based on it being faster instead of it being easier. Worse than all of that, all those optimizations that took forever to do will probably end up making the program *slower*.

Why? Because humans are surprisingly bad at guessing where performance bottlenecks are. The only way to know for sure is by using a specialized sampling tool. This tool will watch the application and figure out what it's doing and for how long. Shark (shown in Figure 25-28), which comes with the free developer tools, is one of the best optimization programs available.

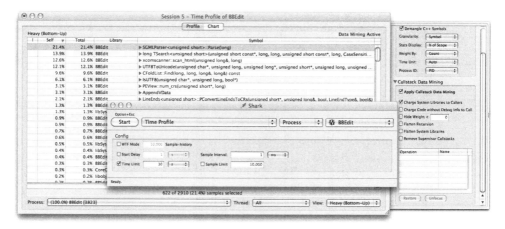

Figure 25-28. Bare Bones's blazing fast BBEdit profiled by Shark

Avoiding blind optimizations makes the development cycle faster, because it lets programmers choose code based on ease of writing and readability. That leaves plenty of time for profiling with Shark, and then pinpointing bottlenecks and performing optimizations only where they will make the biggest difference.

Hard rules are anathema to programmers, but here's one even the most stubborn of hackers should follow: never, ever do something "because it's faster," until you run Shark.

Bug Reporter

Bug Reporter doesn't come with Xcode, but it's one of the most powerful tools available to you as a developer because it allows you to improve Mac OS X itself. The more you use your Mac, the more likely you are to find things about it that annoy you, things that don't work like they're supposed to, or things that Apple could do that would make it even better. These are all kinds of bugs, and they're all filed the same way.

To file a bug, go to Apple Bug Reporter (http://bugreport.apple.com/) and sign in with your Apple ID. Click the New Problem tab and simply fill out the form. Apple provides a link to a description format for those unfamiliar with good bug reporting practices, but here are a few tips for writing good bugs:

- Ninety percent of fixing a bug is reproducing it. Once you can trigger a bug at will, it's relatively easy to find out why it's happening and do something about it. If you notice some unexpected behavior (or lack of behavior), try again to see if it happens again. Try similar things to see if they also trigger the bug. Basically, you want to narrow down the scope of the bug as much as possible, forming a narrative description that an engineer will be able to follow and reproduce, hopefully with the same results.

- Because every system is different, and your system configuration might have something to do with the bug, you should always attach a system profile to your bug reports. To create a system profile, launch the System Profiler application, either by selecting About This Mac from the Apple menu and clicking the More Info... button, or by double-clicking the application icon in /Applications/Utilities. Once in System Profiler, save a profile by selecting Save from the File menu, or by the keyboard shortcut Cmd+S. There is a special button to attach your system profile in the Bug Reporter form.

- If possible, attach some supporting documentation to the bug report as well. It's one thing to describe how to reproduce a bug. It's quite another to demonstrate it directly. If it's a bug in Apple's frameworks, write a trivial test program that shows the bug. If it's a bug in an Apple application, an Instruments recording of the bug being triggered would be a good use of the tools. Zip up any supporting evidence, and attach it using the appropriate button in the Bug Reporter form.

More Information

There's a lot more that could be said about the Mac's development tools. Aside from Xcode's own documentation, there are a few more online resources worth checking out:

Mac OS X Debugging Magic (http://developer.apple.com/technotes/tn2004/tn2124.html): The complexity of Xcode yields all kinds of obscure tips and tricks. Debugging Magic is Apple's documentation of several dozen. My personal favorite is the NSZombie class, which turns your deallocated objects in undead monsters that moan horribly if you try to send them messages. As awful as that sounds, believe you me, when you're trying to track down a crash caused by messaging a floating pointer, NSZombie may just save your brain.

Version Control with Subversion (http://svnbook.red-bean.com/): Subversion is my personal favorite version control program. If you want to learn what version control is, how Subversion works, and every possible detail of making Subversion work for you, you could go to the store and buy this book. Or, you could just read the whole thing for free online.

Solaris Dynamic Tracing Guide (http://docs.sun.com/app/docs/doc/817-6223): This is the ultimate guide to DTrace and the D scripting language. With this knowledge you can create Instruments templates, or just take it straight to the command line. The reading is a bit dry, but if you ever see a demo of what DTrace can do, it's so worth it. This is another real-life book that's available for free online.

Summary

When you bought your Mac, it came loaded with all manner of applications. Some of these you probably use every day. Some of these you not only don't use, but you probably don't even know what they do. The developer tools are the same way. You might use Xcode every day, but never touch Dashcode. You might flex your artistic muscle in Quartz Composer, but never use Interface Builder.

The panoply of developer tools, even more than the bundled applications, is there to ensure that, no matter what kind of development you want to do on your Mac, you'll have the right tools for the job. And as with the Applications folder, if you ever find yourself with some free time, I'd encourage you to open one of these mystery tools and find out what it can do. It might not change your life, but it will definitely expand your mind.

Now that you've spent some time with the tools, you're probably ready to write some code. In the next chapter we'll take a tour of the Objective-C programming language.

## CHAPTER 26

Mac OS X Development: Objective-C

Mac developers have a secret weapon that you're not going to find in the developer tools folder. It's what allows you to do so much with so little, freeing you to think of all the little things that make Mac applications better for your users. It's what makes the Mac the easiest, and yet the most powerful, development platform in the world. It's our language, Objective-C, and it has several advantages:

- An innovative syntax makes it far more readable than any other C-like language.
- It is object-oriented, so projects are organized and understandable.
- It is natively compiled, outperforming any interpreted language.
- It has a dynamic runtime, making it is as flexible as a scripting language.
- It augments, rather than replaces, C, letting programmers get close to the machine if they must.
- It is designed for ease of use, especially Objective-C 2.0.

Objective-C Syntax

Above all else, code must be readable. Elegance, performance, and productivity will follow. The less time you spend figuring out what you wrote yesterday, the more time you'll have to work on it today. The better you can understand what a piece of code is doing, the faster you can add features and fix bugs. If other programmers can understand your code, they can give you constructive criticism, making you and your program better.

The first thing people notice about Objective-C is its syntax. Although standard C syntax remains valid, Objective-C adds new syntax, derived from Smalltalk, the first object-oriented programming language. Many people are at first wary of this alien syntax, but once they get used to it, they can't imagine using anything else. That's because Objective-C is extremely readable. Consider this function call in C syntax:

```
setColor(myObject, 0.4, 0.3, 0.0, 1.0);
```

You can guess it sets a color, but what do those numbers mean? Are those red, green, blue, and alpha? Or alpha, red, green, and blue? Or cyan, yellow, magenta, and black? Or luminosity, hue, and, uh . . . needless to say, most programmers spend a lot of time looking up functions to remember how to write them, let alone ever trying to read them. Now, consider the same thing as an Objective-C method:

```
[myObject setColorWithRed:0.4 green:0.3 blue:0.0 alpha:1.0];
```

It's pretty clear what each of the arguments mean, whether you're writing the code for the first time or you're reading someone else's code three years down the line.

A method's prototype is equally readable, outlining not only the meaning of the method parameters but also their types, the return type, and whether the method belongs to the class or its individual instances:

```
- (void)setColorWithRed:(CGFloat)red green:(CGFloat)green blue:(CGFloat)blue
    alpha:(CGFloat)alpha;
```

This method is of type void, so it returns nothing. All its arguments are of type CGFloat. As detailed in this chapter, CGFloat is a width-neutral floating-point scalar that is converted at compile time into a float on 32-bit systems or a double on 64-bit systems. In this case, the method is an instance method, as indicated by the starting -. Class methods start with +.

This method is, for all intents and purposes, identical to the following function:

```
void setColor(CGFloat red, CGFloat green, CGFloat blue, CGFloat alpha);
```

As would be expected, pointers to objects are represented with the * operator. For example, a class method that took an argument of type NSNumber and returned an NSString would look like this:

```
+ (NSString *)stringWithNumber:(NSNumber *)number;
```

Objective-C Improves C

Although C has its own compiler directives, using the # prefix, Objective-C introduces a new set of its own, using the @ prefix. This is an artifact of Objective-C's origins as a C preprocessor but continues to serve as a convenient sigil of which features are part of Objective-C and which features are just plain C.

Objective-C separates interface from implementation but does so at the preprocessor level with the directives @interface, @implementation, and @end. This allows the use of separate header and implementation files but also allows multiple classes to be defined in a single file, as appropriate.

Finally, many parts of the C standard library have new, upgraded versions in Cocoa that should be used instead. The older C features are still there, and the two can be intermixed.

Memory Management

Object life cycles and interaction complicate memory management, so the entire C memory system has been abstracted. Although malloc and free are still there, they're not used. Instantiation in Objective-C is actually a four-step process: declaration, assignment, allocation, and initialization. These are usually done on one line:

```
NSObject *object = [[NSObject alloc] init];
```

Here it is again, in slow motion:

```
NSObject *object; // Declaration
object = // Assignment
[NSObject alloc]; // Allocation
[object init]; // Initialization
```

> **CAUTION** This is just an example. Apple recommends you never call `alloc` and `init` on two different lines.

Once an object is instantiated, memory management gets a bit more complicated, so we'll have to come back to it. The traditional memory management scheme is discussed in the "Objective-C Memory Management" section. The new garbage collection API is discussed in the "Objective-C 2.0" section.

Scalars

In C, scalars are width specific, but in general, you want to use scalars with the same width as the architecture for which it is compiled. Leopard introduces width-agnostic scalars that resolve into the architecture's native width, as shown in Table 26-1.

Table 26-1. Width-Agnostic Versions of C Scalars

Leopard	C	Description
NSInteger	int, long	Signed integer
NSUInteger	unsigned int, unsigned long	Unsigned integer
CGFloat	float, double	Floating-point number

Logging

C's `printf` and friends have no concept of Objective-C objects, other than that they are pointers. The function `NSLog` has all the tokens and formatting features of `printf` but adds the `%@` token, which calls any object's `description` method.

Strings

In C, a string is just an array of `char` terminated with `NULL`. In Objective-C, you should use the `NSString` class. As an object, `NSString` provides several built-in methods and a mutable subclass, as well as handling things such as Unicode. `NSString` constants can be declared inline with a compiler directive in the form `@"This is a string"`.

Arrays

C arrays are just blocks of memory with the convenience of a bracket operator and pointer arithmetic. There is, for example, absolutely no way of knowing how long an array is, given just the array itself. In Objective-C, use `NSArray`, which, like `NSString`, has convenient methods and a mutable subclass. Beyond this, `NSArray` uses behind-the-scenes optimizations to use the data structure most efficient for the length and operations required.

Booleans

In C, there is no Boolean type. In operations, zero is considered false, while anything other than zero is considered true. Objective-C maintains this convention but adds the scalar type BOOL, whose values are YES and NO.

Equality

Both C and Objective-C use the = operator for assignment and the == operator to represent equality. However, since objects in Objective-C are represented by pointers, comparing two objects with == will not return true unless both are the same pointer.

To work around this problem, NSObject defines the isEqual: method, which compares the objects' hash values. Although it's possible to override isEqual:, it's not easy, because you also have to override hash, and hashing is tricky. Plus, it's often much faster to disqualify equality based on something like the length of a string or the number of objects in an array than it is to generate a hash. As such, many classes have their own equality methods, as shown in Table 26-2.

Table 26-2. Class-Specific Equality Methods

Class	Method
NSArray	isEqualToArray:
NSData	isEqualToData:
NSDate	isEqualToDate:
NSDictionary	isEqualToDictionary:
NSHashTable	isEqualToHashTable:
NSIndexSet	isEqualToIndexSet:
NSNumber	isEqualToNumber:
NSSet	isEqualToSet:
NSValue	isEqualToValue:

It's not as bad as sounds. Aside from the rather obvious pattern, Xcode's autocomplete is there to help. Whenever you type isEqual, instead of typing the colon and the argument, press the Esc key. This will open the autocomplete list, and you can see whether a more specific completion is available.

> **CAUTION** Don't be fooled by isEqualTo:, which is part of AppleScript and should not be used directly.

Void

C functions can return nothing by declaring themselves to be of type void and can accept any pointer by declaring arguments that are pointers to void:

```
void nothingFromSomething(void *anything)
```

Void return types and void pointers can also be used in Objective-C:

```
- (void)nothingFromSomething:(void *)anything;
```

However, any pointer is so rarely what you want, because pointers don't necessarily point to objects. One thing you could do is this:

```
- (void)nothingFromSomeObject:(NSObject *)someObject;
```

Unfortunately, not every object inherits from NSObject, even if most do. There is a middle ground between an NSObject and an object, in the generic sense. As such, Objective-C adds an explicit type, id, that means any object, regardless of inheritance:

```
- (void)nothingFromAnyObject:(id)anyObject;
```

> **NOTE** You're probably wondering why, if id is a pointer, it doesn't use the * operator. In general, primitive types from Objective-C itself don't, while user-level objects from the libraries do. Other types that don't use the * operator include selectors (SEL), implementations (IMP), methods (Method), and the class that represents class itself, Class.

Emptiness

C also uses zero to represent emptiness, generally referred to as NULL. Objective-C has NULL but also has nil, Nil, and NSNull. As opposed to NULL, which means nothing, nil means no object. In other words, nil has type id. The capitalized form Nil means no class, so it has type Class. Finally, NSNull is a singleton object obtained by calling [NSNull null]. This object is an emptiness placeholder for collections such as NSArray, where actual emptiness is not allowed.

All nothing is not created equal, as shown in Table 26-3. NULL, nil, and Nil are all equal to zero, so they are all equal to each other and also the BOOL value NO. However, by convention, sending a message to nil returns nil, so calling [nil isEqual:nil] returns NO, even though it's true. Since NSNull is an object, its pointer is not equal to zero, so its BOOL value is YES, and it never equals anything but itself.

Table 26-3. Boolean Operations on Nothing

Operation	NULL/nil/Nil	NSNull
(BOOL) ____	NO	YES
NULL / nil / Nil== ____	YES	NO
NULL / nil / Nil isEqual: ____	NO	NO
NSNull == ____	NO	YES
NSNull isEqual: ____	NO	YES

Objective-C Memory Management

Because objects can contain other objects and multiple objects might contain the same object, there's a risk of someone freeing an object that someone else is still using. When a program tries to access memory that it no longer owns, the program crashes immediately, as shown in Figure 26-1.

> **NOTE** This section discusses the traditional Objective-C model for manual memory manage-
> ment. Although it is still valid and useful information, Leopard introduces an alternative:
> automatic memory management, also known as *garbage collection*. You can read more about
> garbage collection in the "Objective-C 2.0" section.

To ameliorate this risk, Objective-C uses a system called *retain counting*. Retain counting is
extremely simple, at least in concept. Every object that subclasses NSObject has an instance variable called retainCount. When an object is created by alloc or copy, retainCount is initialized to 1.
Anyone interested in the object sends it a retain message, which increments retainCount. Anyone
no longer interested in the object sends it a release message. When retainCount reaches 0, the
object is freed, as shown in Figure 26-2.

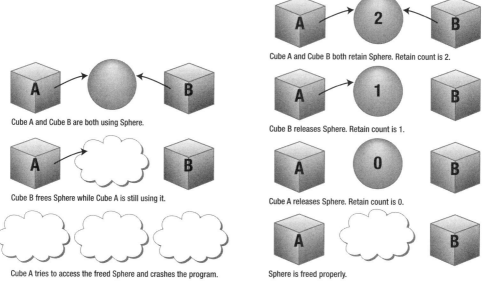

Cube A and Cube B are both using Sphere.

Cube B frees Sphere while Cube A is still using it.

Cube A tries to access the freed Sphere and crashes the program.

Cube A and Cube B both retain Sphere. Retain count is 2.

Cube B releases Sphere. Retain count is 1.

Cube A releases Sphere. Retain count is 0.

Sphere is freed properly.

Figure 26-1. The risk of malloc/free in object-oriented programming

Figure 26-2. Retain counting lets objects be shared safely.

If everyone remembers to retain and release at the appropriate times, this system works perfectly, except for one little problem. What happens if you create an object and then pass it to
someone else, as illustrated in Figure 26-3? The caller can't retain the object until after you
return it. If you release it before you return it, the retain count will drop to zero, and the object
will be freed. If you return it without releasing it, the retain count will never drop to zero, and
the memory will leak!

The solution to this problem is to let a third party retain the object, as shown in Figure 26-4.
That way, the object will not be freed until both the caller and the third party release it. This is
accomplished by sending the object an autorelease message. The system will then place the
object into an autorelease pool. The autorelease pool will keep track of objects on request and
then send them the release message at the bottom of the event loop.

If everyone has released an object before the autorelease pool has released it, the end result
is the same. The object will be freed when the autorelease pool releases it. However, if a lot of
objects are created and released, as in a long loop, the programmer may need to create an inner
autorelease pool and drain it manually. This is easily done; autorelease pools are objects that are
instances of NSAutoreleasePool.

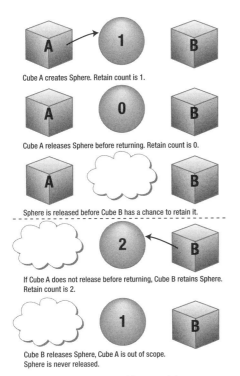

Cube A creates Sphere. Retain count is 1.

Cube A releases Sphere before returning. Retain count is 0.

Sphere is released before Cube B has a chance to retain it.

If Cube A does not release before returning, Cube B retains Sphere. Retain count is 2.

Cube B releases Sphere, Cube A is out of scope.
Sphere is never released.

Figure 26-3. It is impossible to safely return a new object using retain counts alone.

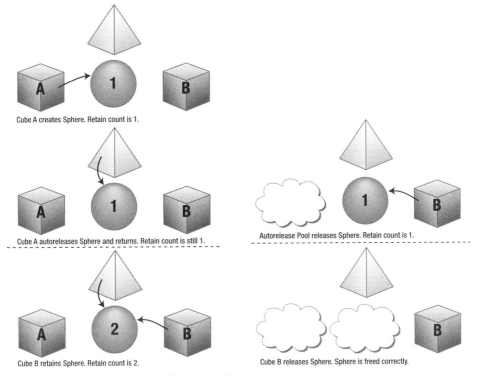

Cube A creates Sphere. Retain count is 1.

Cube A autoreleases Sphere and returns. Retain count is still 1.

Autorelease Pool releases Sphere. Retain count is 1.

Cube B retains Sphere. Retain count is 2.

Cube B releases Sphere. Sphere is freed correctly.

Figure 26-4. An autorelease pool allows safe object creation.

Object-Oriented Programming with Objective-C

Projects written with procedural languages, such as C, become very difficult to understand as they grow larger. Object-oriented programming languages, such as Objective-C, offer a way to organize code into structured units called *classes*. From a C perspective, a class is like a struct, a typedef, and a library of functions all rolled into one. An object is an individual instance of a class.

Other than that broad review, the tenets of object-oriented programming are beyond the scope of this book. Fortunately, it's something most developers should already be familiar with. What's important to the topic at hand are the ways Objective-C implements those tenets and the advantages Objective-C offers, compared to other object-oriented languages.

Declaring an Interface

Let's look at the header of a simple Objective-C class:

```
#import <Cocoa/Cocoa.h>

@interface BMPerson : NSObject {
    NSString *name;
    NSUInteger age;
}

+ (BMPerson *)personWithName:(NSString *)aName age:(NSUInteger)anAge;
- (NSString *)name;
- (void)setName:(NSString *)aName;
- (NSUInteger)age;
- (void)setAge:(NSUInteger)anAge;

@end
```

The first thing you need to do is import your application frameworks. For convenience, you can just import the entirety of Cocoa:

```
#import <Cocoa/Cocoa.h>
```

The #import directive is an improved version of C's #include directive that will add the header files only if they have not already been defined.

You begin the interface with the declaration @interface, name the class BMPerson, and use the : operator to set its superclass to NSObject:

```
@interface BMPerson : NSObject {
```

> **NOTE** Objective-C does not use namespaces, so class names start with a (usually two-letter) prefix to reduce the chance of overlap. Since we're going beyond the manual, we'll go with BM, but you should choose something appropriate, such as your initials, the initials of your company, or something germaine to your project.

The brace opens the composition section, where we declare instance variables, also known as *ivars*. We can use object types by declaring a pointer to the type.

```
NSString *name;
```

We can also use scalars by simple declaration:

```
NSUInteger age;
```

Notice that all lines of code end with a semicolon, whitespace is ignored, and scope is opened and closed with curly braces.

Below the composition section, we declare class and instance methods. We start with a common type of class method, a factory method. This is a convenient shortcut in the allocation and instantiation process:

```
+ (BMPerson *)personWithName:(NSString *)aName age:(NSUInteger)anAge;
```

Note that, as a class method, its declaration begins with +.

Following the class methods, we declare instance methods. These begin with - and follow the same form as our class method:

```
- (NSString *)name;
- (void)setName:(NSString *)aName;
- (NSUInteger)age;
- (void)setAge:(NSUInteger)anAge;
```

Finally, you end the interface with @end and save the file following the traditional format: the class name as the file name and the file extension h, indicating this is a header file.

> **NOTE** Although a class's interface typically goes in a header file and a class's implementation typically goes in an implementation file, this is by no means necessary. For more about the organization of Objective-C classes, read about *categories* in the "Objective-C Dynamic Runtime" section.

Implementing the Class

The implementation of the class looks like this:

```
#import "BMPerson.h"

@implementation BMPerson

+ (BMPerson *)personWithName:(NSString *)aName age:(NSUInteger)anAge;
{
    BMPerson *newPerson = [[self alloc] init];

    [newPerson setName:aName];
    [newPerson setAge:anAge];

    return [newPerson autorelease];
}

- (id)init;
{
    if (![super init])
        return nil;

    name = nil;

    return self;
}
```

```objc
- (void)dealloc;
{
    [name release];
    name = nil;

    [super dealloc];
}

- (NSString *)name;
{
    return name;
}

- (void)setName:(NSString *)aName;
{
    if (name == aName)
        return;

    [name release];
    name = [aName retain];
}

- (NSUInteger)age;
{
    return age;
}

- (void)setAge:(NSUInteger)anAge;
{
    age = anAge;
}

@end
```

As with the interface, you start by importing:

```objc
#import "BMPerson.h"
```

If you recall, you imported the Cocoa framework differently:

```objc
#import <Cocoa/Cocoa.h>
```

Why the change in syntax? When importing system frameworks, use the path notation and the angle brackets. When importing your own headers, use the quote notation.

Incidentally, you don't have to import Cocoa into this implementation, because the header has already imported it. Importing a header also imports any headers it has imported. As you can imagine, that gets complicated quickly, which is why we use #import and not #include.

You open the implementation with the @implementation directive and the name of the class:

```objc
@implementation BMPerson
```

You don't have to rename the superclass or redeclare the instance variables, so you can move right into methods.

Class Methods

The methods are opened with the same declaration as in the header:

```
+ (BMPerson *)personWithName:(NSString *)aName age:(NSUInteger)anAge;
```

That makes starting an implementation as easy as copying and pasting. Technically, method declarations in the implementation section don't require semicolons, but the compiler conveniently ignores them.

The factory method has a simple implementation. You allocate a new person, set its name and age, and return it. The body of a method begins and ends with curly braces:

```
{
    BMPerson *newPerson = [[self alloc] init];

    [newPerson setName:aName];
    [newPerson setAge:anAge];

    return [newPerson autorelease];
}
```

This is just a convenient shortcut for doing the same thing in code, but there are a few subtle differences that are worth noting.

If you actually instantiated a BMPerson externally, you would do so by sending alloc to the class:

```
BMPerson *newPerson = [[BMPerson alloc] init];
```

From within the class method, however, you send the message to self.

Behind the scenes, every method in Objective-C is converted into a function. When you send a message to an object, the messaging system looks up the appropriate function and calls it. Along with the arguments you provided in the message, a few more arguments are slipped in. The first "secret" argument is a pointer to the object on which the function is being called. That argument's name is self.

As such, whenever an object needs to refer to itself, such as to call one of its own methods, it simply sends a message to self. In an instance method, self refers to the instance, which is to say, the object. Six different objects will get six different results by sending the same message to self. In a class method, self refers to the class. Therefore, when a class calls its own class method, such as alloc, it sends a message to itself, using self. It's a fine point, but one to keep in mind.

> **NOTE** Objects also have a secret ivar called isa that refers to its class. Class methods can therefore be called by sending a message to isa. However, runtime considerations make calling isa a gamble, so it's better to get your class indirectly, via [self class].

After setting the name and age that were passed in, you return the new object with the standard C keyword return. Because you created it, you need to release it, but because you're returning it, you send it an autorelease message, as detailed in the previous section on memory management.

To use this method in code, you send a message to the class:

```
BMPerson *worldsToughestProgrammer = [BMPerson personWithName:@"Mike Lee" age:31];
```

This is equivalent to creating an instance on your own, using almost the same code as you used to implement the method.

```
BMPerson *worldsToughestProgrammer = [[BMPerson alloc] init];
[newPerson setName:@"Mike Lee"];
[newPerson setAge:31];
```

The only difference, of course, is that the factory method produces an autoreleased instance, whereas the manually allocated method does not.

> **NOTE** Why bother with factory methods? There are some edge cases where they are useful. Singleton optimizations are one. Teaching people how to write class methods is another. Mostly, though, it's just a way to save three lines of code. For something you aren't using much, it isn't worth the hassle, but if it's something you use a lot, the savings add up. The foundation classes, such as NSString and NSArray, are lousy with factory methods. If you multiply three lines of code by the number of times you instantiate NSArray, we're talking thousands of lines of code. That is why it's commonly said that Objective-C programmers *hate* code.

Init and Dealloc

With the class methods implemented, it's time to fill out the instance methods. The first method declaration you come to looks unfamiliar:

```
- (id)init;
```

A quick visit to the interface reveals no such declaration. Veterans of object-oriented programming are sagely nodding right about now. The init method was inherited from the superclass, NSObject.

> **TIP** In Xcode, you can switch between a class's interface and its implementation with the keystroke Cmd+up arrow.

During the instantiation of an object, you actually call two methods. The first, alloc, is sent to the class you want to instantiate. This returns an object—you hope an instance of the class you just called. However, the object is in a dangerous state. Its instance variables have been declared, but any pointers are not actually pointing to anything. Dereferencing or messaging a floating pointer will cause any program to immediately crash. As such, you immediately call the new object's instance method, init.

If a superclass implements a method, you can call the method on any subclass, and the superclass's implementation will be found and executed. However, if that subclass also implements the method, the subclass's implementation will be used instead. In object-oriented programming, you say that the subclass's implementation *overrides* the superclass's implementation.

Sometimes that's what you want, but sometimes you just want to add something to the superclass's method, rather than replacing it outright. To accomplish this, you call the superclass's implementation from within your own. You do this by sending a message to the superclass via the keyword super.

In Objective-C, as with any language, there are implied contracts. For example, nothing in the language is going to force you to call init right after alloc. You just have to do it to make things work right. Another implied contract is that if you override init, you have to call super, and if that call fails for some reason, you have to return nil. Since nil is equal to the Boolean NO, we can do so with a simple if statement.

```
if (![super init])
    return nil;
```

Only then are you safe to do your own initialization, setting your name pointer safely to nil:

```
name = nil;
```

With that accomplished, you can return your newly instantiated self to be assigned to the waiting pointer:

```
return self;
```

Another way to go about this would have been to create an init method that lets the caller pass in the name and age values in one line, not unlike the factory method example earlier:

```
- (id)initWithName:(NSString *)aName age:(NSNumber)anAge;
{
    if (![super init])
        return nil;

    [self setName:aName];
    [self setAge:anAge];

    return self;
}
```

A new person could then be initialized with custom values:

```
[[BMPerson alloc] initWithName:@"Mike Lee" age:31];
```

Since someone might still call init, it still has to be implemented, but now it can just call the new method:

```
- (id)init;
{
    return [self initWithName:nil age:0];
}
```

Every class will typically have one init method to which all other init methods refer. This is called the *designated initializer*. Subclasses of that class should call the designated initializer, rather than just calling init. The bad news is, you usually can't tell which is the designated initializer without checking the documentation. The good news is, Objective-C doesn't rely on subclassing as much as other languages do, so it's less of a problem in practice.

> **NOTE** Since this new initializer is not declared in the superclass, you would also have to add its declaration to the header file.

As objects are born, so must they die. Just as init gives your objects a chance to get things in order before being used, dealloc gives them a chance to get their affairs in order before they're sent off to that big memory heap in the sky.

```
- (void)dealloc;
{
    [name release];
    name = nil;

    [super dealloc];
}
```

In our case, we've got a pointer, name, that needs to be released. Whenever releasing an object in dealloc, or anywhere else, set the pointer to nil. You never know what might happen, especially in the crazy world of multithreaded, multiprocessor computing. You don't want to leave a dangling pointer around for someone to call and crash.

As with `init`, you're overriding your superclass's implementation. Sending a `dealloc` message to `super` will give everyone in the inheritance tree a chance to take care of their final business as well. With `init`, we typically call `super` first. In `dealloc`, we call `super` last.

With the inherited hassle of memory management out of the way, you can finally get back to all those instance methods you declared.

Instance Methods

The whole point of object-oriented programming is to transfer responsibility to your objects. Whereas a functional programmer might say, "I am going to do something with this," an object-oriented programmer would say, "I am going to ask this to do something." The tasks we can ask our objects to do are their instance methods.

The most common instance methods are for directly accessing and mutating an object's instance variables. In technical terms, we call these methods *accessors* and *mutators*, but Apple prefers the more colloquial *setters* and *getters*. Whatever you call them, these methods follow a standard pattern.

```
- (NSString *)name;
- (void)setName:(NSString *)aName;
```

In Objective-C, a getter has the same name and return type as the ivar it's accessing and takes no arguments. The setter adds the prefix set to the name, takes one argument of the ivar's type, and returns nothing. For the special case of Boolean ivars, the getter may use the prefix is. For example, calling isHidden would access the ivar hidden.

> **NOTE** Some languages will precede the ivar name with the word get, but in Objective-C, you use that pattern for something else.

At its simplest, a getter just returns the value of the ivar:

```
- (NSString *)name;
{
    return name;
}
```

Because of memory management, setters are a bit more complicated:

```
- (void)setName:(NSString *)aName;
{
    if (name == aName)
        return;

    [name release];
    name = [aName retain];
}
```

The first thing you'll notice is a setter's argument cannot have the same name as its ivar. Looking at the first line explains why that is:

```
if (name == aName)
```

If you had given the argument the same name, you'd end up with this:

```
if (name == name)
```

Wouldn't that be confusing?

NOTE In Java, you *can* override ivars with arguments, because you can distinguish them with the keyword this. So, you could say this.name == name. Objective-C doesn't have this nicety (or hassle, depending on your point of view).

In a way, setters are written backward. You're setting the value of the pointer to a new object, which you will retain:

```
name = [aName retain];
```

Doing so will remove your ability to reach the old object, so you must first release it:

```
[name release];
```

However, if the old object and the new object are the same, you might end up causing the object to be freed, which would cause a crash when you tried to use it. As such, before you can do any of this, you need to check that the two objects are, in fact, not the same, and bail out if they are:

```
if (name == aName)
    return;
```

With all the fuss, it seems like it would be a lot easier to just access the variables directly and not hassle with calling methods. However, there's a good reason not to; it's a violation of *encapsulation*.

Encapsulation is an important part of object-oriented programming. It states that implementation details should always be hidden. This prevents objects from becoming entangled and making things just as complicated as they were with procedural programming. It also protects programmers from implementation changes.

For example, consider the setter for age:

```
- (void)setAge:(NSUInteger)anAge;
{
        age = anAge;
}
```

Right now it's very simple. It takes a scalar type rather than a pointer, so we don't even have to worry about memory management. What if you later decide that blithely setting this value is a security risk because of integer overflow exploits? To protect against that, you add some validation logic:

```
- (void)setAge:(NSUInteger)anAge;
{
    if (anAge > 0 && anAge < 100)
        age = anAge;
}
```

If you've been good and respected encapsulation, your work is done. If you've been bad and have been setting the variable directly, you're going to have a lot of implementation work ahead of you. That's why it's always a good idea to use setters and getters, even from within the object itself.

NOTE In the section on Objective-C 2.0, you'll read about Leopard's new property syntax, which makes writing setters and getters yesterday's hassle.

Protocols

Unlike C++, Objective-C uses a single inheritance model by which a class can inherit only from a single superclass. To overcome the restrictions posed by single inheritance while adding a different sort of flexibility, Objective-C classes may inherit additional interface by conforming to any number of protocols.

A *protocol* is like a class, except it does not contain variables or provide any implementation. Rather, it simply defines an interface, which conforming classes are expected to implement. This same concept was later used in Java but renamed *interfaces*.

Classes can then *comply* with a protocol, which tells the compiler they implement any required methods. For example, some objects can be copied by simply sending them the message copy. You don't really care what class the object is; you just care that it implements the appropriate method. To this end, Foundation defines a protocol, NSCopying. If your BMPerson class implements the copy method, you can add the protocol to your class declaration:

```
@interface BMPerson : NSObject <NSCopying>
```

Nothing else in the interface changes, but now you are expected to implement the copy method.

> **NOTE** Technically when you call - (id)copy, you are calling - (id)copyWithZone:(NSZone *)zone with a default value for zone. Zone is largely an obsolete concept, but the upshot is that conforming to NSCopying requires implementing copyWithZone: instead of copy.

You can also define your own protocols. Say you wanted a general interface for providing a unique ID. You start by defining your protocol, much as you would a class:

```
@protocol BMIdentifying
    - (NSString *)uniqueIDString;
@end
```

If BMPerson implements uniqueIDString, you can add that to the protocol list:

```
@interface BMPerson : NSObject <NSCopying, BMIdentifying>
```

Later in your design, you might want to accept some object but need to make sure it complies with your BMIdentifying protocol. You can write method signatures that use protocols as types:

```
- (void)addIdentifyingObject:(id <BMIdentifying>)object;
```

To call this method, you can similarly cast to the protocol:

```
[listOfIdentifyingObjects addIdentifyingObject:(id <BMIdentifying>)object];
```

Cocoa uses formal and informal protocols for several class-agnostic patterns:

Plug-ins: By creating a plug-in architecture, a programmer can open their application to third-party development. For such an architecture to work, the programmer must define an interface. By using protocols, plug-in writers are given total design freedom, as long as they implement the necessary methods.

Delegates and data sources: To be reusable, an object's behavior and content must be configurable. Languages such as Java rely heavily on subclassing to accomplish this. However, this is often too big a tool for the job. The delegate and data source patterns leave behavioral and content decisions to another object. By implementing the necessary methods, programmers can control these classes, without the trouble of subclassing.

Notifications: Often used in conjunction with the delegate pattern, notifications are methods called before and after certain actions occur. By implementing those methods, programmers can synchronize other objects' actions based on what the notifying class is doing. For example, a `didReceiveData` notification might trigger interested objects to act on that data.

Fast enumeration: Objective-C 2.0 introduces a unified, terse, and highly optimized `for...in` loop. Collections become eligible for fast enumeration by conforming to the `NSFastEnumeration` protocol. This makes it easy to add this functionality to existing collection types and lets programmers use fast enumeration with their own collection classes. We discuss fast enumeration in more detail in the "Objective-C 2.0" section.

Key-value coding and key-value observing: In addition to the standard practice of calling explicit methods, objects' properties can be accessed by name. Changes to properties can also be observed, maintaining interobject dependencies with little or no code. We discuss these in more detail in the "Objective-C Runtime" section.

Scripting: To be scriptable, applications require certain additional methods to be implemented. There are also a slew of optional methods that programmers can use to deal with the inherent impedance mismatch between how they use their objects and how a scripter might use them.

Accessibility: By complying with accessibility protocols, applications can not only be used by disabled users but can also participate in user interface scripting, as used by AppleScript, Instruments, and a slew of third-party applications.

Animation: Like fast enumeration, Cocoa's Core Animation wrappings are implemented by protocol, minimizing the need to change existing frameworks while extending usability to developers' own classes.

Spelling: Among the more renowned features of Mac OS X is systemwide spelling and grammar checking. By implementing the spelling protocols, developers can incorporate these into their own applications, customizing behaviors as necessary.

Locking: The locking protocol simply defines a standard interface for thread-safe classes to let themselves be locked and unlocked.

Pasteboard operations: Drag and drop and copy and paste are two sides of the same coin. Dating back to the very first Macintosh, the pasteboard is at the very heart of a modern operating system. Something so basic obviously rises above any class hierarchy. Thus, formal and informal protocols define all parts of a pasteboard operation, from providing data to receiving data to the format of the data itself.

NOTE Prior to Leopard, all protocol methods were required. The interface that was considered optional was implemented as an *informal protocol*, which was really just a category (which we'll get to) on `NSObject`. Objective-C 2.0 introduces the compiler directives `@optional` and `@required`, which eliminate the need for informal protocols.

Objective-C Dynamic Runtime

Simply by being object-oriented, Objective-C is quite dynamic. *Polymorphism*, the ability of different objects to respond to the same message in different ways, follows naturally from the shared interfaces provided by inheritance and protocols. There are limits to the dynamism offered by object-oriented programming, however.

In object-oriented languages such as Java and C++, once classes are compiled, they cease to be dynamic. You can subclass them and do what you like with your subclasses, but you can't change them. Your programming environment is never fully dynamic, because all any programmer can do is create and play in a dynamic sandbox surrounding a static core.

Objective-C doesn't have any such restrictions. Remember that Objective-C is only a very thin layer on top of C. Except for a few compiler directives, notable by their @ prefix, very little above plain C is actually occurring at compile time. With Objective-C, the magic happens at runtime. That means much of what the code is doing is not locked down until right before it happens, and therein lies tremendous power.

At the core of this is Objective-C's unusual messaging syntax. It's not just a readable replacement for dot syntax; it's actually an indirection provided by the runtime that completely separates the act of calling a method from the actual execution of that method.

Consider the previous example:

```
[myObject setColorWithRed:0.4 green:0.3 blue:0.0 alpha:1.0];
```

In the parlance of Objective-C, we call myObject the *receiver* and setColorWithRed:0.4 green:0.3 blue:0.0 alpha:1.0 the *message*. Behind the scenes, the runtime separates the message into a *method signature* and an array of arguments.

Every method signature is resolved into a *selector*, which is represented by the data type SEL. The runtime dynamically pairs selectors with a method *implementation*, represented by the data type IMP. These are tangible data types and can be treated as such. They can be created, examined, changed, and passed around.

> **NOTE** A method's name is the method declaration, including the colons, but without the argument names or types. So, the name of the method being called in setColorWithRed:0.4 green:0.3 blue:0.0 alpha:1.0 is setColorWithRed:green:blue:alpha:.

Categories

Even if it were possible for the designers of a library to consider every possible method programmers might need, it would still be a bad idea. Imagine how hard it would be to use a basic class such as NSString if it implemented every possible method. Even if you managed to page through the thousands of available methods to find the one you need, performance would be awful.

Object-oriented programming gives you the ability to extend existing classes by subclassing them and adding the functionality you need. For example, NSString provides a method that takes a string and appends it to the receiver.

```
NSString *greeting = @"Hello";
greeting = [greeting stringByAppendingString:@", world!"];
NSLog(greeting);
```

```
Hello, world!
```

What if you wanted to prepend a string? That is, append it before the receiver? You can't; there's no such method. However, you could subclass NSString, creating BMString:

```
#import <Cocoa/Cocoa.h>

@interface BMString : NSString
- (NSString *)stringByPrependingString:(NSString *)aString;
@end
```

```
@implementation BMString

- (NSString *)stringByPrependingString:(NSString *)aString;
{
    return [aString stringByAppendingString:self];
}

@end
```

Now you can do what you want:

```
BMString *greeting = [BMString stringWithString:@", world!"];
greeting = [greeting stringByPrependingString:@"Hello"];
NSLog(greeting);
```

```
*** initialization method -initWithCharactersNoCopy:length:freeWhenDone: cannot
be sent to an abstract object of class BMString: Create a concrete instance!
```

Or perhaps not. It turns out there's a lot more to subclassing NSString than meets the eye. For one thing, inheritance is not perfect. Private members, for example, are not inherited. Furthermore, NSString is not an actual class, but rather, it's simply the interface to a *class cluster*, an implementation detail you've been protected from until now.

The NSString documentation provides instructions on subclassing NSString. We'll sum it up for you: it's a lot of work for just adding a simple method. Even if you managed to do all that work, you'd still have to constantly remember to use your custom subclass instead of the standard NSString.

Objective-C Dynamic Runtime to the rescue! Since classes, method signatures, and method implementations are all addressable data, you should be able to create a new method and add it to the NSString class. In fact, this operation is so common, Objective-C gives you a convenient shortcut for doing so: categories.

Categories are additional methods defined on an existing class. As an organizational tool, they let you arrange your code in a way that best fits your needs, and not the needs of the machine. For example, a very large class can be broken into several files, with a separate header for different areas of functionality.

Conversely, functionality can be added to several classes at once. For example, a new feature that affects multiple classes could be implemented in a single file, leaving the original class files untouched. Anyone wanting to use the new features needs to import only the new header, while older classes can simply ignore it.

> **NOTE** Categories are a lot like protocols, except they add implementation in addition to interface. As noted, before Leopard introduced optional protocol methods, *informal protocols* were implemented as categories.

Categories are useful for far more than organization. Categories can be defined on any class, including classes that you did not write and that have already been compiled. That means, if you want to add functionality to a class such as NSString, there's no need to hassle with trying to subclass it. You can simply add the functionality to NSString itself. We declare a category using parentheses after the base class name:

```
#import <Cocoa/Cocoa.h>

@interface NSString (BMString)
- (NSString *)stringByPrependingString:(NSString *)aString;
@end
```

```
@implementation NSString (BMString)

- (NSString *)stringByPrependingString:(NSString *)aString;
{
    return [aString stringByAppendingString:self];
}

@end
```

Now prepending a string works as expected:

```
NSString *greeting = @", world!";
greeting = [greeting stringByPrependingString:@"Hello"];
NSLog(greeting);
```

```
Hello, world!
```

Unlike a subclass, we have access to everything in the NSString class, including private members. Indeed, when you're writing a category, the hardest thing to remember is that you're inside the class you're categorizing. Try not to let the power go to your head, or the next section will really blow your mind.

Method Swizzling

It's one thing to add methods to a class, but the inheritance model offers something categories don't. Namely, a subclass can override a superclass's implementation. That is, it doesn't just add behavior; it can change behavior. Objective-C lets you do this and more. Since method implementations are data, you can swap any class's implementation with your own, a trick called *swizzling*.

For example, consider the description method, as implemented by NSXMLNode. It just spits out raw XML, without any whitespace. I'll show you what I mean. Consider the following snippet of XML, a bit of syndicated web content created by iWeb:

```
<?xml version="1.0" encoding="utf-8"?>
<rss version="2.0">
    <channel>
        <title>My Blog</title>
        <link>http://www.worldofkevin.com/Site/Blog/Blog.html</link>
        <description>Welcome to my blog: Alit, Enit, Laore, Eros Vel, Exer Dolorer,
Niam Lut.</description>
        <generator>iWeb 1.1.2</generator>
        <image>
            <url>http://www.worldofkevin.com/Site/Blog/Blog_files/200206373-3-a.png
</url>
            <title>My Blog</title>
            <link>http://www.worldofkevin.com/Site/Blog/Blog.html</link>
        </image>
        <item>
            <title>Red Vines: the perfect super food</title>
            <link>http://www.worldofkevin.com/Site/Blog/88DD8356-E484-44DD-9419-
AE9F936E8BAD.html</link>
            <guid>http://www.worldofkevin.com/Site/Blog/88DD8356-E484-44DD-9419-
AE9F936E8BAD.html</guid>
            <pubDate>Mon, 20 Aug 2007 10:48:11 -0700</pubDate>
            <description>&lt;a href='http://www.worldofkevin.com/Site/Blog/
88DD8356-E484-44DD-9419-AE9F936E8BAD_files/FD004359-1.jpg'>&lt;img
```

```
src='http://www.worldofkevin.com/Site/Blog/Images/FD004359-1.jpg'
style='float:left; padding-right:10px; padding-bottom:10px; width:109px;
height:79px;'/>&lt;/a>Eliquatuero dip numsan vent lam, conum facillum init lut
doloreet ullametuero od tet adit, commod tatummy feug tiam velit praese exer aute
enit alit, veliqua modit dolorer commod niam onul laore. Uptat prat lut lut
iriliquat, quis alisl irilit am irillum at niam zzrit, verosto consequ ismodit
irius</description>
                <enclosure url="http://www.worldofkevin.com/Site/Blog/88DD8356-E484-
44DD-9419-AE9F936E8BAD_files/FD004359-1.jpg" length="101865" type="image/jpg">
</enclosure>
        </item>
    </channel>
</rss>
```

If you speak XML, it's pretty easy to see what's going on here, because the XML tags are on separate lines and indented to show what goes where. However, if we tried to log this node, NSLog would simply call [NSXMLNode description] behind the scenes and produce an unreadable mess.

```
NSXMLNode *xmlNode;
// ... load the XML document
NSLog(@"Current node: %@", xmlNode);
```

```
Current node: <?xml version="1.0" encoding="utf-8"?><rss version="2.0"><channel><t
itle>My Blog</title><link>http://www.worldofkevin.com/Site/Blog/Blog.html</link><d
escription>Welcome to my blog: Alit, Enit, Laore, Eros Vel, Exer Dolorer, Niam Lut
.</description><generator>iWeb 1.1.2</generator><image><url>http://www.worldofkevi
n.com/Site/Blog/Blog_files/200206373-3-a.png</url><title>My Blog</title><link>http
://www.worldofkevin.com/Site/Blog/Blog.html</link></image><item><title>Red Vines:
the perfect super food</title><link>http://www.worldofkevin.com/Site/Blog/88DD8356
-E484-44DD-9419-AE9F936E8BAD.html</link><guid>http://www.worldofkevin.com/Site/Blo
g/88DD8356-E484-44DD-9419-AE9F936E8BAD.html</guid><pubDate>Mon, 20 Aug 2007 10:48:
11 -0700</pubDate><description>&lt;a href='http://www.worldofkevin.com/Site/Blog/8
8DD8356-E484-44DD-9419-AE9F936E8BAD_files/FD004359-1.jpg'>&lt;img src='http://www.
worldofkevin.com/Site/Blog/Images/FD004359-1.jpg' style='float:left; padding-right
:10px; padding-bottom:10px; width:109px; height:79px;'/>&lt;/a>Eliquatuero dip num
san vent lam, conum facillum init lut doloreet ullametuero od tet adit, commod tat
ummy feug tiam velit praese exer aute enit alit, veliqua modit dolorer commod niam
onul laore. Uptat prat lut lut iriliquat, quis alisl irilit am irillum at niam zzr
it, verosto consequ ismodit irius</description><enclosure url="http://www.worldofk
evin.com/Site/Blog/88DD8356-E484-44DD-9419-AE9F936E8BAD_files/FD004359-1.jpg" leng
th="101865" type="image/jpg"></enclosure></item></channel></rss>
```

Yuck! All the whitespace is gone, and everything is just run together. It's possible, by other means, to output a node using *pretty printing* to make it more readable, but I always forget. It would be a lot more convenient if description would always apply pretty printing.

To accomplish this, we'll create a category on NSXMLNode that defines a new method and then swap that method's implementation with the existing one:

```
#import <Cocoa/Cocoa.h>
#import <objc/runtime.h>

@interface NSXMLNode (BMPrettyDescriptions)
- (NSString *)prettyDescription;
@end

@implementation NSXMLNode (BMPrettyDescriptions)
```

```
+ (void)load;
{
    Method oldMethod = class_getInstanceMethod(self, @selector(description));
    Method newMethod = class_getInstanceMethod(self, @selector(prettyDescription));
    method_exchangeImplementations(oldMethod, newMethod);
}

- (NSString *)prettyDescription;
{
    return [self XMLStringWithOptions:NSXMLNodePrettyPrint];
}

@end
```

Now when we log our XML node, we get the desired results:

```
NSXMLNode *xmlNode;
// ... load above XML document
NSLog(@"Current node: %@", xmlNode);
```

```
Current node: <?xml version="1.0" encoding="utf-8"?>
<rss version="2.0">
    <channel>
        <title>My Blog</title>
        <link>http://www.worldofkevin.com/Site/Blog/Blog.html</link>
        <description>Welcome to my blog: Alit, Enit, Laore, Eros Vel, Exer Dolorer,
Niam Lut.</description>
        <generator>iWeb 1.1.2</generator>
        <image>
            <url>http://www.worldofkevin.com/Site/Blog/Blog_files/200206373-3-a.png
</url>
            <title>My Blog</title>
            <link>http://www.worldofkevin.com/Site/Blog/Blog.html</link>
        </image>
        <item>
            <title>Red Vines: the perfect super food</title>
            <link>http://www.worldofkevin.com/Site/Blog/88DD8356-E484-44DD-9419-
AE9F936E8BAD.html</link>
            <guid>http://www.worldofkevin.com/Site/Blog/88DD8356-E484-44DD-9419-
AE9F936E8BAD.html</guid>
            <pubDate>Mon, 20 Aug 2007 10:48:11 -0700</pubDate>
<description>&lt;a href='http://www.worldofkevin.com/Site/Blog/88DD8356-E484-44DD
-9419-AE9F936E8BAD_files/FD004359-1.jpg'>&lt;img
src='http://www.worldofkevin.com/Site/Blog/Images/FD004359-1.jpg'
style='float:left; padding-right:10px; padding-bottom:10px; width:109px;
height:79px;'/>&lt;/a>Eliquatuero dip numsan vent lam, conum facillum init lut
doloreet ullametuero od tet adit, commod tatummy feug tiam velit praese exer
auteenit alit, veliqua modit dolorer commod niam onul laore. Uptat prat lut
lut iriliquat,quis alisl irilit am irillum at niam zzrit, verosto consequ
ismodit irius</description>
            <enclosure url="http://www.worldofkevin.com/Site/Blog/88DD8356-E484-
44DD-9419-AE9F936E8BAD_files/FD004359-1.jpg" length="101865" type="image/jpg">
</enclosure>
        </item>
    </channel>
</rss>
```

Magic, right? A few lines bear closer examination. First, the functions for directly interacting with the runtime are not part of Cocoa, so they have to be imported separately:

```
#import <objc/runtime.h>
```

To facilitate just this sort of goings on, the runtime sends the load message to any class as it's being loaded but before it's used. This is the perfect place to accomplish what you need to do:

```
+ (void)load;
```

To swap the implementations of the methods, you have to get the methods:

```
Method oldMethod = class_getInstanceMethod(self, @selector(description));
```

The compiler directive @selector converts the name of a method into a SEL, as required by the function class_getInstanceMethod, which returns a Method. The Method is a struct that contains a selector of type SEL, an implementation of type IMP, and some return type encoding information.

With the methods in hand, all you have to do is swap their implementations.

```
method_exchangeImplementations(oldMethod, newMethod);
```

As far as the runtime is concerned, the two methods have literally had their implementations swapped. The message description will now call the implementation you defined for prettyDescription. The inverse is also true; calling prettyDescription will return the original implementation of description. So, to "call super" from within the new implementation, it has to call itself.

```
- (NSString *)prettyDescription;
{
    NSString *oldDescription = [self prettyDescription];
    ...
}
```

Weird, right?

In Objective-C, nothing is ever written in stone. Even without wandering far from the comforts of object-oriented programming, you have the power to pull off staggering feats of engineering brilliance.

Key Value Coding

In recent years, the designers of Objective-C have begun making use of heretofore informal aspects of the language. For example, given a property key, you can assume its getter is key and its setter is setKey:. Alternately, if key is a Boolean property, you can assume its getter is isKey. By making this assumption about the predictability of method names, the system can enable a new level of dynamic behavior known as key value coding (KVC).

KVC treats every property as a named key and introduces a generic form for getting or setting any property by name:

```
id property = [myObject valueForKey:@"property"];
[otherObject setValue:property forKey:@"property"];
```

By allowing you to refer to properties by name, KVC lets you do the following:

- Resolve property names at runtime.
- Deal with unknown or empty keys on the fly.
- Store keys in collections and deal with them en masse without regard to type.

- Create derived properties. For example, you might later decide to derive name from properties called firstName and lastName.

- Create dependent keys, such that a change to one key triggers change notifications in other keys.

- Sync keys to other keys using *bindings*, the zero-code technology that gives Interface Builder much of its power.

- Bridge properties between Objective-C and other technologies such as Core Data and AppleScript.

Objective-C 2.0

Apple has long contributed to the usefulness of Objective-C. Apple has done this directly by contributing to the GNU open source projects that compile, debug, and link Objective-C applications. They've also done this indirectly by providing frameworks such as Cocoa. With Leopard, Apple has finally begun to improve the language itself in an effort known as Objective-C 2.0.

Class Extension

One of the most common uses of Objective-C's method categories is the creation of private headers. These define methods that are used by the internal implementation of a class but should not be called from outside the class.

In a way, this is an abuse of the language. Categories are meant to arrange a class's implementation by functionality. Using a category to define private methods creates an artificial separation in the implementation based on visibility, rather than function.

Class extensions are a new kind of "anonymous" category. Unlike a standard category, which extends both the interface and the implementation, a class extension extends only the interface. The implementation remains with the main class. Thus, a public method and closely related private methods can remain together.

For example, say you had a contrived class whose public interface declared like this:

```
@interface MyClass : NSObject
- (void)publicMethod;
@end
```

Within your implementation file (or private header), you would declare the following:

```
@interface MyClass ()
- (void)privateMethod;
- (void)privateHelper;
@end
```

Then your implementation would look something like this:

```
@implementation MyClass

- (void)publicMethod;
{
    [self privateMethod];
    // ...
}
```

```
- (void)privateMethod;
{
    [self privateHelper];
    // ...
}

- (void)privateHelper;
{
    // ...
}

@end
```

> **NOTE** Class extensions, unlike protocols, are completely anonymous and cannot be adopted by multiple classes.

Fast Enumeration

Iterating over a collection is one of the most common tasks in programming. Traditionally, C accomplishes this via the standard for loop:

```
NSArray *objects = [self methodThatReturnsAnArrayOfObjects];
NSUInteger objectIndex;
for (objectIndex = 0; objectIndex < [objects count]; objectIndex++) {
    NSObject *object = [objects objectAtIndex:objectIndex];
    // ...
}
```

This is effective, but it's a lot to type, it requires an additional method call, and worst of all it works only for arrays. As such, Cocoa provides the NSEnumerator class, which enables the following:

```
NSArray *objects = [self methodThatReturnsAnArrayOfObjects];
NSEnumerator *objectEnumerator = [objects objectEnumerator];
NSObject *object = nil;
while ((object = [objectEnumerator nextObject])) {
    // ...
}
```

For all the object-oriented goodness that enumerators bring, they are slow and require making a copy of every object. They also suffer from the same kind of redundant verbosity as the C iteration loop. Objective-C 2.0 introduces the ultimate solution to the looping problem:

```
NSArray *objects = [self methodThatReturnsAnArrayOfObjects];
for (NSObject *object in objects) {
    // ...
}
```

Fast enumeration is both more concise and more readable than either of the other methods. It is backed by the NSFastEnumeration protocol, so it can work with any collection, including your own. It is also highly optimized, so it is not only faster than traditional enumeration, but it is also faster than C iteration.

Finally, fast enumeration adds the benefit of a mutation check, which ensures collections do not change during enumeration. This makes it possible to perform multiple enumerations simultaneously. This is part of a general move toward thread safety as multiprocessor technology continues to form an important part of the platform.

Garbage Collection

Aside from the syntax, the scariest thing about Objective-C is manual memory management. Even the most experienced programmers are prone to crashes and memory leaks. Memory problems are also among the hardest to debug, taking up a lot of precious development time.

Other languages have solved this problem with automated memory management, generally known as *garbage collection*. Unfortunately, garbage collection is synonymous with poor performance. Collection is typically expensive enough to require pausing general operations, frustrating users. Proponents of garbage collection have hoped computers will eventually get fast enough that this won't matter, but it hasn't happened yet.

Leopard introduces garbage collection done right. The collector in Objective-C 2.0 is built on the collective knowledge of the almost 50 years since garbage collection was invented. It was also designed with a solid foundation in the real world, mindful of the patterns and habits of Objective-C programmers.

- Avoid expensive memory optimization operations such as compacting the heap or moving objects around.

- Concentrate on new objects, which tend to live short lives, rather than old objects, which tend to live forever.

- Don't stop all operations for collection. Wait for opportune moments, only collect on the main thread, and yield to user events.

- Retain the dual nature of Objective-C by not breaking compatibility with other frameworks or the use of inline C code.

- Give the programmer control, where needed, to optimize garbage collection, or opt out of it altogether.

This last point is important. It's possible to write your code for both automatic and manual memory management.

Toggling garbage collection is a project option in Xcode, as shown in Figure 26-5. When garbage collection is on, the compiler ignores retain, release, and autorelease operations, except for the NSAutoreleasePool instance method drain, which serves as a hint to the collector. The dealloc method is also ignored, though a finalize method may be implemented if there's somehow something in dealloc that is not made moot by garbage collection.

TIP Switching between automated and manual memory management is a great way to debug crashes. If one mode crashes and the other doesn't, you know there's something wrong in your implementation.

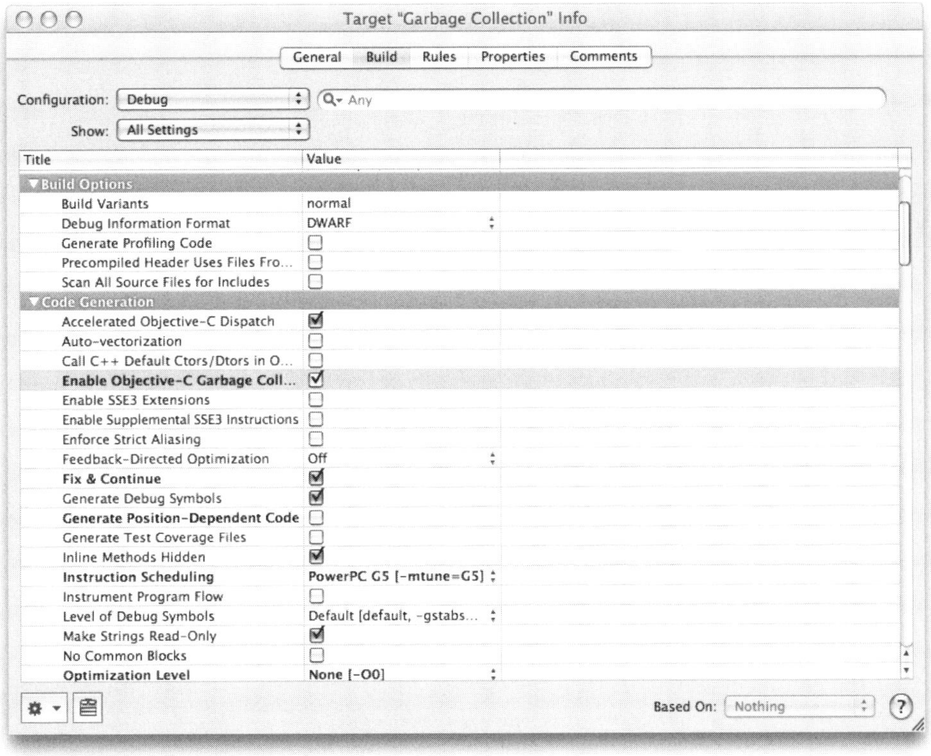

Figure 26-5. Xcode's garbage collection option

Properties

Dealing with ivars, getters, and setters takes an enormous amount of time and code. Consider the BMPerson class. All of the instance methods, except for init and dealloc, were concerned with accessing and mutating our instance variables.

```
#import <Cocoa/Cocoa.h>

@interface BMPerson : NSObject {
    NSString *name;
    NSUInteger age;
}

+ (BMPerson *)personWithName:(NSString *)aName age:(NSUInteger)anAge;
- (NSString *)name;
- (void)setName:(NSString *)aName;
- (NSUInteger)age;
- (void)setAge:(NSUInteger)anAge;

@end
```

Every time you add an ivar, you have to add two lines to your interface and as many as 14 lines to your implementation:

```objc
#import "BMPerson.h"

@implementation BMPerson

+ (BMPerson *)personWithName:(NSString *)aName age:(NSUInteger)anAge;
{
    BMPerson *newPerson = [[self alloc] init];

    [newPerson setName:aName];
    [newPerson setAge:anAge];

    return [newPerson autorelease];
}

- (id)init;
{
    if (![super init])
    return nil;

    name = nil;

    return self;
}

- (void)dealloc;
{
    [name release];
    name = nil;

    [super dealloc];
}

- (NSString *)name;
{
    return name;
}

- (void)setName:(NSString *)aName;
{
    if (name == aName)
        return;

    [name release];
    name = [aName retain];
}

- (NSUInteger)age;
{
    return age;

}

- (void)setAge:(NSUInteger)anAge;
{
    age = anAge;
}

@end
```

Worse yet, the more ivars you add, the more you're writing the same code over and over again.

Objective-C 2.0 introduces explicitly named properties via a compact header syntax:

```
#import <Cocoa/Cocoa.h>

@interface BMPerson : NSObject {
    NSString *name;
    NSUInteger age;
}

+ (BMPerson *)personWithName:(NSString *)aName age:(NSUInteger)anAge;

@property (retain) NSString *name;
@property (assign) NSUInteger age;

@end
```

That's nice, but what's really amazing is what this does for your implementation:

```
#import "BMPerson.h"

@implementation BMPerson

+ (BMPerson *)personWithName:(NSString *)aName age:(NSUInteger)anAge;
{
    BMPerson *newPerson = [[self alloc] init];
    newPerson.name = aName;
    newPerson.age = age;

    return [newPerson autorelease];
}

- (void)dealloc;
{
    self.name = nil;

    [super dealloc];
}

@synthesize name, age;

@end
```

That's a lot less code. For one thing, all the setter and getter method implementations have been replaced by one line:

```
@synthesize name, age;
```

That compiler directive inserts the standard implementations, keeping you from having to type them over and over again. The generated implementations are faster than the handwritten ones and are executed atomically, meaning they are thread-safe. Better results for less work? That's the Objective-C way.

Dot syntax, on the other hand, is decidedly not the Objective-C way, yet when it comes to accessing and mutating property values, the compactness of dot syntax is actually nicer than the readability of Objective-C syntax. Objective-C 2.0 gives you the best of both worlds. Now you can use dot notation and simple assignment to get and set properties:

```
BMPerson *worldsToughestProgrammer = [[BMPerson alloc] init];
worldsToughestProgrammer.name = @"Mike Lee";
NSLog(@"%@ is the world's toughest programmer.", worldsToughestProgrammer.name);
```

```
Mike Lee is the world's toughest programmer.
```

Notably, properties do not prevent you from using standard syntax:

```
[worldsToughestProgrammer setName:@"Mike Lee"];
```

Nor do they prevent you from using KVC syntax:

```
[worldsToughestProgrammer setValue:@"Mike Lee" forKey:@"name"];
```

Properties, like scalars, are automatically initialized to nil, so you don't have to do that in init, which means, in this case, you don't need init at all. You also don't have to explicitly release your pointers or remember to set them to nil. You can just set the property to nil, which will do both.

Should you decide to change the way a property behaves, you can just change the property attributes themselves. The compiler will do the right thing when it comes to the @synthesize directive. There are three classes of property behavior; see Table 26-4.

Table 26-4. Objective-C 2.0 Property Attributes

Behavior	Values	Notes
Memory management	retain, assign, copy	The default is assign.
Mutability	readonly, readwrite	The default is readwrite.
Thread safety	nonatomic	atomic is assumed.

The Objective-C way is to make things easy but to allow you to do things the hard way if necessary. Properties are the same way. If, for example, you have a property whose instance variable does not have the same name, you can connect the two explicitly. For example, if, in BMPerson, you called the property age but the ivar years, you could note this in your @synthesize directive:

```
@synthesize name, age = years;
```

If you wanted to override the setter of the age property to provide validation, all you have to do is implement it:

```
- (void)setAge:(NSUInteger)anAge;
{
    if (anAge > 0 && anAge < 100)
        age = anAge;
}
```

Even though you've asked the compiler to synthesize this property, it will see that you've implemented it yourself and do the right thing.

In the converse of assigning an ivar, you can also, if necessary, explicitly assign a setter or getter in the property declaration:

```
@property (assign, getter=ageInYears) NSUInteger age;
```

Properties can be redeclared in subclasses or class extensions to, for example, change a property from readonly to readwrite. Properties can be marked with the garbage collector hints __weak and __strong. Finally, properties can be implemented with the directive @dynamic, which tells the compiler that the implementation will be provided at runtime. Core Data, for example, will dynamically generate property implementations.

64-bit Changes

Macintosh processors are capable of operating in both 32-bit and 64-bit modes, and Leopard includes both 32-bit and 64-bit versions of the system frameworks. Developers can compile their applications as both 32-bit and 64-bit, thanks to the same Universal binary technology that allows applications to be compiled for both Intel and PowerPC.

Although many of the improvements of Objective-C 2.0 were able to be added in a completely backward-compatible way, other wish-list items were not possible without breaking binary compatibility. However, since the move to 64-bit was going to break compatibility anyway, the language designers added them to the 64-bit version of Objective-C 2.0.

- Subclasses are not reliant on the offsets of their superclasses, which is an esoteric issue known as the "fragile base class" problem.

- Instance variables can be synthesized, eliminating the need to explicitly declare them for use in properties.

- The runtime has been improved with an optimized messaging system, which reduces overhead for increased performance.

Learn More

This quick-and-dirty review of Objective-C barely scratches the surface. There are several places to find a more in-depth study of Objective-C and Mac development in general. Depending on your own programming background, there are likely several resources aimed directly at helping you explore Objective-C.

Apple's own free documentation is a good place to start. Available online and in Xcode's documentation manager, the Apple Developer Connection library contains several documents worth reading:

Introduction to the Objective-C 2.0 Programming Language: As the title suggests, this document talks about the language and has been updated with the latest changes brought by Objective-C 2.0. It relates Objective-C to C and C++, including an extensive section on Objective-C++. It also discusses the runtime, the messaging system, and how Objective-C accomplishes much of its magic.

Introduction to Coding Guidelines for Cocoa: This is a style guide of accepted conventions for naming methods, functions, and variables. It also goes over acceptable abbreviations and acronyms and offers tips for developing your own frameworks. Whether you want to produce readable code, read someone else's code, or just generally look like you know what you're doing, this is a must-read.

Object-Oriented Programming with Objective-C: This relates object-oriented programming and Objective-C, giving each a fair explanation in terms of the other. It also discusses the Cocoa frameworks and how and why they relate to Objective-C.

Objective-C 2.0 Runtime Reference: This is detailed and specific documentation of the Mac OS X Objective-C runtime. Rather than discussing the high-level metaphors and philosophies of the runtime, its topics include changes to underlying structure and functions and incompatibilities and deprecations between the 32-bit and 64-bit versions of the Application Binary Interface.

Introduction to Memory Management Programming Guide for Cocoa: This is an in-depth look at manual memory management in Objective-C. It looks at object ownership conventions, autorelease pools, how memory is managed in the API, and how memory management should be implemented in your own classes.

Introduction to Garbage Collection: This is a complete description of automated memory management in Objective-C 2.0. It discusses the essential things any Cocoa programmer must know about garbage collection, the architecture of the garbage collector, issues you're likely to discover while adopting garbage collection, and a summary of the garbage collection API.

There are also several good books on Objective-C and Mac programming. We recommend *Programming in Objective-C* by Stephen Kochan (Sams, 2003) as unique, in that it doesn't assume you already know C or some other language, as well as being a pretty decent book.

Summary

Lots of languages can be used to develop applications for the Mac, and even more can be used to develop applications on the Mac. Yet Objective-C is Apple's choice for the future of native Mac programming. That's because, increasingly, Objective-C has been designed for exactly that purpose.

Since its origins at NeXT, Mac OS X has never been afraid to do things differently in its quest to do things better. Objective-C is an extension of this spirit. Yes, it takes a little bit of extra time to learn to do things this way, but that investment is quickly repaid many times over. Objective-C is to programming languages as the Macintosh is to computers: simply the best combination of speed, power, and productivity.

## PART 8

Cross-Platform Solutions

## CHAPTER 27

Working with Microsoft Windows and Other Operating Systems

Occasionally while using Leopard, you may find it necessary to utilize resources intended for other operating systems. With Apple's new Intel-based computers combined with Leopard's ability to work with different file systems and networks protocols, today your Mac can run just about any software, including entire other operating systems. This chapter will show you how your Mac can do the following:

- Work with a wide range of files and file systems
- Run Microsoft Windows or other operating systems and applications on your Mac
- Access Microsoft Windows systems remotely

Working with Other File Types and File Systems

Long ago, working with files created on another operating system was troublesome. First, the files created by one application were often unreadable in any other application, so if an application was available only on one operating system, that file would be unreadable on another. The second problem was that each operating system stored files in a way that made it difficult to move a file from one operating system to another. (This was back in the days when the most popular way to move a file from one computer to another was a good ol' floppy disk.)

Today things are significantly better but not perfect. The most popular applications currently in use have both Microsoft Windows and Mac OS X counterparts that can freely share files back and forth. If a particular application isn't cross-platform, then it's possible either that the host application can save files in a format that is accessible by some other common application or that some native application can import a foreign file type.

> **NOTE** For example, Apple's Pages application could open Microsoft Office 2007 files before Microsoft's own Office:mac could open them.

File systems are a bit trickier. Although OS X is quite good at reading file systems used by other operating systems, other operating systems aren't quite as capable.

Sharing Files with Windows

With the prevalence of Microsoft Windows computers, unless you work and live in a very enlightened Mac-only universe, it's likely that sooner or later you'll need to share a file or two with a Windows system.

The file type you choose is fairly straightforward. Microsoft Office formats tend to work fine on both Macs and Windows computers. Any standard graphics formats such as JPEG, GIF, PNG, and TIFF files (along with numerous others) will transfer from one system to another just fine. PDF files are also common among most operating systems. When it comes to audio files, MP3, ACC, and WAV are all just fine (FLAC and a number of other audio formats are equally cross-platform but require third-party software to play them). Video is a bit trickier since video is generally comprised of mixing both audio and video formats. Apple's QuickTime is the best option for cross-platform video with a few important considerations. First, QuickTime movies created on a Mac must be "flattened" to work on the Web or on a Windows computer. This is done by using the Save As... command in QuickTime Pro or using the Lillipot utility (www.qtbridge.com/lillipot/lillipot.html). Movies exported from iMovie and most other video-editing software will be flattened automatically. Second, QuickTime must be installed for them to play back properly. This isn't a big issue for most Windows computers, because many computer manufacturers include QuickTime by default, and it's a free and easy install for any Windows computers that don't already have it. QuickTime, however, isn't available for Linux or other alternative operating systems. MPEG4 files (which is the default video format for Quick-Time movies these days) work just fine too.

> **NOTE** Windows Media files are popular; however, they pose a number of tricky problems. First, you will likely need a third-party QuickTime plug-in or stand-alone application to play them on your Mac. Filp4Mac WMV (www.flip4mac.com/) is a third-party QuickTime plug-in that today is endorsed by Microsoft for playing Windows Media files, and VLC Media Player (www.videolan.org/vlc/) is an open source stand-alone media player that supports many formats, including WMV. The bigger problem is that at this time neither of these products will support Windows Media protected by DRM (which is quite popular).

> **NOTE** A new QuickTime plug-in called Perian (http://perian.org/) will greatly enhance QuickTime's abilities to play back a number of media types. QuickTime combined with Flip4Mac and Perian should enable you to play back the majority of video files you find on the Internet with the notable exceptions of RealVideo and protected Windows Media files.

Once you have your file, transferring it from one computer to another is the next trick. Transferring your file over a network circumvents most file system problems. By enabling Windows sharing on your Mac, you can allow a Windows system to simply browse your shared directory and copy the file from your Mac to a Windows computer. Also, your Mac can utilize any Windows file servers or shared directories. If you have .Mac, you can place your file in your public iDisk folder that is accessible from Windows using Apple's iDisk Utility for Windows (www.mac.com/1/idiskutility_download.html), or you can set up our Public iDisk folder to be accessible from the Web. Also, you can use any standard Internet file-sharing protocol. If, rather than using the network, you want to use a physical means of file transfer (such as external hard drive, thumb drive, and so on), then you will likely want to format the drive using the FAT32 file system, which will work with both Macs and Windows computers.

> **NOTE** Windows computers do not support Apple's default file system (HFS+) without special third-party software. Additionally, Macs support NTFS (the Windows default file system) as read-only only, which makes it a bit limiting for file sharing. The FAT32 file system, however, is the old Windows default file system and has had good Mac support for many years.

Running Microsoft Windows on Your Mac

Unfortunately, since about 90 percent of the world's desktops run Microsoft Windows, sometimes you may need to use a Windows-only application or feature (Figure 27-1).

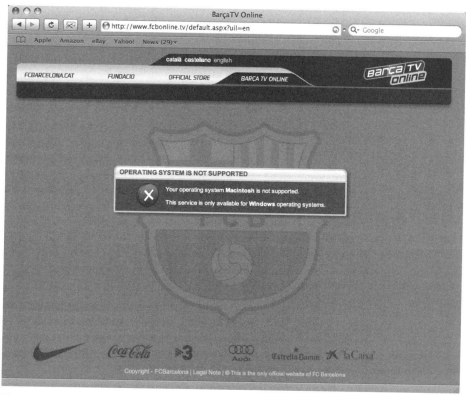

Figure 27-1. Ugggh! World's best football (aka soccer) team needs better web developers!

More than 10 years ago a highly innovative company called Connectix created a product called Virtual PC that allowed your Mac to run an emulated x86 system as a separate application. This x86 system allowed Mac users to run Microsoft Windows on their Macs. Although the performance was notably slow, it worked and ushered in the era of emulation on the Mac. Eventually, Virtual PC was purchased from Connectix by Microsoft (which continues to support Virtual PC but only for Windows hosts).

> **NOTE** Besides Virtual PC, Connectix also invented the QuickCam, which it sold to Logitech. After selling off QuickCam and Virtual PC (as well as selling its Virtual Play Station product to Sony, which promptly killed it), the company effectively called it quits in 2003. During its 15 years of existence, the company also introduced memory and innovative techniques for RAM use to the pre–OS X Mac platform.

NOTE Emulation and virtualization seem similar in many cases but are quite different. *Emulation* (like the original Virtual PC) requires that the code being run actually needs to be translated before being used. (Virtual PC used *dynamic recompilation* to translate x86 code to PowerPC code before the code could be run.) *Virtualization*, on the other hand, allows concurrent computer processes to run using the same hardware by partitioning the hardware's memory and processing power so that each process runs entirely independently of every other. Common "virtualization" software that runs on your Mac today actually is a hybrid of both virtualization and emulation.

NOTE Leopard (and Tiger before that) actually contains its own emulation software that, like the original Virtual PC, uses dynamic recompilation. This software (called Rosetta) does the opposite, though. Rather than translate x86 code into PowerPC code, it makes sure old PowerPC code on your Mac runs on the new x86 architecture.

Upon switching to an Intel-based platform, Apple changed everything. Today not only is it possible to run Windows natively on your Apple computer, but a new range of virtualization products are now available to Mac users that run extremely well with little performance loss.

As a Mac user (provided you are using an Intel-based Mac), you have a number of options for running Windows on your computer. We'll quickly go over each of these and point out the pros and cons of each of them.

Boot Camp

Shortly after Apple started shipping Intel-based computers, it released a utility called Boot Camp (which you had to seek out on its web site and download as a beta). Beginning with Leopard, Boot Camp is included along with Mac OS X. To get it up and running, you can use the Boot Camp Assistant that is located in the `Applications/Utilities` folder.

Running Boot Camp allows you to effectively turn your Mac computer into a full-fledged Windows machine. The advantage of this is that all your Mac's hardware will become dedicated to running Windows. The significant issue here, which is not available through any current virtualization or emulation methods, is that running in Boot Camp gives you full video acceleration, which is a must for certain applications (including most Windows gaming).

Boot Camp has a few disadvantages as well, though:

- You must reboot your computer to switch between OS X and Windows.
- You must create a dedicated partition on an *internal* hard drive to install Windows on.

NOTE You cannot install Windows on an external hard drive right now using Boot Camp.

- You must have a full version of Windows XP SP2 or newer to install Windows with Boot Camp.

Parallels Desktop and VMware Fusion

Shortly after the release of Intel-based Macs, the buzz started increasing about a company called Parallels (`www.parallels.com/en/products/desktop/`) that was making a virtualization product for the new Macs that would allow one to run Windows and other x86 operating systems on the new Macs under OS X with exceptional performance. Sure enough, when Parallels Desktop for the Mac was released, it did what it said it would. Soon, VMware, a company (now owned by EMC) that has a long history of virtualization, announced it too was building a product for the Mac; VMware has since released Fusion (`www.vmware.com/products/fusion/`; Figure 27-2) with similar capabilities to Parallels Desktop. These two products, although slightly different, work (from a user's perspective) so similarly that it's hard to pick one to recommend over the other. Overall, they are both excellent.

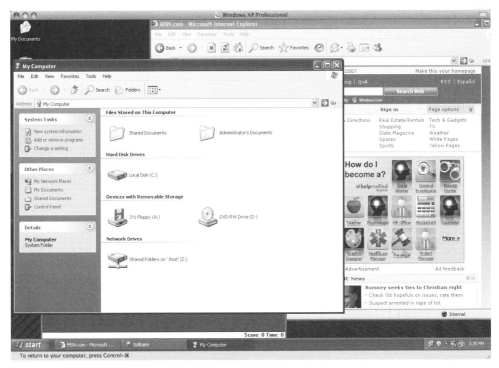

Figure 27-2. Microsoft Windows XP Professional running in VMware

Running either Parallels Desktop or VMware Fusion has some obvious advantages:

- They run on top of Mac OS X, providing you with the ability to switch quickly and easily from one environment to another without rebooting; in fact, both Parallels Desktop and VMware Fusion have modes that actually will integrate the running Windows applications into your Mac OS X desktop.

- They can both run other operating systems besides Windows, allowing you to run Linux, Free BSD, Solaris x86, and many other operating systems (Figure 27-3).

- You can run multiple instances of one or many operating systems at the same time.

- They are both reasonably priced, well-supported, easy-to-use products that are quickly evolving with new features and better performance.

Despite the overwhelming advantages, there are a few disadvantages to both of these virtualization products:

- To allow them to run on top of Mac OS X, many hardware devices need to be emulated. Although this largely doesn't affect performance much for most devices, it has a very big effect on video acceleration performance.

> **NOTE** VMware Fusion 1.1 and Parallels Desktop 3.0 finally both support DirectX 9, making it possible to use applications that require it. However, there is still a rather significant performance hit. As both of these products evolve, it is likely that video performance will continue to improve, but it's still a big consideration for some.

- You will need a copy of Windows or whatever operating system you choose to run, though unlike Boot Camp these will allow you to use older products and upgrades.

Figure 27-3. Ubuntu Linux running in Parallels Desktop

> **NOTE** One issue with Windows Vista is that Microsoft's licensing agreement for the Windows Vista Home Edition products specifically disallows the use of those versions of Windows Vista for use with virtualization products, so if you plan on running Windows Vista on either of these products, you will need to purchase the more expensive Business Edition or Ultimate Edition to comply.

CodeWeaver's CrossOver (and Wine)

One other option for running Windows applications (without Windows!) is CodeWeaver's CrossOver (www.codeweavers.com/products/cxmac/). CrossOver is a commercially enhanced and supported product based on the open source Wine (Wine Is Not an Emulator) project (www.winehq.org/). What's interesting about this is that rather than rely on Windows to run Windows-based applications, Wine attempts to duplicate the underlying libraries and frameworks used by the applications in order to run them natively on a different host operating system. The advantages of CrossOver over other options are as follows:

- It's a less expensive option since it doesn't require you to purchase Windows as well.
- Nothing is emulated, so the overall performance is very good, even for applications requiring video acceleration.
- It fairly easy to install and use.

> **NOTE** The ease of use claim is made specifically for the commercial CrossOver product. Wine requires some work to get up and running, and it isn't as easy to use once it's set up either (but it is free and does work).

That said, it has some significant disadvantages. The biggest one is that not all Windows apps will work with CrossOver, and some that do exhibit some significant bugs. So if you need to run one or two Windows applications that are supported by CrossOver (or Wine), then this is a good way to go; if, however, you need to run a wide range of Windows applications, one of the other solutions is likely a better option.

Accessing a Windows Computer Remotely

Another, very different way of using Windows on your Mac is to actually connect to another computer running Windows using Microsoft's Remote Desktop Connection (RDC). With RDC (available for free from www.microsoft.com/mac/), you can actually use a remote Windows computer from your Mac as if you were sitting right in front of it (Figure 27-4).

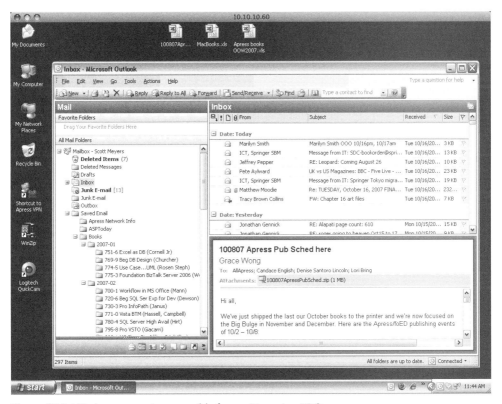

Figure 27-4. Windows computer accessible from a Mac using RDC

Not only does RDC allow you to access a remote Windows computer, but it will allow you to copy and paste files and move them back and forth from your Mac to the connected Windows computer. You can even print items on your connected Windows computer to the printer connected to your Mac. Of course, you can also take full advantage of any application installed on the remote Windows computer.

The downside to RDC is that you need to have access to a computer running Windows. And of course, depending on the network connection between your Mac and the Windows computer, your performance may vary.

Summary

As any Mac user will tell you, Macs are just better computers with a better operating system. With the switch to an Intel architecture, a Mac not only can run the best operating system (Leopard, of course) but is more than capable of slipping over into the world of Windows when necessary. Not only do apps such as Boot Camp, Fusion, and Parallels Desktop provide compatibility when necessary, but for people switching from Windows computers to Macs, they provide a way to maintain your investment in Windows software while you discover the advantages of using a Mac.

Appendixes

What's New with Leopard?

Apple boasts "300-plus innovations" in Leopard. Even if you are an experienced OS X user, that sounds like a lot of new stuff to learn. The truth is, many of these innovations are buried deep in the system, and while they in subtle ways improve how OS X behaves and interacts with the user, it's often in ways that you may never consciously notice. This chapter aims to outline a few of the more significant changes in OS X, broken down into a few areas:

- The Finder and the desktop
- Safety features
- Application enhancements
- Developer tools
- Darwin
- Under the hood
- Others

New Finder and Desktop Features

The first thing an experienced OS X user will notice upon using Leopard (Figure A-1) is that while things are somewhat similar to OS X of the past, a number of things just look different. Window borders have changed, the Dock is certainly different, and the Finder and its contents appear to be different, too.

Figure A-1. The default Leopard desktop

Superficial Changes

Many of the changes seem to be purely superficial, including the following:

- The menu bar is translucent now.
- The Apple and the Spotlight icons in the menu bar are now black.
- The Dock now seems to be a 3D shelf with the icons sitting upon it rather than in it.
- The active applications in the Dock now seem to have a light shining on them to indicate they are active, rather than the small black triangle of old.
- The Window borders have changed to a more consistent, slightly different, "smoother" gray metal theme.
- The drop-down menus now have slightly curved corners.
- The system folders have a new look to them.
- The drop shadows on everything seem a bit different.

These changes, however, are fairly insignificant. They don't make using Leopard any different, they just change how it looks. If we delve deeper, we can find a number of things that can actually change how Leopard works, and more importantly how you can work with Leopard.

Stacks

Beyond changing its overall appearance, the Dock has added the Stack feature, which allows you to create "stacks" of files and place them on the Dock for easy access. This feature makes all the files in a directory easily accessible from the Dock. Figure A-2 shows the Stack feature.

Figure A-2. Applications folder expanded as a stack

Cover Flow

The Finder has integrated a few new features from other Apple applications. The first one, Cover Flow, represents a whole new way of browsing your computer. Cover Flow lets you browse through the files of a directory visually by either showing an icon or a Quick Look preview of the actual file in the same way that iTunes allows you to browse through album covers. Within the Finder, Cover Flow will display previews of most file types it understands, including MS Office files, text files, PDFs, most image formats, and even HTML previews (where it will display the actual rendered web page complete with images and styles!). This ability makes Cover Flow ideal for identifying a specific file from a large collection where the file itself has specific visual elements. An example of Cover Flow used in a large collection of images is shown in Figure A-3.

> **NOTE** By default, selecting Show All from a Spotlight search will open all the search results in a Cover View window. This makes finding things from a Spotlight search even easier!

Figure A-3. Cover Flow in action

Quick Look

While Quick Look is responsible for Cover Flow's preview ability, it goes way beyond just displaying simple thumbnail images of a file. Selecting a file in the Finder and clicking the Quick Look icon (the eye on the Finder's toolbar), or using the keyboard shortcut Cmd+Y (or just pressing the spacebar), will open any supported file in a window for viewing. The cool thing is that it opens the entire file for viewing almost immediately, without the need to launch any other application. A Word file open in Quick Look is shown in Figure A-4.

> **NOTE** Quick Look relies on plug-ins for displaying items. Depending on the plug-in, what you see in the preview may not exactly match what you see in the application.

Improved Smart Folders

Like Cover Flow, *smart folders* are another Apple technology that was used in the past that has really matured nicely in Leopard. You can create a smart folder anywhere you have permission to do so. To create a smart folder, either select File ➤ New Smart Folder from the Finder's menu bar, use the Option+Cmd+N keyboard shortcut, or select the New Smart Folder option from the contextual menu (via mouse button 2, Ctrl+click, or a two-finger trackpad click, if that option is selected in the Trackpad preferences). This will bring up the window shown in Figure A-5, where you can set the parameters for your smart folder. Once you are done setting up your smart folder, click the Save button and choose a location for your smart folder.

You can create a smart folder from any Spotlight search as well.

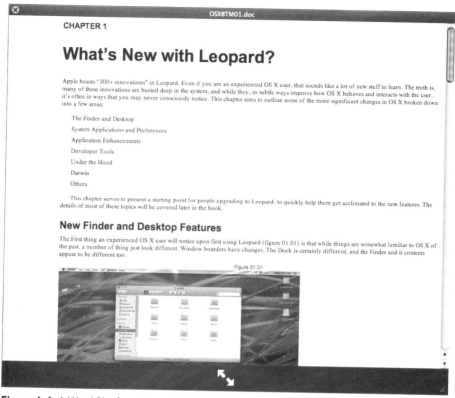

Figure A-4. A Word file (from this book, actually) open in Quick Look

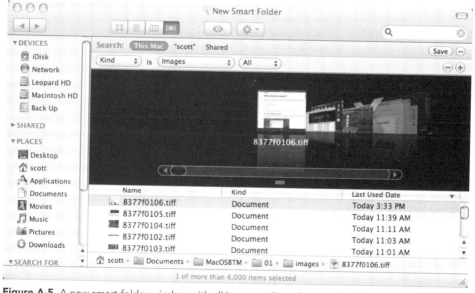

Figure A-5. A new smart folder window with all images selected as one (and the only) search criterion

Spaces

Another feature new to OS X is Spaces. Spaces allows you to set up multiple desktops that are all active concurrently and can be switched between as needed (this ability is more commonly know as *virtual desktops*). This is very nice if you are the sort of person who works on many different activities at the same time (or are at least running a large number of applications at the same time). For example, you could use one desktop for your normal workspace, one for your web browser and e-mail, one for iTunes, and one for iChat. This sort of setup is shown in Figure A-6. By selecting any open application from the Dock, you will be "teleported" to the appropriate "space."

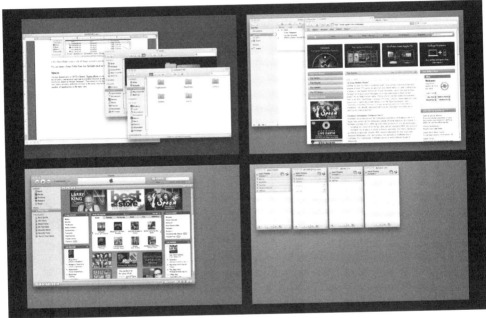

Figure A-6. Spaces configured with four different virtual desktops

> **NOTE** There are a number of third-party add-ons that have provided virtual desktops for OS X for a while. Spaces is merely Apple's built-in solution to providing this ability, and it seems to do the job admirably. Other means of accomplishing virtual desktops on OS X include, most notably, CodeTek's VirtualDesktop (www.codetek.com/ctvd/), as well as a number of less-polished projects.

System Safety

Leopard also introduces a number of new system-level safety enhancements for your family and your data. The two big improvements here are the Parental Controls preference and Time Machine.

Time Machine

Time Machine is a revolutionary backup system that keeps track of your data over a period of time. In order to use Time Machine, you must have a separate hard drive for backups, but once configured, Time Machine will automatically keep track of your data should you ever need to recover from a hard drive failure or accidental data loss. Additionally, since Time Machine keeps track of changes over a period of time, you can recover lost or deleted files (or versions of files) from the past. The Time Machine interface is shown in Figure A-7.

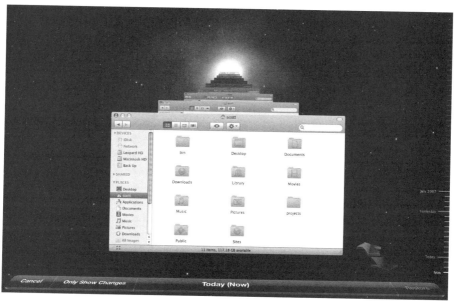

Figure A-7. Time Machine in action

Besides just working on the file system, Time Machine, when launched within certain applications, can also help recover files specific to that app. For example, when launched from Mail, Time Machine can recover old messages that have been deleted from your mailbox.

Improved Parental Controls

Besides protecting your data, Leopard also includes parental controls to allow you to control the activities of specified users on the computer. The parental controls in Leopard allow you to do the following:

- Choose what applications a specific user can use
- Filter what content a user has access to on the Internet using built-in filters, or by explicitly allowing or denying specific web sites
- Keep logs of a user's activities
- Set time limits for what times the computer is available to a specific user, and how much time per day it's acceptable for them to use it (Figure A-8)

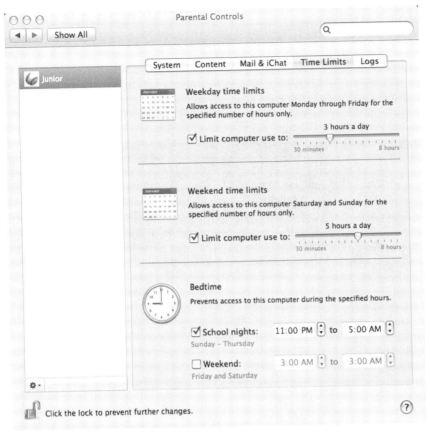

Figure A-8. Parental control preferences: time limits

Application Enhancements

All of the applications that ship with OS X have been updated, and a number of them include some significant new features.

Preview

In Leopard, Preview (shown in Figure A-9) adds the following:

- An improved ability to mark up and annotate documents
- Image rotating, resizing, cropping, and converting capabilities
- Improved preview, index, bookmark, and search features

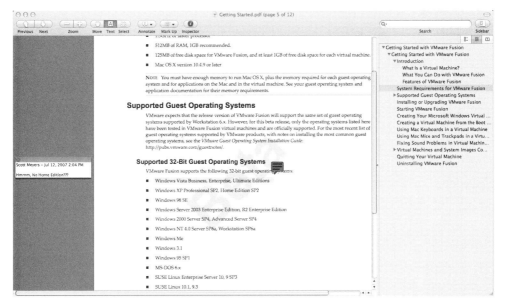

Figure A-9. The Preview application in Leopard

Mail

The Mail application in Leopard (Figure A-10) comes with the following enhancements:

- Notes and To Do list access from within the Mail app (with links to iCal)
- The ability to view RSS feeds in Mail
- New ways to add appointments into iCal from Mail
- Improved mail searches
- Automatic backup with Time Machine
- Stationary templates for e-mail

Safari

Leopard ships with the latest version of the Safari web browser (version 3), which includes the following:

- A noticeable performance boost over version 2
- An improved Find feature, which makes searching for text in a web page fast and easy
- Tabs that are movable across Safari and generally improved across the board
- Better PDF viewing from within Safari
- The ability to restore a browsing session from the last time Safari was closed

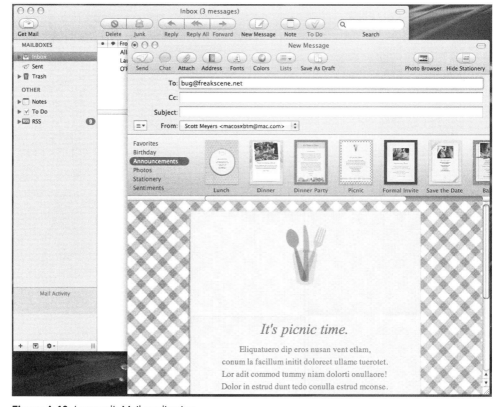

Figure A-10. Leopard's Mail application

iChat

The Leopard version of iChat has added a number of cool features not only for communicating, but also for sharing. These new features include the following:

- iChat Theater, which allows you to share movies, slideshows, and document previews via iChat
- iChat effects, which allow you to utilize photo booth effects for video chats, and even create false, animated backgrounds (Figure A-11)
- Tabbed chats
- Improved file transfers
- SMS forwarding

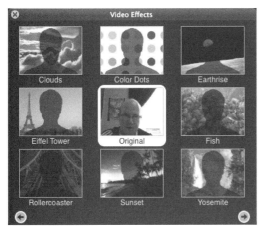

Figure A-11. Video effects are now available for iChat.

iCal

iCal in Leopard has a much more streamlined look to it, which makes it quite a bit friendlier to use. Besides the improved interface, iCal adds some cool new features:

- Inline appointment editing (Figure A-12)
- The ability to attach items to events to help keep event-related data together
- The ability to schedule group meetings, check attendee availability, and perform other enterprise-level calendaring tasks when used with a CalDAV standards-based calendar server (like iCal Server)

DVD Player

DVD Player (Figure A-13) includes a new streamlined interface along with some cool full-screen features, including the following capabilities:

- "Sliding" to any part of the movie using the time slider (as in QuickTime)
- Selecting DVD titles visually with dynamically created movie images
- Creating your own bookmarks within the DVD
- Creating your own clips from your DVDs and accessing them instantly
- Zooming in and out of your movies

Figure A-12. Viewing and editing Calendar event info inline

Figure A-13. DVD Player, full-screen

Photo Booth

Photo Booth (Figure A-14) adds a few new features as well. They include the following:

- A number of new effects (the same effects available for iChat)
- The ability to open up Photo Booth photos directly in iPhoto
- An icon to mail photos from Photo Booth
- The ability to develop your own backgrounds and effects

Figure A-14. Photo Booth with some improved features in Leopard

Development and Automation Tools

Whether you develop full-fledged applications or simple workflows, Apple has made a number of changes to the development tools in Leopard to make development faster and easier, and to allow your results to be more powerful.

Automator

In Leopard, on top of a new interface, Automator adds the following:

- A series of starting points for common workflows (Figure A-15)
- The ability to create and use variables inside of workflows
- A new record feature that allows you to record actions in applications to become actions within Automator

Figure A-15. Automator with workflow starting points shown

Xcode

Leopard introduces Xcode 3 (Figure A-16). This new version of Xcode includes many enhancements—a few of the key ones include the following:

- A greatly enhanced text editor with the ability to highlight ranges of code for easy editing, code completion, and inline messages
- Improved debugging from within the Xcode editor as well as through a new HUD (heads-up display), which allows you to debug programs without launching Xcode

- Project snapshots, which will save the state of a project and allow you to return to that state at a later date
- Tools to assist you with refactoring your code to improve readability and maintainability
- An improved document reader and a research assistant window for easy access to reference documentation
- Built-in support for Ruby and Python
- A new GUI to browse SCM (source code management) repositories from Xcode (supporting CVS, Subversion, and Perforce repositories)

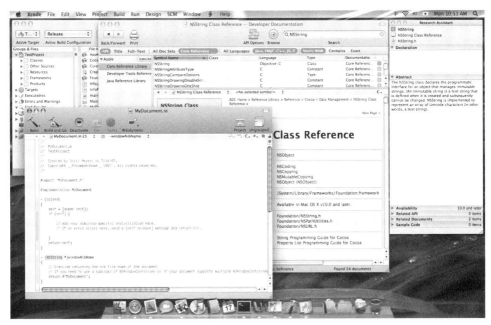

Figure A-16. Xcode 3 with various windows open

Interface Builder

The Leopard version of Interface Builder (Figure A-17) supports a new interface as well as the ability to add new behaviors to your applications.

Instruments

Along with the new Xcode tools, Apple includes a new application, Instruments (Figure A-18). Instruments is a tool that utilizes the newly included DTrace framework to allow developers an inside look at the execution of an application or the system itself. This allows the developer to see potential issues within the application that would otherwise be difficult to identify.

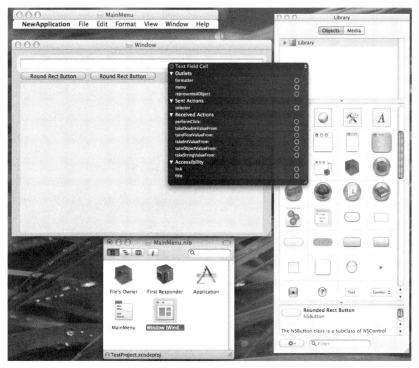

Figure A-17. Interface Builder 3

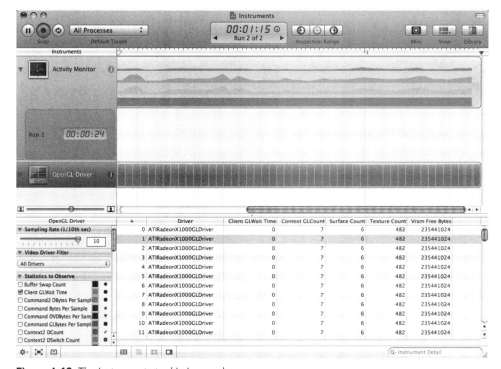

Figure A-18. The Instruments tool in Leopard

Dashcode

Dashcode (Figure A-19) is another new developer application included in Leopard. Dashcode is an IDE designed for creating Dashboard widgets. It includes a number of templates for popular types of widgets, an extensible code snippet library, an integrated text editor, and drag-and-drop widget-design facilities.

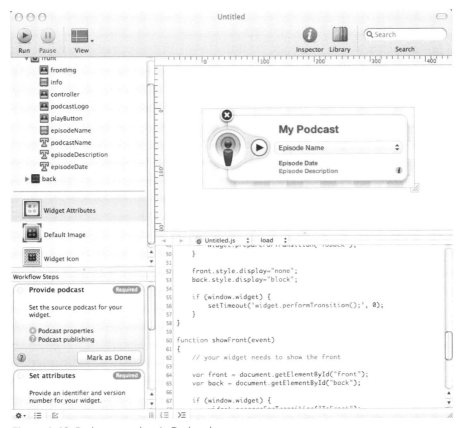

Figure A-19. Podcast template in Dashcode

Darwin (UNIX)

Behind the Aqua interface, Apple made a number of improvements to the UNIX underpinnings of Leopard as well. Rather than covering them all (which would be a lot), here are a few highlights:

- The Terminal app for accessing Darwin is greatly improved, and includes tabbed windows.
- Apache2 is now the default web server in Leopard.
- Perl, Python, and Ruby have all been updated to current versions.
- Ruby on Rails is now included as part of Leopard.

Under the Hood

A number of new features in Leopard exist behind the scenes to improve your day-to-day computing experience. These include the following:

- Full 64-bit, multi-core support in Leopard to fully unleash the power of modern hardware capabilities.
- Improved security throughout the system to unobtrusively keep your computer safe and under your control.
- Updated Cocoa frameworks and the inclusion of Core Animation, which allows full-motion animation capabilities to be easily included into new applications.

NOTE Make no mistake, Leopard is a developer's release. Just the bullet points in the "Under the Hood" section would take up an entire chapter.

Working with Others

Some additional features included with Leopard can help you work with other computers and other operating systems. These include the following:

- Boot Camp, which allows you to install and run Microsoft Windows OSs on your Macintosh
- Directory Utility and the Directory application, which allow your Leopard system to access a variety of directory servers including LDAP, NIS, and Active Directory.

Installing Mac OS X Leopard

Whether you are doing a clean install or upgrading, installing Leopard isn't too complicated. However, a number of options are available to you when installing, so you should consider several issues. This short appendix will help guide you through this process.

To begin the installation, you must insert the Leopard Install DVD and restart your computer so that it boots from the DVD. To do this, you can just restart your computer and hold down the C key while it starts. (If you try to run the installer while the DVD is not your start-up disk, then the installer will automatically restart your computer from the DVD.)

When the computer restarts from the DVD, the installation will begin automatically. The first thing you will be asked is what language you want to run the installer in (Figure B-1).

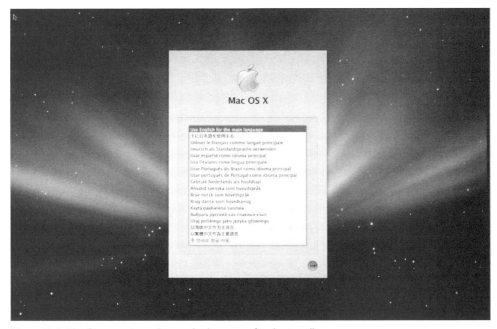

Figure B-1. The first step is to choose the language for the installer.

After you select your language choice, you will be presented with a Welcome screen (Figure B-2). If you click the More Information button, the Welcome screen will expand (Figure B-3) to include installation requirements and other installation information. It is not a bad idea to read through this.

Figure B-2. A message welcoming you to the Leopard installer

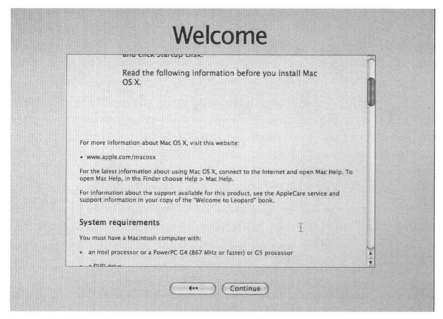

Figure B-3. Clicking the More Information button on the Welcome screen provides you with a lot of additional installation information that can help you with your install.

Clicking the Continue button on the Welcome screen will take you to the Select Destination screen. Here you select the disk volume on which you want to install Leopard. If the volume has a previous eligible version of OS X installed on it, the default behavior of the installer will be to update that volume with Leopard. Otherwise, the default action will be to install a fresh copy of Leopard on the selected volume.

> **NOTE** If you'd like to prepare volumes beforehand, the OS X Disk Utility is accessible from the Utilities menu on the menu bar.

Once you have selected the install volume, you can click Continue to go ahead with the default install/upgrade, or you can click the Options button, which will present you with a pane of additional install types (Figure B-4).

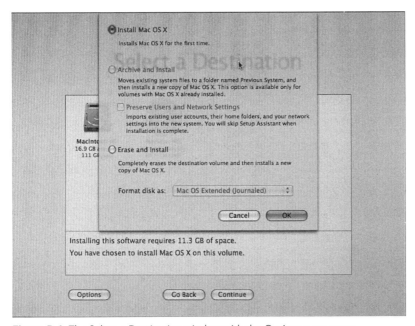

Figure B-4. The Select a Destination window with the Options pane open

The Options pane will provide you with three types of installs you can perform on the selected volume:

- *Install (or Upgrade) Mac OS X*: This is the default option and will either install or upgrade the selected volume.
- *Archive and Install*: This is a handy option, which, rather than upgrading an existing OS X volume, will install a fresh OS X system on the volume; however, it will save all your previous system information in a `Previous System` folder. The Preserve Users and Network Settings option will keep all of your user and network information intact and available to use on the new system.

> **NOTE** The Archive and Install option will not be available (will be grayed out) if your volume doesn't have a previous version of OS X installed on it.

> **NOTE** Since the Archive and Install option starts you out with a clean system, some applications that have installed items in the System Library or Library folder may not function properly since those items will not be present in the fresh system. To solve this problem, you can either reinstall the application or find the missing item in the Previous System folder and move it to the proper folder in the active system.

> **NOTE** Using the Archive and Install option is also referred to as a *clean install* like in older Mac OS systems before OS X.

- *Erase and Install*: This option will format the selected volume and then install a fresh copy of OS X on it. With this option, all applications, user data, and settings will be wiped out.

Once you have selected your volume and options and you click the Continue button, you will be presented with the dreaded software licensing agreement (Figure B-5). You must click the Agree button to continue with your installation.

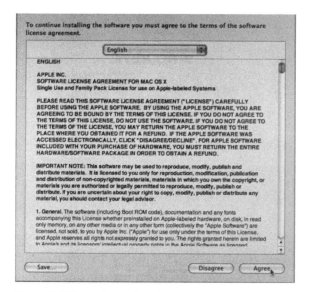

Figure B-5. The software licensing agreement; you must agree in order to continue.

After accepting the license agreement, you will be presented with an Install Summary screen (Figure B-6).

One important installation feature available on the Install Summary screen is the ability to customize what components are installed with the OS. This is available by clicking the Customize button that will open a pane allowing you to customize some of the components that get installed (Figure B-7).

Unlike previous versions of OS X, all of the customizable components are installed by default; this pane, however, allows you to deselect items that you may never need, saving you significant disk space. Some things that people may choose not to install are language translations and additional fonts for languages that you are likely never going to need. For a desktop computer, there are likely a large number of printer drivers you can dispense with (if you travel with a laptop, you may just want to keep all the printer drivers since you never know when you may need one to print to a random printer in some remote location). Information about each item is available when you select the item.

NOTE There is certainly nothing wrong with installing everything; in fact, it's probably a good idea for most users. That said, if you have a smaller hard drive (say less than 100GB), saving a few extra gigabytes may be a priority for you.

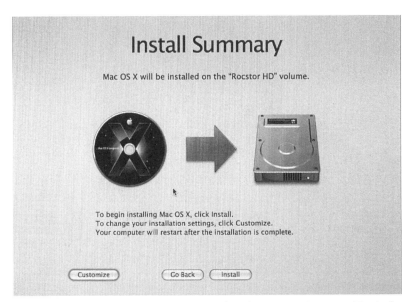

Figure B-6. The Install Summary screen: your last chance to review everything before the install takes place

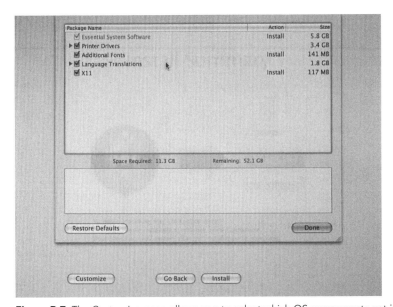

Figure B-7. The Customize pane allows you to select which OS components get installed.

When you are done reviewing your installation, click the Install button to begin the installation. When the installation is going, the screen will provide you with the progress of your install (Figure B-8). Generally, installing Leopard can take anywhere from 15 minutes to an hour depending on your system configuration and install type.

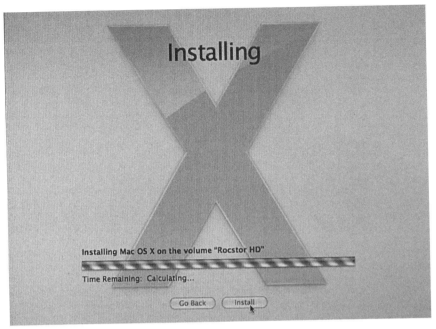

Figure B-8. Leopard is installing.

After the installer is done installing Leopard, your computer will automatically restart from your newly installed OS. Upon restarting, you will be presented with a brief *Welcome to Leopard* movie. When the movie ends, you will be presented with a Welcome screen (Figure B-9) that begins a number of post-install tasks.

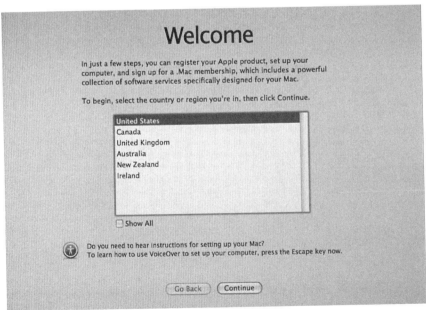

Figure B-9. After your install is finished, your computer will reboot, play a movie, and then begin some post-install tasks.

NOTE All of these tasks are shown for a new install; if you have performed an upgrade or pre-served your user and networking information while doing an Archive and Install, many of these post-installation steps will be skipped.

On the Welcome screen, you must first select your country and then click Continue. (The list of countries initially presented is based on the language you selected when initially installing Leopard; if your country isn't shown, click the Show All option to reveal a much larger choice of countries.) After that, click Continue, and you will be given a number of options for importing existing computer data from another Mac or Mac OS volume (Figure B-10).

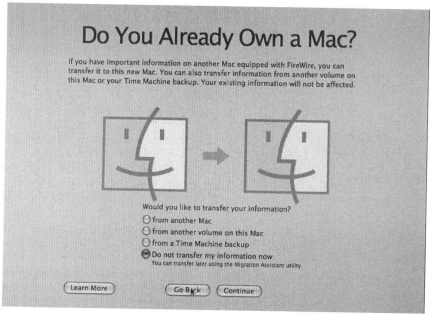

Figure B-10. If you have another Mac or Mac volume, you can import information to your newly installed OS.

If you choose not to transfer any information now, you may do so at any time using the Migration Assistant utility (in your Utilities folder).

Next, you are asked what type of keyboard you are using (Figure B-11). The list of key-boards shown by default depends on the language and country you selected previously; click the Show All option if your keyboard layout is not shown.

NOTE Your keyboard layout does more than just select a specific physical keyboard layout; it also is used by the system to determine measurements and other system-wide settings. For example, Canada and the United States use the same keyboard but have other important dif-ferences (such as default measurement standards—the United States still uses the "standard" measurement system rather than the metric system used by the rest of the world).

Once you select your keyboard, you will be asked to set up your networking. By default OS X asks you to select a wireless network (Figure B-12). If you connect to the Internet by some other means, you should click the Different Network Setup button, which will open a different window (Figure B-13) to walk you through setting up all types of network connections.

NOTE If you have questions about setting up your networking, please refer to Chapter 9 or Chapter 20.

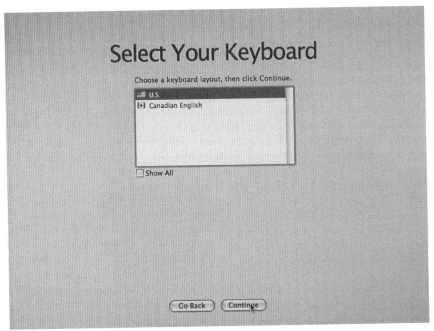

Figure B-11. Next you must select your keyboard layout.

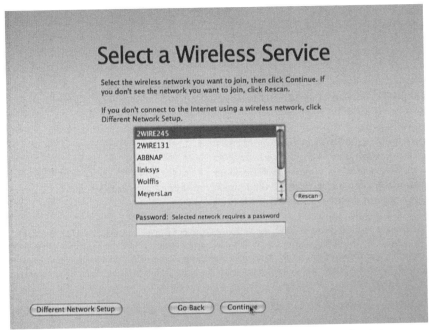

Figure B-12. If you connect to the Internet through a wireless network, select it here.

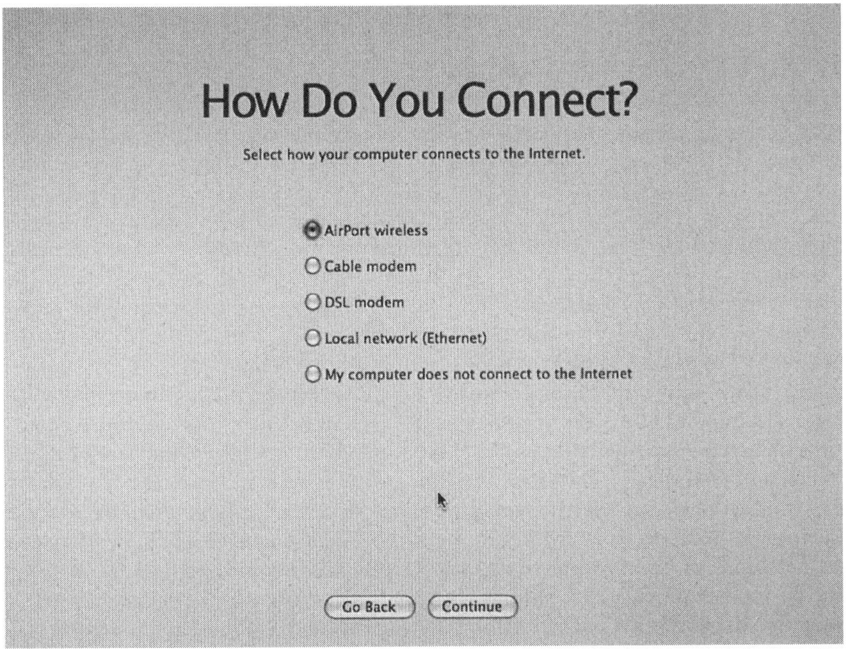

Figure B-13. If you connect to a network through a wired connection, there are post-install options that will walk you through that as well.

After you have successfully set up your networking, you will be prompted to enter your Apple ID if you have one (Figure B-14). If you don't have one, just click Continue.

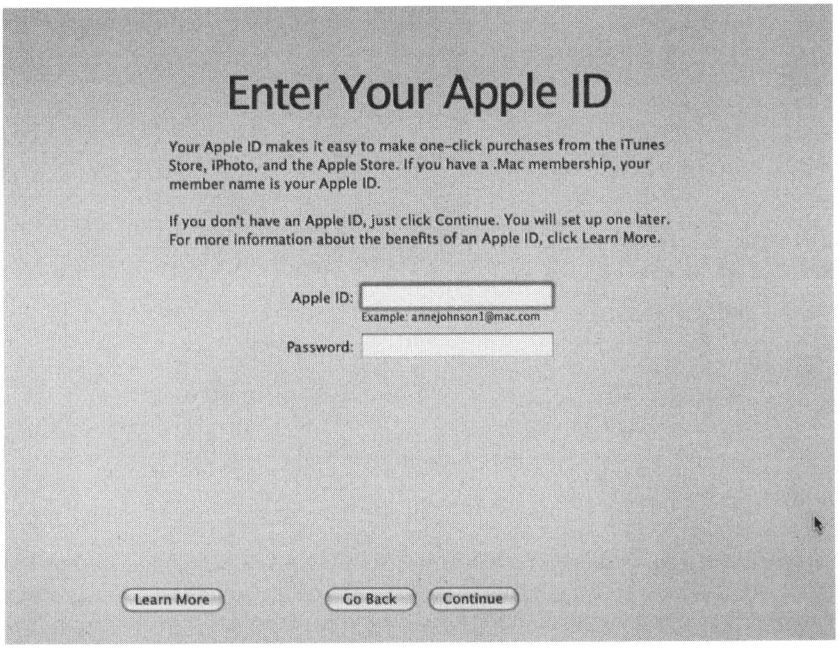

Figure B-14. Enter your Apple ID if you have one.

After the Apple ID screen you will be presented with a Registration screen to register your copy of Leopard. If you entered an Apple ID, most of this information will be filled in automatically for you; otherwise, you can enter it here.

NOTE If the registration information was filled in with old information, you may want to update it.

After you enter your information and click Continue, you will be asked a few more questions about how you use your computer. Once you have answered those, your registration will be sent to Apple.

After the registration process, you will be asked to create your user account for your system. You will be asked for a name, a short name, and a password (plus you may optionally enter a password hint). The name and short name will be filled in by default based on previously entered information; however, you may edit these as you see fit. Once the account is created, you cannot change the short name. After selecting your names, you must enter your password twice (strong passwords are encouraged here; they should be a minimum of eight characters of mixed numbers, letters, and symbols).

After you're done with selecting your usernames and password, you will be presented with a screen to select an account picture (Figure B-15). If you have an iSight camera attached to your computer, it will turn on allowing you to snap a picture of yourself. If you'd rather, you can select the "Choose from the picture library" option to select one of many generic user icons (you can change or customize this at any time in the Accounts panel of System Preferences).

Figure B-15. You can use your iSight camera to snap a photo to use as your account image.

After you create your account, you will be asked to either try, sign up for, or enter your current information for .Mac. If you don't have a .Mac account, it's definitely worth at least signing up for the trial here. (You can read about the benefits of .Mac in Chapter 15 and in various places throughout the book.)

Finally, after the .Mac stuff, you will receive one more screen—a Thank You screen (Figure B-16)—letting you know your Mac is all set up and ready to go. Just click the Go button to begin.

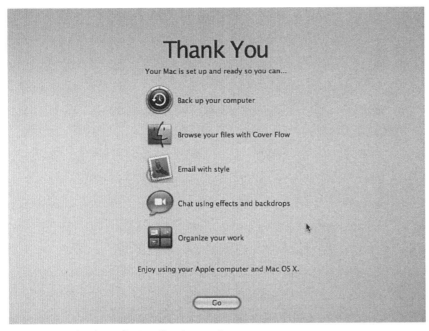

Figure B-16. Thank you for installing Leopard!

Index

You Need the Companion eBook

Your purchase of this book entitles you to buy the companion PDF-version eBook for only $10. Take the weightless companion with you anywhere.

We believe this Apress title will prove so indispensable that you'll want to carry it with you everywhere, which is why we are offering the companion eBook (in PDF format) for $10 to customers who purchase this book now. Convenient and fully searchable, the PDF version of any content-rich, page-heavy Apress book makes a valuable addition to your programming library. You can easily find and copy code—or perform examples by quickly toggling between instructions and the application. Even simultaneously tackling a donut, diet soda, and complex code becomes simplified with hands-free eBooks!

Once you purchase your book, getting the $10 companion eBook is simple:

❶ Visit **www.apress.com/promo/tendollars/**.

❷ Complete a basic registration form to receive a randomly generated question about this title.

❸ Answer the question correctly in 60 seconds, and you will receive a promotional code to redeem for the $10.00 eBook.

THE EXPERT'S VOICE™

2855 TELEGRAPH AVENUE │ SUITE 600 │ BERKELEY, CA 94705

Offer valid through 6/17/08.